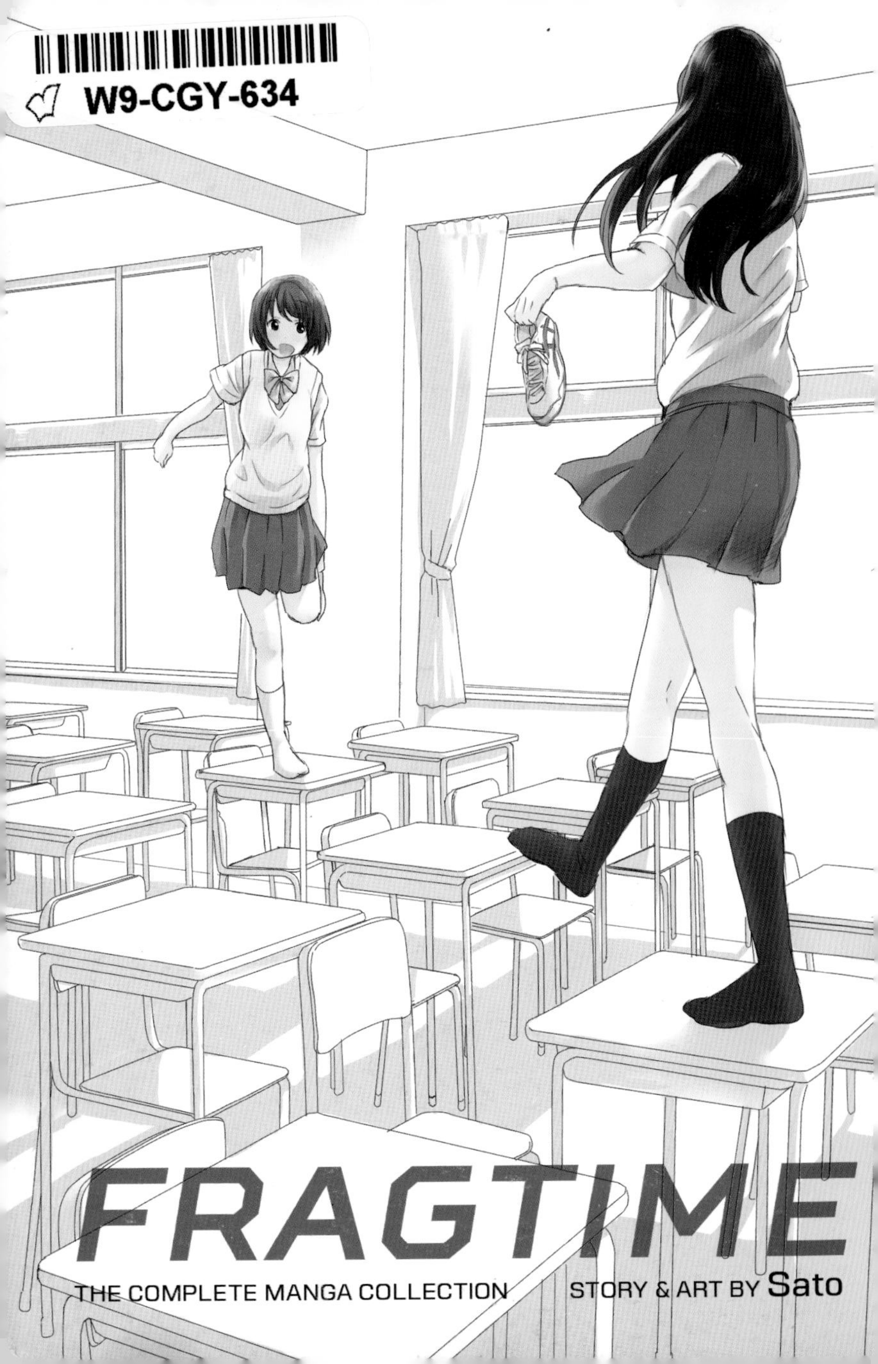

FRAGTIME

THE COMPLETE MANGA COLLECTION

STORY & ART BY Sato

CONTENTS

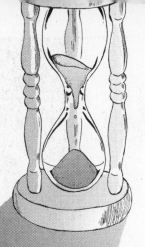

WHAT WOULD *YOU* DO IF YOU COULD STOP TIME?

STEAL ALL YOU WANT?

CHEAT ON A TEST?

BUT, AT LEAST...

I, MORITANI MISUZU, AM A CHICKEN. I CAN'T DO STUFF LIKE THAT.

3

fragtime

#1 What Would You Do If You Could Stop Time?

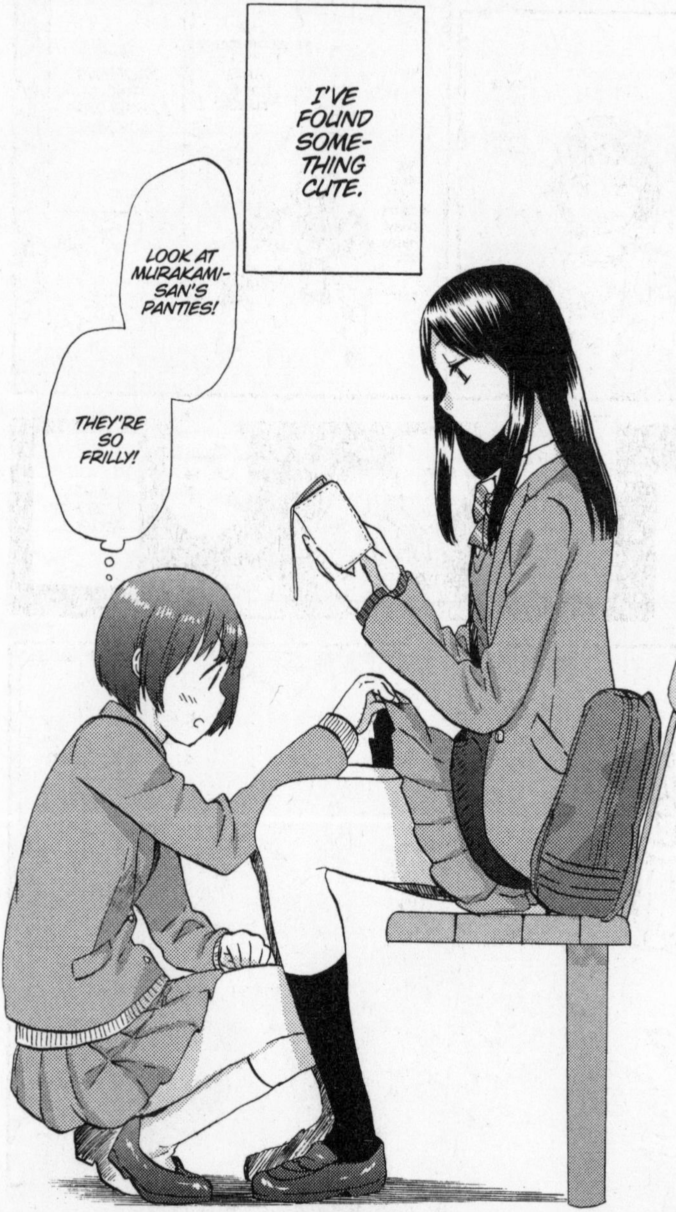
I'VE FOUND SOMETHING CUTE.
LOOK AT MURAKAMI-SAN'S PANTIES!
THEY'RE SO FRILLY!

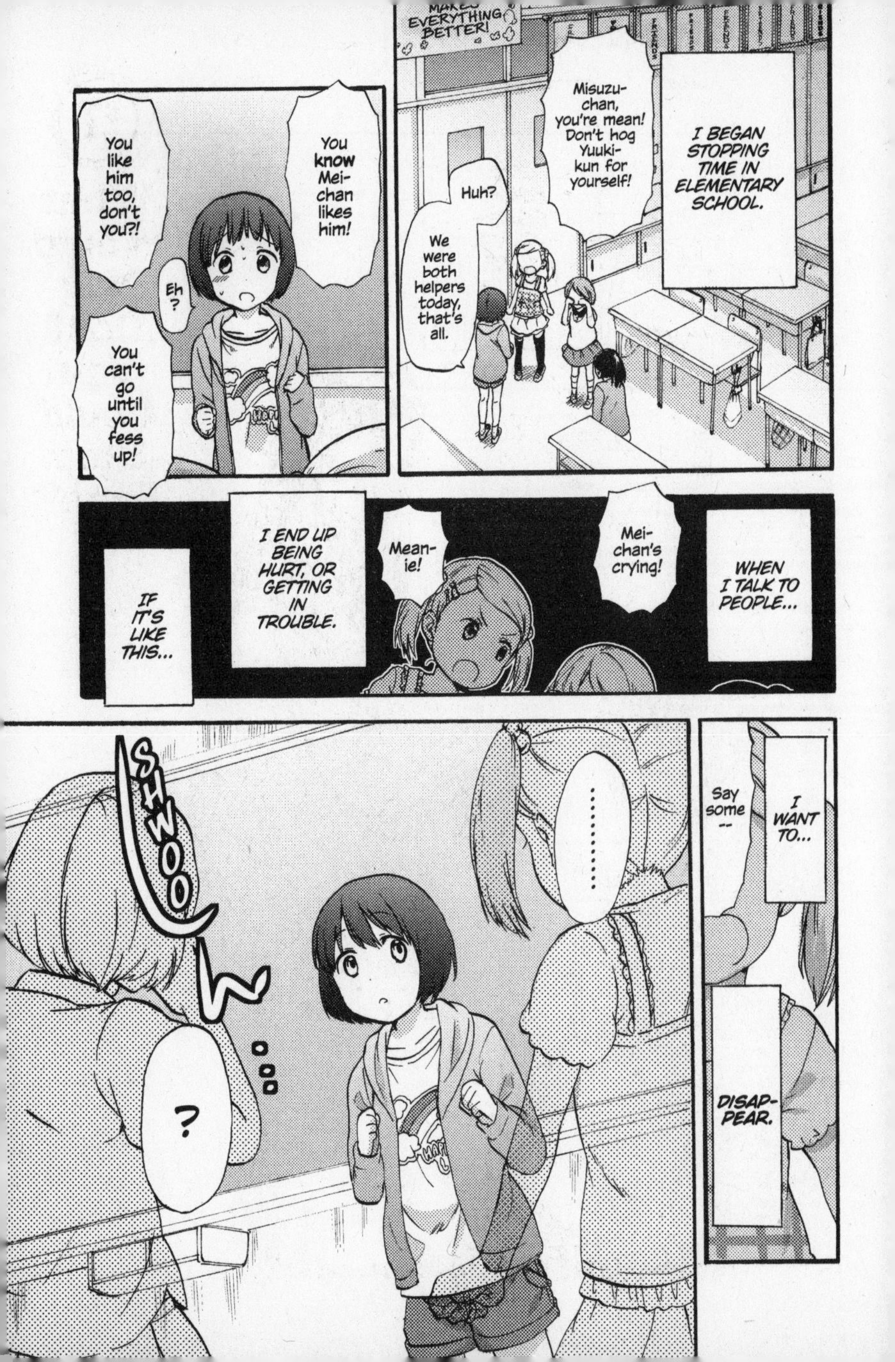

EVERYTHING BETTER!
I BEGAN STOPPING TIME IN ELEMENTARY SCHOOL.
Misuzu-chan, you're mean! Don't hog Yuuki-kun for yourself!
Huh?
We were both helpers today, that's all.
You know Mei-chan likes him!
You like him too, don't you?!
Eh?
You can't go until you fess up!
WHEN I TALK TO PEOPLE...
Mei-chan's crying!
Mean-ie!
I END UP BEING HURT, OR GETTING IN TROUBLE.
IF IT'S LIKE THIS...
I WANT TO...
Say some--
DISAPPEAR.
......
SHWOOO
...
?

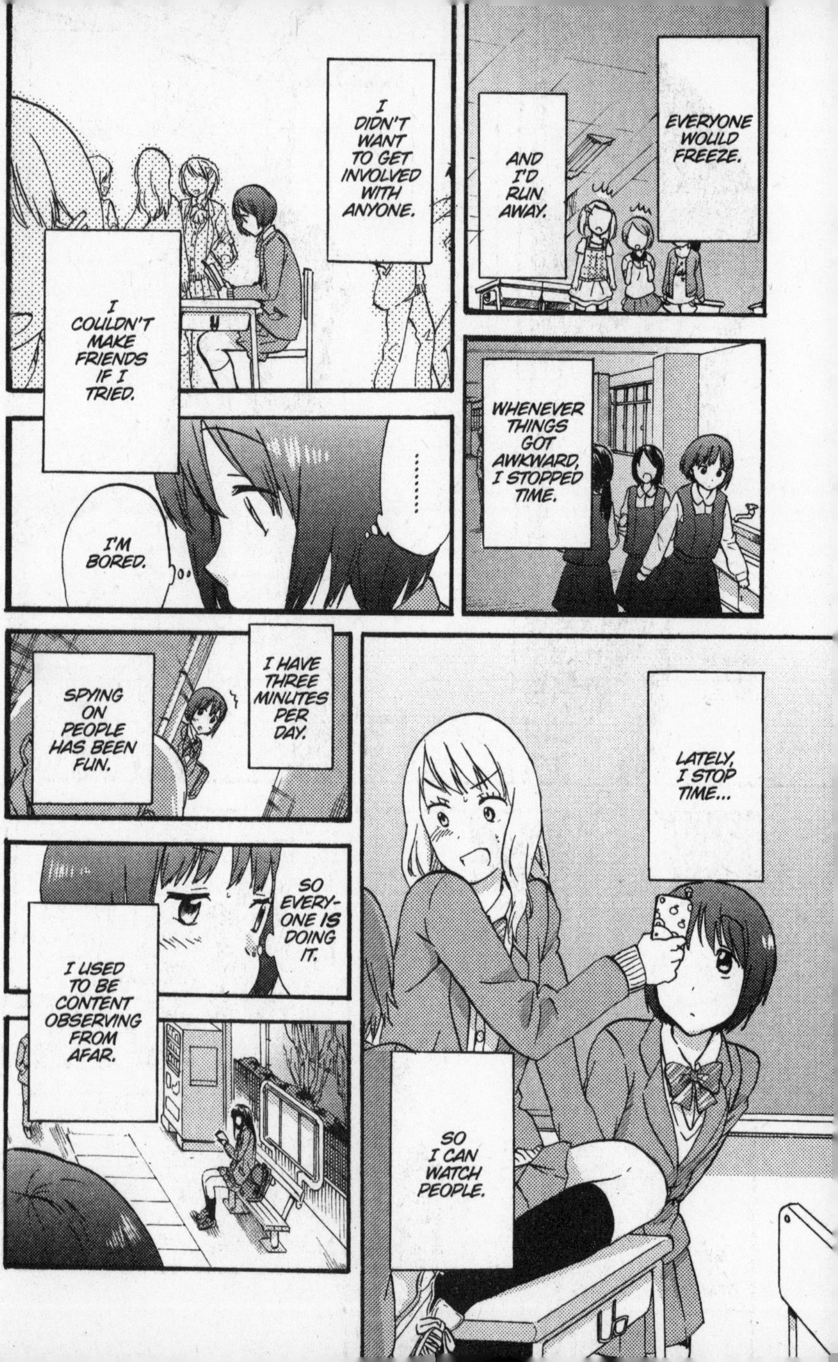
EVERYONE WOULD FREEZE.
AND I'D RUN AWAY.
WHENEVER THINGS GOT AWKWARD, I STOPPED TIME.
I DIDN'T WANT TO GET INVOLVED WITH ANYONE.
I COULDN'T MAKE FRIENDS IF I TRIED.
......
I'M BORED.
LATELY, I STOP TIME...
SO I CAN WATCH PEOPLE.
I HAVE THREE MINUTES PER DAY.
SPYING ON PEOPLE HAS BEEN FUN.
SO EVERY-ONE IS DOING IT.
I USED TO BE CONTENT OBSERVING FROM AFAR.

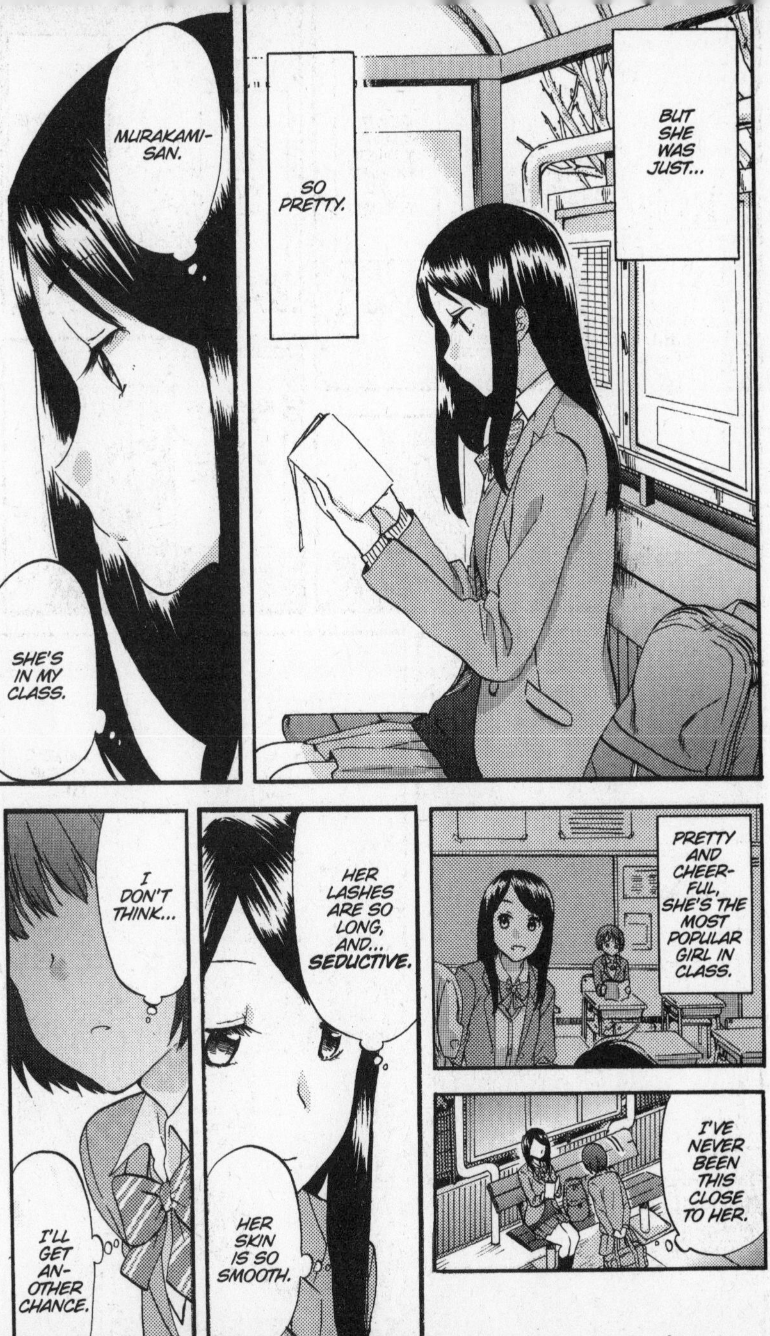
BUT SHE WAS JUST...
SO PRETTY.
MURAKAMI-SAN.
SHE'S IN MY CLASS.
PRETTY AND CHEER-FUL, SHE'S THE MOST POPULAR GIRL IN CLASS.
I'VE NEVER BEEN THIS CLOSE TO HER.
HER LASHES ARE SO LONG, AND... SEDUCTIVE.
HER SKIN IS SO SMOOTH.
I DON'T THINK...
I'LL GET AN-OTHER CHANCE.

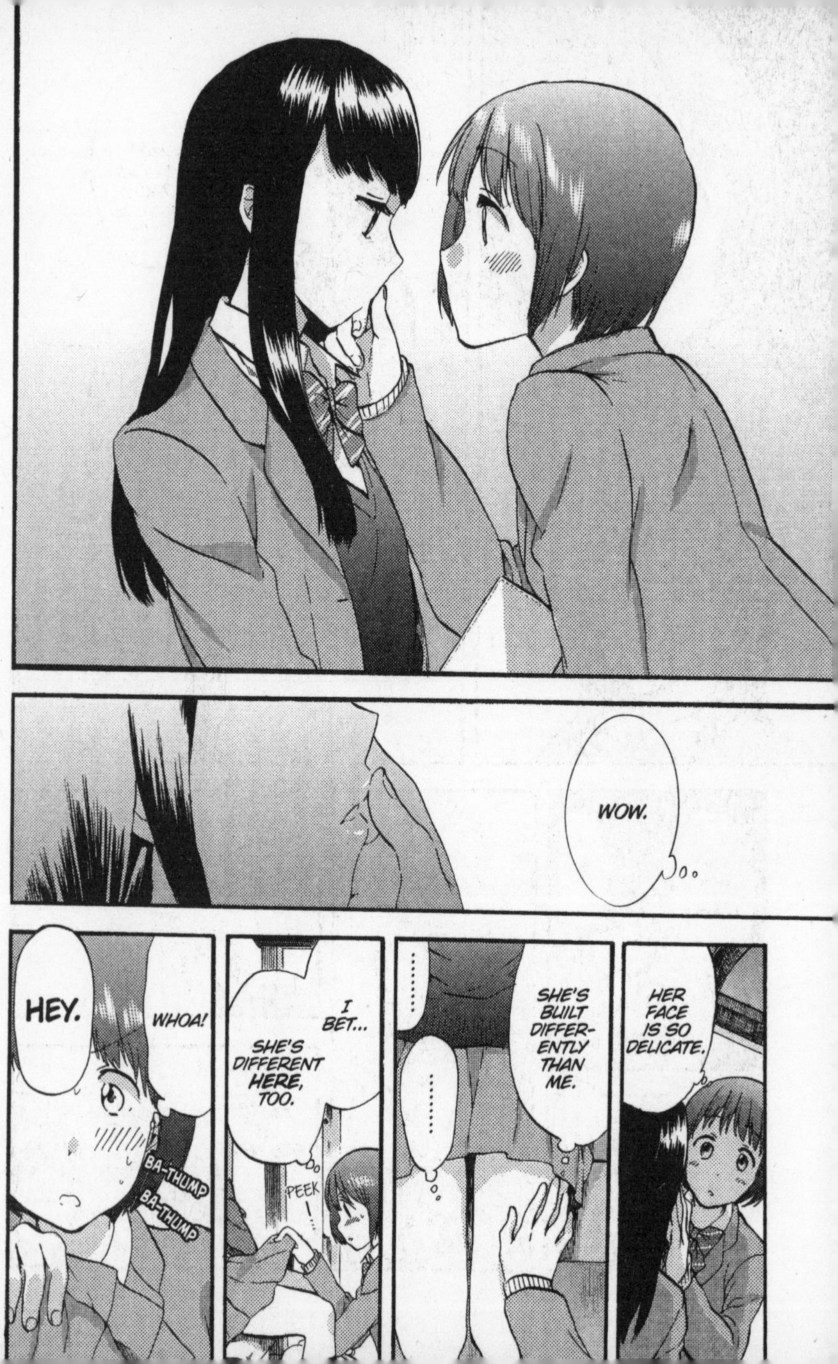
WOW.
HER FACE IS SO DELICATE.
SHE'S BUILT DIFFERENTLY THAN ME.
......
......
I BET...
SHE'S DIFFERENT HERE, TOO.
PEEK!
HEY.
WHOA!
BA-THUMP
BA-THUMP

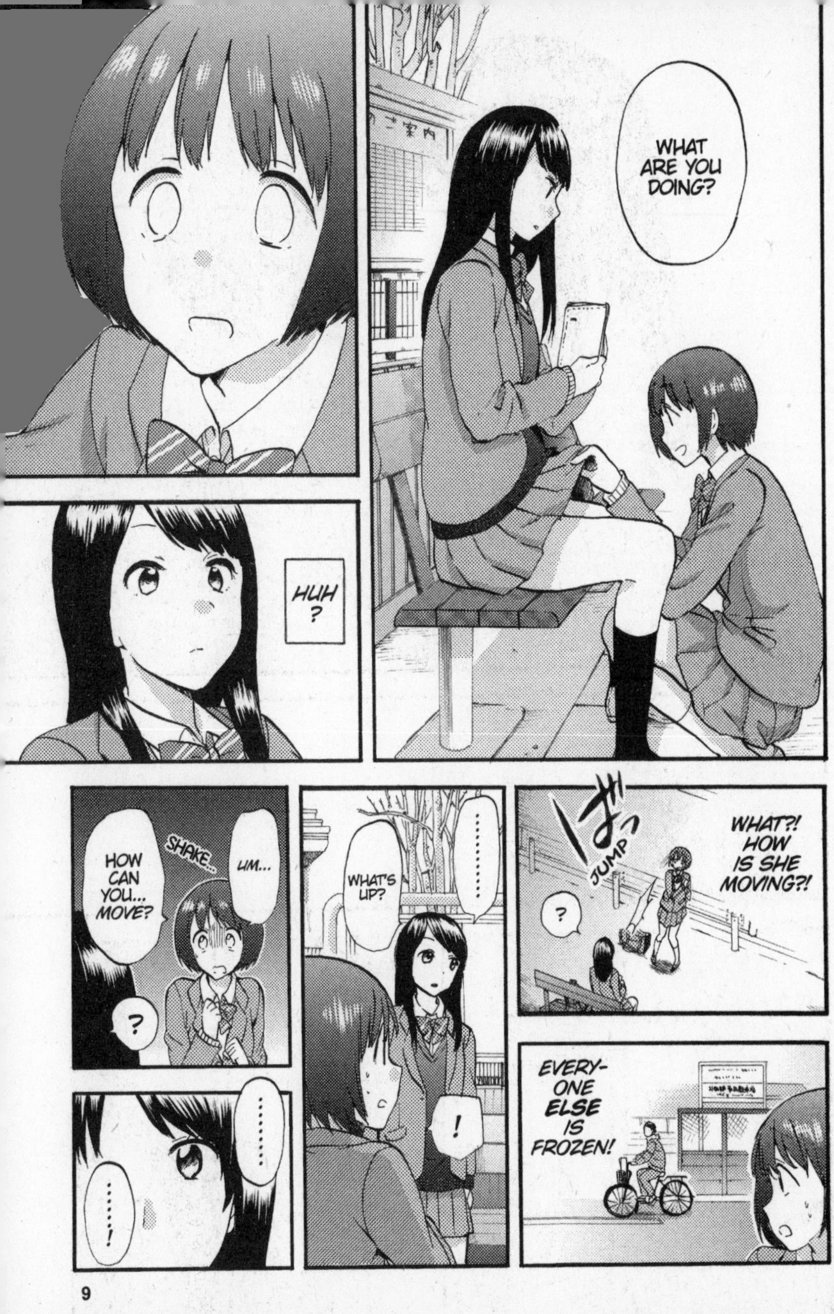
WHAT ARE YOU DOING?
HUH ?
ぱっ
JUMP
WHAT?! HOW IS SHE MOVING?!
?
EVERY-ONE ELSE IS FROZEN!
......
WHAT'S UP?
!
UM...
SHAKE...
HOW CAN YOU... MOVE?
?
......
......!

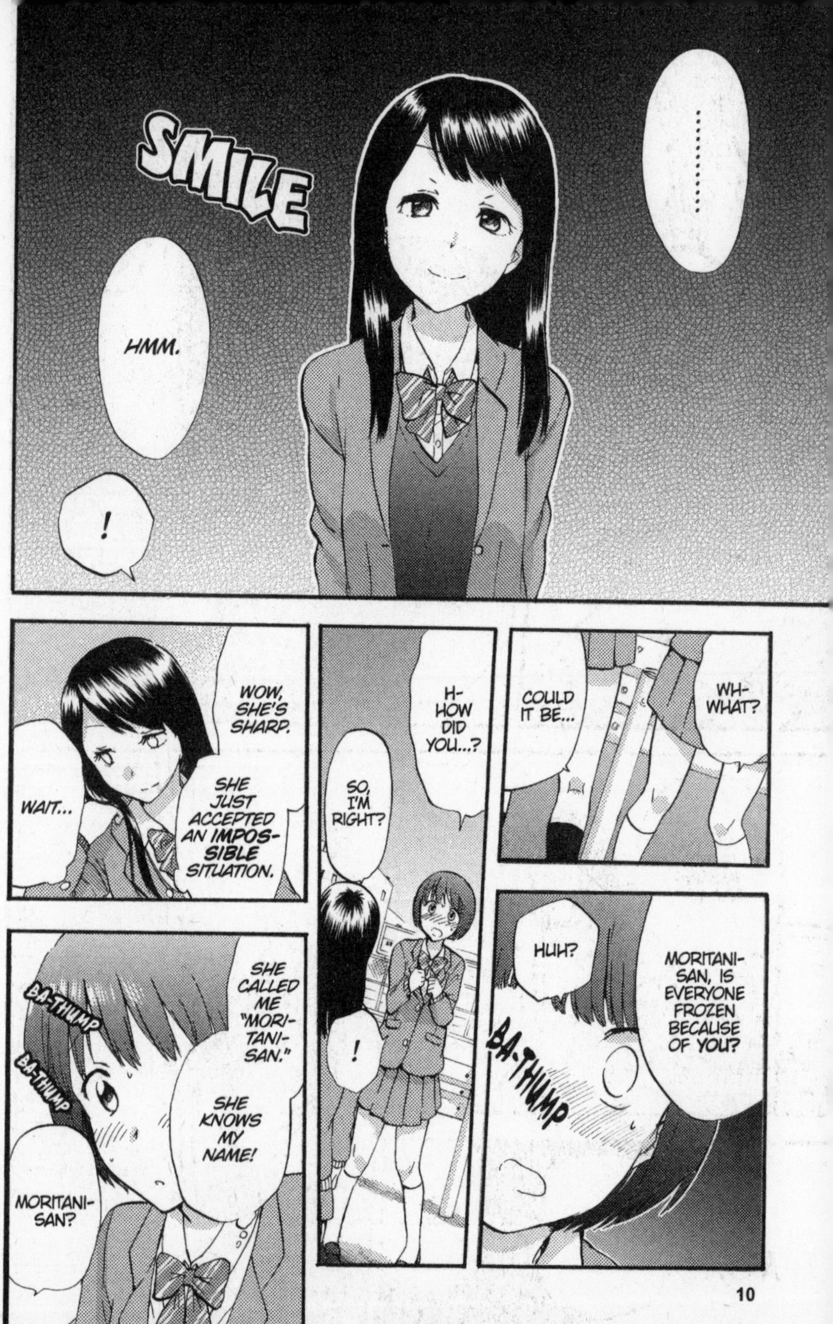
......
SMILE
HMM.
!
WH-WHAT?
COULD IT BE...
MORITANI-SAN, IS EVERYONE FROZEN BECAUSE OF YOU?
HUH?
BA-THUMP
H-HOW DID YOU...?
SO, I'M RIGHT?
!
WOW, SHE'S SHARP.
SHE JUST ACCEPTED AN IMPOSSIBLE SITUATION.
WAIT...
SHE CALLED ME "MORITANI-SAN."
SHE KNOWS MY NAME!
BA-THUMP
BA-THUMP
MORITANI-SAN?

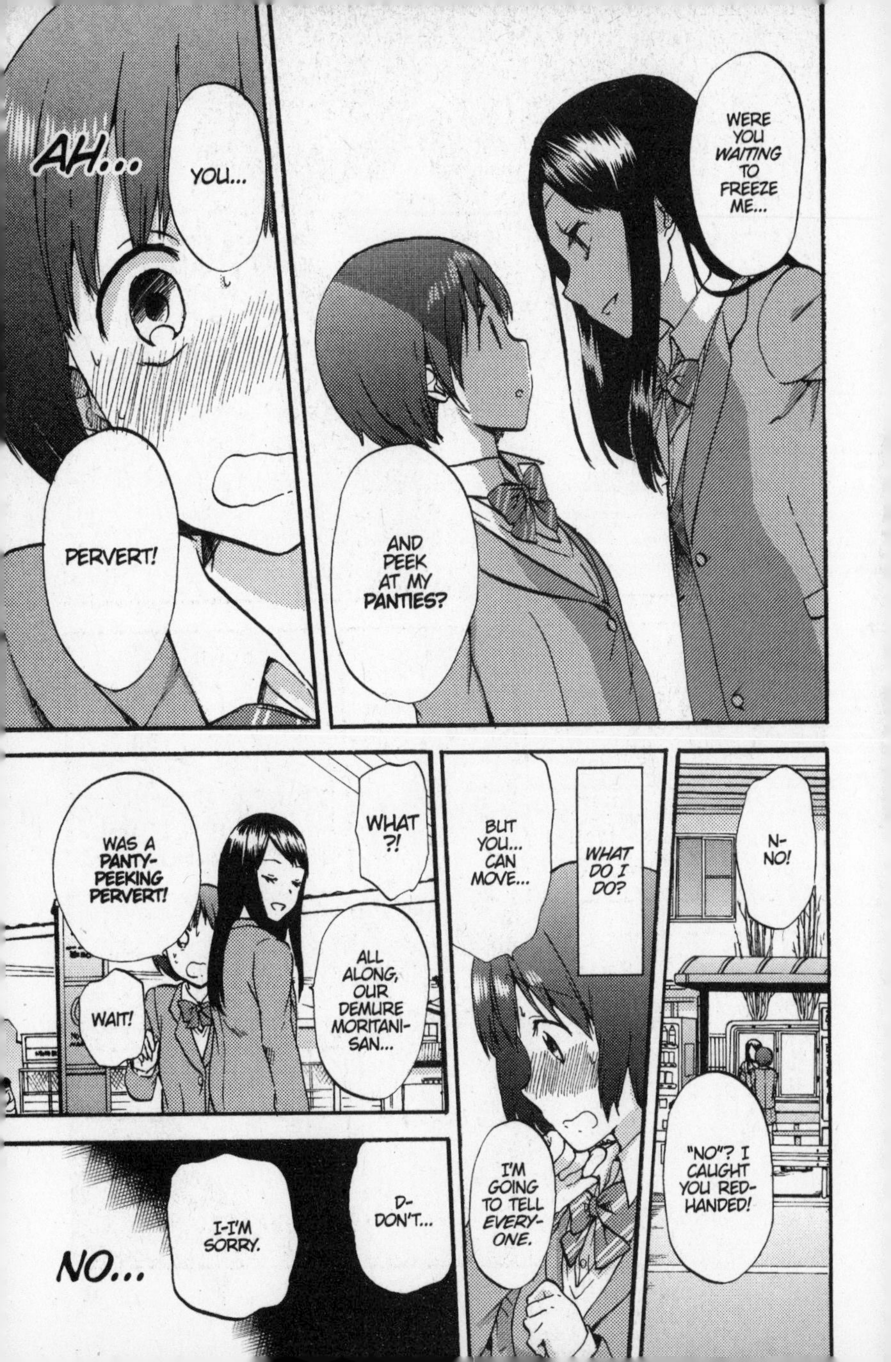
WERE YOU WAITING TO FREEZE ME...
AND PEEK AT MY PANTIES?
AH...
YOU...
PERVERT!
N-NO!
"NO"? I CAUGHT YOU RED-HANDED!
BUT YOU... CAN MOVE...
WHAT DO I DO?
I'M GOING TO TELL EVERYONE.
WHAT?!
ALL ALONG, OUR DEMURE MORITANI-SAN...
WAS A PANTY-PEEKING PERVERT!
WAIT!
D-DON'T...
I-I'M SORRY.
NO...

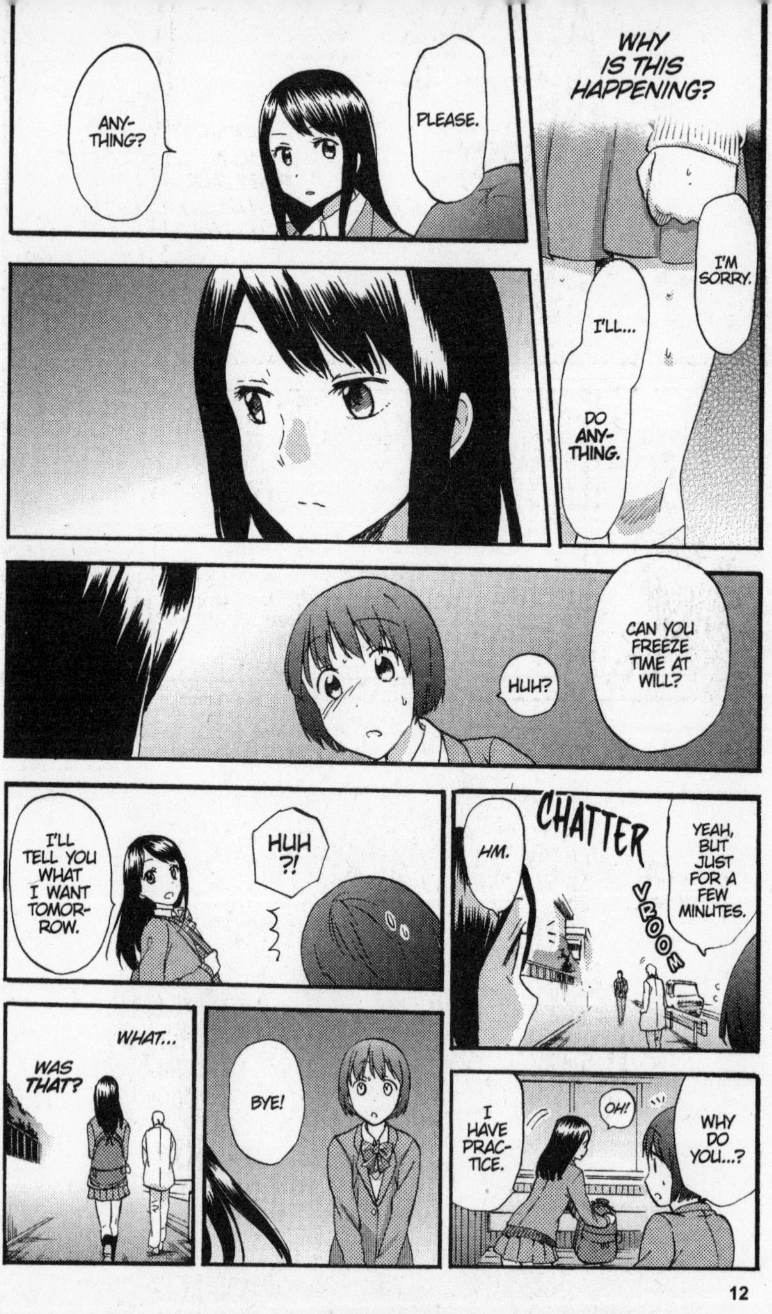
WHY IS THIS HAPPENING?
I'M SORRY.
I'LL...
DO ANY-THING.
PLEASE.
ANY-THING?
CAN YOU FREEZE TIME AT WILL?
HUH?
YEAH, BUT JUST FOR A FEW MINUTES.
CHATTER
HM.
VROOM
HUH ?!
I'LL TELL YOU WHAT I WANT TOMOR-ROW.
WHY DO YOU...?
OH!
I HAVE PRAC-TICE.
BYE!
WHAT...
WAS THAT?

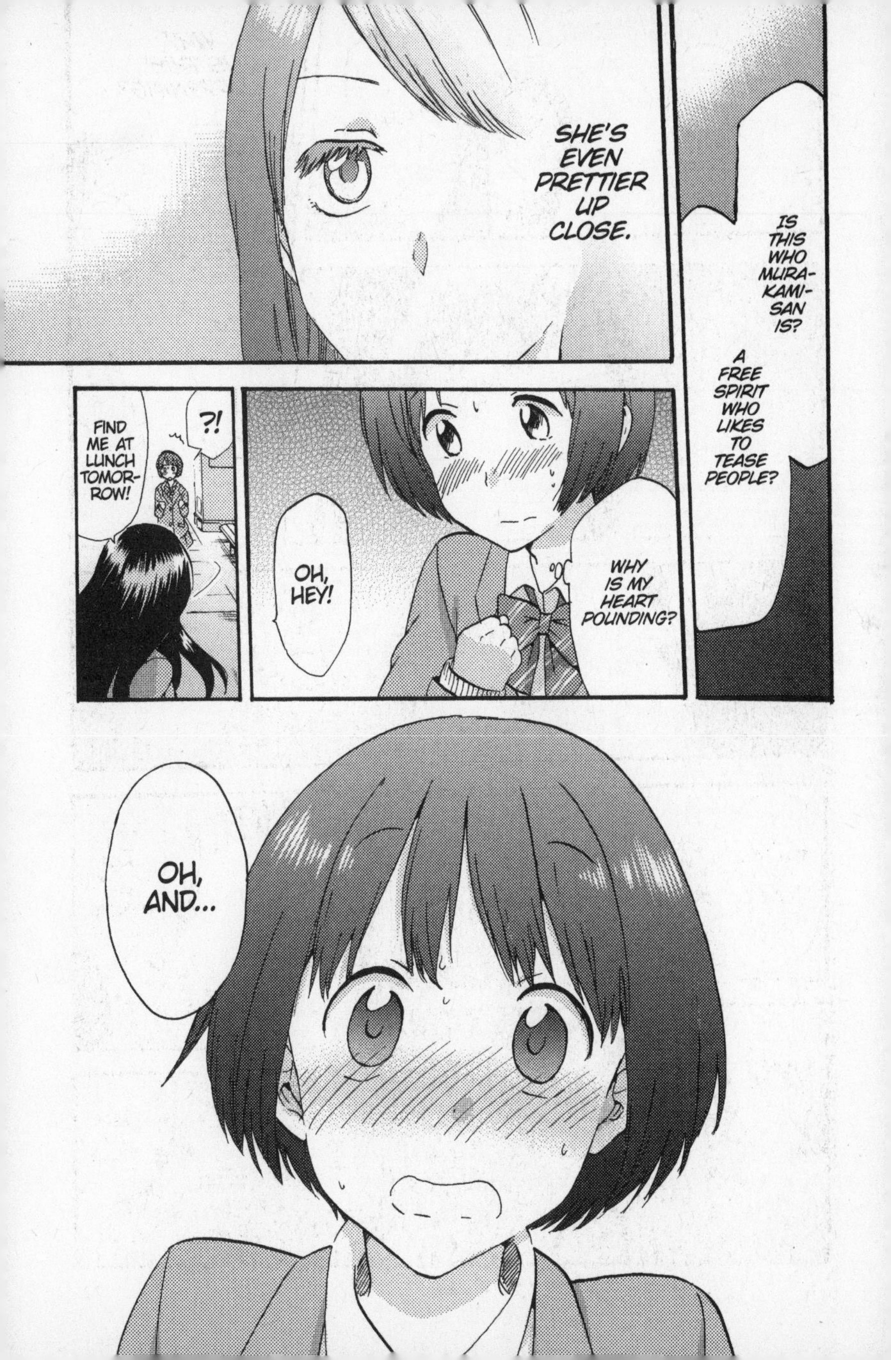
IS THIS WHO MURAKAMI-SAN IS?
A FREE SPIRIT WHO LIKES TO TEASE PEOPLE?
SHE'S EVEN PRETTIER UP CLOSE.
WHY IS MY HEART POUNDING?
OH, HEY!
?!
FIND ME AT LUNCH TOMORROW!
OH, AND...

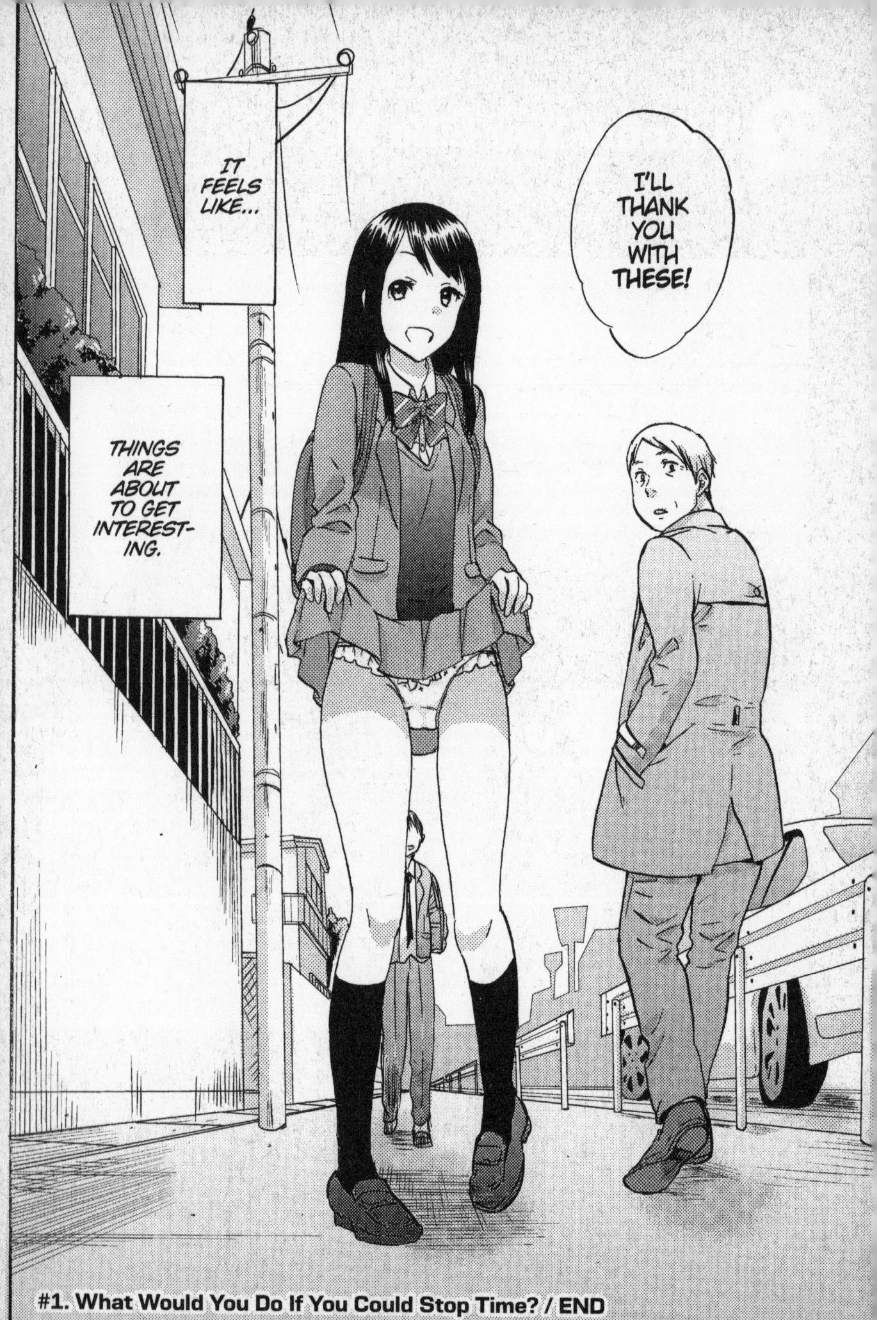
I'LL THANK YOU WITH THESE!
IT FEELS LIKE...
THINGS ARE ABOUT TO GET INTERESTING.

#1. What Would You Do If You Could Stop Time? / END

fragtime

#2 I Know You Like Me

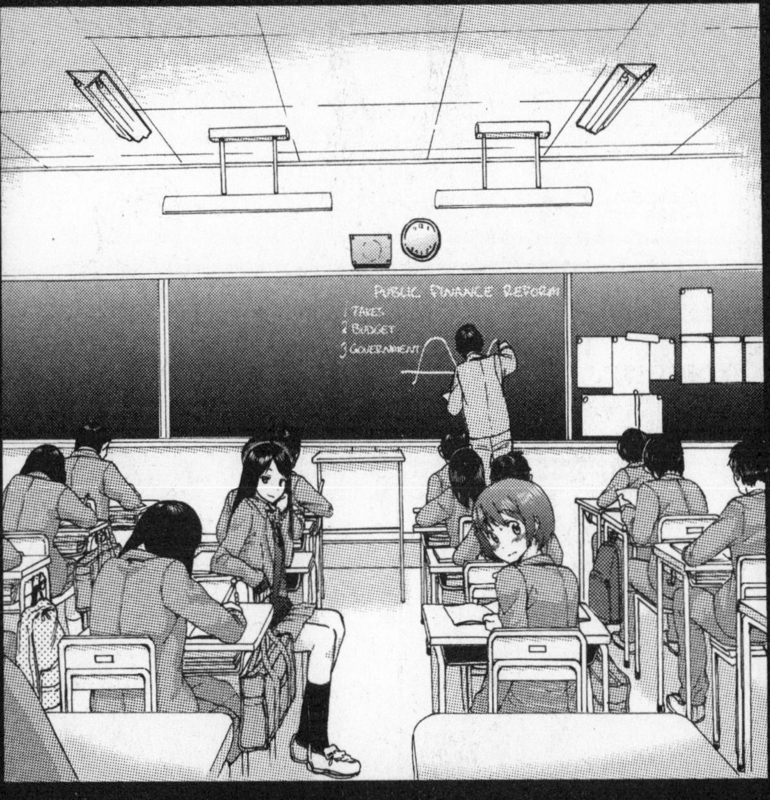
PUBLIC FINANCE REFORM
1 TAXES
2 BUDGET
3 GOVERNMENT

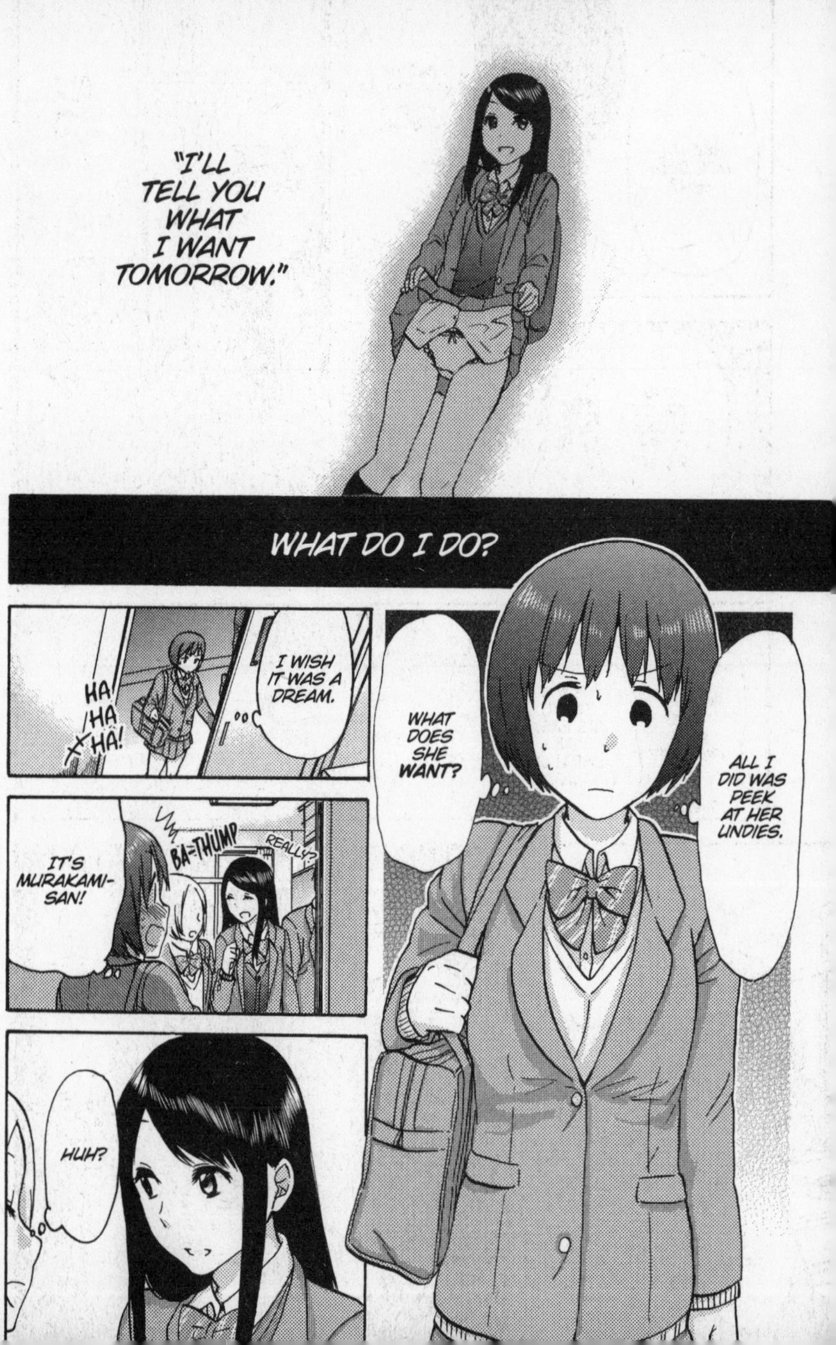
"I'LL TELL YOU WHAT I WANT TOMORROW."
WHAT DO I DO?
ALL I DID WAS PEEK AT HER UNDIES.
WHAT DOES SHE WANT?
I WISH IT WAS A DREAM.
HA HA HA!
REALLY?
BA-THUMP
IT'S MURAKAMI-SAN!
HUH?

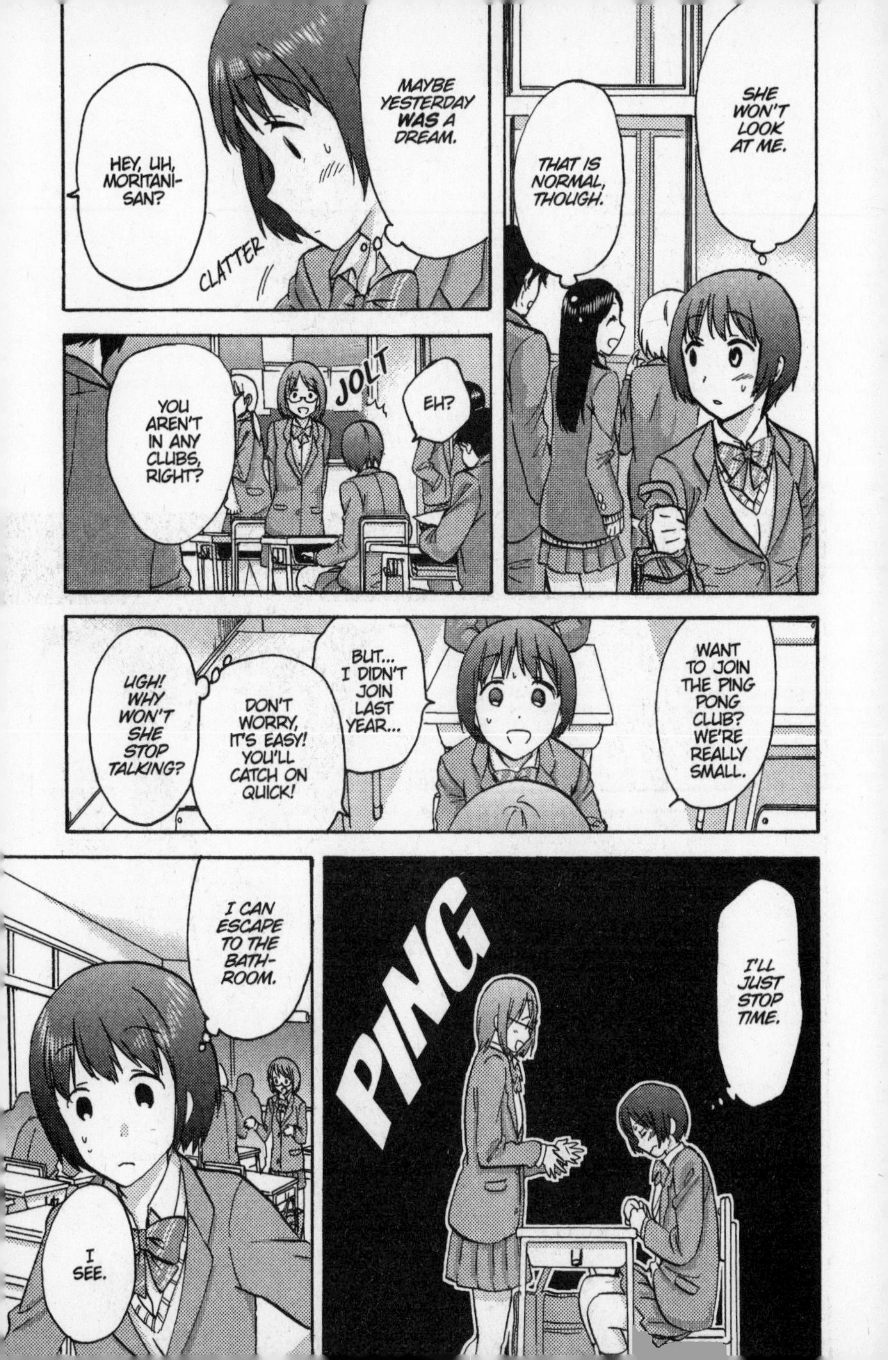
SHE WON'T LOOK AT ME.
THAT IS NORMAL, THOUGH.
MAYBE YESTERDAY WAS A DREAM.
HEY, UH, MORITANI-SAN?
CLATTER
EH?
JOLT
YOU AREN'T IN ANY CLUBS, RIGHT?
WANT TO JOIN THE PING PONG CLUB? WE'RE REALLY SMALL.
BUT... I DIDN'T JOIN LAST YEAR...
DON'T WORRY, IT'S EASY! YOU'LL CATCH ON QUICK!
UGH! WHY WON'T SHE STOP TALKING?
I'LL JUST STOP TIME.
PING
I CAN ESCAPE TO THE BATH-ROOM.
I SEE.

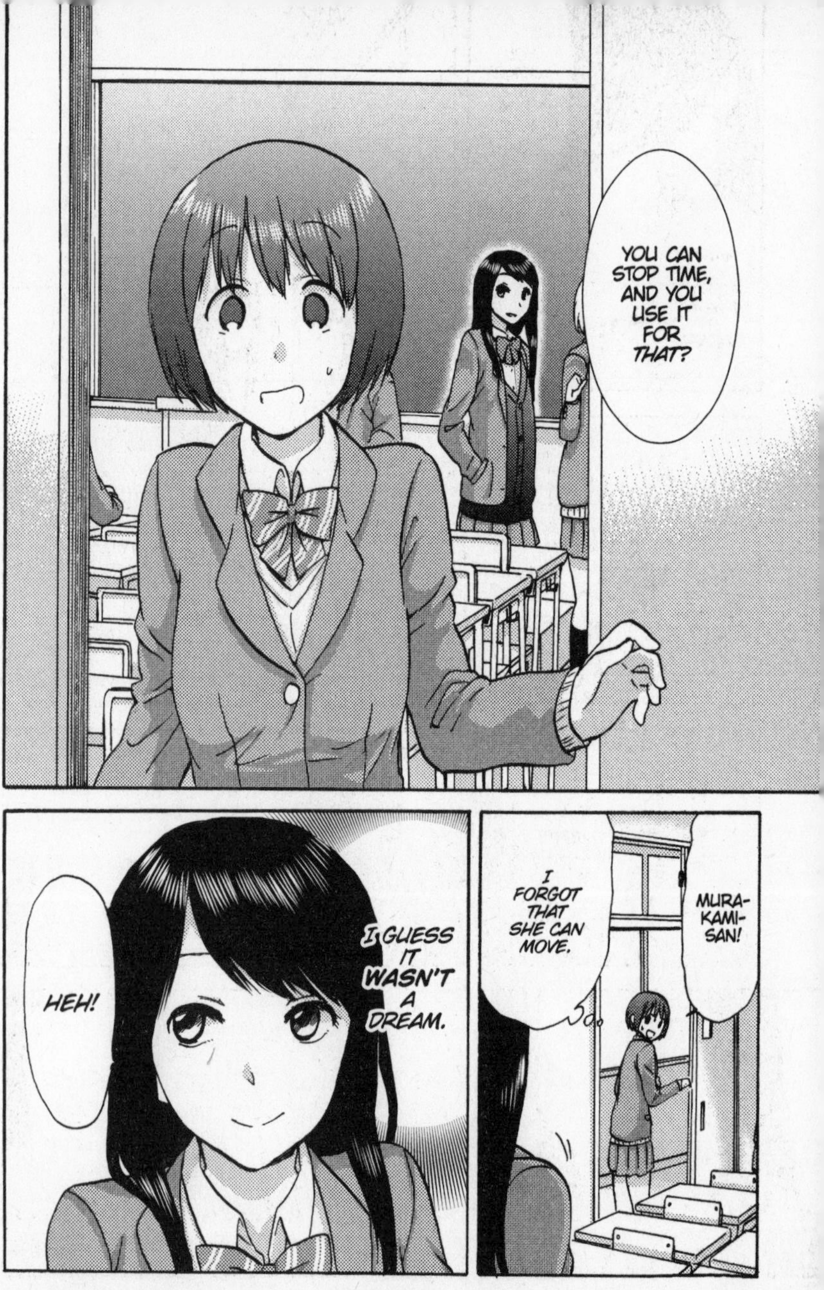
YOU CAN STOP TIME, AND YOU USE IT FOR THAT?
MURA-KAMI-SAN!
I FORGOT THAT SHE CAN MOVE.
I GUESS IT WASN'T A DREAM.
HEH!

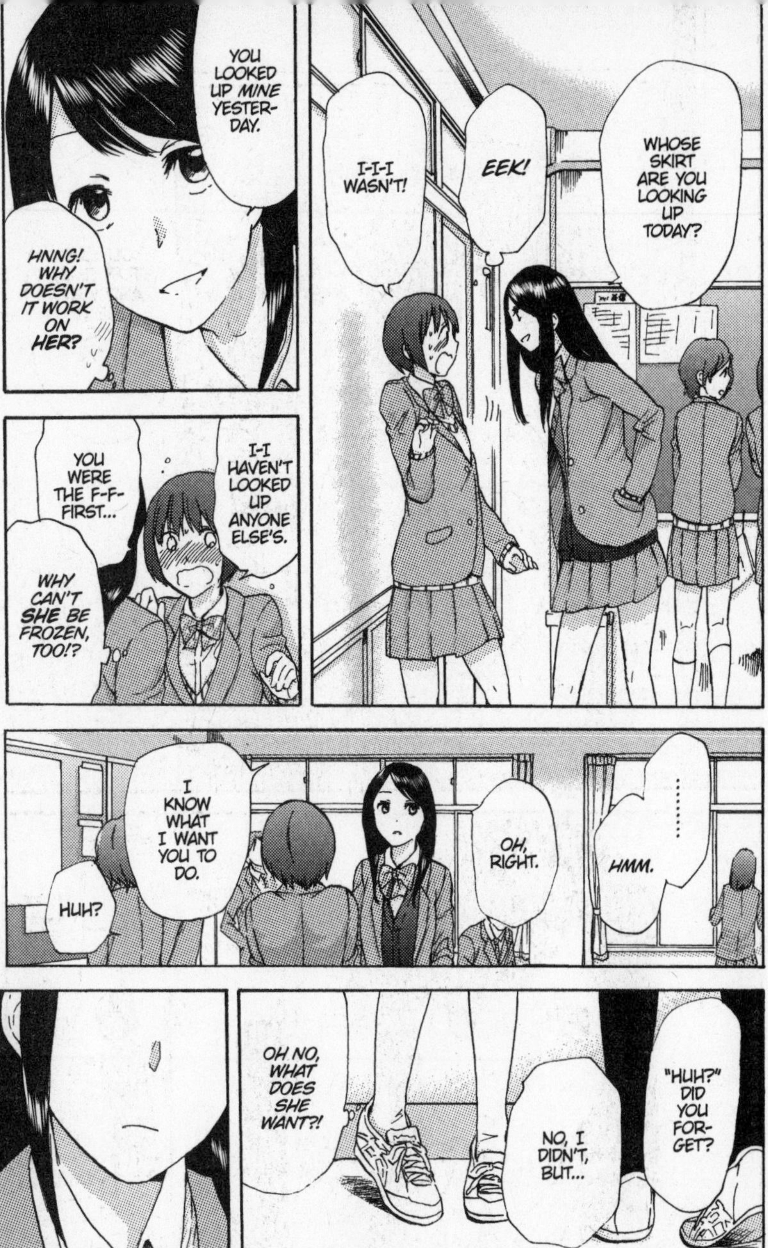
WHOSE SKIRT ARE YOU LOOKING UP TODAY?
EEK!
I-I-I WASN'T!
YOU LOOKED UP MINE YESTER-DAY.
HNNG! WHY DOESN'T IT WORK ON HER?
I-I HAVEN'T LOOKED UP ANYONE ELSE'S.
YOU WERE THE F-F-FIRST...
WHY CAN'T SHE BE FROZEN, TOO!?
......
HMM.
OH, RIGHT.
I KNOW WHAT I WANT YOU TO DO.
HUH?
"HUH?" DID YOU FOR-GET?
NO, I DIDN'T, BUT...
OH NO, WHAT DOES SHE WANT?!

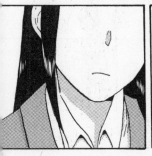

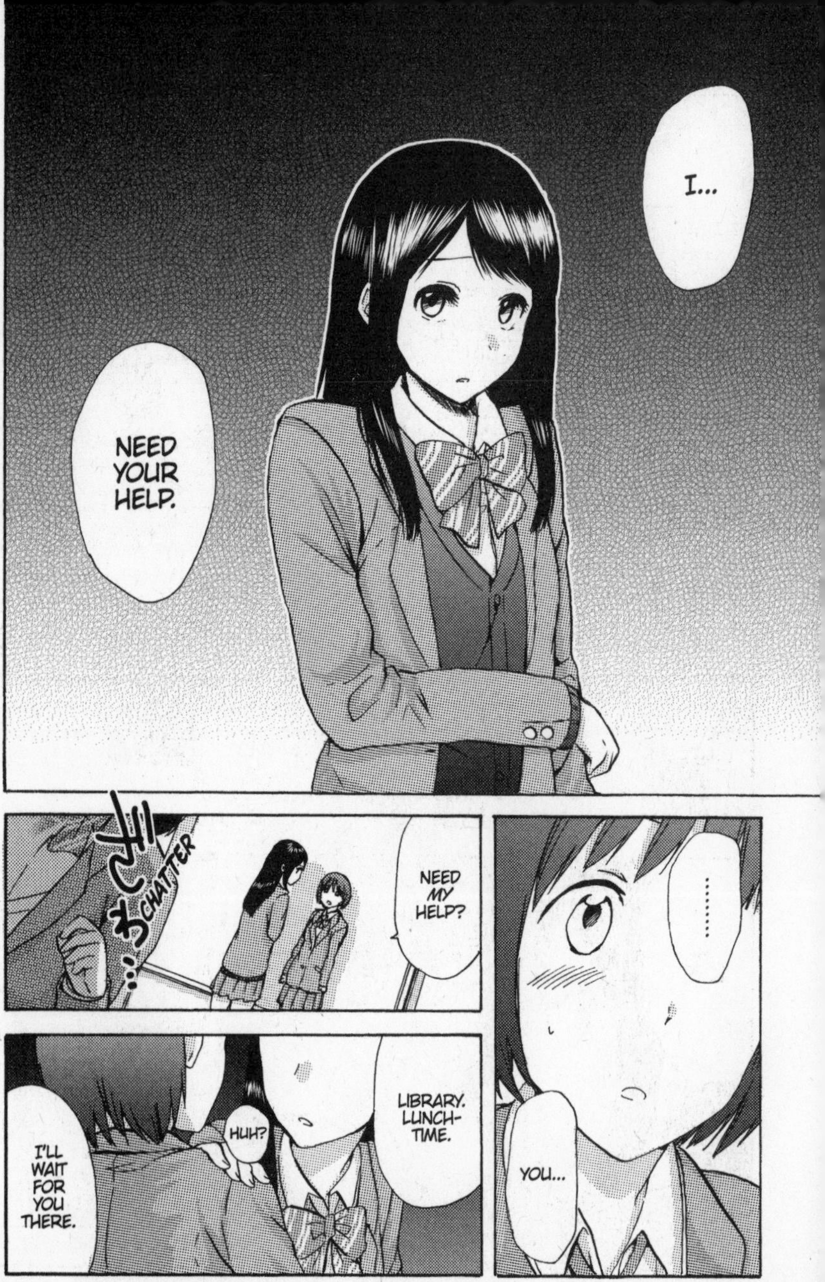
I...
NEED YOUR HELP.
......
YOU...
NEED MY HELP?
CHATTER
LIBRARY. LUNCH-TIME.
HUH?
I'LL WAIT FOR YOU THERE.

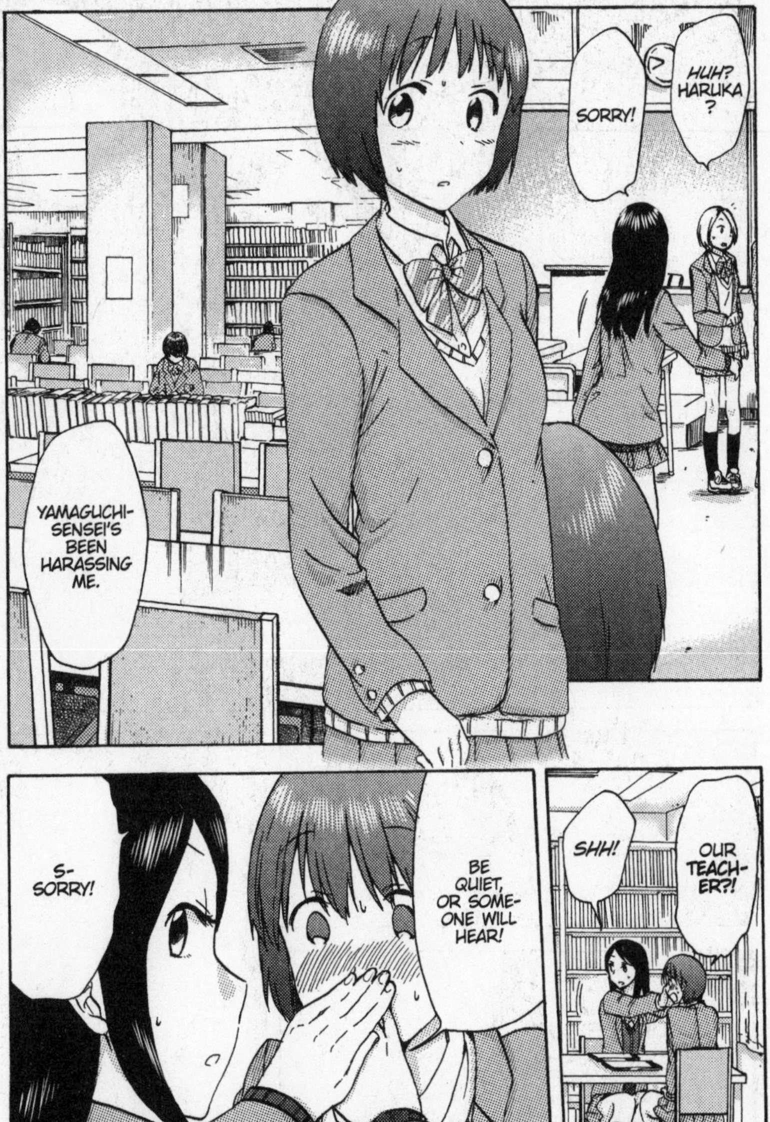
HUH? HARUKA?
SORRY!
YAMAGUCHI-SENSEI'S BEEN HARASSING ME.
OUR TEACHER?!
SHH!
BE QUIET, OR SOME-ONE WILL HEAR!
S-SORRY!

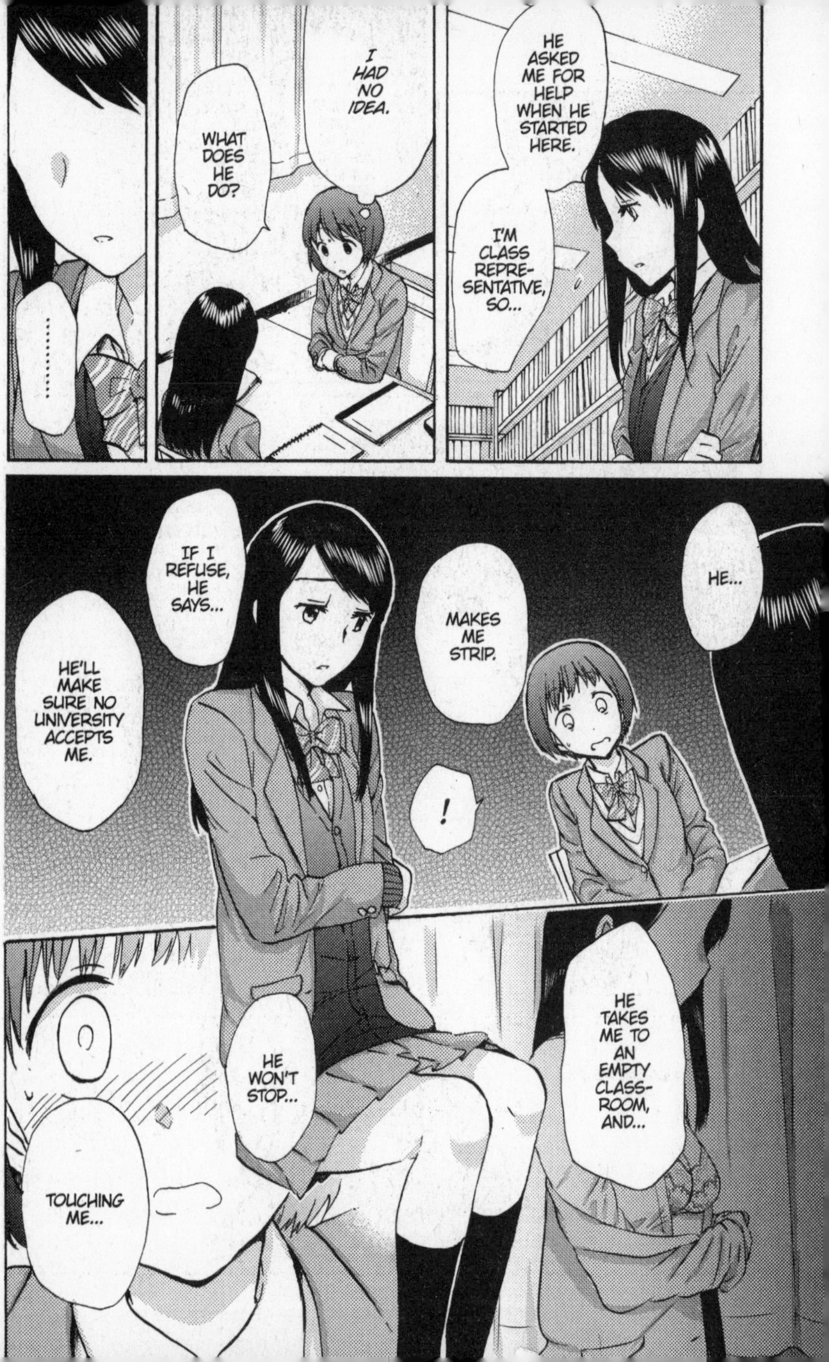
HE ASKED ME FOR HELP WHEN HE STARTED HERE.
I'M CLASS REPRESENTATIVE, SO...
I HAD NO IDEA.
WHAT DOES HE DO?
......
HE...
MAKES ME STRIP.
!
IF I REFUSE, HE SAYS...
HE'LL MAKE SURE NO UNIVERSITY ACCEPTS ME.
HE TAKES ME TO AN EMPTY CLASSROOM, AND...
HE WON'T STOP...
TOUCHING ME...

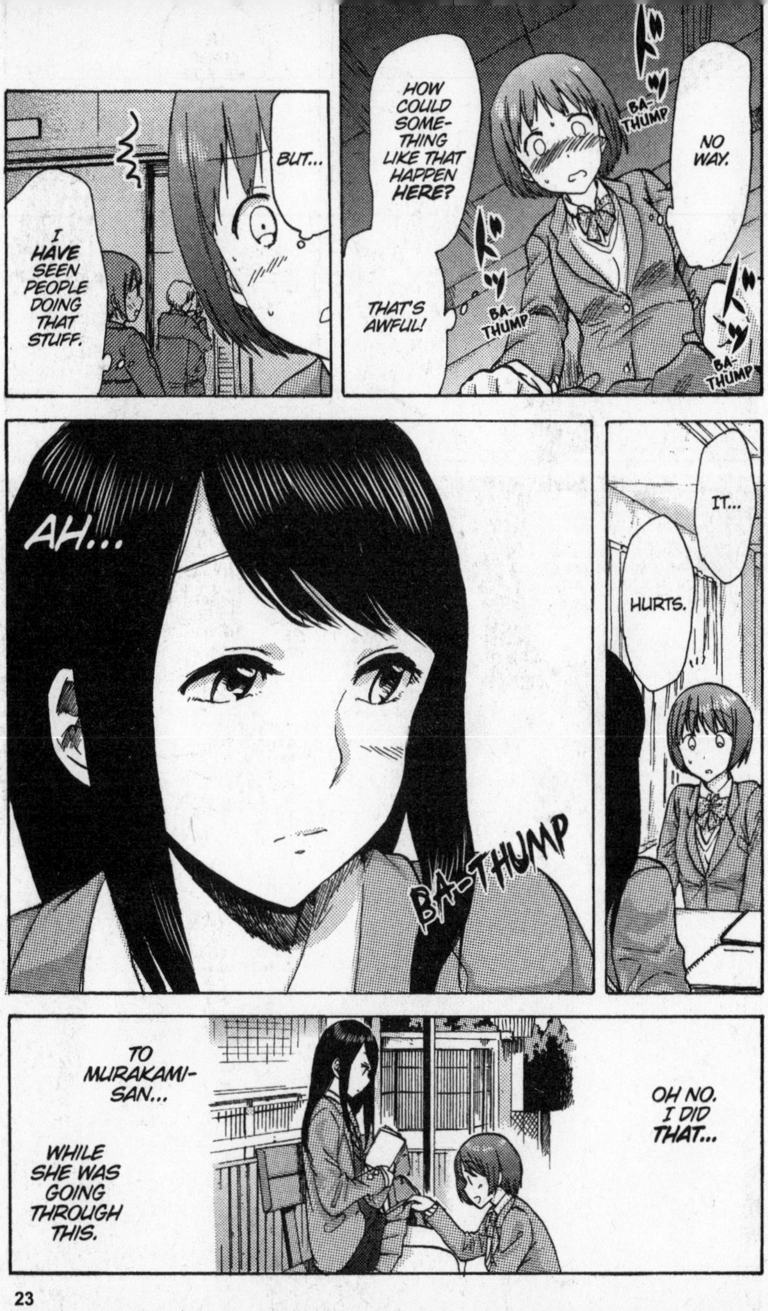
BA-THUMP
NO WAY.
HOW COULD SOMETHING LIKE THAT HAPPEN HERE?
BA-THUMP
BA-THUMP
THAT'S AWFUL!
BUT...
I HAVE SEEN PEOPLE DOING THAT STUFF.
IT...
HURTS.
AH...
BA-THUMP
OH NO. I DID THAT...
TO MURAKAMI-SAN...
WHILE SHE WAS GOING THROUGH THIS.

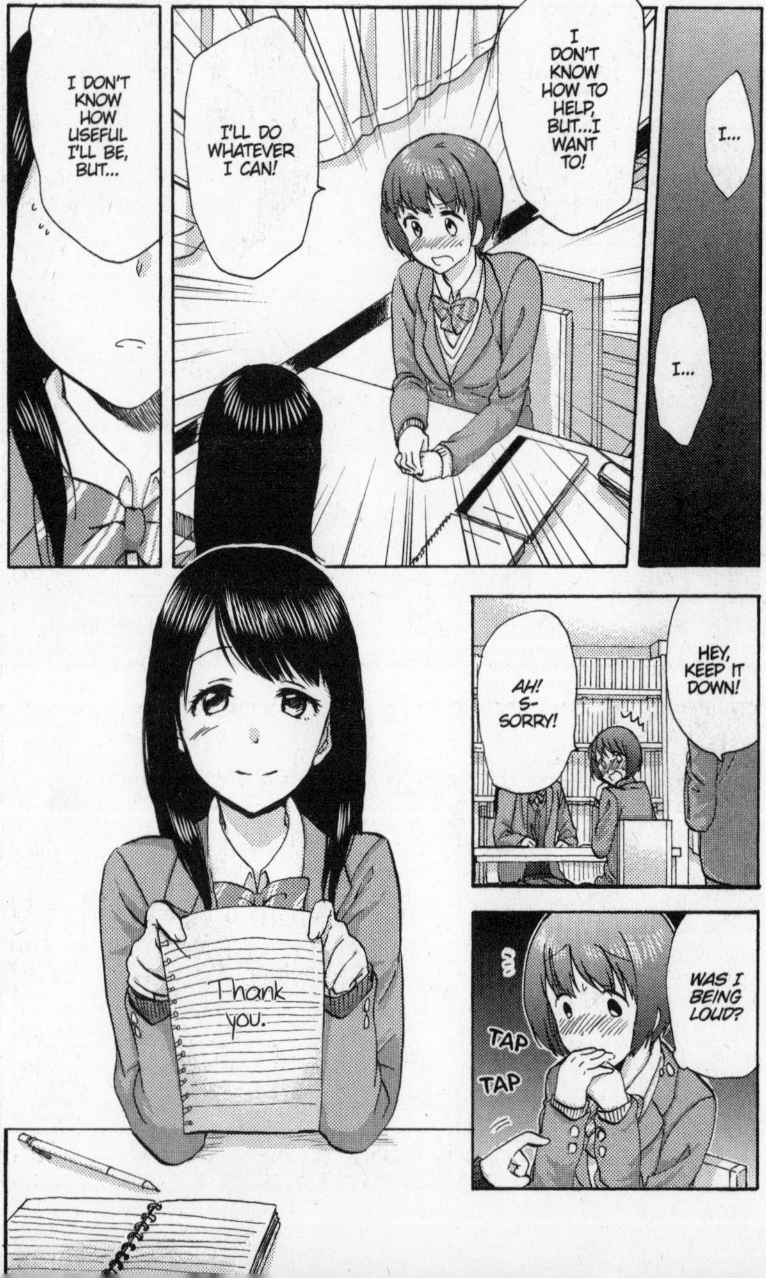
I...
I...
I DON'T KNOW HOW TO HELP, BUT...I WANT TO!
I'LL DO WHATEVER I CAN!
I DON'T KNOW HOW USEFUL I'LL BE, BUT...
HEY, KEEP IT DOWN!
AH! S-SORRY!
WAS I BEING LOUD?
TAP
TAP
Thank you.

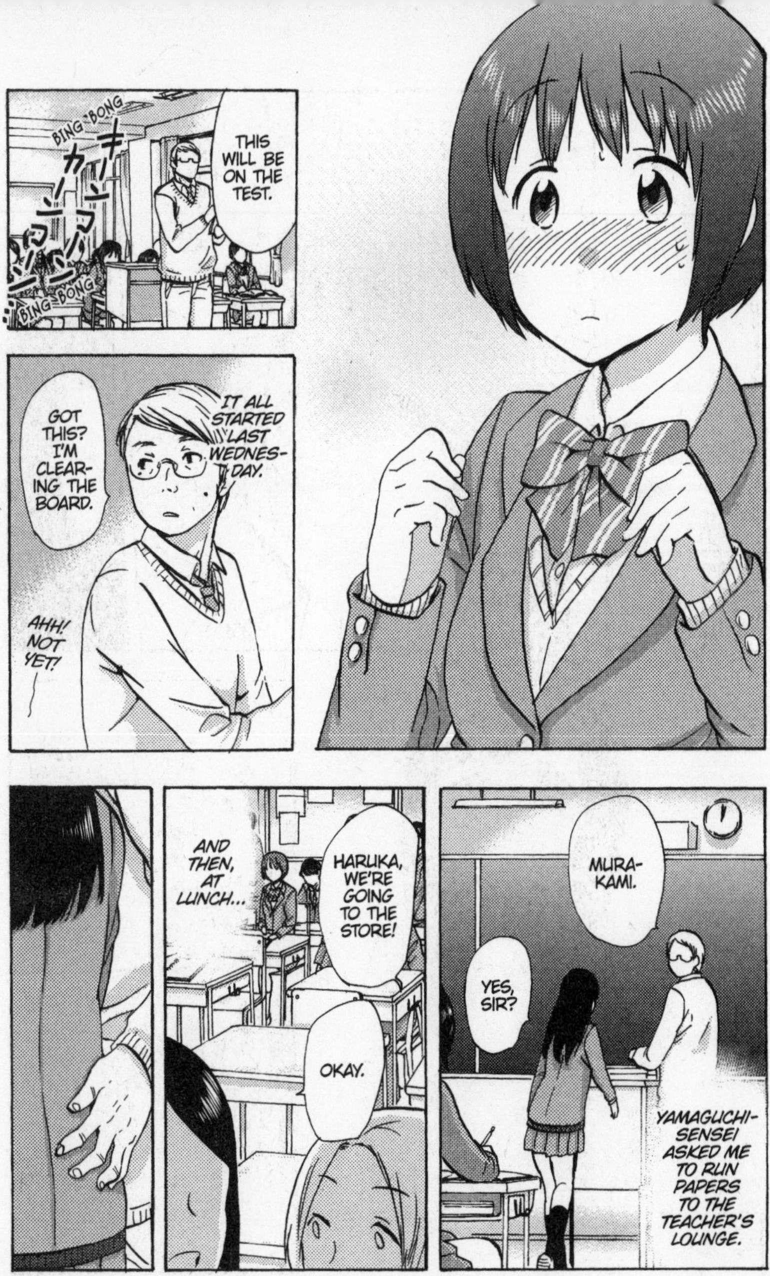
BING BONG
THIS WILL BE ON THE TEST.
BING BONG
IT ALL STARTED LAST WEDNES-DAY.
GOT THIS? I'M CLEAR-ING THE BOARD.
AHH! NOT YET!
MURA-KAMI.
YES, SIR?
YAMAGUCHI-SENSEI ASKED ME TO RUN PAPERS TO THE TEACHER'S LOUNGE.
AND THEN, AT LUNCH...
HARUKA, WE'RE GOING TO THE STORE!
OKAY.

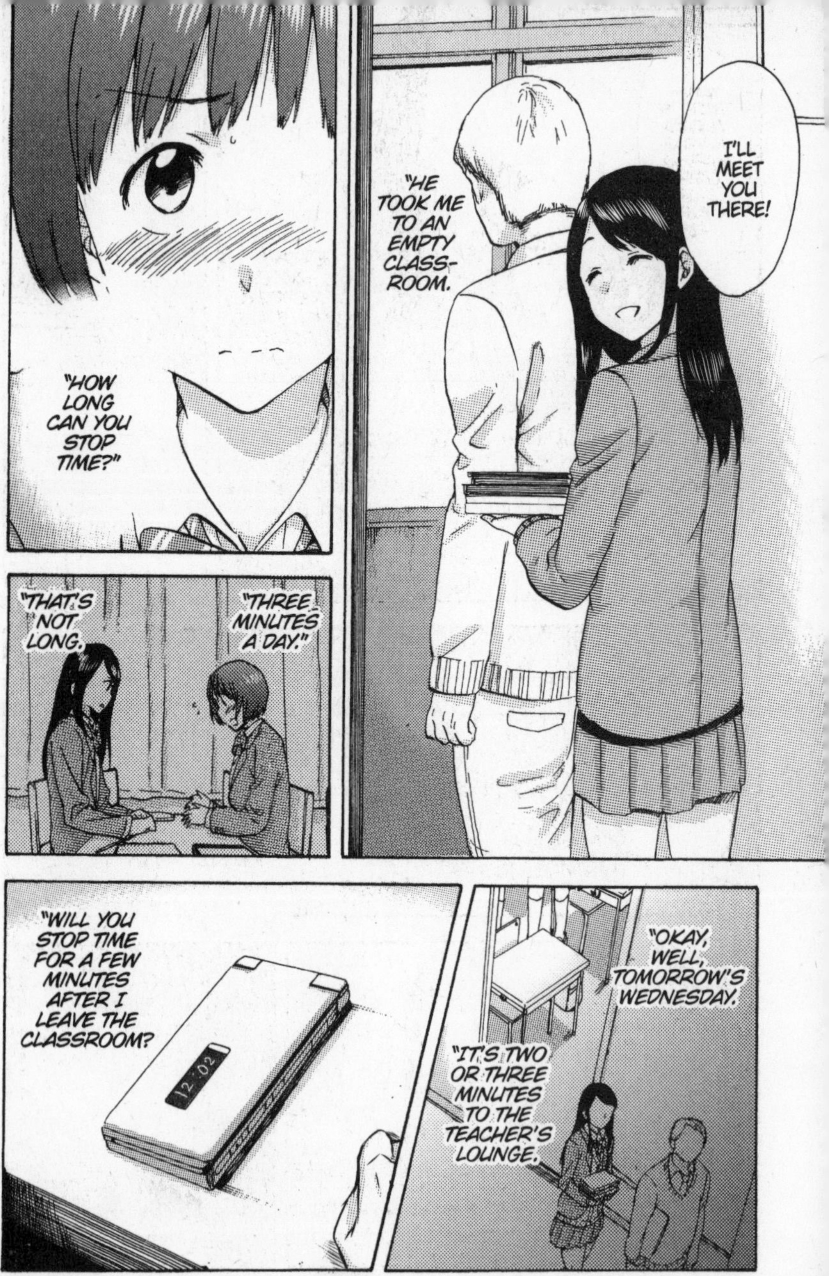
I'LL MEET YOU THERE!
"HE TOOK ME TO AN EMPTY CLASS-ROOM.
"HOW LONG CAN YOU STOP TIME?"
"THREE MINUTES A DAY."
"THAT'S NOT LONG.
"OKAY, WELL, TOMORROW'S WEDNESDAY.
"IT'S TWO OR THREE MINUTES TO THE TEACHER'S LOUNGE.
"WILL YOU STOP TIME FOR A FEW MINUTES AFTER I LEAVE THE CLASSROOM?
12:02

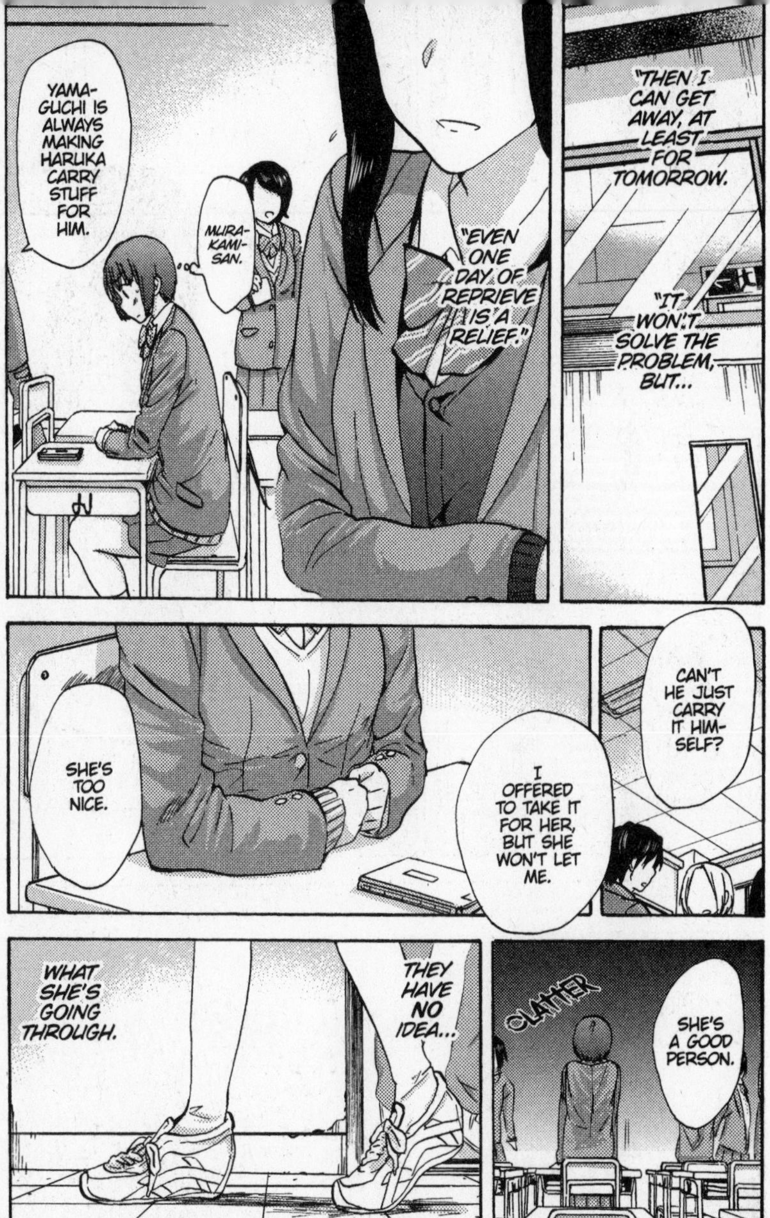
"THEN I CAN GET AWAY, AT LEAST FOR TOMORROW.
"IT WON'T SOLVE THE PROBLEM, BUT...
"EVEN ONE DAY OF REPRIEVE IS A RELIEF."
MURA-KAMI-SAN.
YAMA-GUCHI IS ALWAYS MAKING HARUKA CARRY STUFF FOR HIM.
CAN'T HE JUST CARRY IT HIM-SELF?
I OFFERED TO TAKE IT FOR HER, BUT SHE WON'T LET ME.
SHE'S TOO NICE.
CLATTER
SHE'S A GOOD PERSON.
THEY HAVE NO IDEA...
WHAT SHE'S GOING THROUGH.

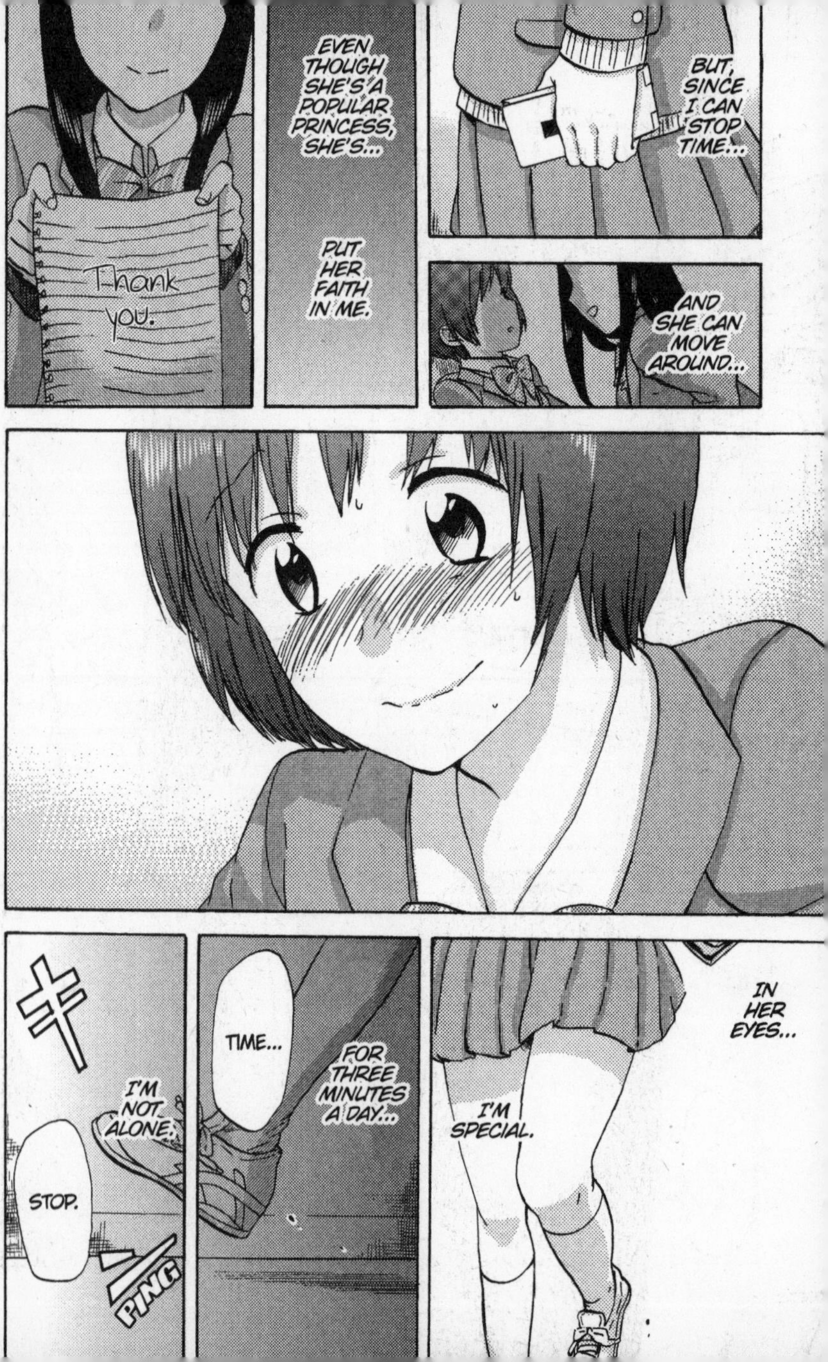

BUT, SINCE I CAN STOP TIME...
AND SHE CAN MOVE AROUND...
EVEN THOUGH SHE'S A POPULAR PRINCESS, SHE'S...
PUT HER FAITH IN ME.
Thank you.
IN HER EYES...
I'M SPECIAL.
TIME...
FOR THREE MINUTES A DAY...
キ
I'M NOT ALONE.
STOP.
PING

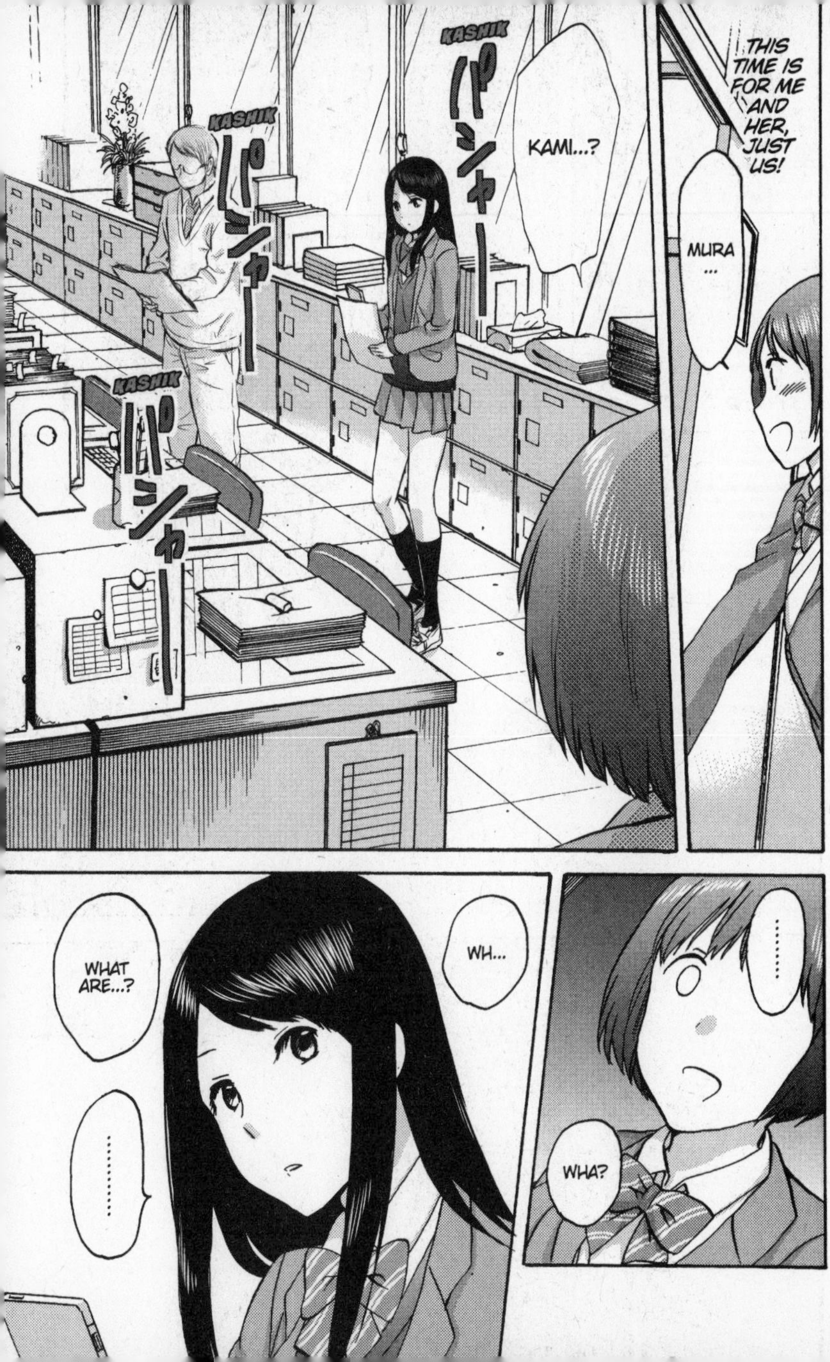
THIS TIME IS FOR ME AND HER, JUST US!
MURA ...
KAMI...?
KASHIK
パシャー
KASHIK
パシャー
KASHIK
パシャー
......
WHA?
WH...
WHAT ARE...?
......

PICTURES ...?

YOU WANT TO TAKE PICTURES OF THESE, TOO?

HUH? WHAT?

OH, YOU FOLLOWED.

· · · · ·
!

World History

I. For section
I. Humanity
and in PB[?]
in the de[?]
was cons[?]
Emperor Qin[?]
nomads were dispatche[?]
to attack the nomad[?]
With the arrival of th[?]
[?]nasty came-

IT'S OUR MID-TERMS.

WHY NOT?

YOU ASKED ME TO PROTECT YOU FROM HARASSMENT...

THAT'S WHY I--

OH, THAT?

YOU CAN'T DO THAT!

GRAB

WHAT ARE YOU DOING?!

30

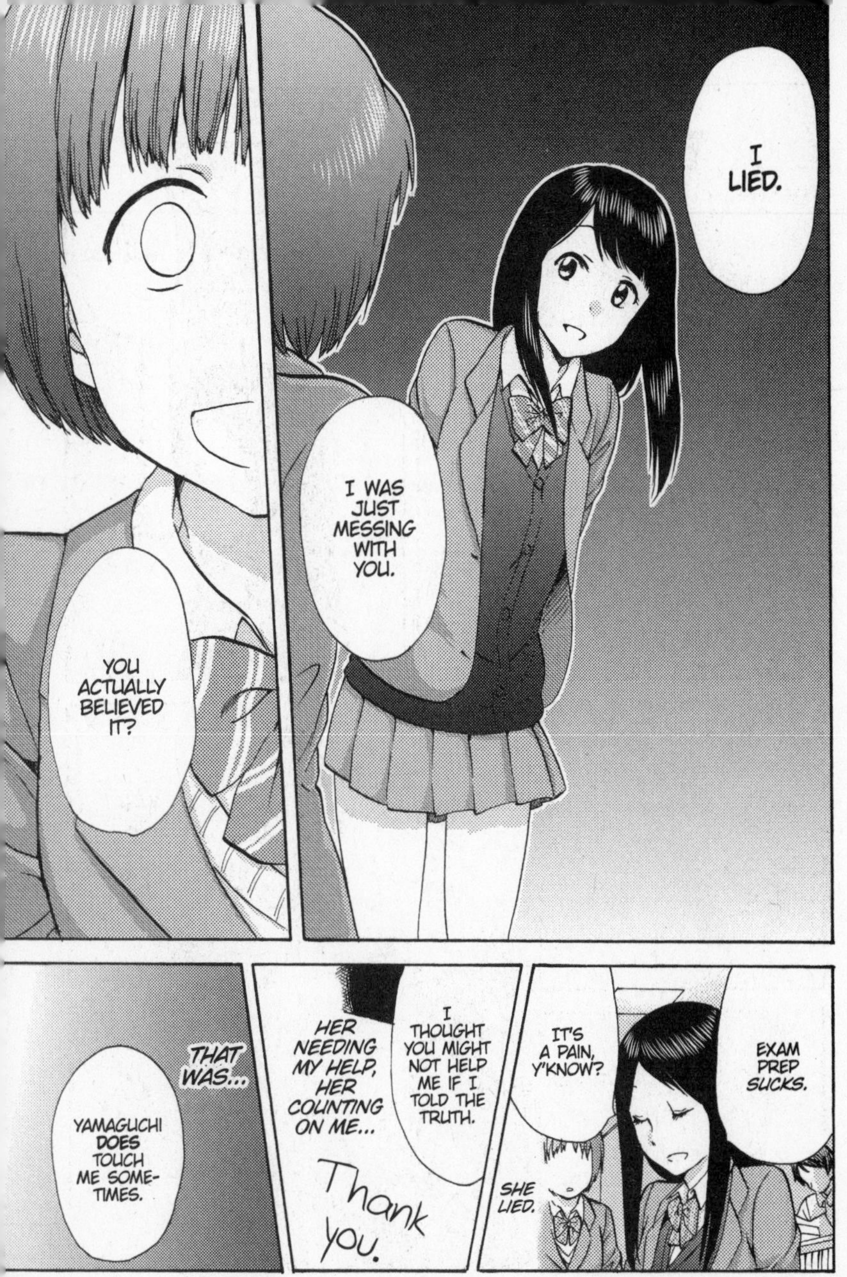
I LIED.
I WAS JUST MESSING WITH YOU.
YOU ACTUALLY BELIEVED IT?
EXAM PREP SUCKS.
IT'S A PAIN, Y'KNOW?
SHE LIED.
I THOUGHT YOU MIGHT NOT HELP ME IF I TOLD THE TRUTH.
HER NEEDING MY HELP, HER COUNTING ON ME...
Thank you.
THAT WAS...
YAMAGUCHI DOES TOUCH ME SOME-TIMES.

PLIP

PLIP

BUT IT DOESN'T...

MAKE ME STOP TIME FOR THIS?

WHY WOULD YOU...

WHY AM I SO UPSET?

IT'S ...

CHEAT... OR COPY...

WHAT'S WITH ME?

DON'T...

HM?

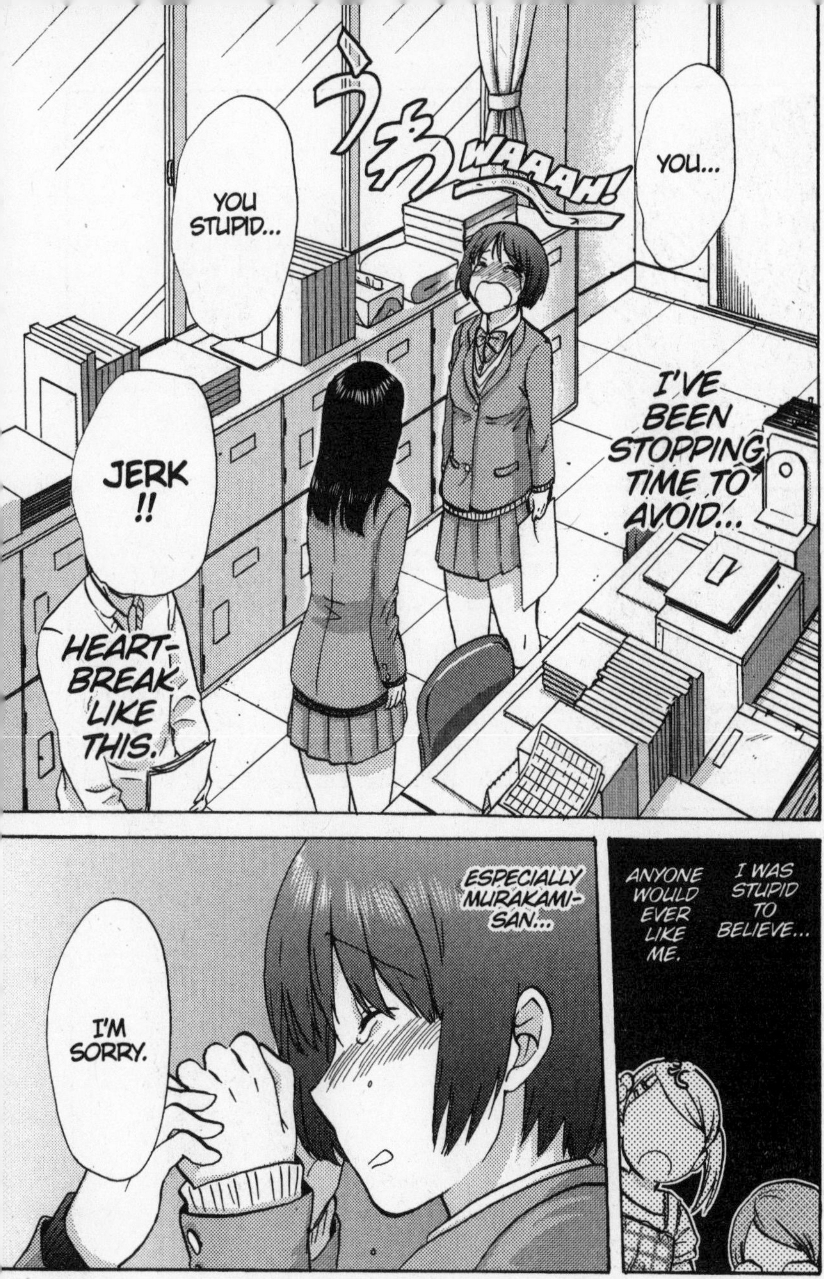
YOU...
WAAAAH!
YOU STUPID...
I'VE BEEN STOPPING TIME TO AVOID...
JERK!!
HEART-BREAK LIKE THIS.
I WAS STUPID TO BELIEVE...
ANYONE WOULD EVER LIKE ME.
ESPECIALLY MURAKAMI-SAN...
I'M SORRY.

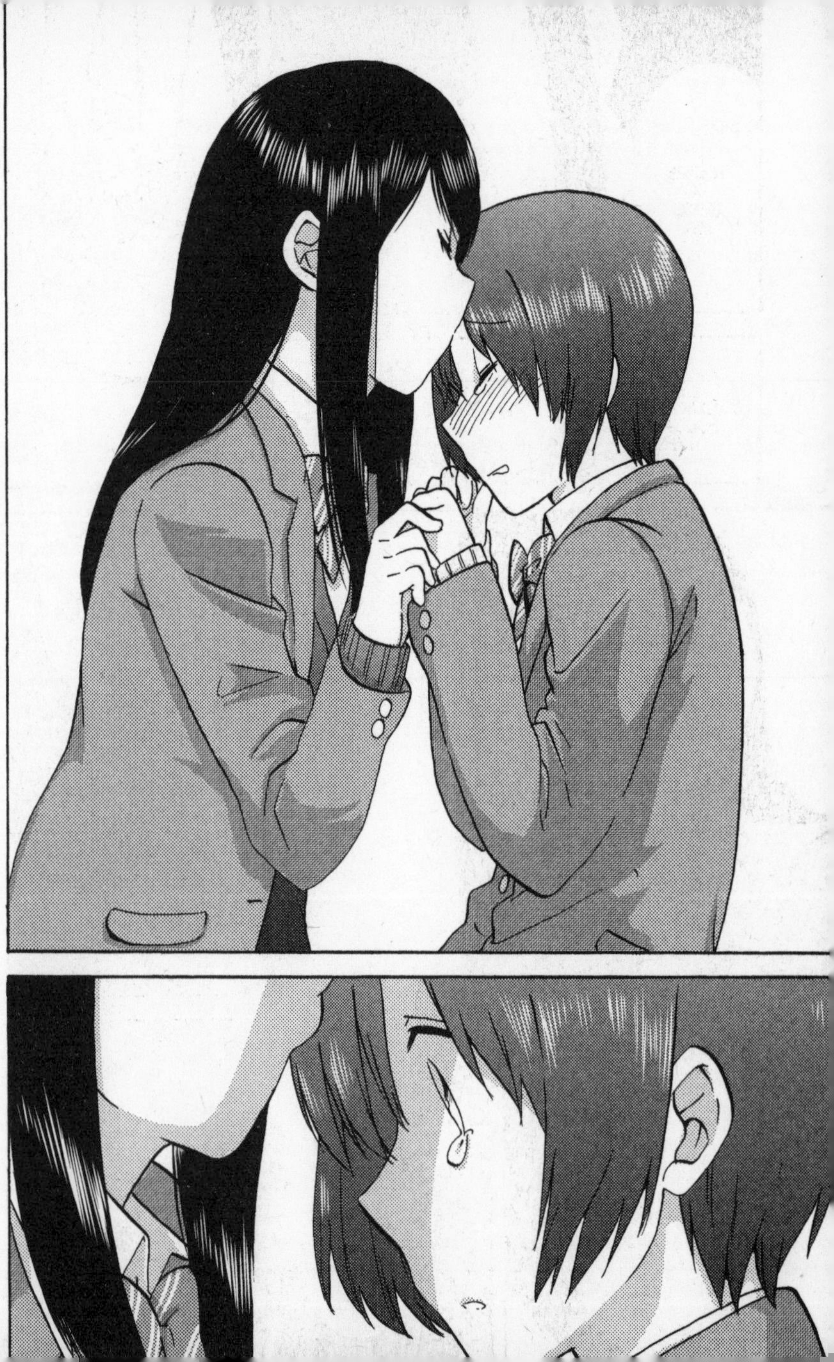

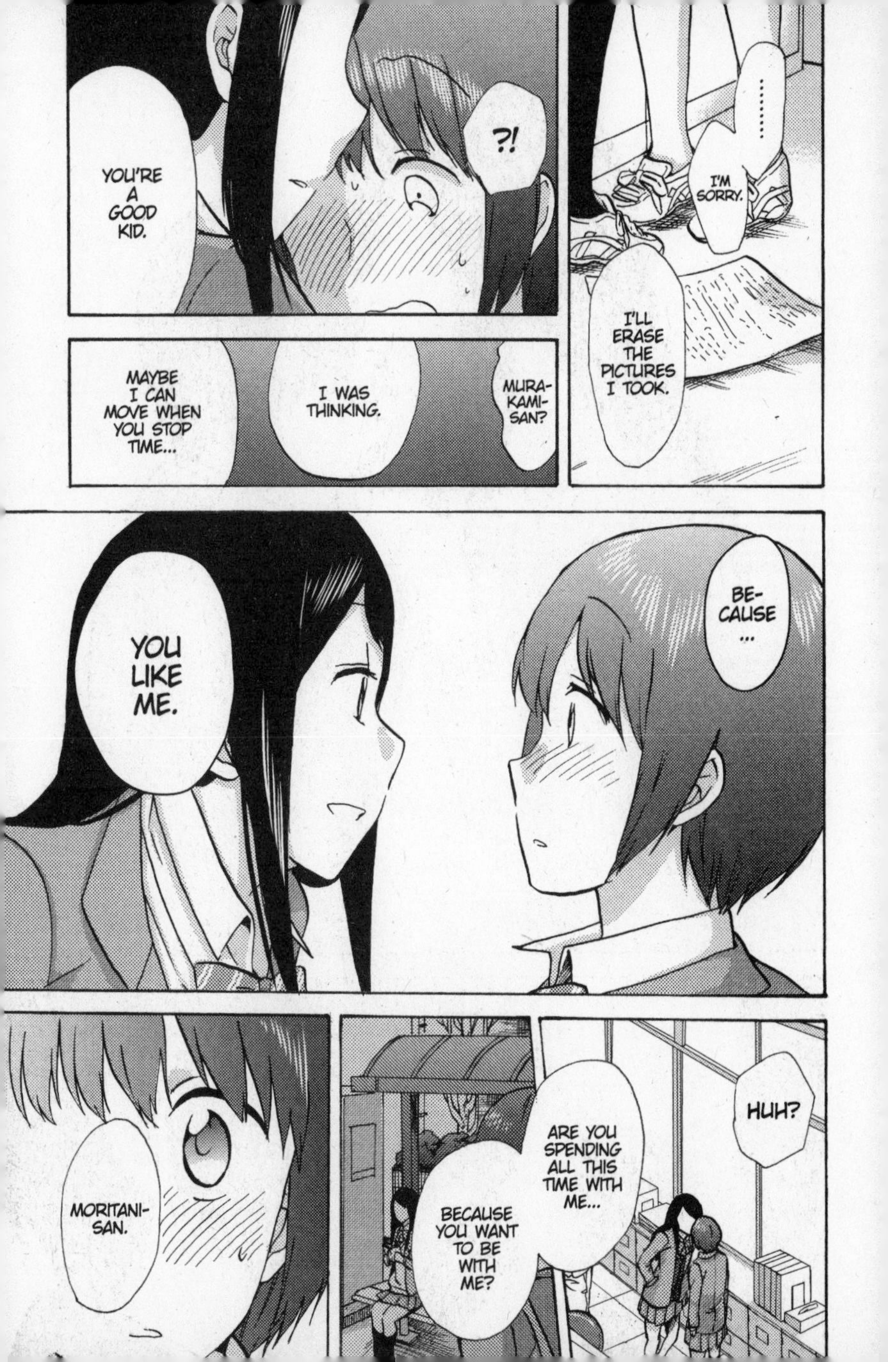
......
I'M SORRY.
I'LL ERASE THE PICTURES I TOOK.
?!
YOU'RE A GOOD KID.
MURA-KAMI-SAN?
I WAS THINKING.
MAYBE I CAN MOVE WHEN YOU STOP TIME...
BE-CAUSE ...
YOU LIKE ME.
HUH?
ARE YOU SPENDING ALL THIS TIME WITH ME...
BECAUSE YOU WANT TO BE WITH ME?
MORITANI-SAN.

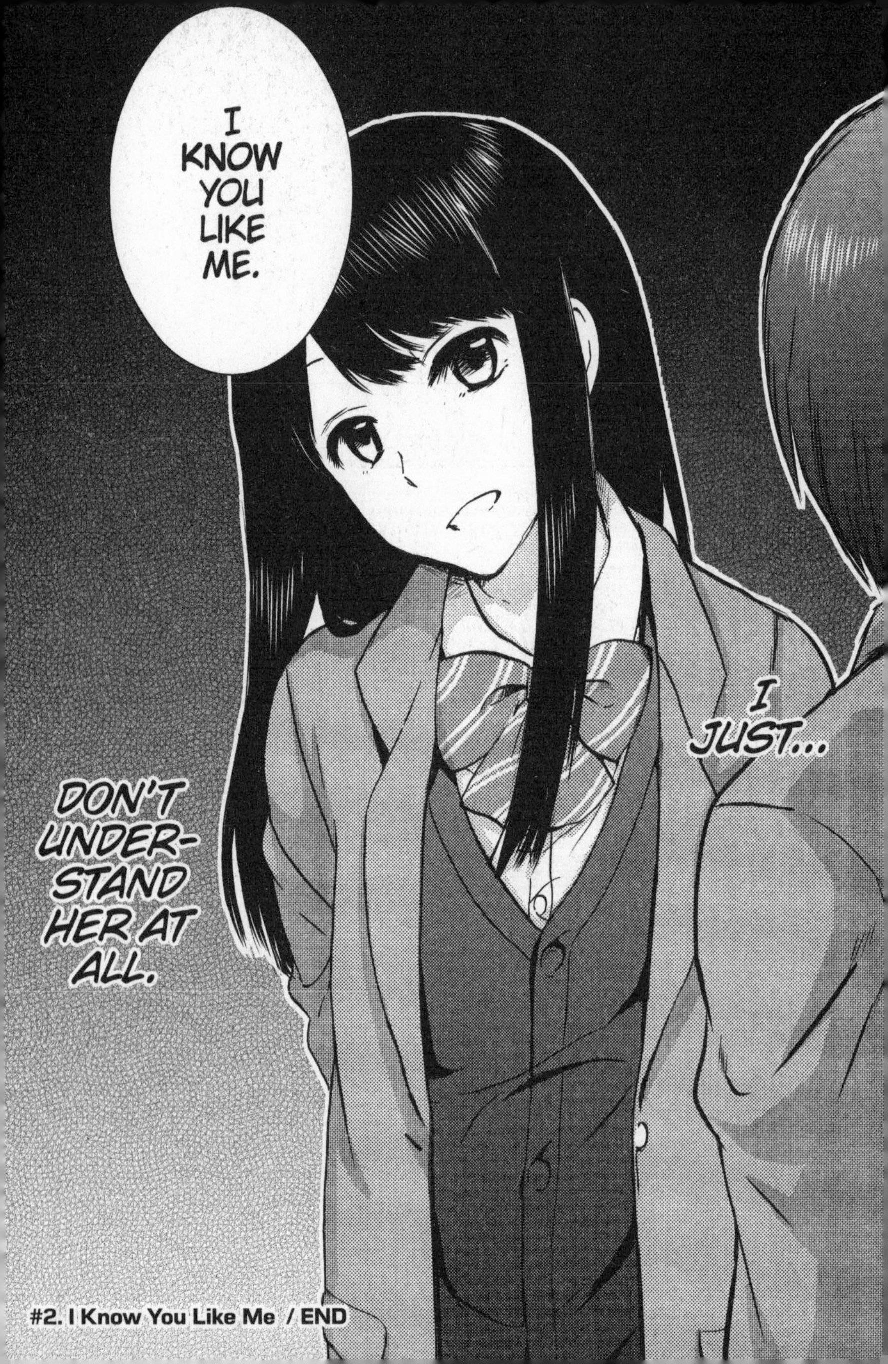
I KNOW YOU LIKE ME.
I JUST...
DON'T UNDER-STAND HER AT ALL.

#2. I Know You Like Me / END

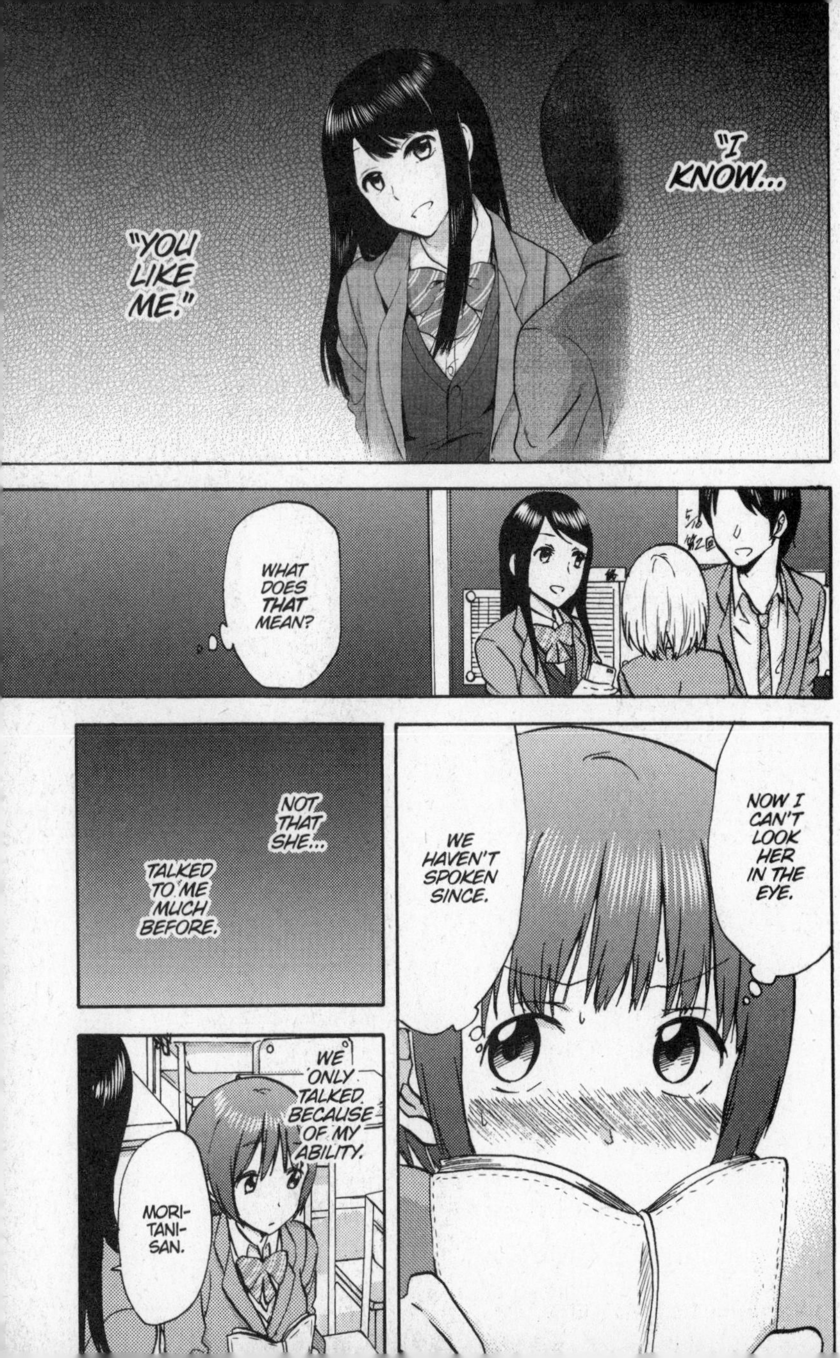
"I KNOW...
"YOU LIKE ME."
WHAT DOES THAT MEAN?
NOW I CAN'T LOOK HER IN THE EYE.
WE HAVEN'T SPOKEN SINCE.
NOT THAT SHE...
TALKED TO ME MUCH BEFORE.
WE ONLY TALKED BECAUSE OF MY ABILITY.
MORI-TANI-SAN.

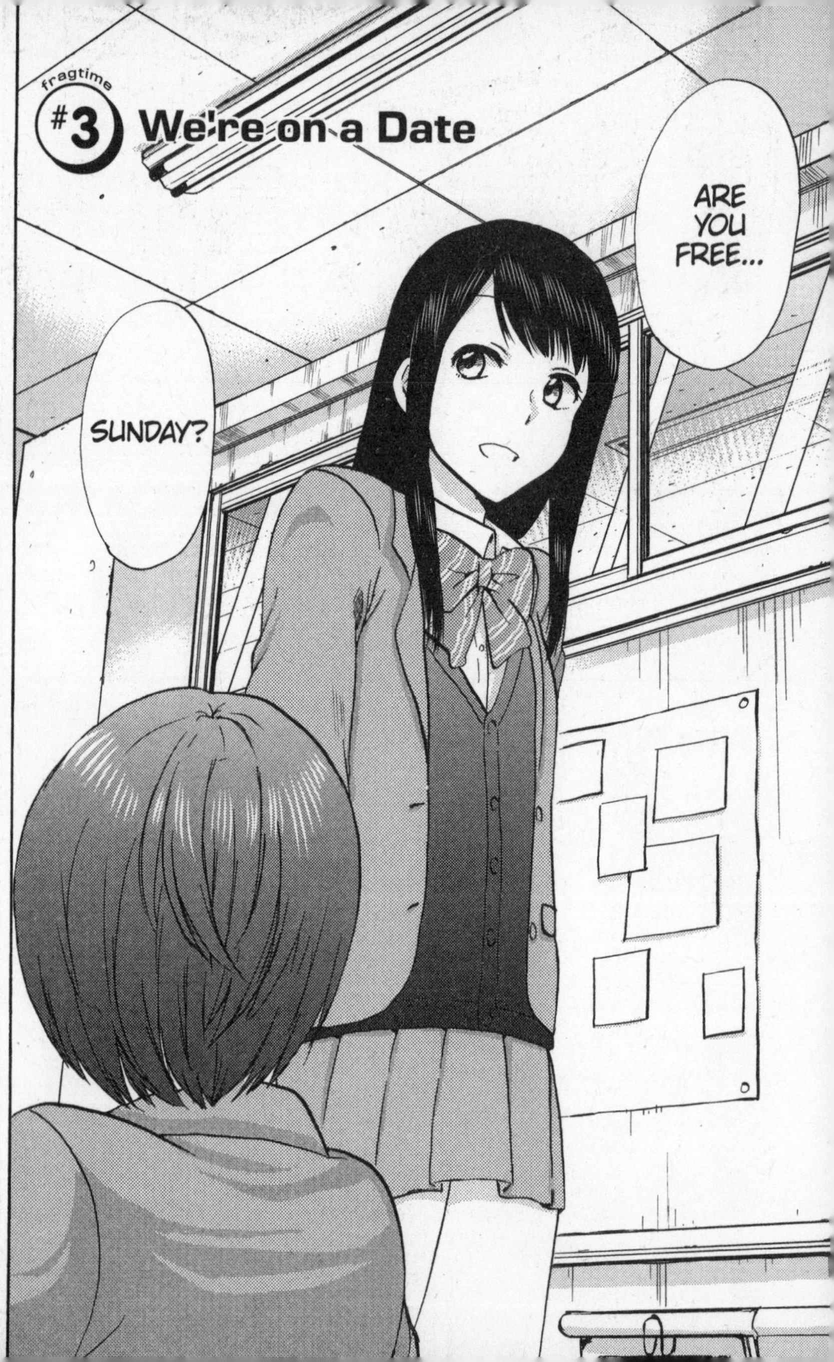
fragtime
#3 We're on a Date
ARE YOU FREE...
SUNDAY?

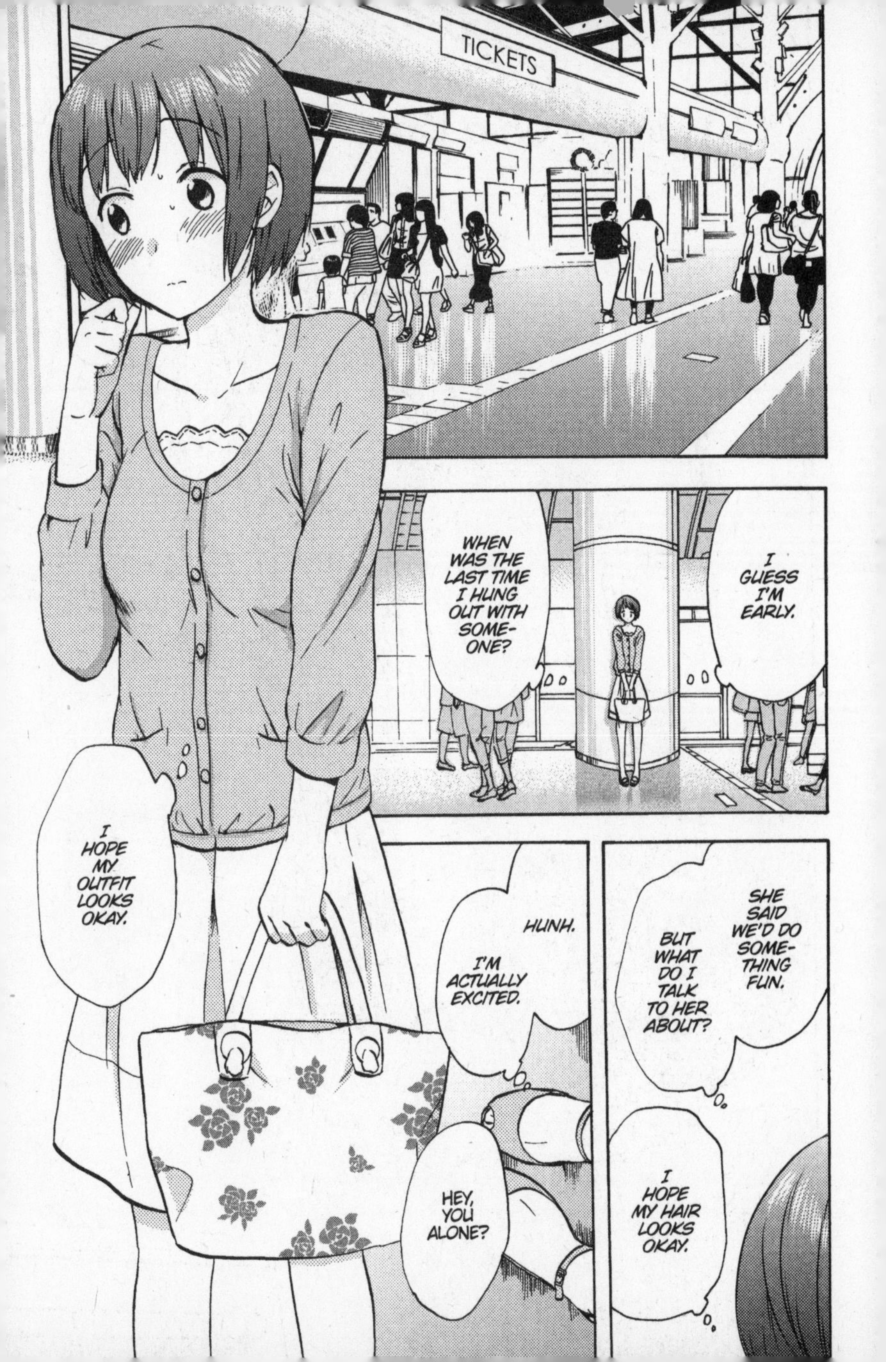
TICKETS
I GUESS I'M EARLY.
WHEN WAS THE LAST TIME I HUNG OUT WITH SOME-ONE?
SHE SAID WE'D DO SOME-THING FUN.
BUT WHAT DO I TALK TO HER ABOUT?
I HOPE MY HAIR LOOKS OKAY.
HUNH.
I'M ACTUALLY EXCITED.
HEY, YOU ALONE?
I HOPE MY OUTFIT LOOKS OKAY.

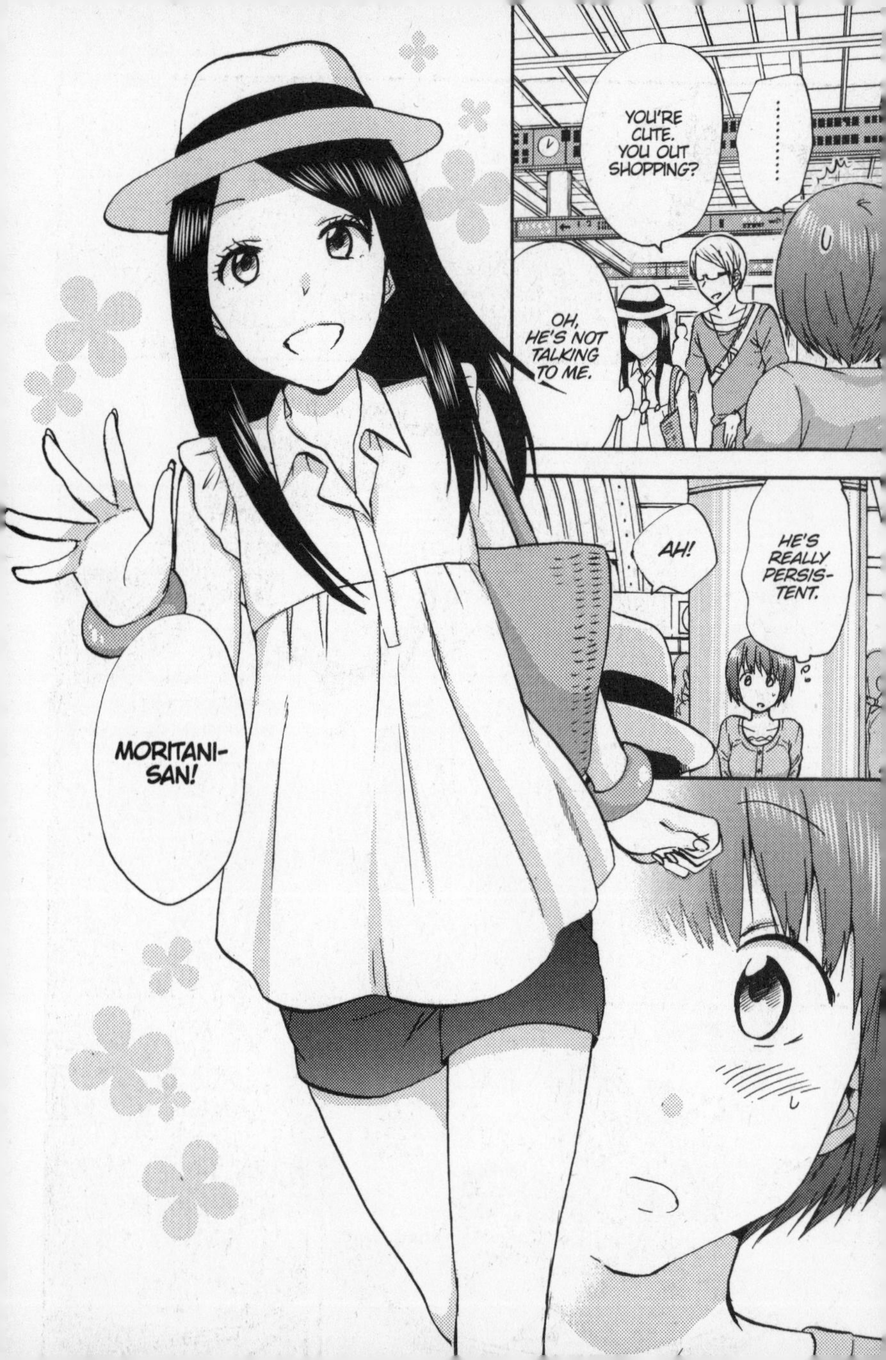

......
YOU'RE CUTE. YOU OUT SHOPPING?
OH, HE'S NOT TALKING TO ME.
HE'S REALLY PERSIS-TENT.
AH!
MORITANI-SAN!

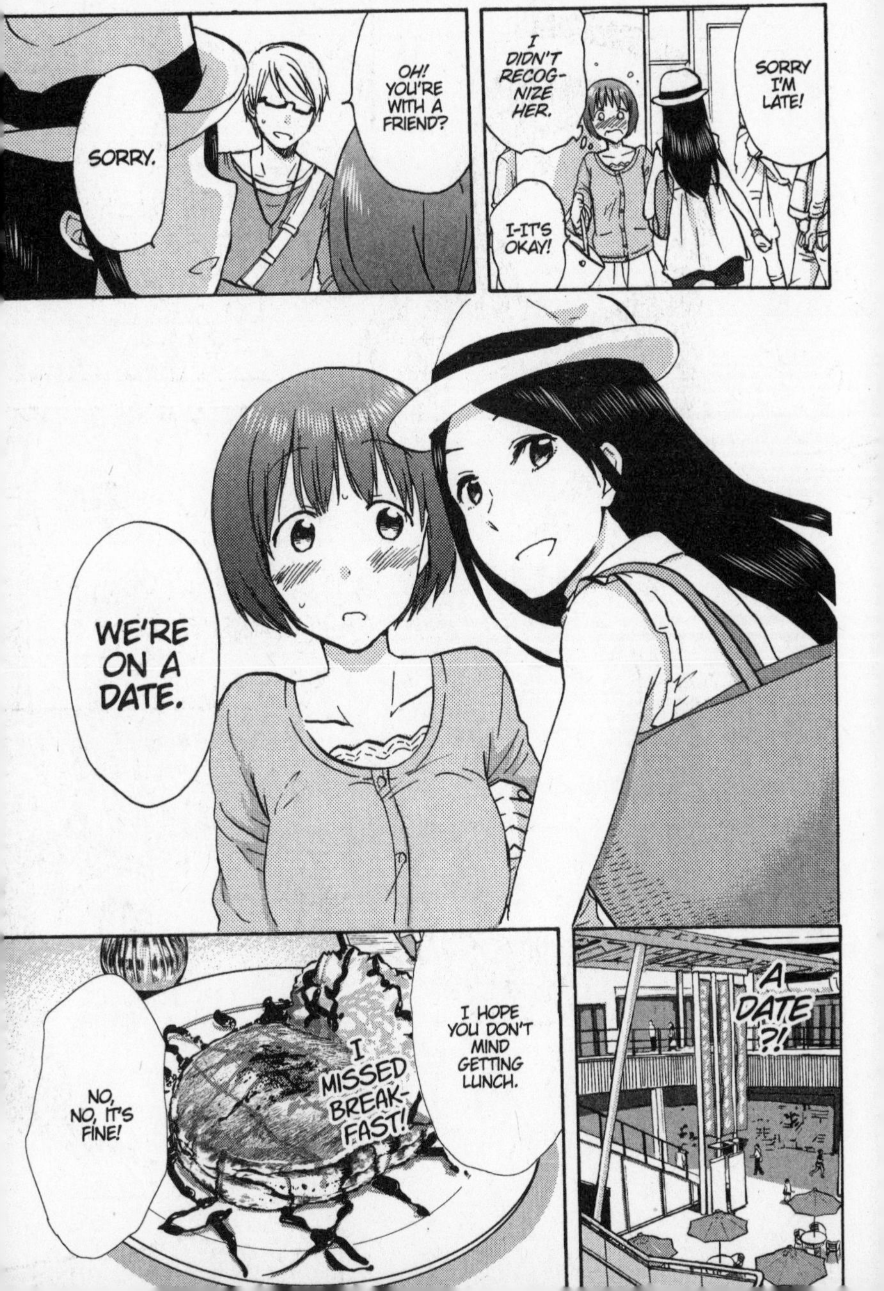
SORRY I'M LATE!
I DIDN'T RECOG-NIZE HER.
I-IT'S OKAY!
OH! YOU'RE WITH A FRIEND?
SORRY.
WE'RE ON A DATE.
A DATE ?!
I HOPE YOU DON'T MIND GETTING LUNCH.
I MISSED BREAK-FAST!
NO, NO, IT'S FINE!

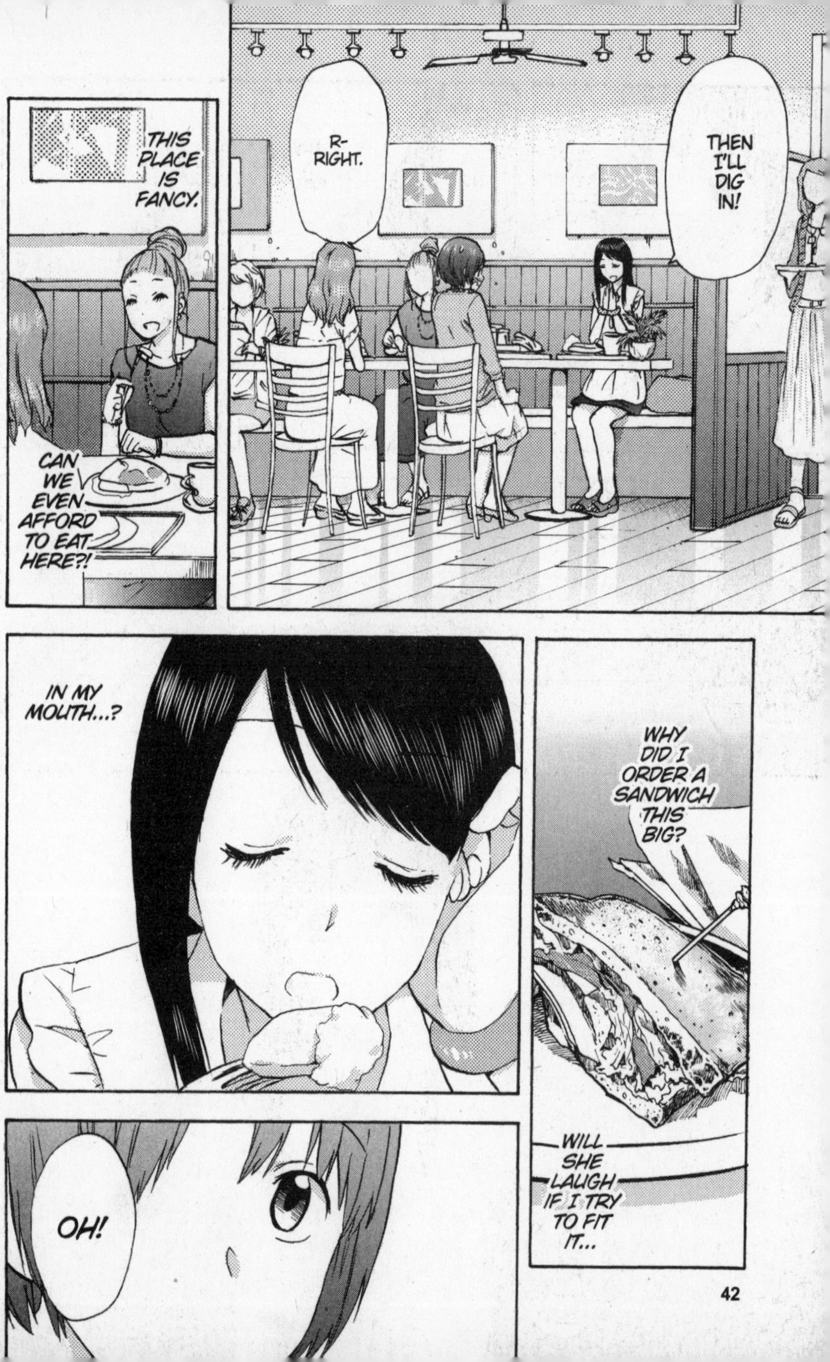
THEN I'LL DIG IN!
R-RIGHT.
THIS PLACE IS FANCY.
CAN WE EVEN AFFORD TO EAT HERE?!
WHY DID I ORDER A SANDWICH THIS BIG?
WILL SHE LAUGH IF I TRY TO FIT IT...
IN MY MOUTH...?
OH!

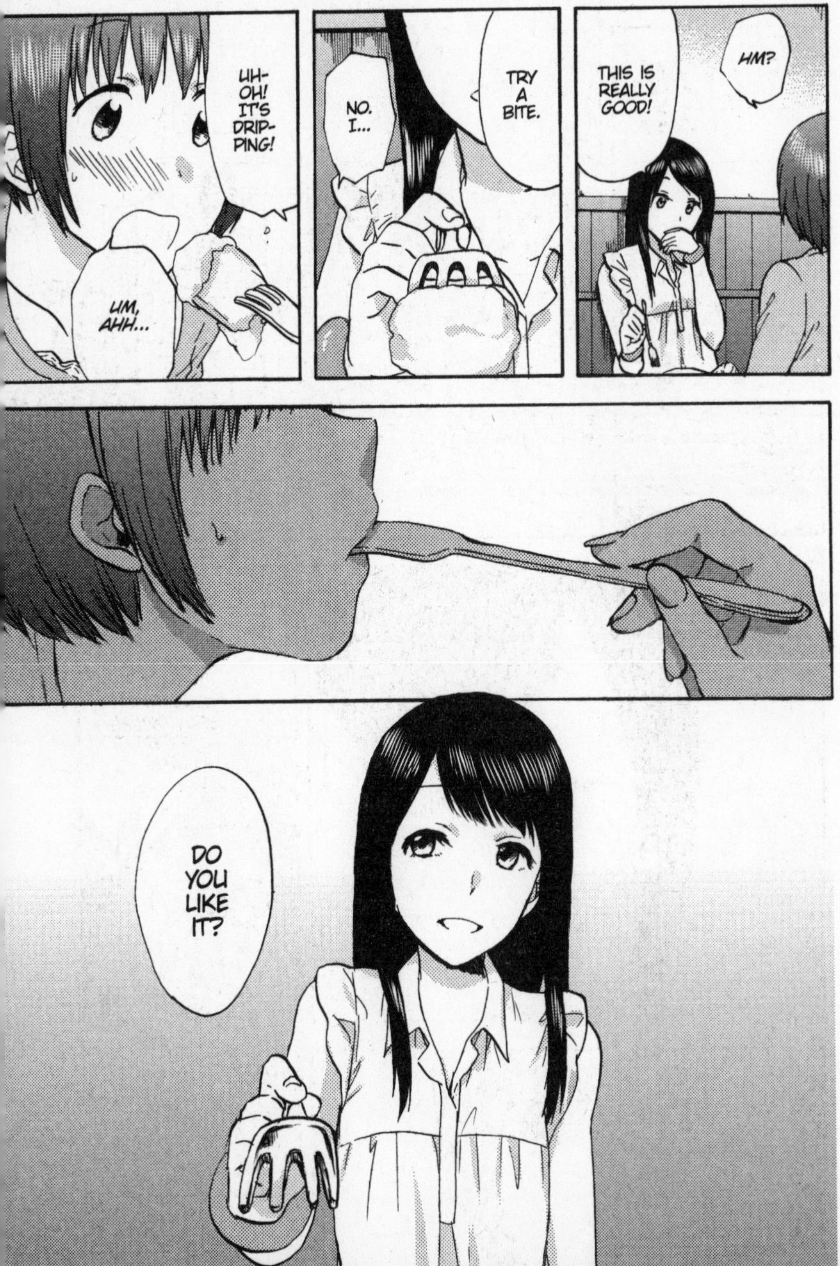
HM?
THIS IS REALLY GOOD!
TRY A BITE.
NO. I...
UH-OH! IT'S DRIP-PING!
UM, AHH...
DO YOU LIKE IT?

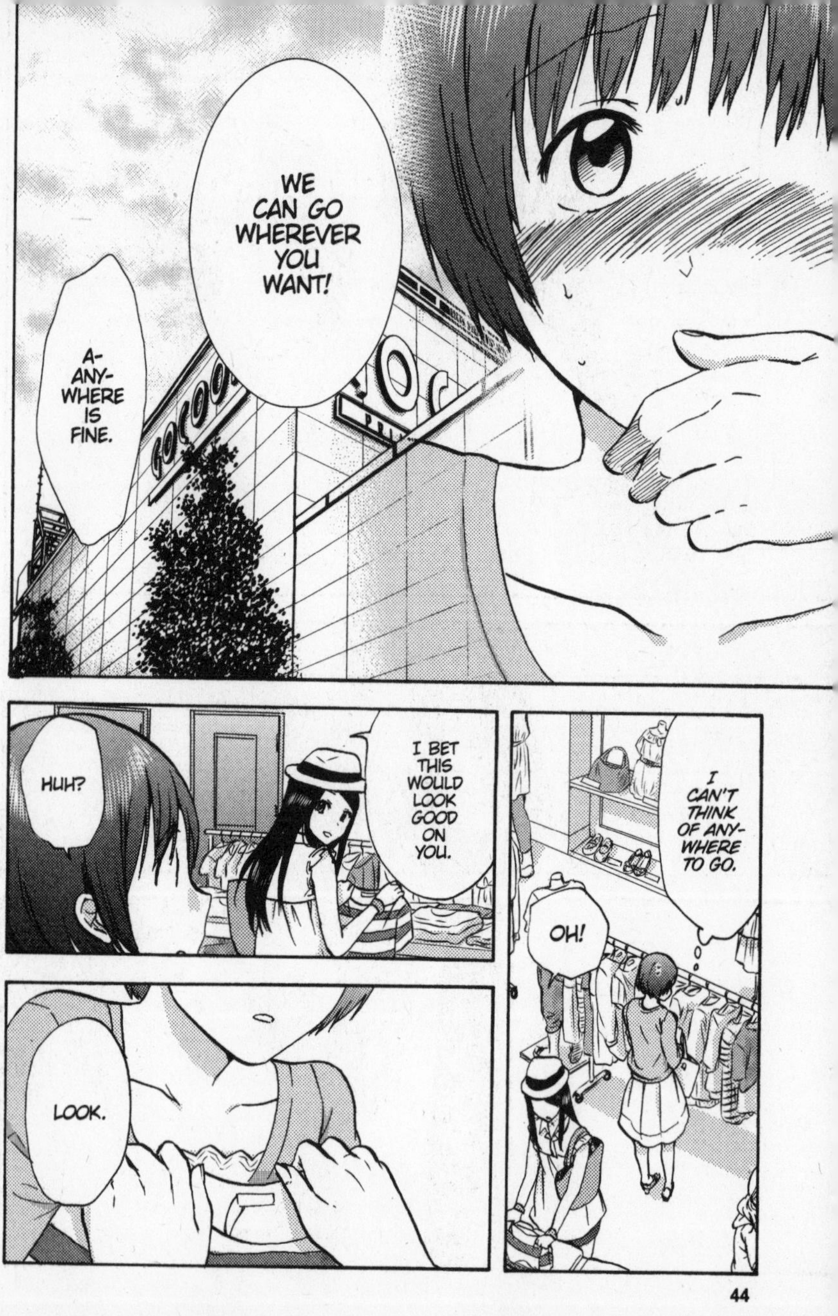
WE CAN GO WHEREVER YOU WANT!
A- ANY-WHERE IS FINE.
I CAN'T THINK OF ANY-WHERE TO GO.
OH!
I BET THIS WOULD LOOK GOOD ON YOU.
HUH?
LOOK.

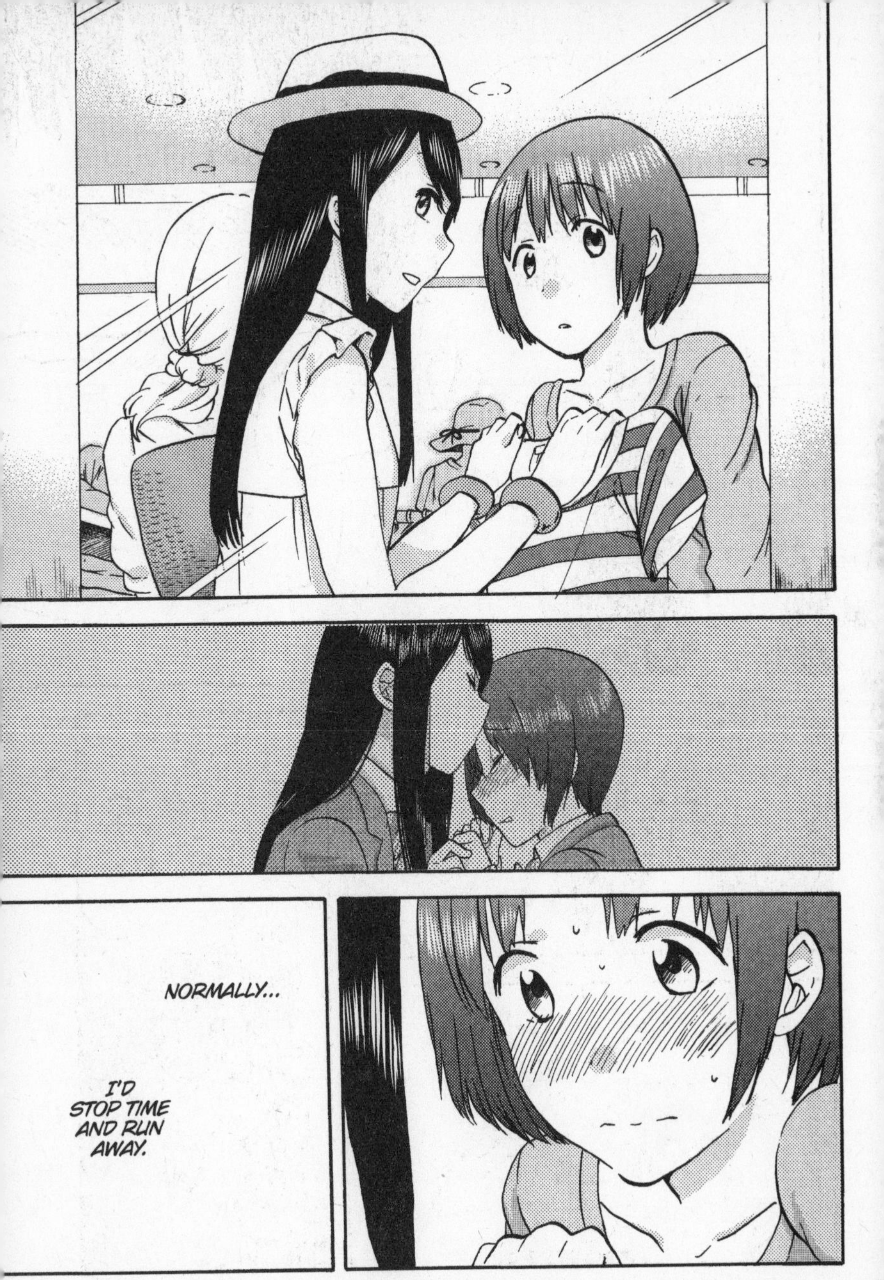
NORMALLY...
I'D STOP TIME AND RUN AWAY.

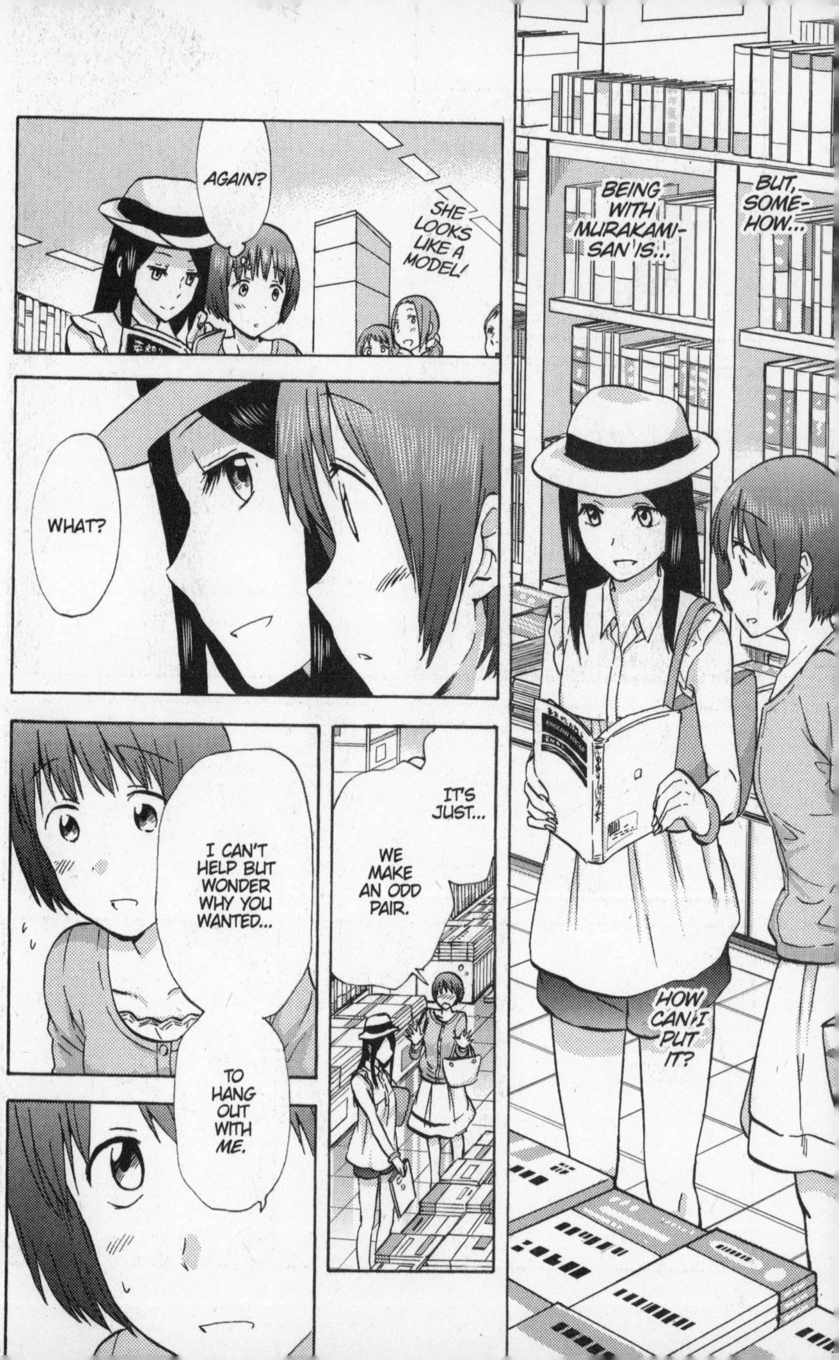
BUT, SOMEHOW...
BEING WITH MURAKAMI-SAN IS...
HOW CAN I PUT IT?
SHE LOOKS LIKE A MODEL!
AGAIN?
WHAT?
IT'S JUST...
WE MAKE AN ODD PAIR.
I CAN'T HELP BUT WONDER WHY YOU WANTED...
TO HANG OUT WITH ME.

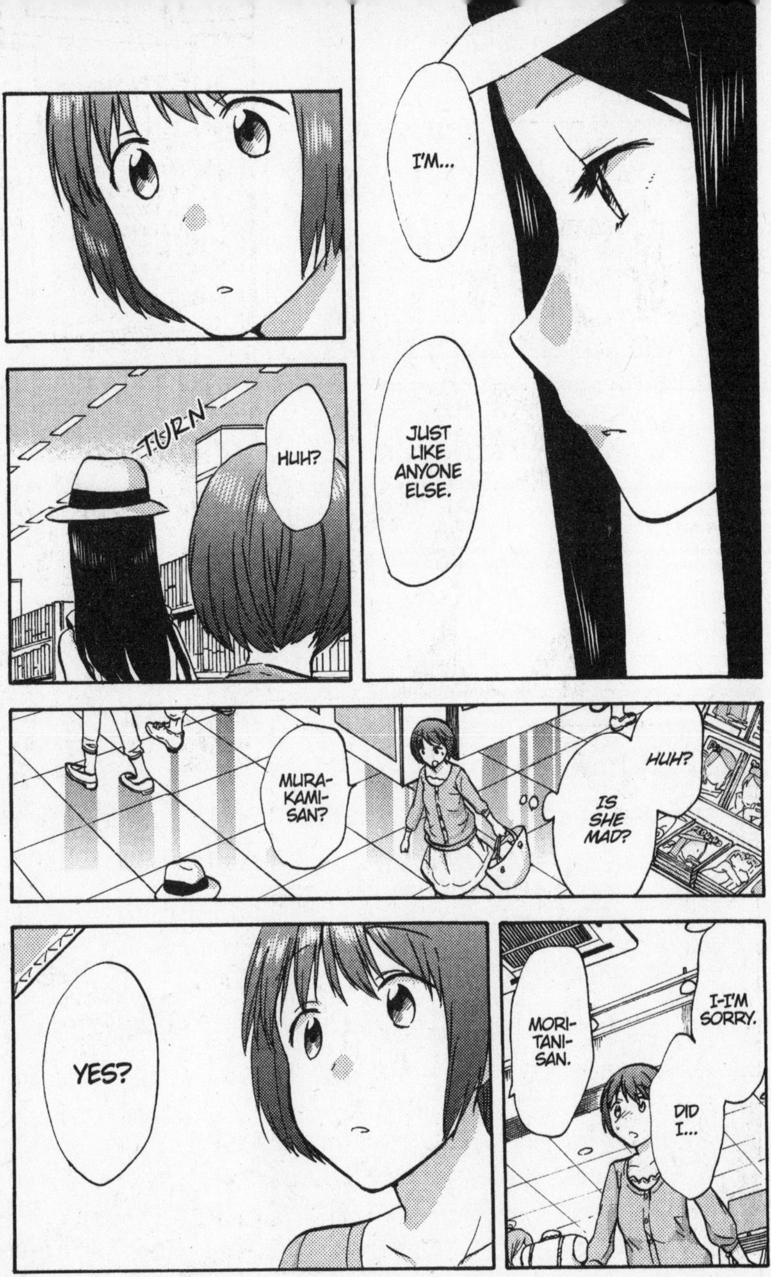
I'M...
JUST LIKE ANYONE ELSE.
TURN
HUH?
HUH?
IS SHE MAD?
MURA-KAMI-SAN?
I-I'M SORRY.
MORI-TANI-SAN.
DID I...
YES?

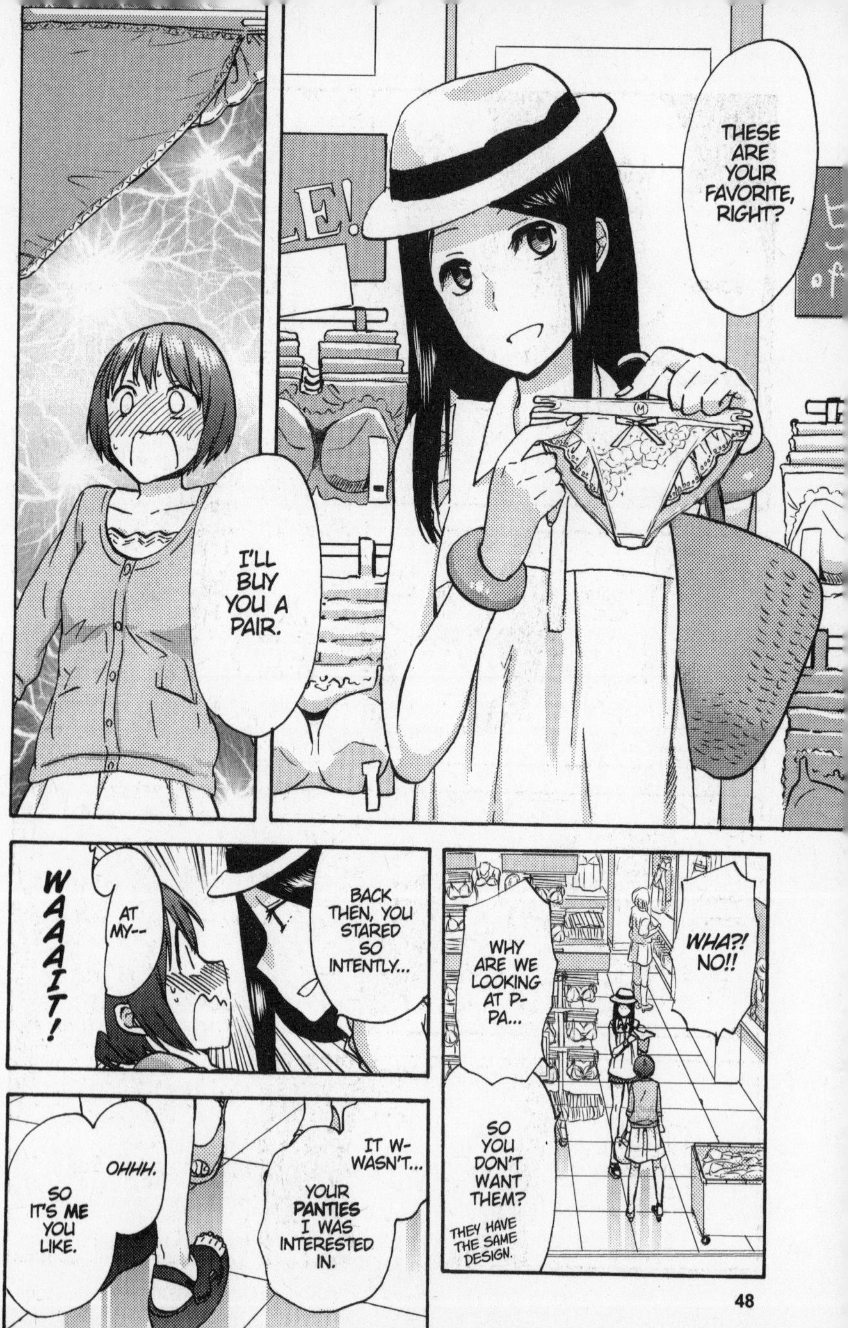
THESE ARE YOUR FAVORITE, RIGHT?
I'LL BUY YOU A PAIR.
WHA?! NO!!
WHY ARE WE LOOKING AT P-PA...
SO YOU DON'T WANT THEM?
THEY HAVE THE SAME DESIGN.
BACK THEN, YOU STARED SO INTENTLY...
AT MY--
WAAAIT!
IT W-WASN'T... YOUR PANTIES I WAS INTERESTED IN.
OHHH.
SO IT'S ME YOU LIKE.

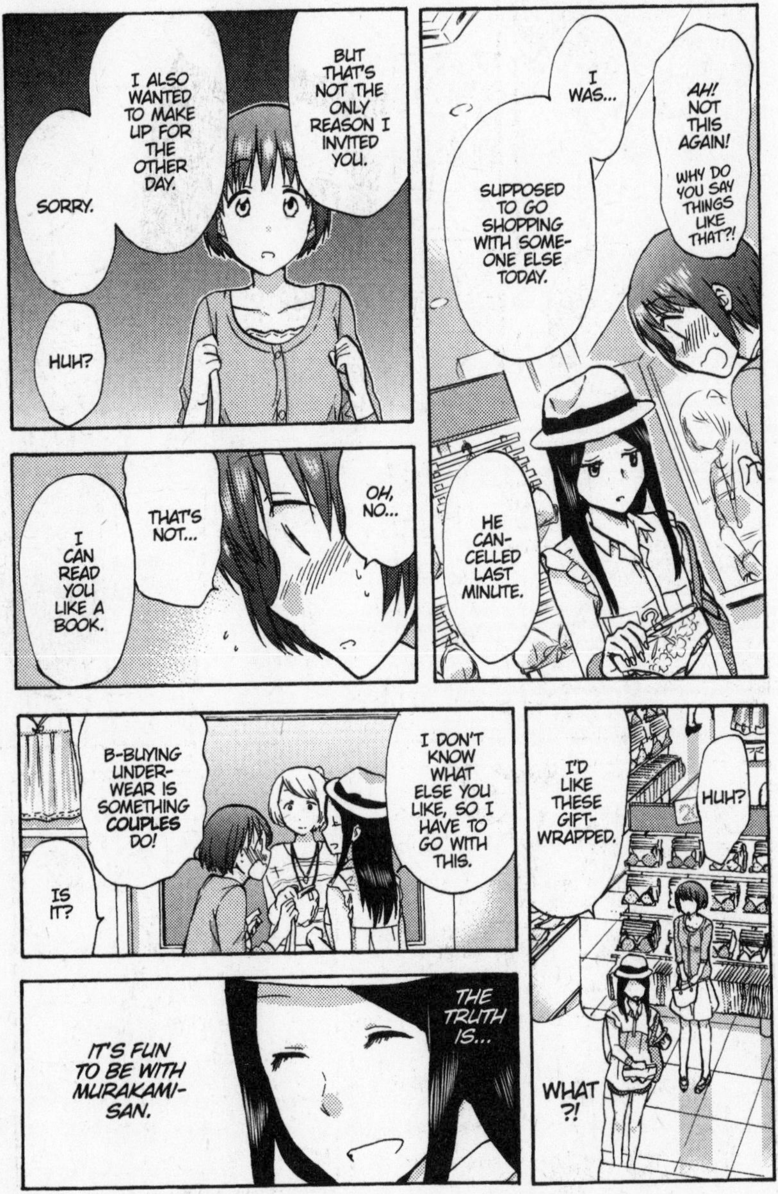
AH! NOT THIS AGAIN!
WHY DO YOU SAY THINGS LIKE THAT?!
I WAS...
SUPPOSED TO GO SHOPPING WITH SOME-ONE ELSE TODAY.
HE CAN-CELLED LAST MINUTE.
BUT THAT'S NOT THE ONLY REASON I INVITED YOU.
I ALSO WANTED TO MAKE UP FOR THE OTHER DAY.
SORRY.
HUH?
OH, NO...
THAT'S NOT...
I CAN READ YOU LIKE A BOOK.
HUH?
I'D LIKE THESE GIFT-WRAPPED.
WHAT ?!
I DON'T KNOW WHAT ELSE YOU LIKE, SO I HAVE TO GO WITH THIS.
B-BUYING UNDER-WEAR IS SOMETHING COUPLES DO!
IS IT?
THE TRUTH IS...
IT'S FUN TO BE WITH MURAKAMI-SAN.

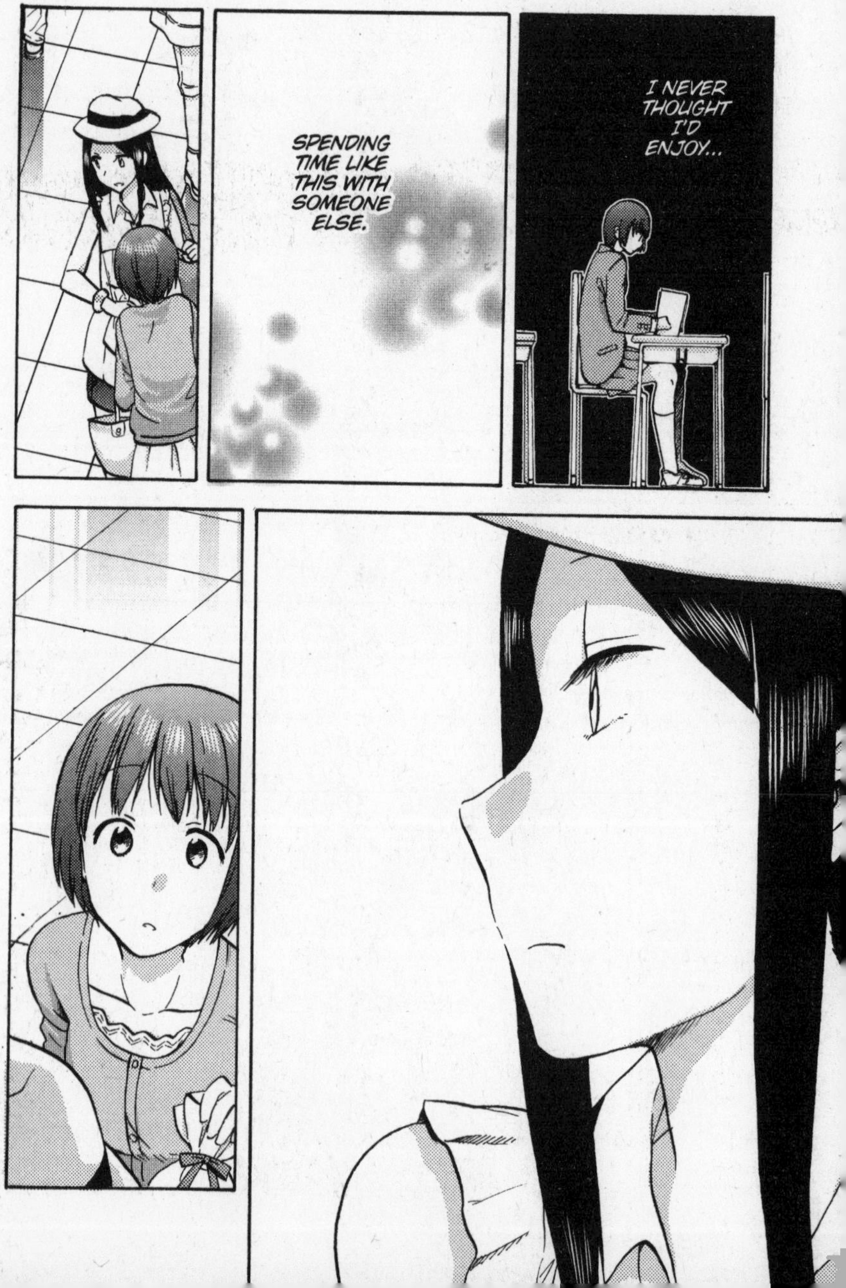
I NEVER THOUGHT I'D ENJOY...
SPENDING TIME LIKE THIS WITH SOMEONE ELSE.

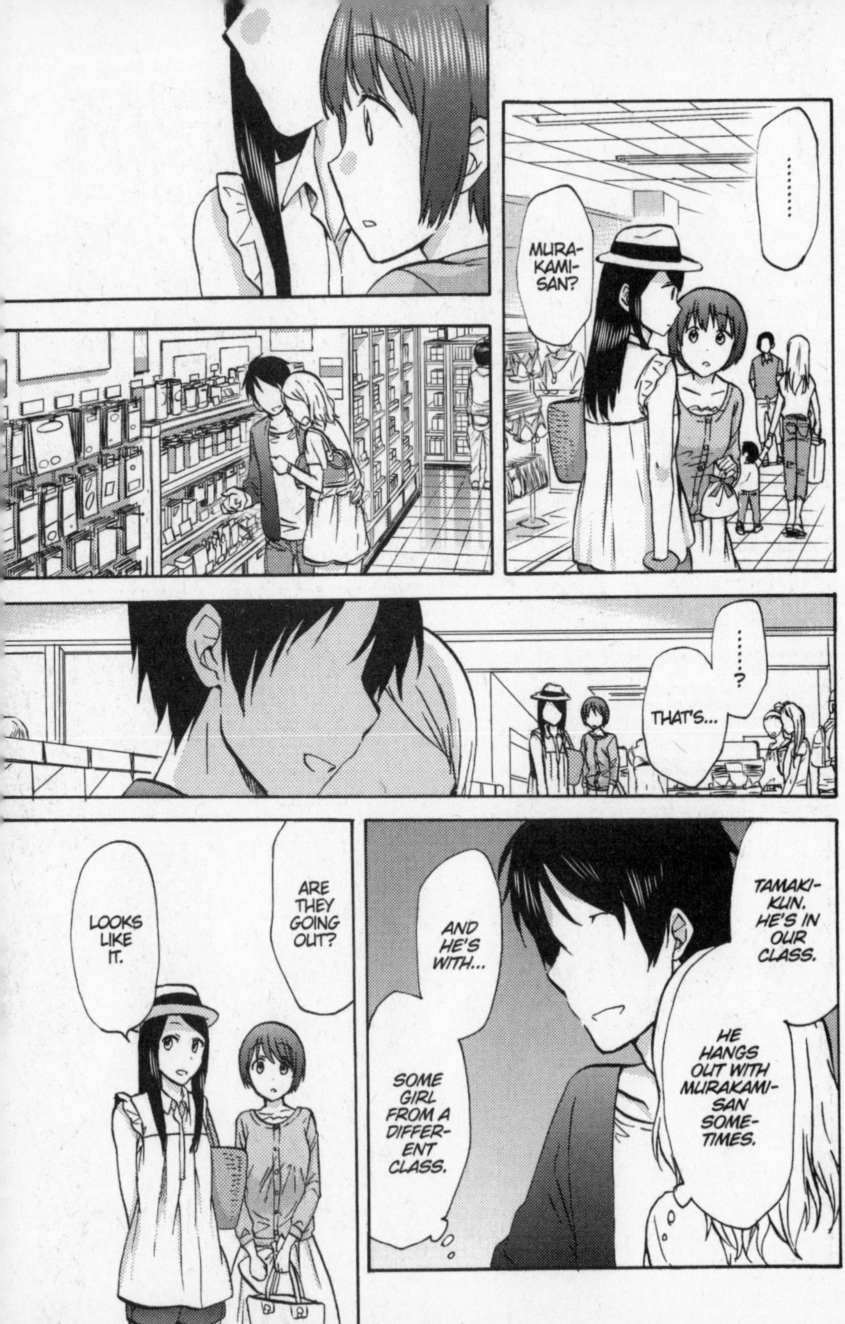
......
MURA-KAMI-SAN?
......?
THAT'S...
TAMAKI-KUN. HE'S IN OUR CLASS.
HE HANGS OUT WITH MURAKAMI-SAN SOME-TIMES.
AND HE'S WITH...
SOME GIRL FROM A DIFFER-ENT CLASS.
ARE THEY GOING OUT?
LOOKS LIKE IT.

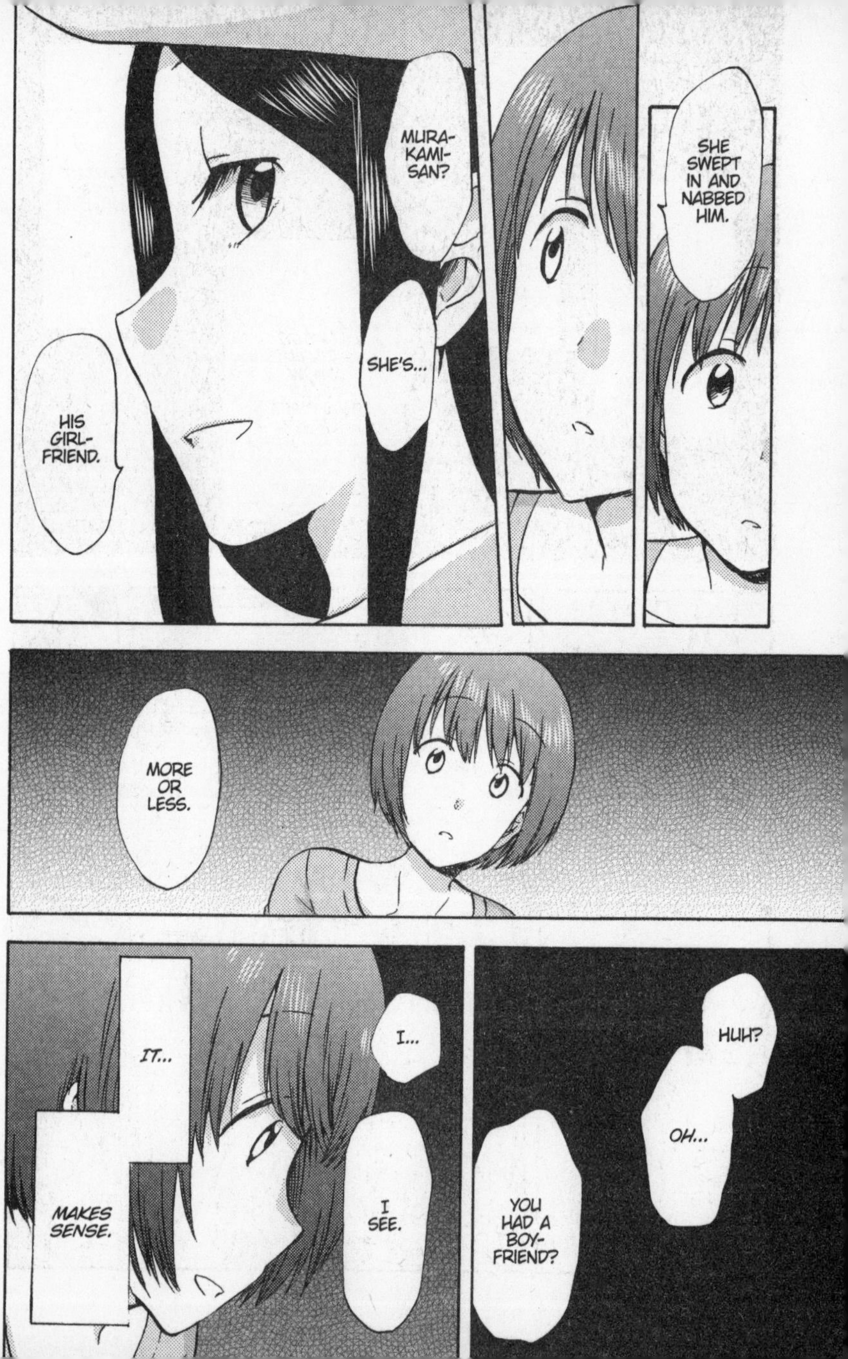
SHE SWEPT IN AND NABBED HIM.
MURA-KAMI-SAN?
SHE'S...
HIS GIRL-FRIEND.
MORE OR LESS.
HUH?
OH...
YOU HAD A BOY-FRIEND?
I...
I SEE.
IT...
MAKES SENSE.

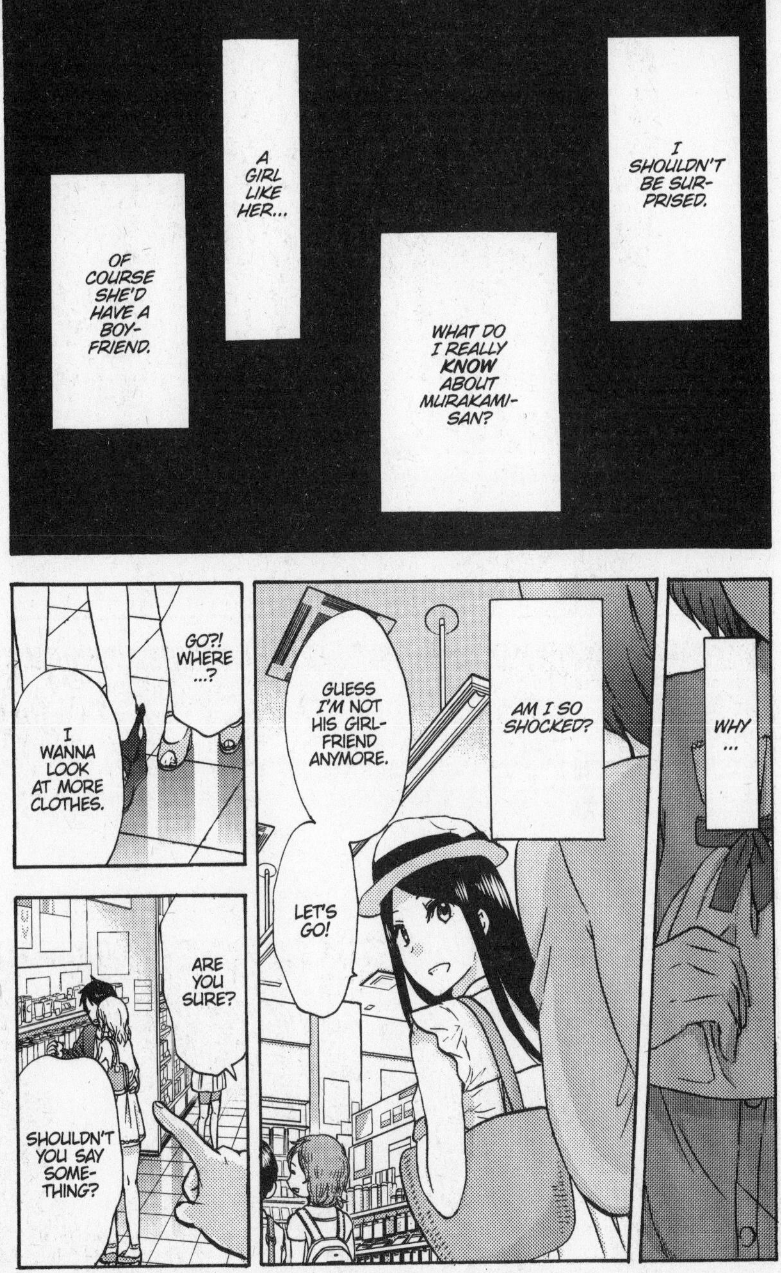
I SHOULDN'T BE SURPRISED.
WHAT DO I REALLY **KNOW** ABOUT MURAKAMI-SAN?
A GIRL LIKE HER...
OF COURSE SHE'D HAVE A BOYFRIEND.
WHY...
AM I SO SHOCKED?
GUESS I'M NOT HIS GIRLFRIEND ANYMORE.
LET'S GO!
GO?! WHERE ...?
I WANNA LOOK AT MORE CLOTHES.
ARE YOU SURE?
SHOULDN'T YOU SAY SOMETHING?

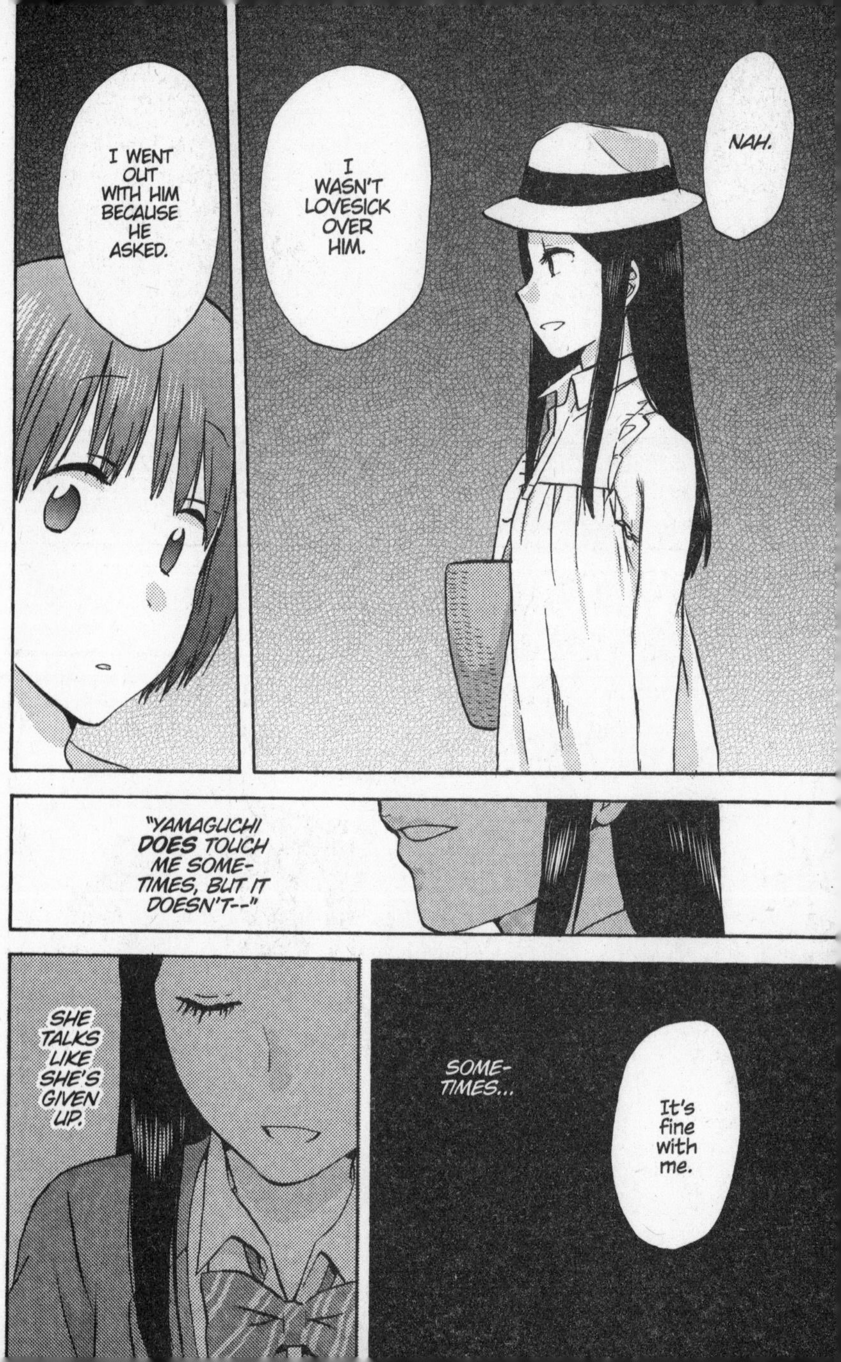
NAH.
I WASN'T LOVESICK OVER HIM.
I WENT OUT WITH HIM BECAUSE HE ASKED.
"YAMAGUCHI DOES TOUCH ME SOME-TIMES, BUT IT DOESN'T--"
It's fine with me.
SOME-TIMES...
SHE TALKS LIKE SHE'S GIVEN UP.

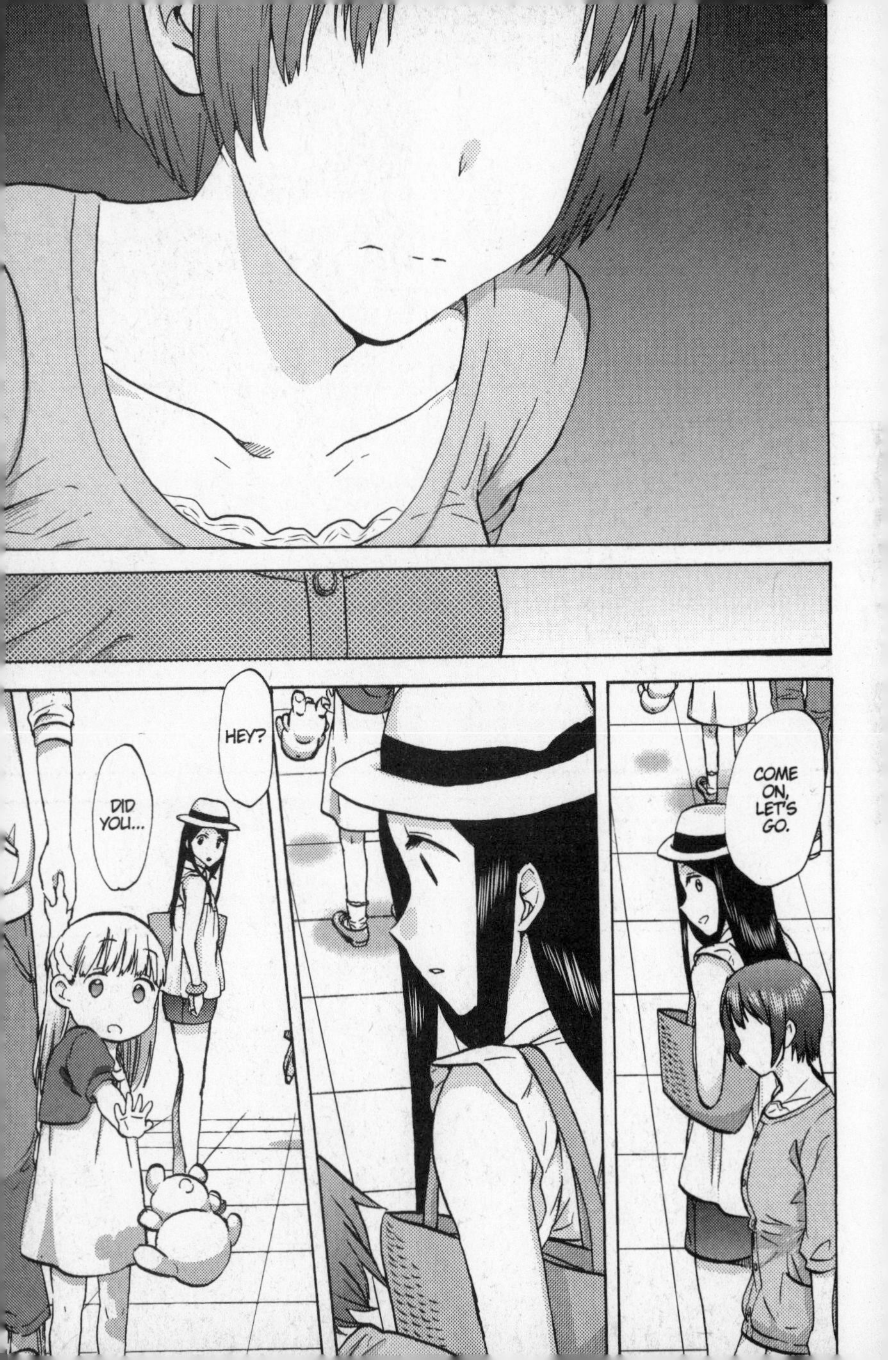
COME ON, LET'S GO.
HEY?
DID YOU...

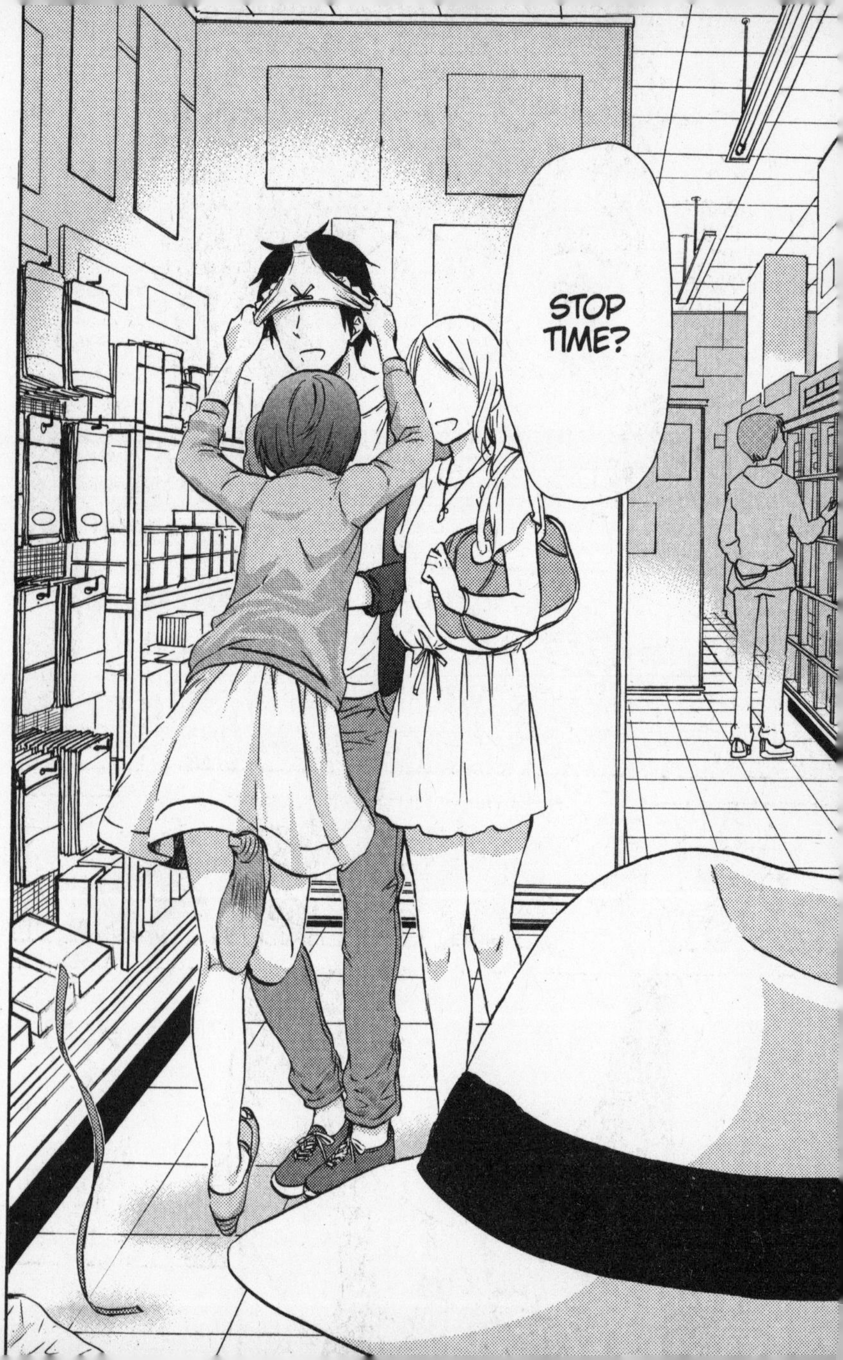
STOP TIME?

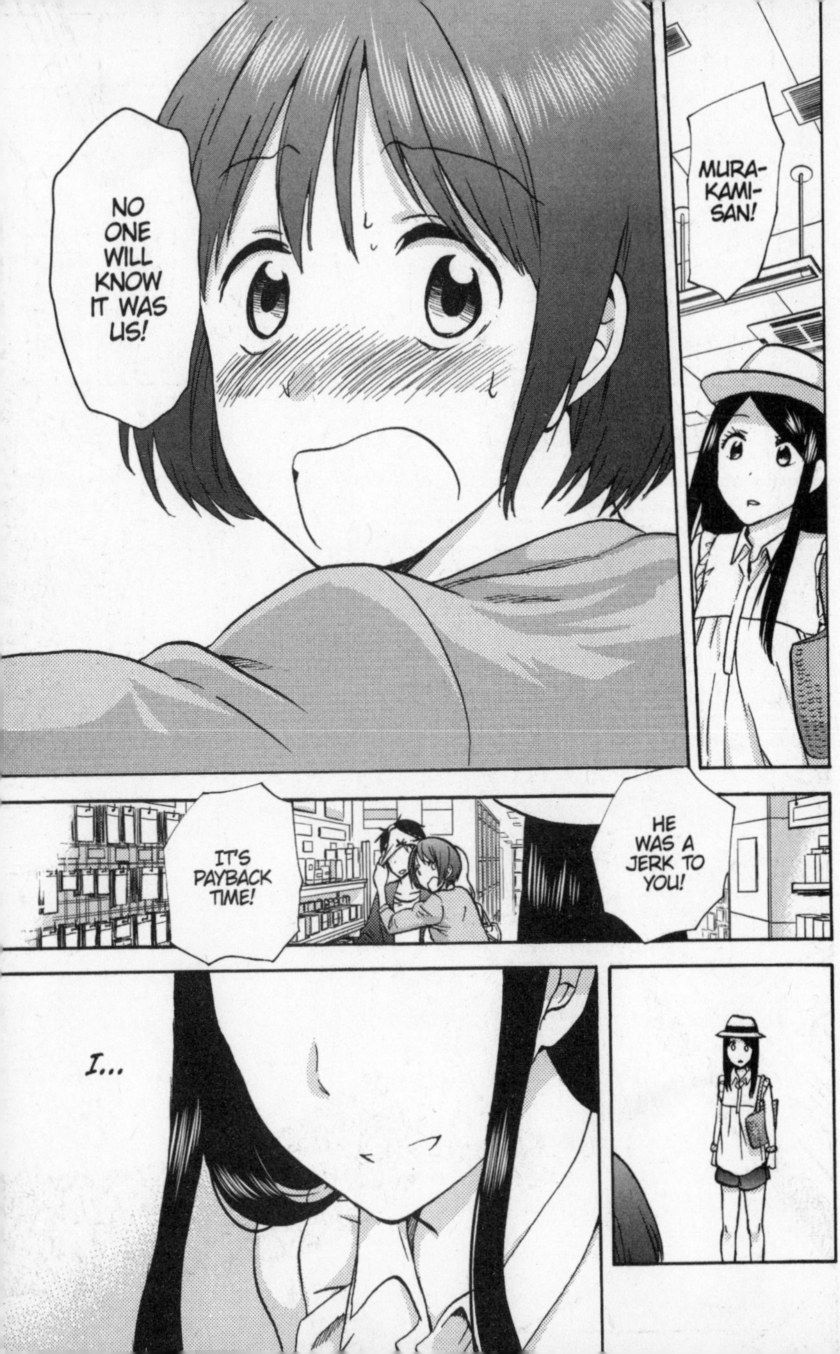
MURA-KAMI-SAN!
NO ONE WILL KNOW IT WAS US!
HE WAS A JERK TO YOU!
IT'S PAYBACK TIME!
I...

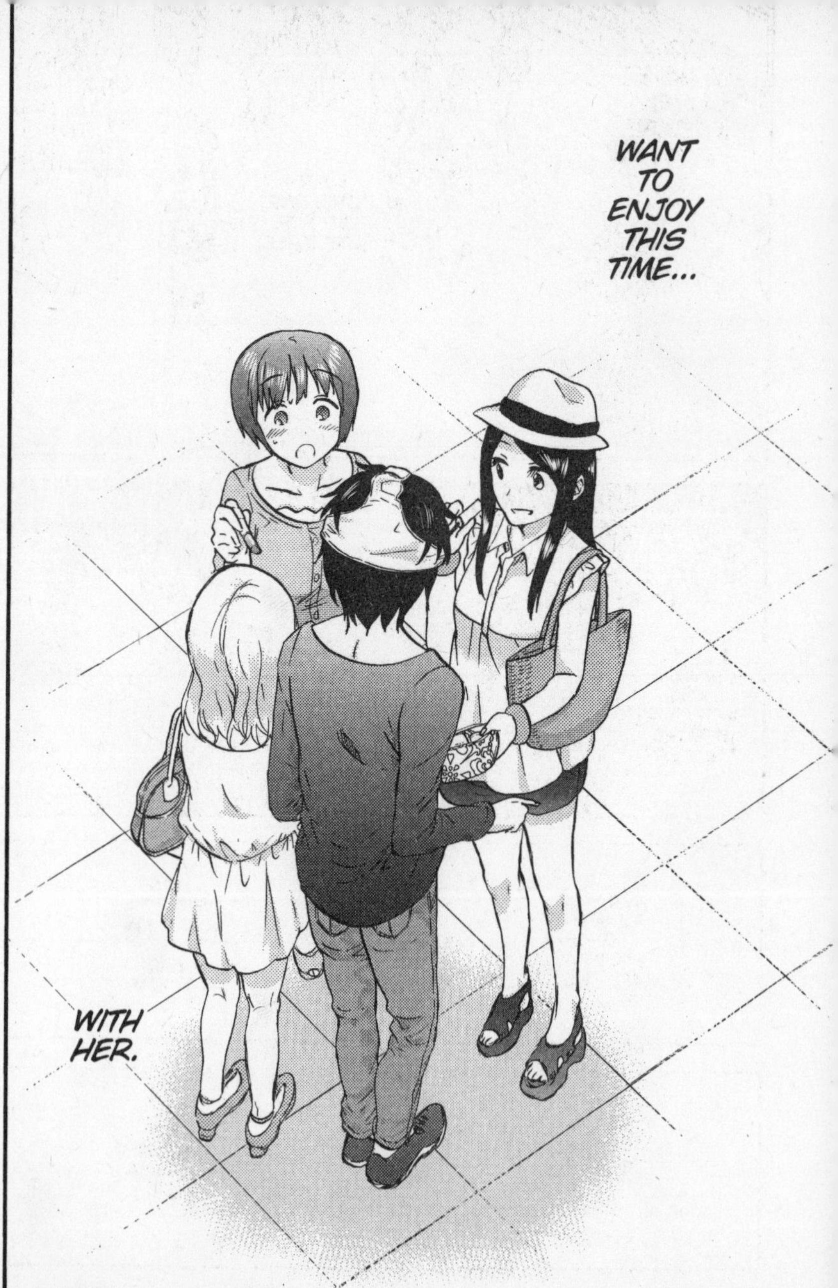
WANT TO ENJOY THIS TIME...
WITH HER.

#3. We're on a Date / END

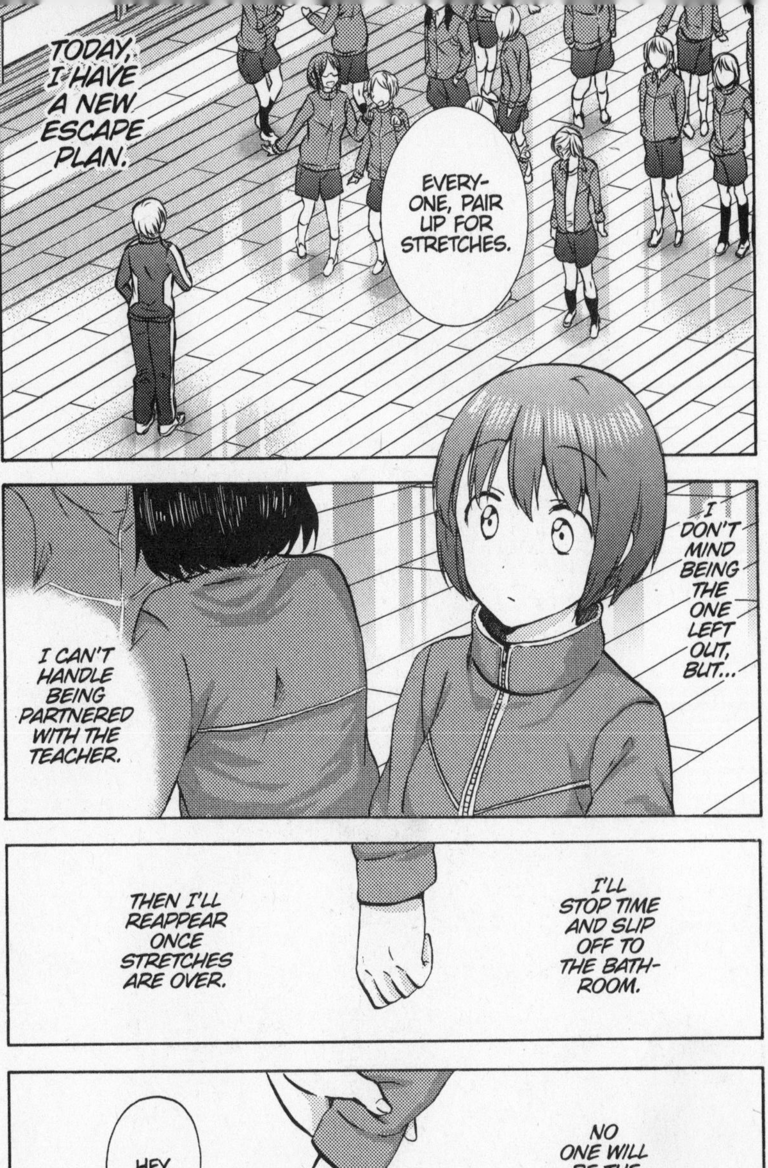
EVERY-ONE, PAIR UP FOR STRETCHES.
TODAY, I HAVE A NEW ESCAPE PLAN.
I DON'T MIND BEING THE ONE LEFT OUT, BUT...
I CAN'T HANDLE BEING PARTNERED WITH THE TEACHER.
I'LL STOP TIME AND SLIP OFF TO THE BATH-ROOM.
THEN I'LL REAPPEAR ONCE STRETCHES ARE OVER.
NO ONE WILL BE THE WISER.
HEY.

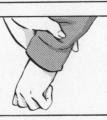

fragtime #4 You're Such a Prude

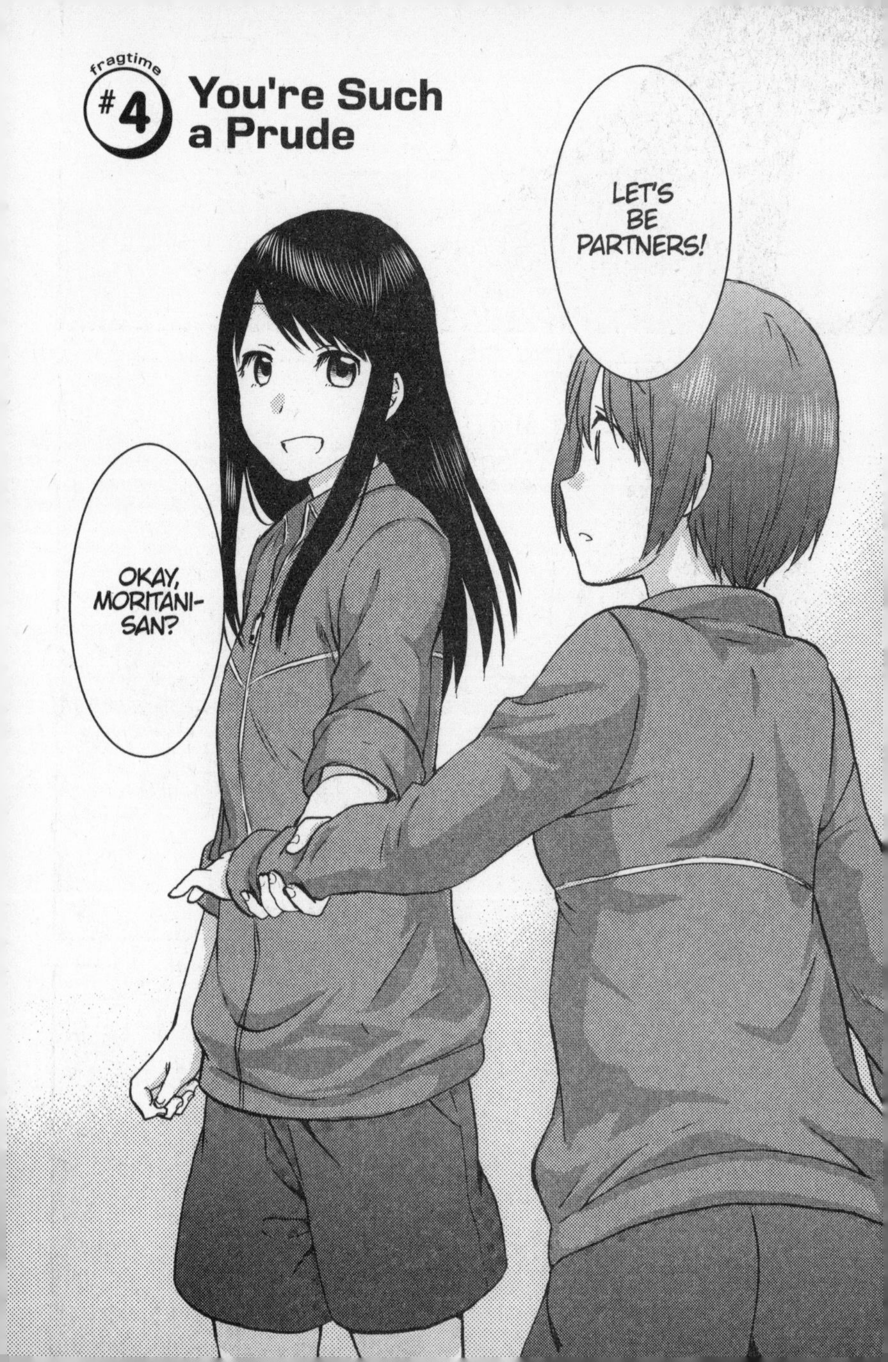
LET'S BE PARTNERS!
OKAY, MORITANI-SAN?

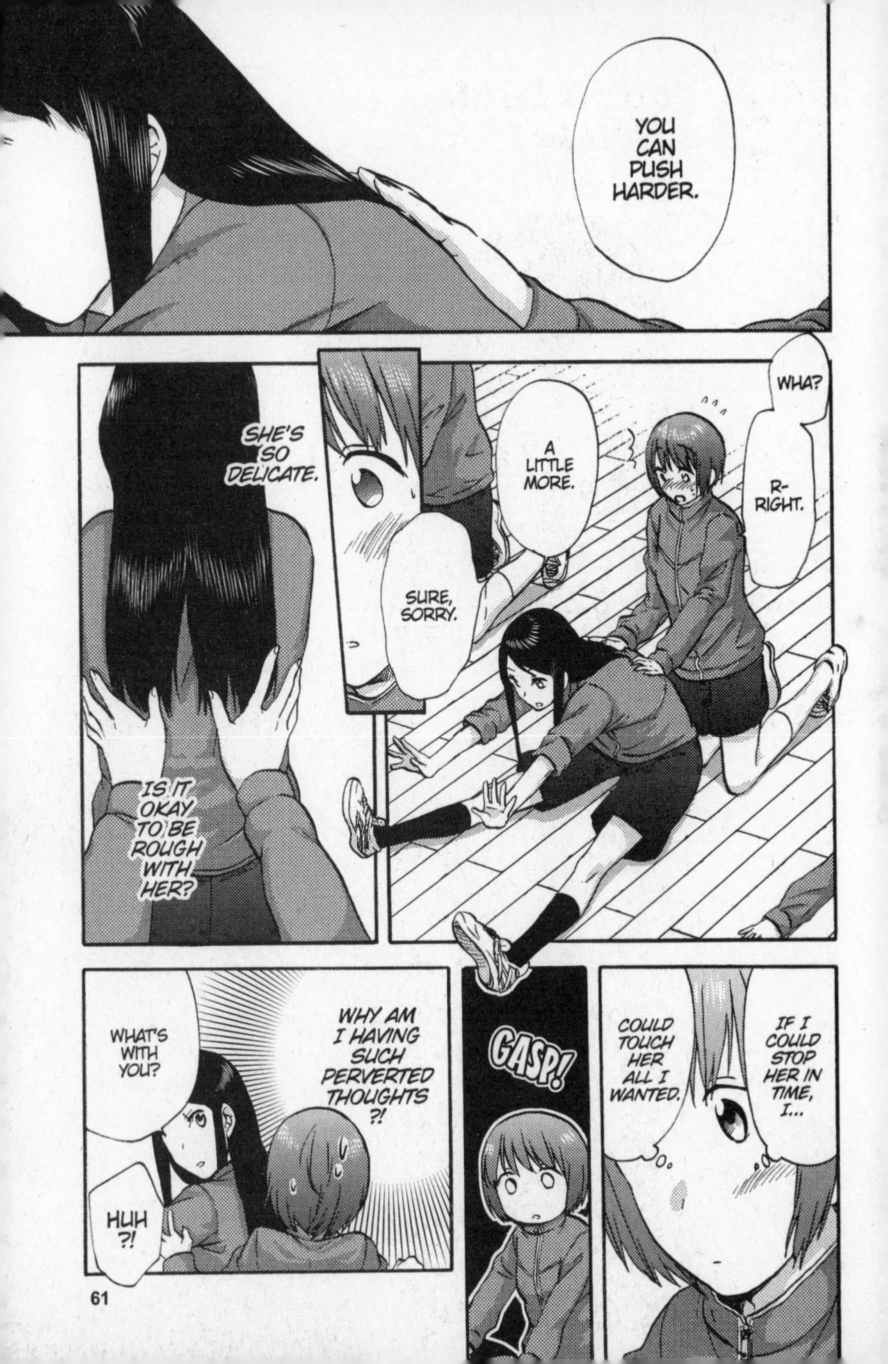
YOU CAN PUSH HARDER.
WHA?
R-RIGHT.
A LITTLE MORE.
SURE, SORRY.
SHE'S SO DELICATE.
IS IT OKAY TO BE ROUGH WITH HER?
IF I COULD STOP HER IN TIME, I...
COULD TOUCH HER ALL I WANTED.
GASP!
WHY AM I HAVING SUCH PERVERTED THOUGHTS?!
WHAT'S WITH YOU?
HUH?!

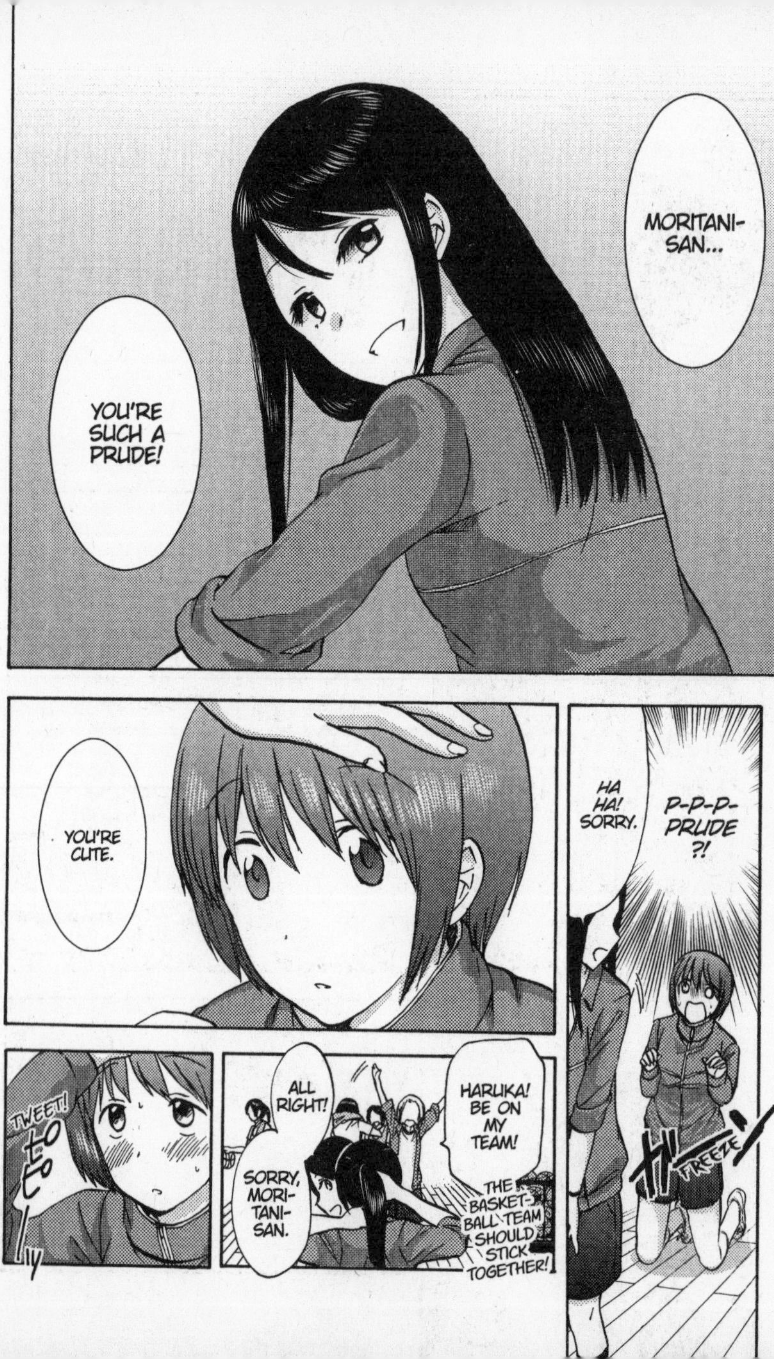
MORITANI-SAN...
YOU'RE SUCH A PRUDE!
P-P-P-PRUDE ?!
HA HA! SORRY.
FREEZE
YOU'RE CUTE.
HARUKA! BE ON MY TEAM!
ALL RIGHT!
THE BASKET-BALL TEAM SHOULD STICK TOGETHER!
SORRY, MORITANI-SAN.
TWEET!

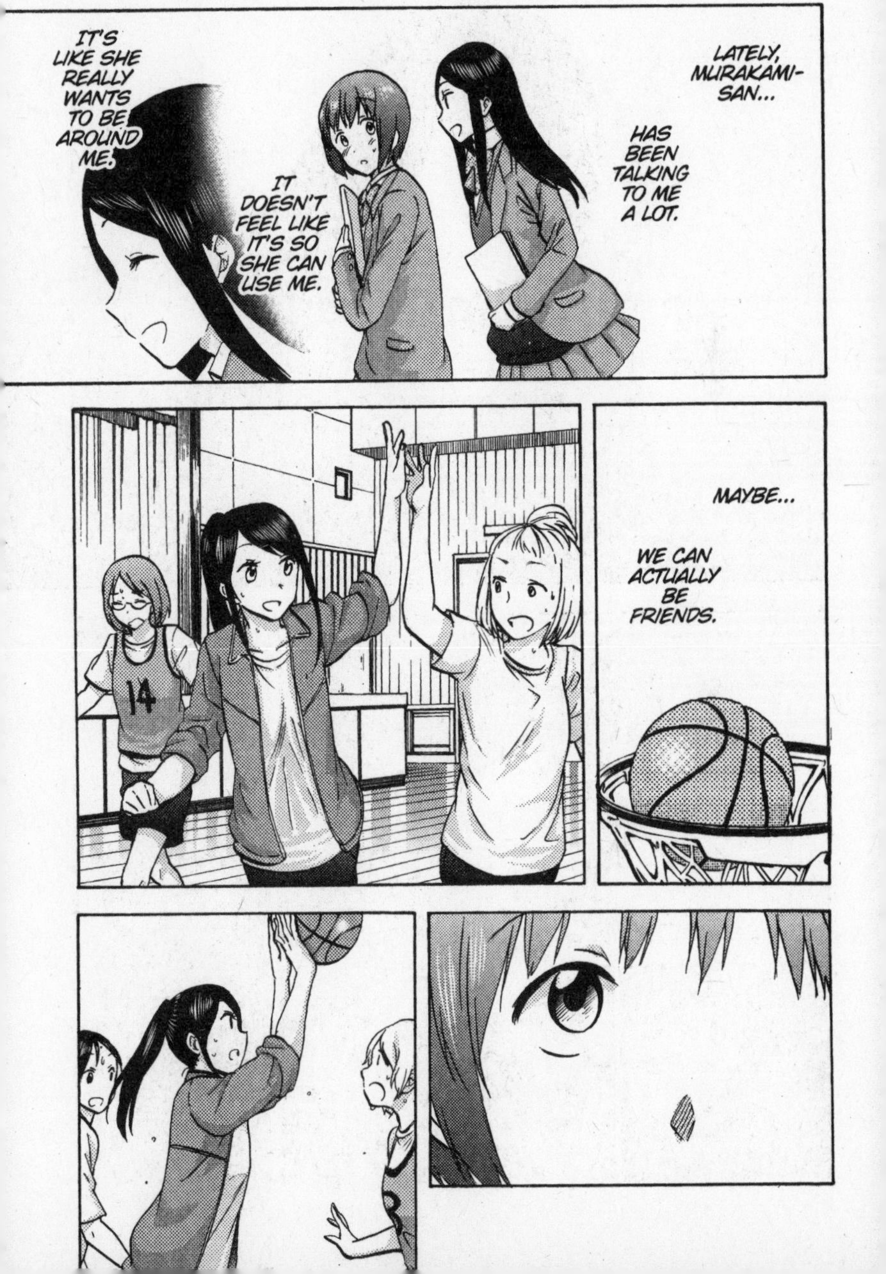
LATELY, MURAKAMI-SAN...
HAS BEEN TALKING TO ME A LOT.
IT DOESN'T FEEL LIKE IT'S SO SHE CAN USE ME.
IT'S LIKE SHE REALLY WANTS TO BE AROUND ME.
MAYBE...
WE CAN ACTUALLY BE FRIENDS.

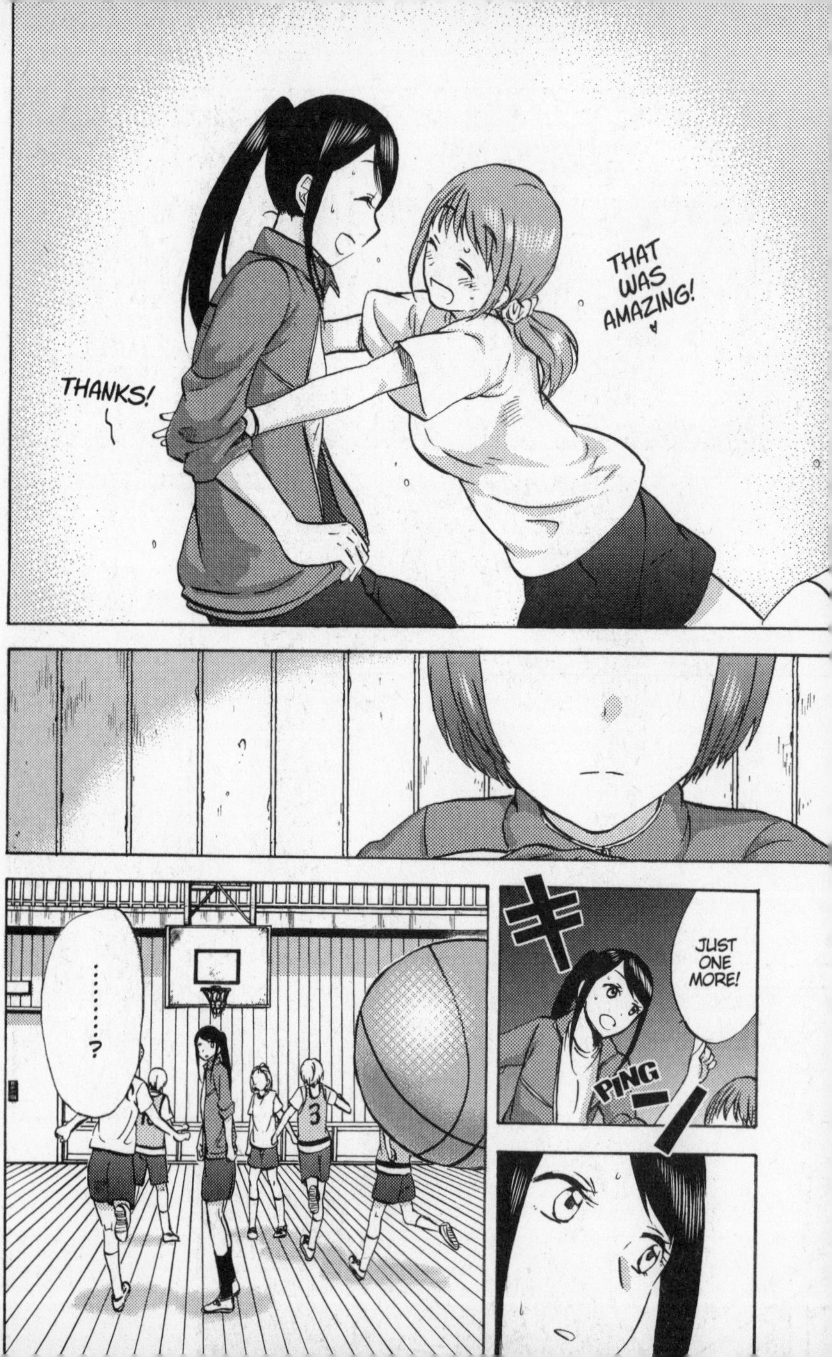
THAT WAS AMAZING!
THANKS!
JUST ONE MORE!
PING
......?

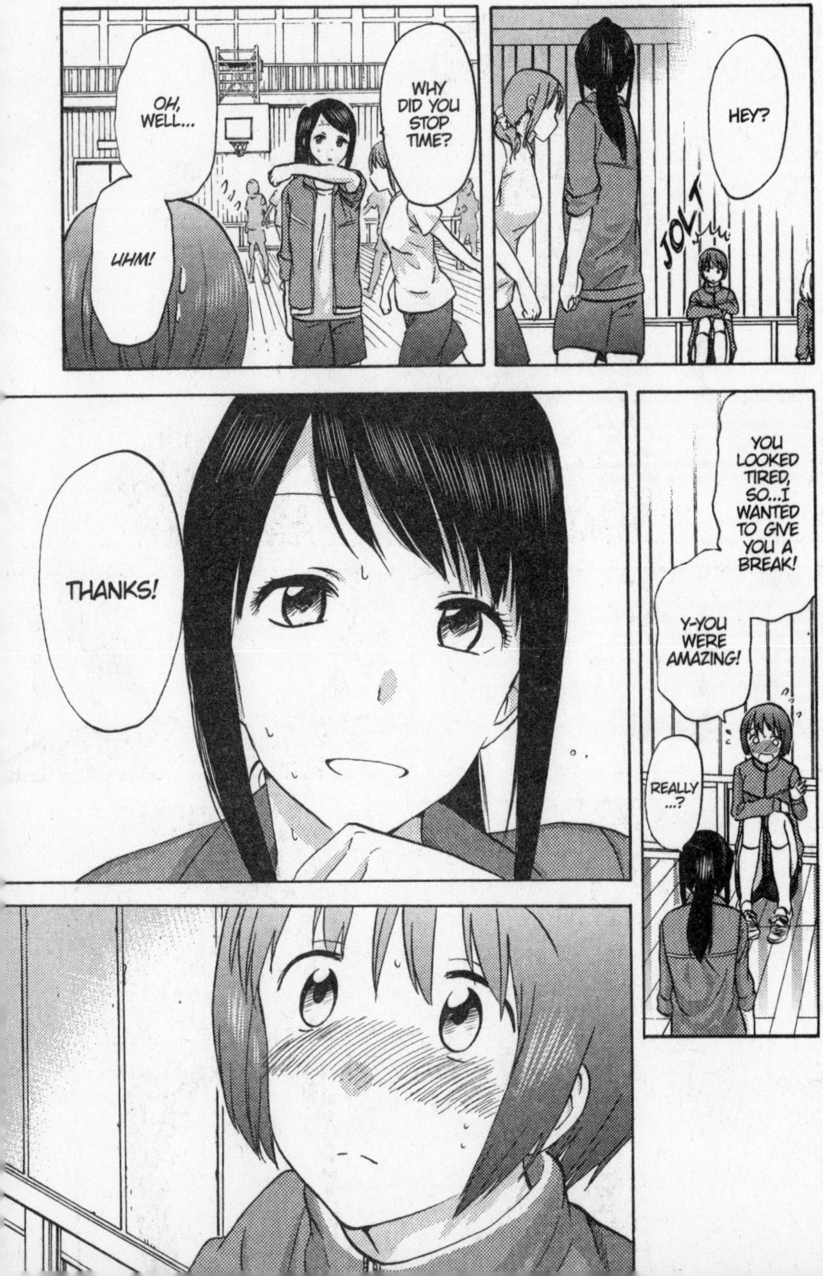
HEY?
JOLT
WHY DID YOU STOP TIME?
OH, WELL...
UHM!
YOU LOOKED TIRED, SO...I WANTED TO GIVE YOU A BREAK!
Y-YOU WERE AMAZING!
REALLY ...?
THANKS!

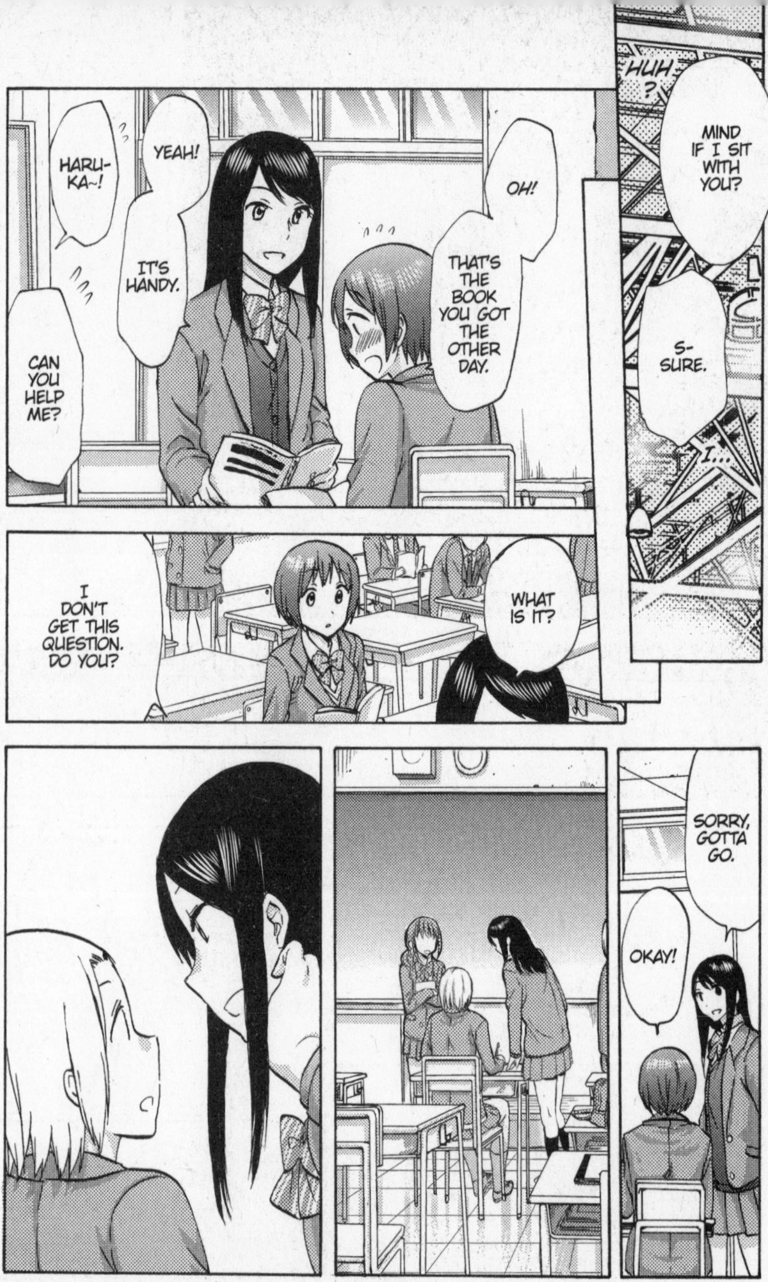
HUH?
MIND IF I SIT WITH YOU?
S-SURE.
I...
OH!
THAT'S THE BOOK YOU GOT THE OTHER DAY.
YEAH!
IT'S HANDY.
HARU-KA~!
CAN YOU HELP ME?
WHAT IS IT?
I DON'T GET THIS QUESTION. DO YOU?
SORRY, GOTTA GO.
OKAY!

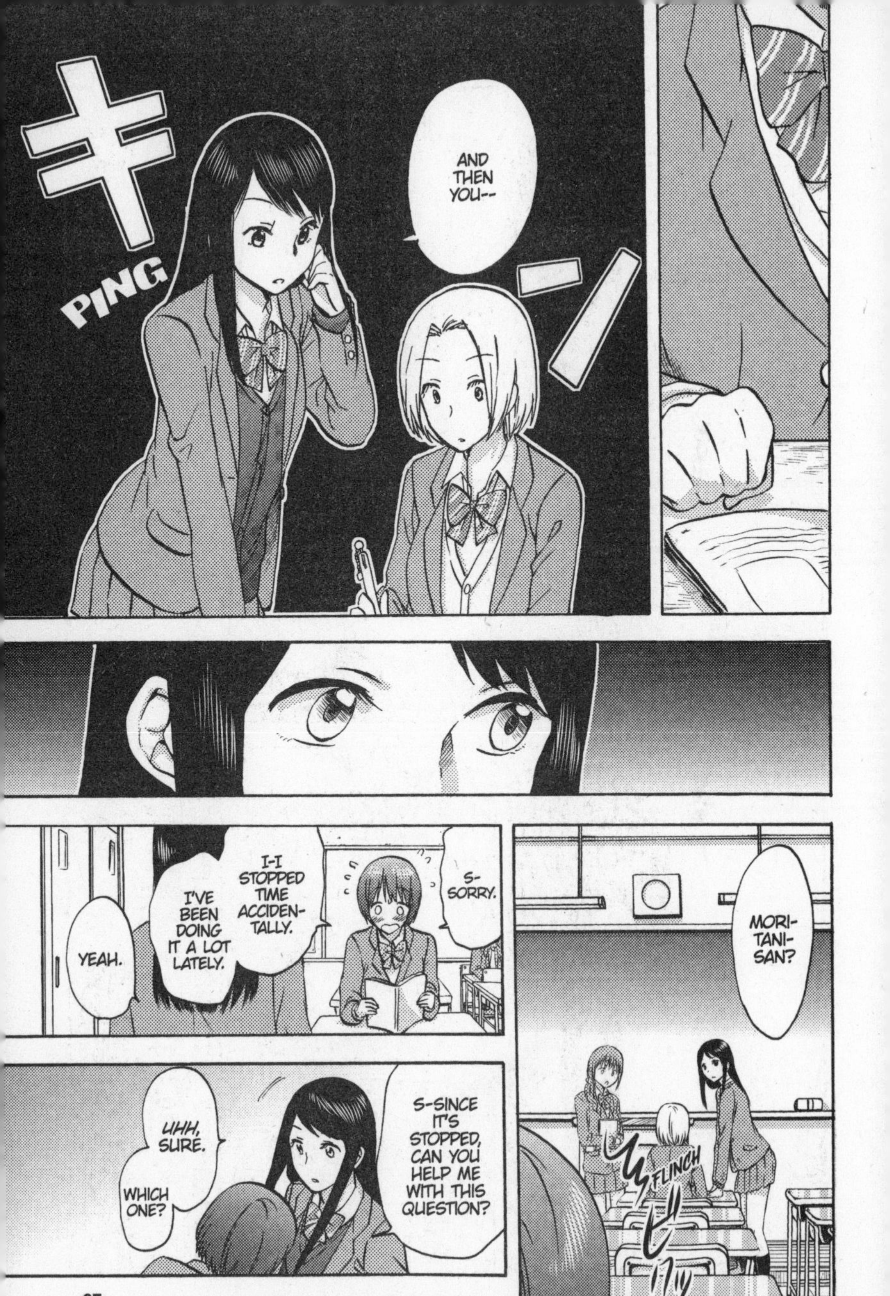
PING
AND THEN YOU--
MORI-TANI-SAN?
FLINCH
S-SORRY.
I-I STOPPED TIME ACCIDENTALLY.
I'VE BEEN DOING IT A LOT LATELY.
YEAH.
S-SINCE IT'S STOPPED, CAN YOU HELP ME WITH THIS QUESTION?
UHH, SURE.
WHICH ONE?

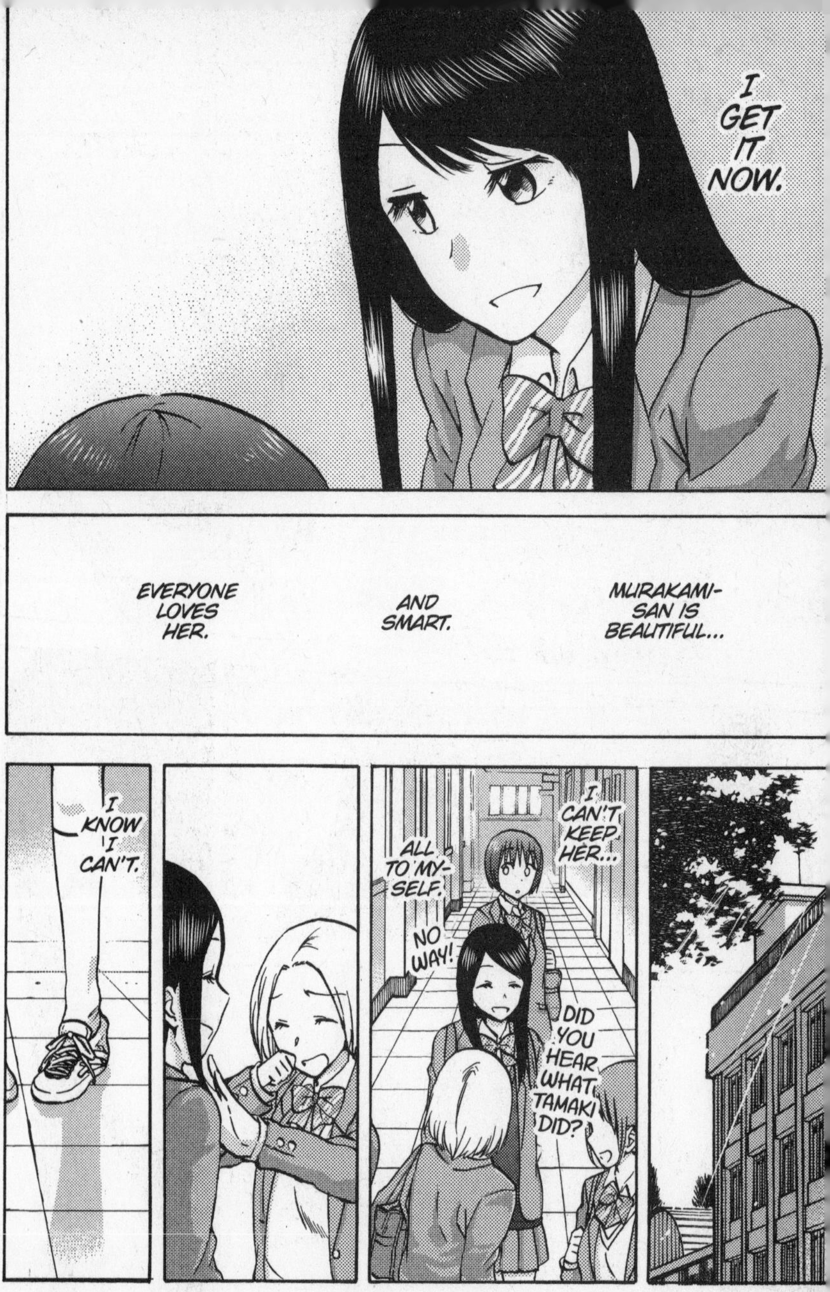
I GET IT NOW.
MURAKAMI-SAN IS BEAUTIFUL...
AND SMART.
EVERYONE LOVES HER.
I CAN'T KEEP HER...
ALL TO MY-SELF.
DID YOU HEAR WHAT TAMAKI DID?
NO WAY!
I KNOW I CAN'T.

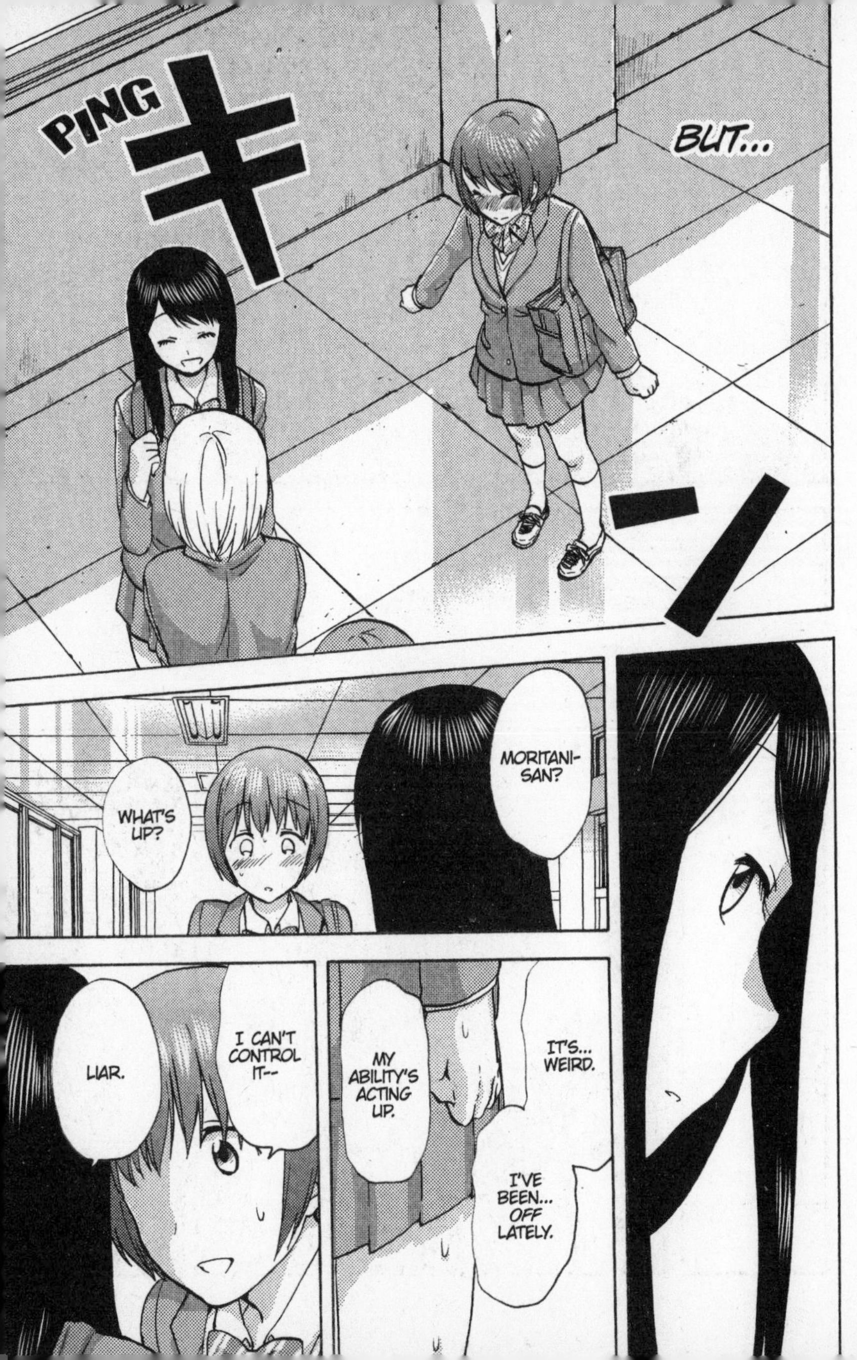
BUT...
PING
MORITANI-SAN?
WHAT'S UP?
IT'S... WEIRD.
MY ABILITY'S ACTING UP.
I'VE BEEN... OFF LATELY.
I CAN'T CONTROL IT--
LIAR.

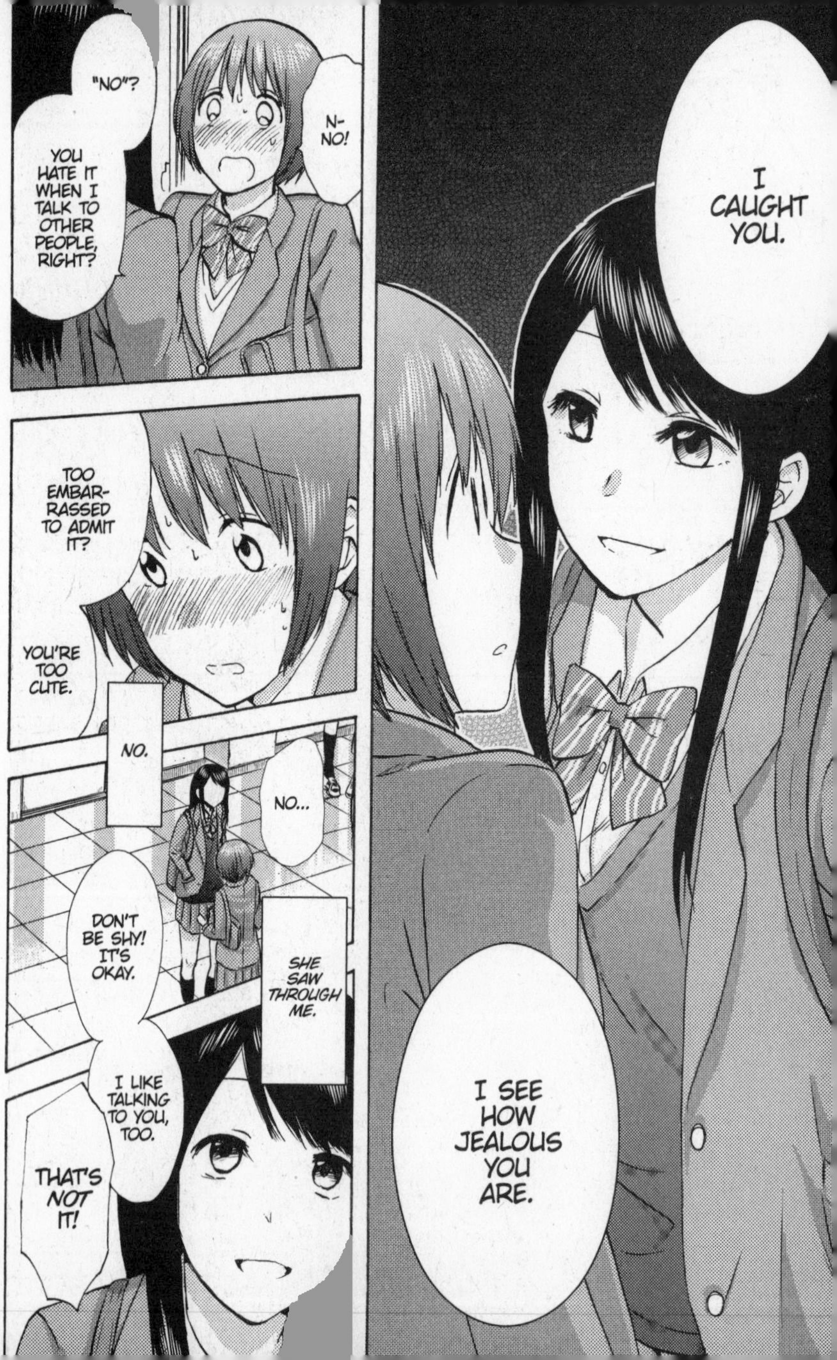
I CAUGHT YOU.
I SEE HOW JEALOUS YOU ARE.
N-NO!
"NO"?
YOU HATE IT WHEN I TALK TO OTHER PEOPLE, RIGHT?
TOO EMBARRASSED TO ADMIT IT?
YOU'RE TOO CUTE.
NO...
NO.
DON'T BE SHY! IT'S OKAY.
SHE SAW THROUGH ME.
I LIKE TALKING TO YOU, TOO.
THAT'S NOT IT!

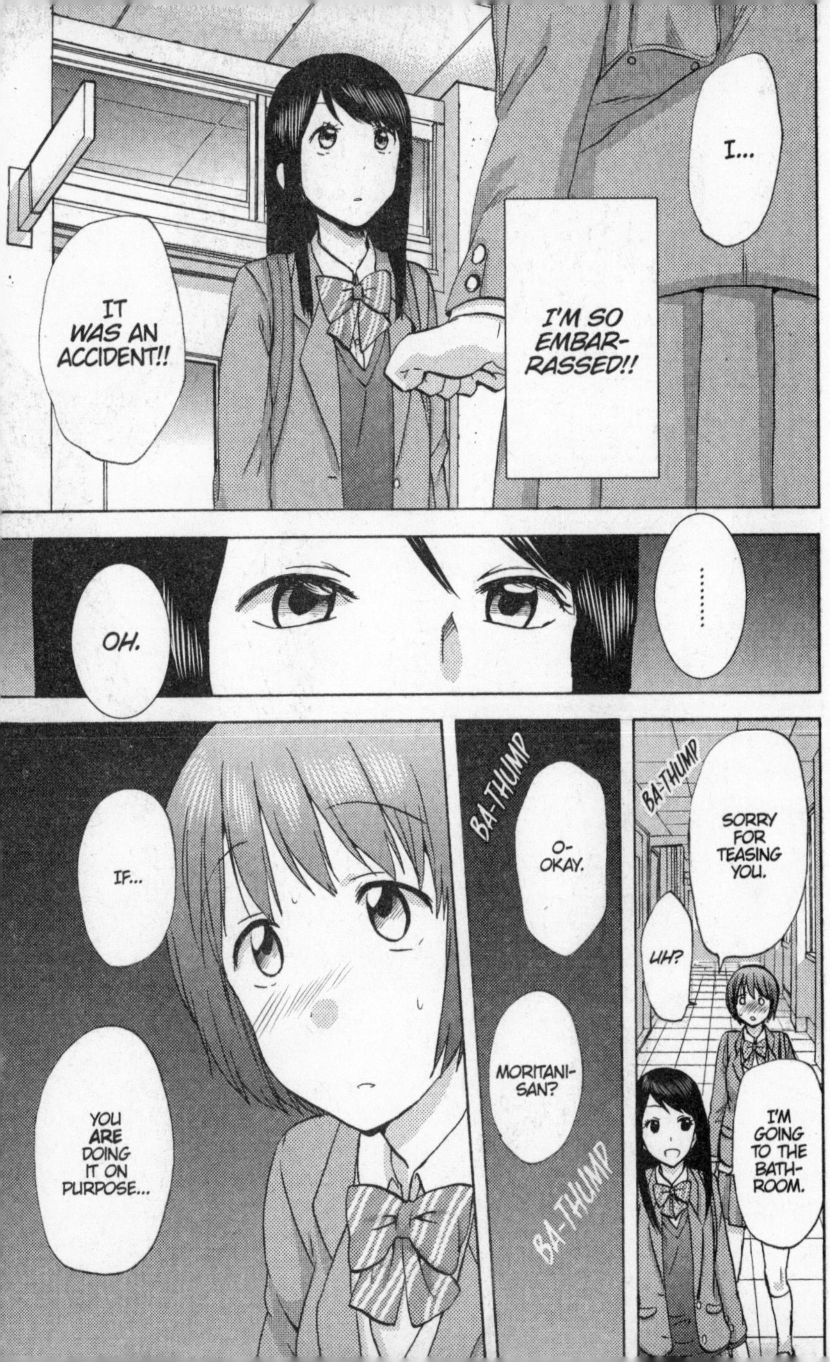
I...
I'M SO EMBAR-RASSED!!
IT WAS AN ACCIDENT!!
......
OH.
BA-THUMP
SORRY FOR TEASING YOU.
UH?
I'M GOING TO THE BATH-ROOM.
BA-THUMP
O-OKAY.
MORITANI-SAN?
BA-THUMP
IF...
YOU ARE DOING IT ON PURPOSE...

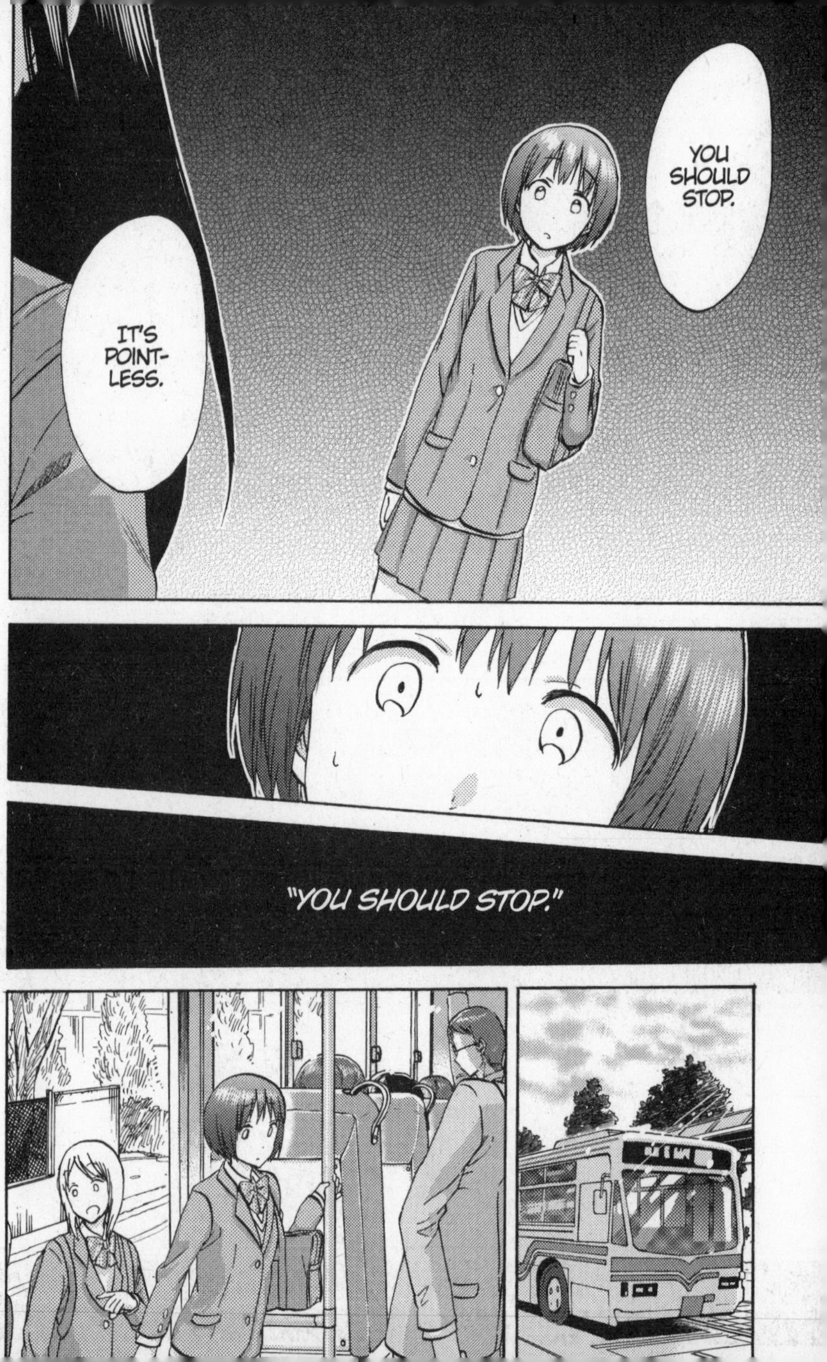
YOU SHOULD STOP.
IT'S POINT-LESS.
"YOU SHOULD STOP."

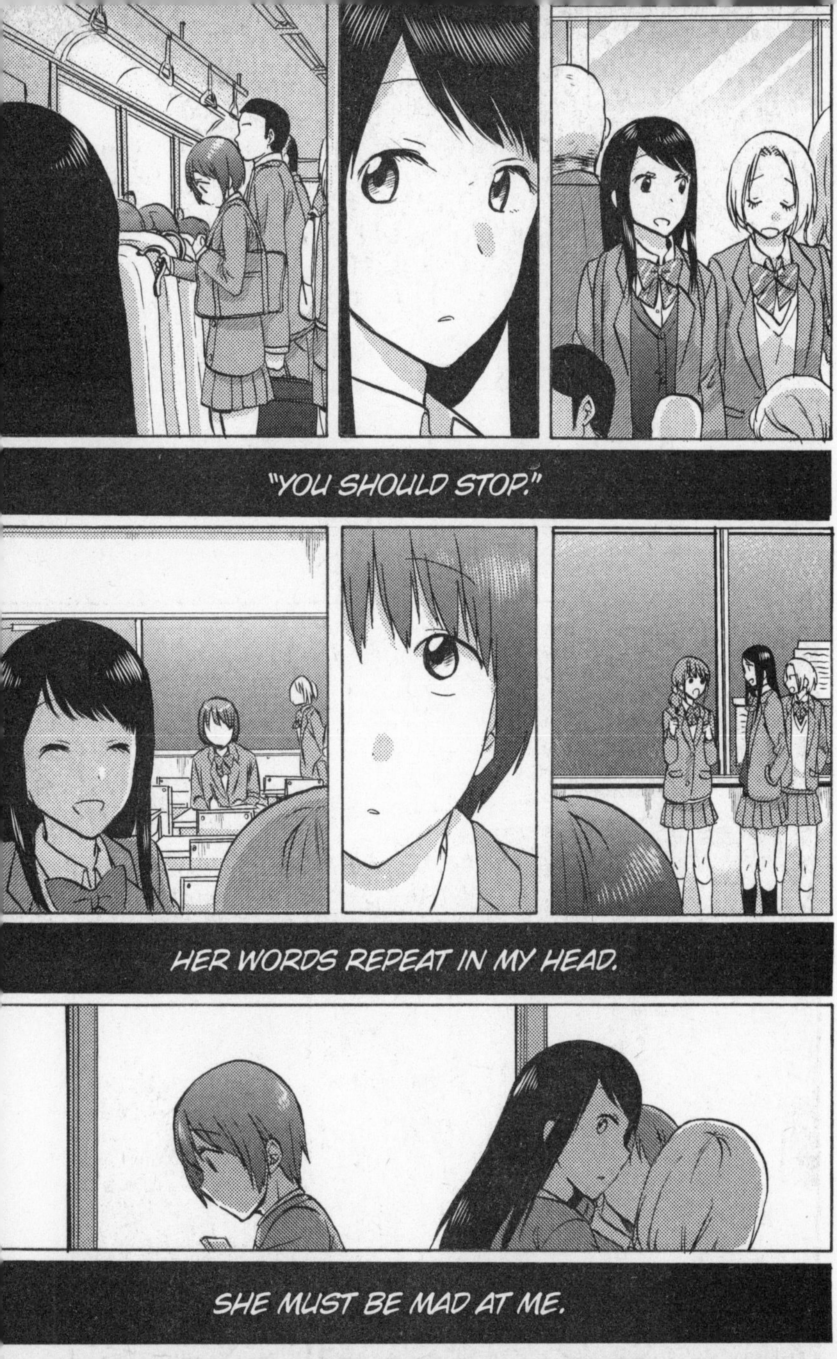
"YOU SHOULD STOP."
HER WORDS REPEAT IN MY HEAD.
SHE MUST BE MAD AT ME.

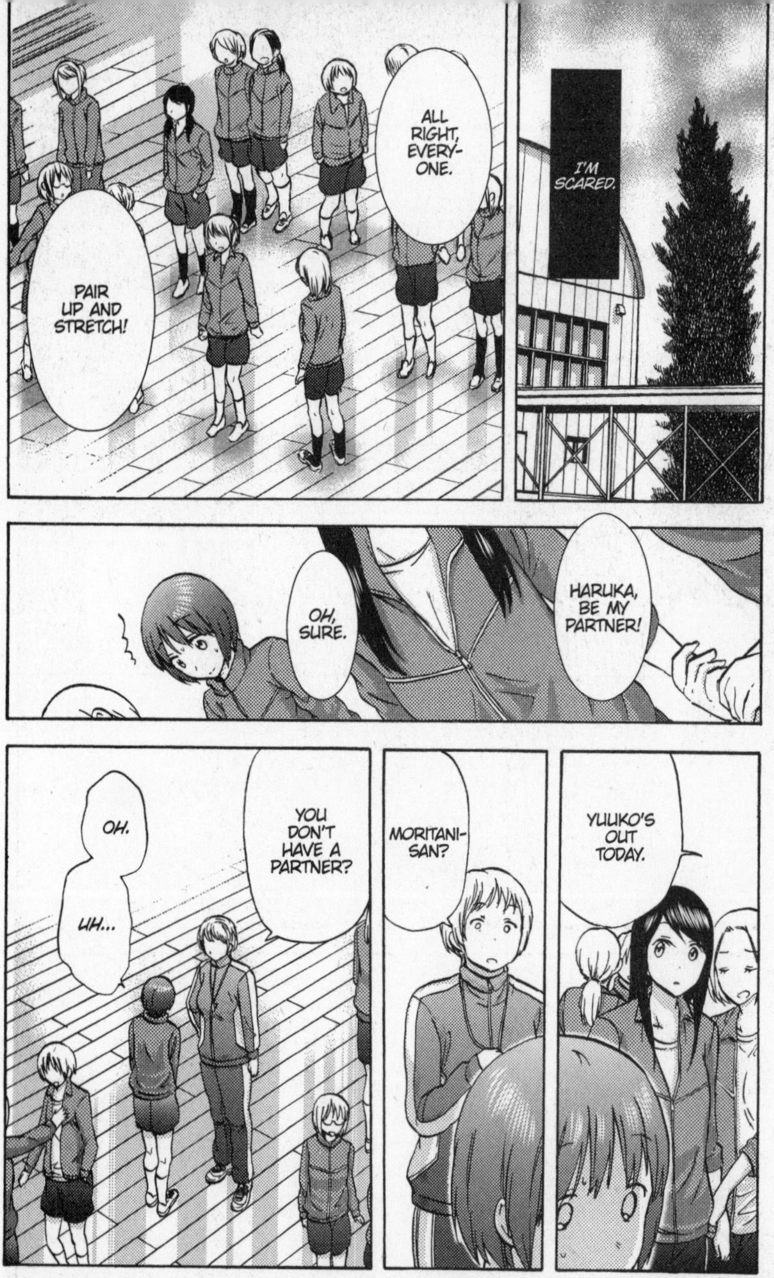
I'M SCARED.
ALL RIGHT, EVERYONE.
PAIR UP AND STRETCH!
HARUKA, BE MY PARTNER!
OH, SURE.
YUUKO'S OUT TODAY.
MORITANI-SAN?
YOU DON'T HAVE A PARTNER?
OH.
UH...

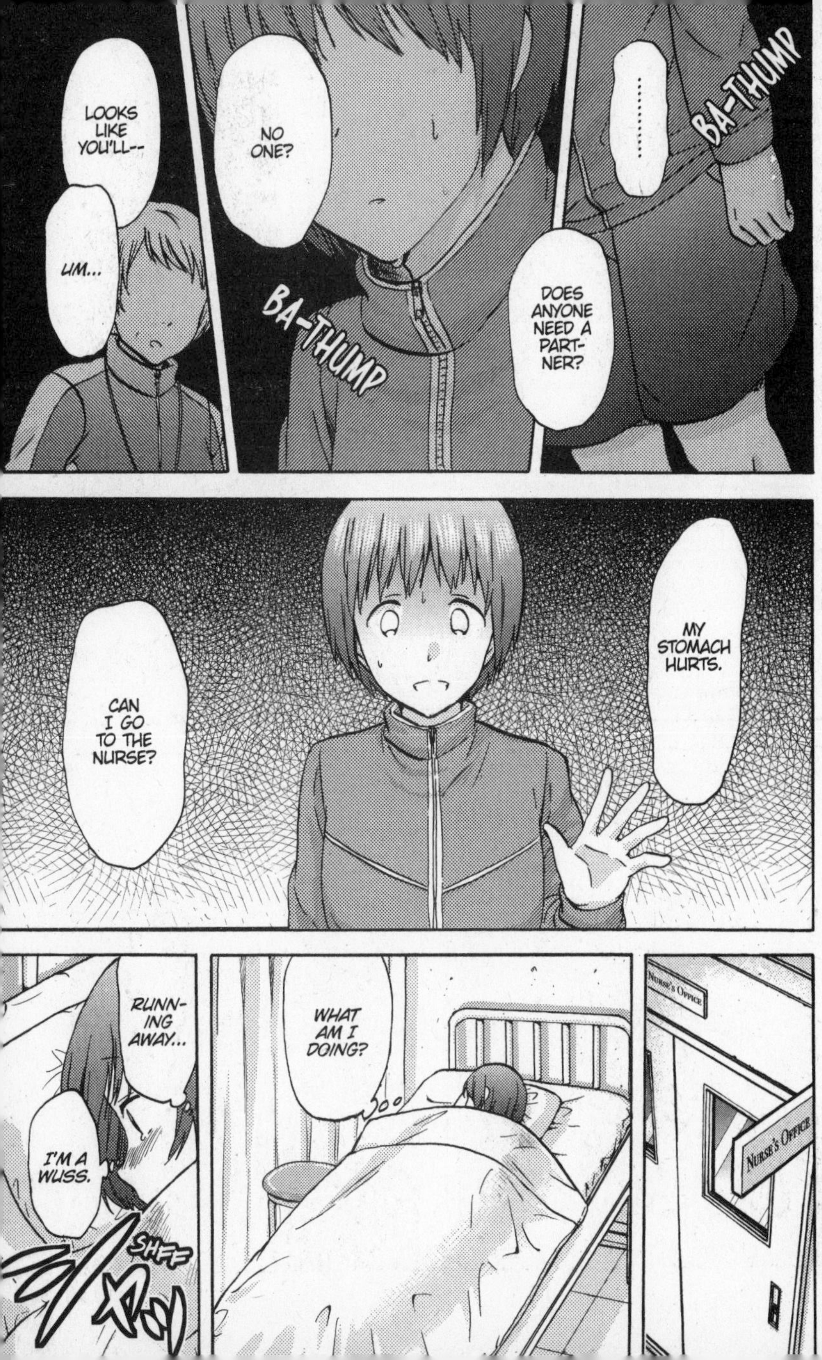
......
BA-THUMP
DOES ANYONE NEED A PART-NER?
NO ONE?
BA-THUMP
LOOKS LIKE YOU'LL--
UM...
MY STOMACH HURTS.
CAN I GO TO THE NURSE?
NURSE'S OFFICE
NURSE'S OFFICE
WHAT AM I DOING?
RUNN-ING AWAY...
I'M A WUSS.
SHFF

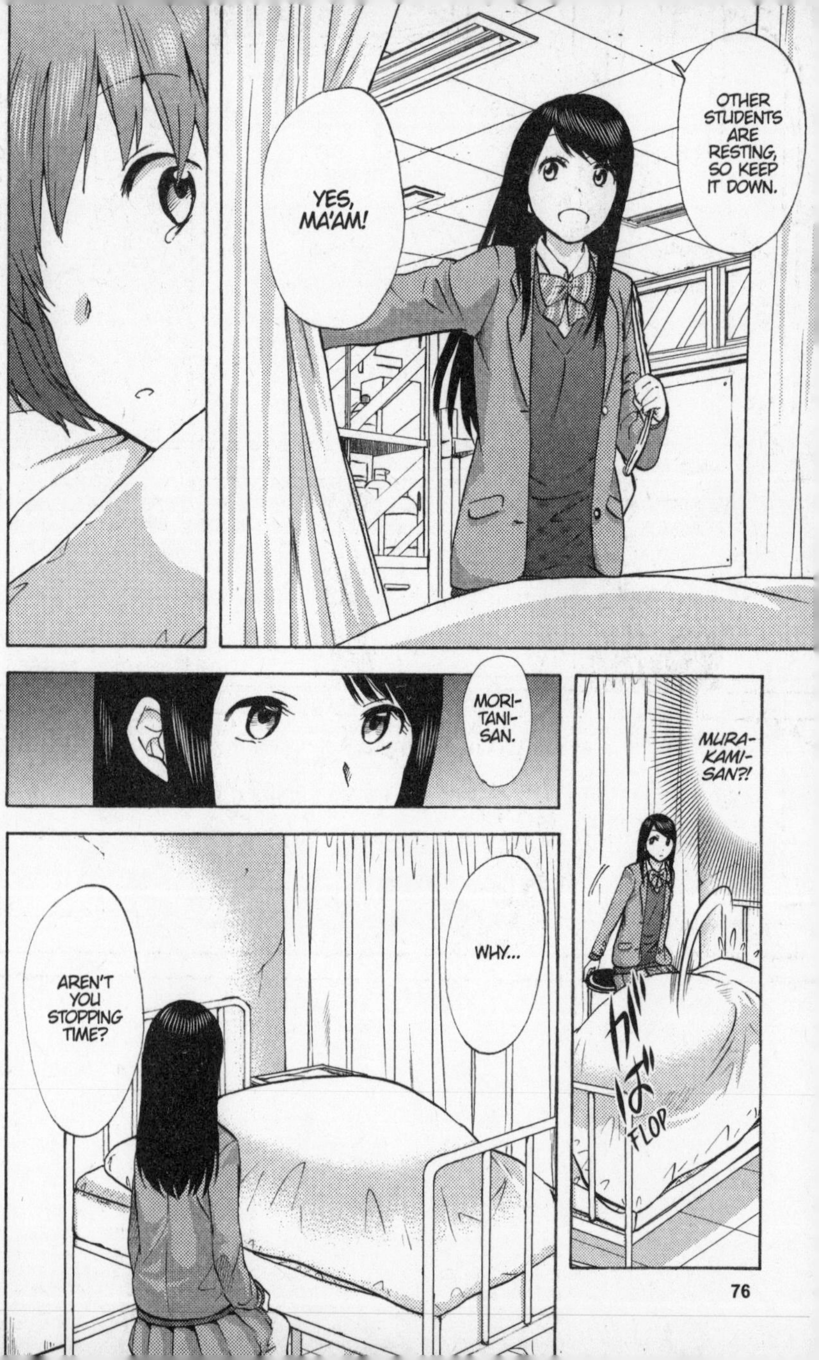
OTHER STUDENTS ARE RESTING, SO KEEP IT DOWN.
YES, MA'AM!
MURA-KAMI-SAN?!
FLOP
MORI-TANI-SAN.
WHY...
AREN'T YOU STOPPING TIME?

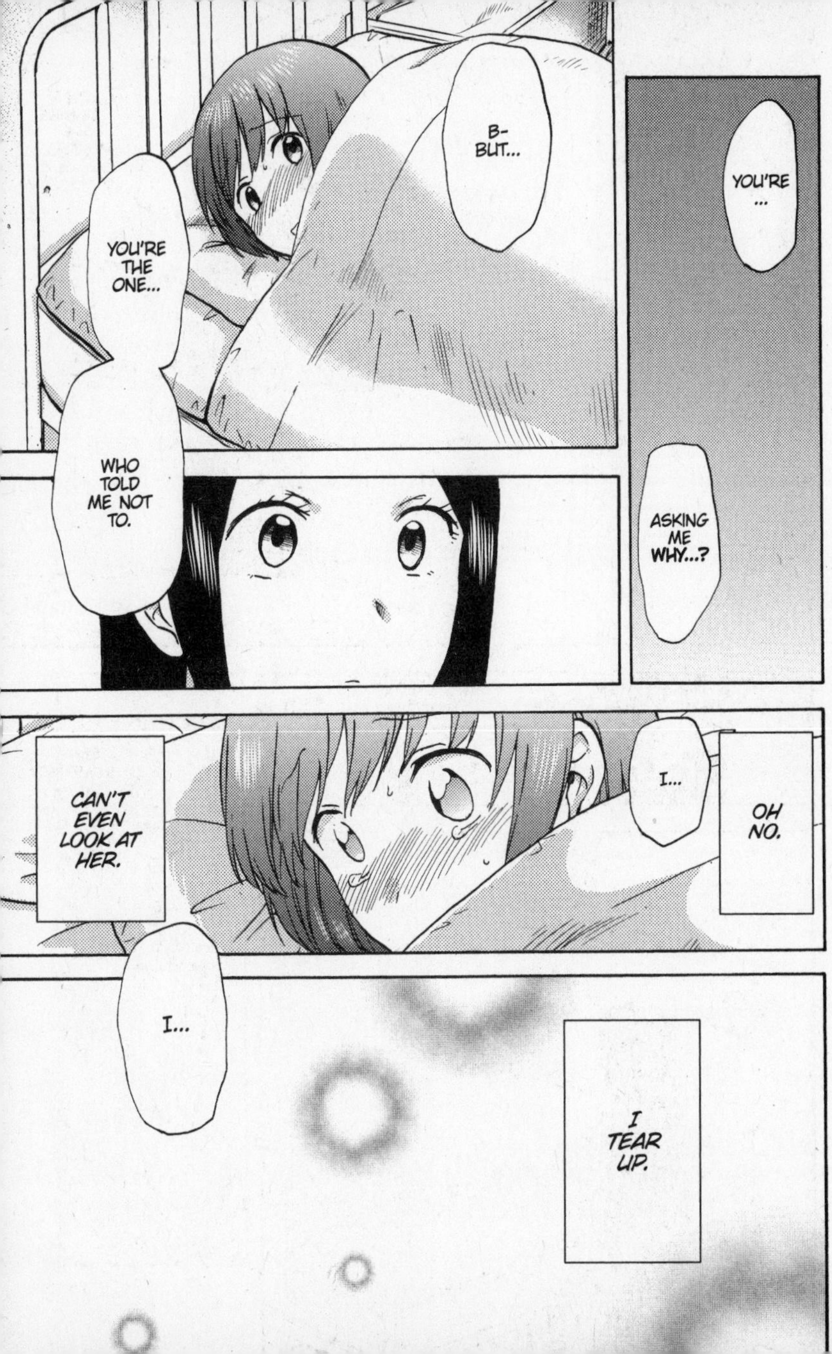
YOU'RE ...
ASKING ME WHY...?
B-BUT...
YOU'RE THE ONE...
WHO TOLD ME NOT TO.
OH NO.
I...
CAN'T EVEN LOOK AT HER.
I TEAR UP.
I...

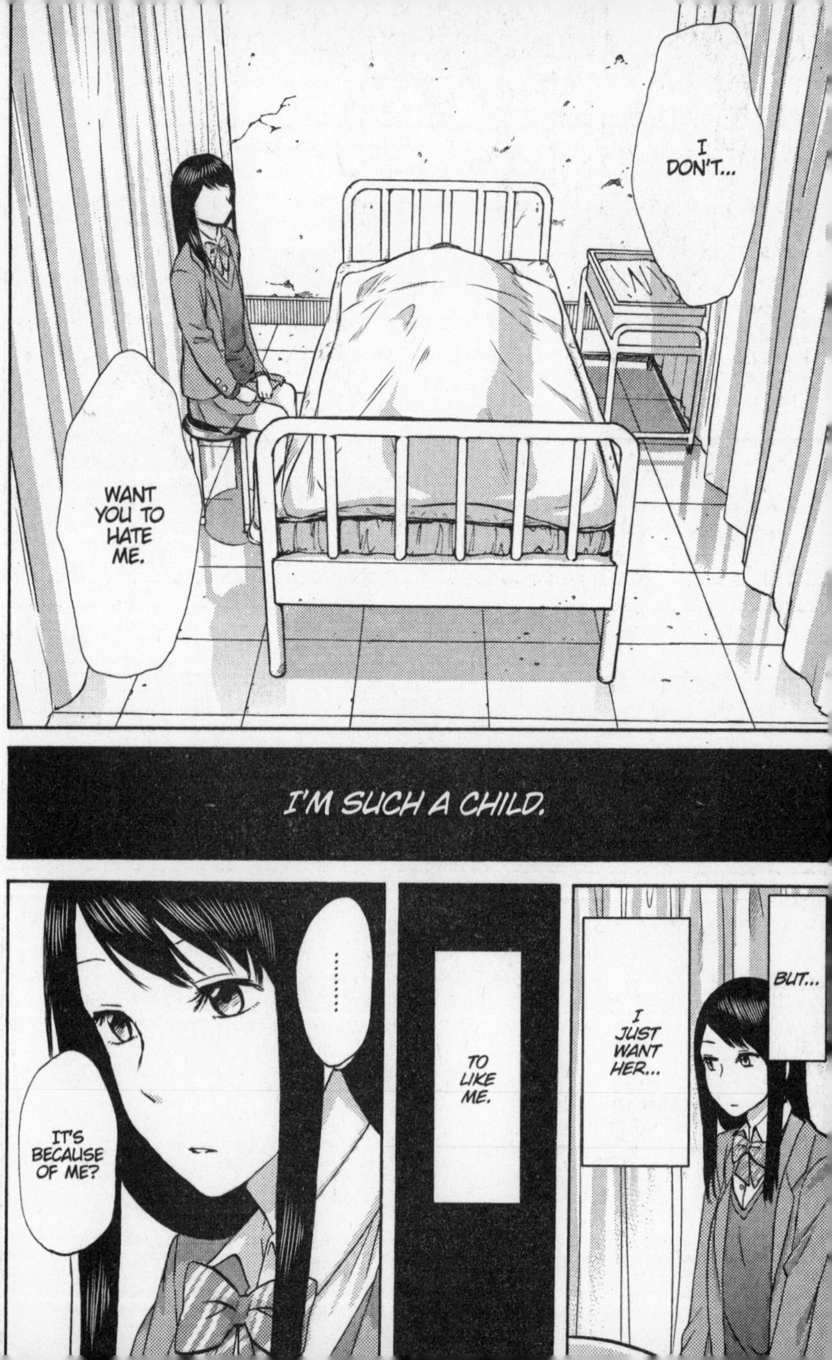
I DON'T...
WANT YOU TO HATE ME.
I'M SUCH A CHILD.
BUT...
I JUST WANT HER...
TO LIKE ME.
......
IT'S BECAUSE OF ME?

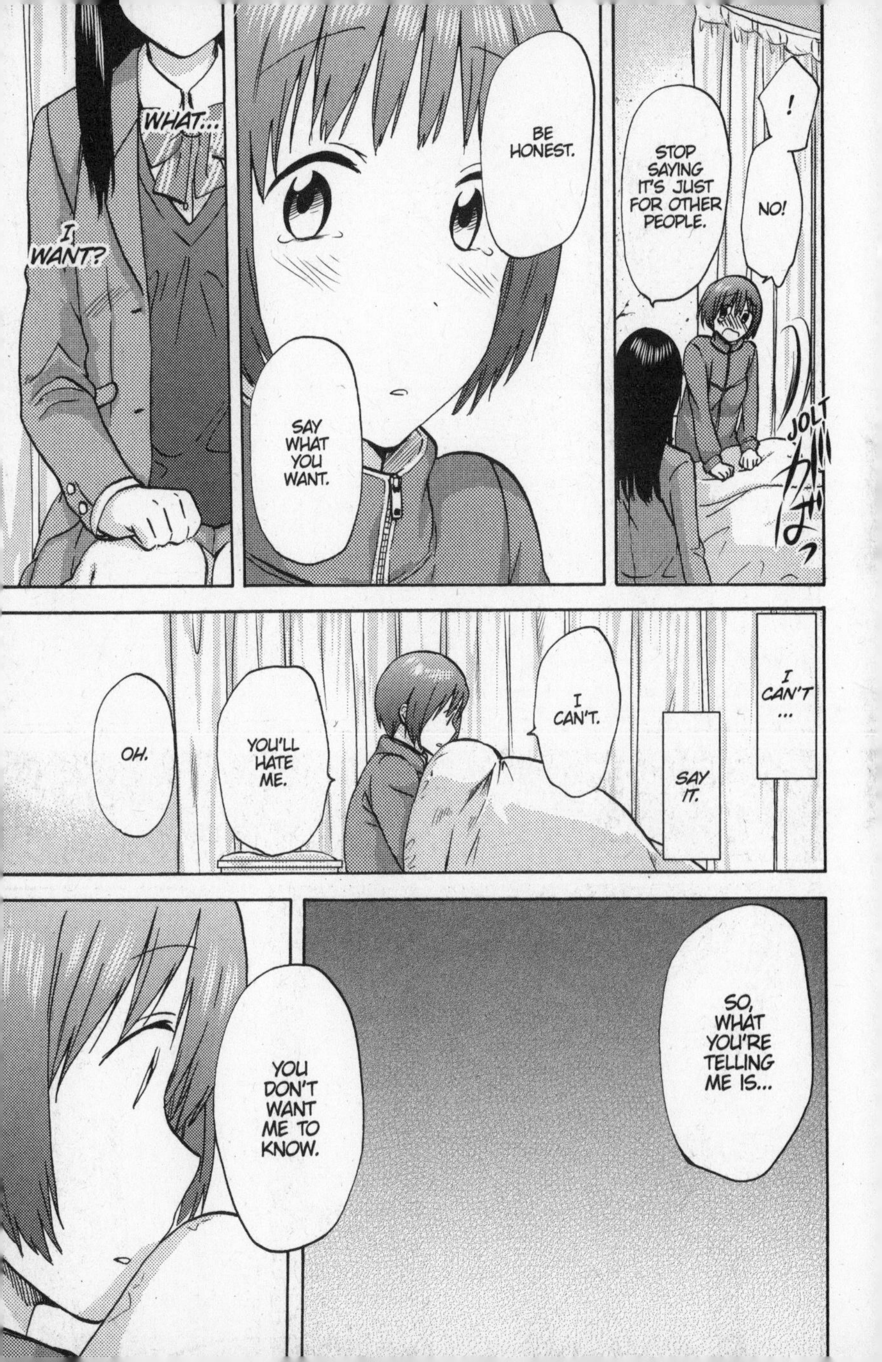
!
NO!
STOP SAYING IT'S JUST FOR OTHER PEOPLE.
JOLT
BE HONEST.
SAY WHAT YOU WANT.
WHAT...
I WANT?
I CAN'T...
SAY IT.
I CAN'T.
YOU'LL HATE ME.
OH.
SO, WHAT YOU'RE TELLING ME IS...
YOU DON'T WANT ME TO KNOW.

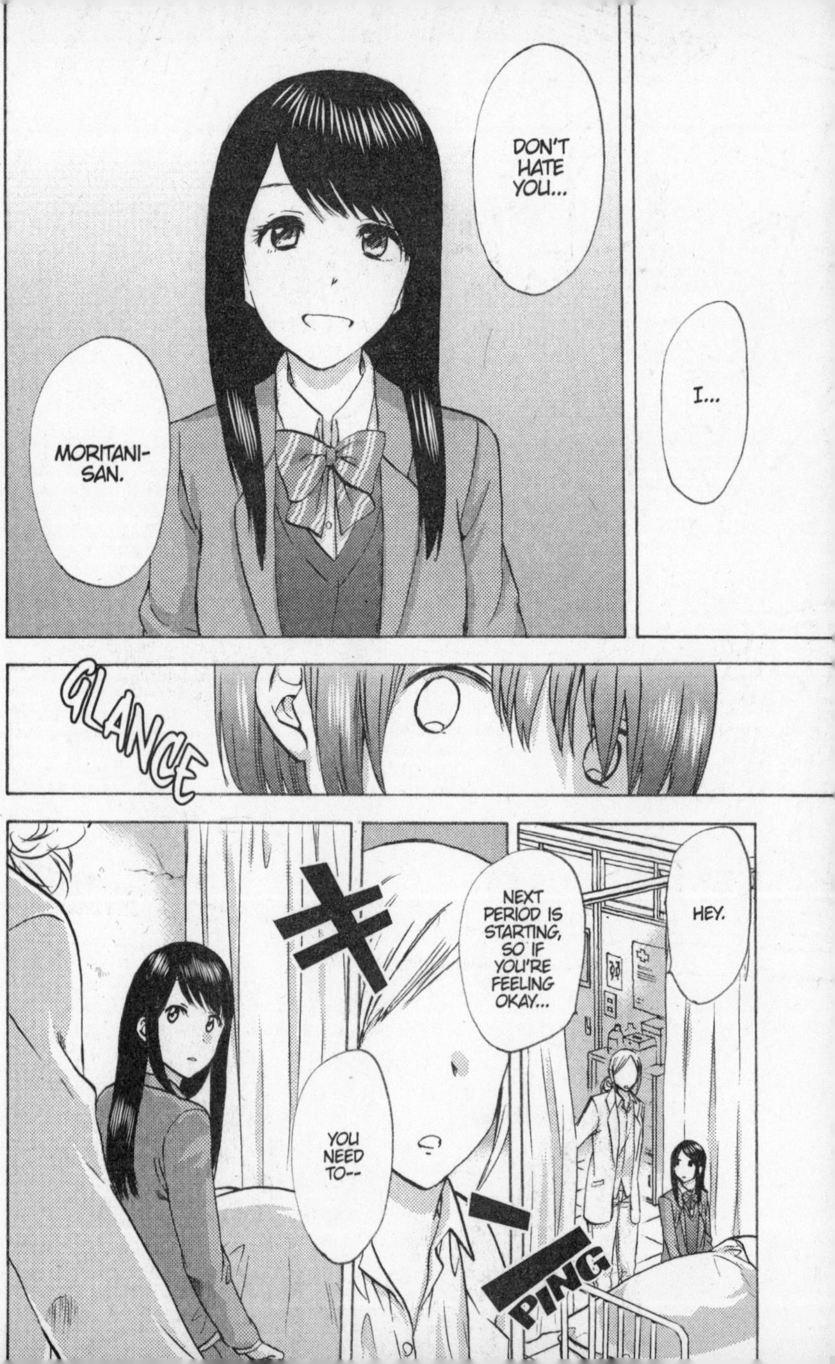

I...
DON'T HATE YOU...
MORITANI-SAN.
GLANCE
HEY.
NEXT PERIOD IS STARTING, SO IF YOU'RE FEELING OKAY...
YOU NEED TO--
PING

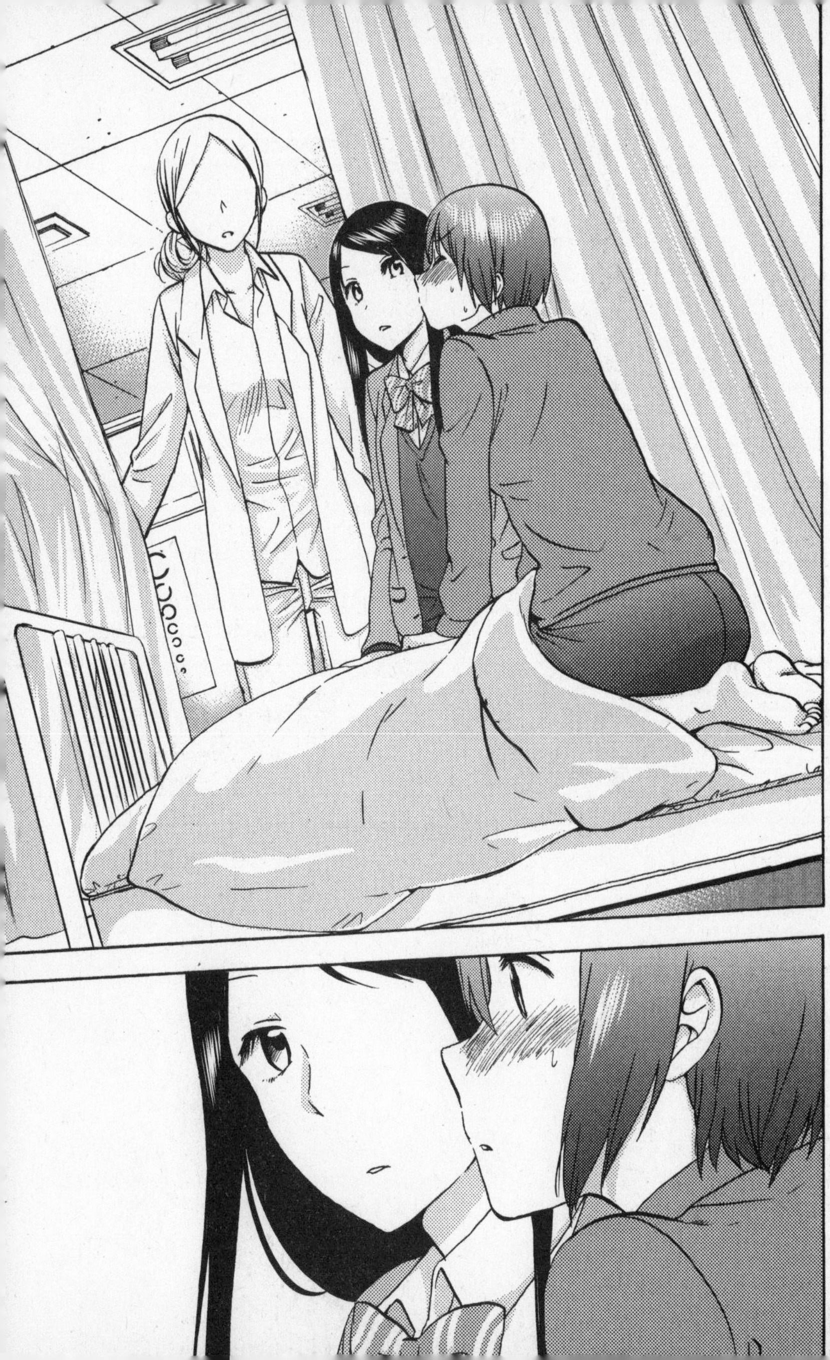

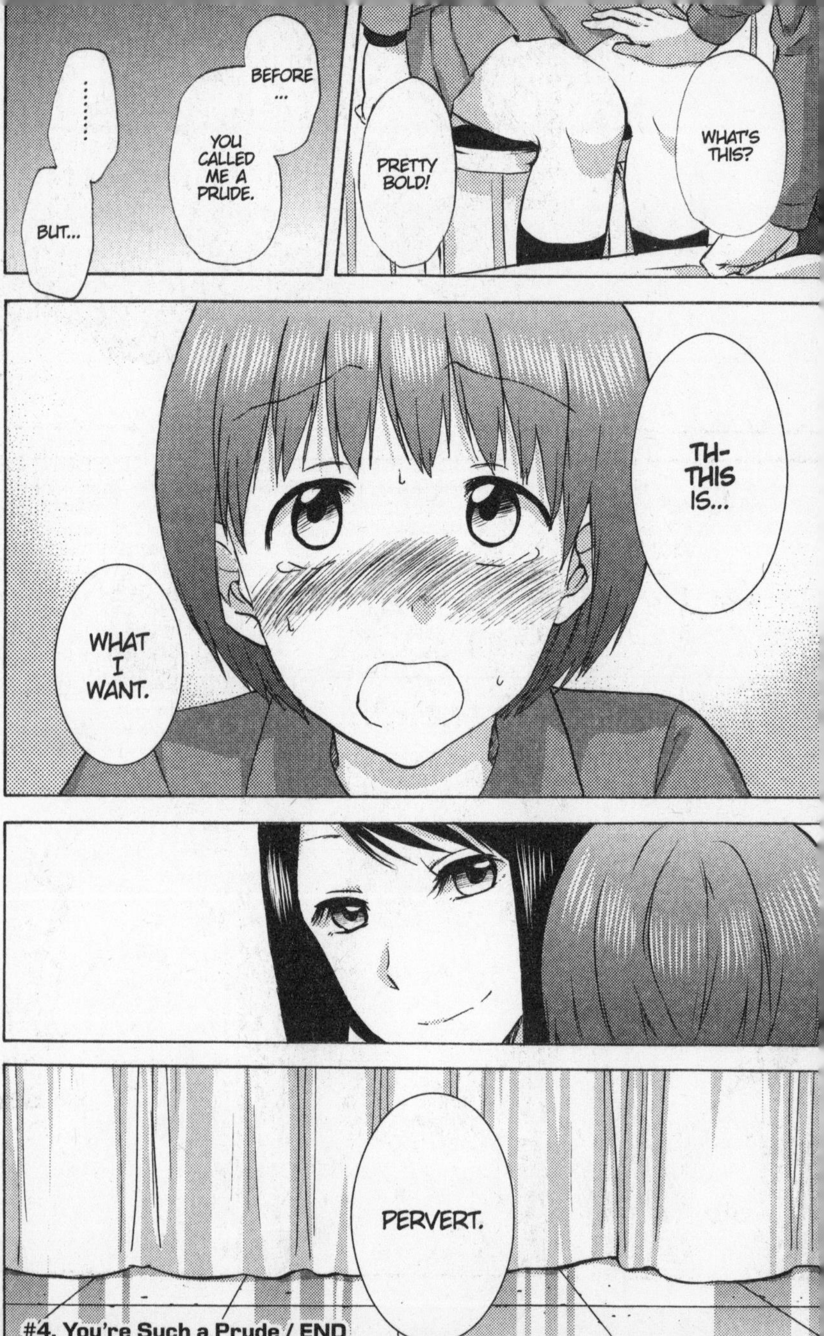
WHAT'S THIS?
PRETTY BOLD!
BEFORE ...
YOU CALLED ME A PRUDE.
......
BUT...
TH-THIS IS...
WHAT I WANT.
PERVERT.

#4. You're Such a Prude / END

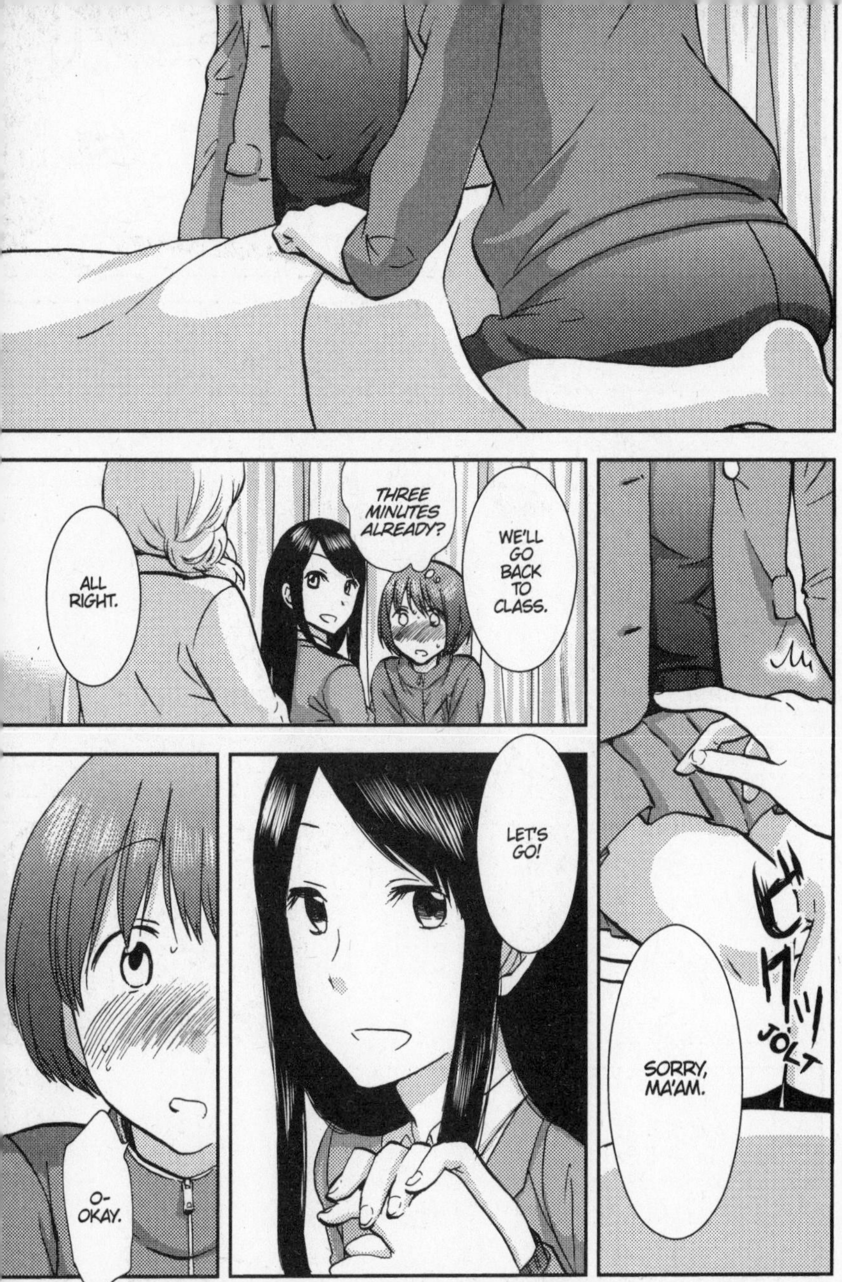
JOLT
SORRY, MA'AM.
WE'LL GO BACK TO CLASS.
THREE MINUTES ALREADY?
ALL RIGHT.
LET'S GO!
O-OKAY.

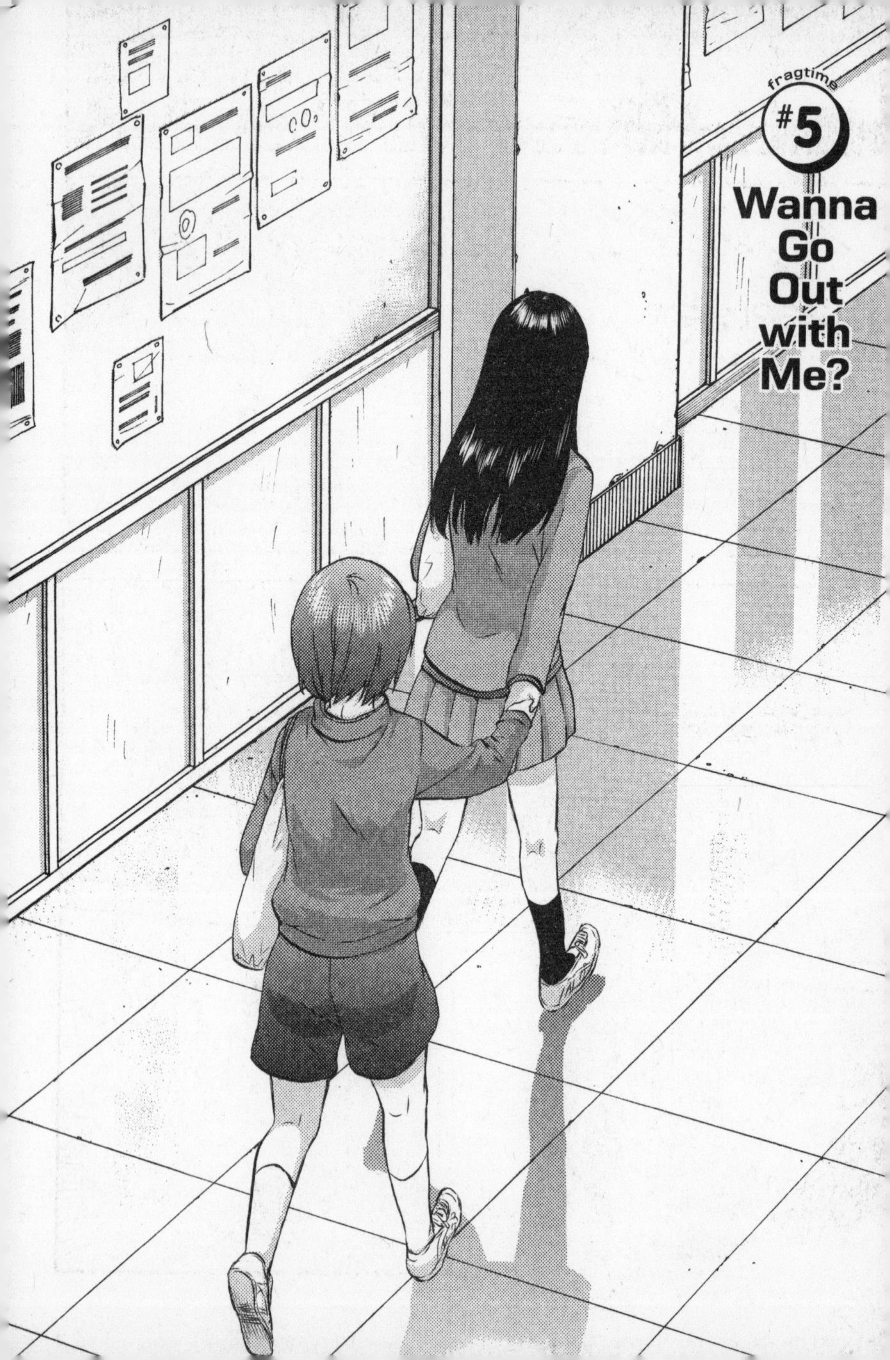
fragtime
#5
Wanna Go Out with Me?

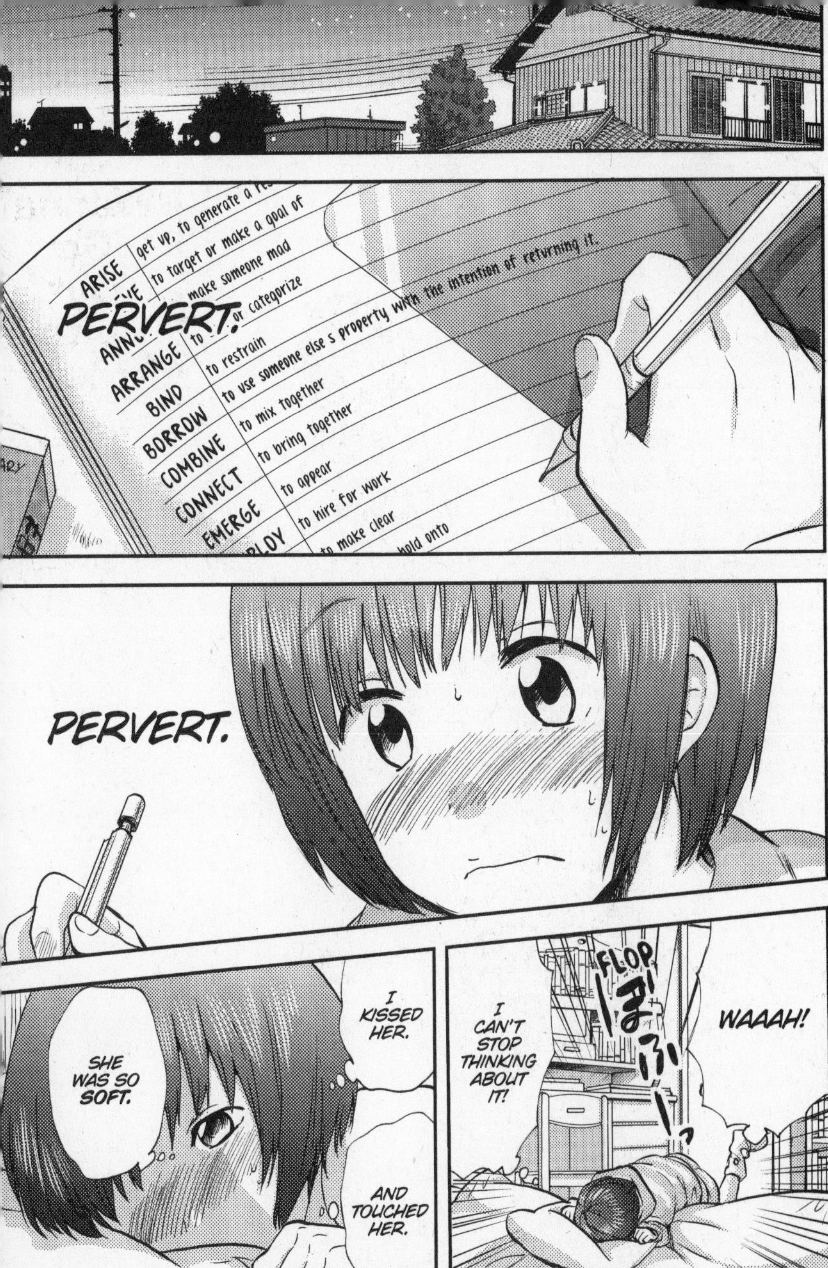

ARISE get up, to generate a
to target or make a goal of
make someone mad
or categorize
PERVERT.
ARRANGE
BIND to restrain
BORROW to use someone else s property with the intention of returning it.
COMBINE to mix together
CONNECT to bring together
EMERGE to appear
to hire for work
to make clear
hold onto
PERVERT.
WAAAH!
FLOP
ぼふーっ
I CAN'T STOP THINKING ABOUT IT!
I KISSED HER.
SHE WAS SO SOFT.
AND TOUCHED HER.

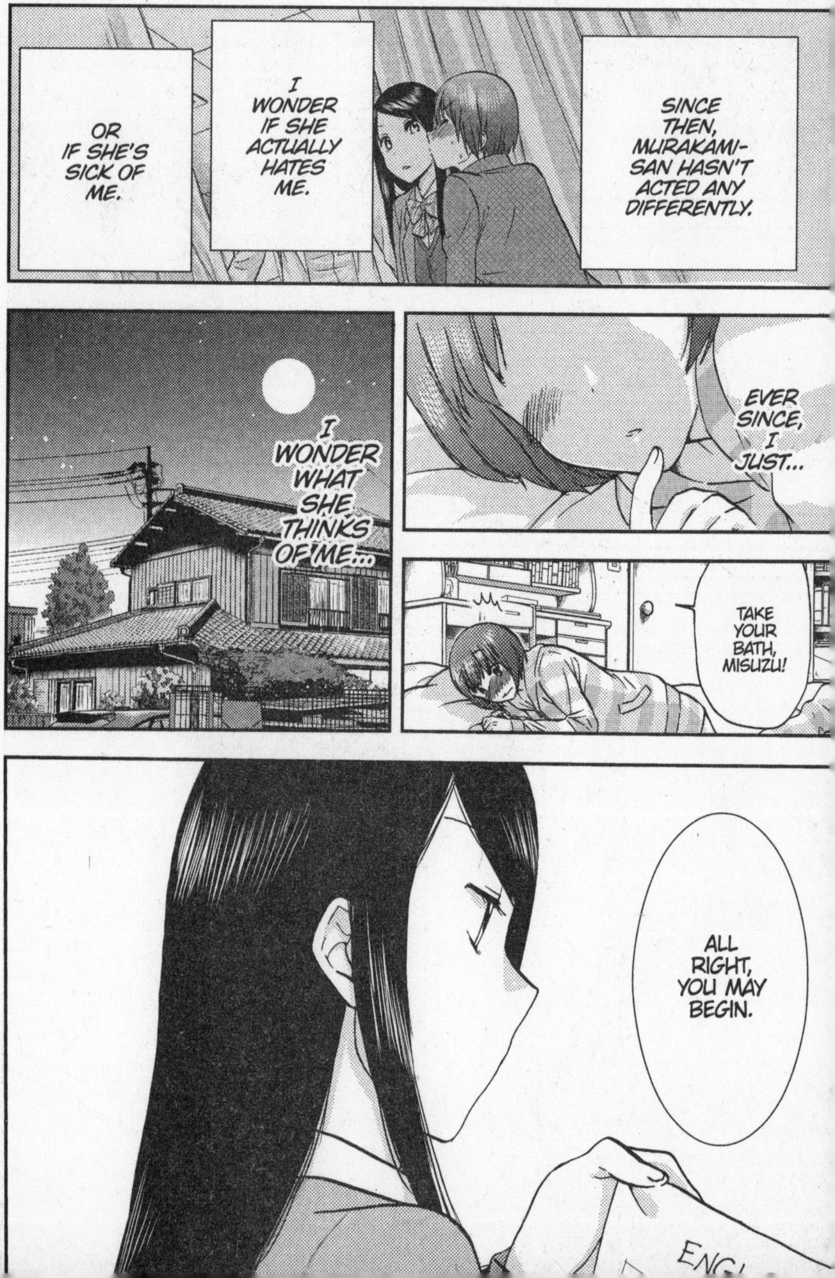
SINCE THEN, MURAKAMI-SAN HASN'T ACTED ANY DIFFERENTLY.
I WONDER IF SHE ACTUALLY HATES ME.
OR IF SHE'S SICK OF ME.
EVER SINCE, I JUST...
TAKE YOUR BATH, MISUZU!
I WONDER WHAT SHE THINKS OF ME...
ALL RIGHT, YOU MAY BEGIN.
ENGL

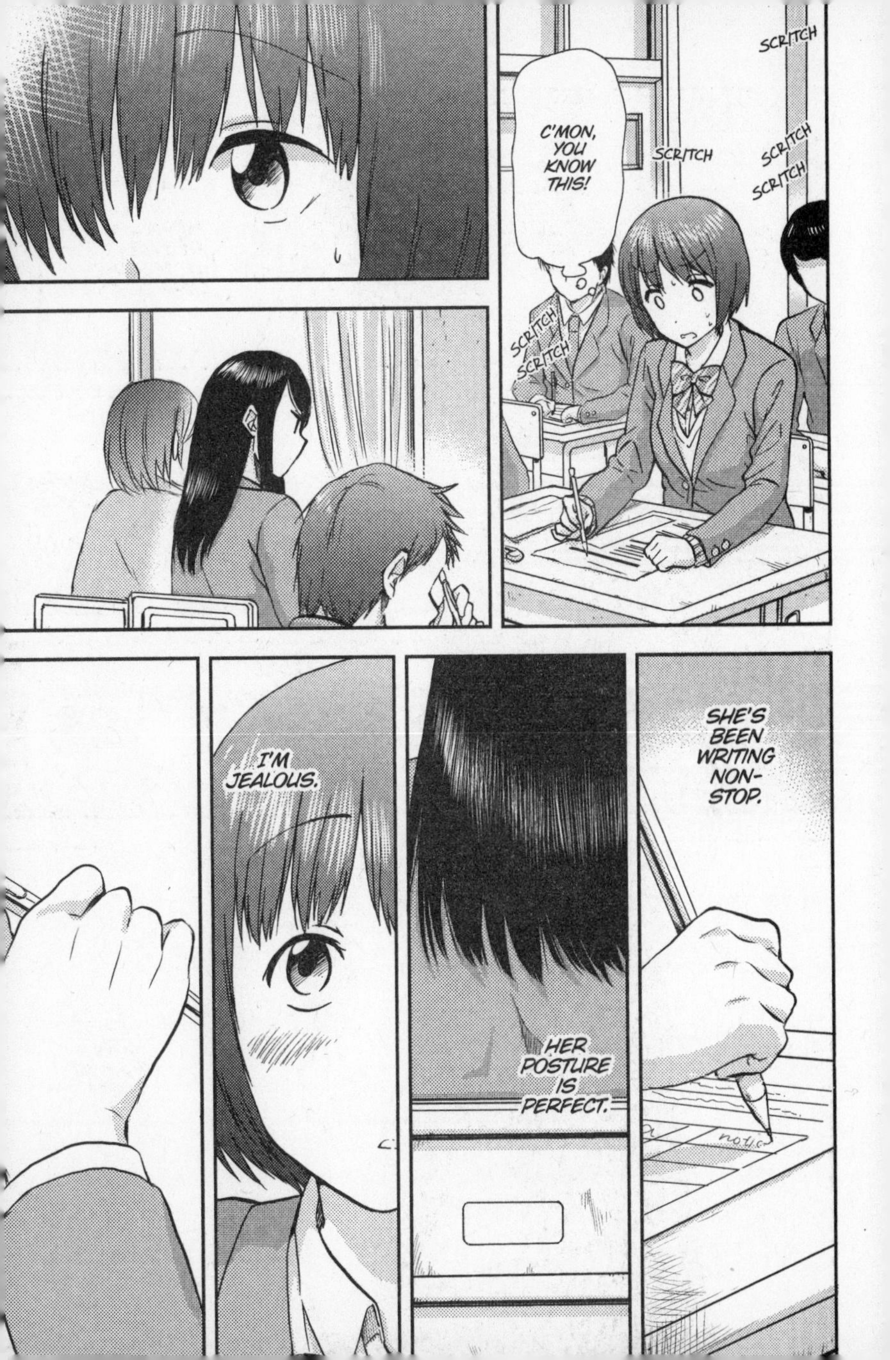
SCRITCH
SCRITCH
SCRITCH
SCRITCH
C'MON, YOU KNOW THIS!
SCRITCH
SCRITCH
SHE'S BEEN WRITING NON-STOP.
HER POSTURE IS PERFECT.
I'M JEALOUS.

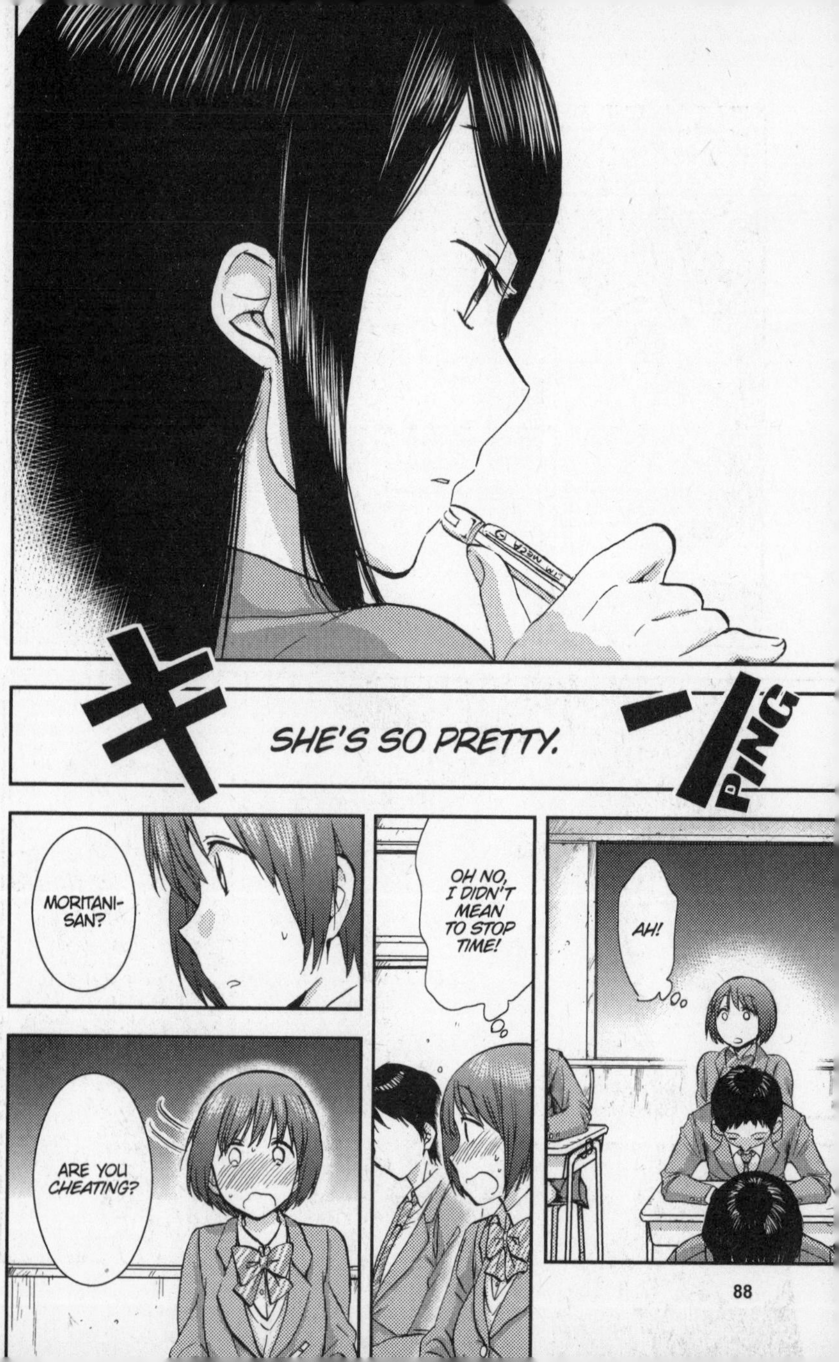
SHE'S SO PRETTY.
PING
AH!
OH NO, I DIDN'T MEAN TO STOP TIME!
MORITANI-SAN?
ARE YOU CHEATING?

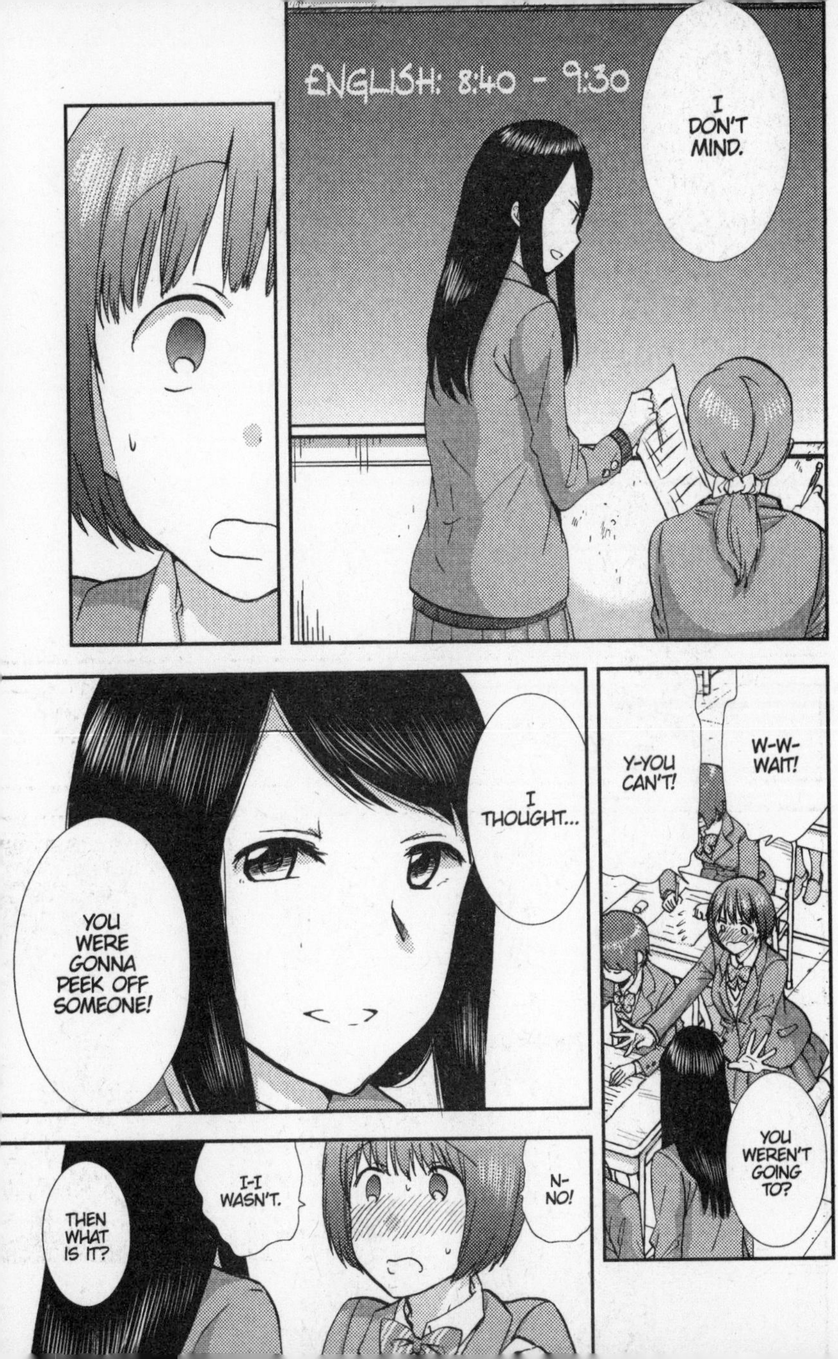
ENGLISH: 8:40 - 9:30
I DON'T MIND.
W-W-WAIT!
Y-YOU CAN'T!
YOU WEREN'T GOING TO?
I THOUGHT...
YOU WERE GONNA PEEK OFF SOMEONE!
N-NO!
I-I WASN'T.
THEN WHAT IS IT?

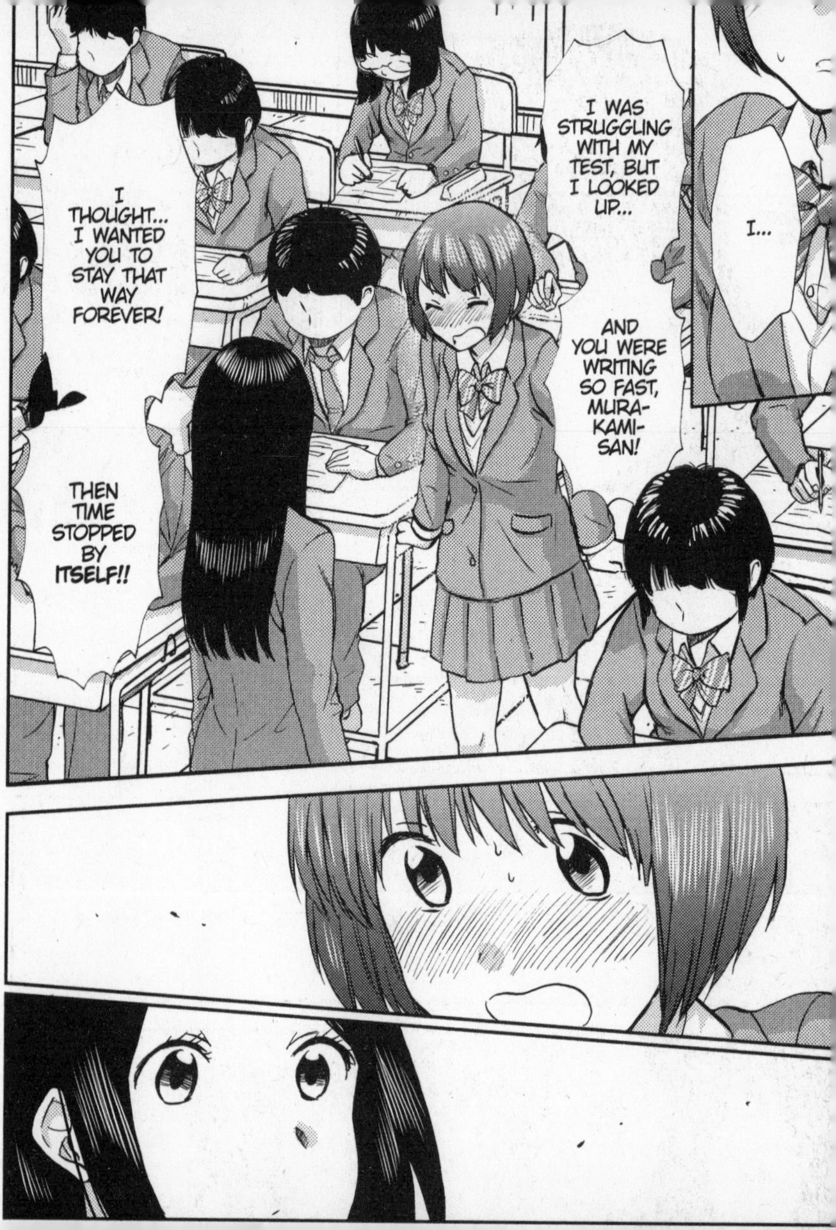
I...
I WAS STRUGGLING WITH MY TEST, BUT I LOOKED UP...
AND YOU WERE WRITING SO FAST, MURA-KAMI-SAN!
I THOUGHT... I WANTED YOU TO STAY THAT WAY FOREVER!
THEN TIME STOPPED BY ITSELF!!

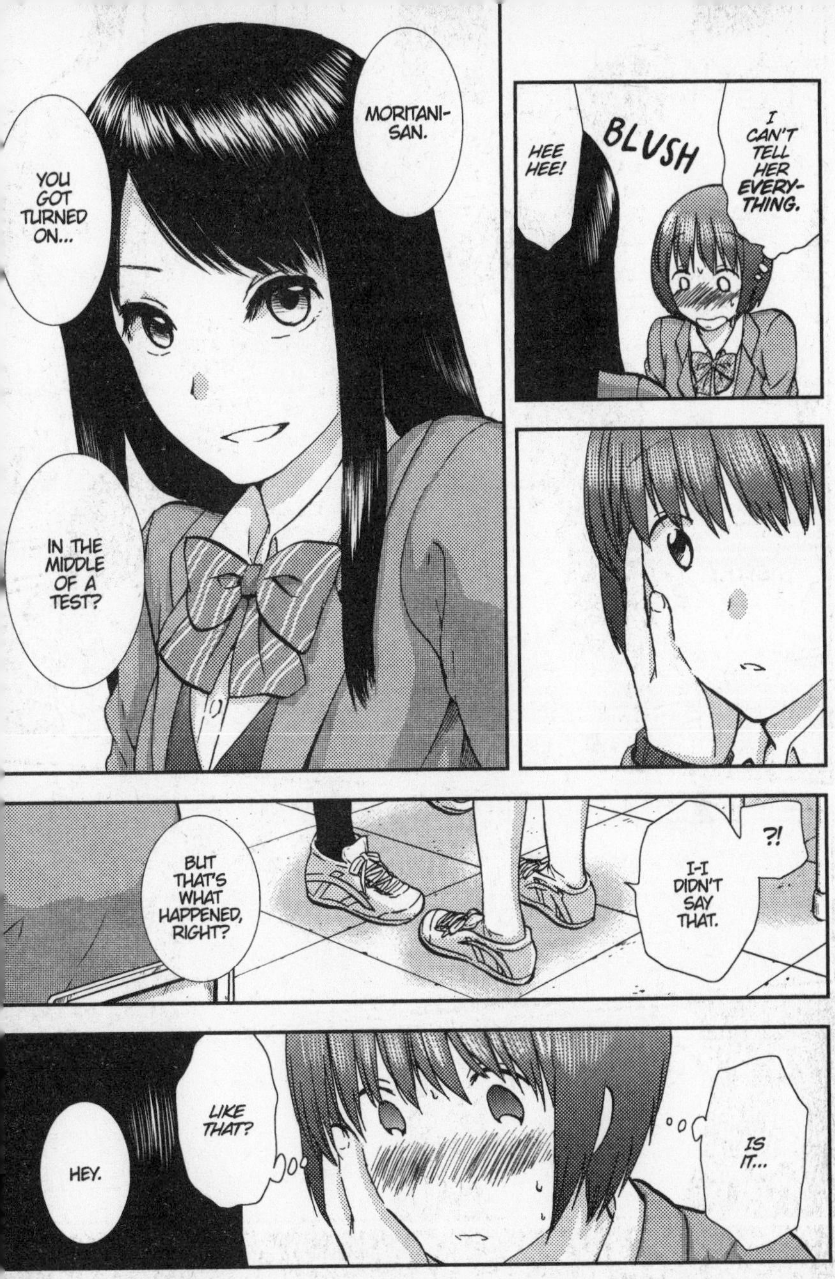
I CAN'T TELL HER EVERYTHING.
BLUSH
HEE HEE!
MORITANI-SAN.
YOU GOT TURNED ON...
IN THE MIDDLE OF A TEST?
?!
I-I DIDN'T SAY THAT.
BUT THAT'S WHAT HAPPENED, RIGHT?
IS IT...
LIKE THAT?
HEY.

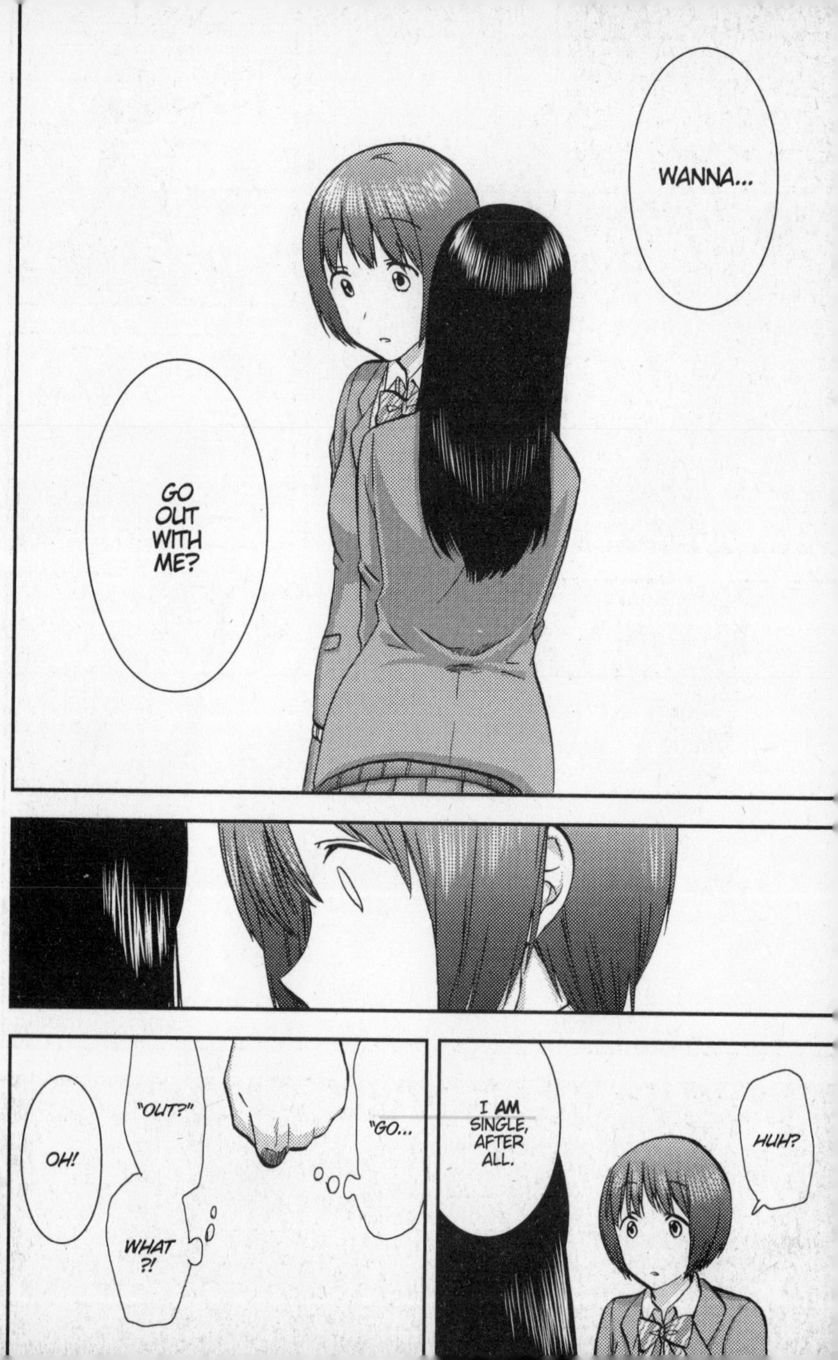
WANNA...
GO OUT WITH ME?
HUH?
I AM SINGLE, AFTER ALL.
"GO...
"OUT?"
WHAT ?!
OH!

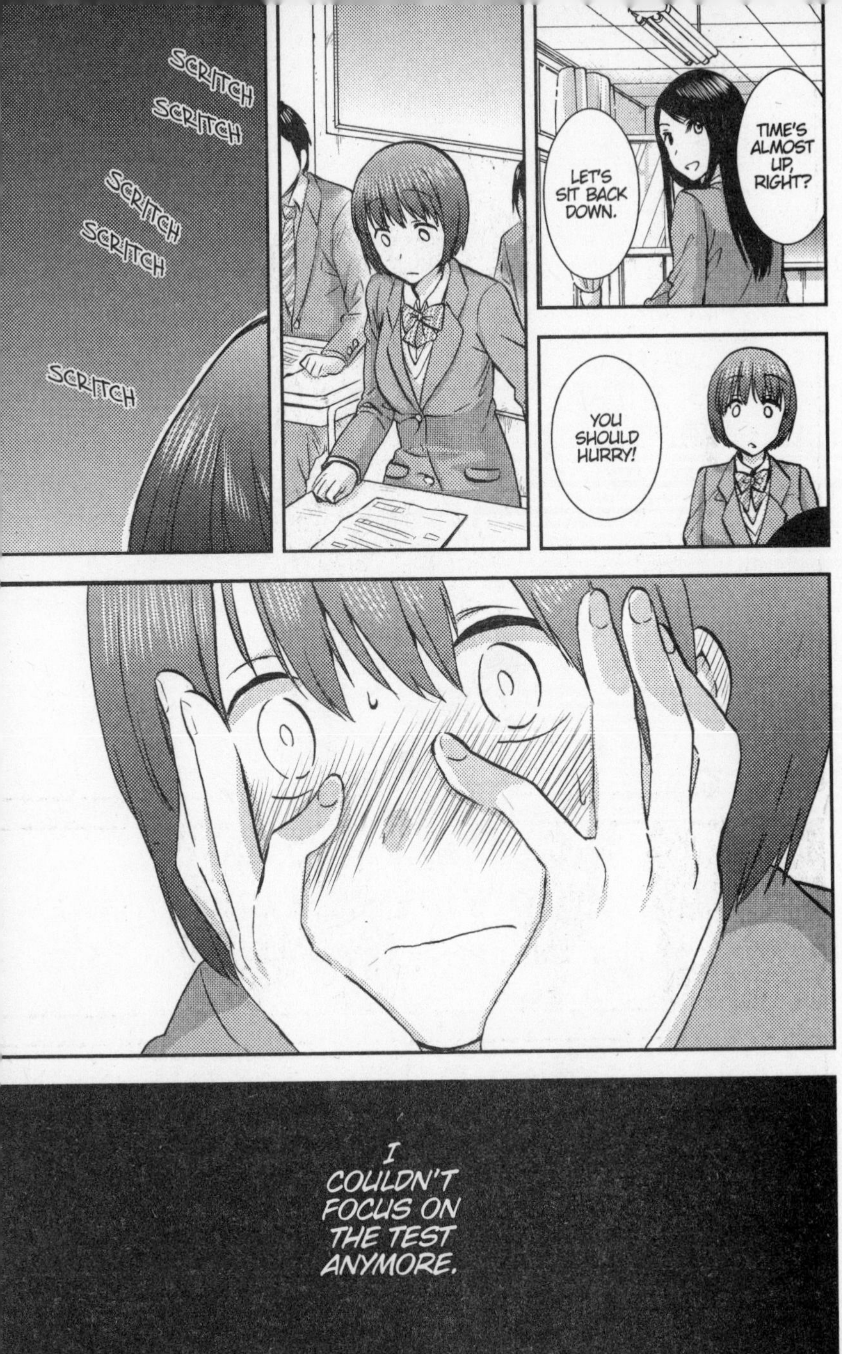
TIME'S ALMOST UP, RIGHT?
LET'S SIT BACK DOWN.
YOU SHOULD HURRY!
SCRITCH
SCRITCH
SCRITCH
SCRITCH
SCRITCH
I COULDN'T FOCUS ON THE TEST ANYMORE.

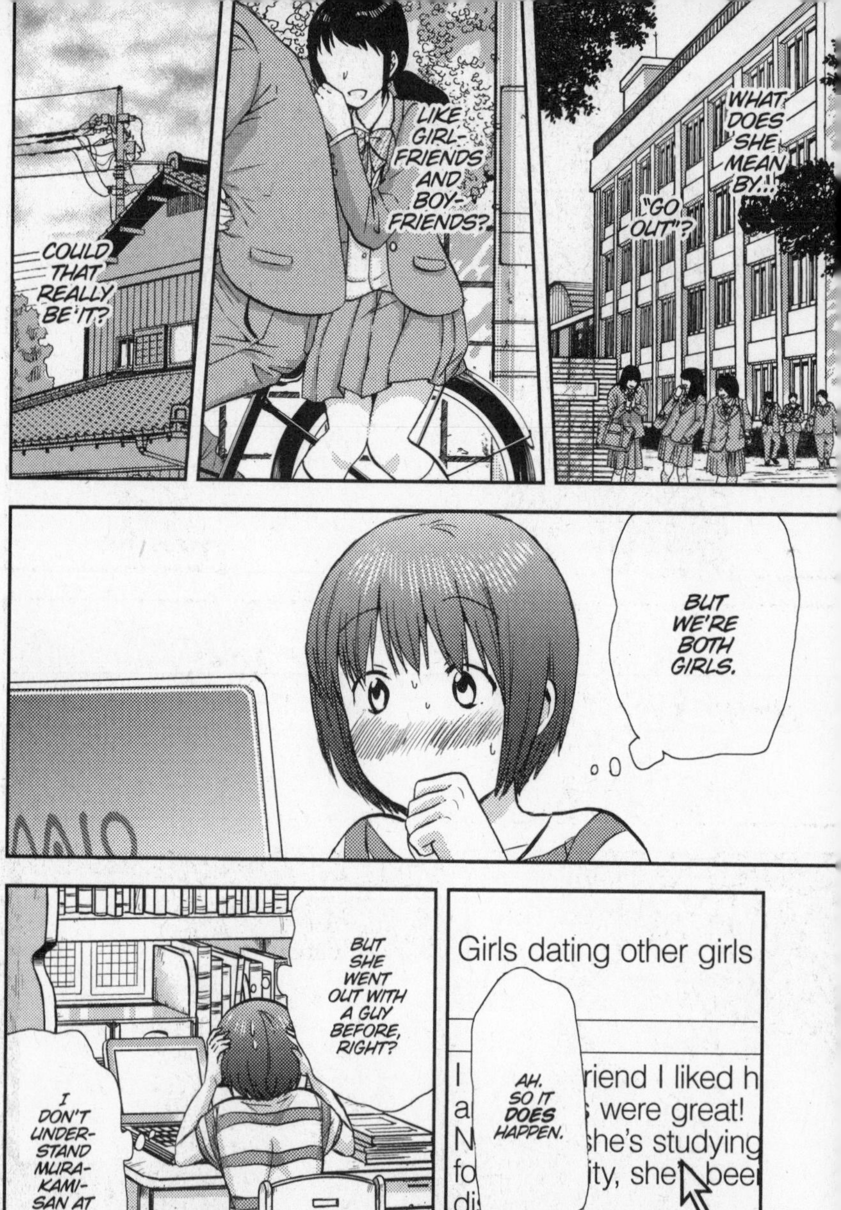
WHAT DOES SHE MEAN BY...
"GO OUT"?
LIKE GIRL-FRIENDS AND BOY-FRIENDS?
COULD THAT REALLY BE IT?
BUT WE'RE BOTH GIRLS.
Girls dating other girls
AH. SO IT DOES HAPPEN.
BUT SHE WENT OUT WITH A GUY BEFORE, RIGHT?
I DON'T UNDER-STAND MURA-KAMI-SAN AT ALL!!

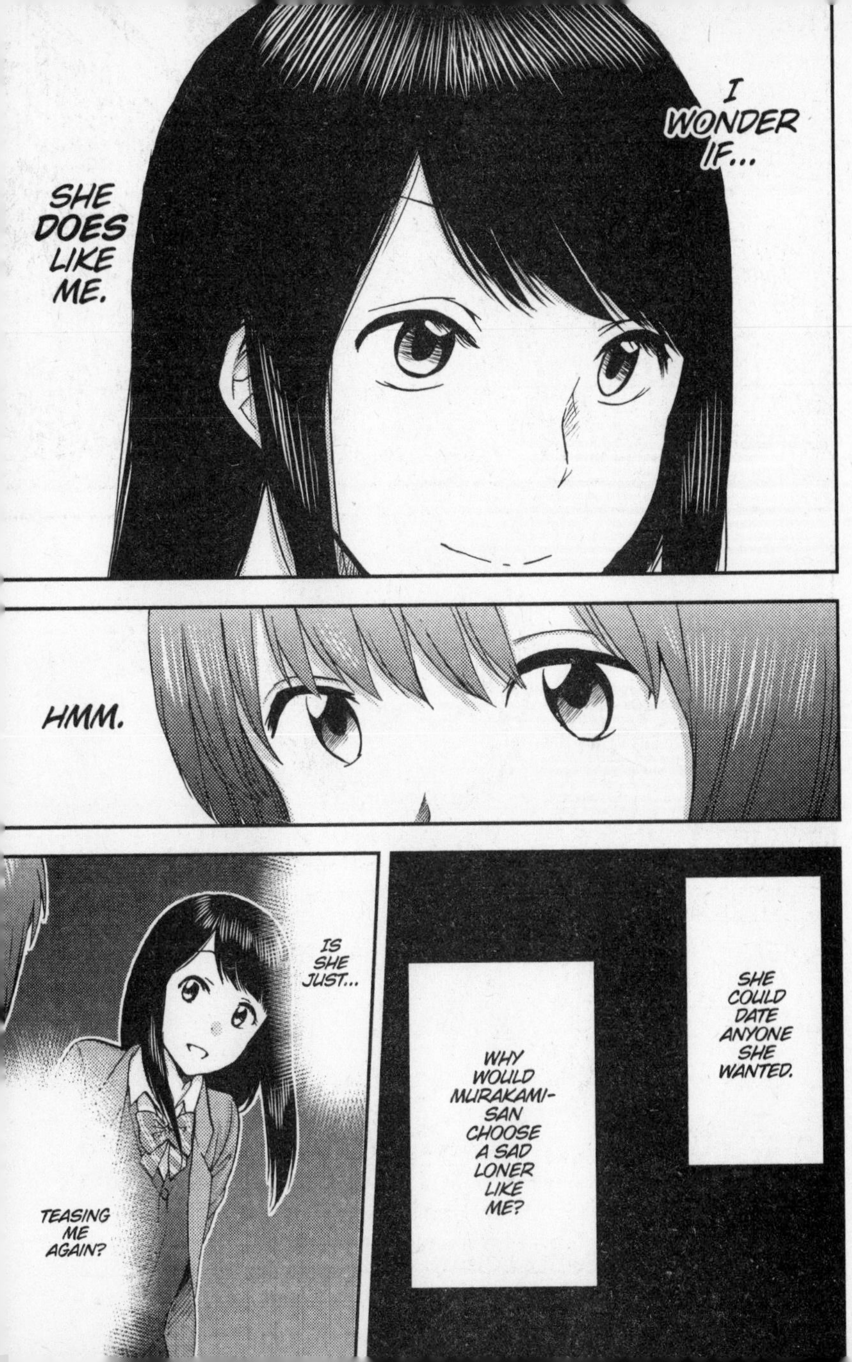
I WONDER IF...
SHE DOES LIKE ME.
HMM.
SHE COULD DATE ANYONE SHE WANTED.
WHY WOULD MURAKAMI-SAN CHOOSE A SAD LONER LIKE ME?
IS SHE JUST...
TEASING ME AGAIN?

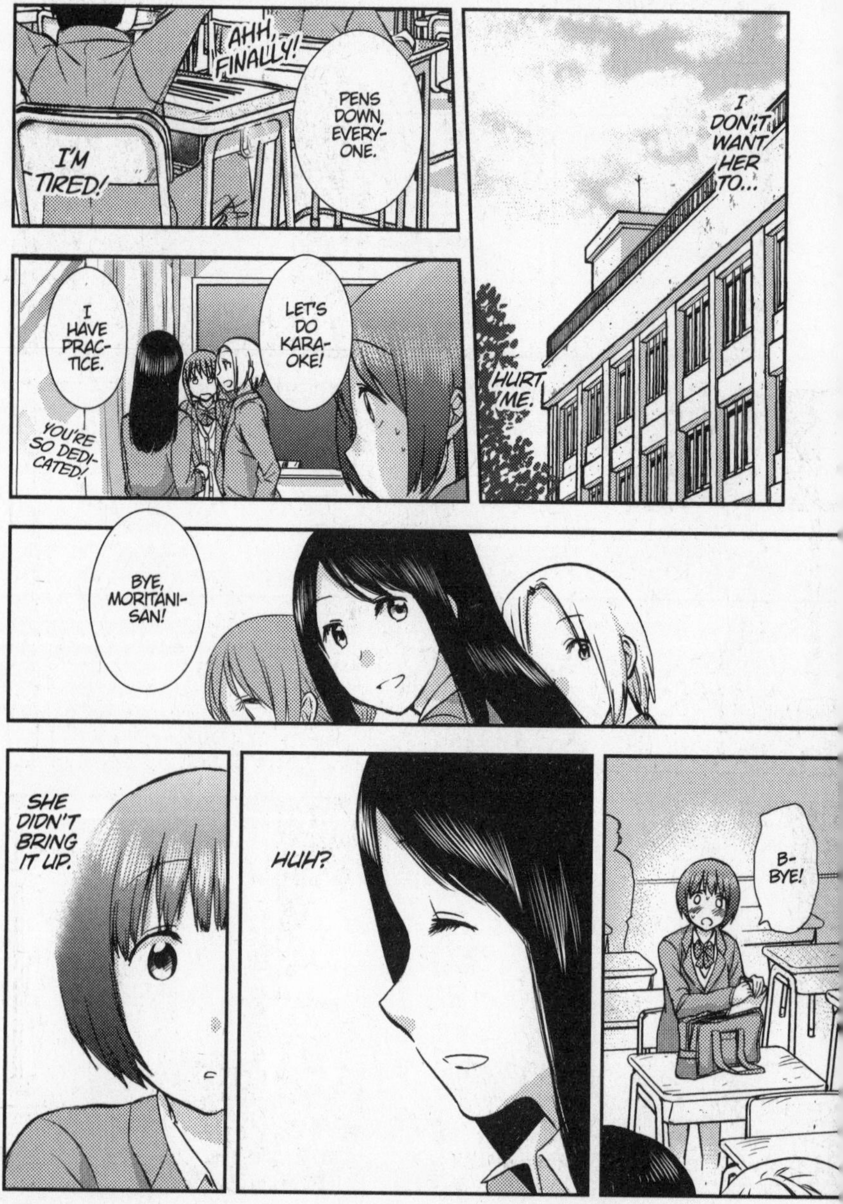
I DON'T WANT HER TO...
HURT ME.
PENS DOWN, EVERY-ONE.
AHH, FINALLY!
I'M TIRED!
LET'S DO KARA-OKE!
I HAVE PRAC-TICE.
YOU'RE SO DEDI-CATED!
BYE, MORITANI-SAN!
B-BYE!
HUH?
SHE DIDN'T BRING IT UP.

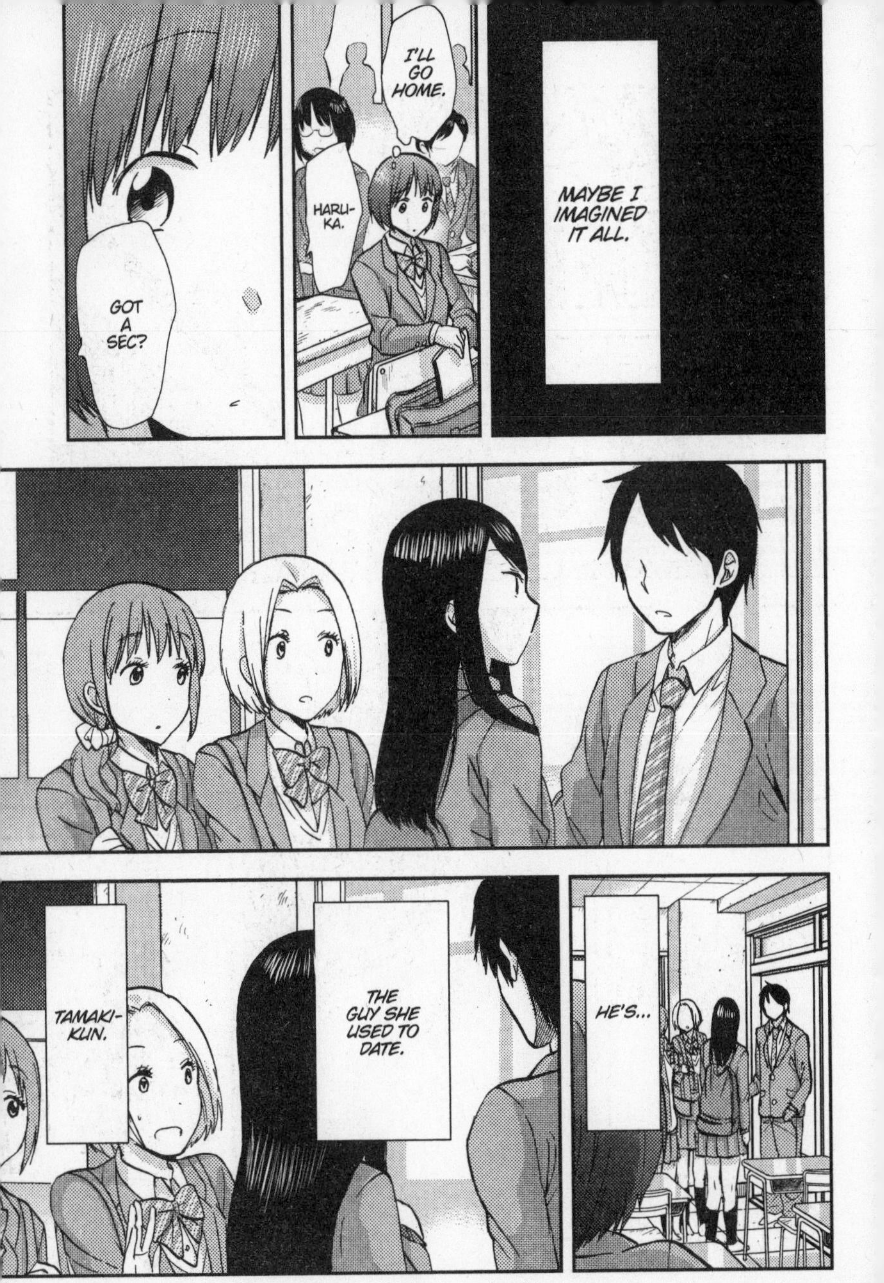
MAYBE I IMAGINED IT ALL.
I'LL GO HOME.
HARU-KA.
GOT A SEC?
HE'S...
THE GUY SHE USED TO DATE.
TAMAKI-KUN.

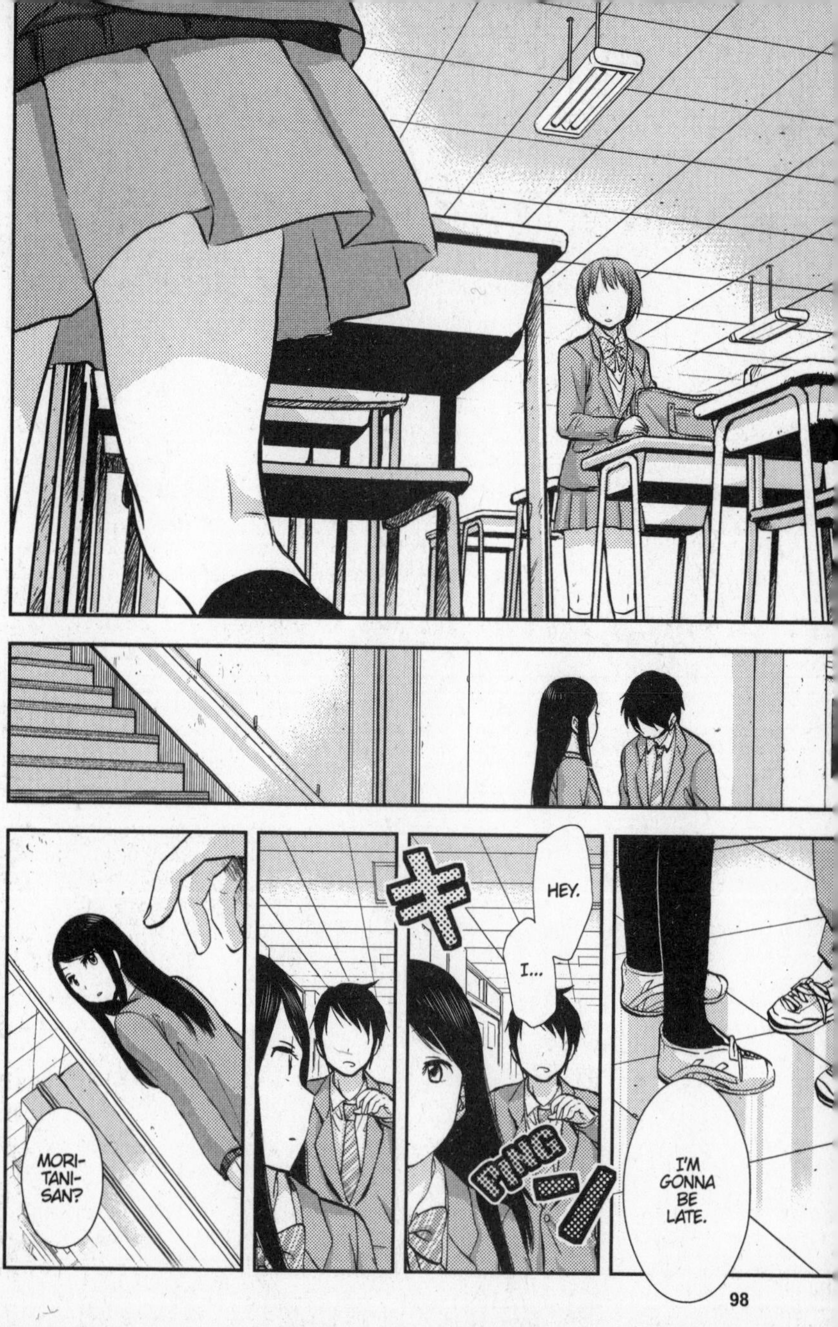
I'M GONNA BE LATE.
HEY.
I...
DING-
MORI-TANI-SAN?

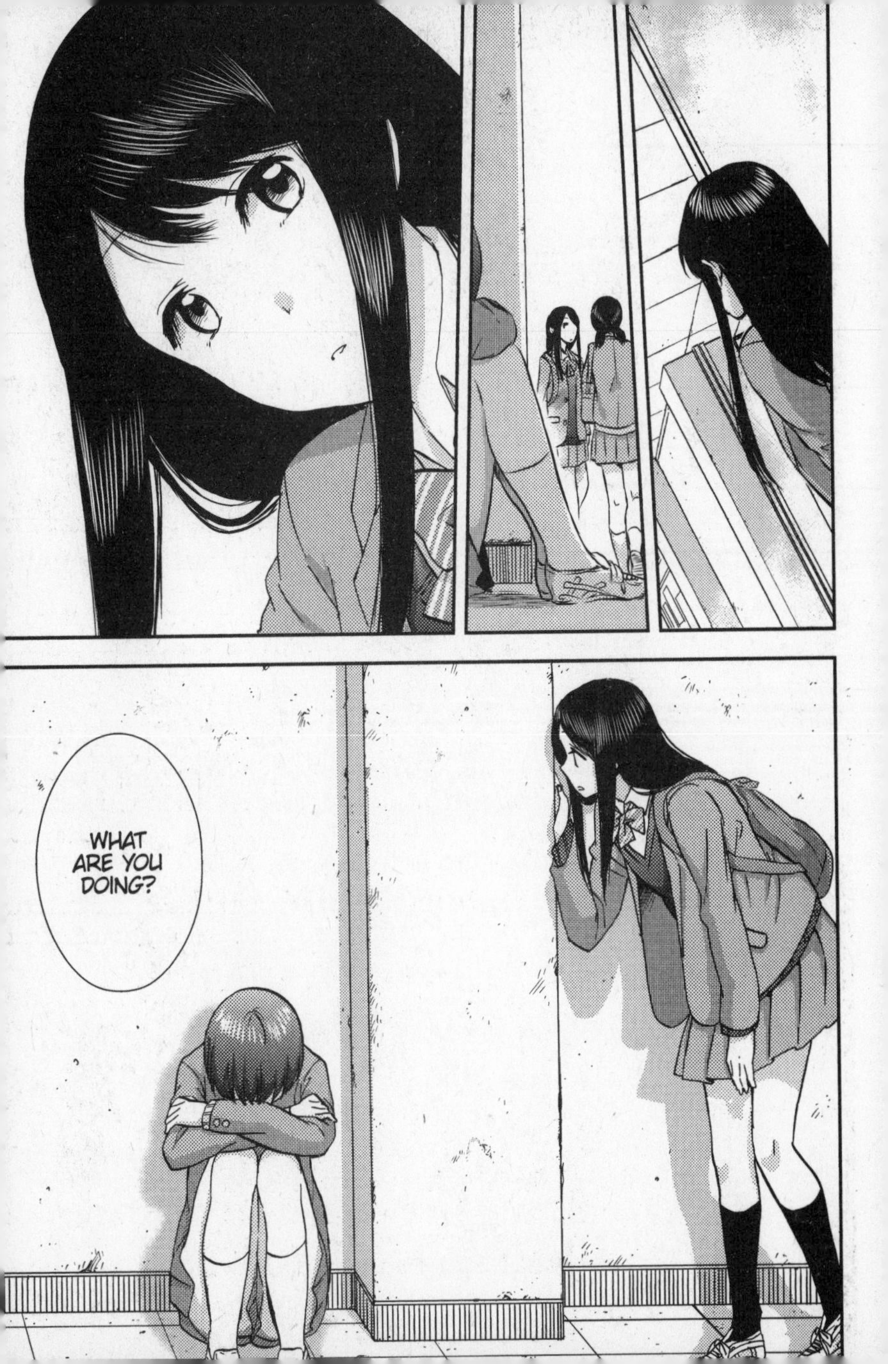
WHAT ARE YOU DOING?

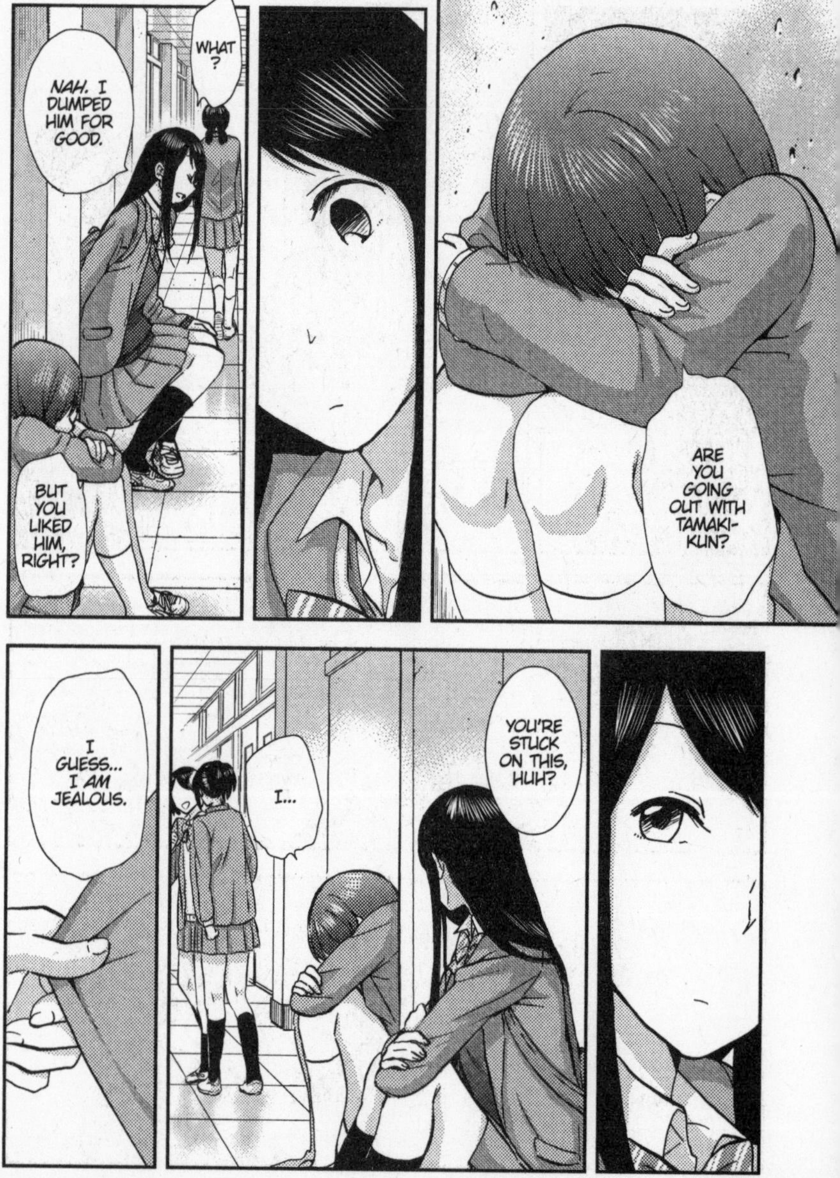
ARE YOU GOING OUT WITH TAMAKI-KUN?
WHAT?
NAH. I DUMPED HIM FOR GOOD.
BUT YOU LIKED HIM, RIGHT?
YOU'RE STUCK ON THIS, HUH?
I...
I GUESS... I AM JEALOUS.

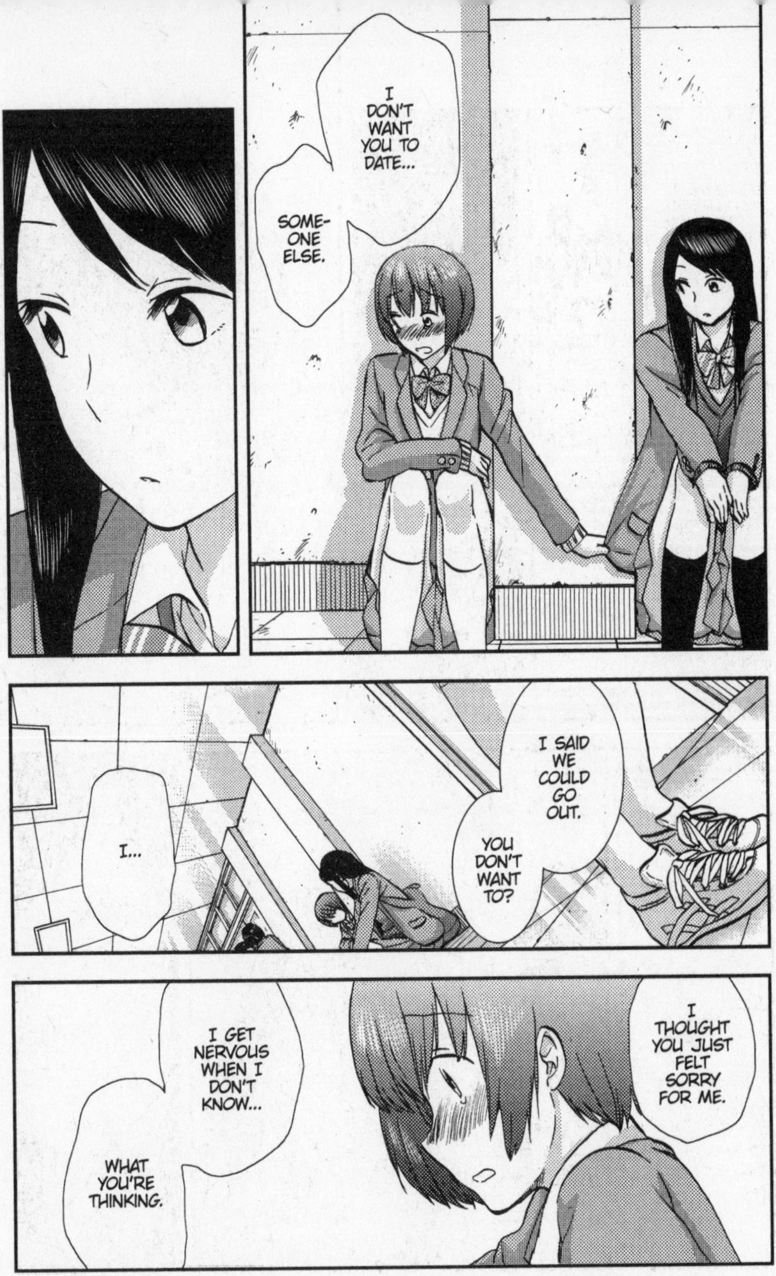
I DON'T WANT YOU TO DATE...
SOME-ONE ELSE.
I SAID WE COULD GO OUT.
YOU DON'T WANT TO?
I...
I THOUGHT YOU JUST FELT SORRY FOR ME.
I GET NERVOUS WHEN I DON'T KNOW...
WHAT YOU'RE THINKING.

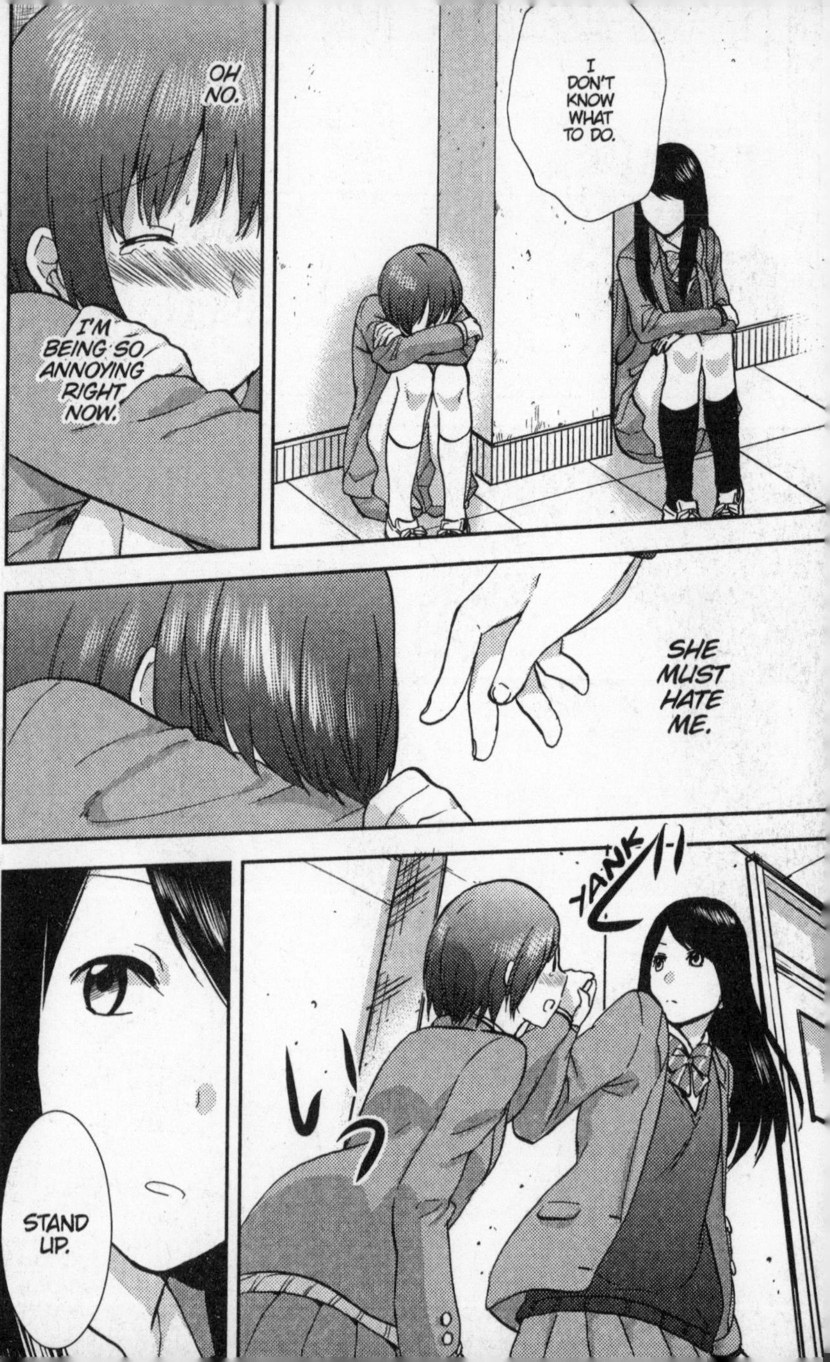
I DON'T KNOW WHAT TO DO.
OH NO.
I'M BEING SO ANNOYING RIGHT NOW.
SHE MUST HATE ME.
YANK
STAND UP.

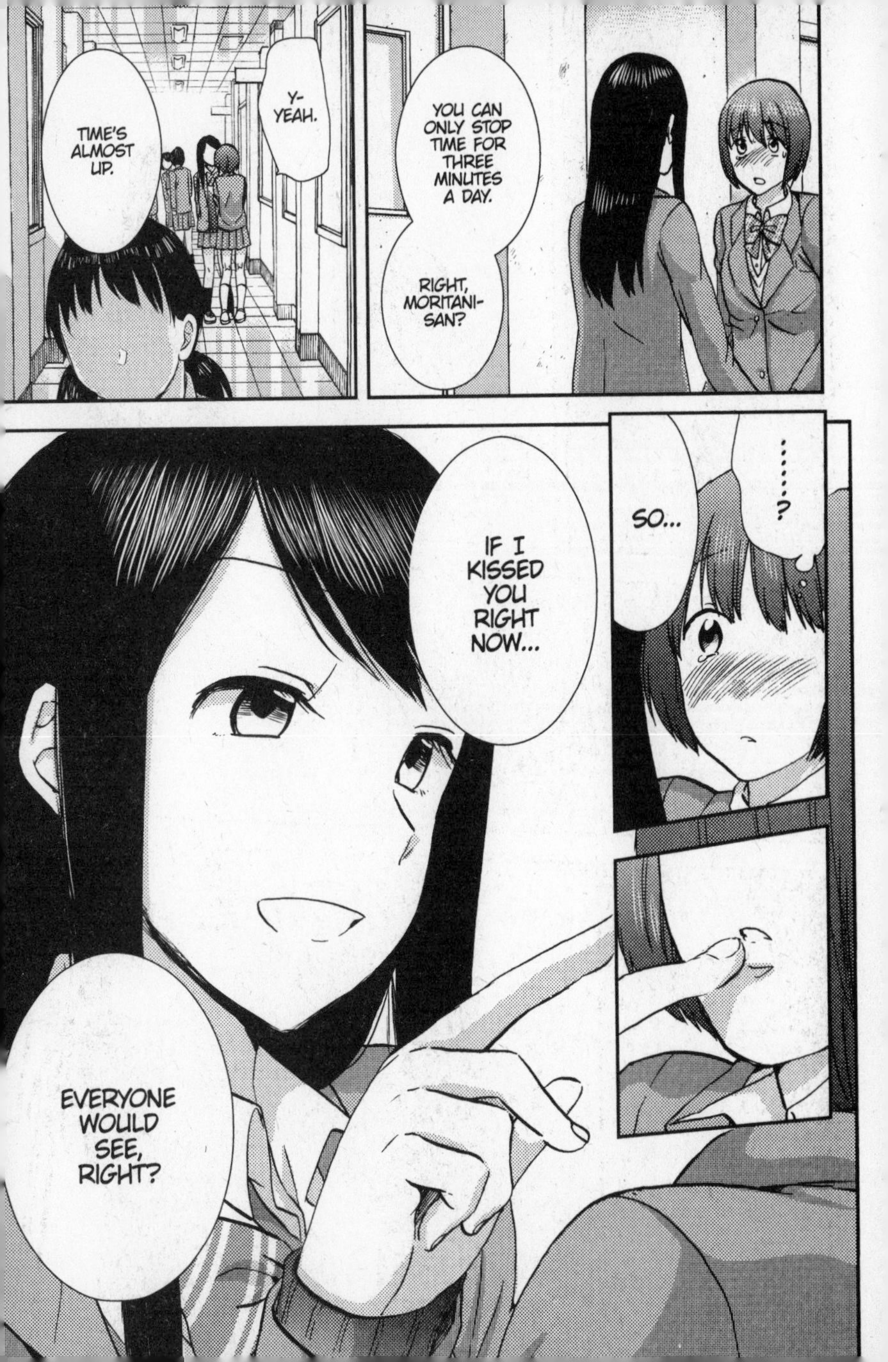
YOU CAN ONLY STOP TIME FOR THREE MINUTES A DAY.
RIGHT, MORITANI-SAN?
Y-YEAH.
TIME'S ALMOST UP.
......?
SO...
IF I KISSED YOU RIGHT NOW...
EVERYONE WOULD SEE, RIGHT?

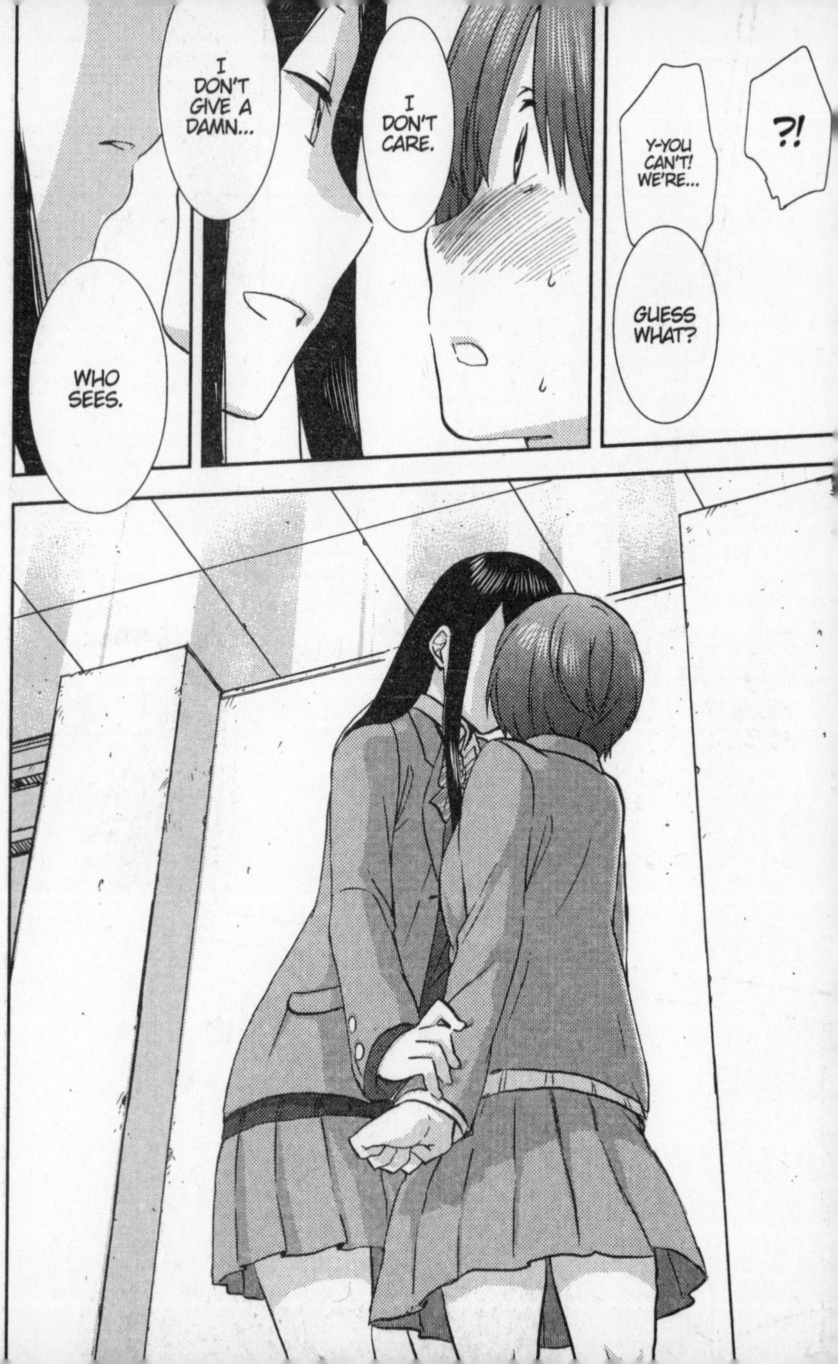
?!
Y-YOU CAN'T! WE'RE...
GUESS WHAT?
I DON'T CARE.
I DON'T GIVE A DAMN...
WHO SEES.

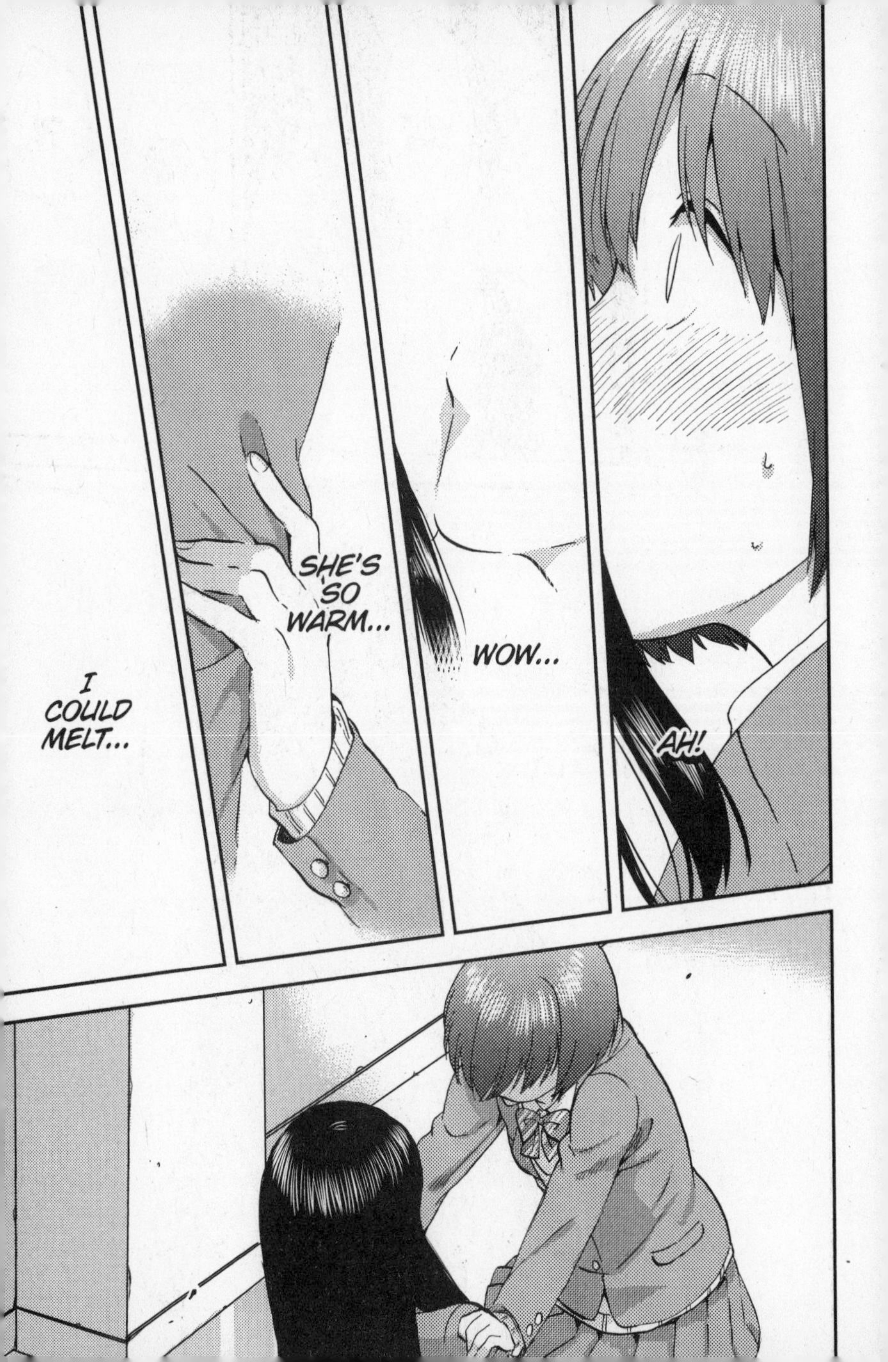
AH!
WOW...
SHE'S SO WARM...
I COULD MELT...

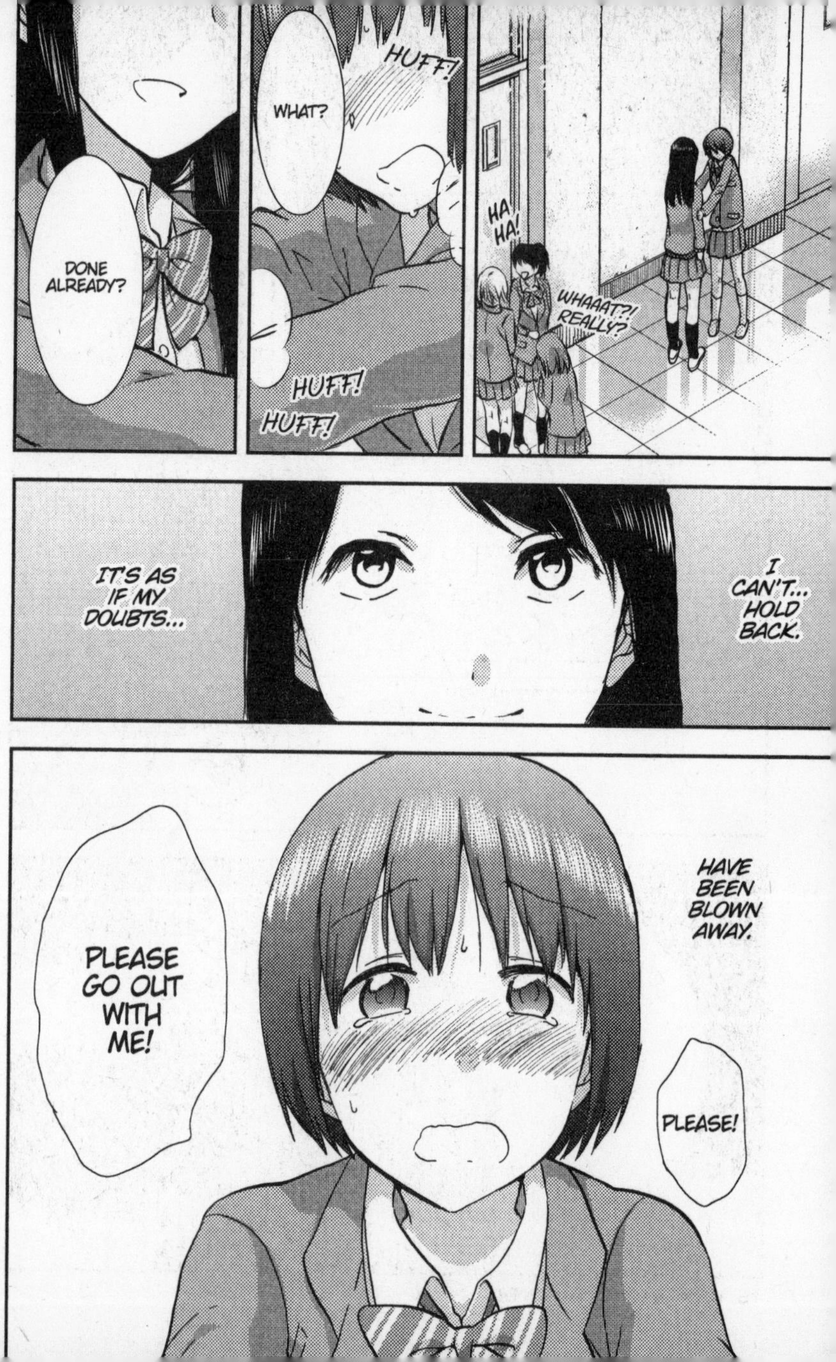
HA HA!
WHAAAT?! REALLY?
HUFF!
WHAT?
HUFF!
HUFF!
DONE ALREADY?
I CAN'T... HOLD BACK.
IT'S AS IF MY DOUBTS...
HAVE BEEN BLOWN AWAY.
PLEASE!
PLEASE GO OUT WITH ME!

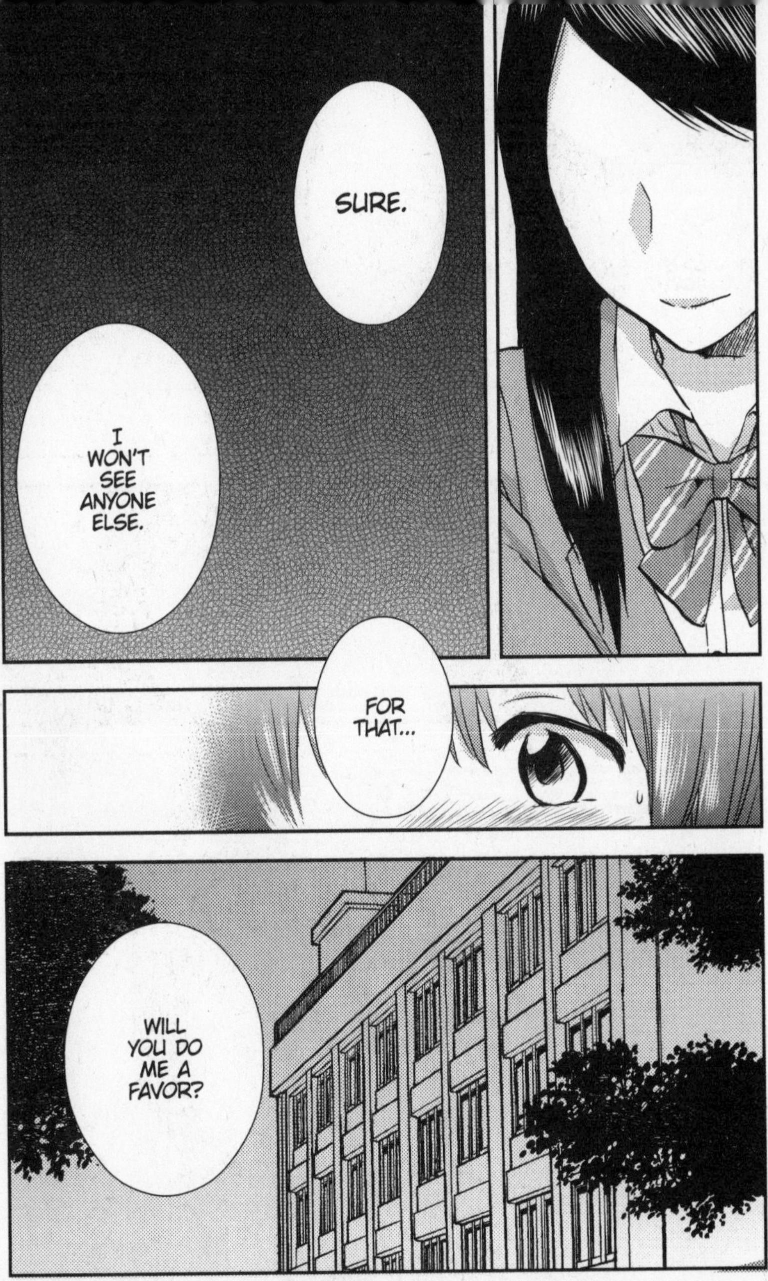
SURE.
I WON'T SEE ANYONE ELSE.
FOR THAT...
WILL YOU DO ME A FAVOR?

#5. Wanna Go Out with Me? / END

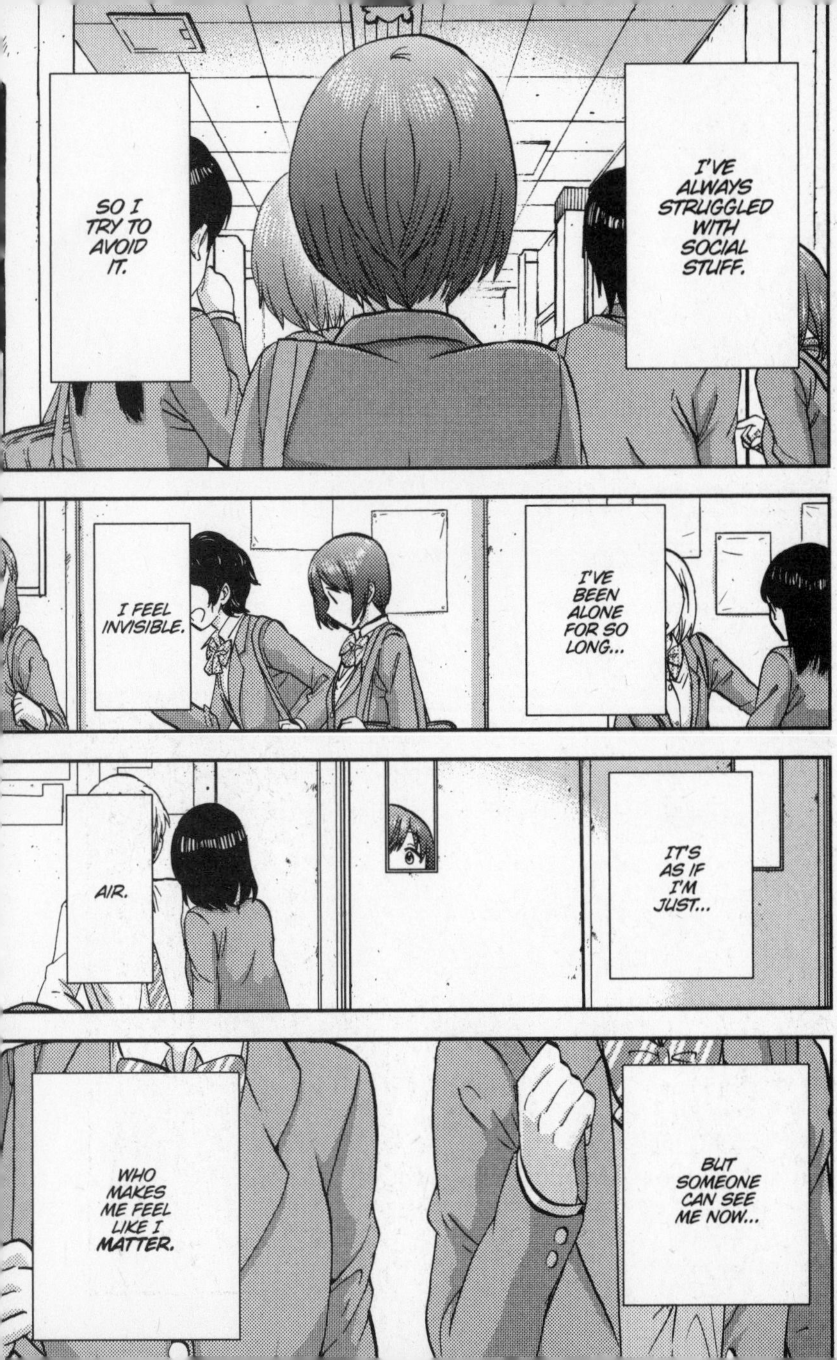
I'VE ALWAYS STRUGGLED WITH SOCIAL STUFF.
SO I TRY TO AVOID IT.
I'VE BEEN ALONE FOR SO LONG...
I FEEL INVISIBLE.
IT'S AS IF I'M JUST...
AIR.
BUT SOMEONE CAN SEE ME NOW...
WHO MAKES ME FEEL LIKE I **MATTER.**

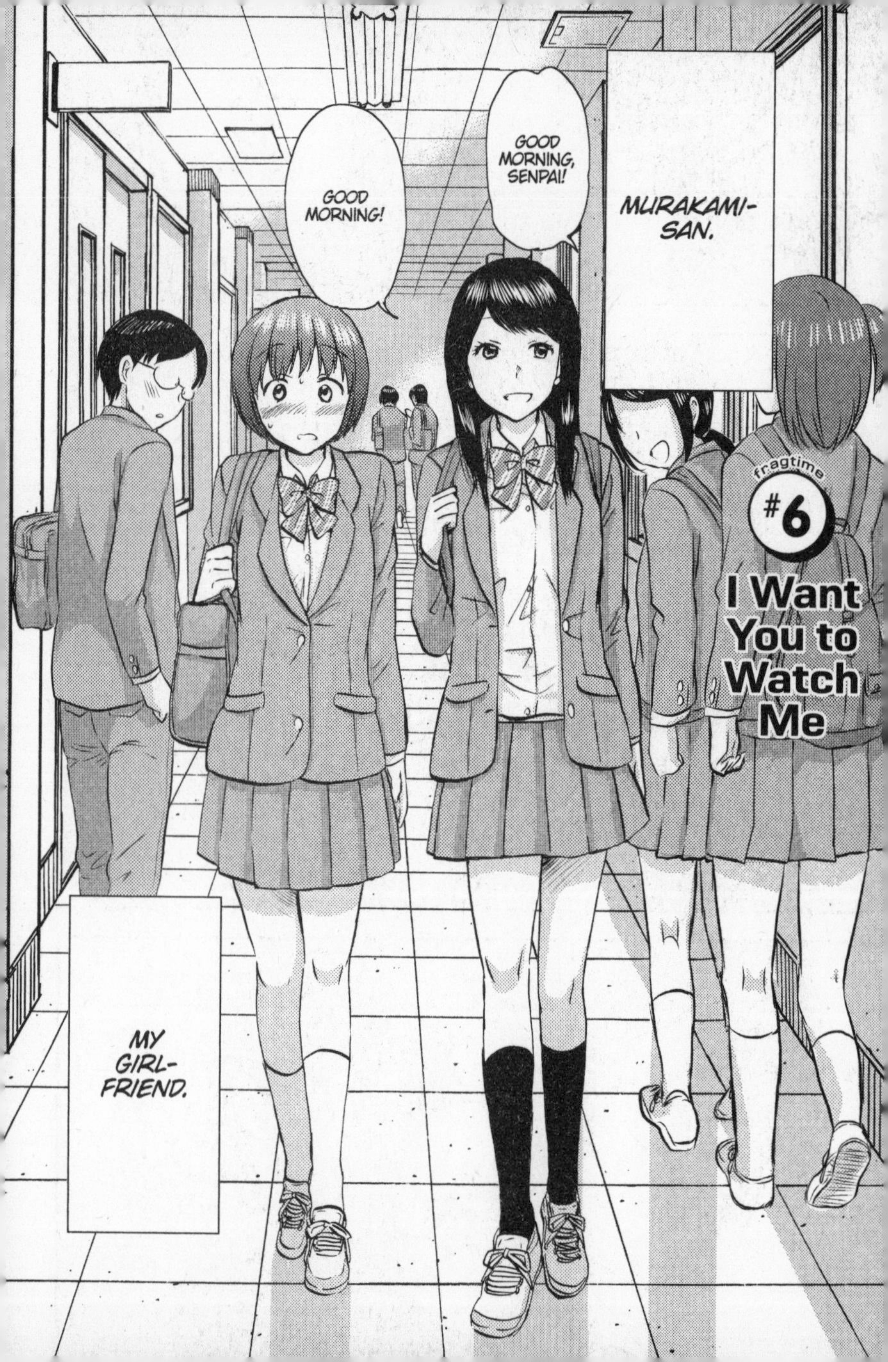
MURAKAMI-SAN.
GOOD MORNING, SENPAI!
GOOD MORNING!
fragtime
#6
I Want You to Watch Me
MY GIRLFRIEND.

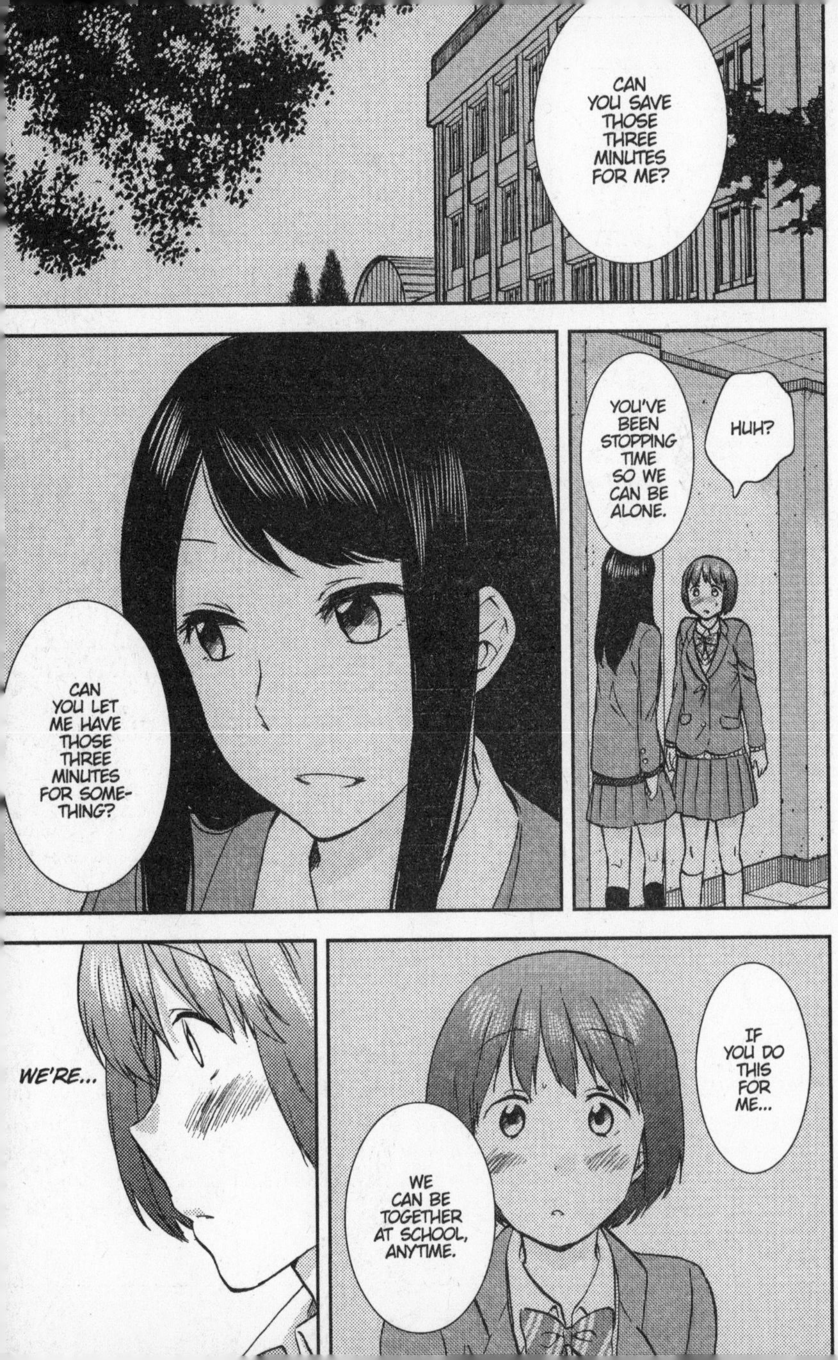
CAN YOU SAVE THOSE THREE MINUTES FOR ME?
HUH?
YOU'VE BEEN STOPPING TIME SO WE CAN BE ALONE.
CAN YOU LET ME HAVE THOSE THREE MINUTES FOR SOME-THING?
IF YOU DO THIS FOR ME...
WE CAN BE TOGETHER AT SCHOOL, ANYTIME.
WE'RE...

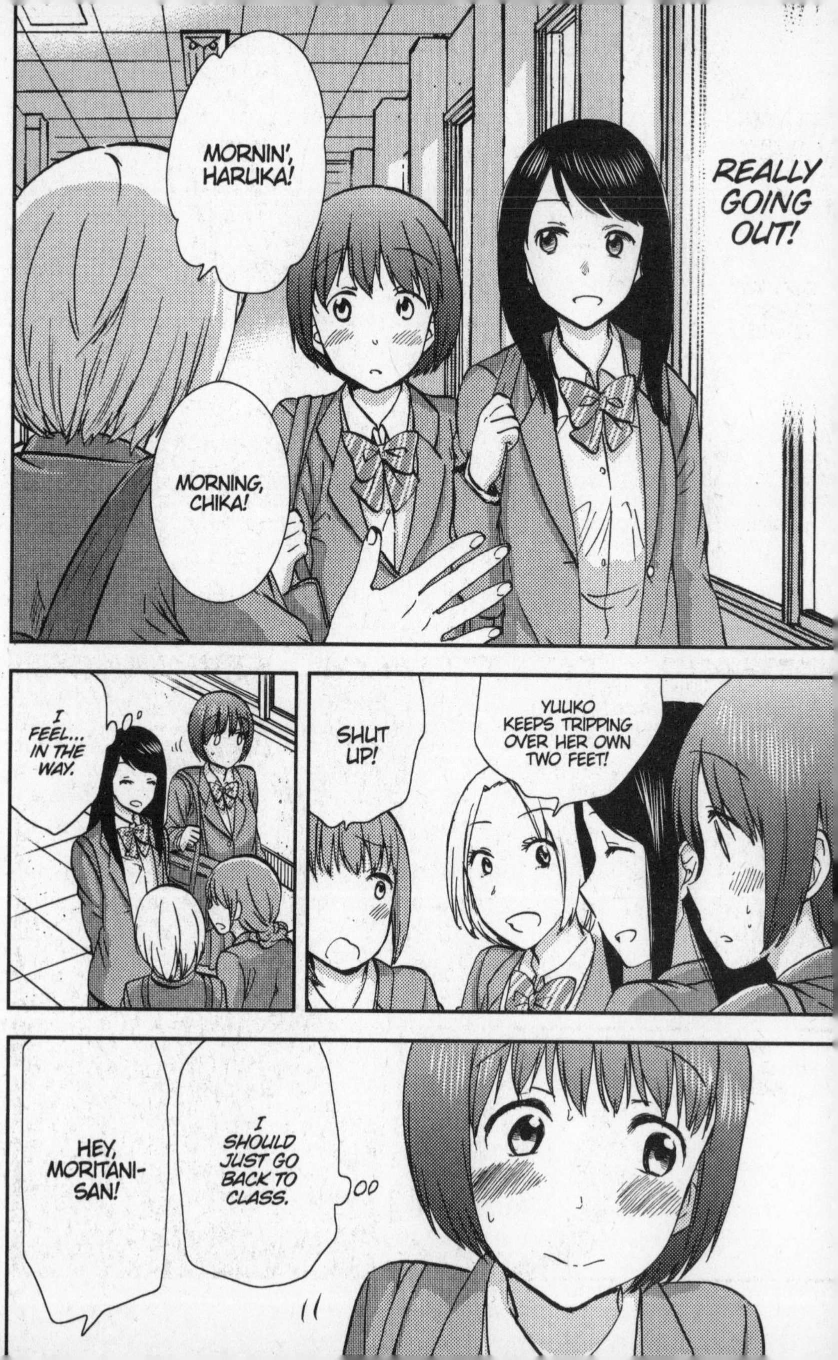
REALLY GOING OUT!
MORNIN', HARUKA!
MORNING, CHIKA!
YUUKO KEEPS TRIPPING OVER HER OWN TWO FEET!
SHUT UP!
I FEEL... IN THE WAY.
I SHOULD JUST GO BACK TO CLASS.
HEY, MORITANI-SAN!

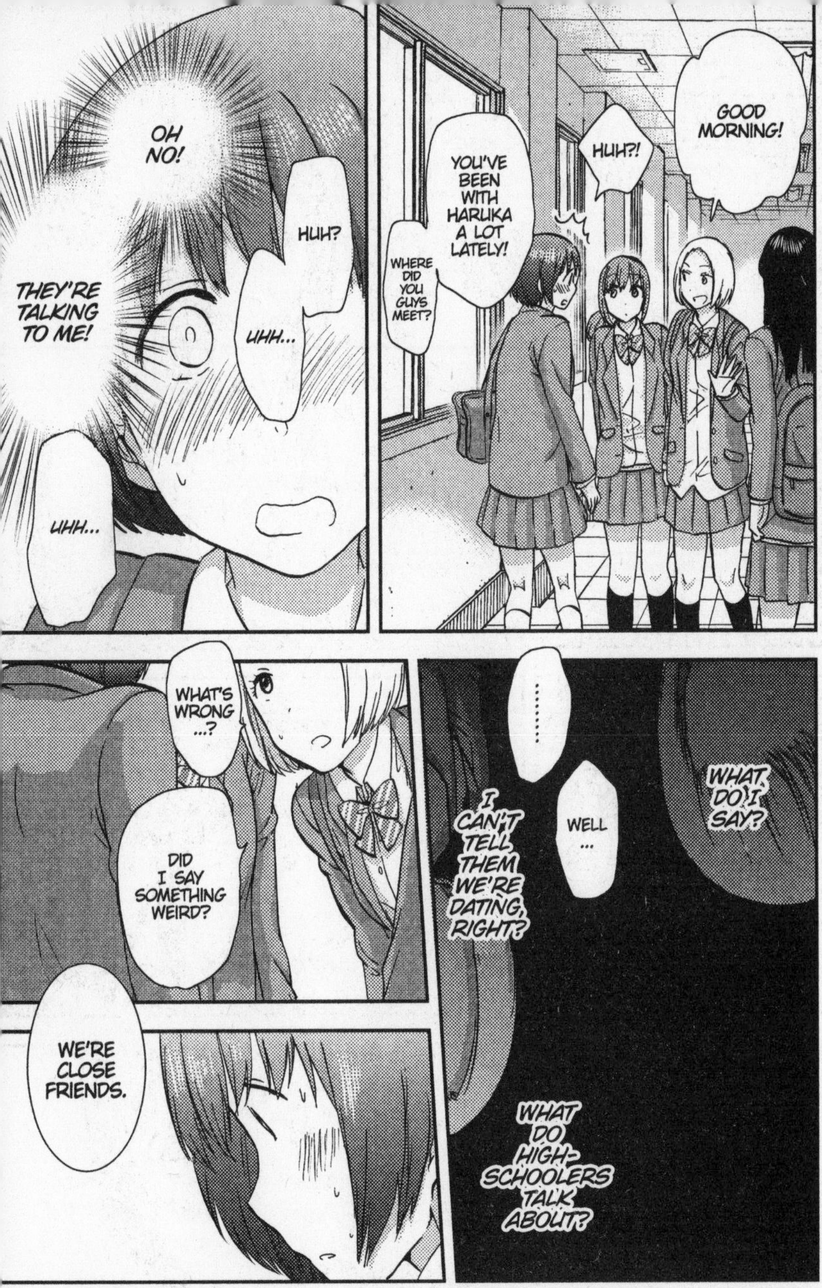
GOOD MORNING!
HUH?!
YOU'VE BEEN WITH HARUKA A LOT LATELY!
WHERE DID YOU GUYS MEET?
HUH?
UHH...
OH NO!
THEY'RE TALKING TO ME!
UHH...
......
WELL ...
WHAT DO I SAY?
I CAN'T TELL THEM WE'RE DATING, RIGHT?
WHAT DO HIGH-SCHOOLERS TALK ABOUT?
WHAT'S WRONG ...?
DID I SAY SOMETHING WEIRD?
WE'RE CLOSE FRIENDS.

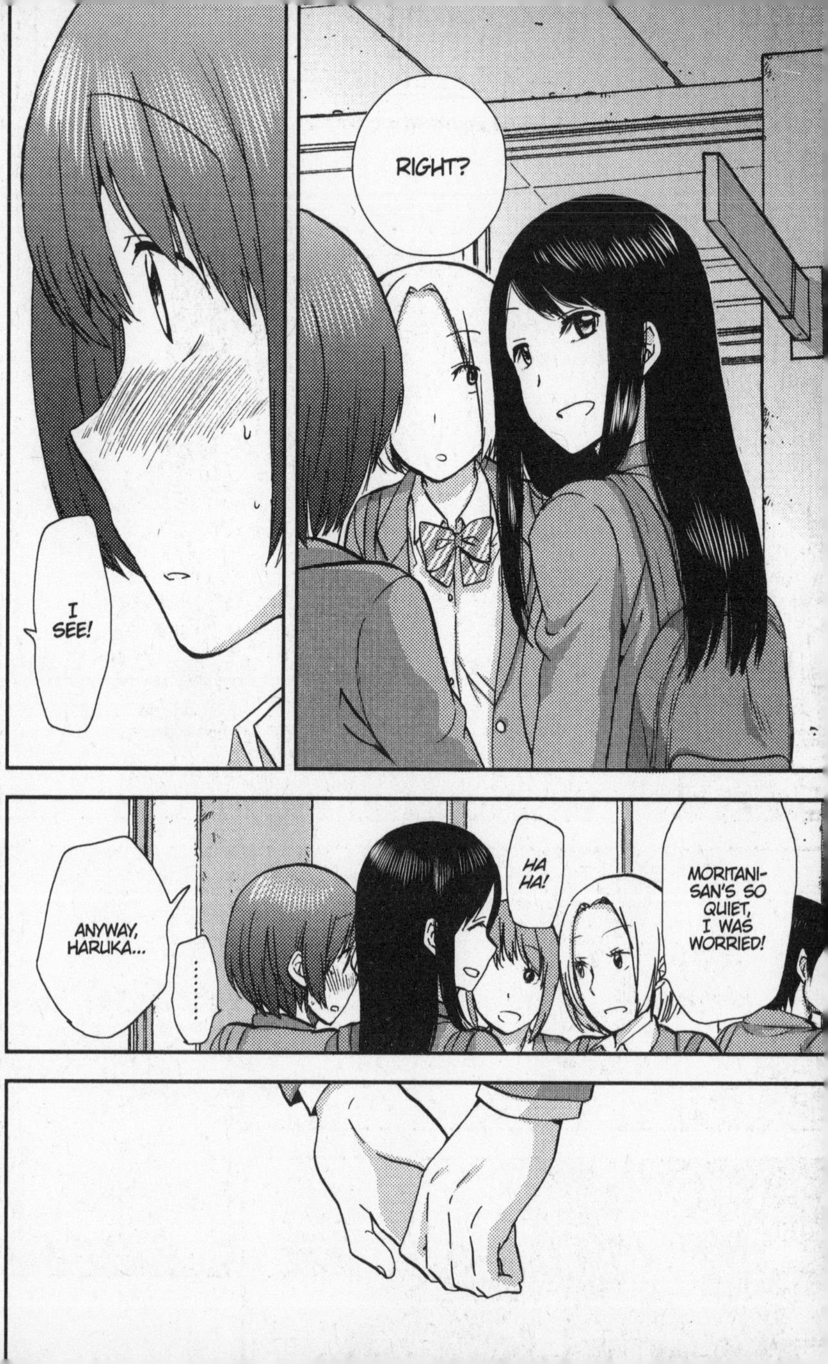
RIGHT?
I SEE!
MORITANI-SAN'S SO QUIET, I WAS WORRIED!
HA HA!
......
ANYWAY, HARUKA...

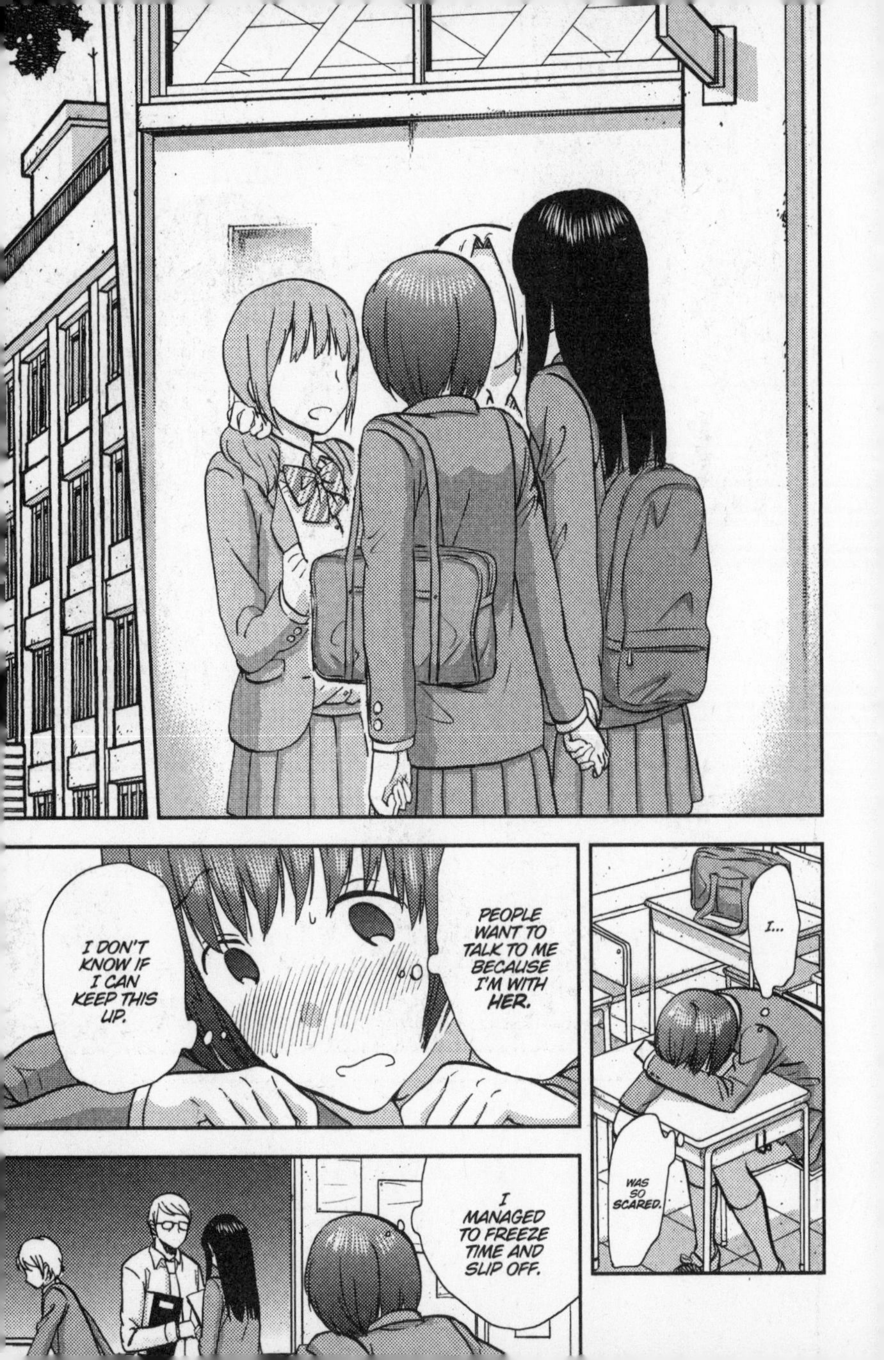
I...
WAS SO SCARED.
PEOPLE WANT TO TALK TO ME BECAUSE I'M WITH HER.
I DON'T KNOW IF I CAN KEEP THIS UP.
I MANAGED TO FREEZE TIME AND SLIP OFF.

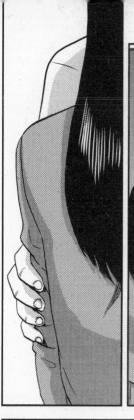

SHE SAID YAMAGUCHI-SENSEI TOUCHES HER...

I SHOULD STOP TIME.

WHAT DO I DO?

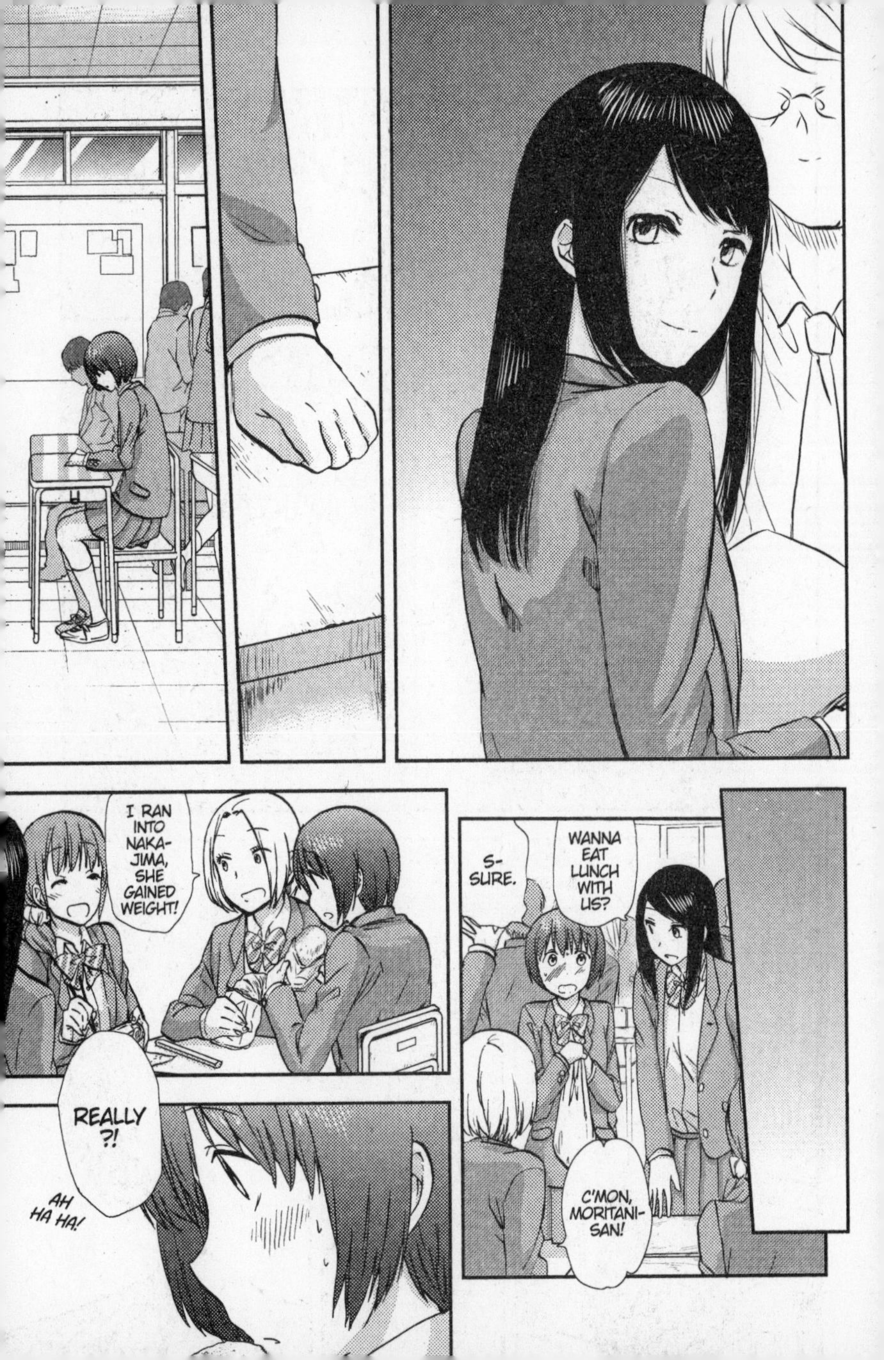
WANNA EAT LUNCH WITH US?
S-SURE.
C'MON, MORITANI-SAN!
I RAN INTO NAKAJIMA, SHE GAINED WEIGHT!
REALLY?!
AH HA HA!

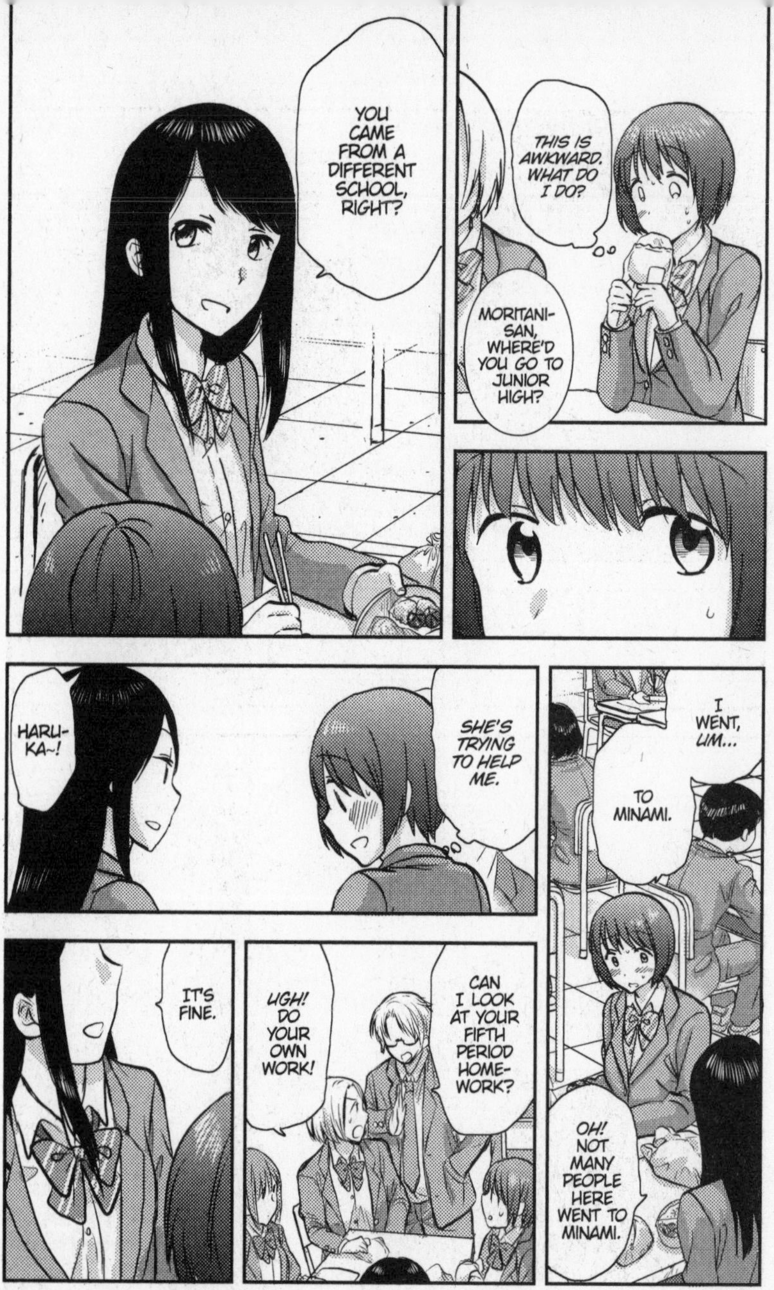
THIS IS AWKWARD. WHAT DO I DO?
MORITANI-SAN, WHERE'D YOU GO TO JUNIOR HIGH?
YOU CAME FROM A DIFFERENT SCHOOL, RIGHT?
I WENT, UM...
TO MINAMI.
OH! NOT MANY PEOPLE HERE WENT TO MINAMI.
SHE'S TRYING TO HELP ME.
HARU-KA~!
CAN I LOOK AT YOUR FIFTH PERIOD HOME-WORK?
UGH! DO YOUR OWN WORK!
IT'S FINE.

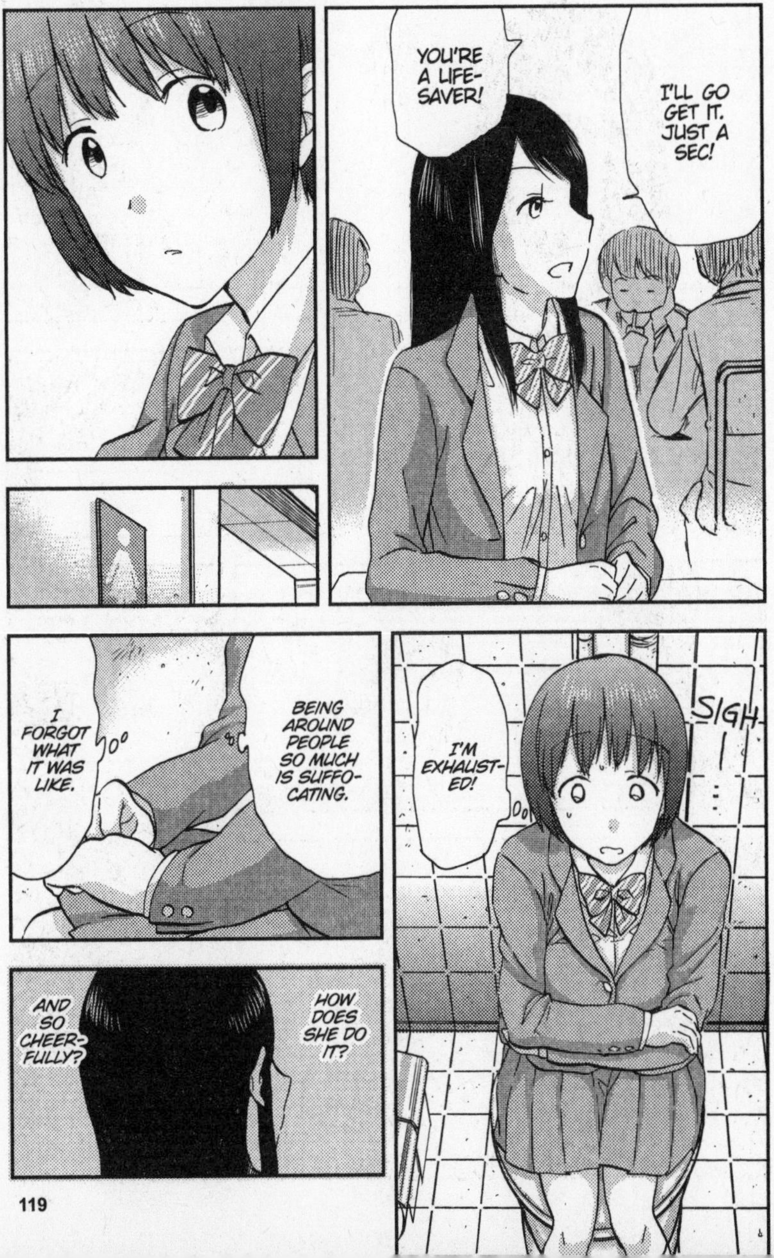
I'LL GO GET IT. JUST A SEC!
YOU'RE A LIFE-SAVER!
SIGH
I'M EXHAUSTED!
BEING AROUND PEOPLE SO MUCH IS SUFFOCATING.
I FORGOT WHAT IT WAS LIKE.
HOW DOES SHE DO IT?
AND SO CHEERFULLY?

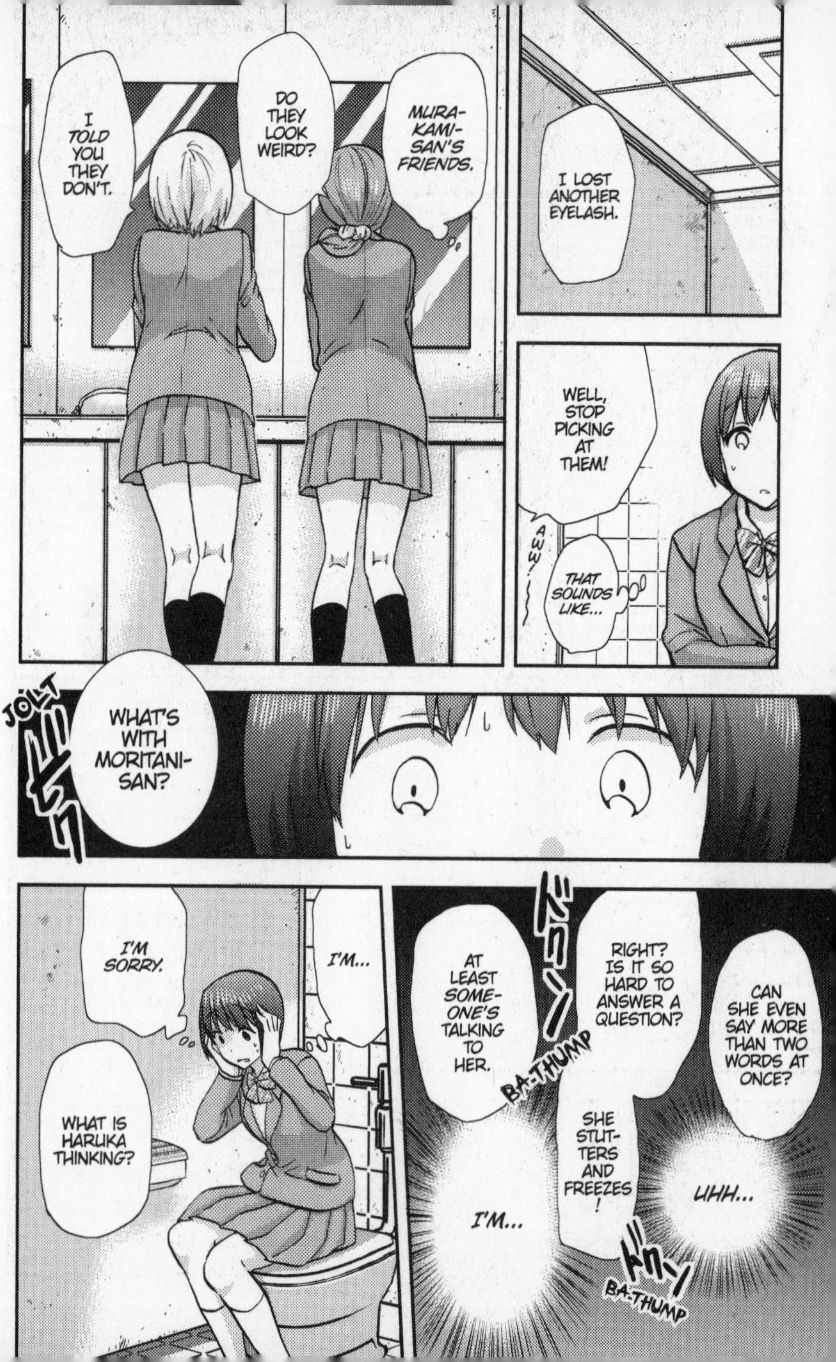
I LOST ANOTHER EYELASH.
WELL, STOP PICKING AT THEM!
AWW...
THAT SOUNDS LIKE...
MURA-KAMI-SAN'S FRIENDS.
DO THEY LOOK WEIRD?
I TOLD YOU THEY DON'T.
WHAT'S WITH MORITANI-SAN?
JOLT
CAN SHE EVEN SAY MORE THAN TWO WORDS AT ONCE?
RIGHT? IS IT SO HARD TO ANSWER A QUESTION?
AT LEAST SOME-ONE'S TALKING TO HER.
BA-THUMP
UHH...
SHE STUT-TERS AND FREEZES!
I'M...
BA-THUMP
I'M...
I'M SORRY.
WHAT IS HARUKA THINKING?

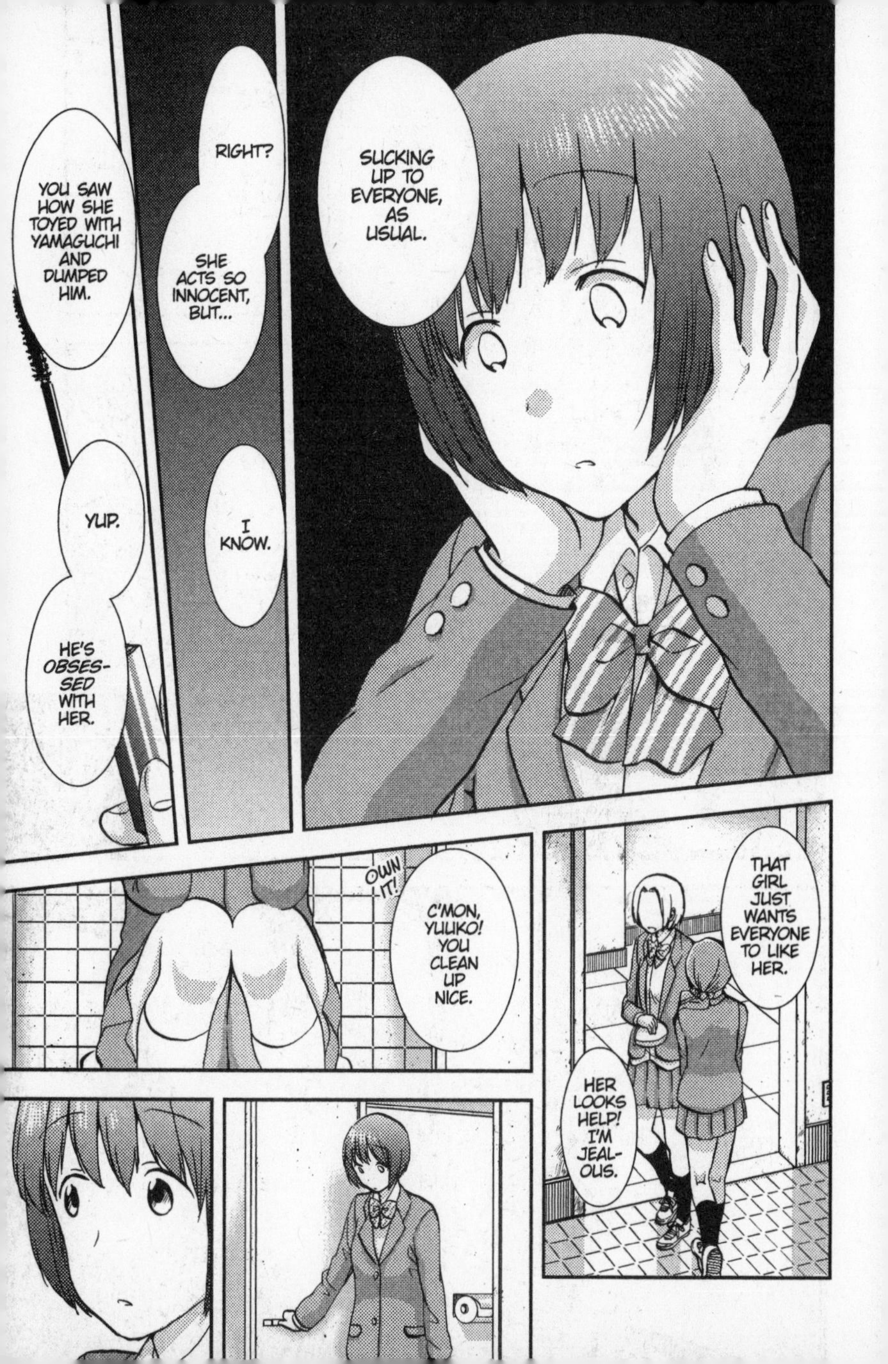
SUCKING UP TO EVERYONE, AS USUAL.
RIGHT?
SHE ACTS SO INNOCENT, BUT...
I KNOW.
YOU SAW HOW SHE TOYED WITH YAMAGUCHI AND DUMPED HIM.
YUP.
HE'S OBSES-SED WITH HER.
THAT GIRL JUST WANTS EVERYONE TO LIKE HER.
HER LOOKS HELP! I'M JEAL-OUS.
OWN IT!
C'MON, YUUKO! YOU CLEAN UP NICE.

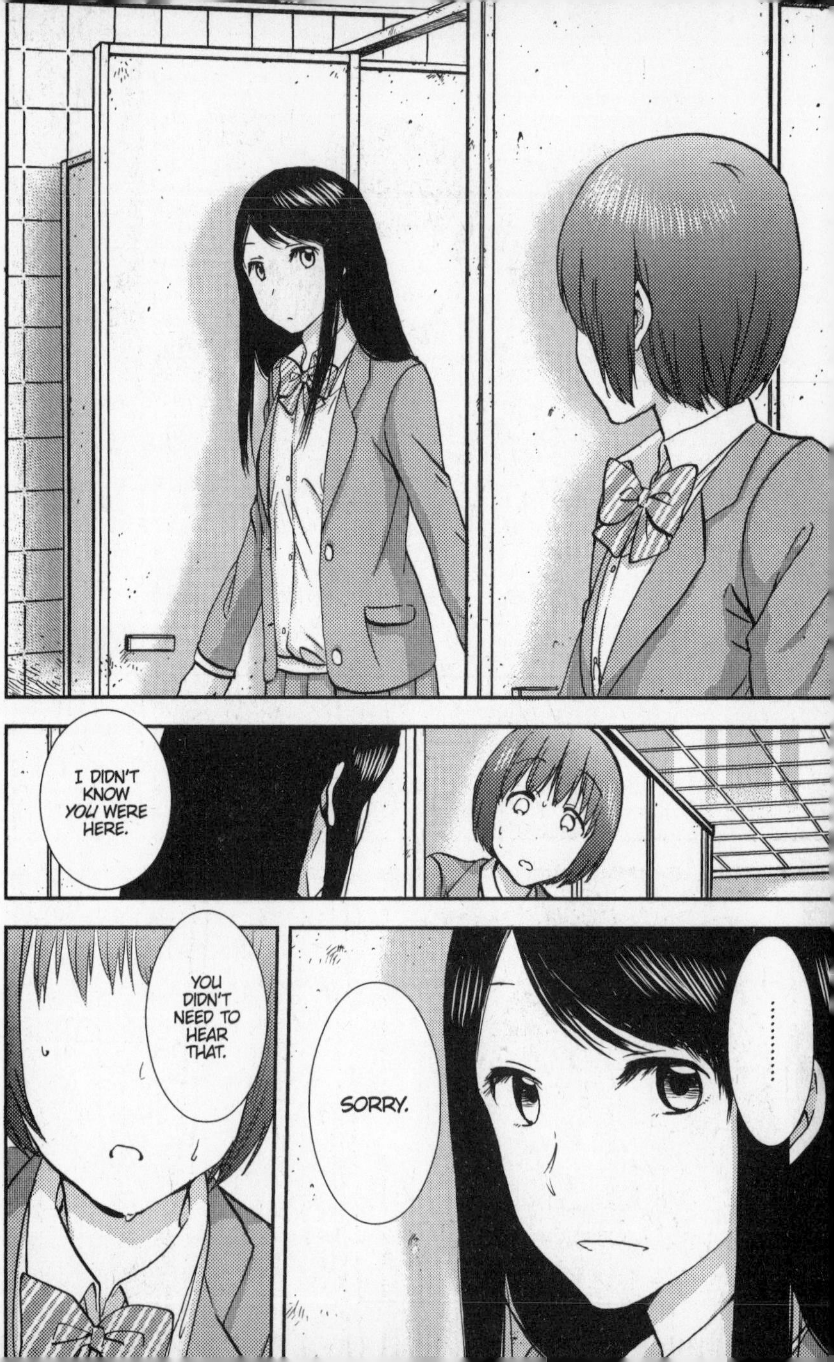
I DIDN'T KNOW YOU WERE HERE.
......
SORRY.
YOU DIDN'T NEED TO HEAR THAT.

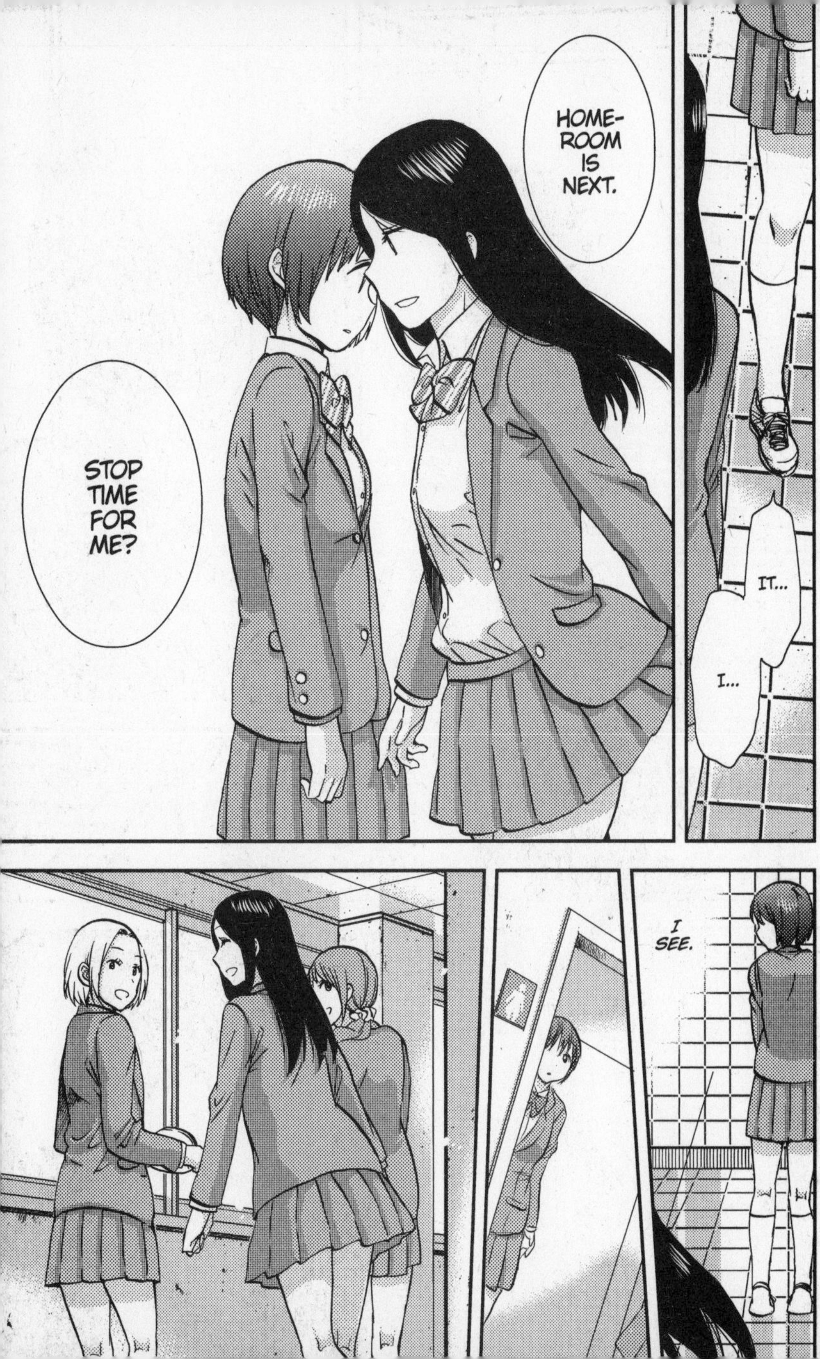
IT...
I...
HOME-ROOM IS NEXT.
STOP TIME FOR ME?
I SEE.

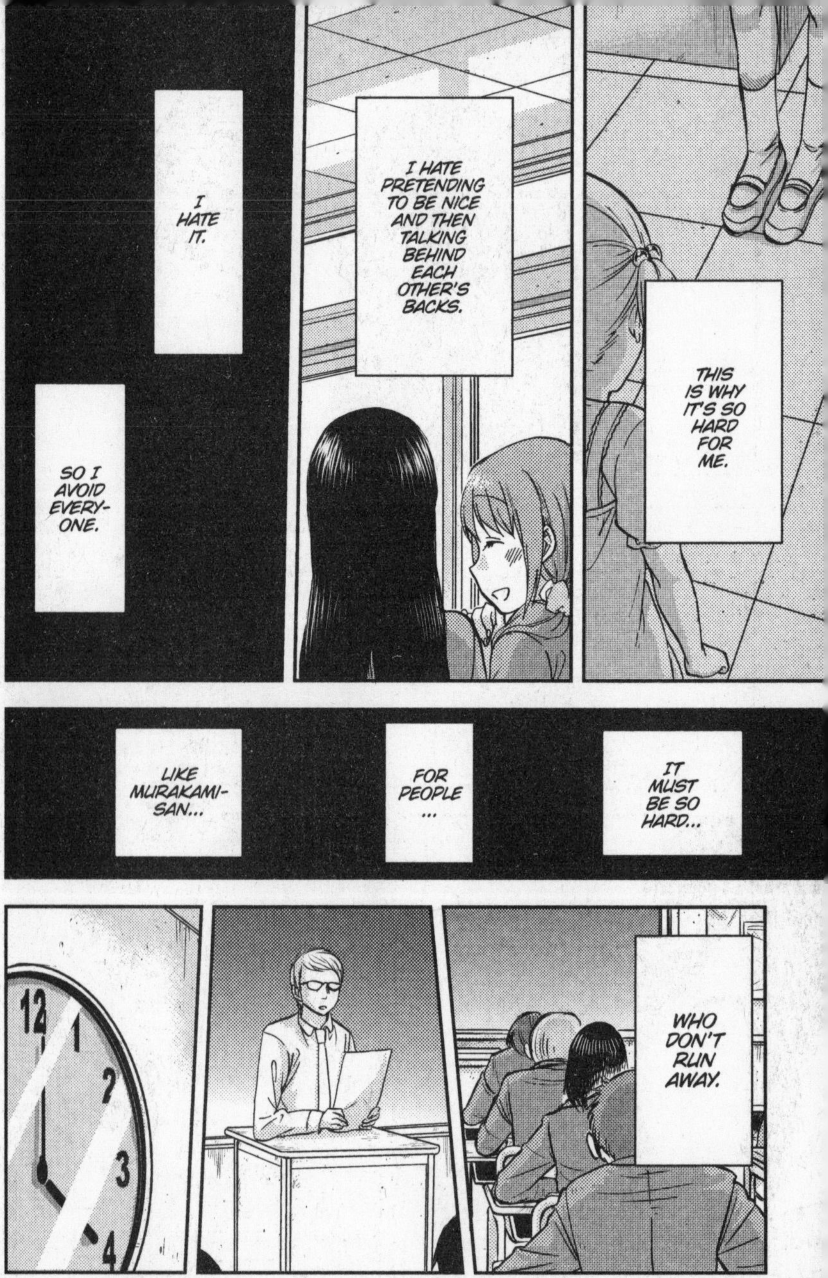
THIS IS WHY IT'S SO HARD FOR ME.
I HATE PRETENDING TO BE NICE AND THEN TALKING BEHIND EACH OTHER'S BACKS.
I HATE IT.
SO I AVOID EVERY-ONE.
IT MUST BE SO HARD...
FOR PEOPLE ...
LIKE MURAKAMI-SAN...
WHO DON'T RUN AWAY.

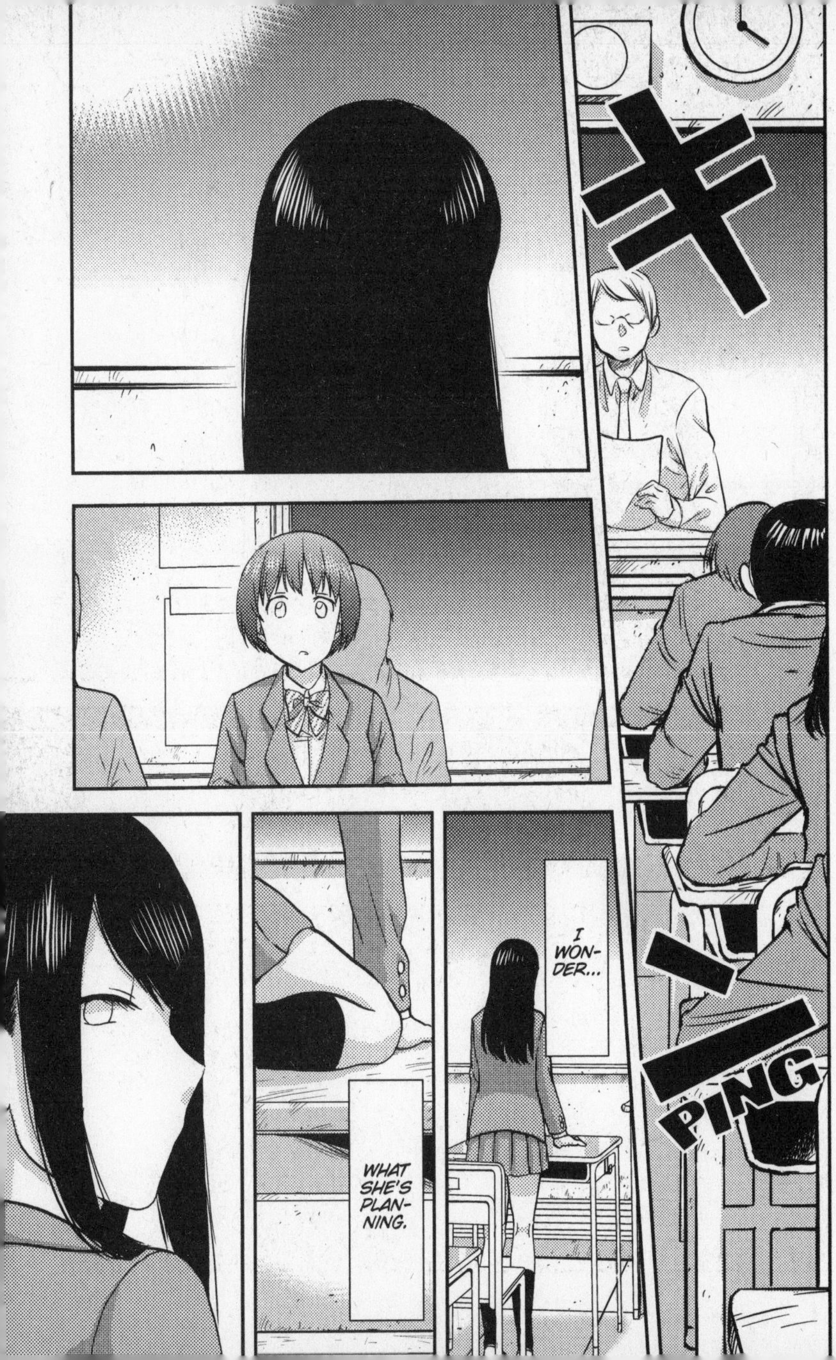
PING
I WONDER...
WHAT SHE'S PLANNING.

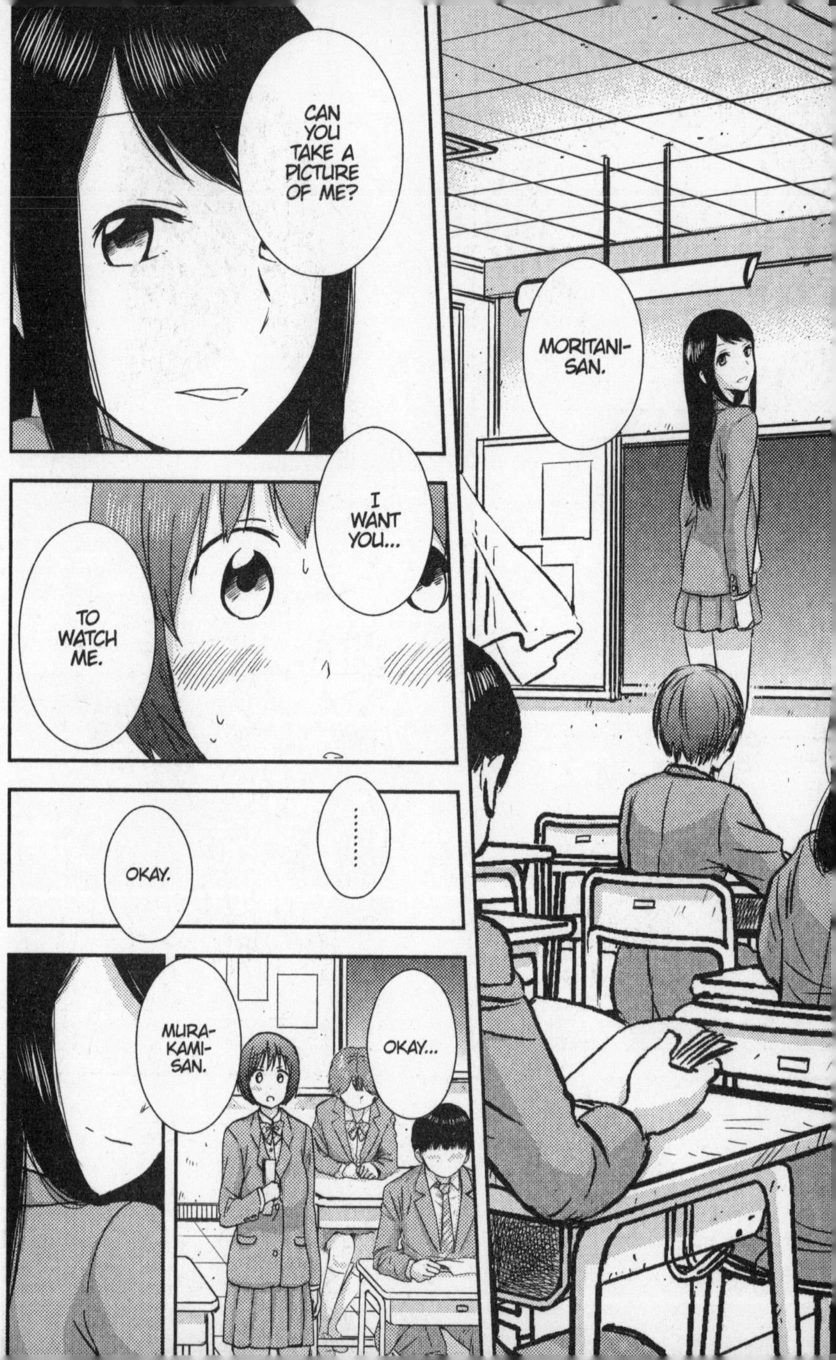
MORITANI-SAN.
CAN YOU TAKE A PICTURE OF ME?
I WANT YOU...
TO WATCH ME.
......
OKAY.
OKAY...
MURA-KAMI-SAN.

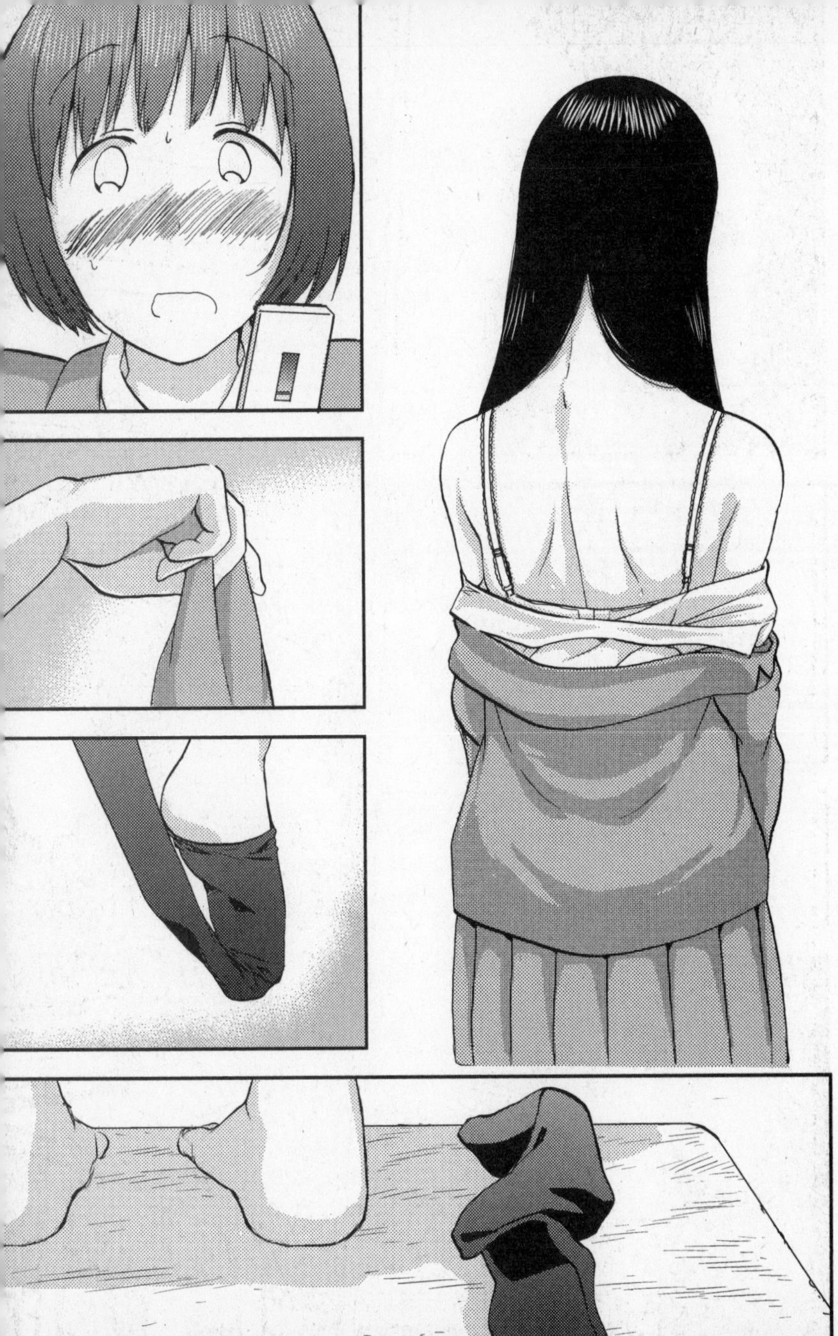

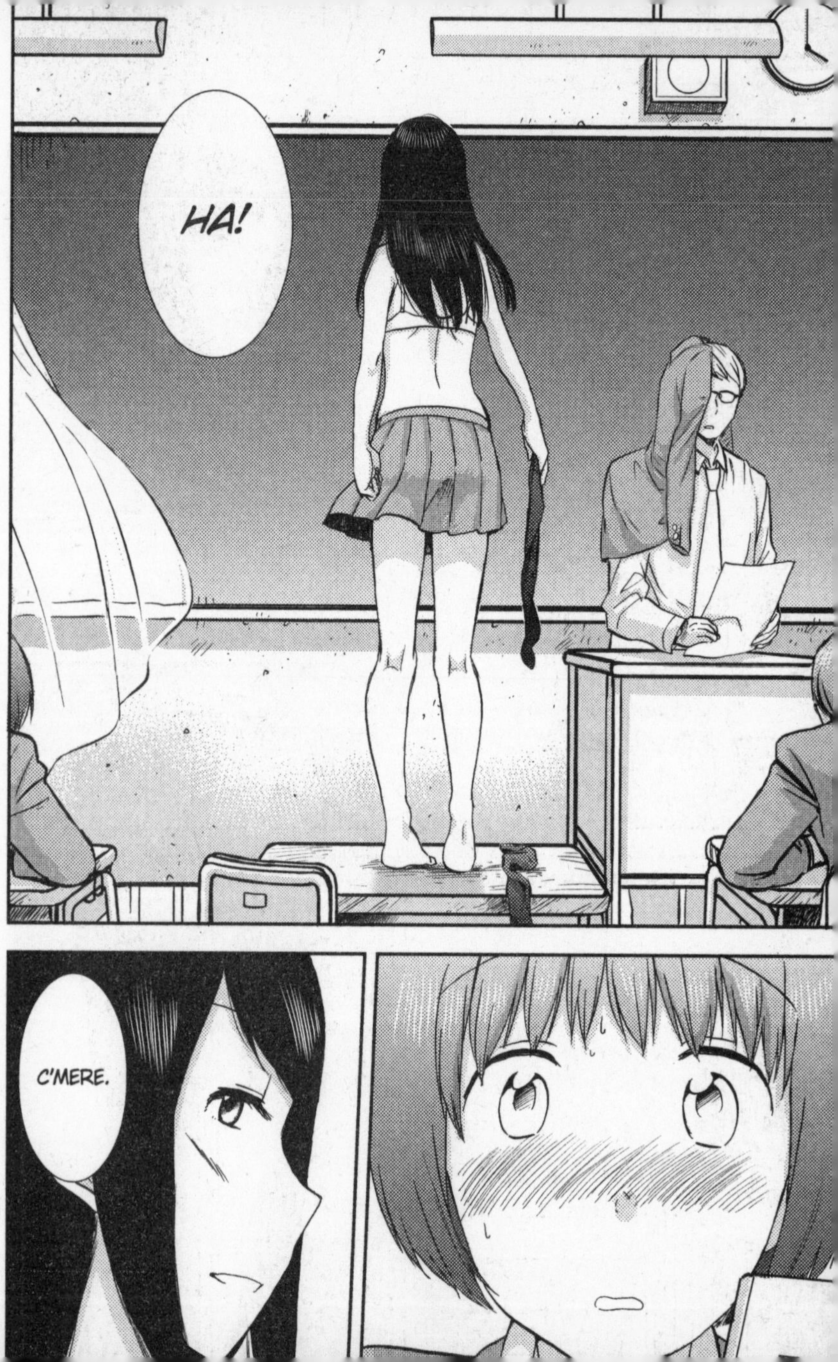
HA!
C'MERE.

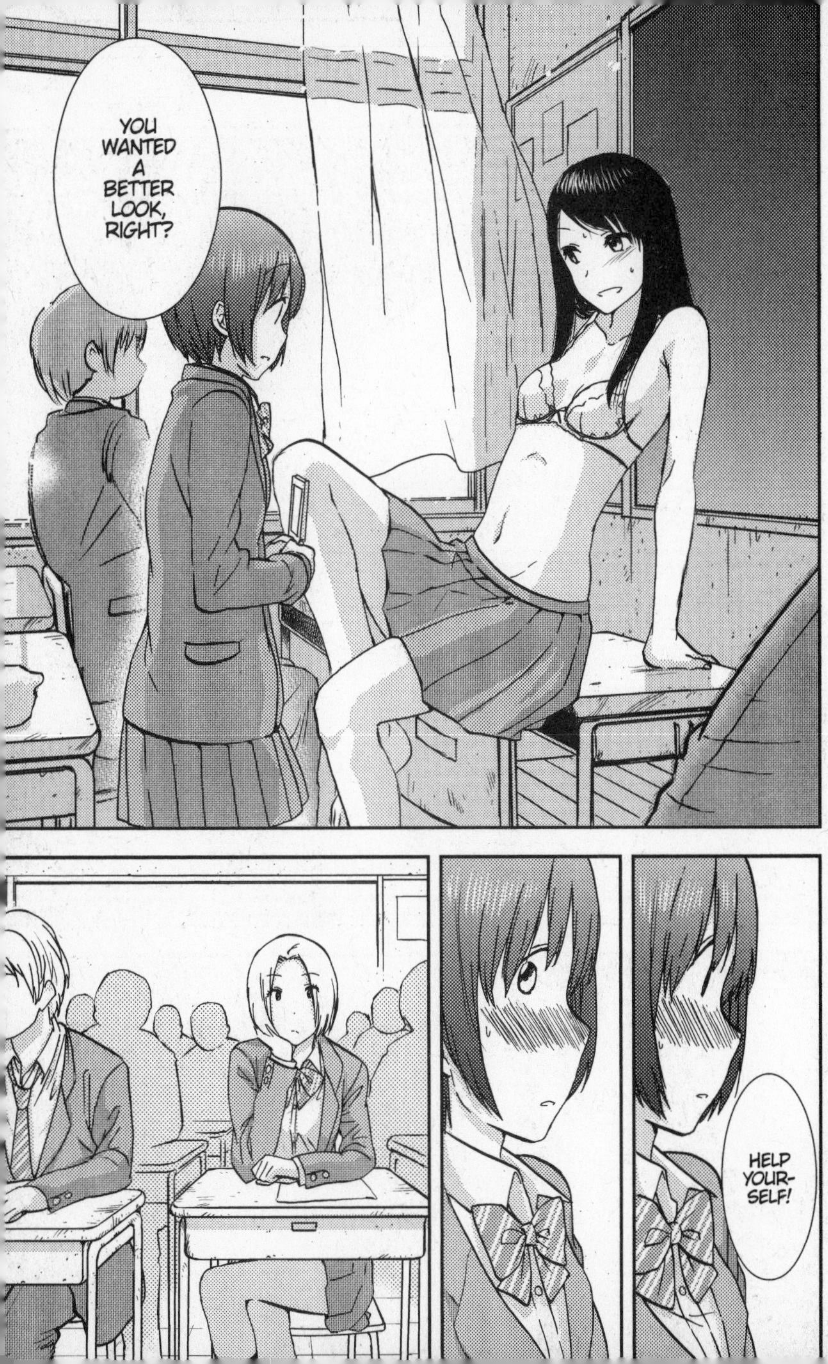
YOU WANTED A BETTER LOOK, RIGHT?
HELP YOUR-SELF!

NO
ONE
CAN
SEE
US.

FOR
NOW,
ANYWAY.

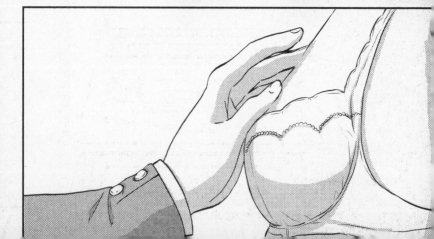

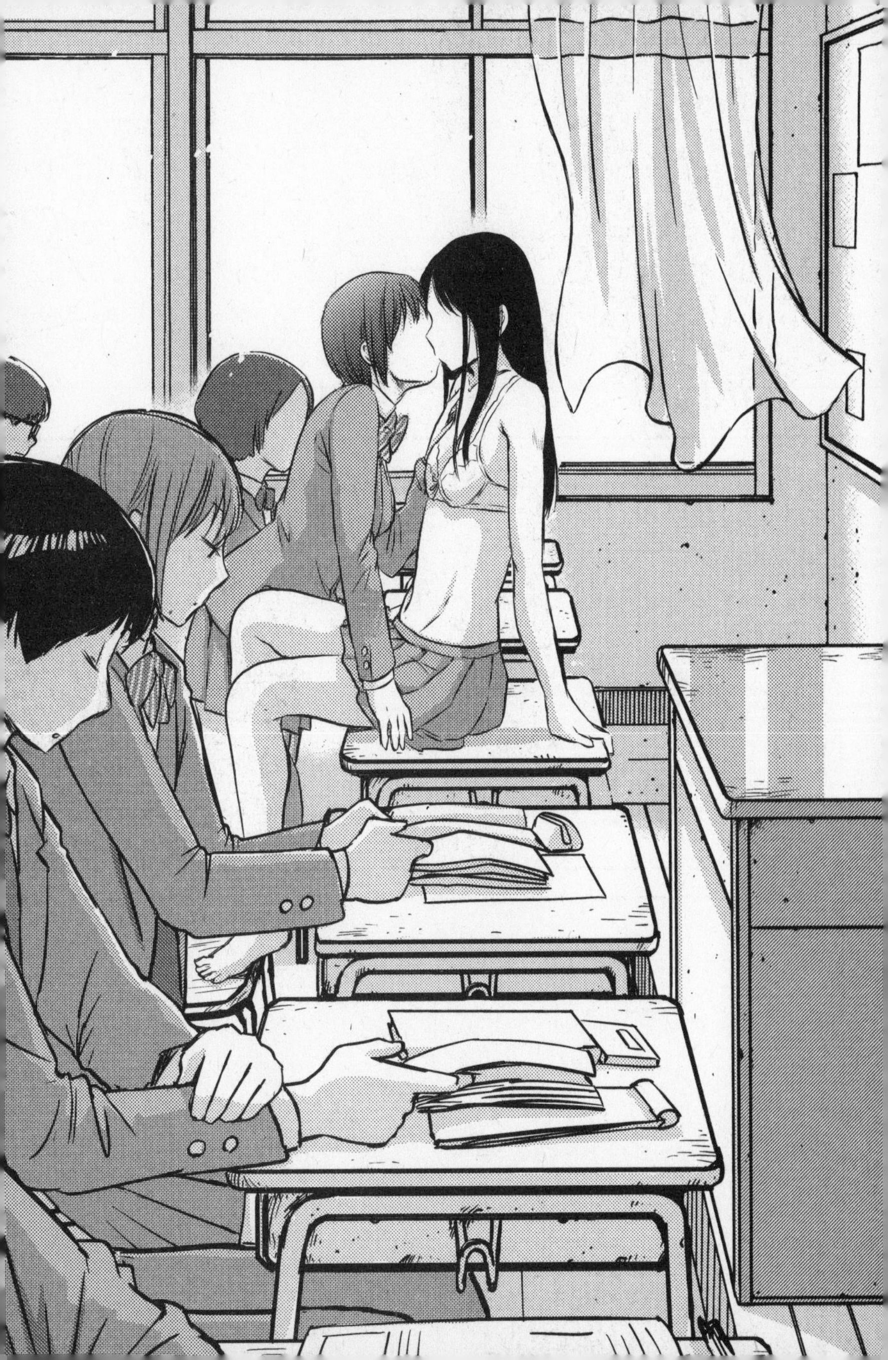

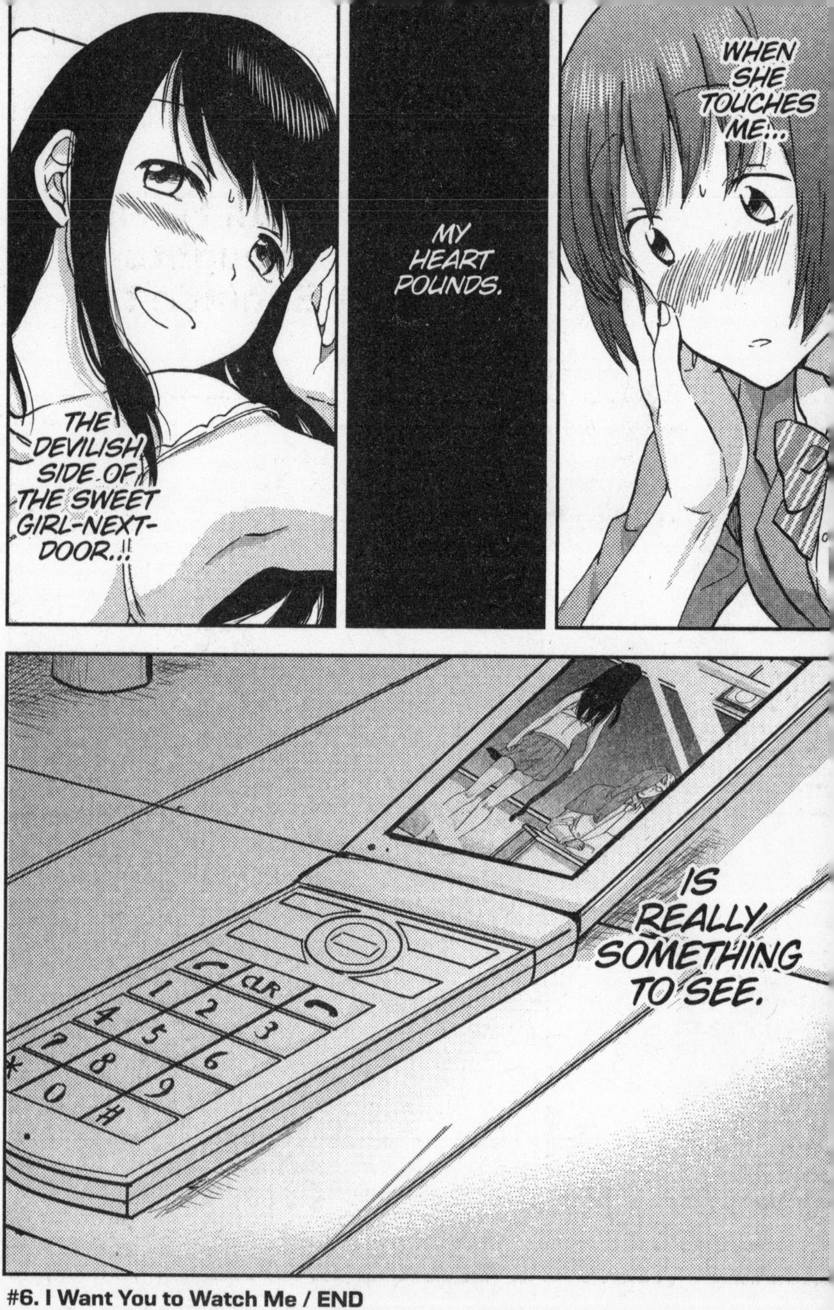
WHEN SHE TOUCHES ME...
MY HEART POUNDS.
THE DEVILISH SIDE OF THE SWEET GIRL-NEXT-DOOR...!
IS REALLY SOMETHING TO SEE.

#6. I Want You to Watch Me / END

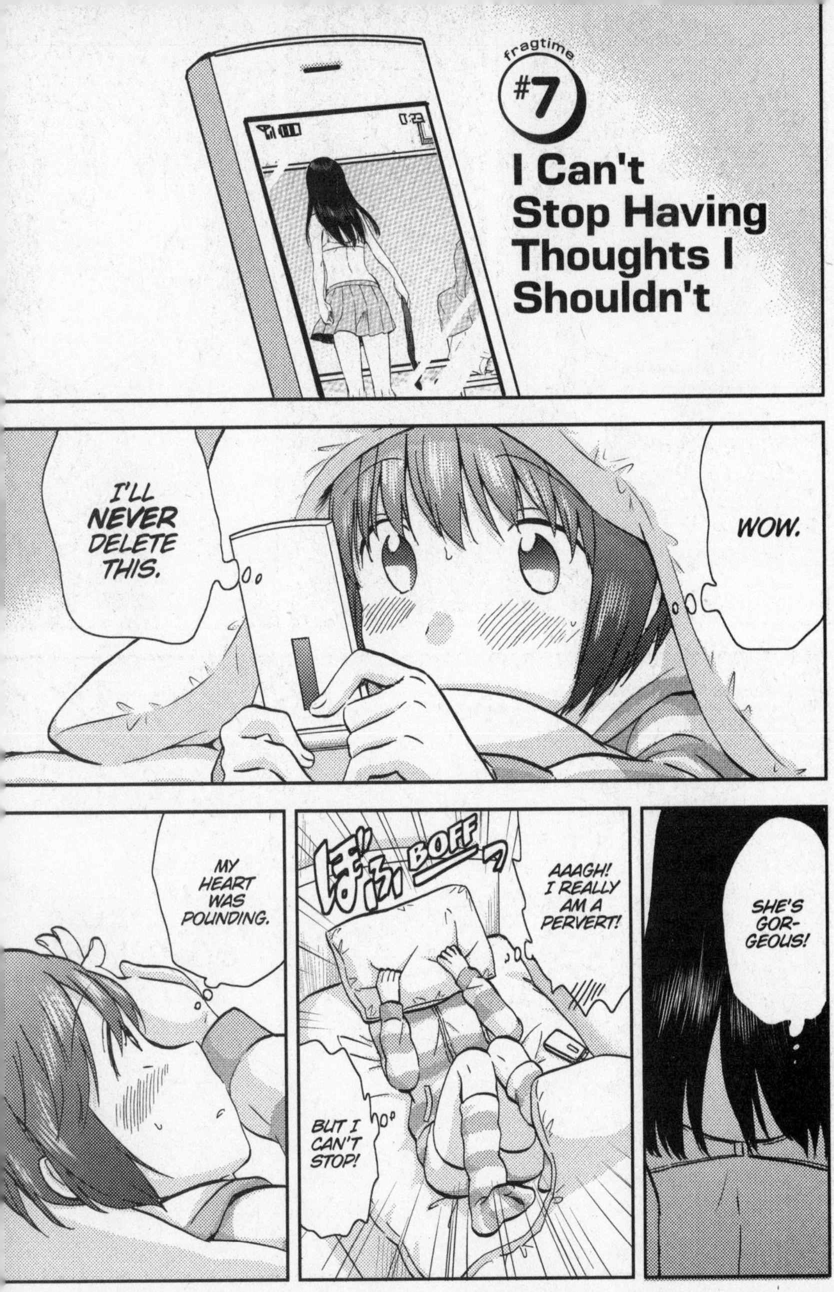
fragtime
#7
I Can't Stop Having Thoughts I Shouldn't
WOW.
I'LL NEVER DELETE THIS.
SHE'S GOR-GEOUS!
AAAGH! I REALLY AM A PERVERT!
ぼふっ BOFF
BUT I CAN'T STOP!
MY HEART WAS POUNDING.

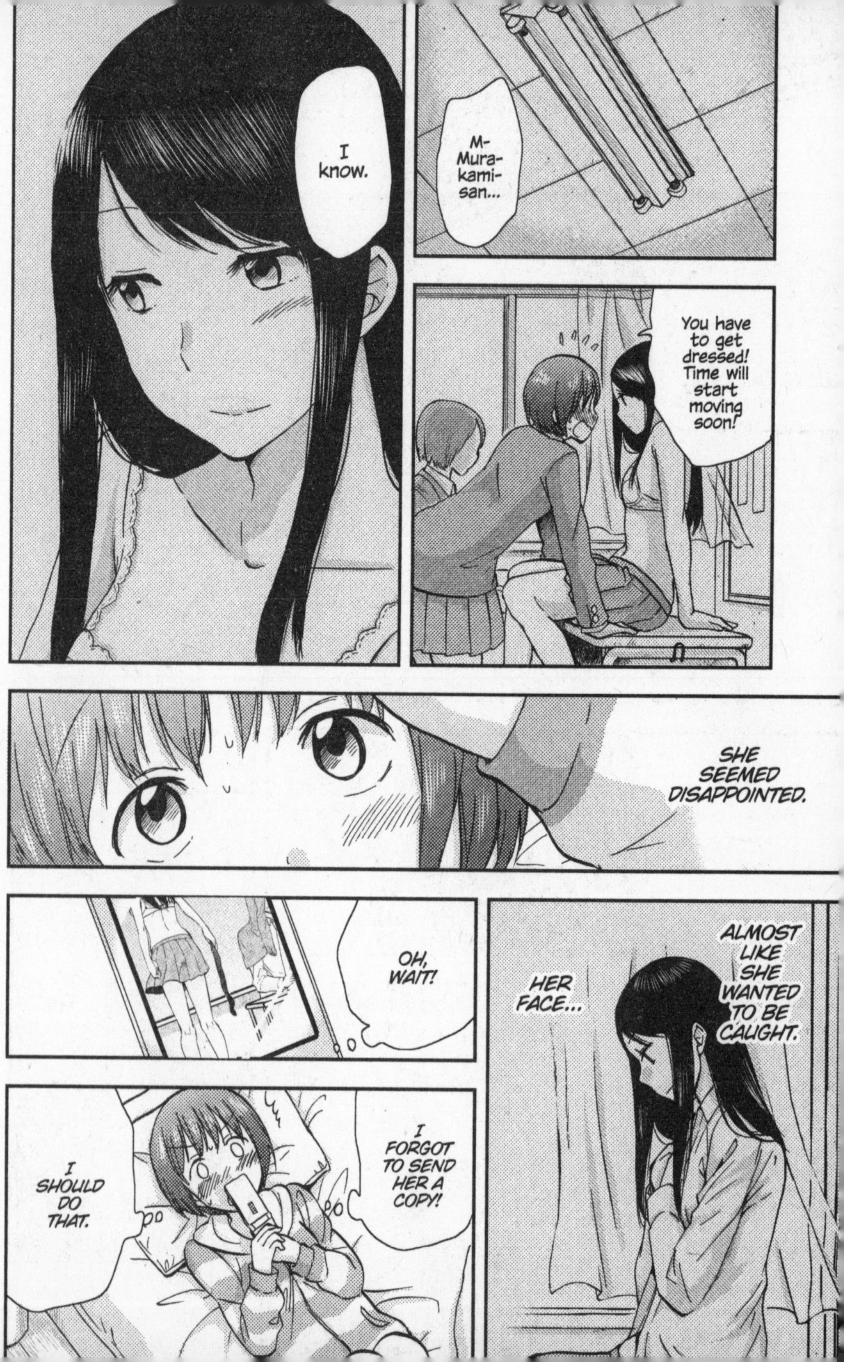
M-Mura-kami-san...
You have to get dressed! Time will start moving soon!
I know.
SHE SEEMED DISAPPOINTED.
ALMOST LIKE SHE WANTED TO BE CAUGHT.
HER FACE...
OH, WAIT!
I FORGOT TO SEND HER A COPY!
I SHOULD DO THAT.

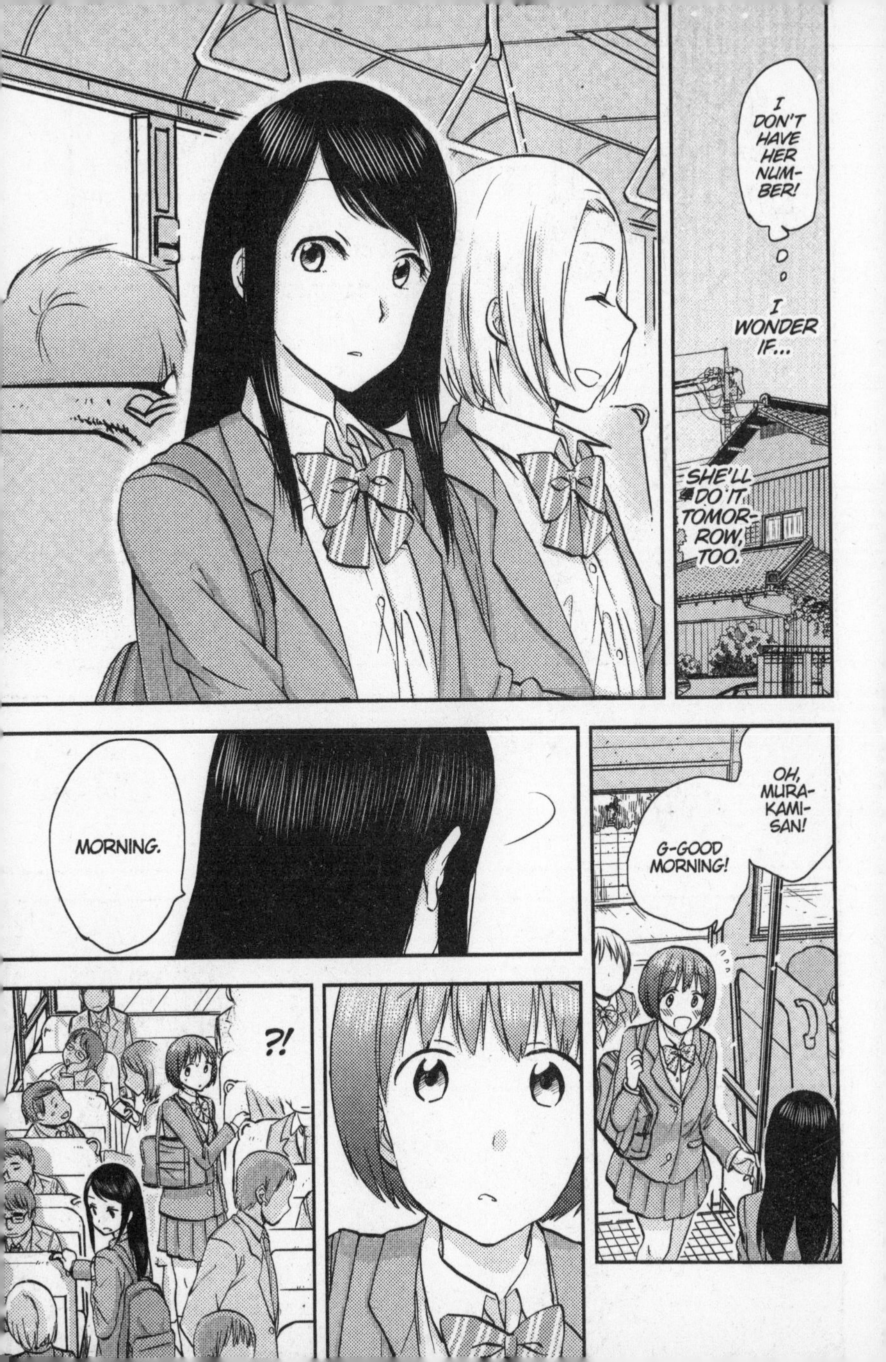
I DON'T HAVE HER NUM-BER!
I WONDER IF...
SHE'LL DO IT TOMOR-ROW, TOO.
OH, MURA-KAMI-SAN!
G-GOOD MORNING!
MORNING.
?!

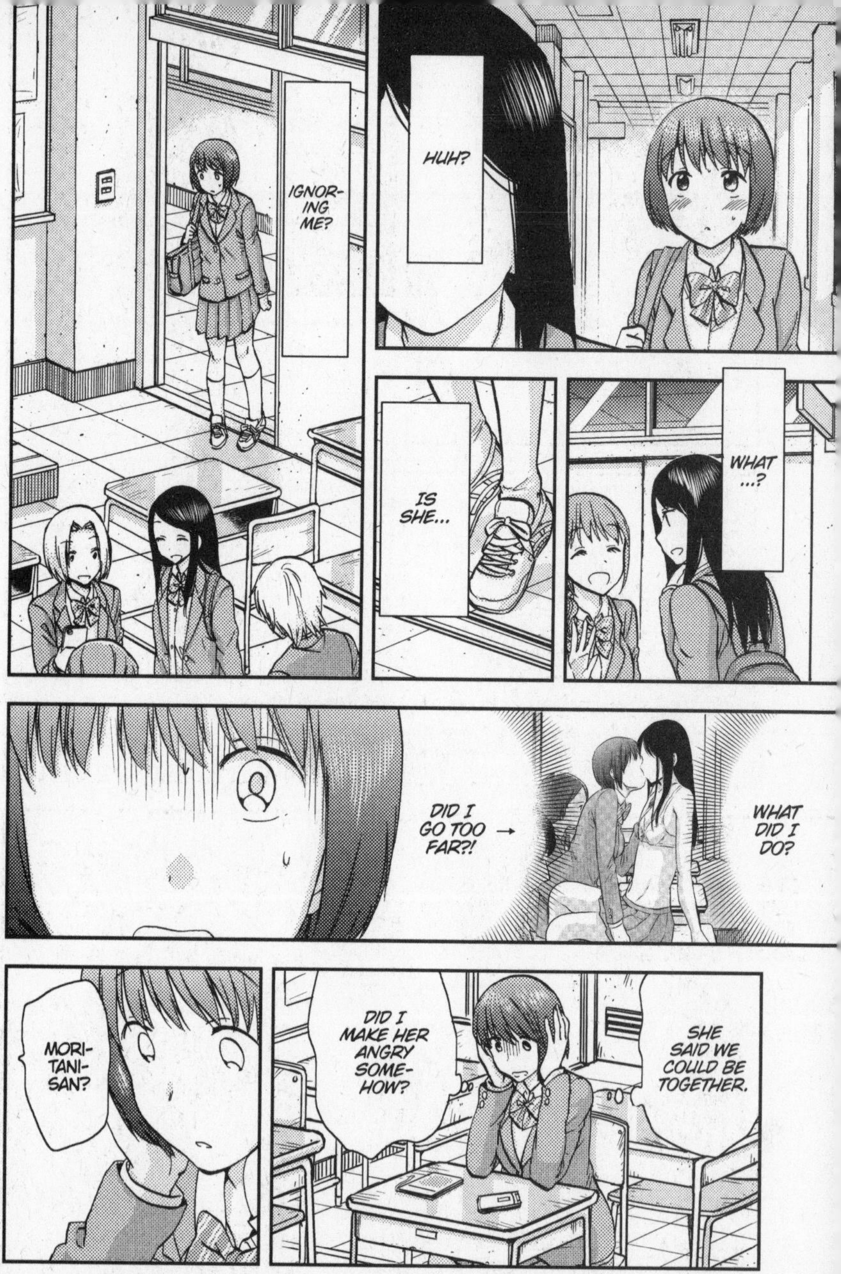
HUH?
WHAT ...?
IS SHE...
IGNOR-ING ME?
WHAT DID I DO?
DID I GO TOO FAR?! →
SHE SAID WE COULD BE TOGETHER.
DID I MAKE HER ANGRY SOME-HOW?
MORI-TANI-SAN?

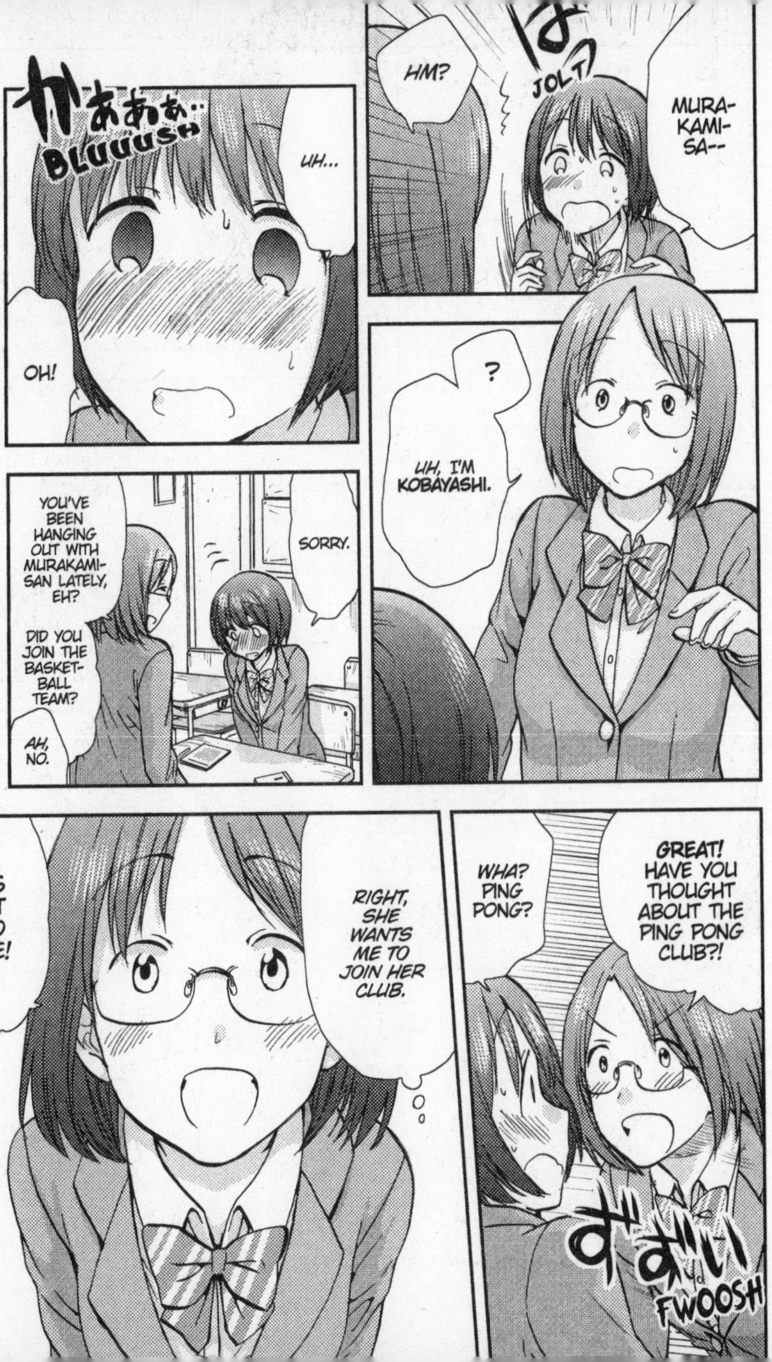
MURA-KAMI-SA--
JOLT
HM?
BLUUUSH
UH...
OH!
?
UH, I'M KOBAYASHI.
SORRY.
YOU'VE BEEN HANGING OUT WITH MURAKAMI-SAN LATELY, EH?
DID YOU JOIN THE BASKET-BALL TEAM?
AH, NO.
GREAT! HAVE YOU THOUGHT ABOUT THE PING PONG CLUB?!
WHA? PING PONG?
FWOOSH
RIGHT, SHE WANTS ME TO JOIN HER CLUB.
IT'S NOT TOO LATE!

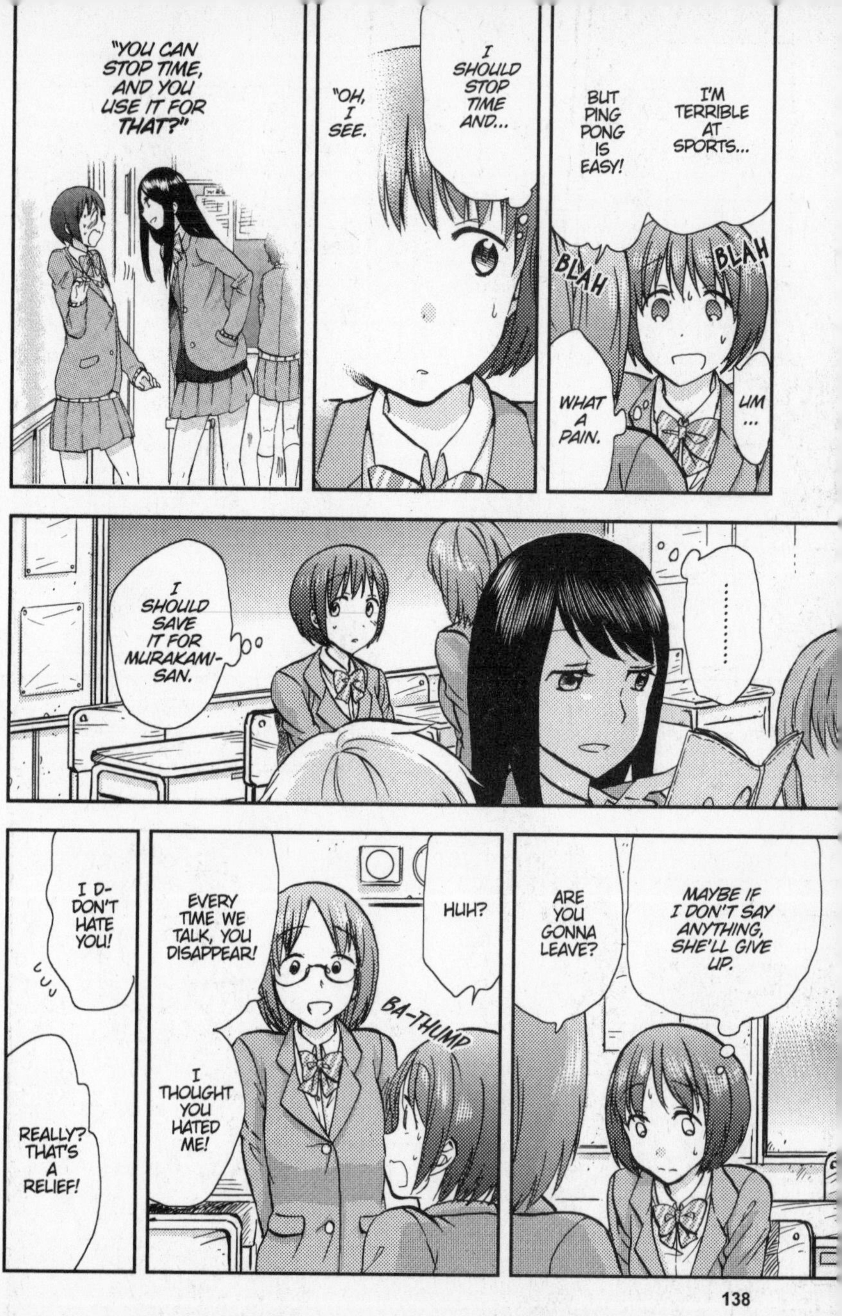
I'M TERRIBLE AT SPORTS...
BLAH
BLAH
BUT PING PONG IS EASY!
UM ...
WHAT A PAIN.
I SHOULD STOP TIME AND...
"OH, I SEE.
"YOU CAN STOP TIME, AND YOU USE IT FOR THAT?"
......
I SHOULD SAVE IT FOR MURAKAMI-SAN.
MAYBE IF I DON'T SAY ANYTHING, SHE'LL GIVE UP.
ARE YOU GONNA LEAVE?
HUH?
EVERY TIME WE TALK, YOU DISAPPEAR!
BA-THUMP
I THOUGHT YOU HATED ME!
I D-DON'T HATE YOU!
REALLY? THAT'S A RELIEF!

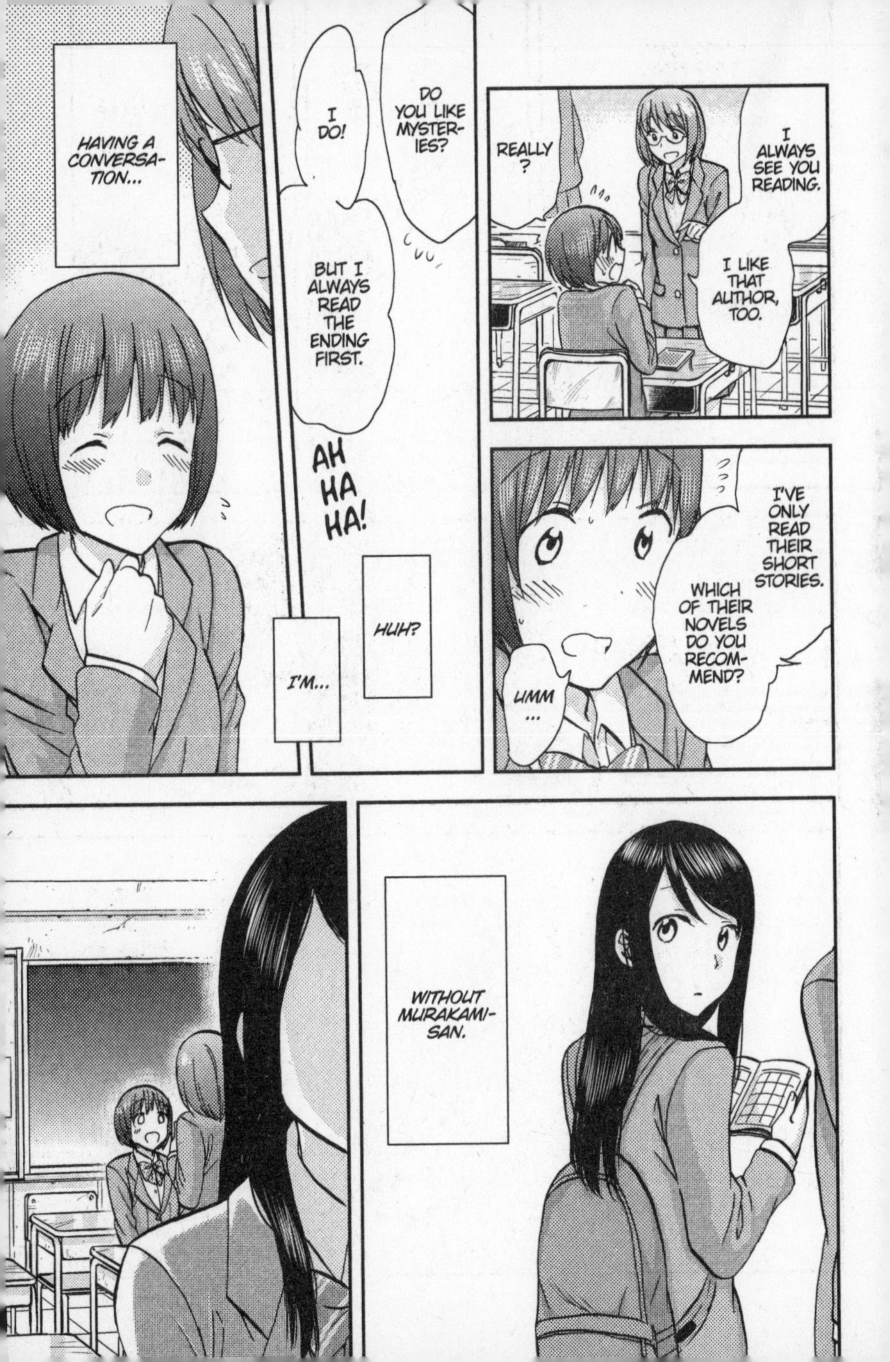
I ALWAYS SEE YOU READING.
REALLY?
I LIKE THAT AUTHOR, TOO.
I'VE ONLY READ THEIR SHORT STORIES.
WHICH OF THEIR NOVELS DO YOU RECOMMEND?
UMM...
DO YOU LIKE MYSTERIES?
I DO!
BUT I ALWAYS READ THE ENDING FIRST.
AH HA HA!
HUH?
I'M...
HAVING A CONVERSATION...
WITHOUT MURAKAMI-SAN.

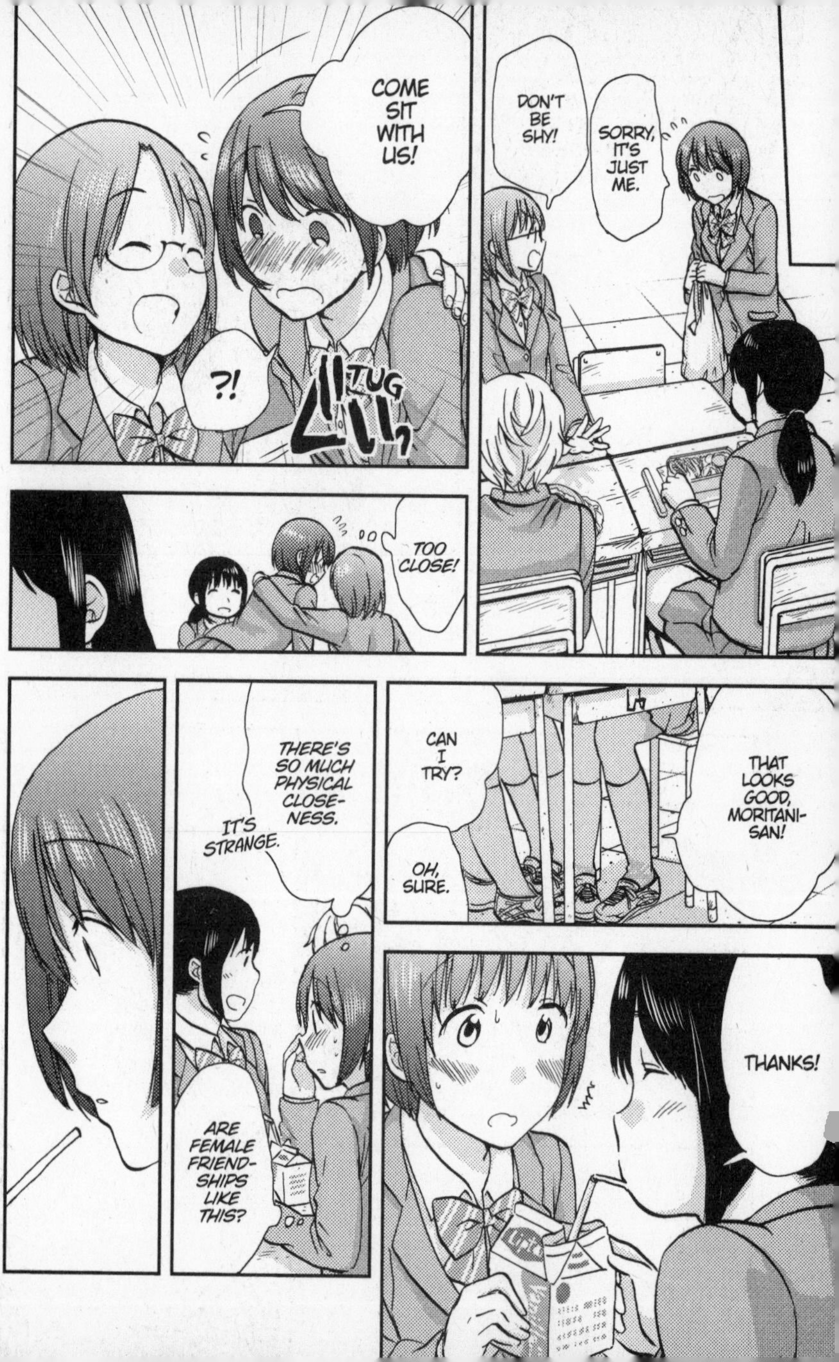
SORRY, IT'S JUST ME.
DON'T BE SHY!
COME SIT WITH US!
TUG
?!
TOO CLOSE!
THAT LOOKS GOOD, MORITANI-SAN!
CAN I TRY?
OH, SURE.
THANKS!
THERE'S SO MUCH PHYSICAL CLOSE-NESS.
IT'S STRANGE.
ARE FEMALE FRIEND-SHIPS LIKE THIS?

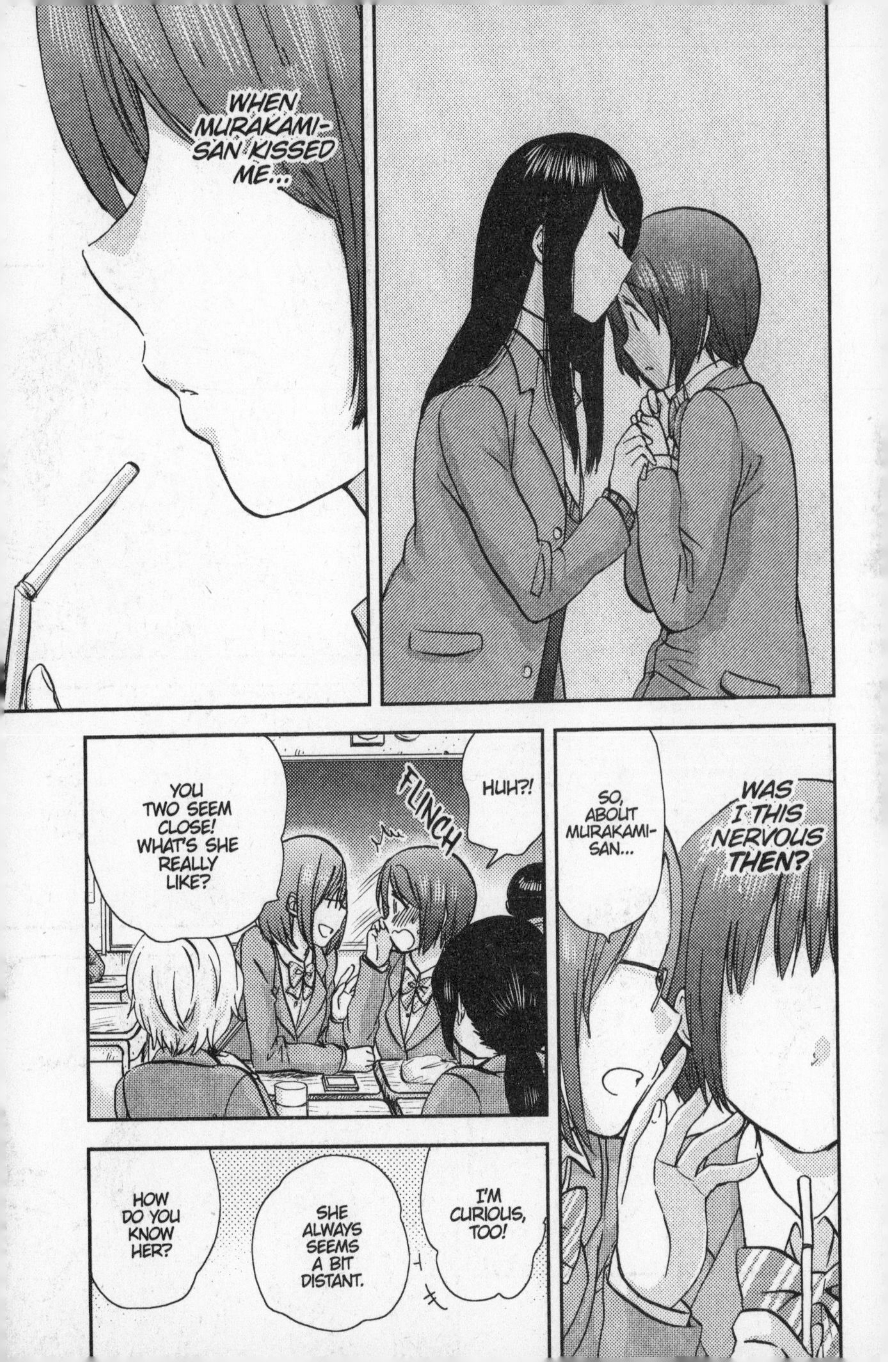
WHEN MURAKAMI-SAN KISSED ME...
WAS I THIS NERVOUS THEN?
SO, ABOUT MURAKAMI-SAN...
HUH?!
FLINCH
YOU TWO SEEM CLOSE! WHAT'S SHE REALLY LIKE?
I'M CURIOUS, TOO!
SHE ALWAYS SEEMS A BIT DISTANT.
HOW DO YOU KNOW HER?

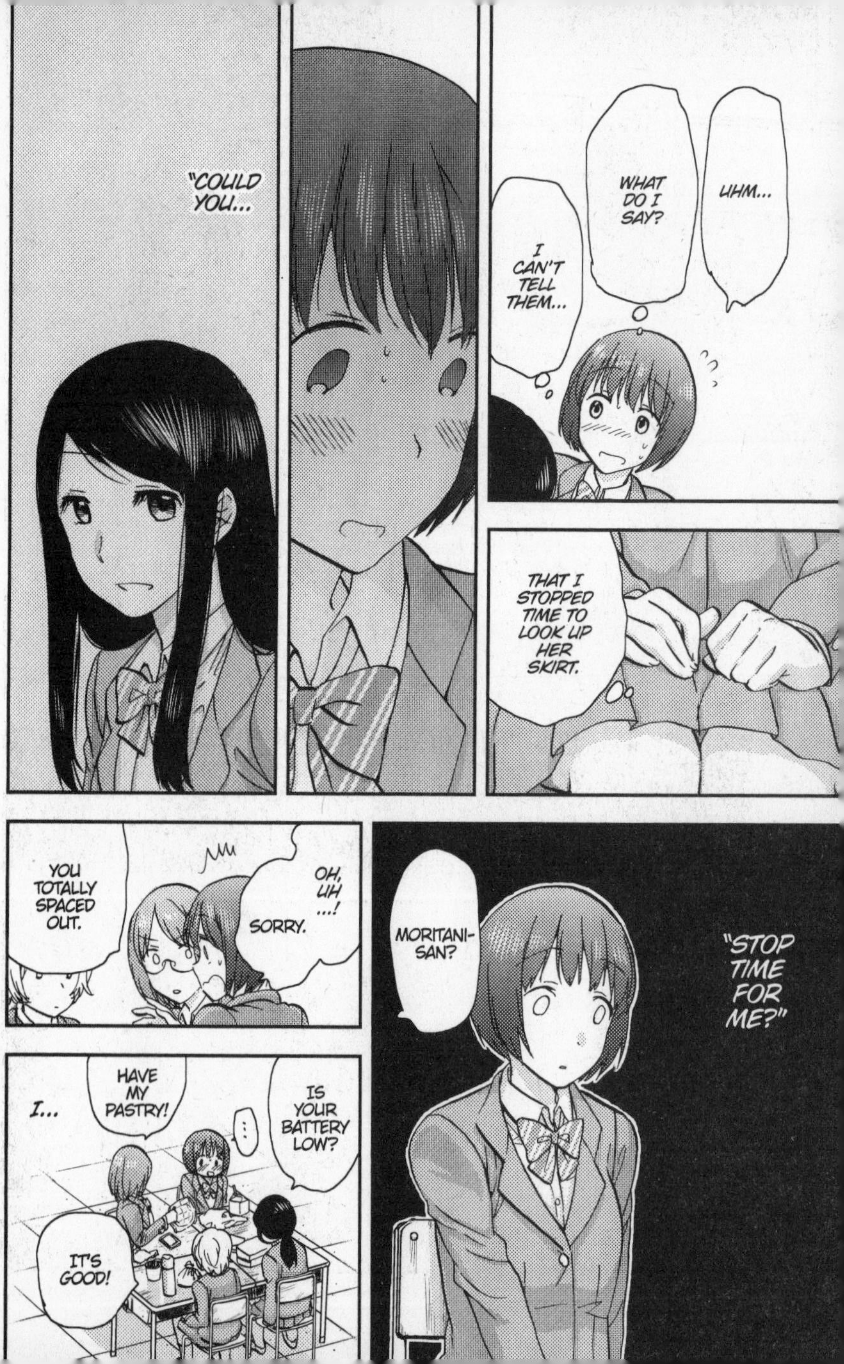
UHM...
WHAT DO I SAY?
I CAN'T TELL THEM...
THAT I STOPPED TIME TO LOOK UP HER SKIRT.
"COULD YOU...
"STOP TIME FOR ME?"
MORITANI-SAN?
OH, UH ...!
SORRY.
YOU TOTALLY SPACED OUT.
IS YOUR BATTERY LOW?
...
HAVE MY PASTRY!
I...
IT'S GOOD!

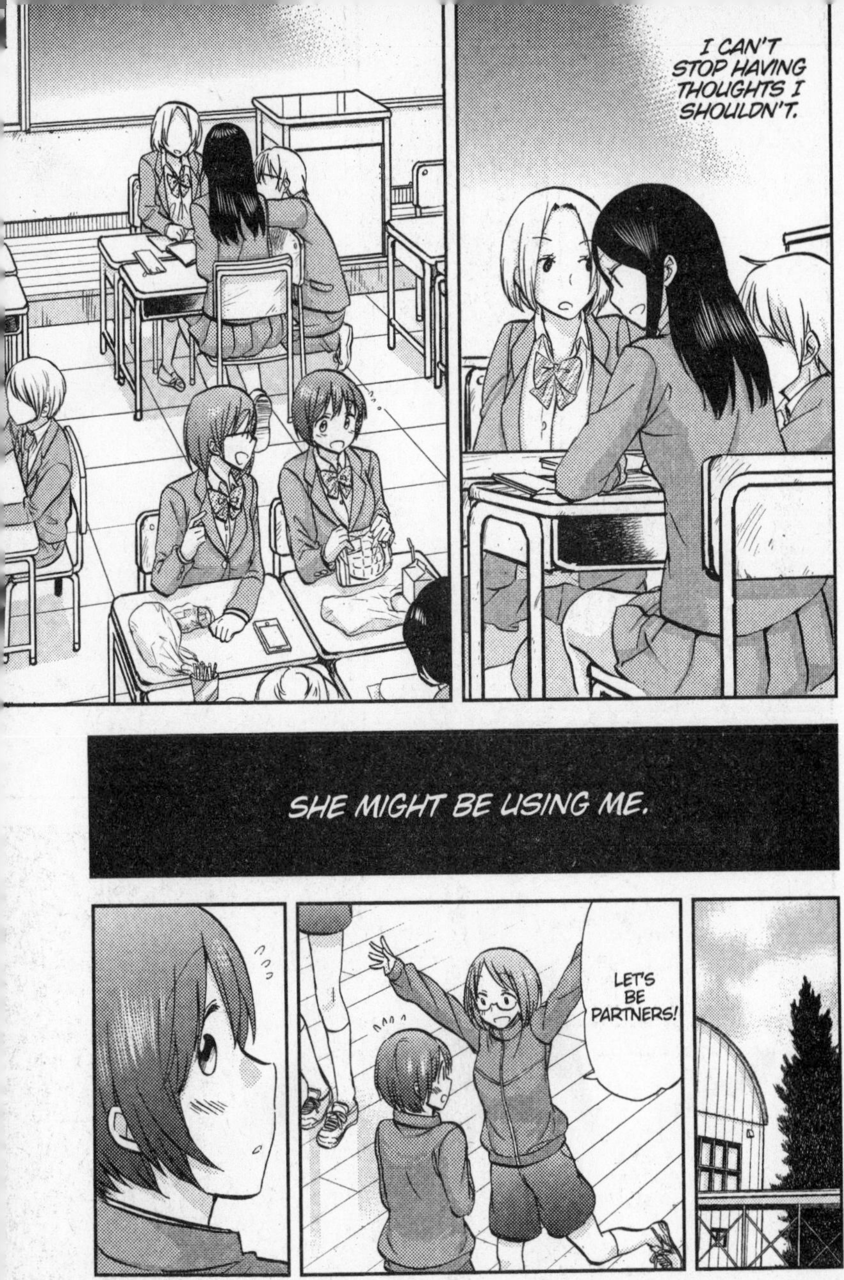
I CAN'T STOP HAVING THOUGHTS I SHOULDN'T.
SHE MIGHT BE USING ME.
LET'S BE PARTNERS!

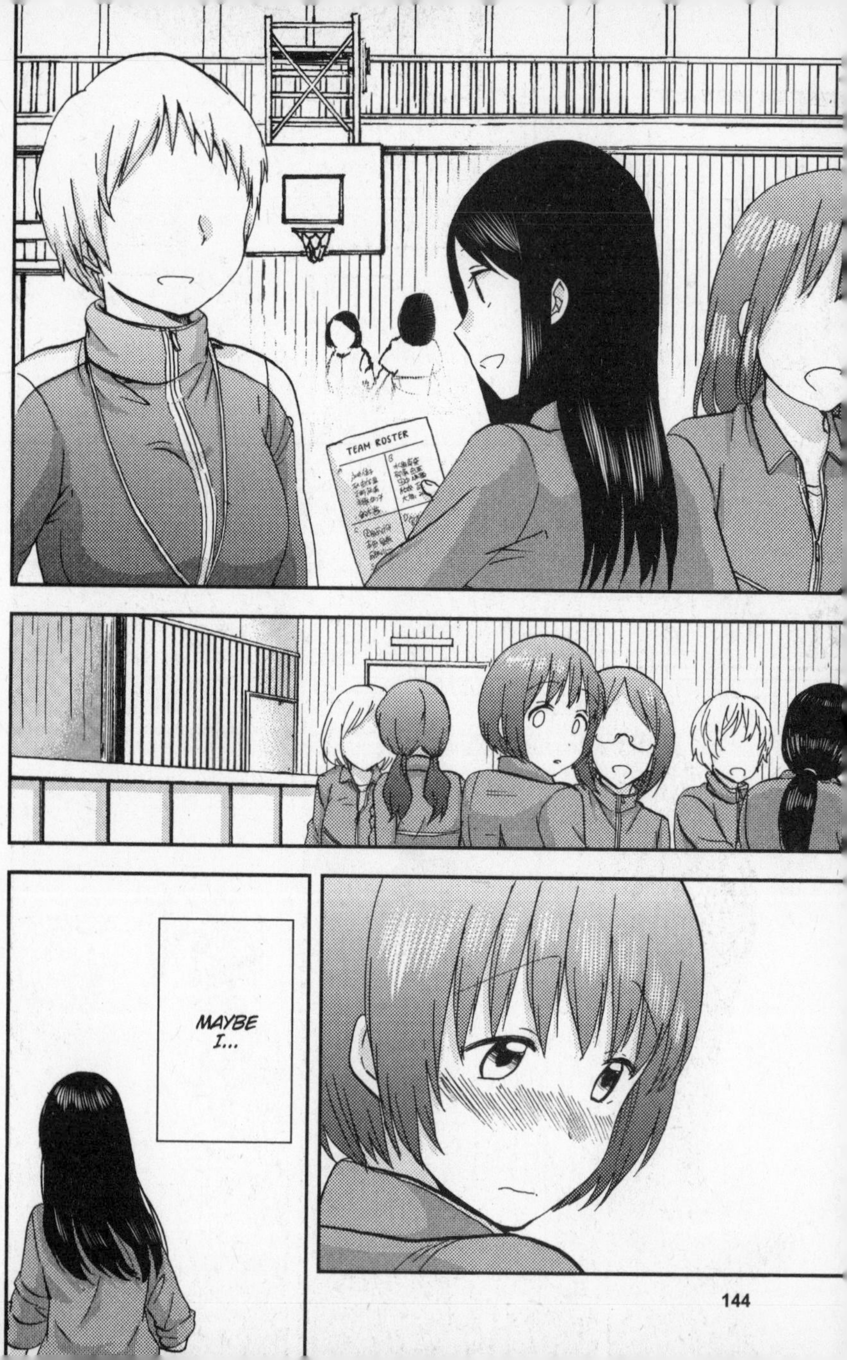
TEAM ROSTER
MAYBE I...

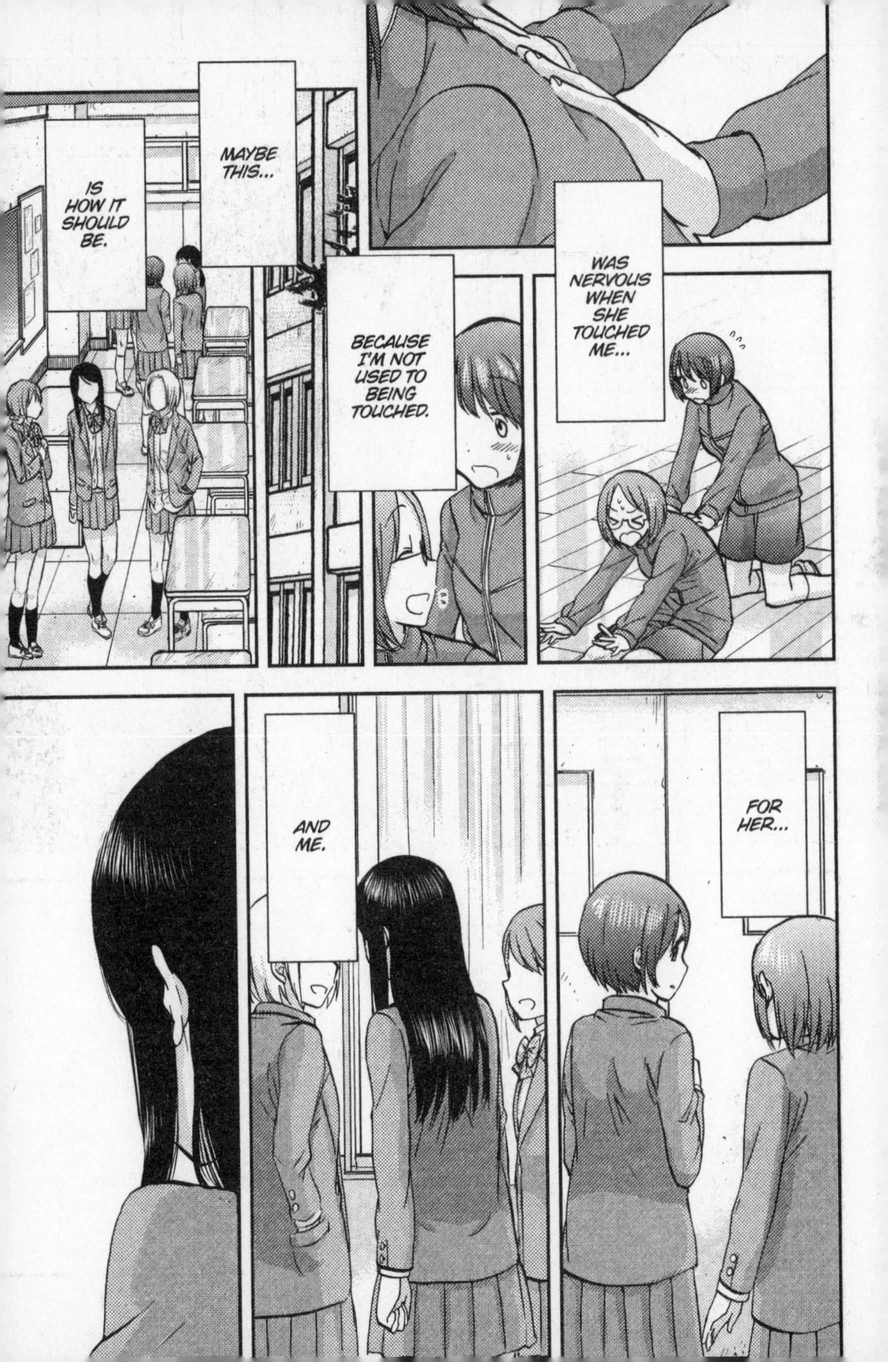
WAS NERVOUS WHEN SHE TOUCHED ME...
BECAUSE I'M NOT USED TO BEING TOUCHED.
MAYBE THIS...
IS HOW IT SHOULD BE.
FOR HER...
AND ME.

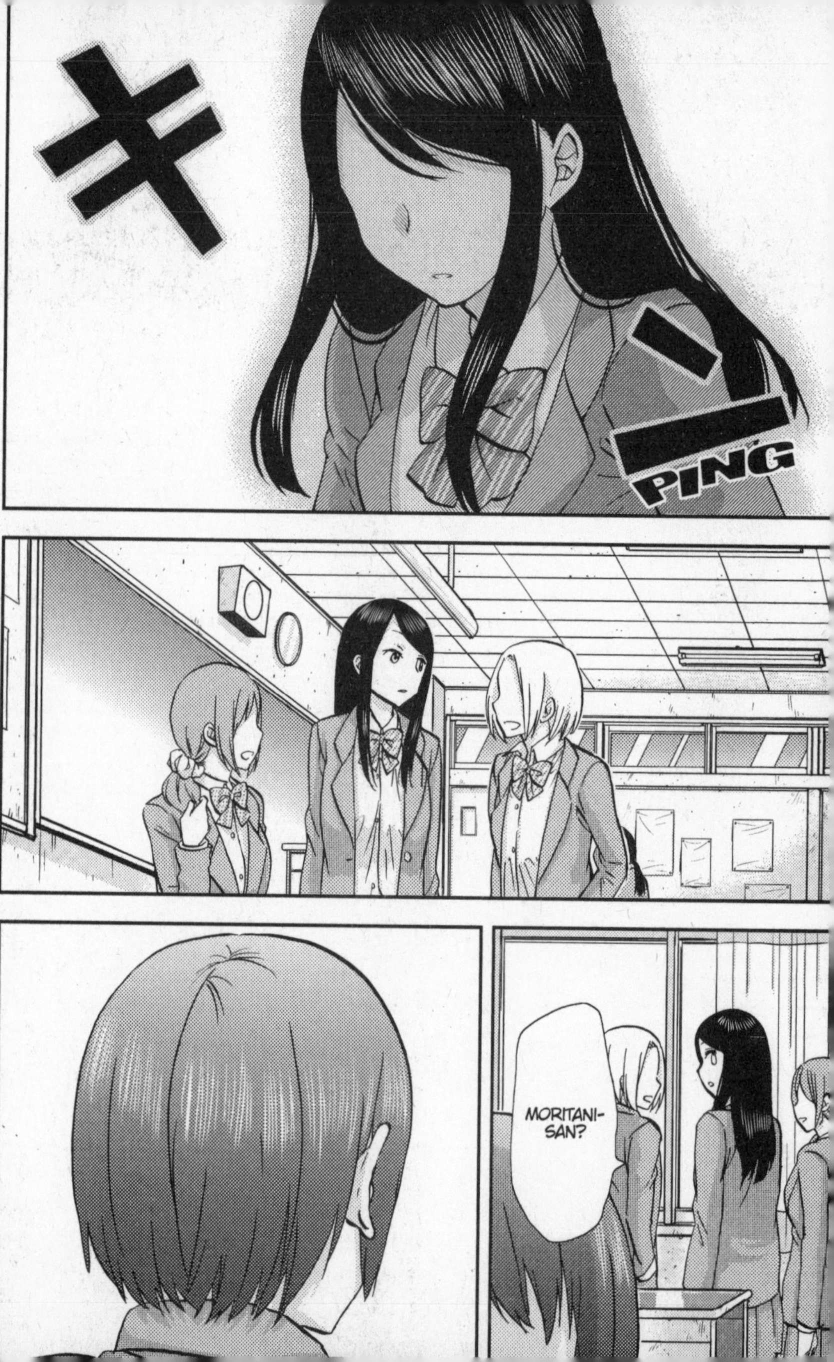
PING
MORITANI-SAN?

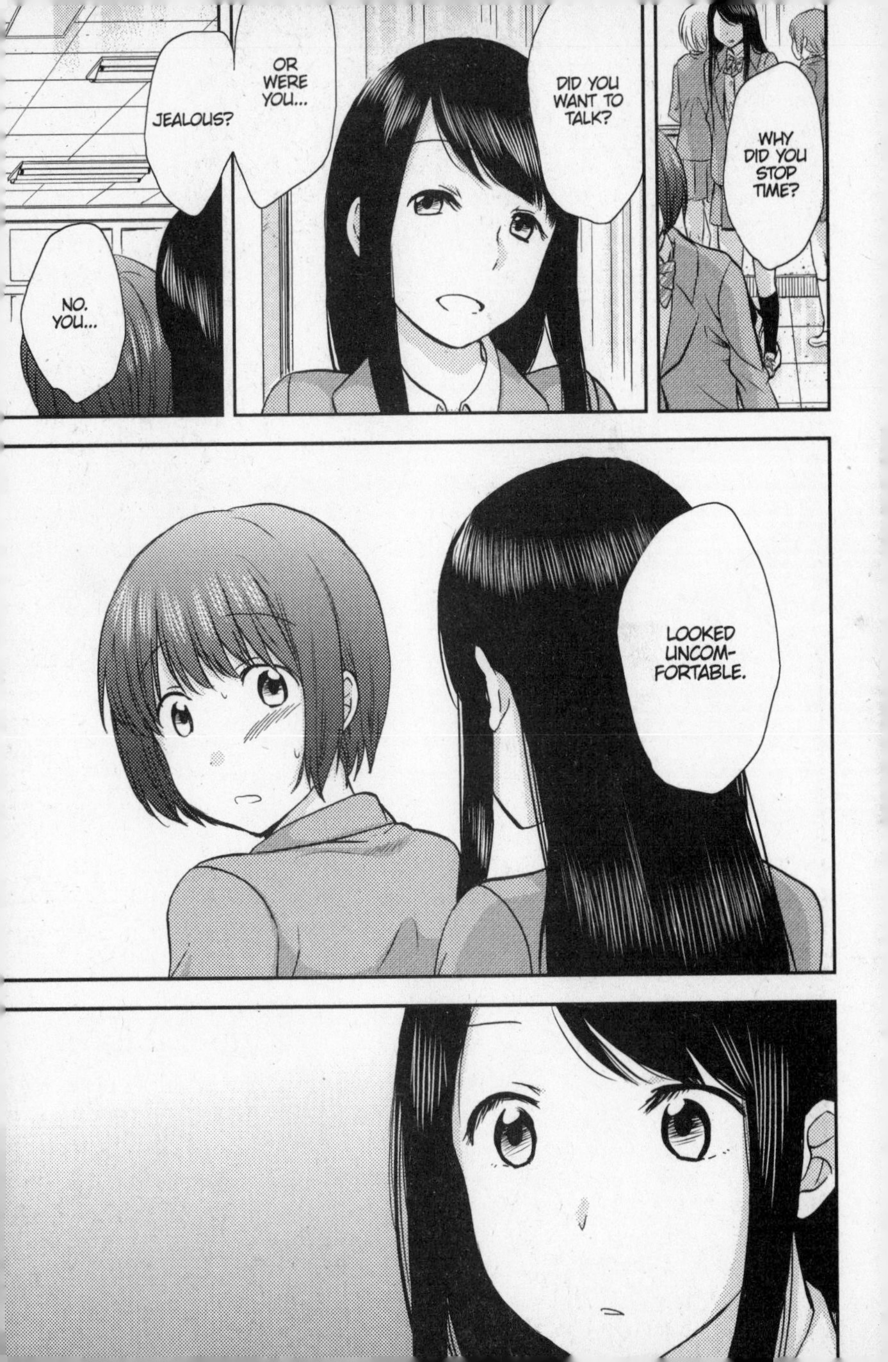
WHY DID YOU STOP TIME?
DID YOU WANT TO TALK?
OR WERE YOU...
JEALOUS?
NO. YOU...
LOOKED UNCOMFORTABLE.

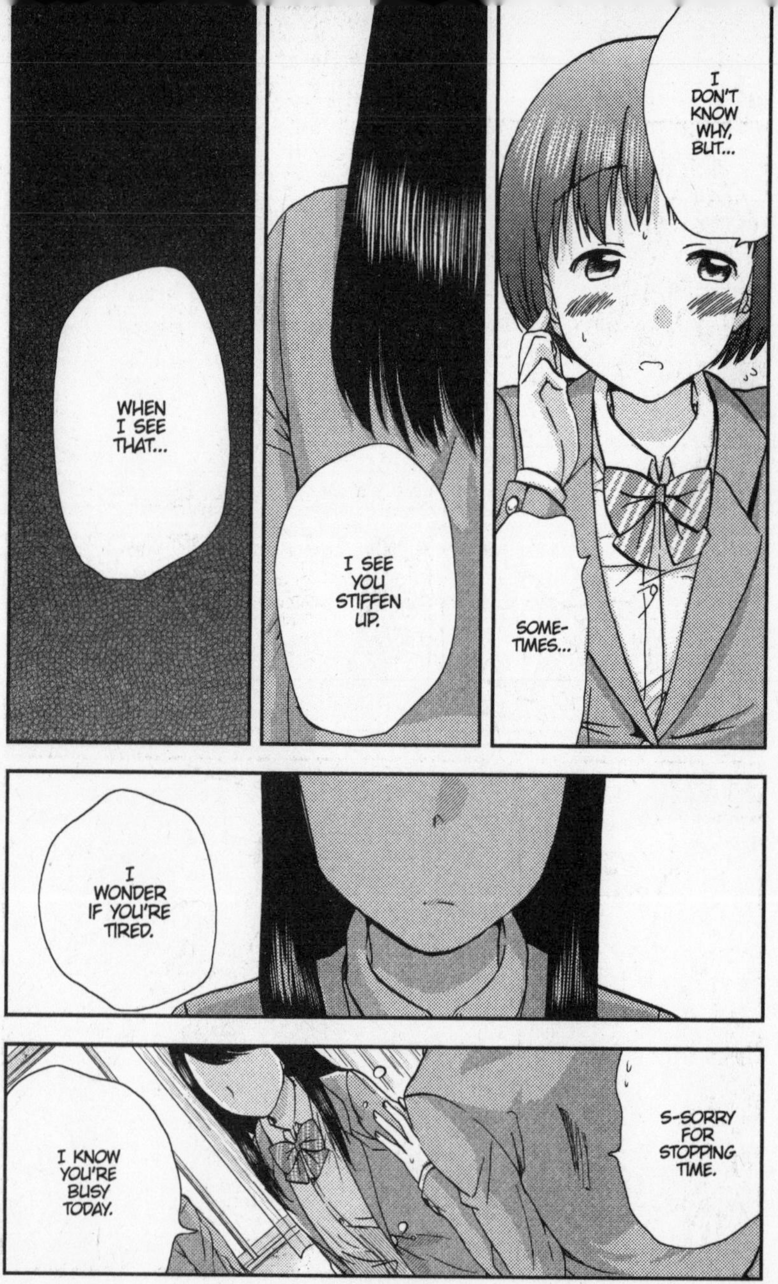
I DON'T KNOW WHY, BUT...
SOME-TIMES...
I SEE YOU STIFFEN UP.
WHEN I SEE THAT...
I WONDER IF YOU'RE TIRED.
S-SORRY FOR STOPPING TIME.
I KNOW YOU'RE BUSY TODAY.

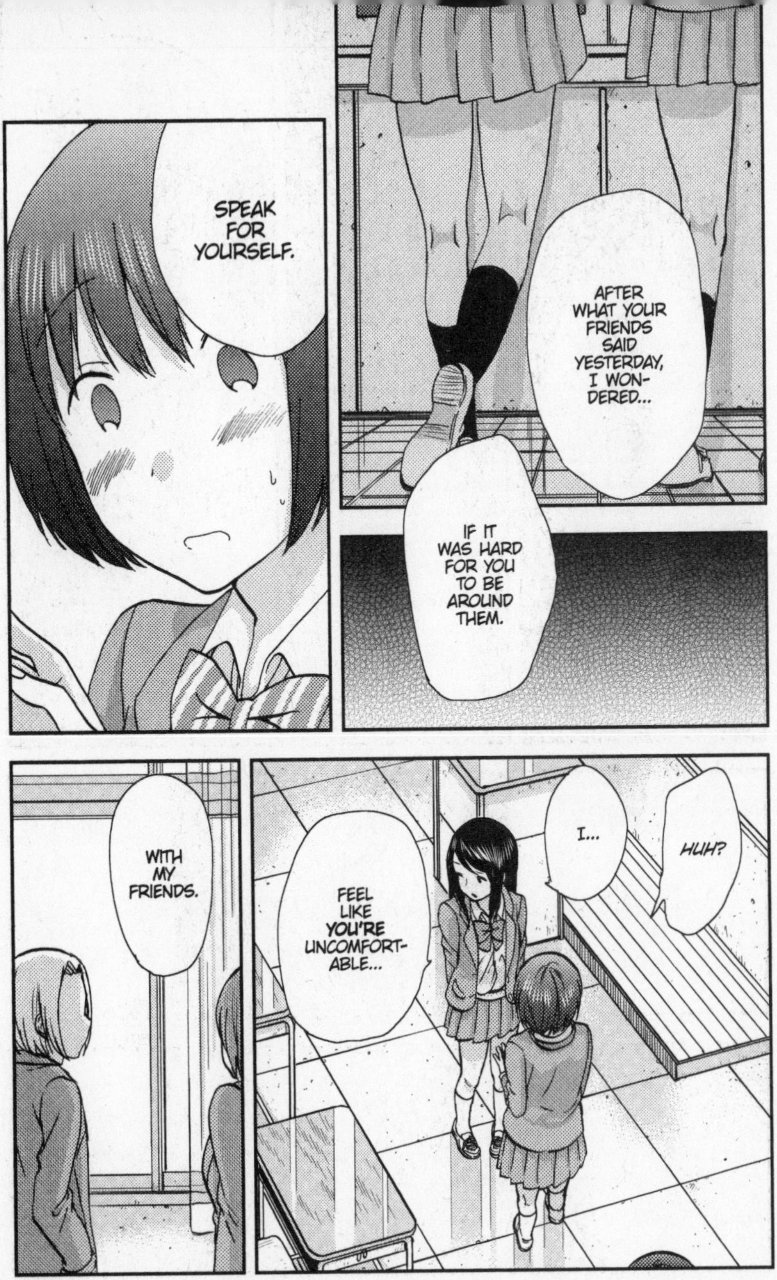
AFTER WHAT YOUR FRIENDS SAID YESTERDAY, I WONDERED...
IF IT WAS HARD FOR YOU TO BE AROUND THEM.
SPEAK FOR YOURSELF.
HUH?
I...
FEEL LIKE YOU'RE UNCOMFORTABLE...
WITH MY FRIENDS.

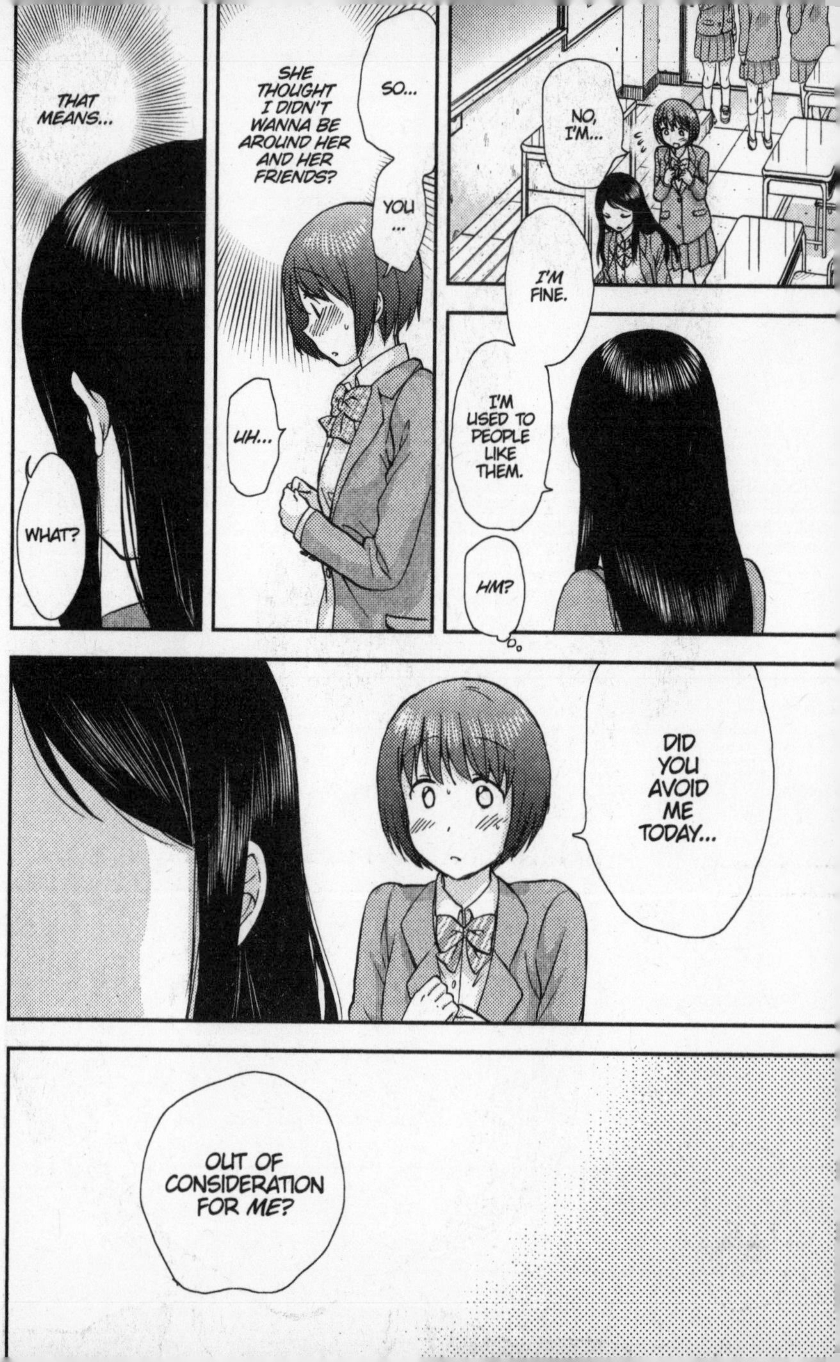
NO, I'M...
I'M FINE.
I'M USED TO PEOPLE LIKE THEM.
HM?
SO...
SHE THOUGHT I DIDN'T WANNA BE AROUND HER AND HER FRIENDS?
YOU...
UH...
THAT MEANS...
WHAT?
DID YOU AVOID ME TODAY...
OUT OF CONSIDERATION FOR ME?

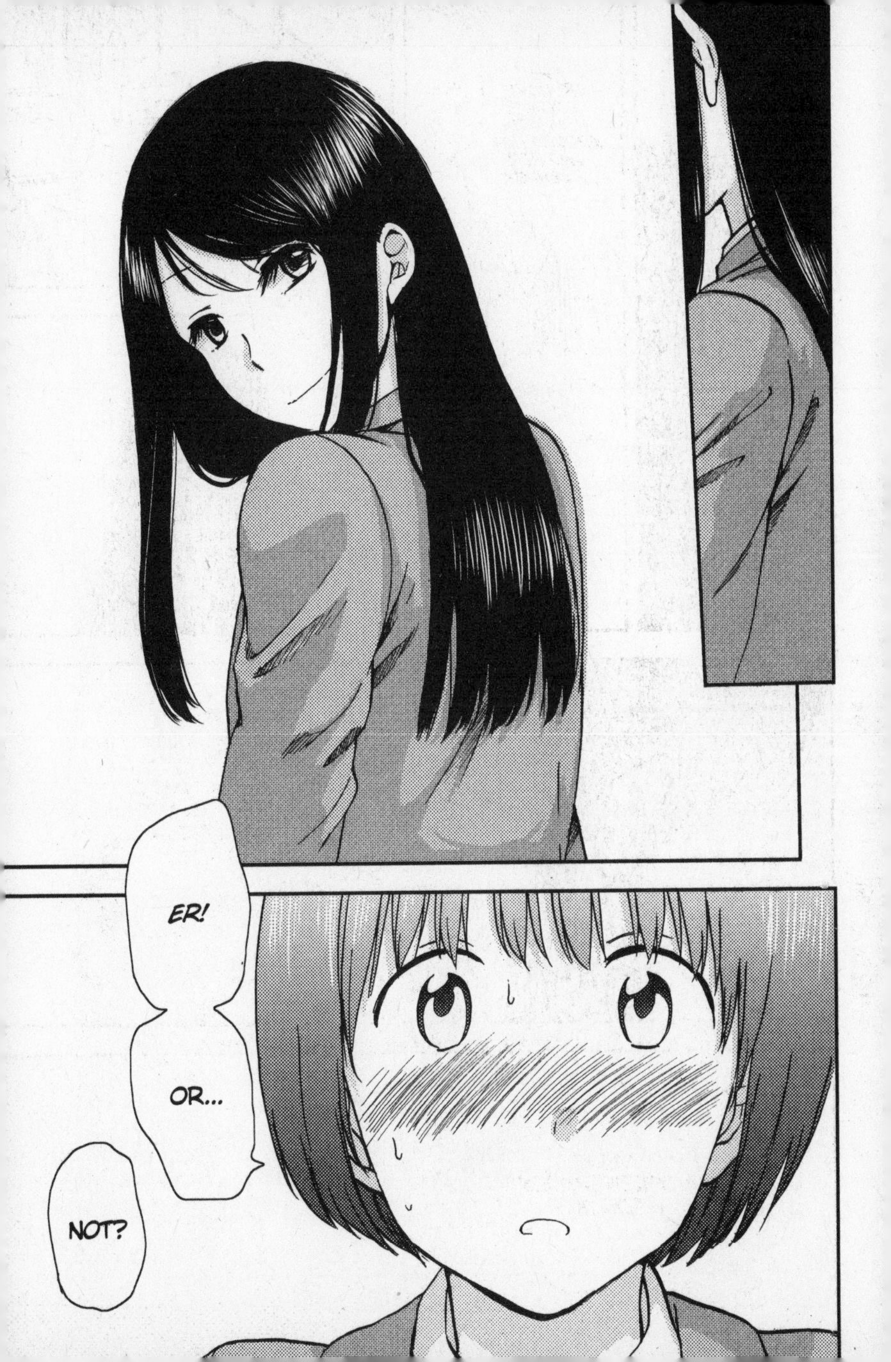
ER!
OR...
NOT?

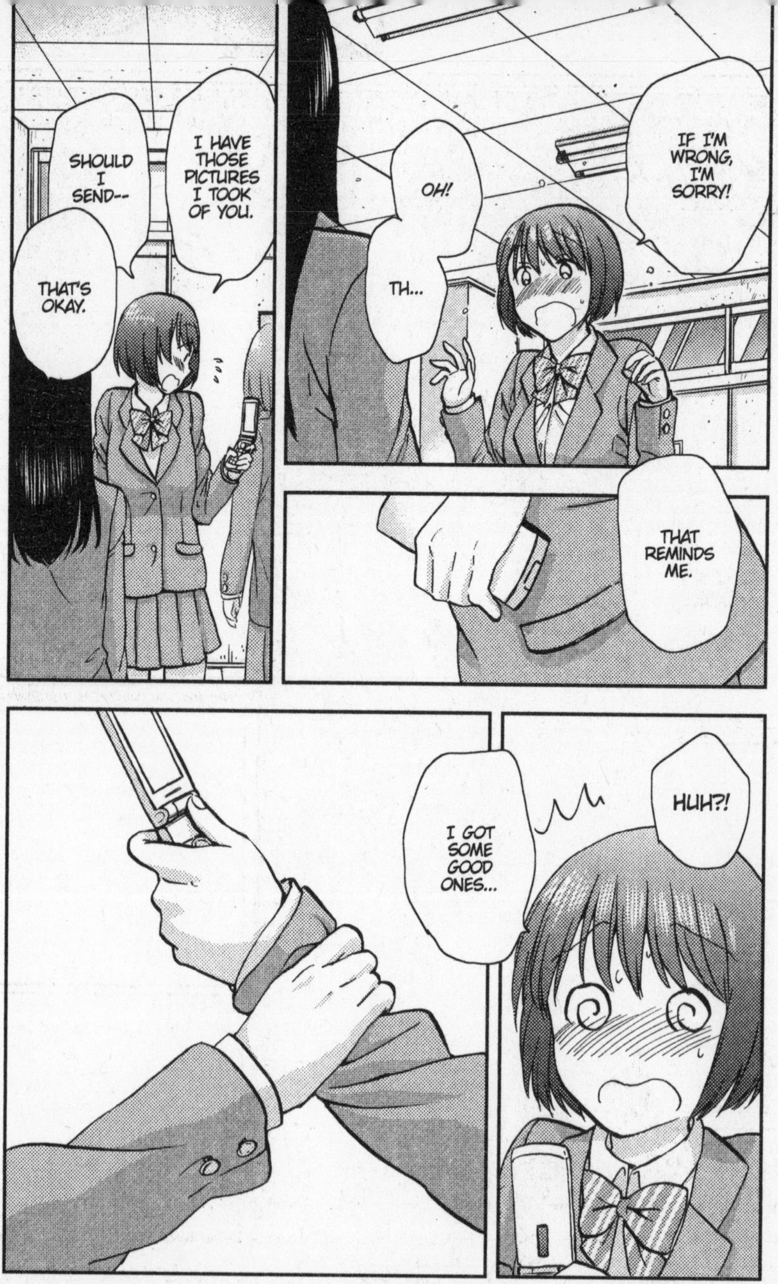
IF I'M WRONG, I'M SORRY!
OH!
TH...
THAT REMINDS ME.
I HAVE THOSE PICTURES I TOOK OF YOU.
SHOULD I SEND--
THAT'S OKAY.
HUH?!
I GOT SOME GOOD ONES...

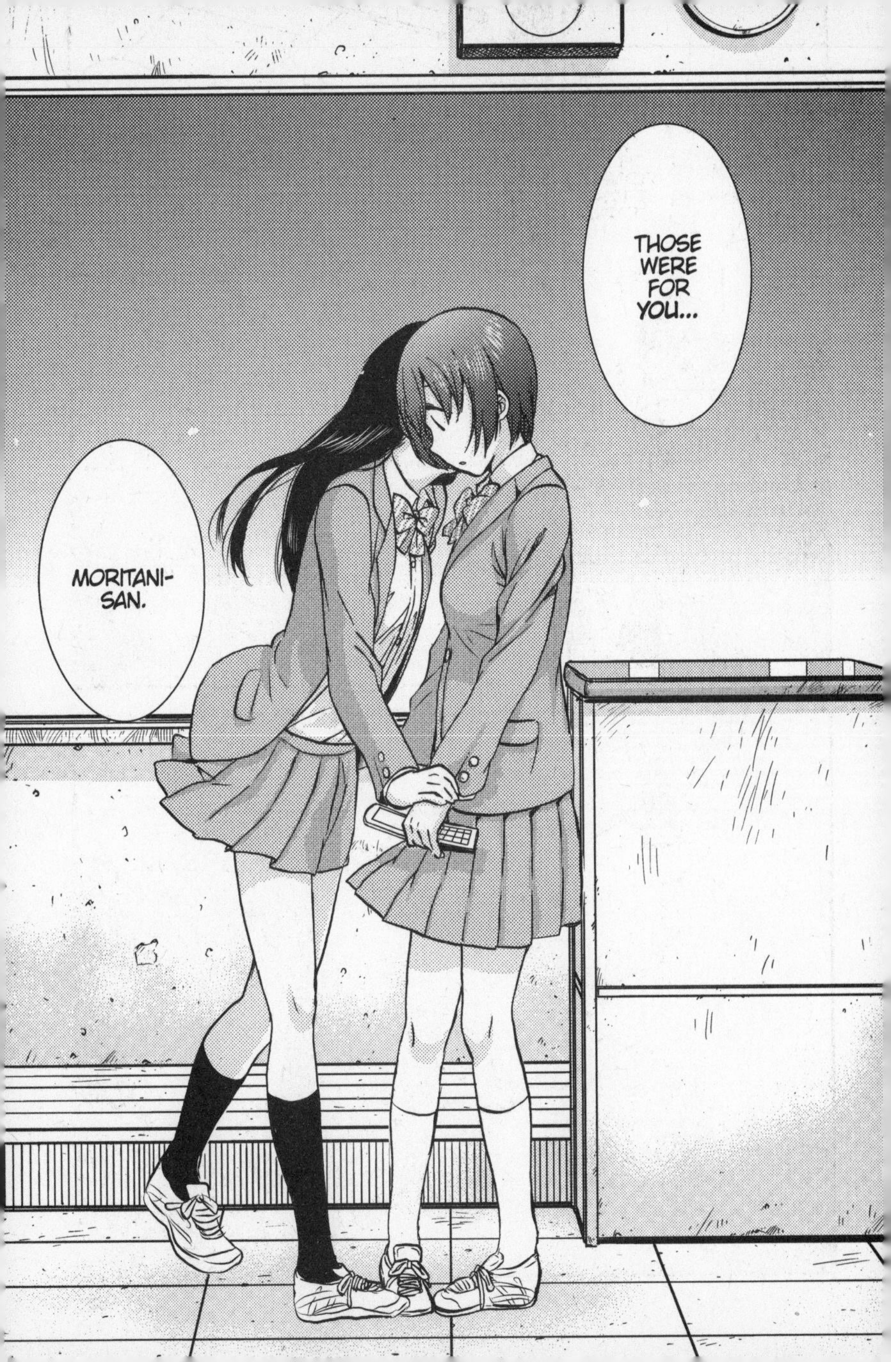
THOSE WERE FOR YOU...
MORITANI-SAN.

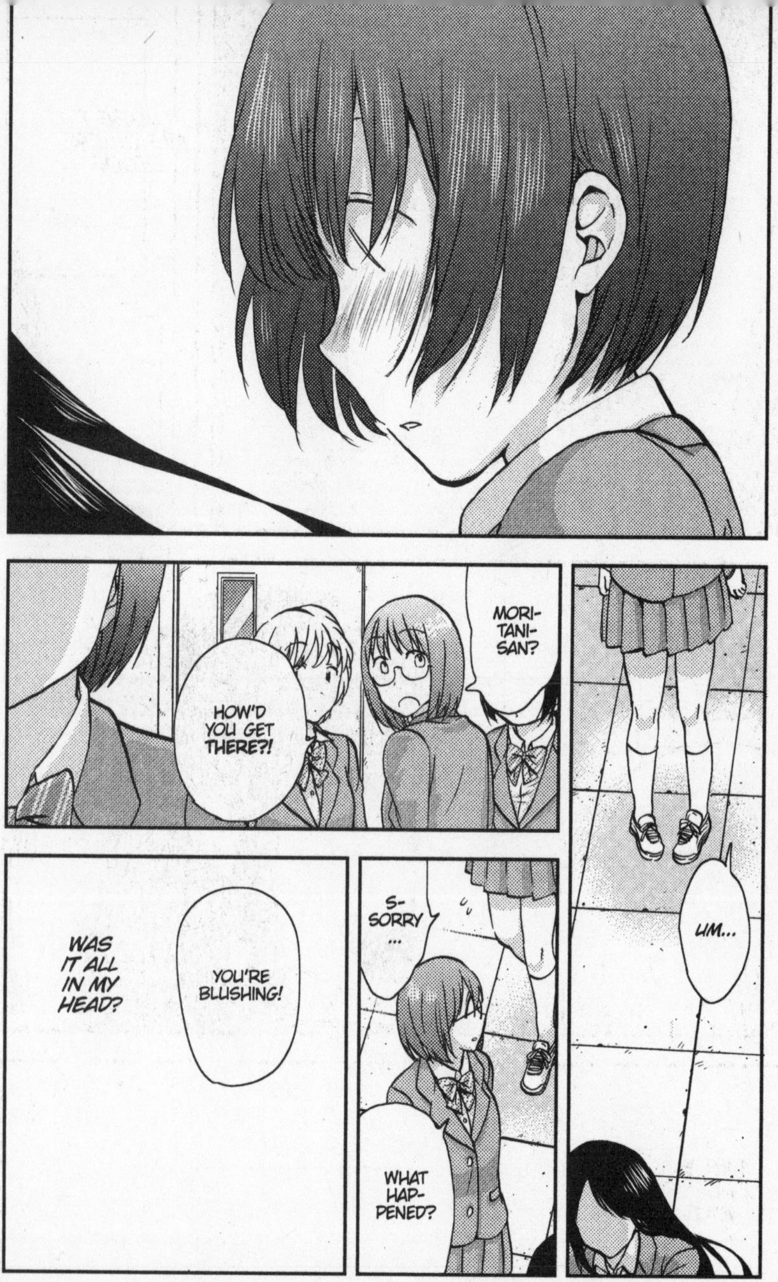
UM...
MORI-TANI-SAN?
HOW'D YOU GET THERE?!
S-SORRY ...
WHAT HAP-PENED?
YOU'RE BLUSHING!
WAS IT ALL IN MY HEAD?

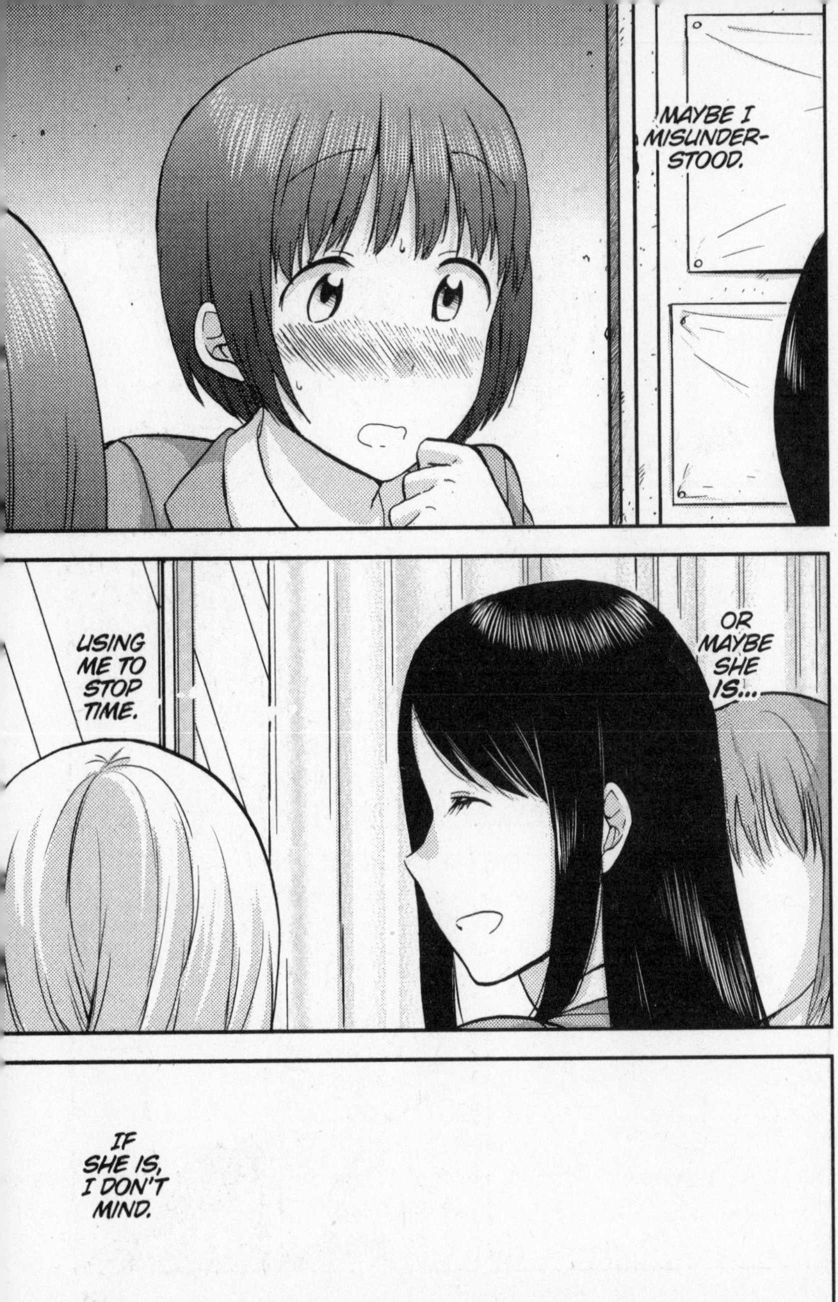
MAYBE I MISUNDER-STOOD.
OR MAYBE SHE IS...
USING ME TO STOP TIME.
IF SHE IS, I DON'T MIND.

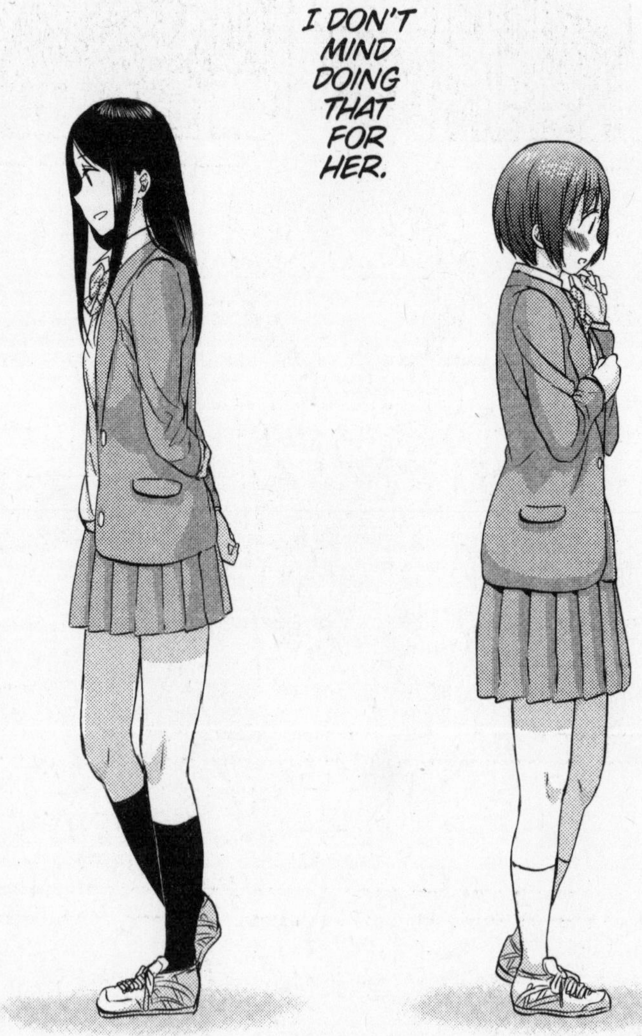
I DON'T MIND DOING THAT FOR HER.

#7. I Can't Stop Having Thoughts I Shouldn't / END

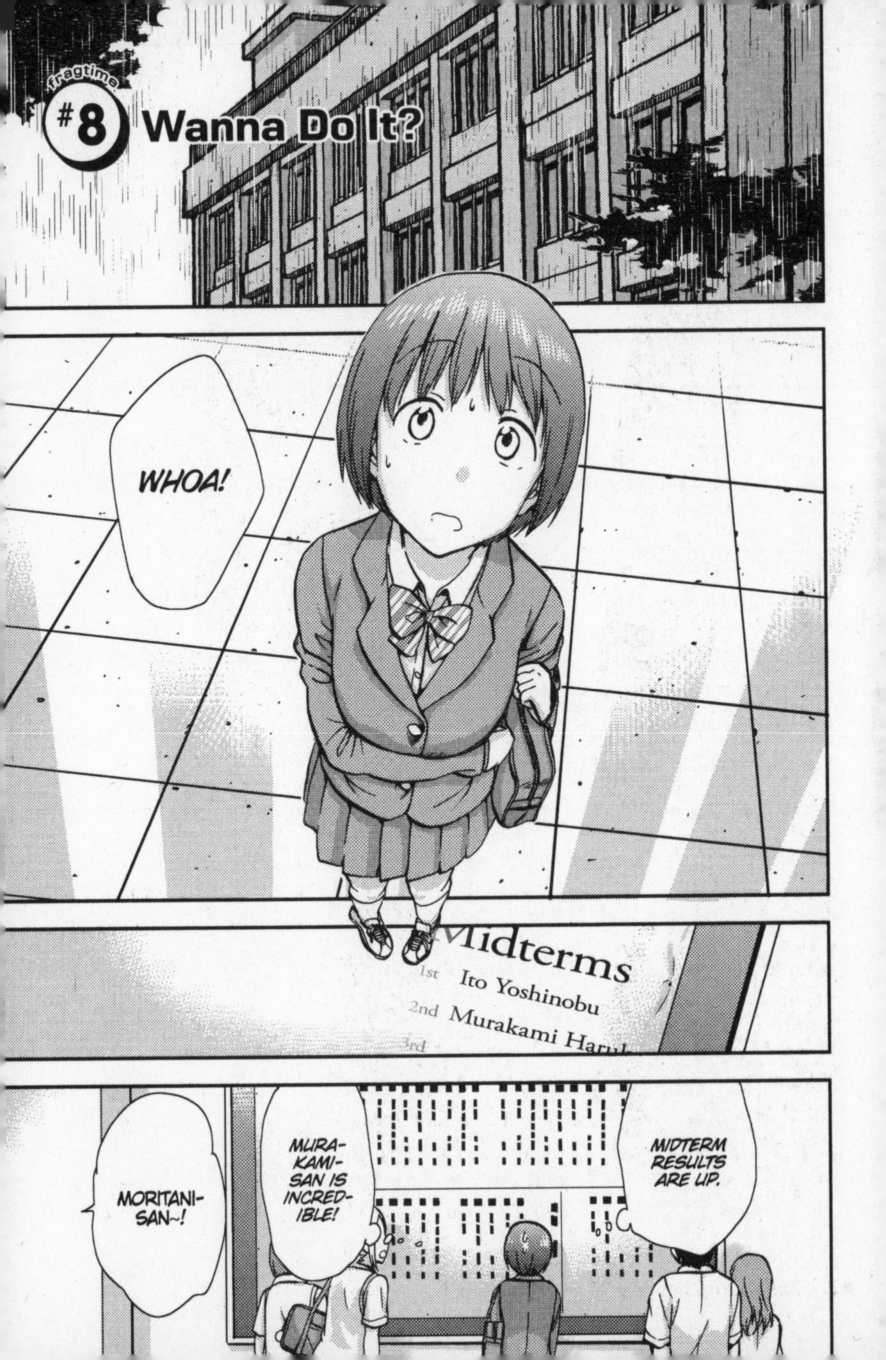
fragtime
#8 Wanna Do It?
WHOA!
Midterms
1st Ito Yoshinobu
2nd Murakami
3rd
MIDTERM RESULTS ARE UP.
MURAKAMI-SAN IS INCREDIBLE!
MORITANI-SAN~!

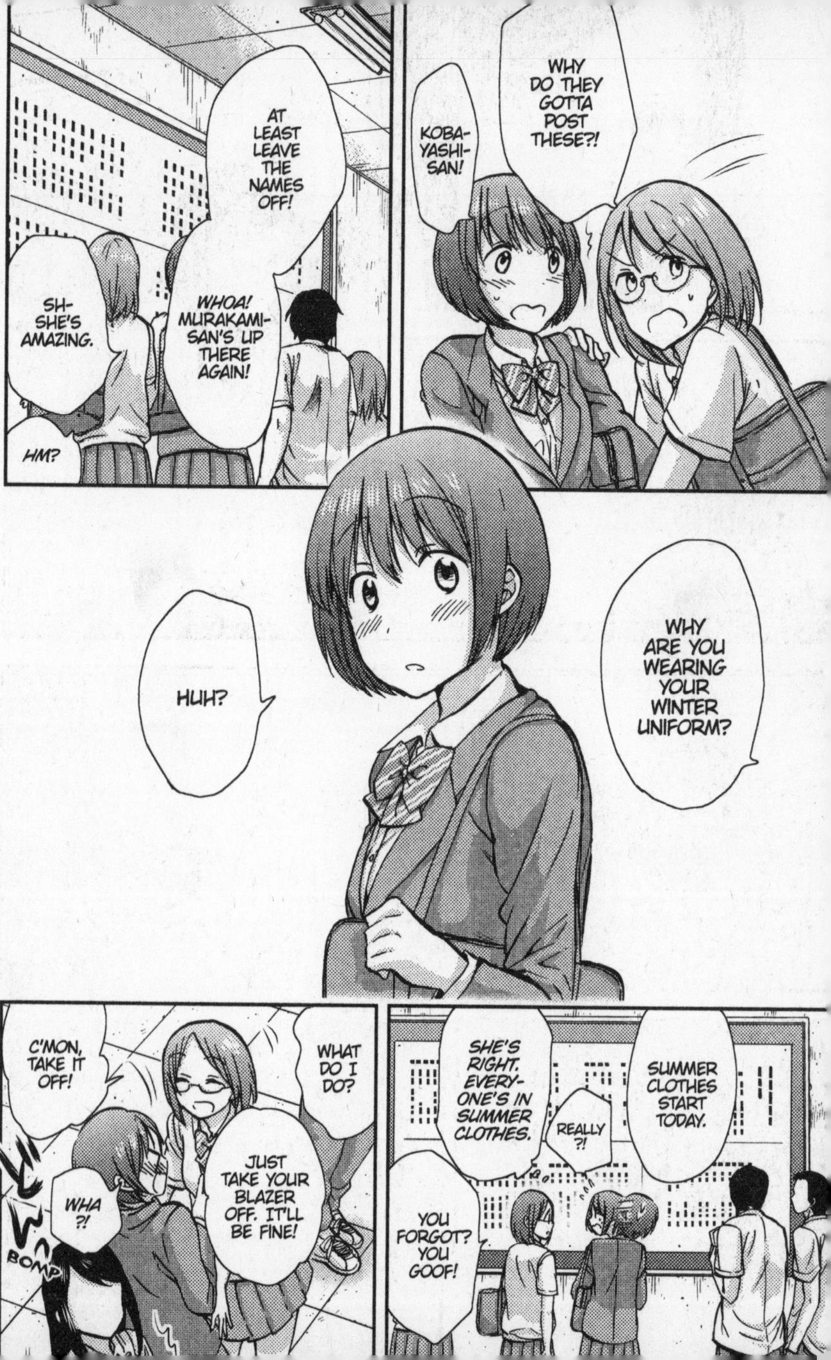
WHY DO THEY GOTTA POST THESE?!
KOBA-YASHI-SAN!
AT LEAST LEAVE THE NAMES OFF!
WHOA! MURAKAMI-SAN'S UP THERE AGAIN!
SH-SHE'S AMAZING.
HM?
WHY ARE YOU WEARING YOUR WINTER UNIFORM?
HUH?
SUMMER CLOTHES START TODAY.
REALLY?!
SHE'S RIGHT. EVERY-ONE'S IN SUMMER CLOTHES.
YOU FORGOT? YOU GOOF!
WHAT DO I DO?
C'MON, TAKE IT OFF!
JUST TAKE YOUR BLAZER OFF. IT'LL BE FINE!
WHA?!
BOMP

IT'S OKAY.

OH, SORRY!

YOU OKAY?

WHAT?

YEAH.

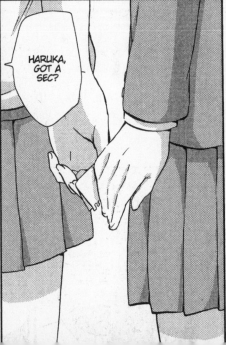

HARUKA, GOT A SEC?

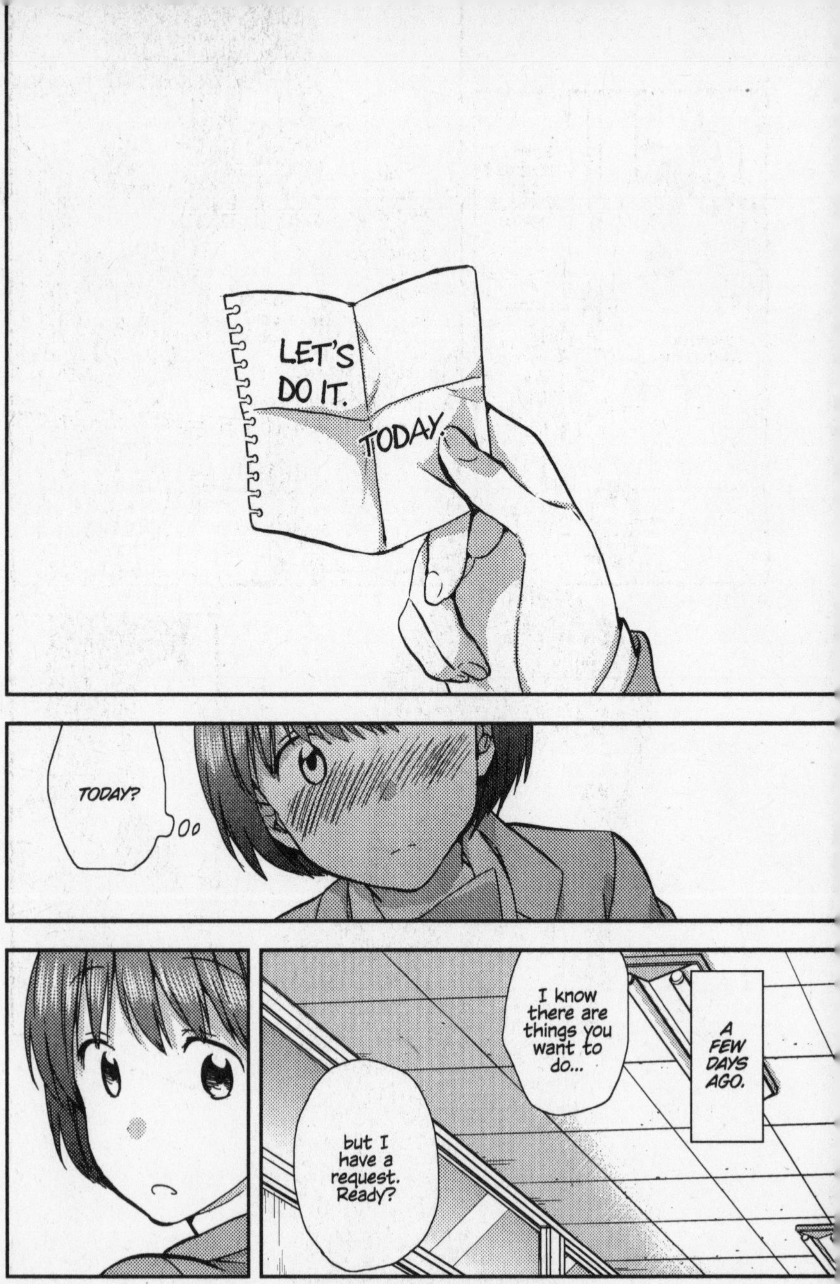
LET'S DO IT.
TODAY.
TODAY?
Oo
A FEW DAYS AGO.
I know there are things you want to do...
but I have a request. Ready?

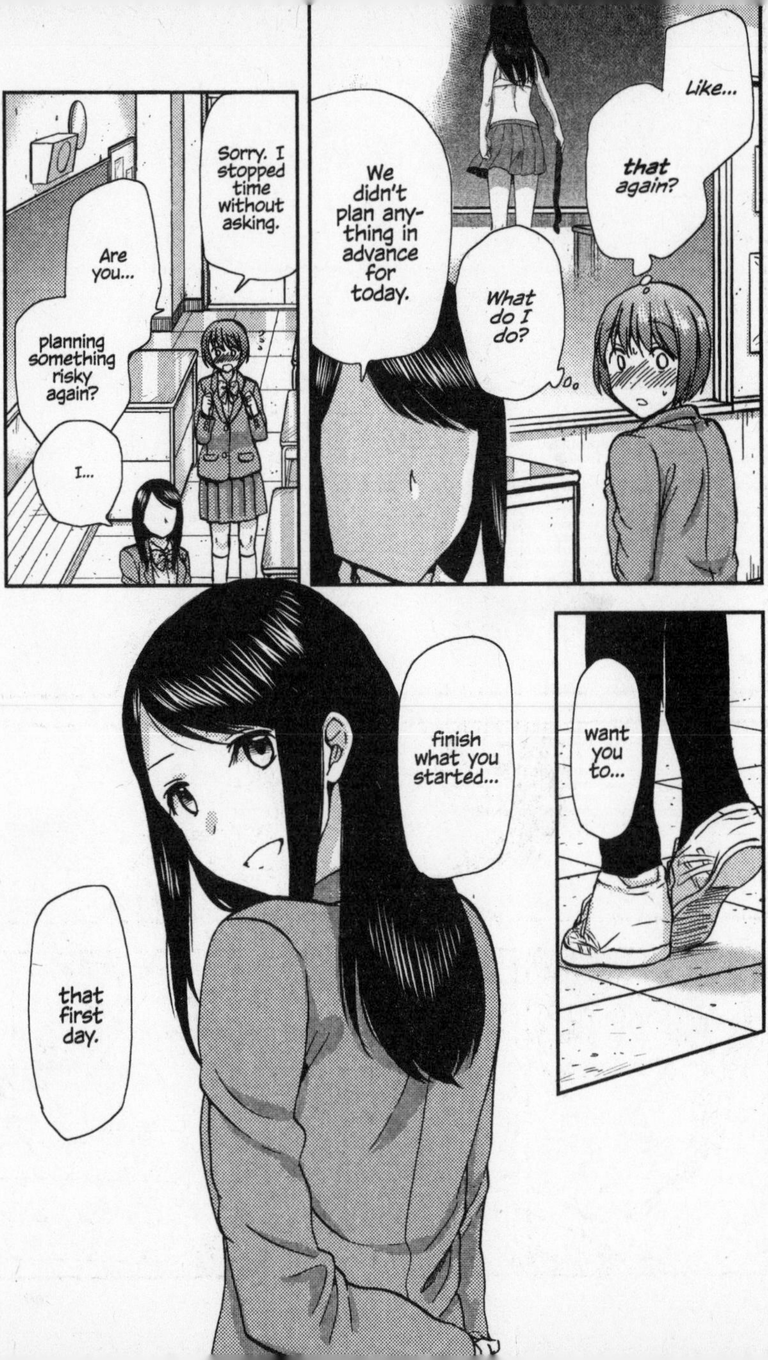
Like...
that again?
We didn't plan any-thing in advance for today.
What do I do?
Sorry. I stopped time without asking.
Are you...
planning something risky again?
I...
want you to...
finish what you started...
that first day.

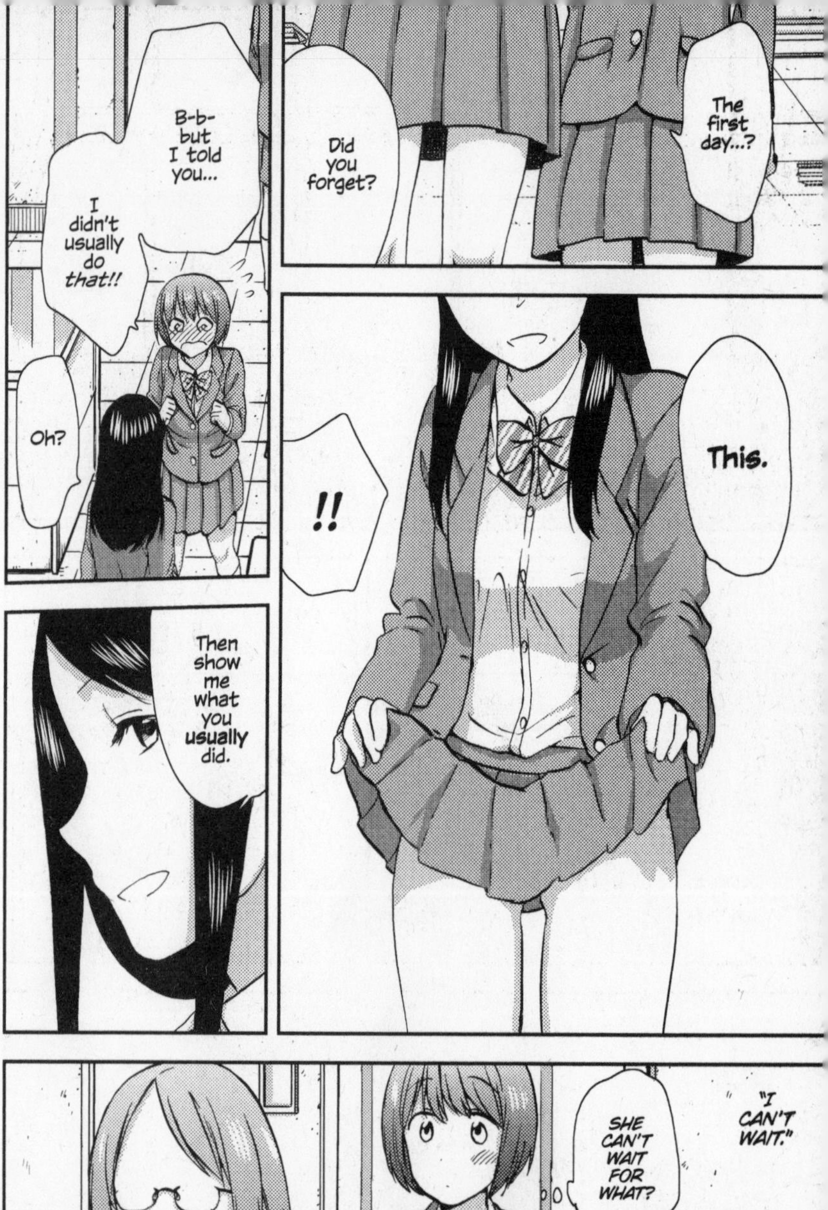
The first day...?
Did you forget?
B-b-but I told you...
I didn't usually do *that!!*
Oh?
Then show me what you usually did.
!!
This.
"I CAN'T WAIT."
SHE CAN'T WAIT FOR WHAT?

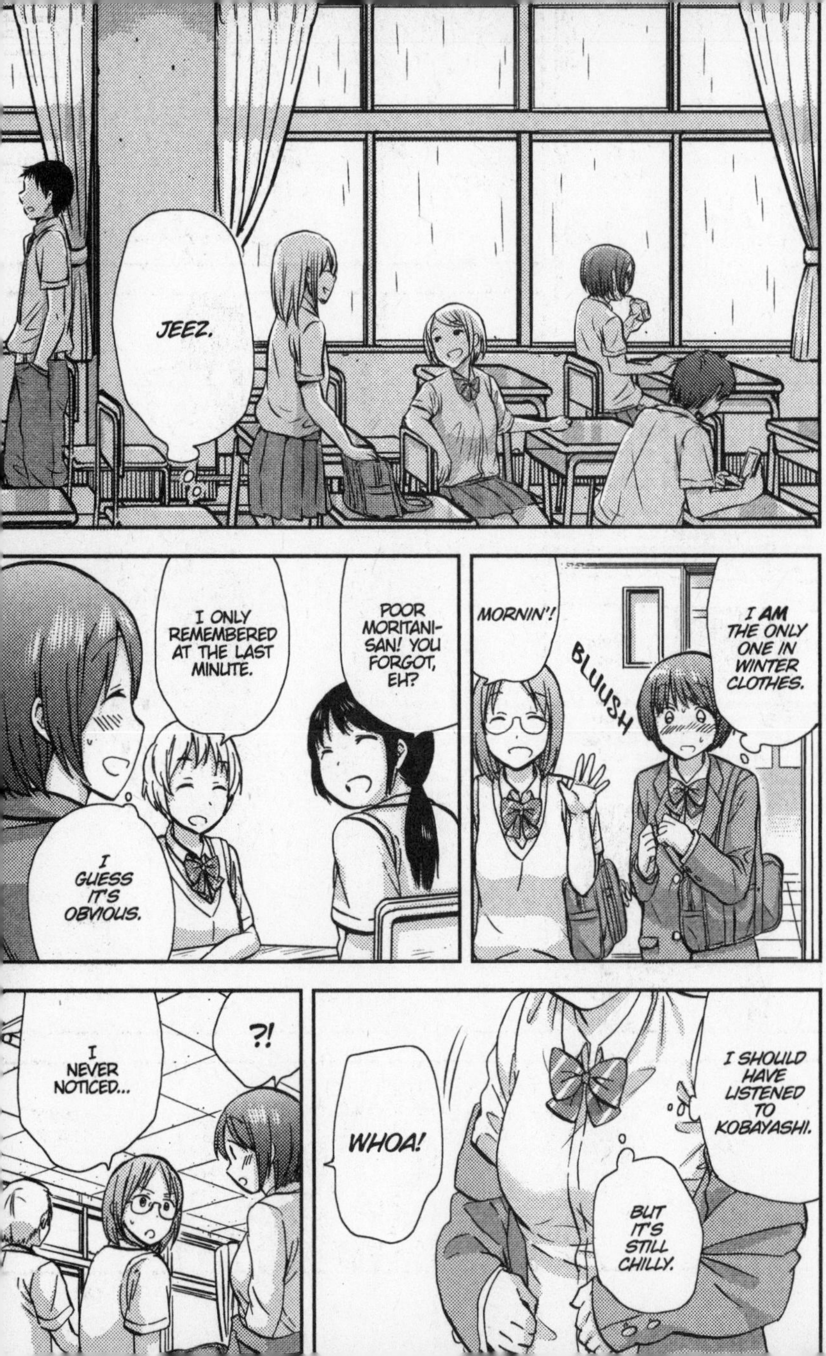
JEEZ.
I AM THE ONLY ONE IN WINTER CLOTHES.
MORNIN'!
BLUUSH
POOR MORITANI-SAN! YOU FORGOT, EH?
I ONLY REMEMBERED AT THE LAST MINUTE.
I GUESS IT'S OBVIOUS.
I SHOULD HAVE LISTENED TO KOBAYASHI.
WHOA!
BUT IT'S STILL CHILLY.
?!
I NEVER NOTICED...

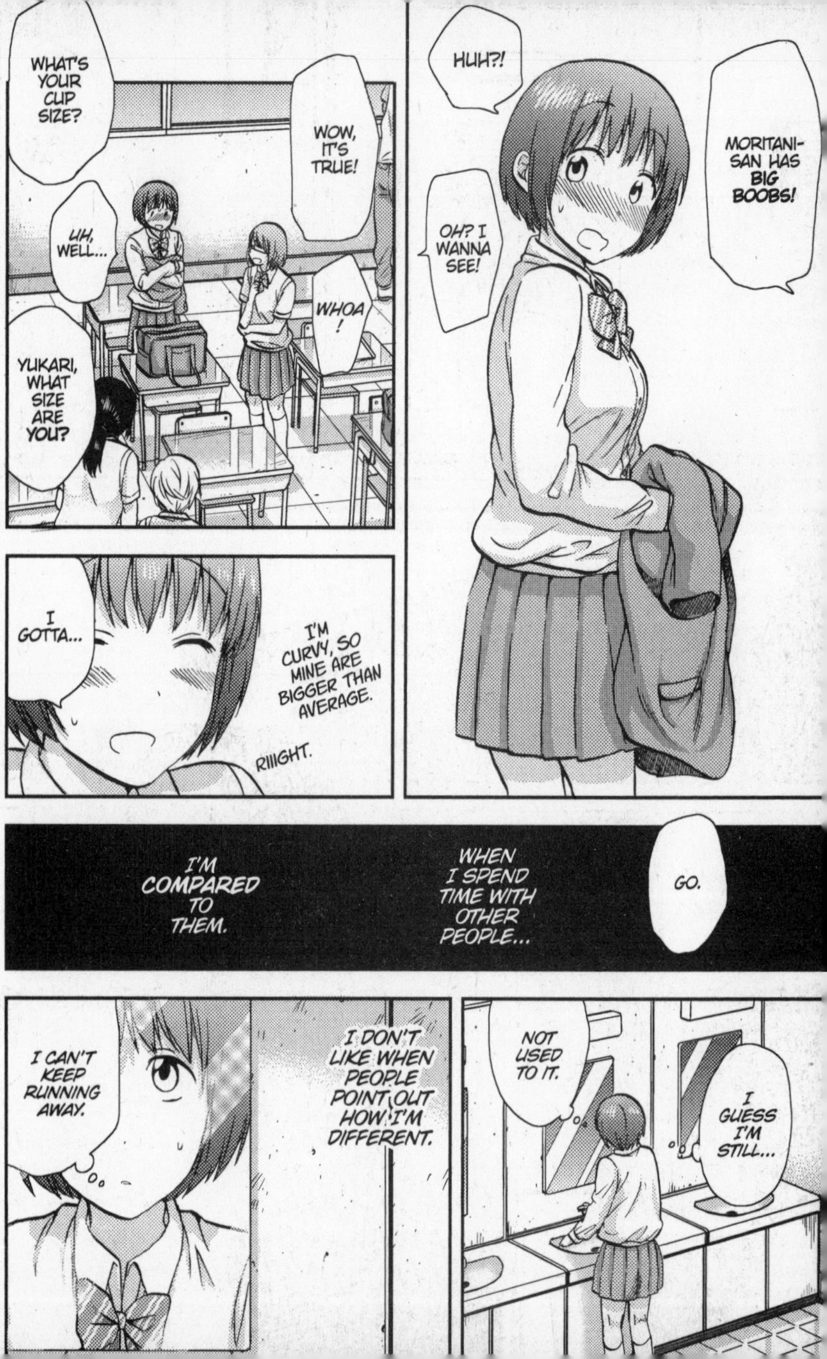
MORITANI-SAN HAS BIG BOOBS!
OH? I WANNA SEE!
HUH?!
WOW, IT'S TRUE!
WHAT'S YOUR CUP SIZE?
UH, WELL...
WHOA!
YUKARI, WHAT SIZE ARE YOU?
I'M CURVY, SO MINE ARE BIGGER THAN AVERAGE.
RIIIGHT.
I GOTTA...
GO.
WHEN I SPEND TIME WITH OTHER PEOPLE...
I'M COMPARED TO THEM.
I GUESS I'M STILL...
NOT USED TO IT.
I DON'T LIKE WHEN PEOPLE POINT OUT HOW I'M DIFFERENT.
I CAN'T KEEP RUNNING AWAY.

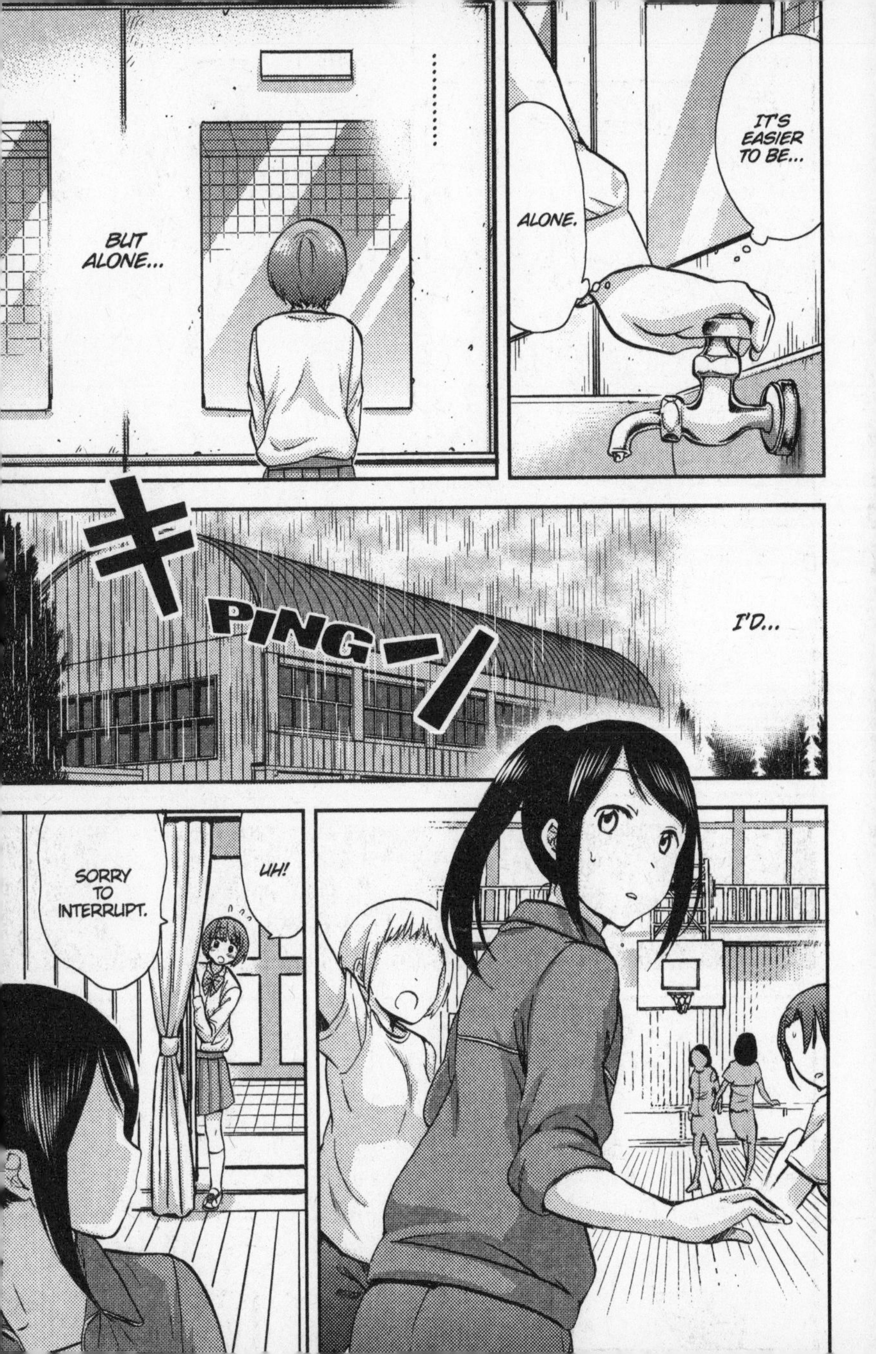
IT'S EASIER TO BE...
ALONE.
......
BUT ALONE...
キ
PING—!
I'D...
UH!
SORRY TO INTERRUPT.

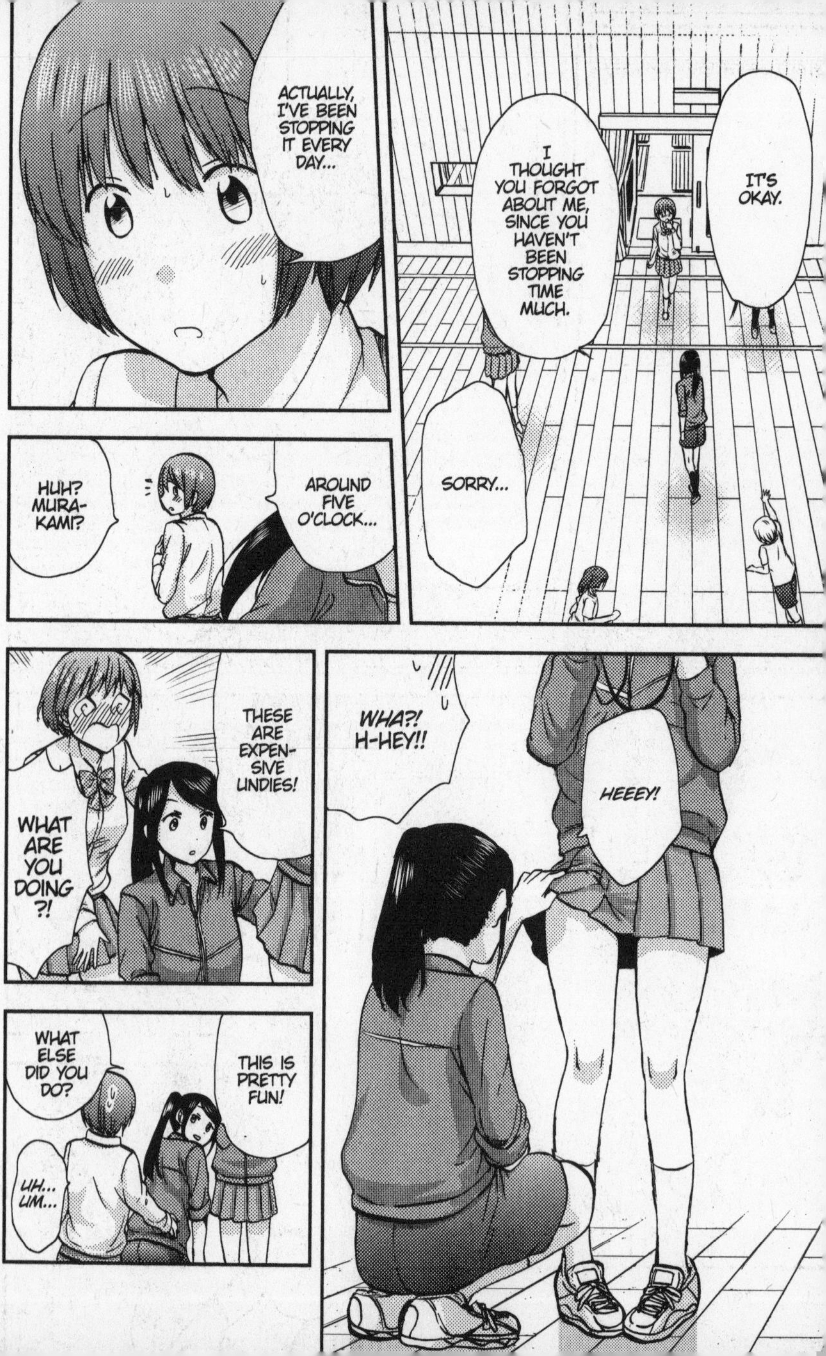
IT'S OKAY.
I THOUGHT YOU FORGOT ABOUT ME, SINCE YOU HAVEN'T BEEN STOPPING TIME MUCH.
SORRY...
ACTUALLY, I'VE BEEN STOPPING IT EVERY DAY...
AROUND FIVE O'CLOCK...
HUH? MURA-KAMI?
WHA?! H-HEY!!
HEEEY!
THESE ARE EXPEN-SIVE UNDIES!
WHAT ARE YOU DOING?!
THIS IS PRETTY FUN!
WHAT ELSE DID YOU DO?
UH... UM...

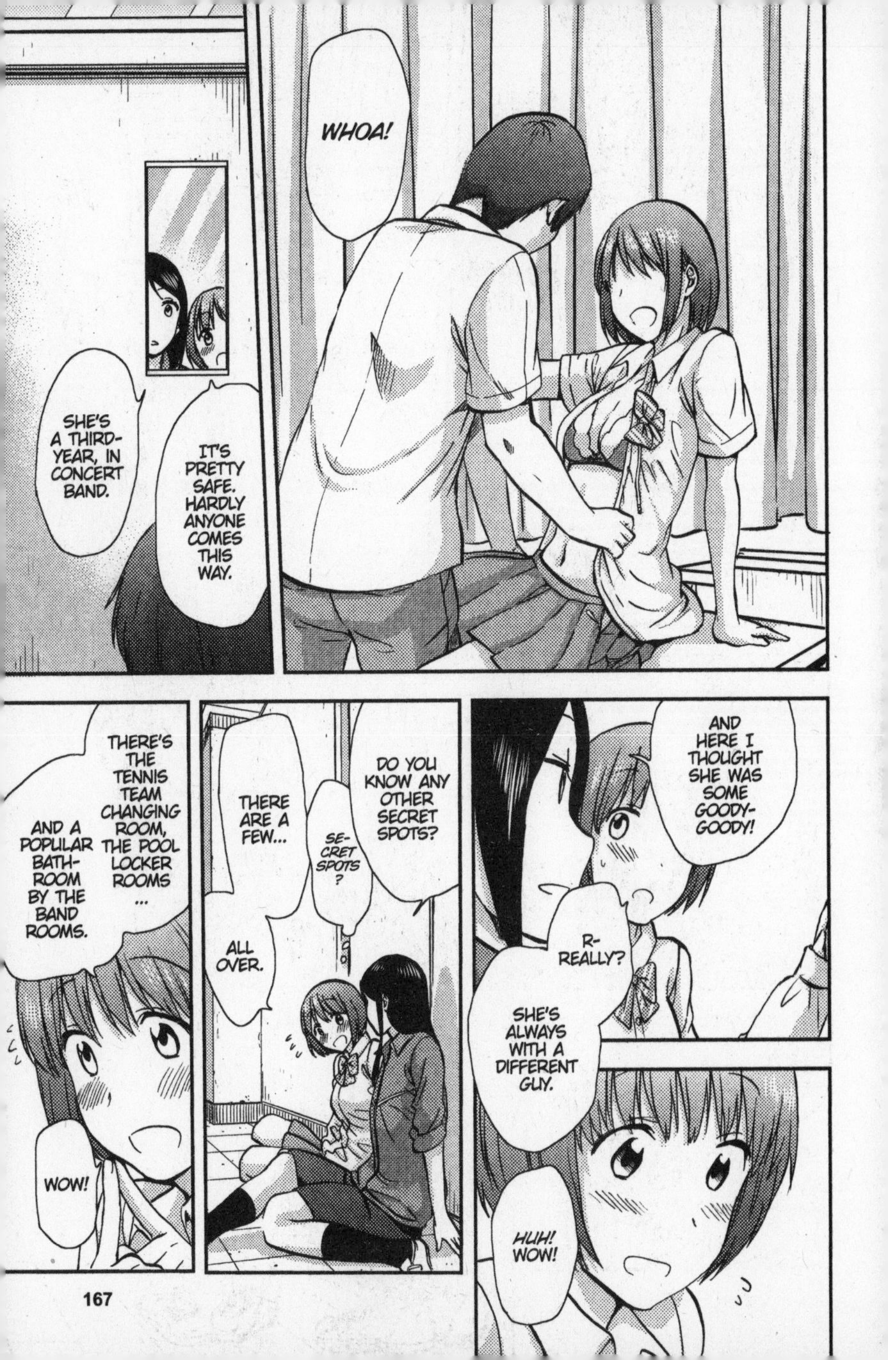
WHOA!
IT'S PRETTY SAFE. HARDLY ANYONE COMES THIS WAY.
SHE'S A THIRD-YEAR, IN CONCERT BAND.
AND HERE I THOUGHT SHE WAS SOME GOODY-GOODY!
R-REALLY?
SHE'S ALWAYS WITH A DIFFERENT GUY.
HUH! WOW!
DO YOU KNOW ANY OTHER SECRET SPOTS?
SE-CRET SPOTS?
THERE ARE A FEW...
ALL OVER.
THERE'S THE TENNIS TEAM CHANGING ROOM, THE POOL LOCKER ROOMS...
AND A POPULAR BATH-ROOM BY THE BAND ROOMS.
WOW!

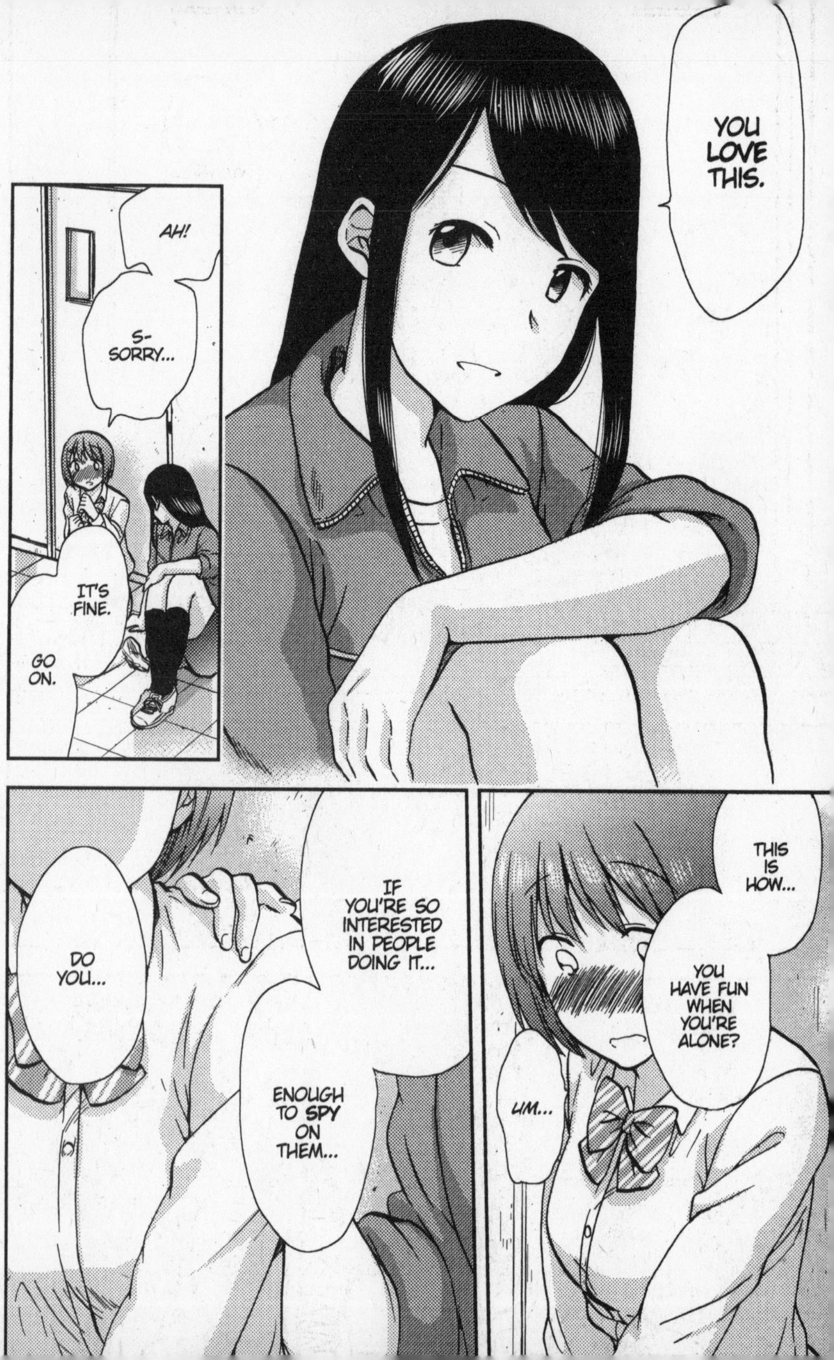
YOU LOVE THIS.
AH!
S-SORRY...
IT'S FINE.
GO ON.
THIS IS HOW...
YOU HAVE FUN WHEN YOU'RE ALONE?
UM...
IF YOU'RE SO INTERESTED IN PEOPLE DOING IT...
DO YOU...
ENOUGH TO SPY ON THEM...

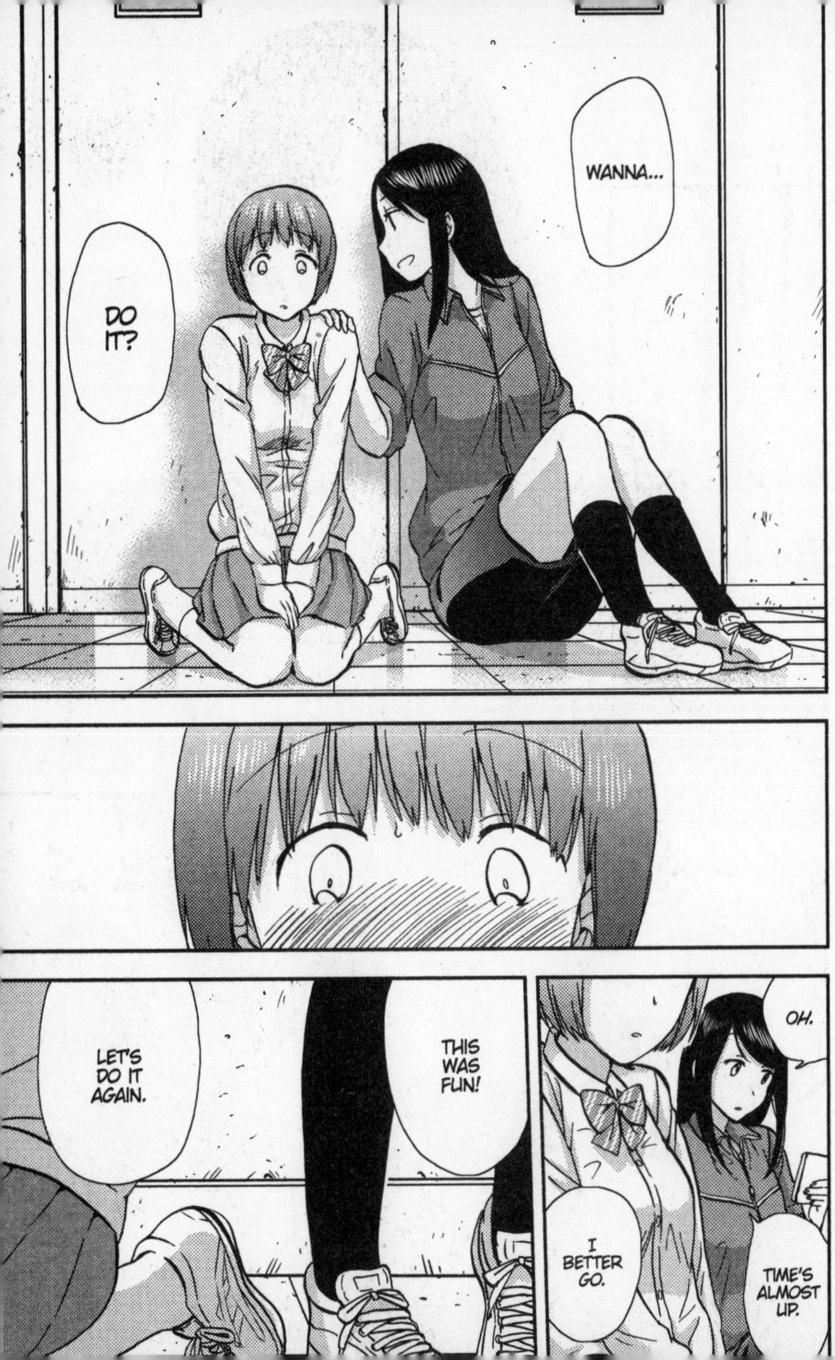
WANNA...
DO IT?
OH.
TIME'S ALMOST UP.
I BETTER GO.
THIS WAS FUN!
LET'S DO IT AGAIN.

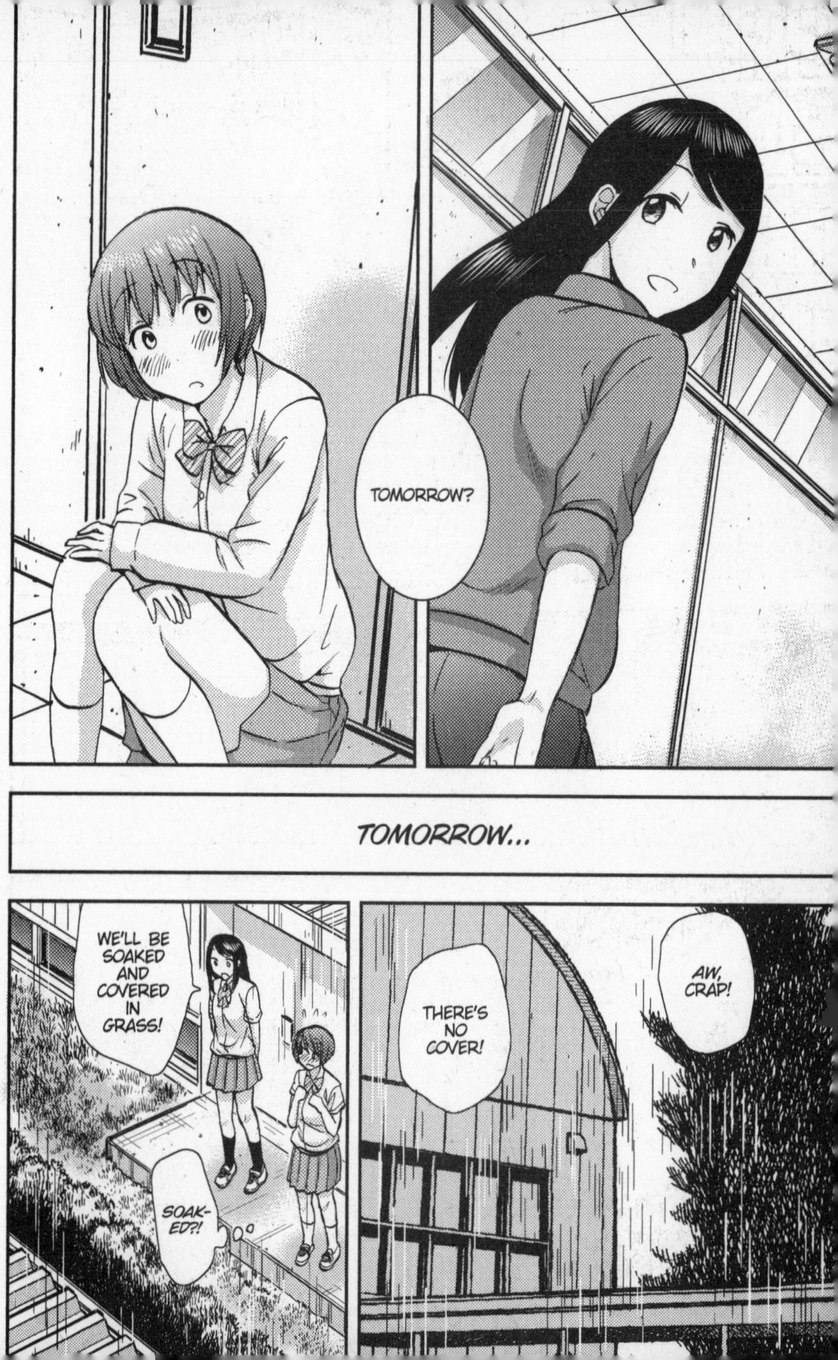
TOMORROW?
TOMORROW...
AW, CRAP!
THERE'S NO COVER!
WE'LL BE SOAKED AND COVERED IN GRASS!
SOAK-ED?!

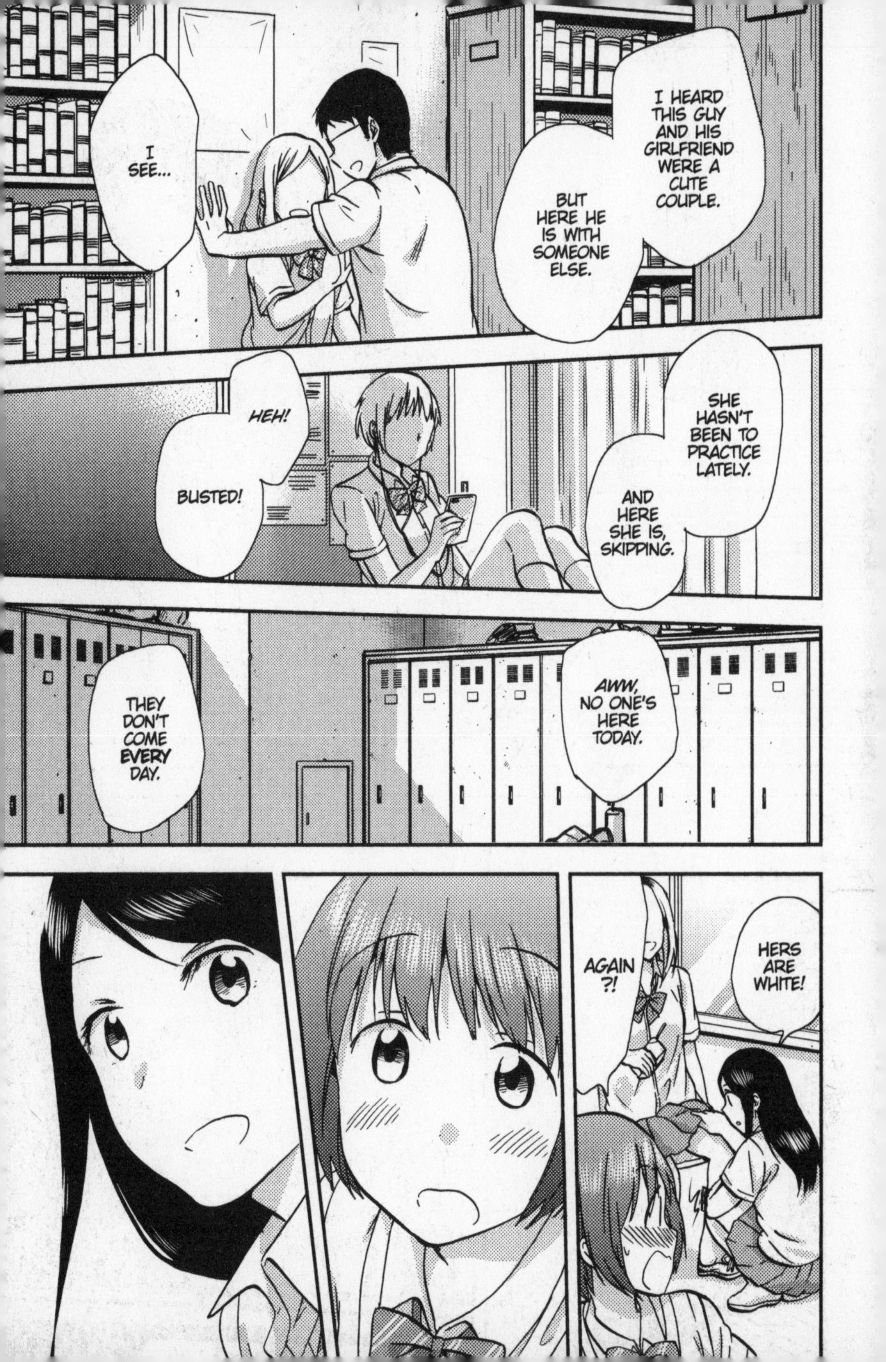
I HEARD THIS GUY AND HIS GIRLFRIEND WERE A CUTE COUPLE.
BUT HERE HE IS WITH SOMEONE ELSE.
I SEE...
SHE HASN'T BEEN TO PRACTICE LATELY.
AND HERE SHE IS, SKIPPING.
HEH!
BUSTED!
AWW, NO ONE'S HERE TODAY.
THEY DON'T COME EVERY DAY.
HERS ARE WHITE!
AGAIN?!

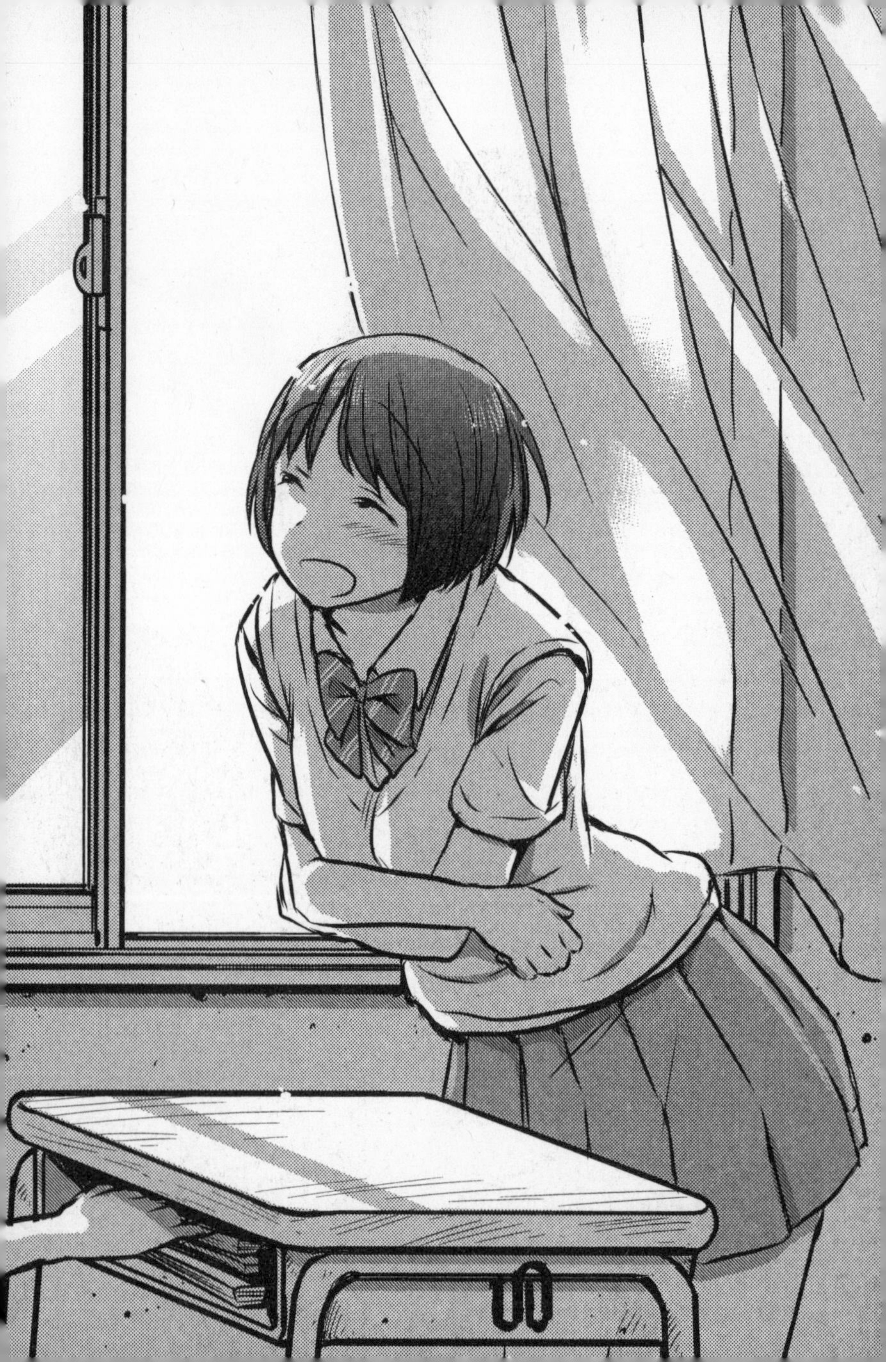

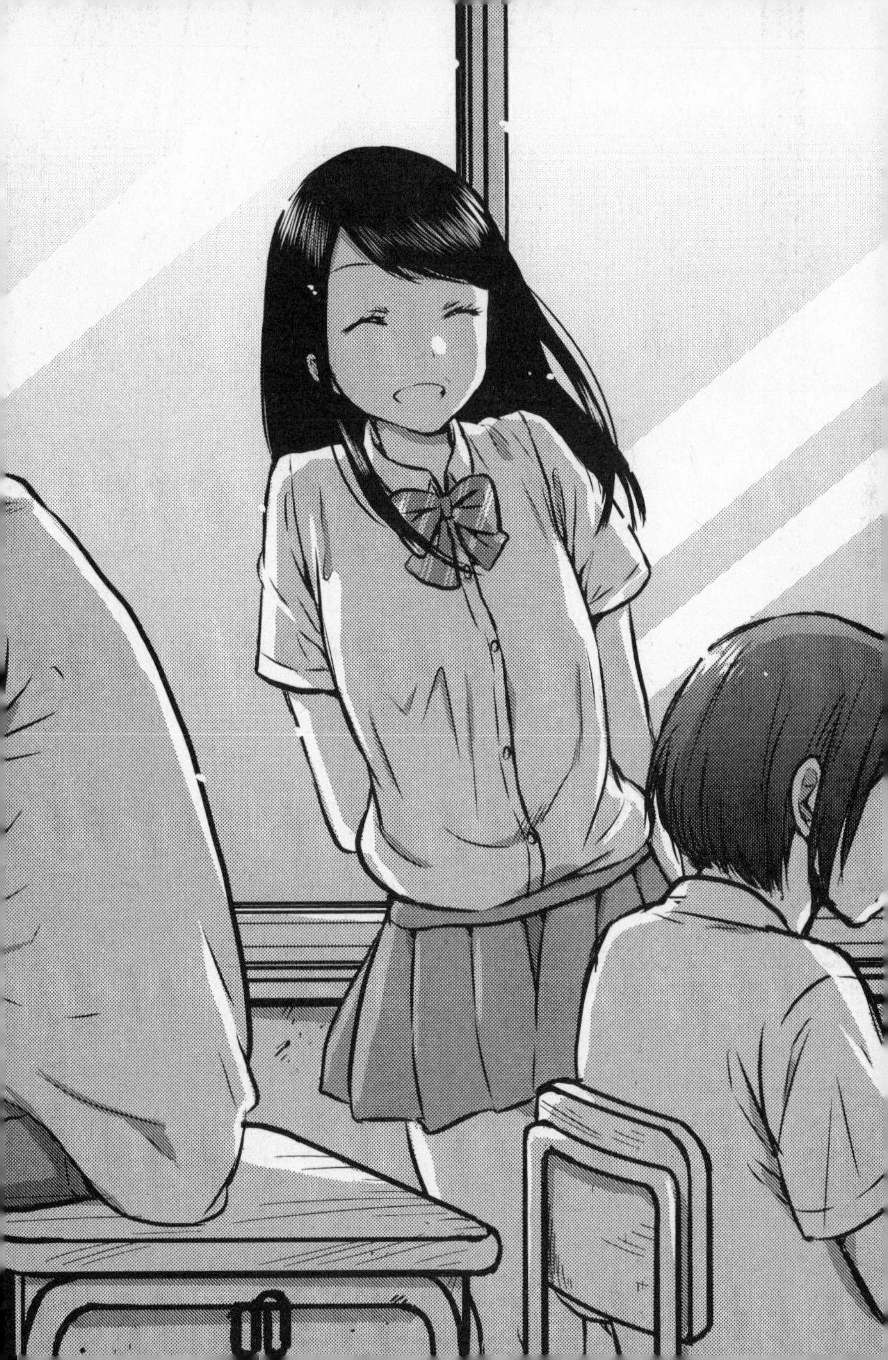

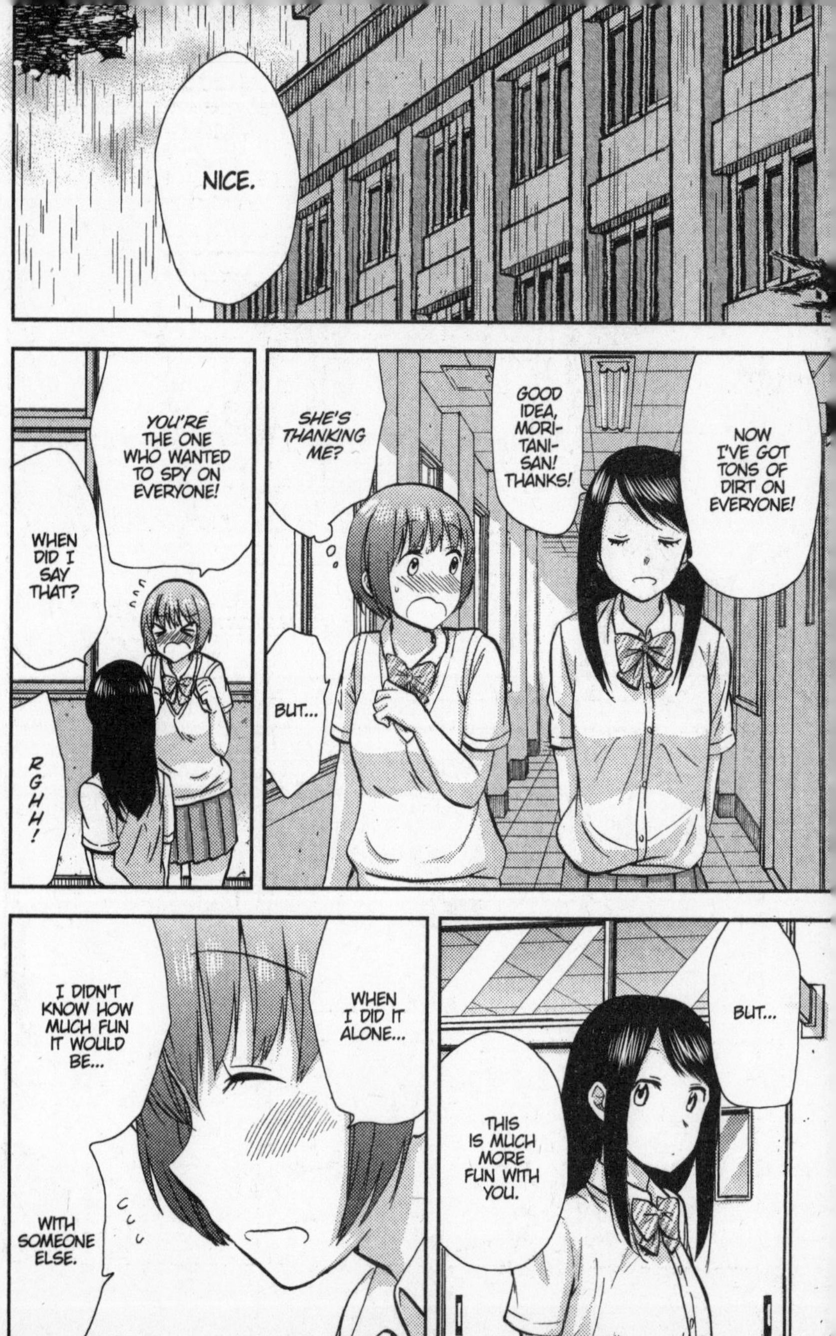
NICE.
NOW I'VE GOT TONS OF DIRT ON EVERYONE!
GOOD IDEA, MORI-TANI-SAN! THANKS!
SHE'S THANKING ME?
BUT...
YOU'RE THE ONE WHO WANTED TO SPY ON EVERYONE!
WHEN DID I SAY THAT?
RGHH!
BUT...
THIS IS MUCH MORE FUN WITH YOU.
WHEN I DID IT ALONE...
I DIDN'T KNOW HOW MUCH FUN IT WOULD BE...
WITH SOMEONE ELSE.

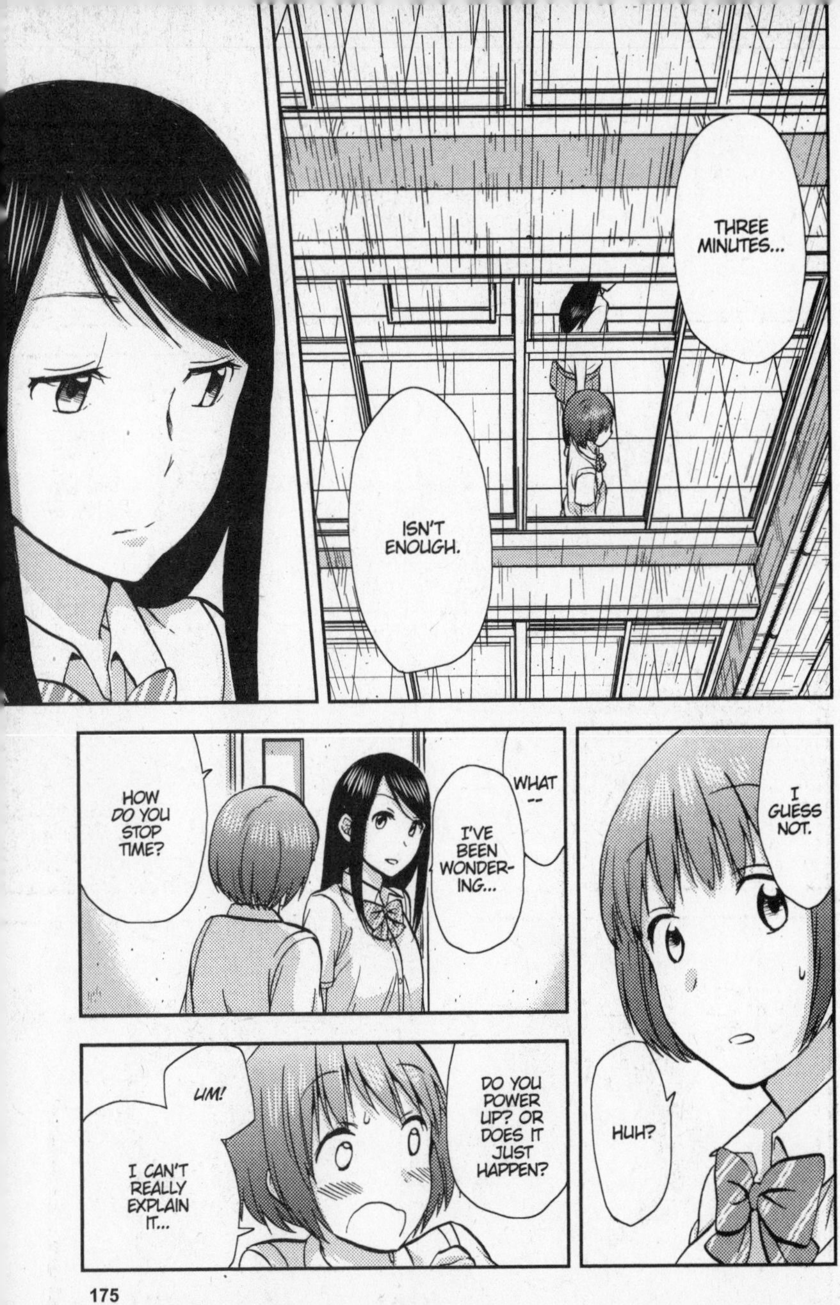
THREE MINUTES...
ISN'T ENOUGH.
I GUESS NOT.
HUH?
WHAT --
I'VE BEEN WONDERING...
HOW DO YOU STOP TIME?
DO YOU POWER UP? OR DOES IT JUST HAPPEN?
UM!
I CAN'T REALLY EXPLAIN IT...

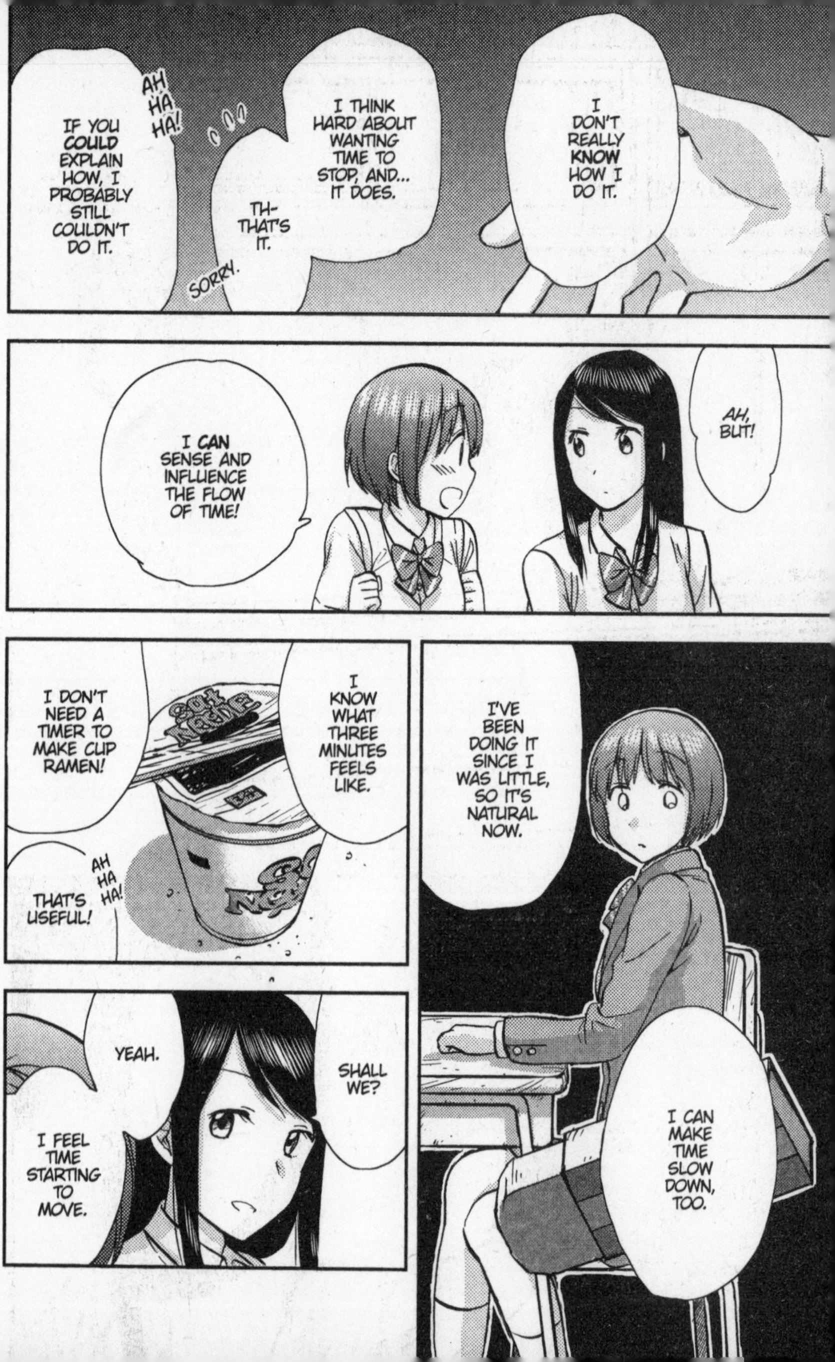
I DON'T REALLY KNOW HOW I DO IT.
I THINK HARD ABOUT WANTING TIME TO STOP, AND... IT DOES.
TH-THAT'S IT.
SORRY.
AH HA HA!
IF YOU COULD EXPLAIN HOW, I PROBABLY STILL COULDN'T DO IT.
AH, BUT!
I CAN SENSE AND INFLUENCE THE FLOW OF TIME!
I'VE BEEN DOING IT SINCE I WAS LITTLE, SO IT'S NATURAL NOW.
I CAN MAKE TIME SLOW DOWN, TOO.
I KNOW WHAT THREE MINUTES FEELS LIKE.
I DON'T NEED A TIMER TO MAKE CUP RAMEN!
AH HA HA!
THAT'S USEFUL!
SHALL WE?
YEAH.
I FEEL TIME STARTING TO MOVE.

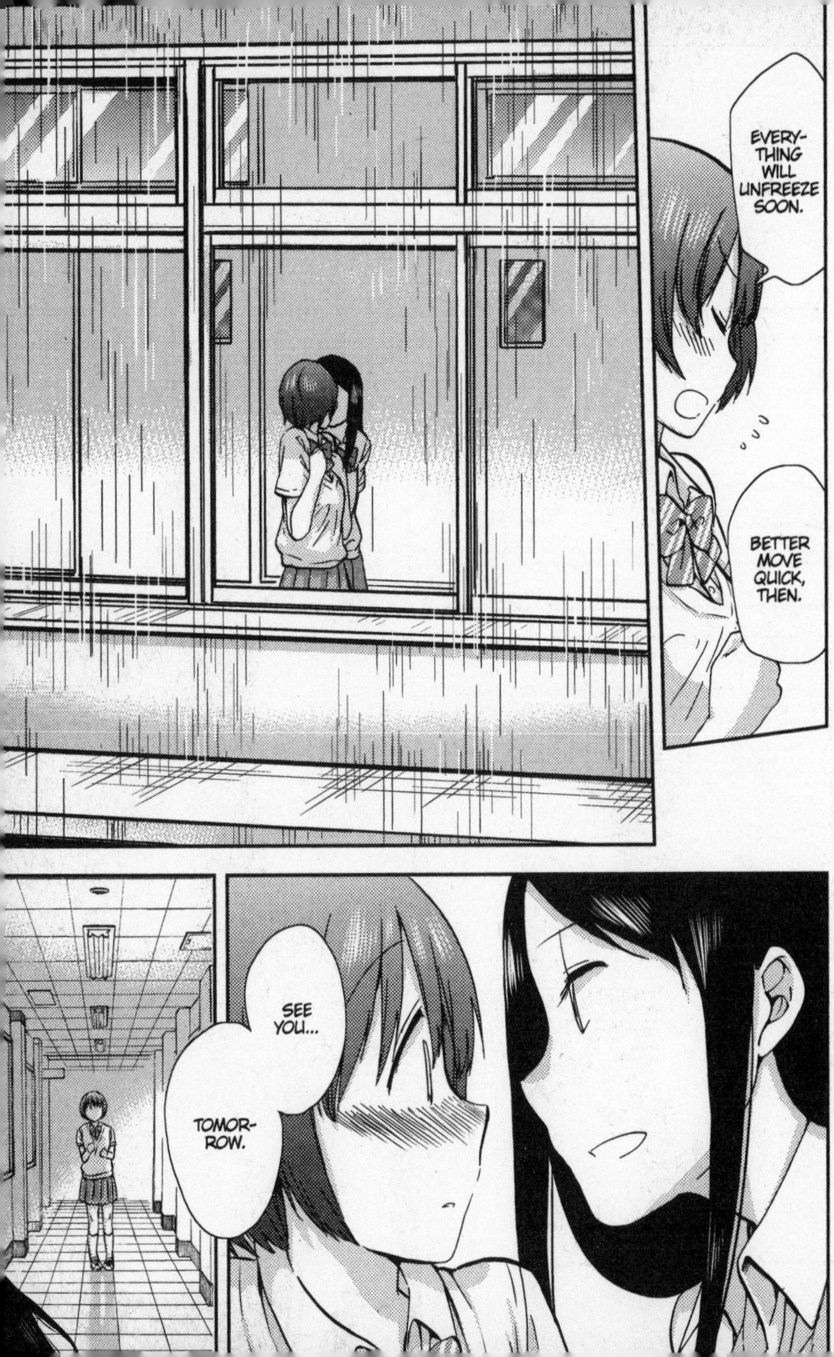
EVERY-THING WILL UNFREEZE SOON.
BETTER MOVE QUICK, THEN.
SEE YOU...
TOMOR-ROW.

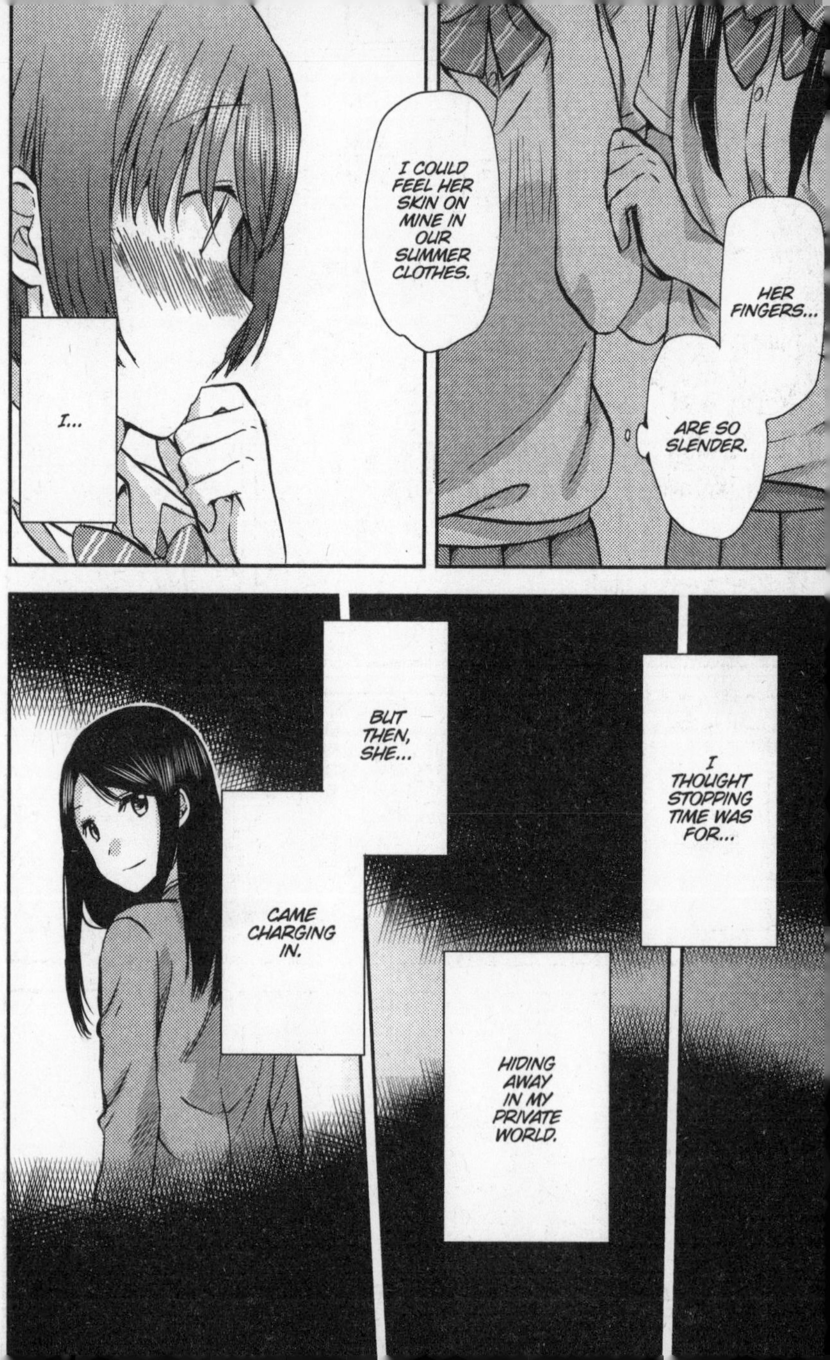
HER FINGERS...
ARE SO SLENDER.
I COULD FEEL HER SKIN ON MINE IN OUR SUMMER CLOTHES.
I...
I THOUGHT STOPPING TIME WAS FOR...
HIDING AWAY IN MY PRIVATE WORLD.
BUT THEN, SHE...
CAME CHARGING IN.

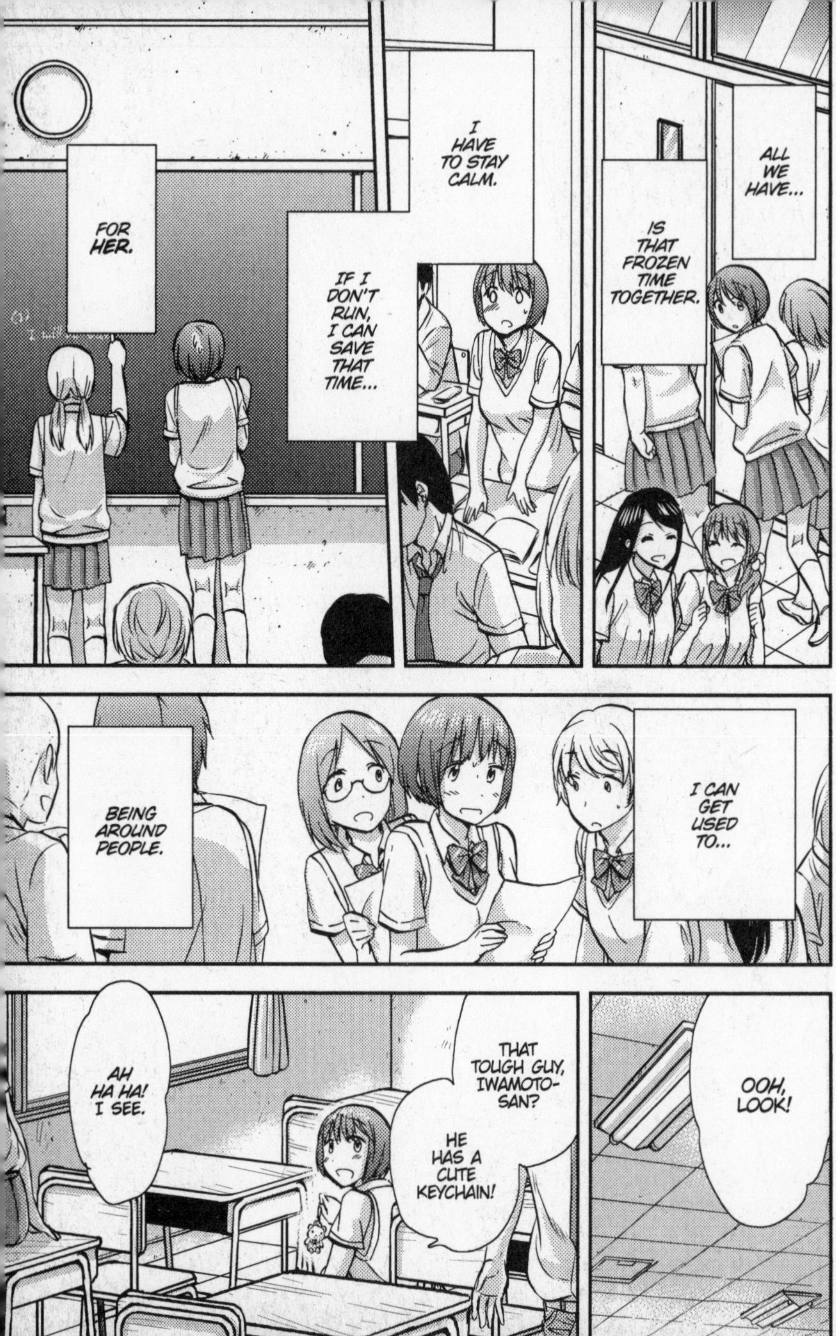
ALL WE HAVE...
IS THAT FROZEN TIME TOGETHER.
I HAVE TO STAY CALM.
IF I DON'T RUN, I CAN SAVE THAT TIME...
FOR HER.
I CAN GET USED TO...
BEING AROUND PEOPLE.
OOH, LOOK!
THAT TOUGH GUY, IWAMOTO-SAN?
HE HAS A CUTE KEYCHAIN!
AH HA HA! I SEE.

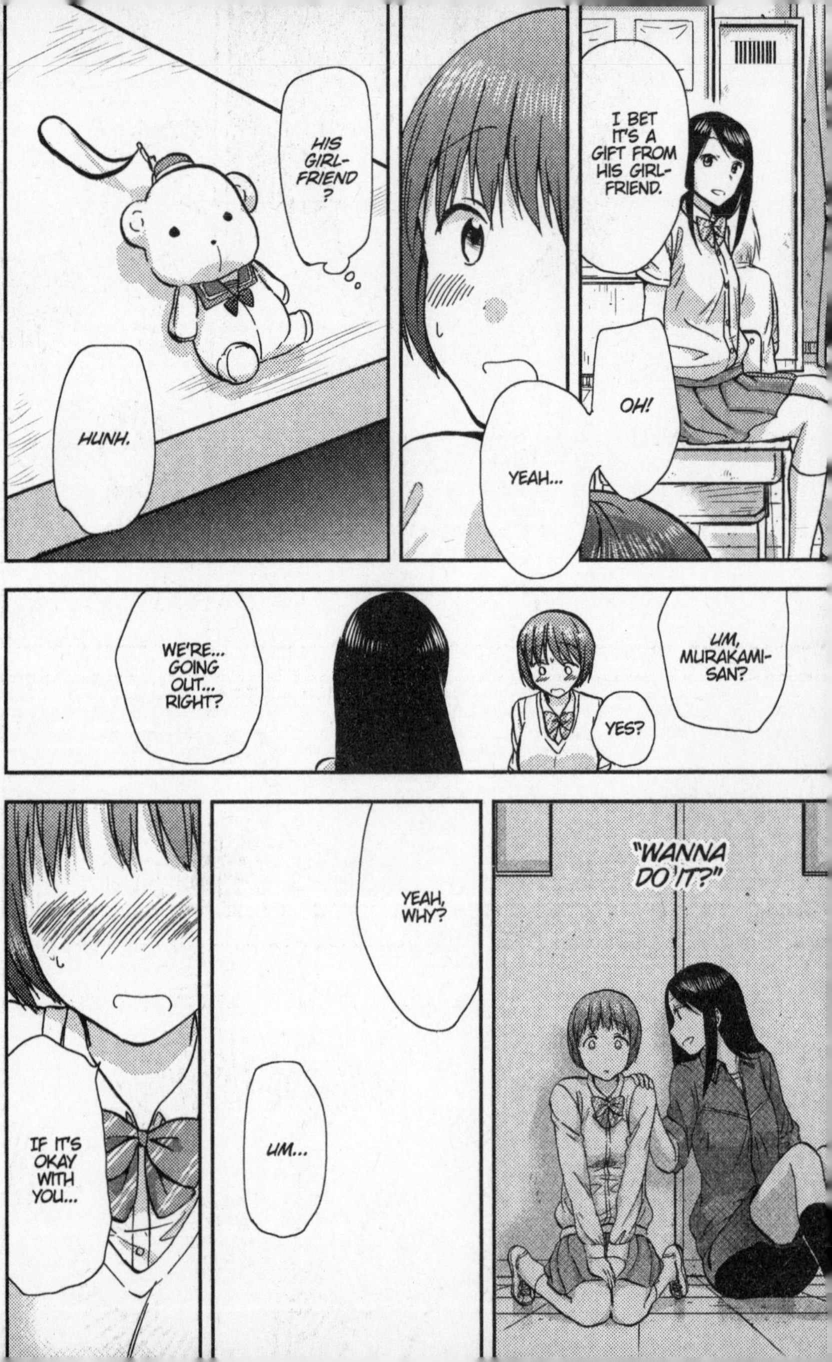
I BET IT'S A GIFT FROM HIS GIRL-FRIEND.
OH!
YEAH...
HIS GIRL-FRIEND?
HUNH.
UM, MURAKAMI-SAN?
YES?
WE'RE... GOING OUT... RIGHT?
"WANNA DO IT?"
YEAH, WHY?
UM...
IF IT'S OKAY WITH YOU...

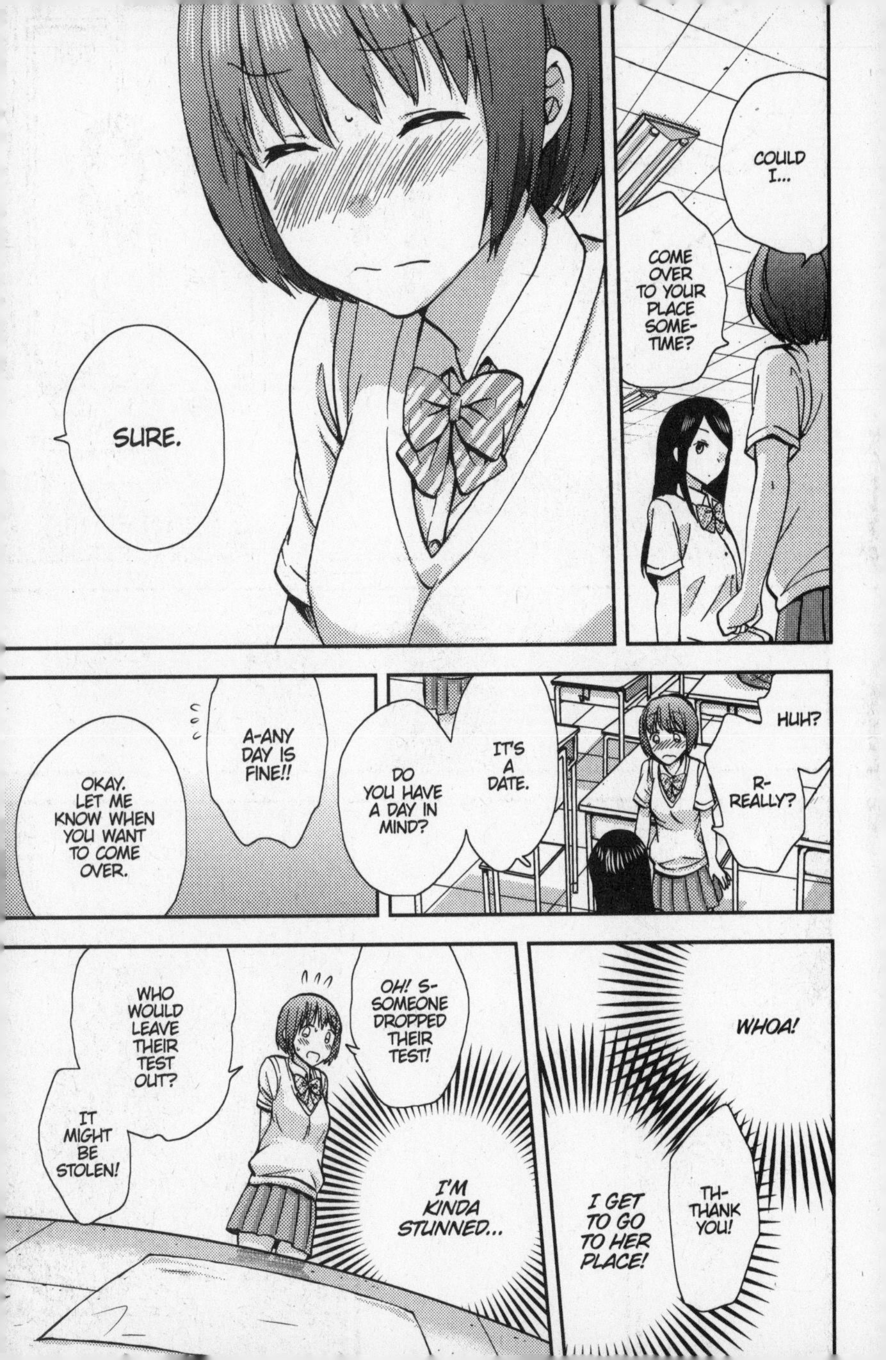
COULD I...
COME OVER TO YOUR PLACE SOME-TIME?
SURE.
HUH?
R-REALLY?
IT'S A DATE.
DO YOU HAVE A DAY IN MIND?
A-ANY DAY IS FINE!!
OKAY. LET ME KNOW WHEN YOU WANT TO COME OVER.
WHOA!
TH-THANK YOU!
I GET TO GO TO HER PLACE!
I'M KINDA STUNNED...
OH! S-SOMEONE DROPPED THEIR TEST!
WHO WOULD LEAVE THEIR TEST OUT?
IT MIGHT BE STOLEN!

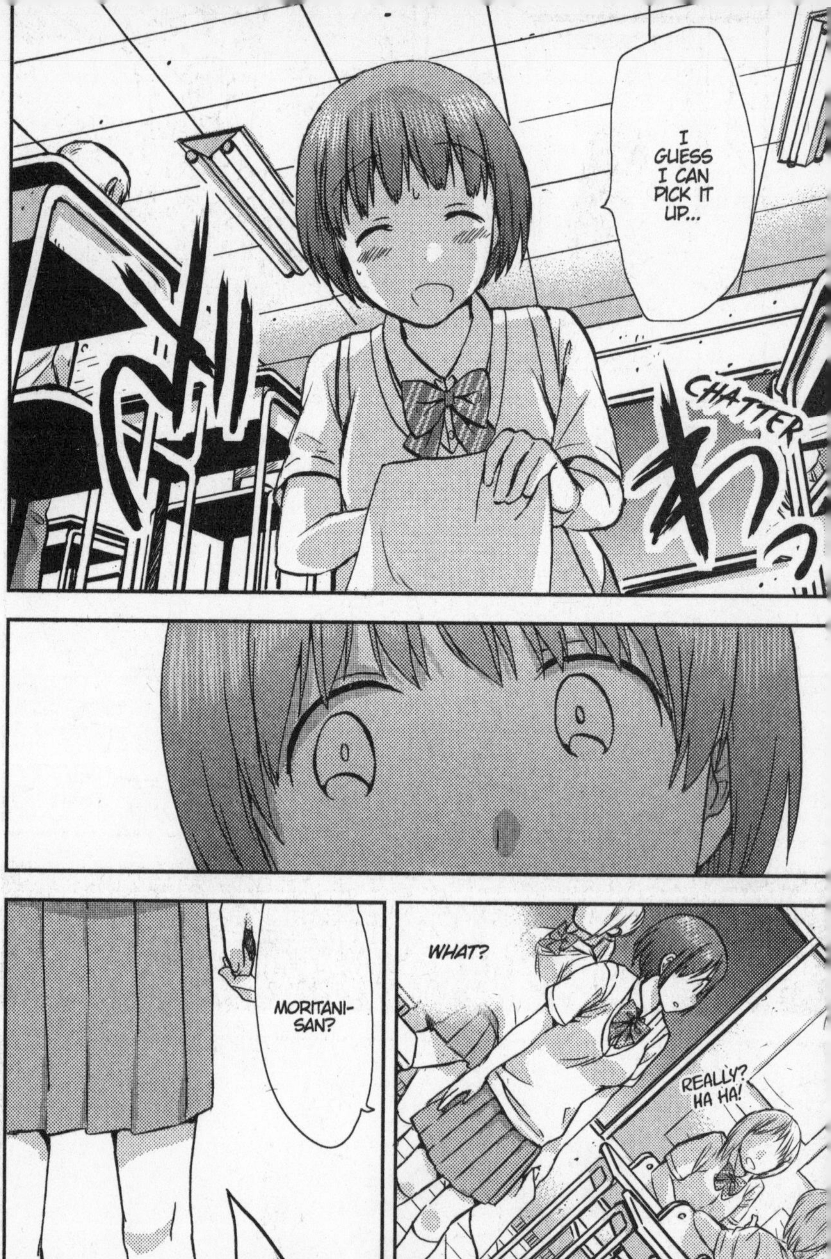
I GUESS I CAN PICK IT UP...
CHATTER
わっ
WHAT?
REALLY? HA HA!
MORITANI-SAN?

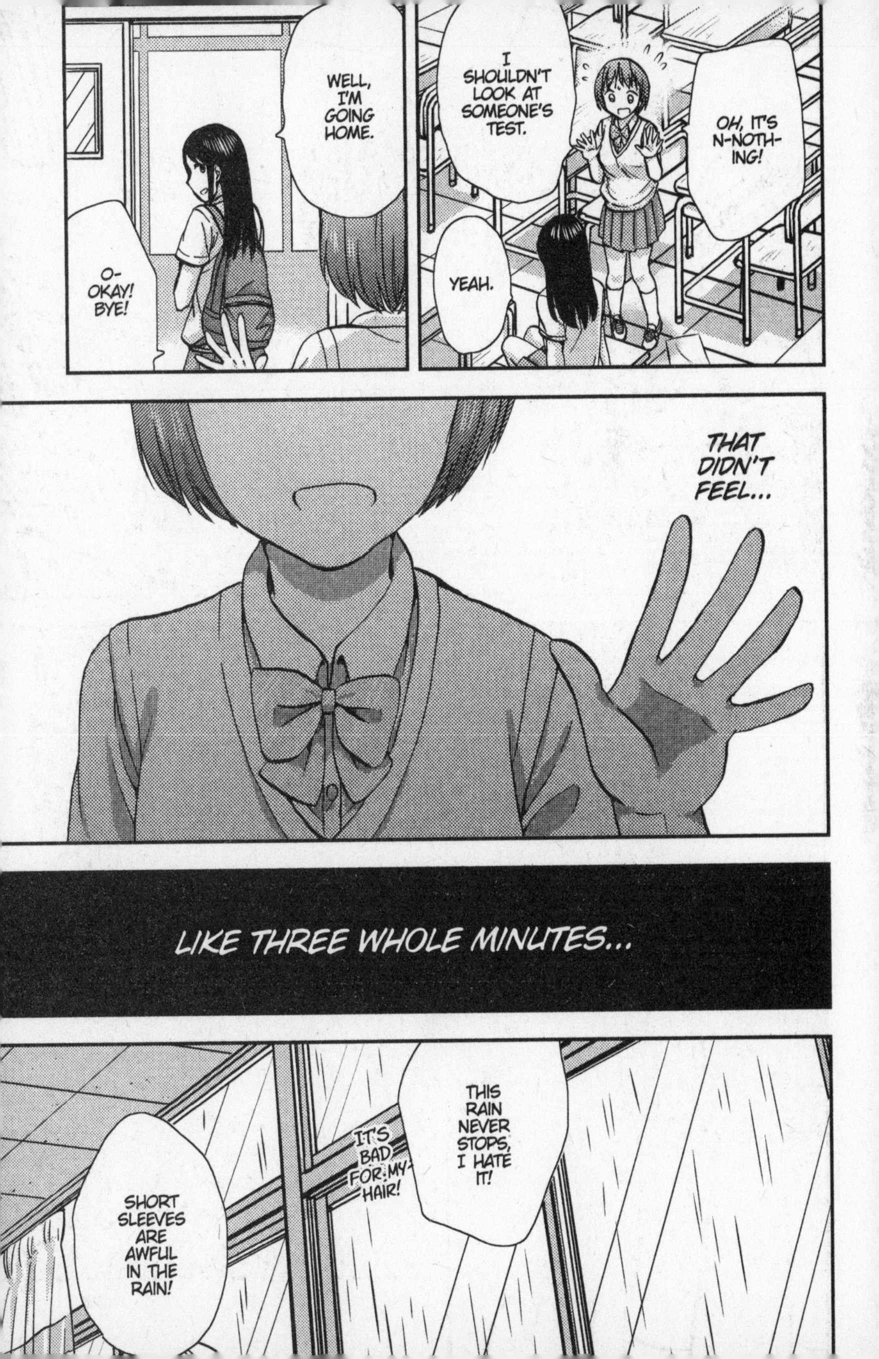
OH, IT'S N-NOTHING!
I SHOULDN'T LOOK AT SOMEONE'S TEST.
YEAH.
WELL, I'M GOING HOME.
O-OKAY! BYE!
THAT DIDN'T FEEL...
LIKE THREE WHOLE MINUTES...
THIS RAIN NEVER STOPS, I HATE IT!
IT'S BAD FOR MY HAIR!
SHORT SLEEVES ARE AWFUL IN THE RAIN!

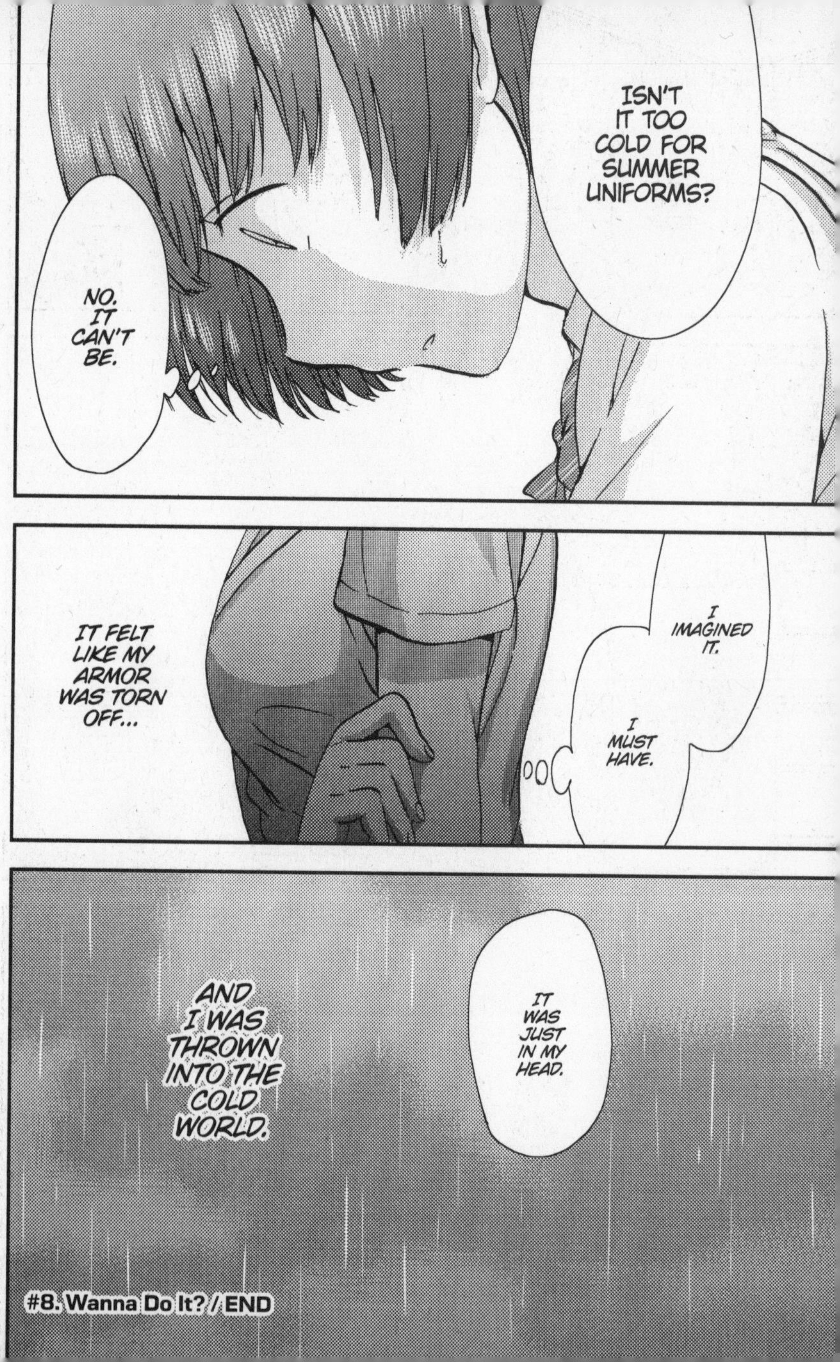
ISN'T IT TOO COLD FOR SUMMER UNIFORMS?
NO. IT CAN'T BE.
I IMAGINED IT.
I MUST HAVE.
IT FELT LIKE MY ARMOR WAS TORN OFF...
IT WAS JUST IN MY HEAD.
AND I WAS THROWN INTO THE COLD WORLD.
#8. Wanna Do It? / END

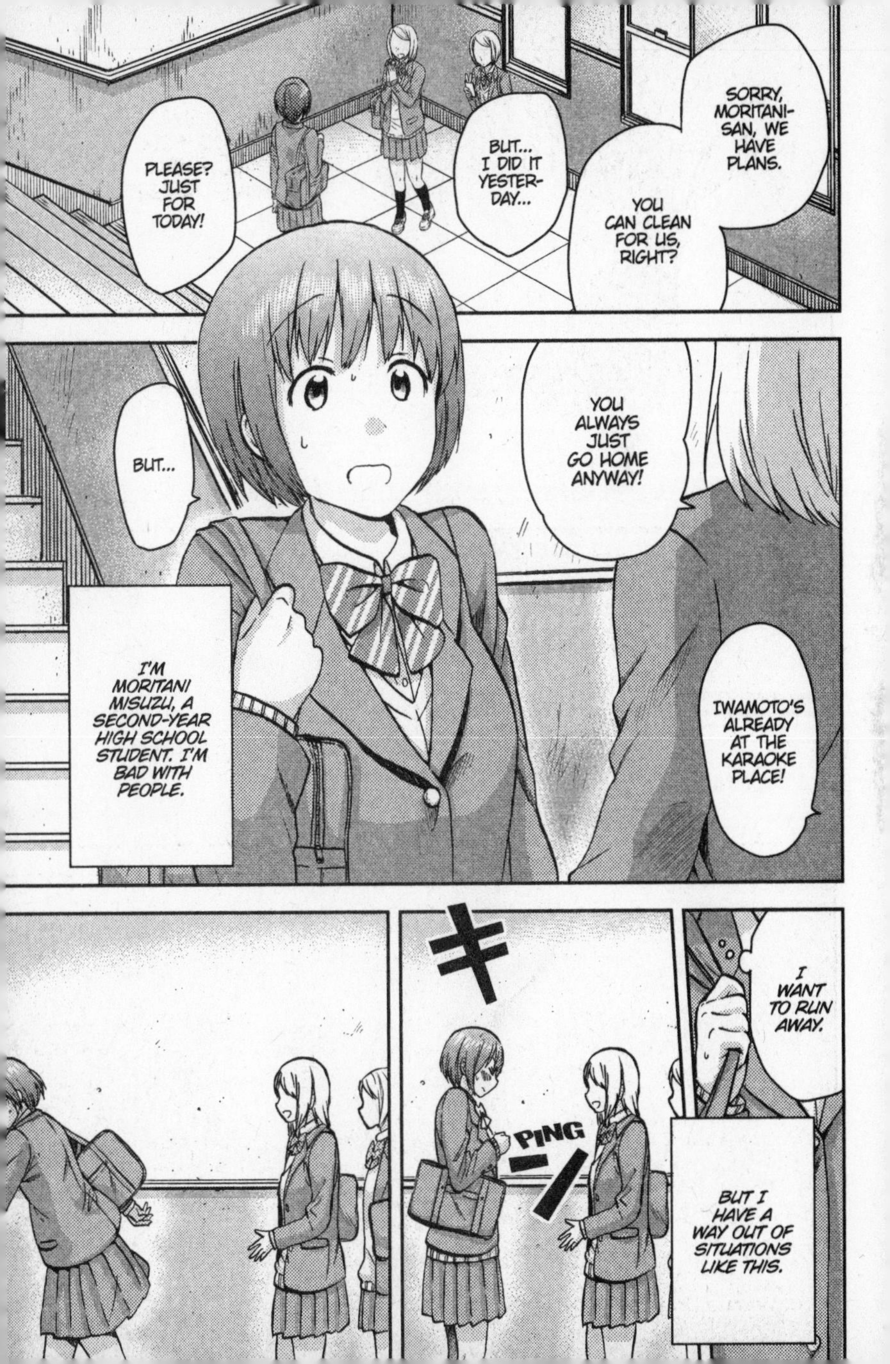
SORRY, MORITANI-SAN, WE HAVE PLANS.
YOU CAN CLEAN FOR US, RIGHT?
BUT... I DID IT YESTERDAY...
PLEASE? JUST FOR TODAY!
YOU ALWAYS JUST GO HOME ANYWAY!
IWAMOTO'S ALREADY AT THE KARAOKE PLACE!
BUT...
I'M MORITANI MISUZU, A SECOND-YEAR HIGH SCHOOL STUDENT. I'M BAD WITH PEOPLE.
I WANT TO RUN AWAY.
BUT I HAVE A WAY OUT OF SITUATIONS LIKE THIS.
キ
PING

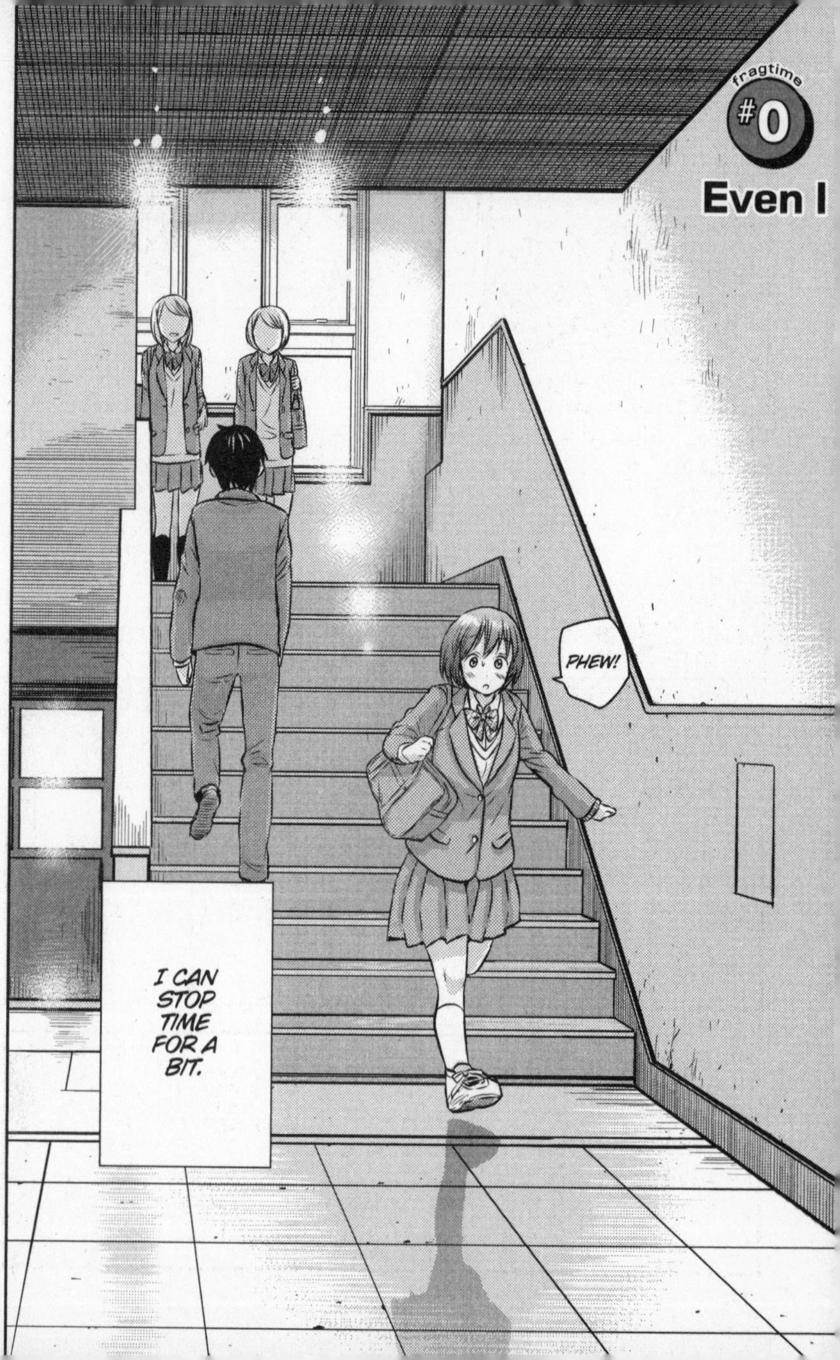
fragtime
#0
Even I
PHEW!
I CAN STOP TIME FOR A BIT.

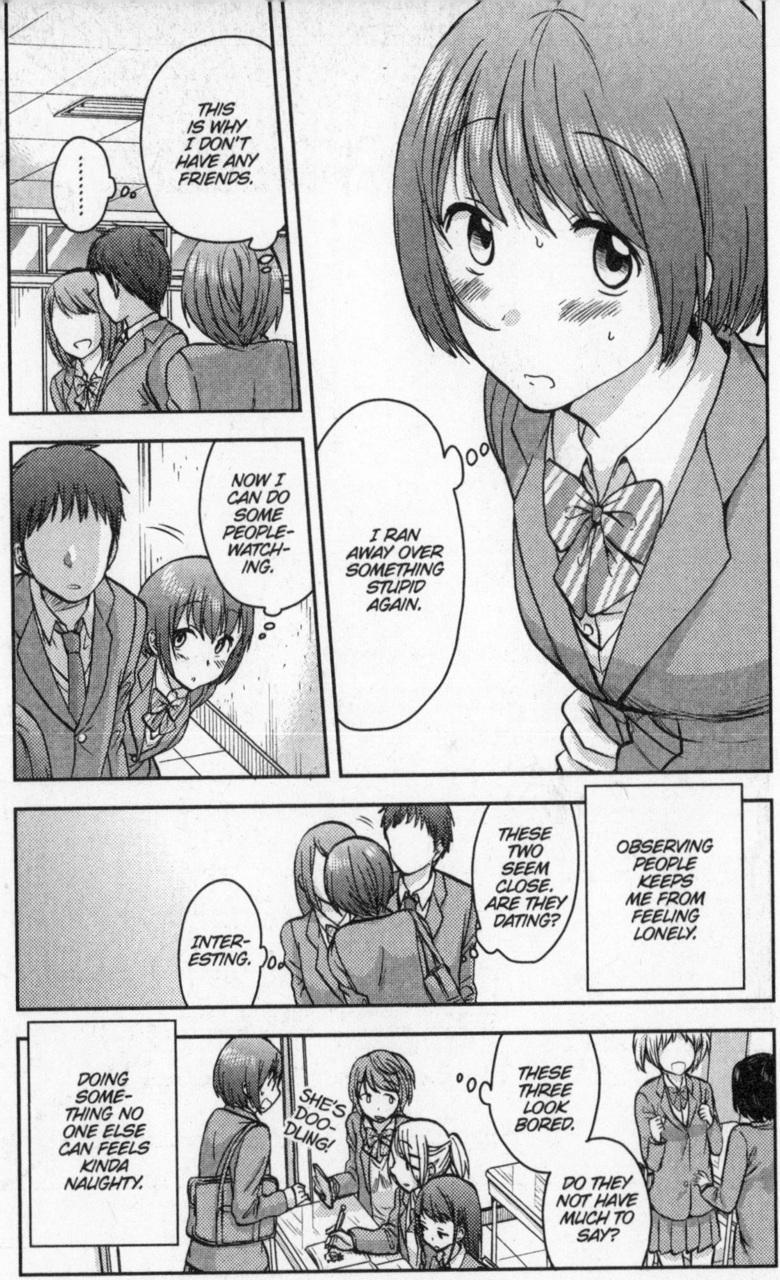
I RAN AWAY OVER SOMETHING STUPID AGAIN.
THIS IS WHY I DON'T HAVE ANY FRIENDS.
......
NOW I CAN DO SOME PEOPLE-WATCHING.
OBSERVING PEOPLE KEEPS ME FROM FEELING LONELY.
THESE TWO SEEM CLOSE. ARE THEY DATING?
INTERESTING.
THESE THREE LOOK BORED.
DO THEY NOT HAVE MUCH TO SAY?
SHE'S DOODLING!
DOING SOMETHING NO ONE ELSE CAN FEELS KINDA NAUGHTY.

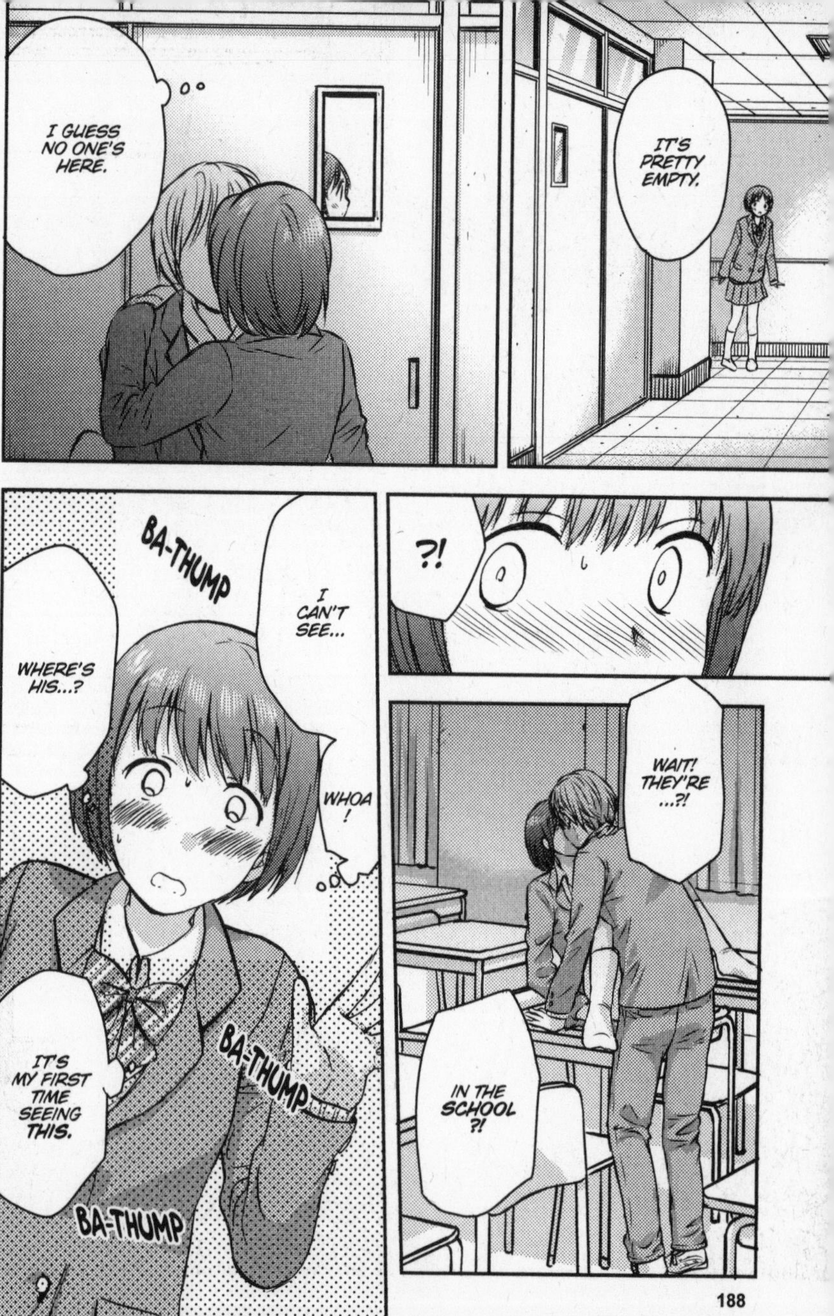
IT'S PRETTY EMPTY.
I GUESS NO ONE'S HERE.
?!
WAIT! THEY'RE ...?!
IN THE SCHOOL ?!
I CAN'T SEE...
BA-THUMP
WHERE'S HIS...?
WHOA!
BA-THUMP
IT'S MY FIRST TIME SEEING THIS.
BA-THUMP

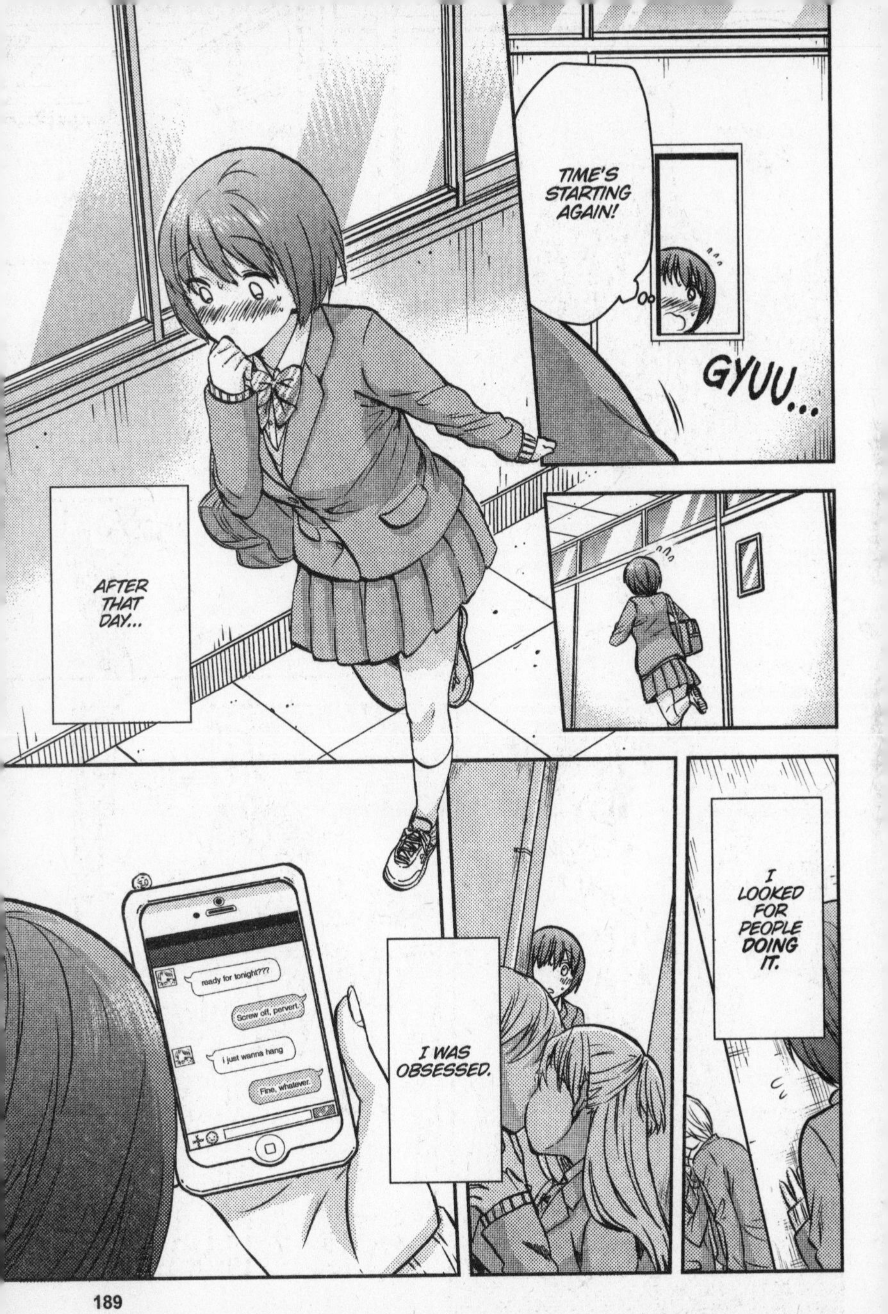

TIME'S STARTING AGAIN!
GYUU...
AFTER THAT DAY...
I LOOKED FOR PEOPLE DOING IT.
I WAS OBSESSED.
ready for tonight???
Screw off, pervert.
i just wanna hang
Fine, whatever.

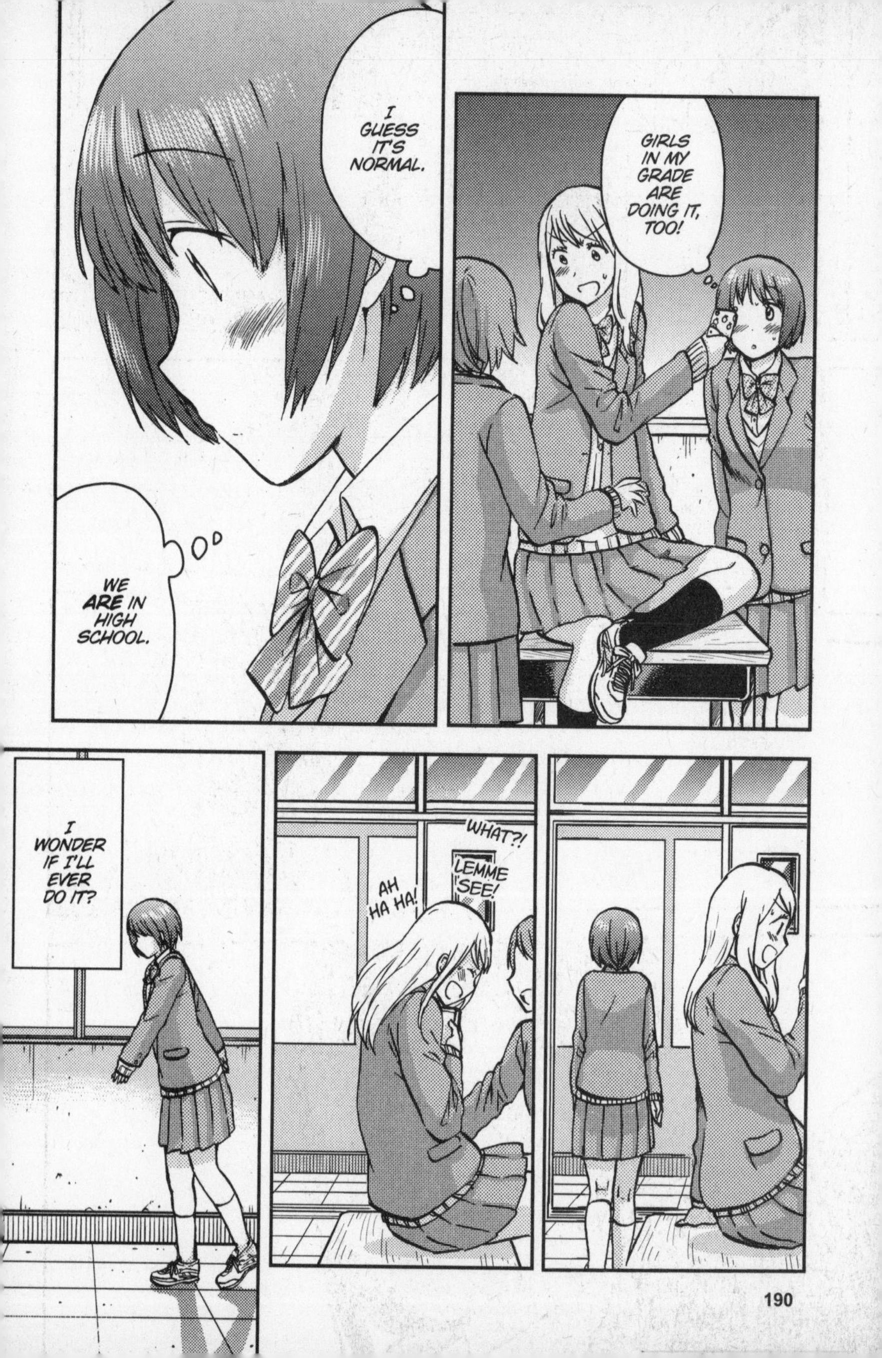
GIRLS IN MY GRADE ARE DOING IT, TOO!
I GUESS IT'S NORMAL.
WE **ARE** IN HIGH SCHOOL.
WHAT?!
LEMME SEE!
AH HA HA!
I WONDER IF I'LL EVER DO IT?

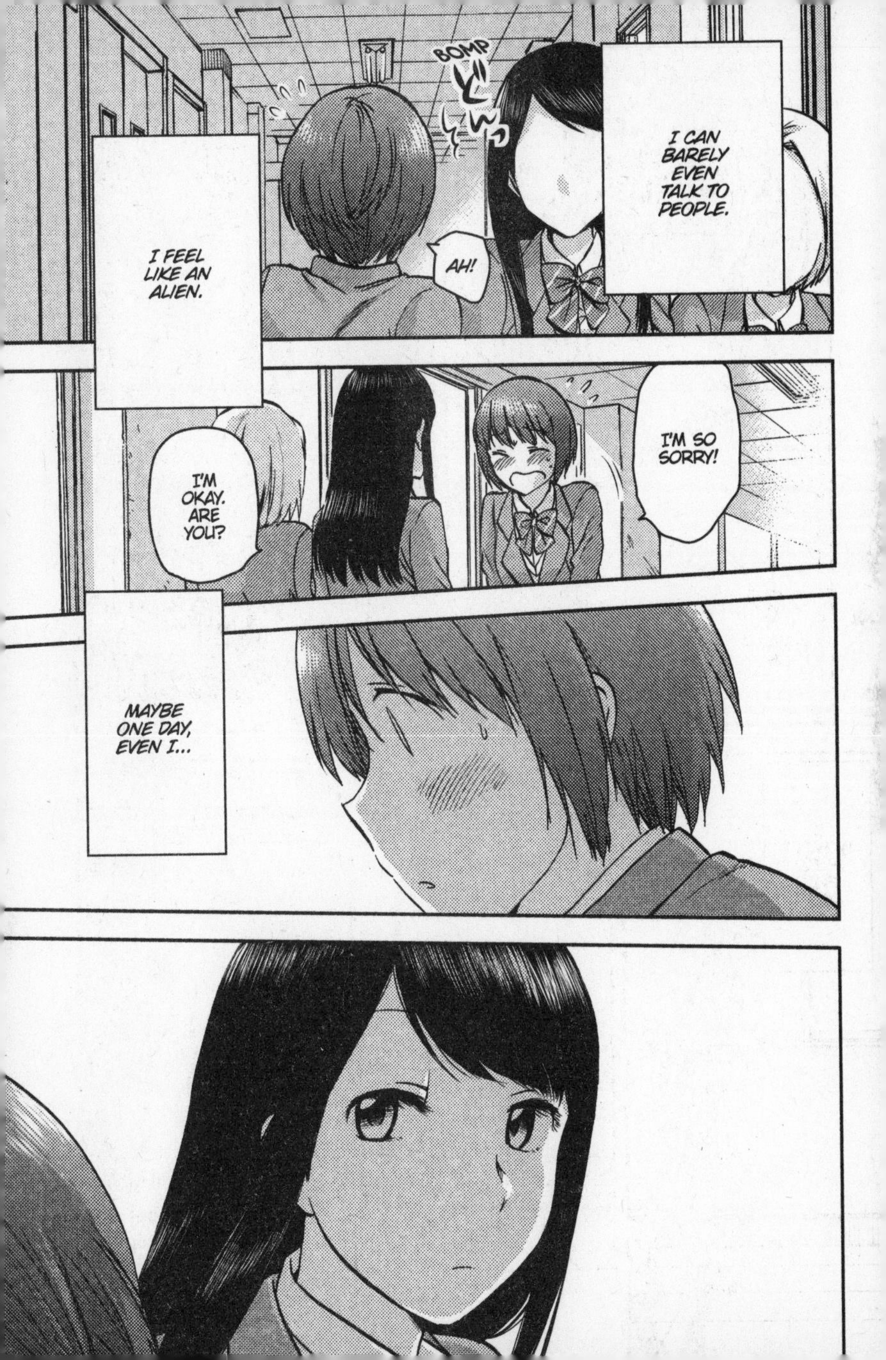
I CAN BARELY EVEN TALK TO PEOPLE.
BOMP
AH!
I FEEL LIKE AN ALIEN.
I'M SO SORRY!
I'M OKAY. ARE YOU?
MAYBE ONE DAY, EVEN I...

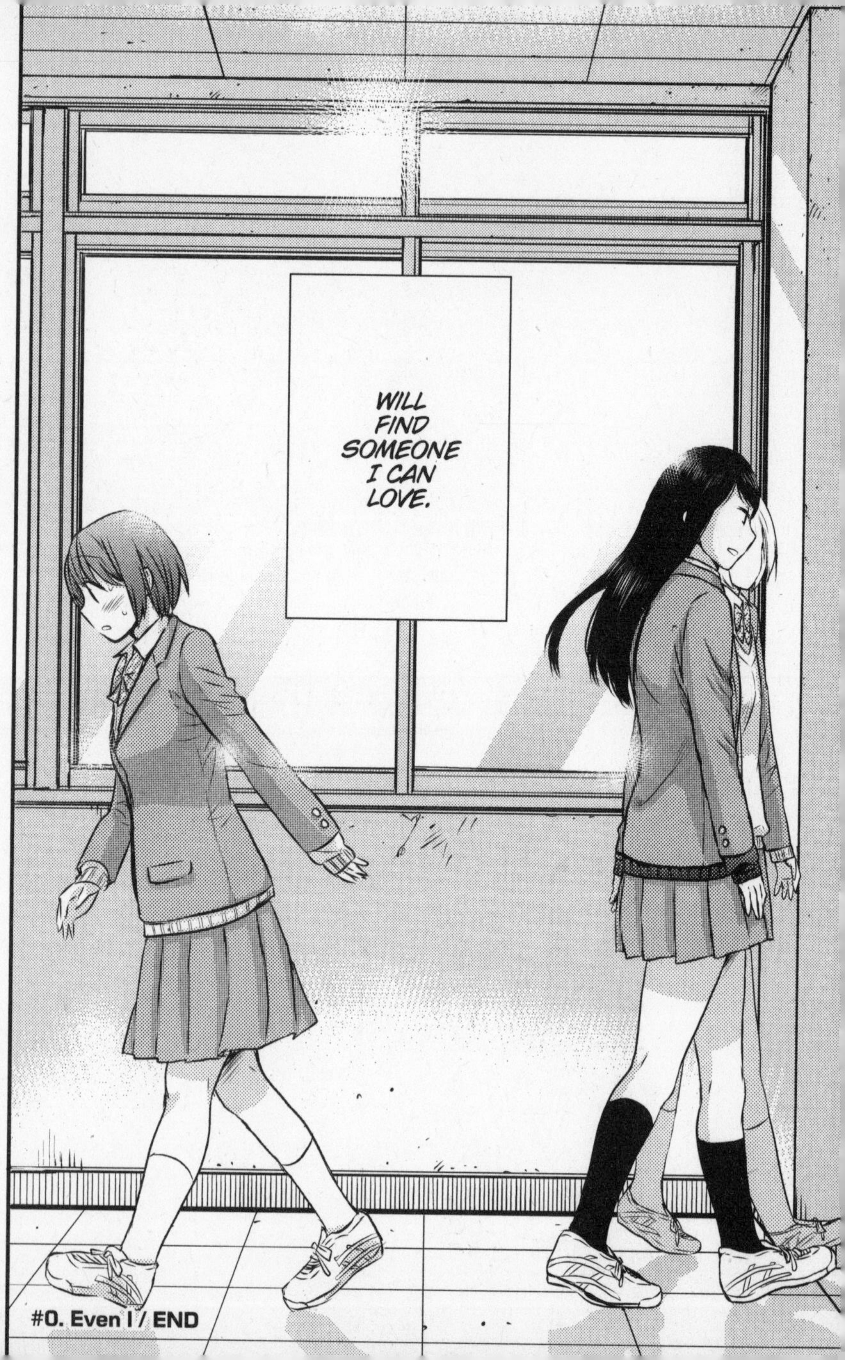
WILL FIND SOMEONE I CAN LOVE.
#0. Even I / END

FRAGTIME

THE COMPLETE MANGA COLLECTION

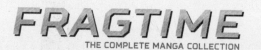

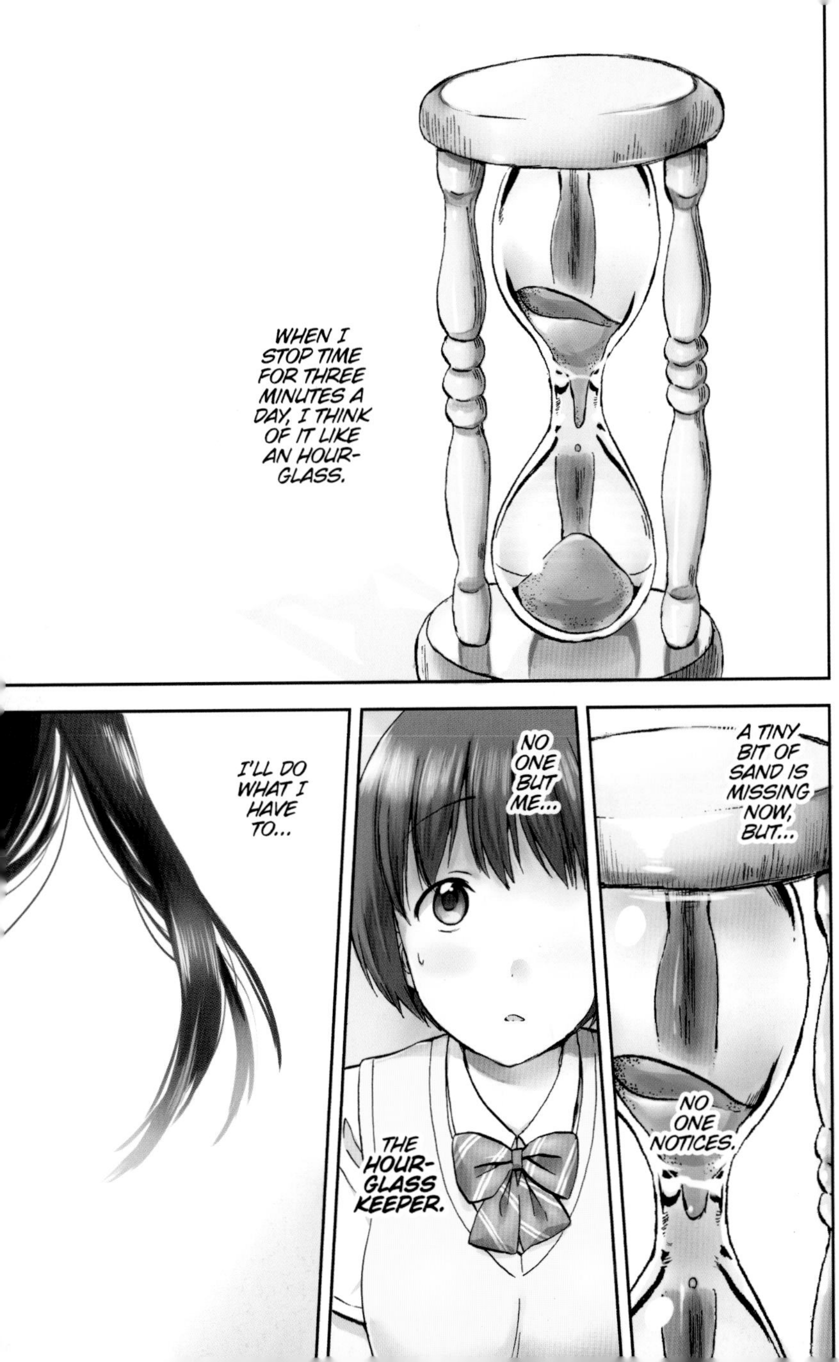
WHEN I STOP TIME FOR THREE MINUTES A DAY, I THINK OF IT LIKE AN HOUR-GLASS.
A TINY BIT OF SAND IS MISSING NOW, BUT...
NO ONE NOTICES.
NO ONE BUT ME...
THE HOUR-GLASS KEEPER.
I'LL DO WHAT I HAVE TO...

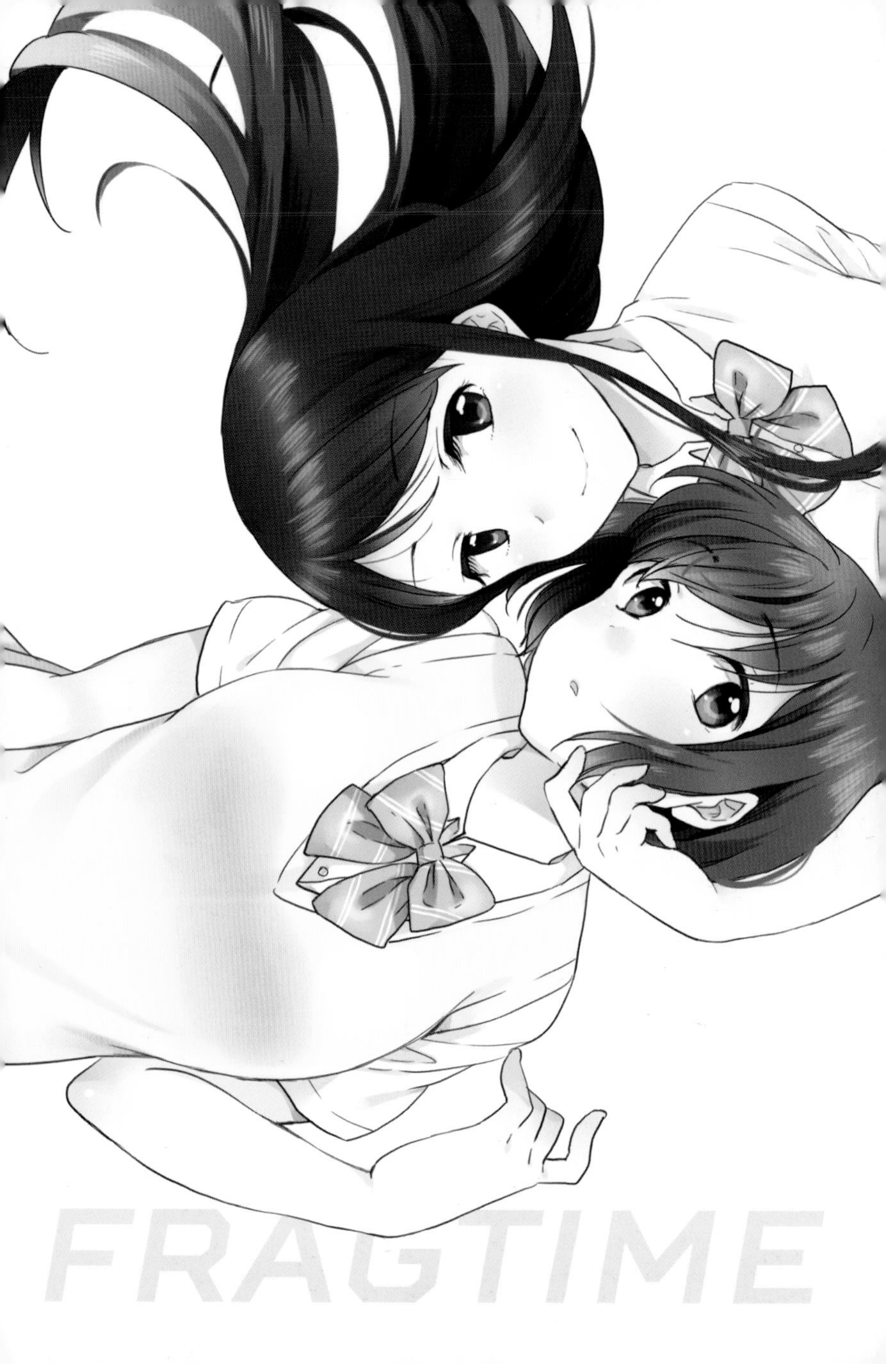
FRAGTIME

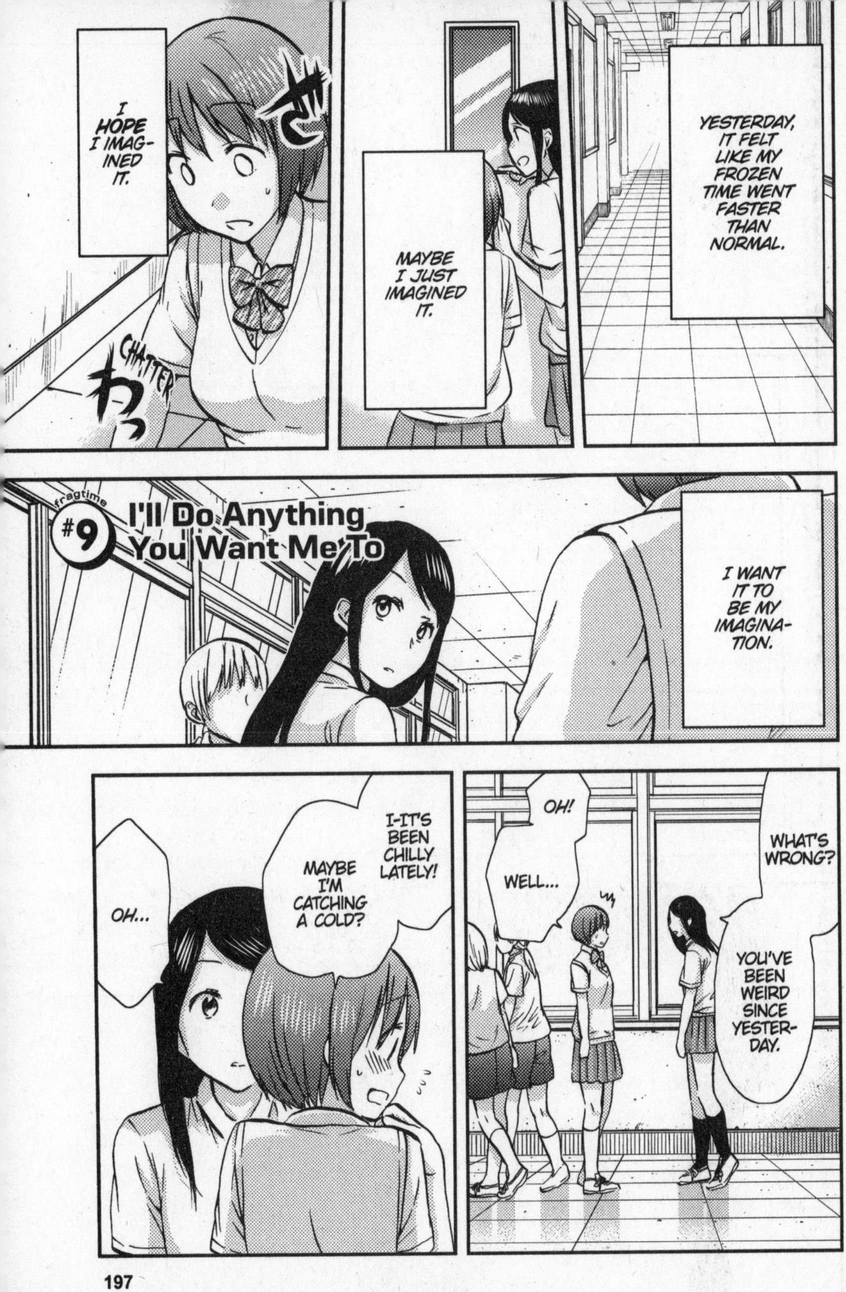
YESTERDAY, IT FELT LIKE MY FROZEN TIME WENT FASTER THAN NORMAL.
MAYBE I JUST IMAGINED IT.
I HOPE I IMAGINED IT.
CHATTER
fragtime
#9 I'll Do Anything You Want Me To
I WANT IT TO BE MY IMAGINATION.
WHAT'S WRONG?
YOU'VE BEEN WEIRD SINCE YESTERDAY.
OH!
WELL...
I-IT'S BEEN CHILLY LATELY!
MAYBE I'M CATCHING A COLD?
OH...

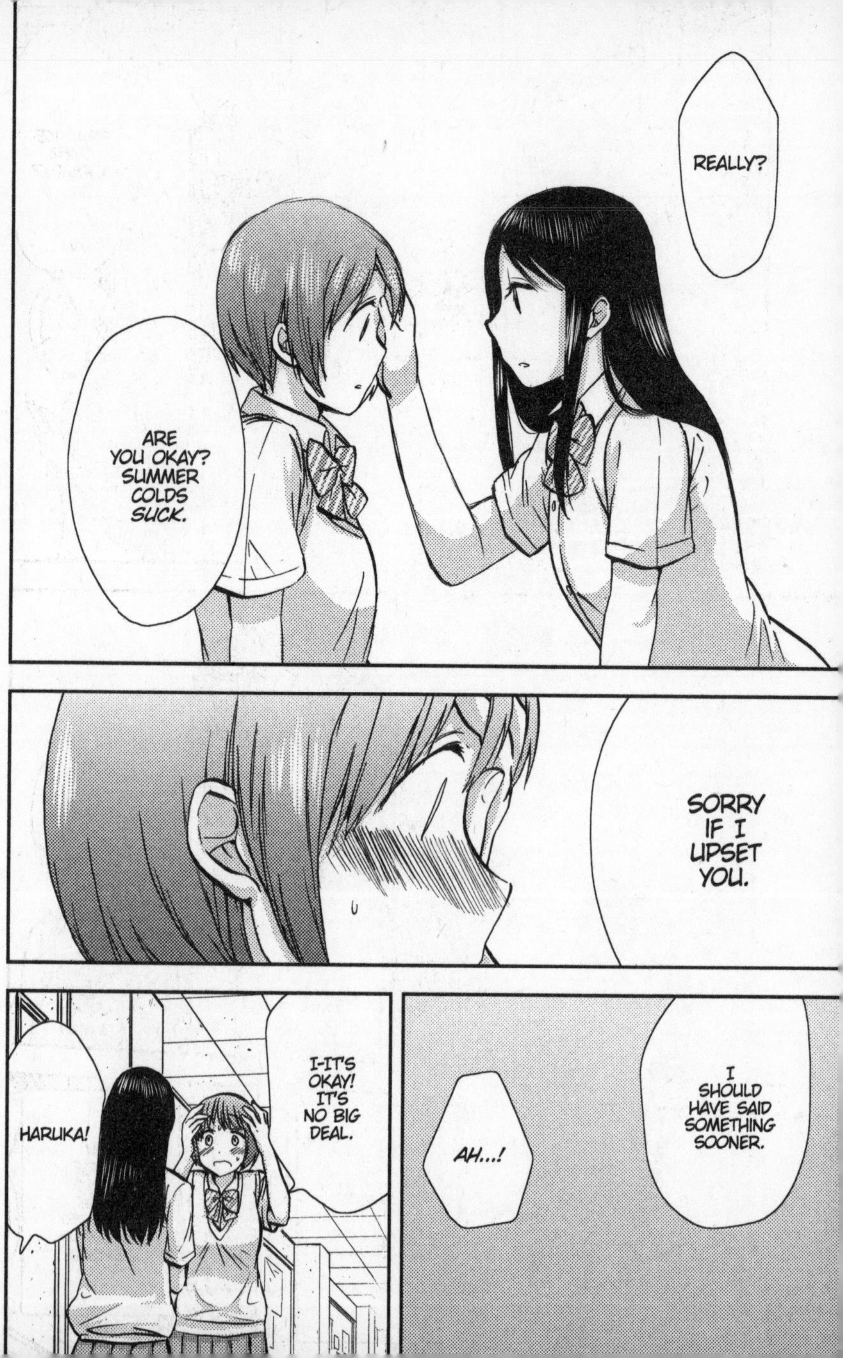
REALLY?
ARE YOU OKAY? SUMMER COLDS SUCK.
SORRY IF I UPSET YOU.
I SHOULD HAVE SAID SOMETHING SOONER.
AH...!
I-IT'S OKAY! IT'S NO BIG DEAL.
HARUKA!

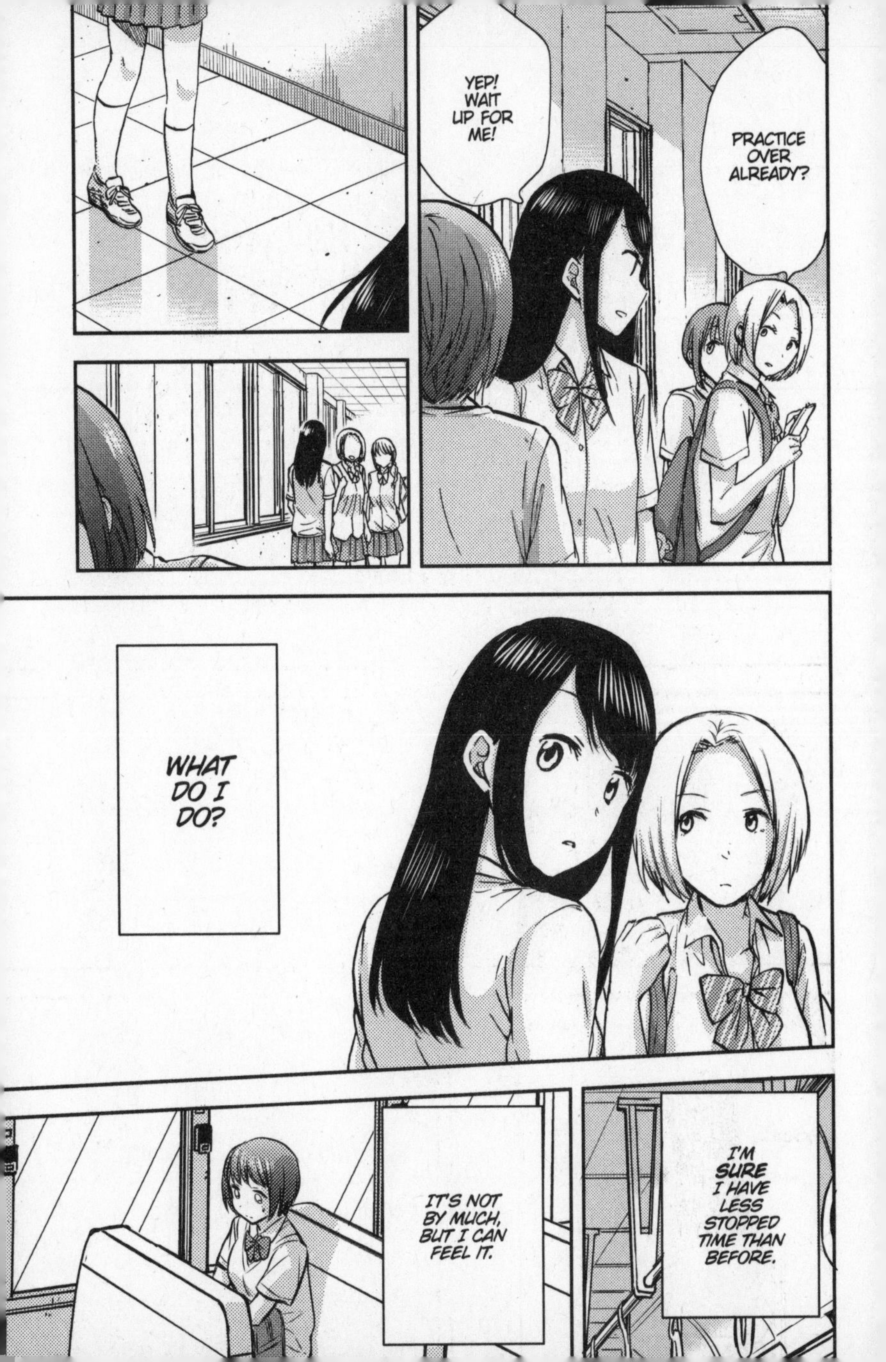
PRACTICE OVER ALREADY?
YEP! WAIT UP FOR ME!
WHAT DO I DO?
I'M SURE I HAVE LESS STOPPED TIME THAN BEFORE.
IT'S NOT BY MUCH, BUT I CAN FEEL IT.

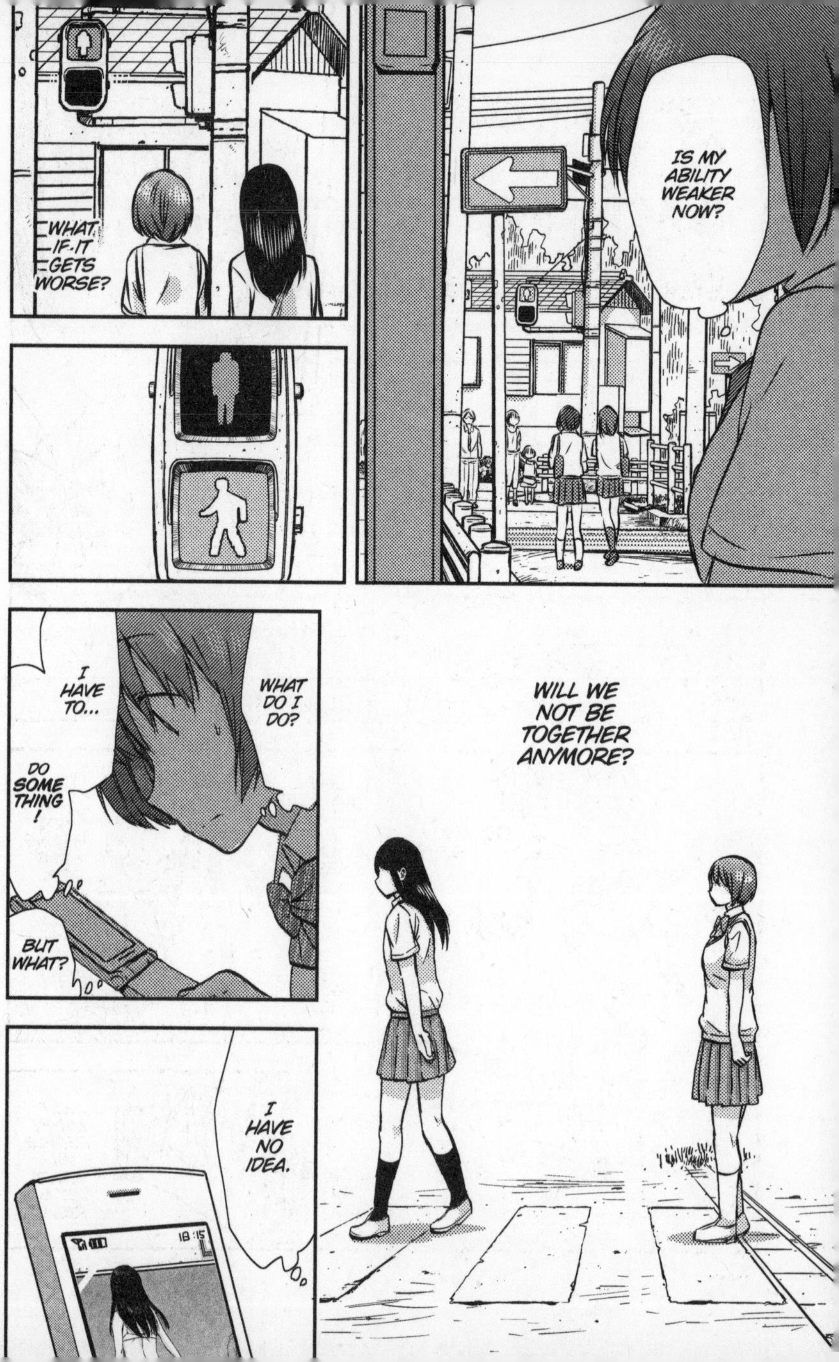
IS MY ABILITY WEAKER NOW?
WHAT IF IT GETS WORSE?
WILL WE NOT BE TOGETHER ANYMORE?
WHAT DO I DO?
I HAVE TO...
DO SOME THING!
BUT WHAT?
I HAVE NO IDEA.
18:15

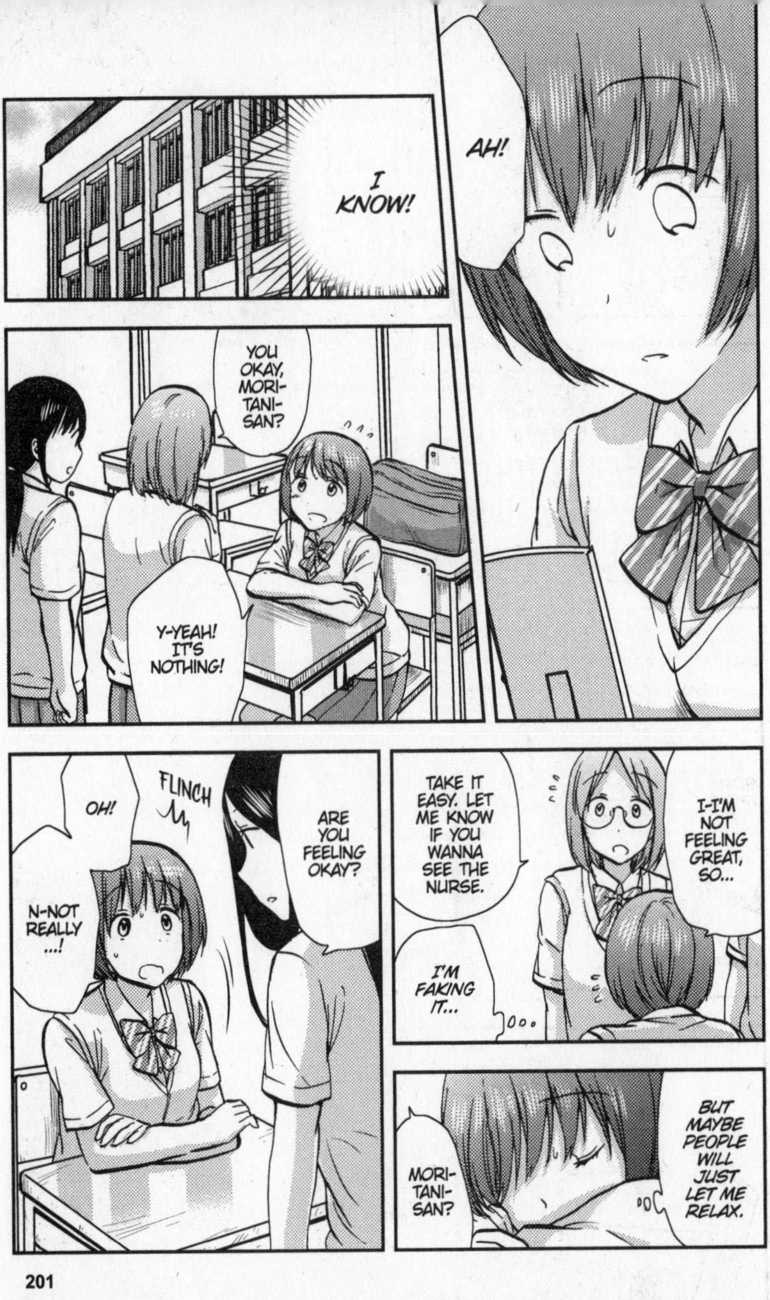
AH!
I KNOW!
YOU OKAY, MORI-TANI-SAN?
Y-YEAH! IT'S NOTHING!
I-I'M NOT FEELING GREAT, SO...
TAKE IT EASY. LET ME KNOW IF YOU WANNA SEE THE NURSE.
I'M FAKING IT...
BUT MAYBE PEOPLE WILL JUST LET ME RELAX.
MORI-TANI-SAN?
ARE YOU FEELING OKAY?
FLINCH
OH!
N-NOT REALLY ...!

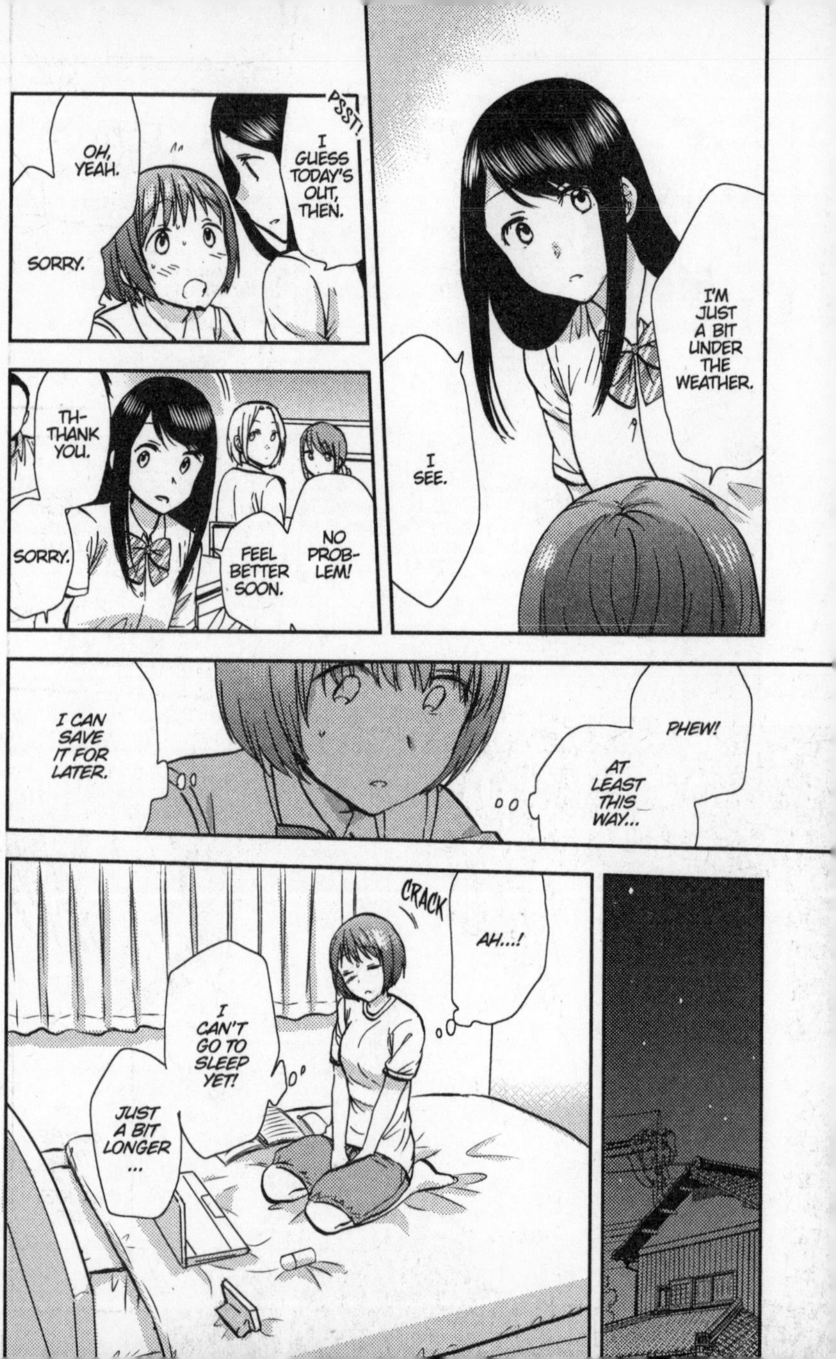
I'M JUST A BIT UNDER THE WEATHER.
I SEE.
PSST!
I GUESS TODAY'S OUT, THEN.
OH, YEAH.
SORRY.
NO PROB-LEM!
FEEL BETTER SOON.
TH-THANK YOU.
SORRY.
PHEW!
AT LEAST THIS WAY...
I CAN SAVE IT FOR LATER.
CRACK
AH...!
I CAN'T GO TO SLEEP YET!
JUST A BIT LONGER ...

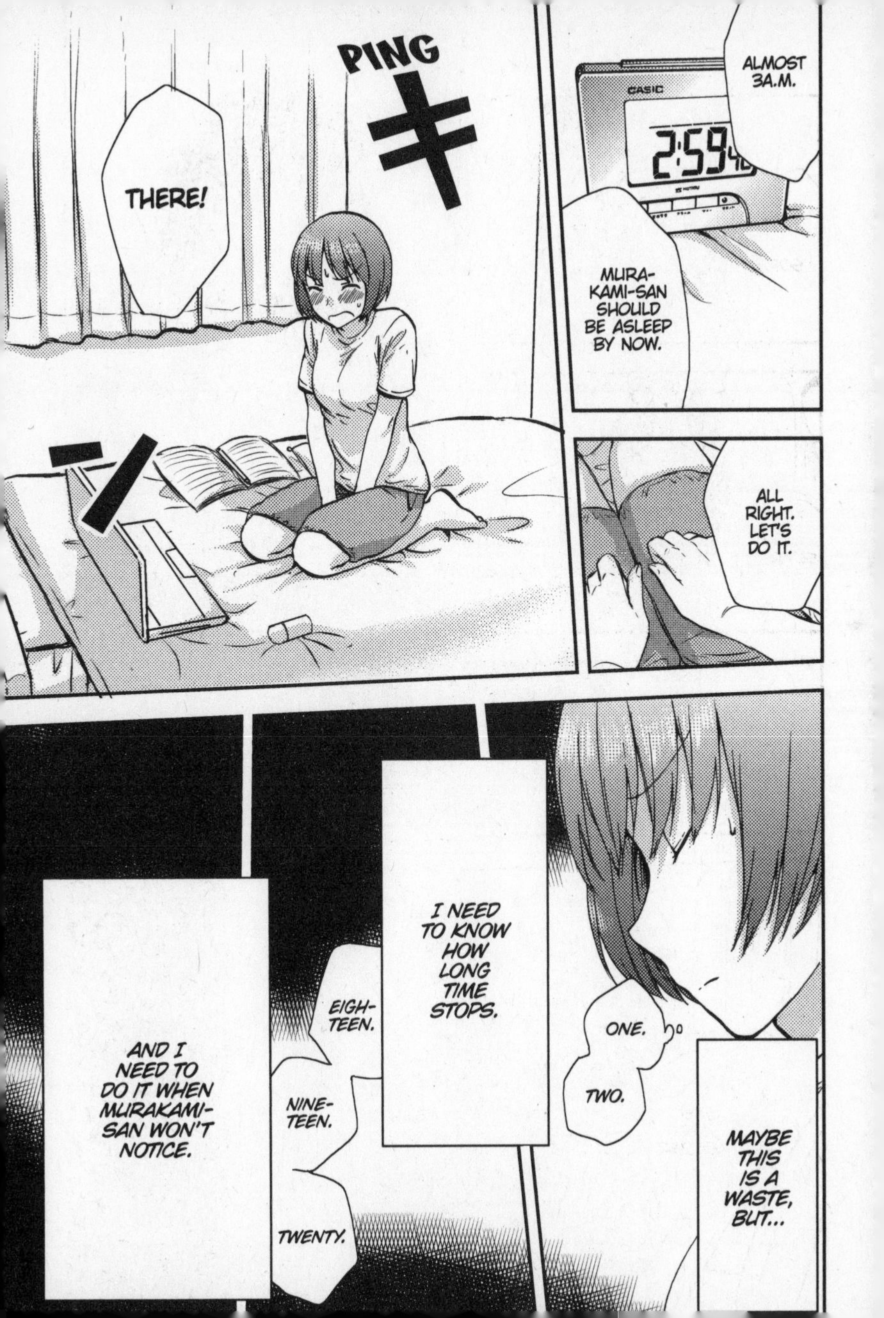
ALMOST 3A.M.
MURA-KAMI-SAN SHOULD BE ASLEEP BY NOW.
ALL RIGHT. LET'S DO IT.
PING
キ
THERE!
ONE.
TWO.
MAYBE THIS IS A WASTE, BUT...
I NEED TO KNOW HOW LONG TIME STOPS.
EIGH-TEEN.
NINE-TEEN.
TWENTY.
AND I NEED TO DO IT WHEN MURAKAMI-SAN WON'T NOTICE.

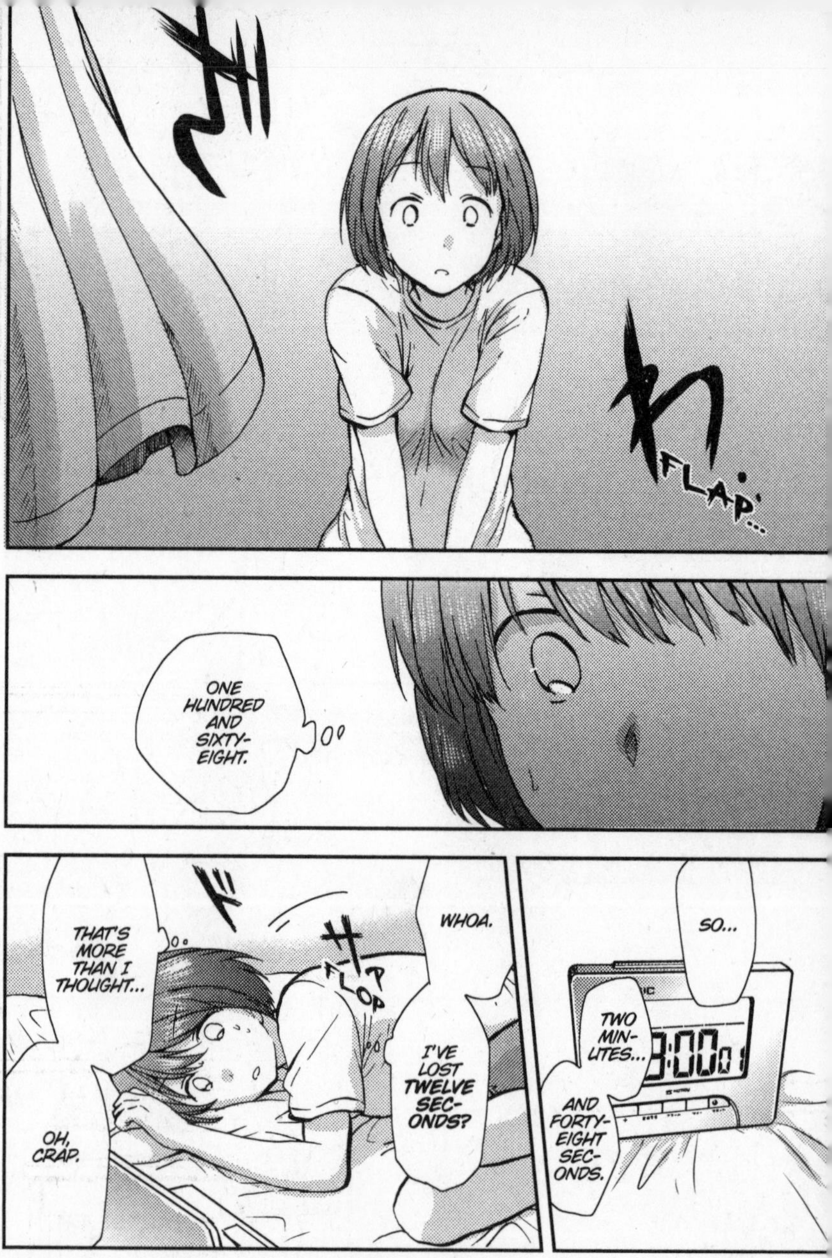
FLAP...
ONE HUNDRED AND SIXTY-EIGHT.
SO...
TWO MINUTES...
AND FORTY-EIGHT SECONDS.
WHOA.
FLOP
I'VE LOST TWELVE SECONDS?
THAT'S MORE THAN I THOUGHT...
OH, CRAP.

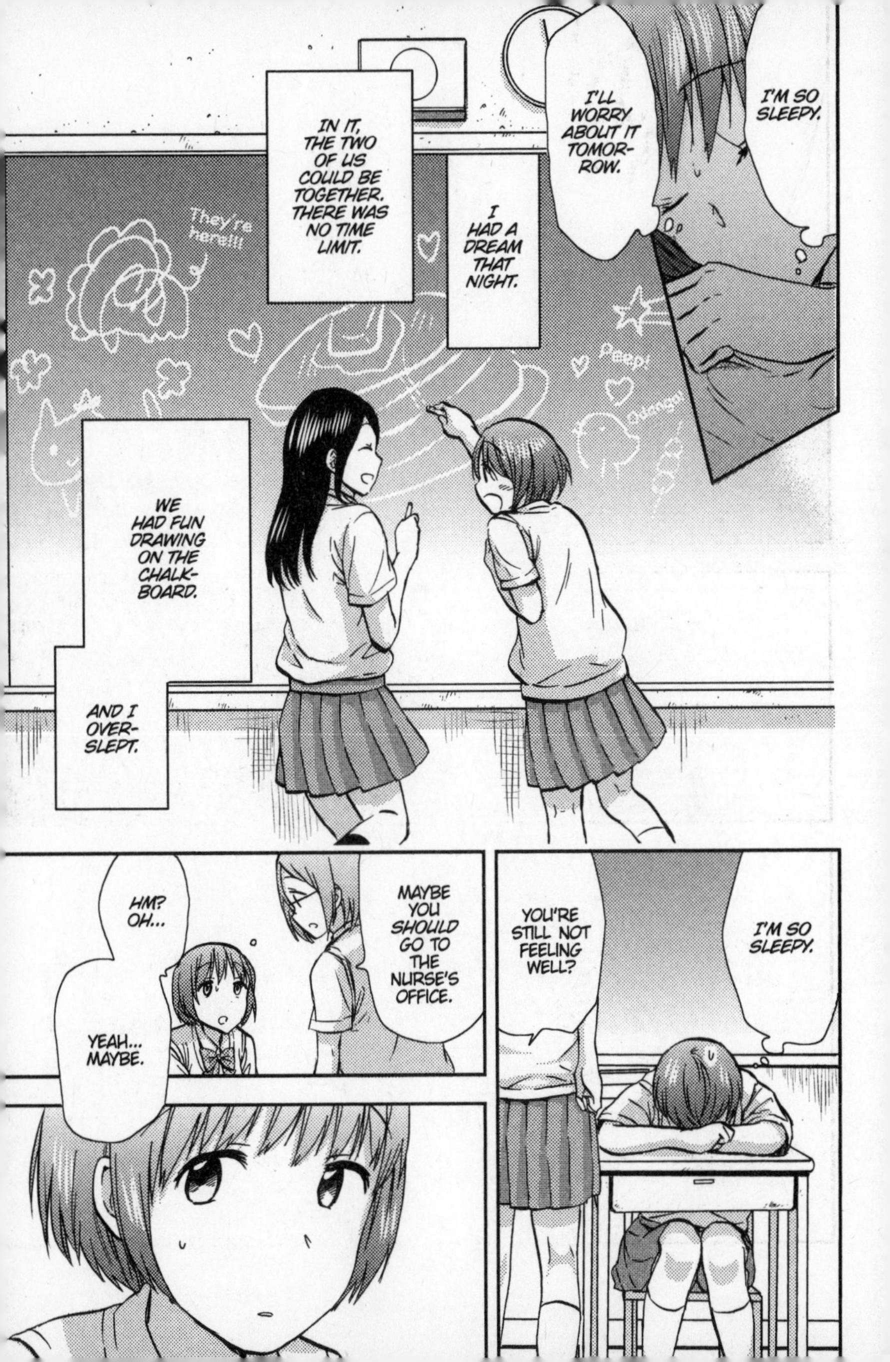
I'M SO SLEEPY.
I'LL WORRY ABOUT IT TOMORROW.
I HAD A DREAM THAT NIGHT.
IN IT, THE TWO OF US COULD BE TOGETHER. THERE WAS NO TIME LIMIT.
They're here!!!
Peep!
WE HAD FUN DRAWING ON THE CHALKBOARD.
AND I OVERSLEPT.
I'M SO SLEEPY.
YOU'RE STILL NOT FEELING WELL?
MAYBE YOU SHOULD GO TO THE NURSE'S OFFICE.
HM? OH...
YEAH... MAYBE.

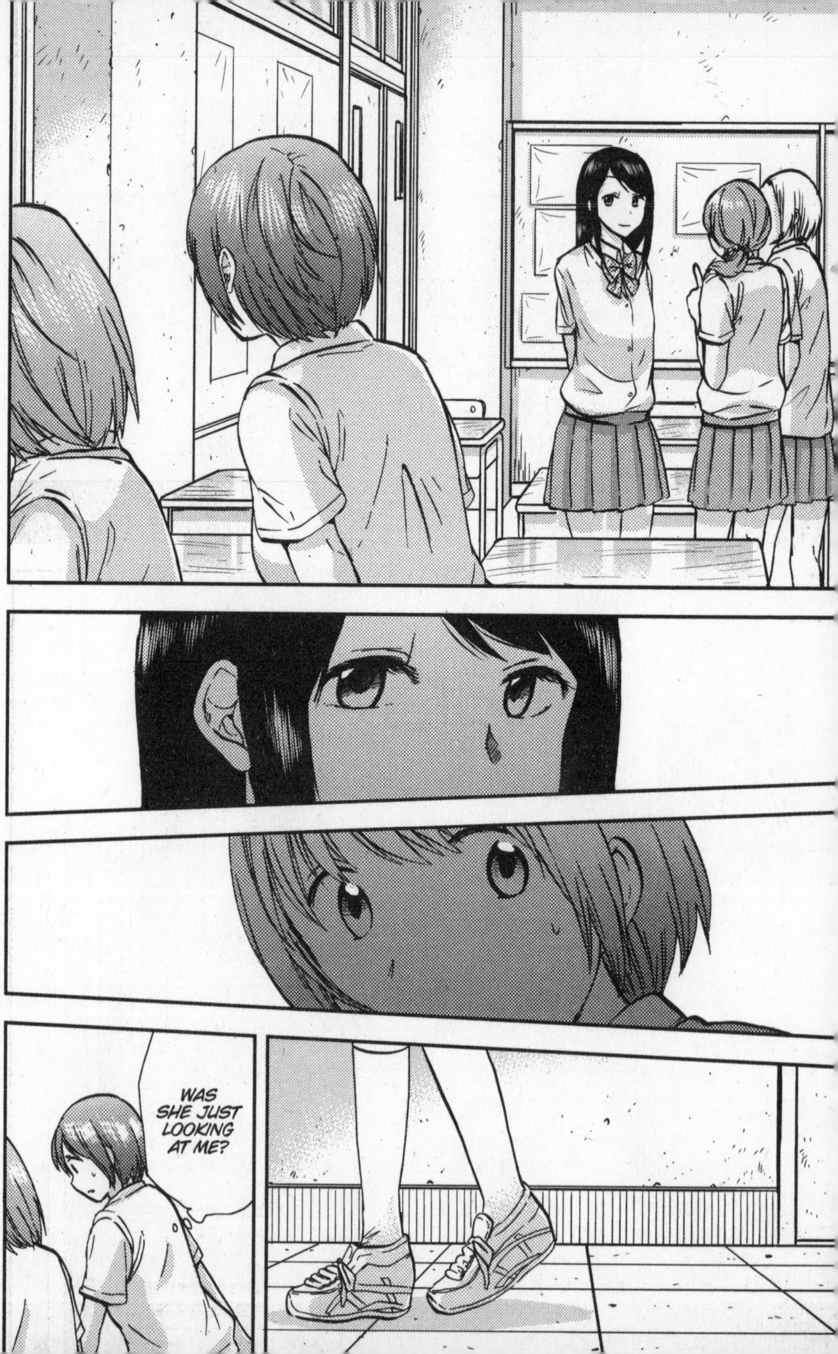
WAS SHE JUST LOOKING AT ME?

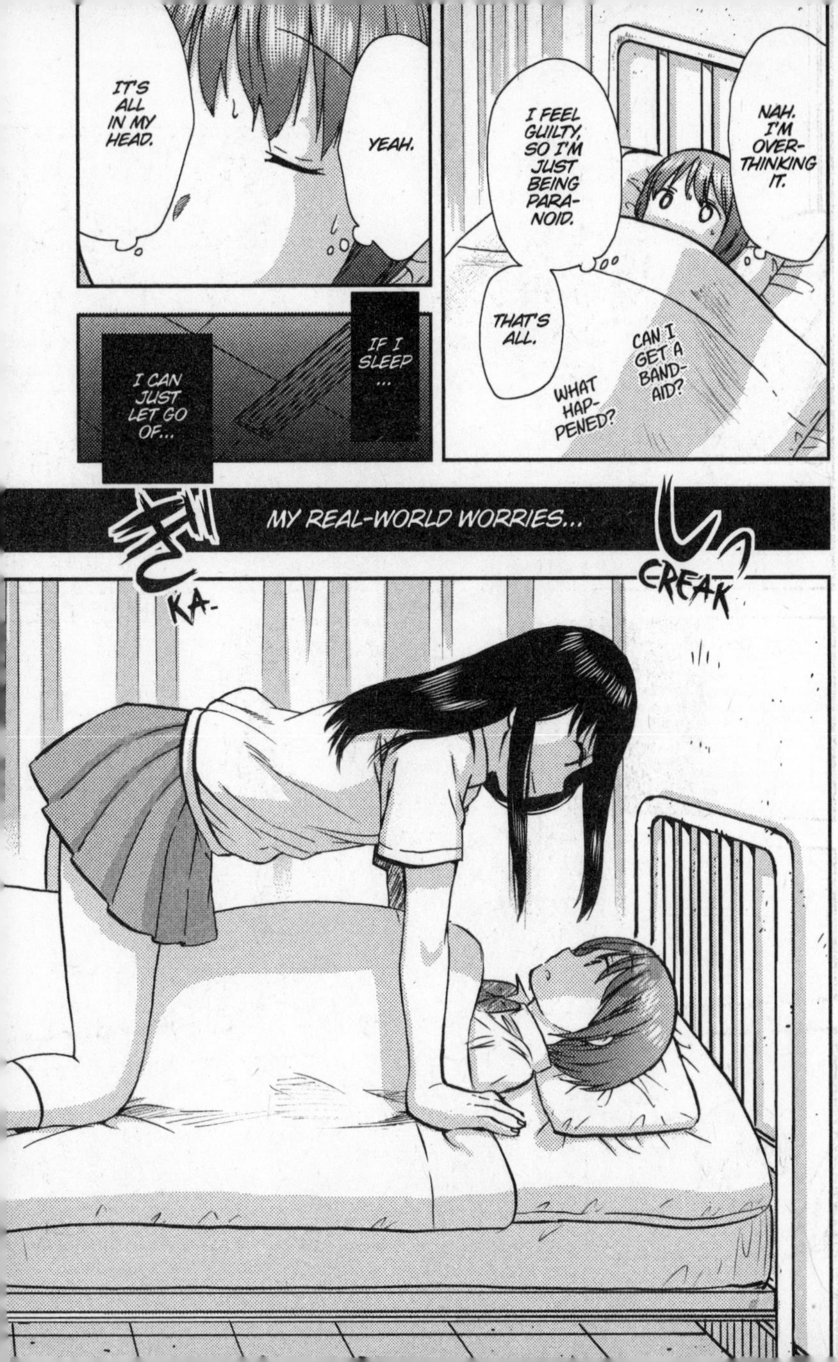
NAH. I'M OVER-THINKING IT.
I FEEL GUILTY, SO I'M JUST BEING PARA-NOID.
THAT'S ALL.
CAN I GET A BAND-AID?
WHAT HAP-PENED?
YEAH.
IT'S ALL IN MY HEAD.
IF I SLEEP ...
I CAN JUST LET GO OF...
MY REAL-WORLD WORRIES...
CREAK
KA-

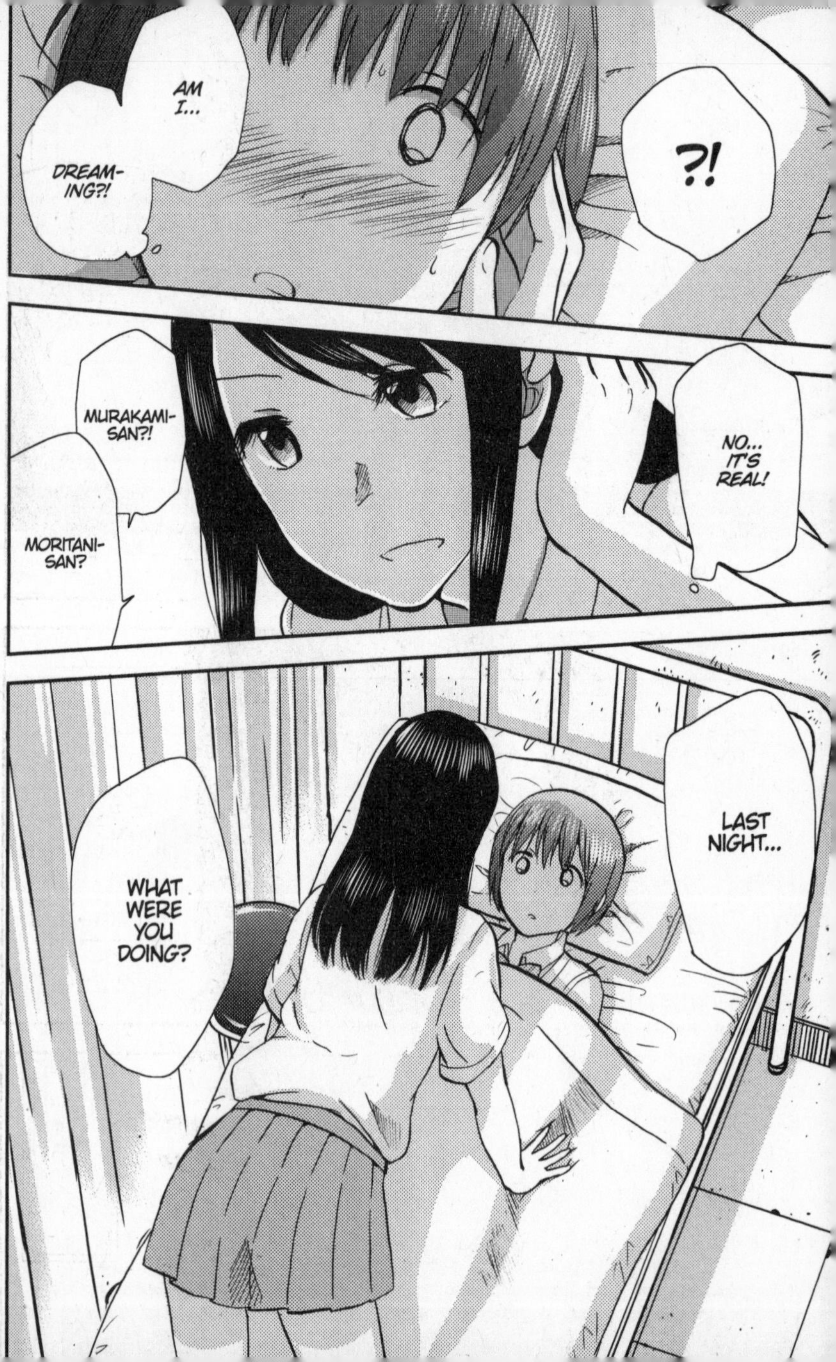
?!
AM I... DREAMING?!
NO... IT'S REAL!
MURAKAMI-SAN?!
MORITANI-SAN?
LAST NIGHT...
WHAT WERE YOU DOING?

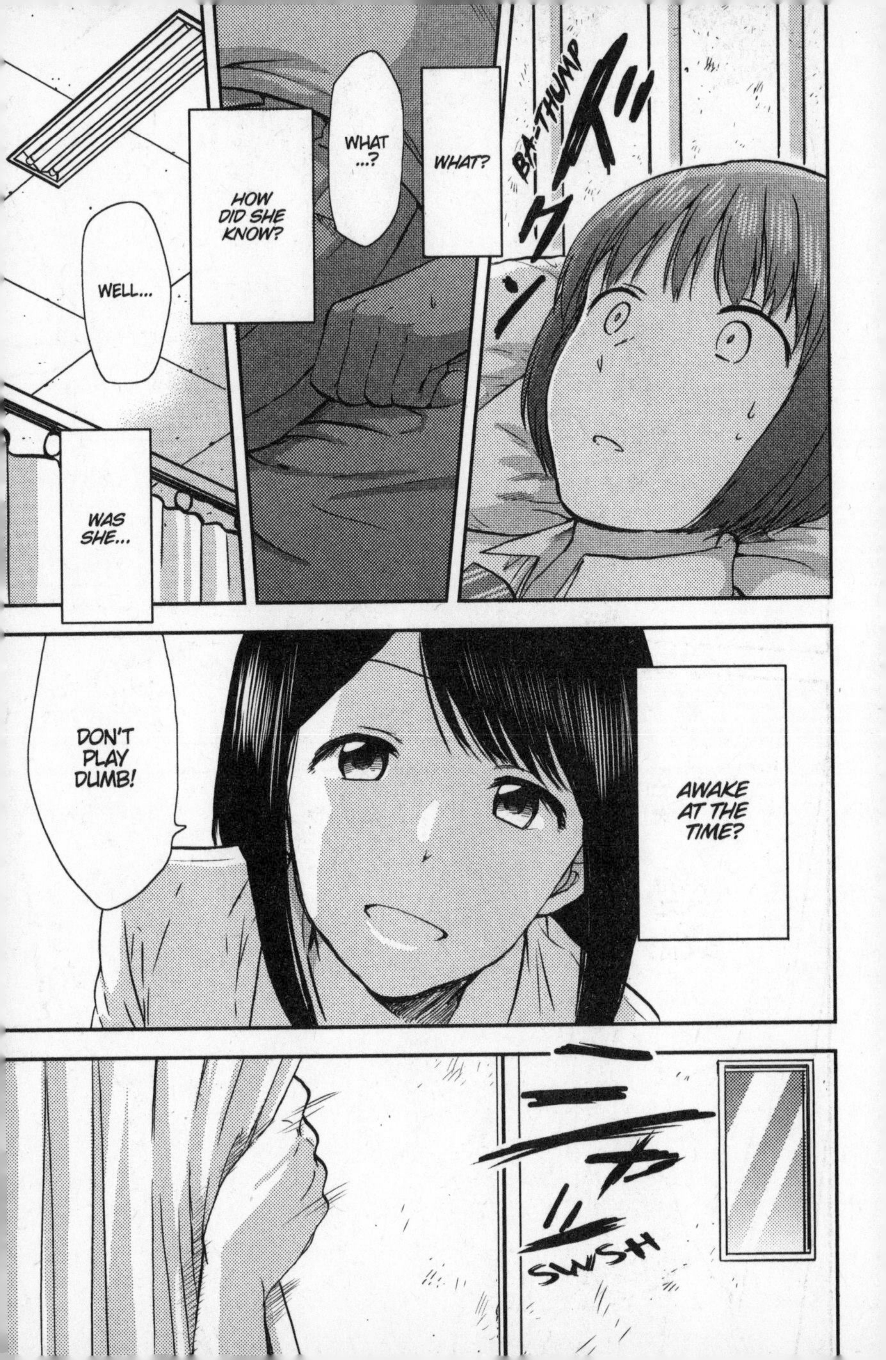
BA-THUMP
WHAT?
WHAT ...?
HOW DID SHE KNOW?
WELL...
WAS SHE...
AWAKE AT THE TIME?
DON'T PLAY DUMB!
SWISH

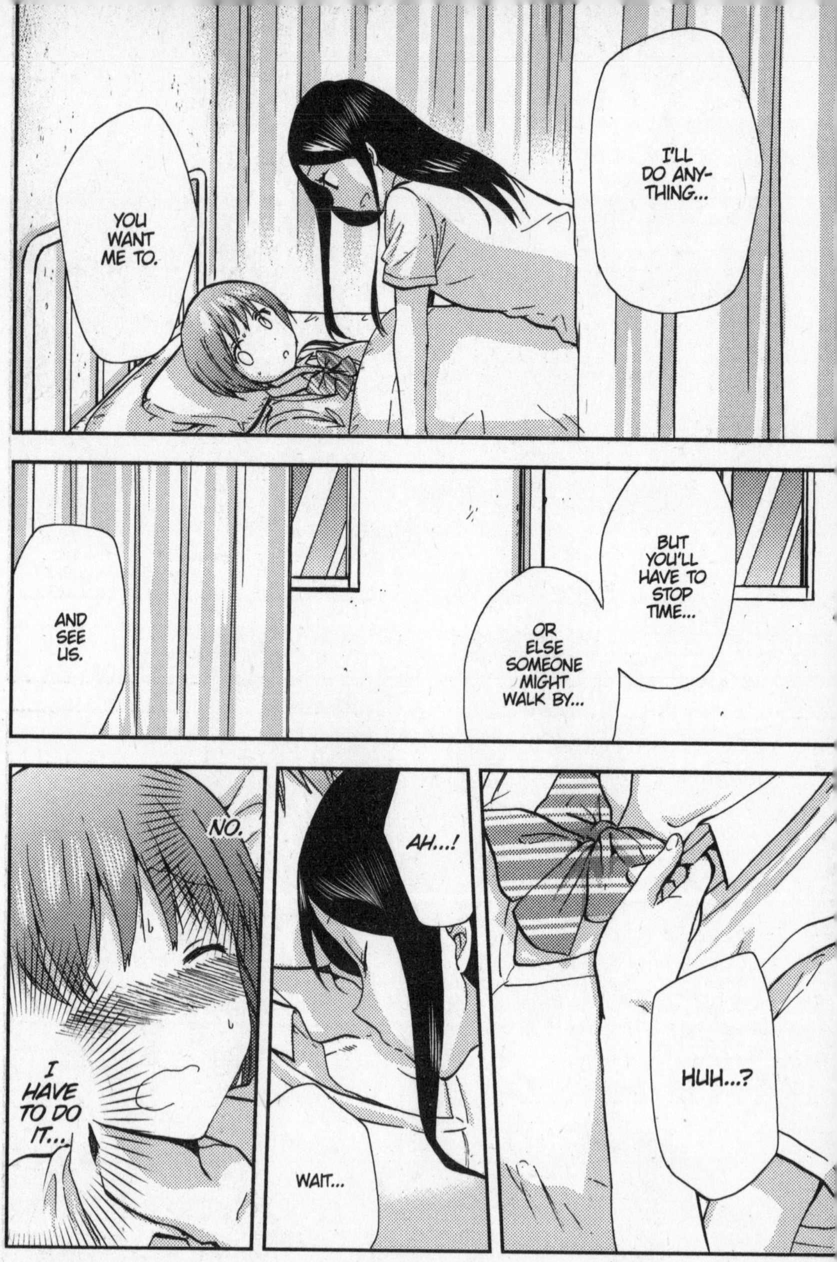
I'LL DO ANY-THING...
YOU WANT ME TO.
BUT YOU'LL HAVE TO STOP TIME...
OR ELSE SOMEONE MIGHT WALK BY...
AND SEE US.
HUH...?
AH...!
WAIT...
NO.
I HAVE TO DO IT...

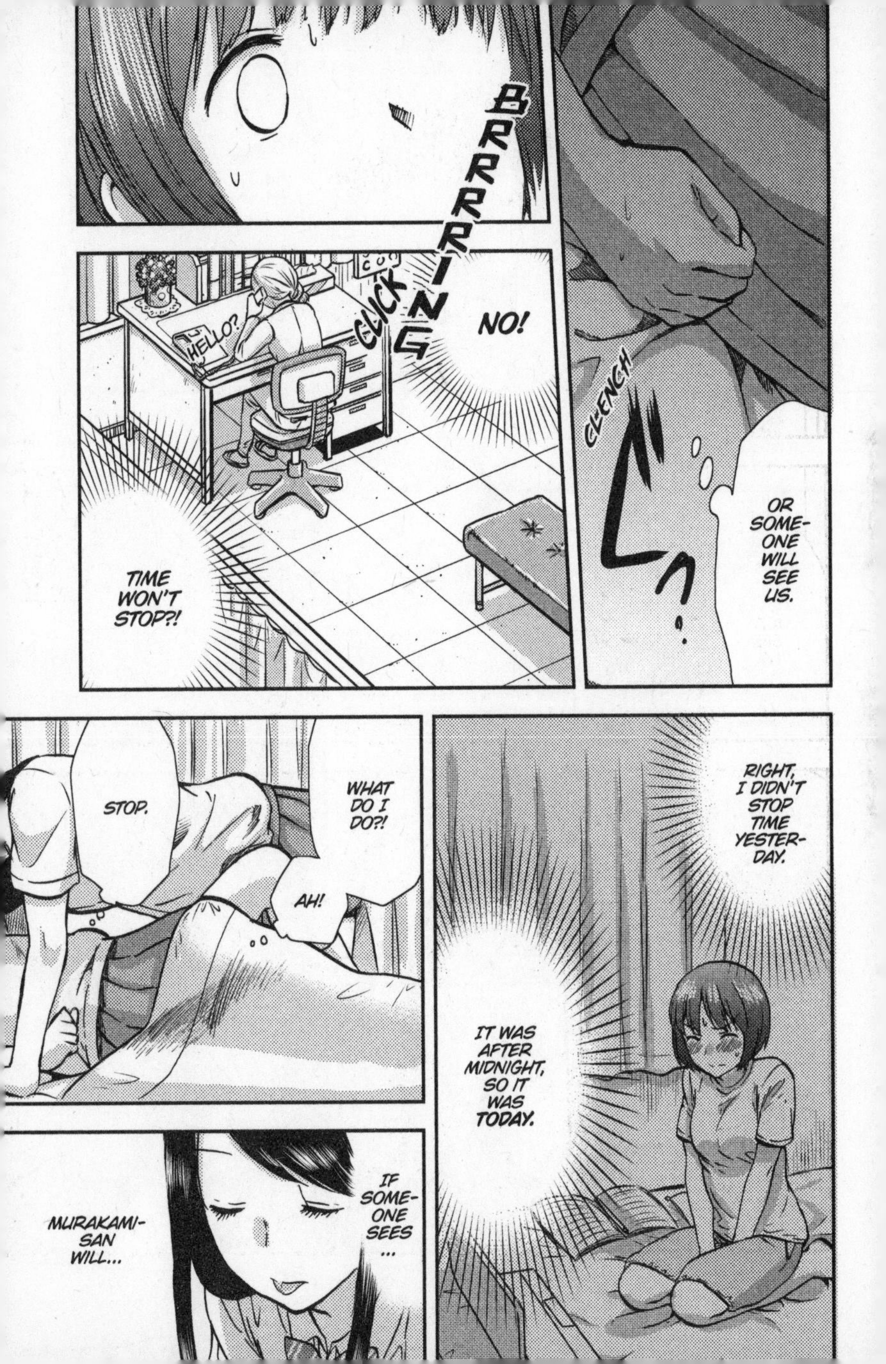
CLENCH
OR SOME-ONE WILL SEE US.
BRRRRING
CLICK
HELLO?
NO!
TIME WON'T STOP?!
RIGHT, I DIDN'T STOP TIME YESTER-DAY.
IT WAS AFTER MIDNIGHT, SO IT WAS TODAY.
WHAT DO I DO?!
STOP.
AH!
IF SOME-ONE SEES...
MURAKAMI-SAN WILL...

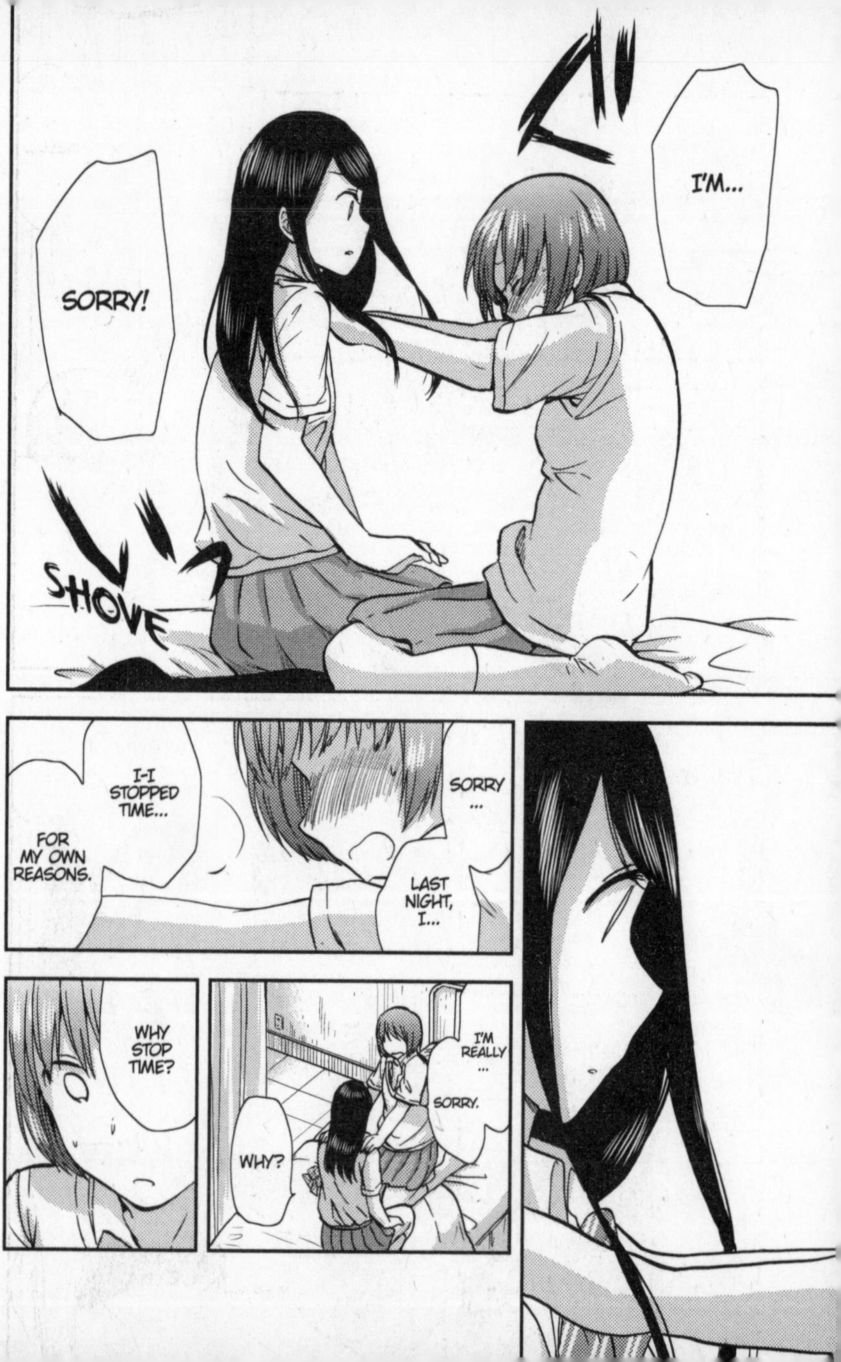
I'M...
SORRY!
SHOVE
SORRY ...
LAST NIGHT, I...
I-I STOPPED TIME...
FOR MY OWN REASONS.
I'M REALLY ...
SORRY.
WHY?
WHY STOP TIME?

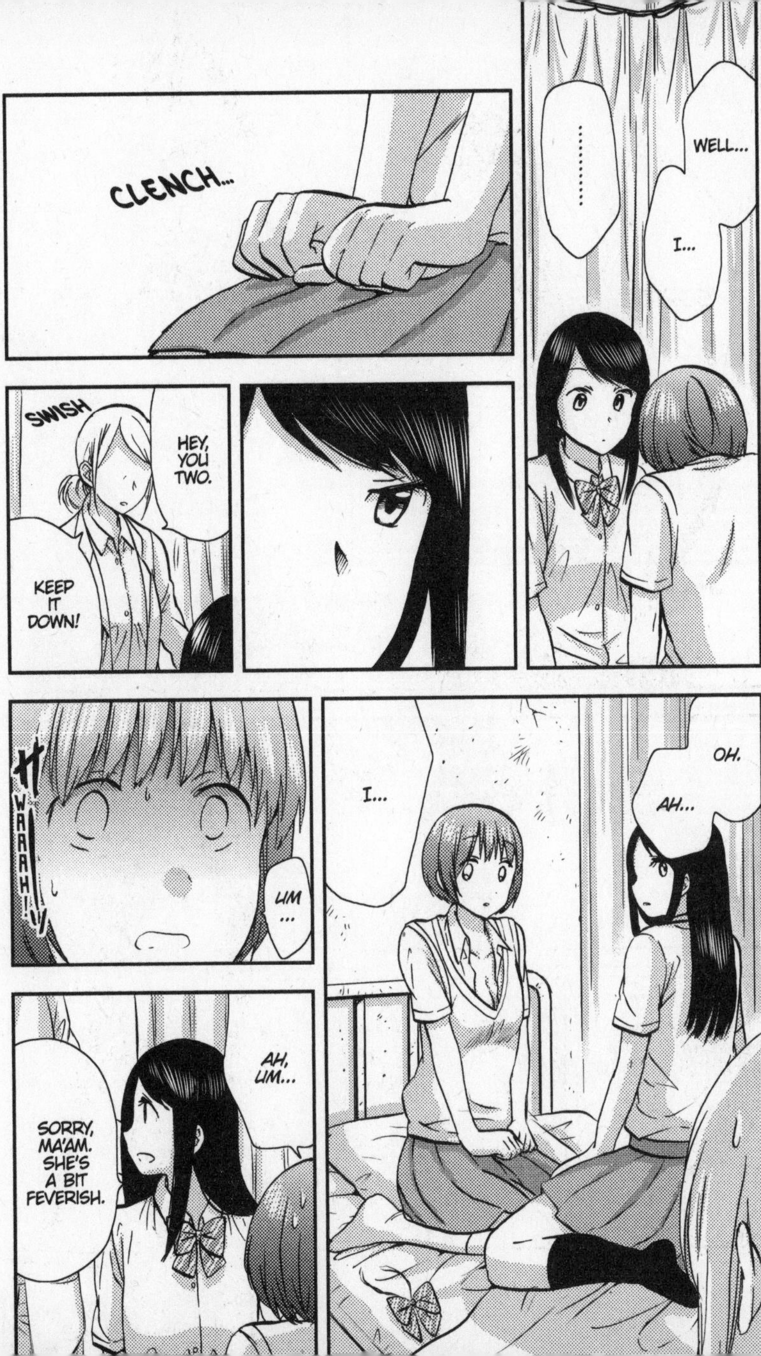
WELL...
I...
......
CLENCH...
SWISH
HEY, YOU TWO.
KEEP IT DOWN!
OH.
AH...
I...
HWAAAH!
UM...
AH, UM...
SORRY, MA'AM. SHE'S A BIT FEVERISH.

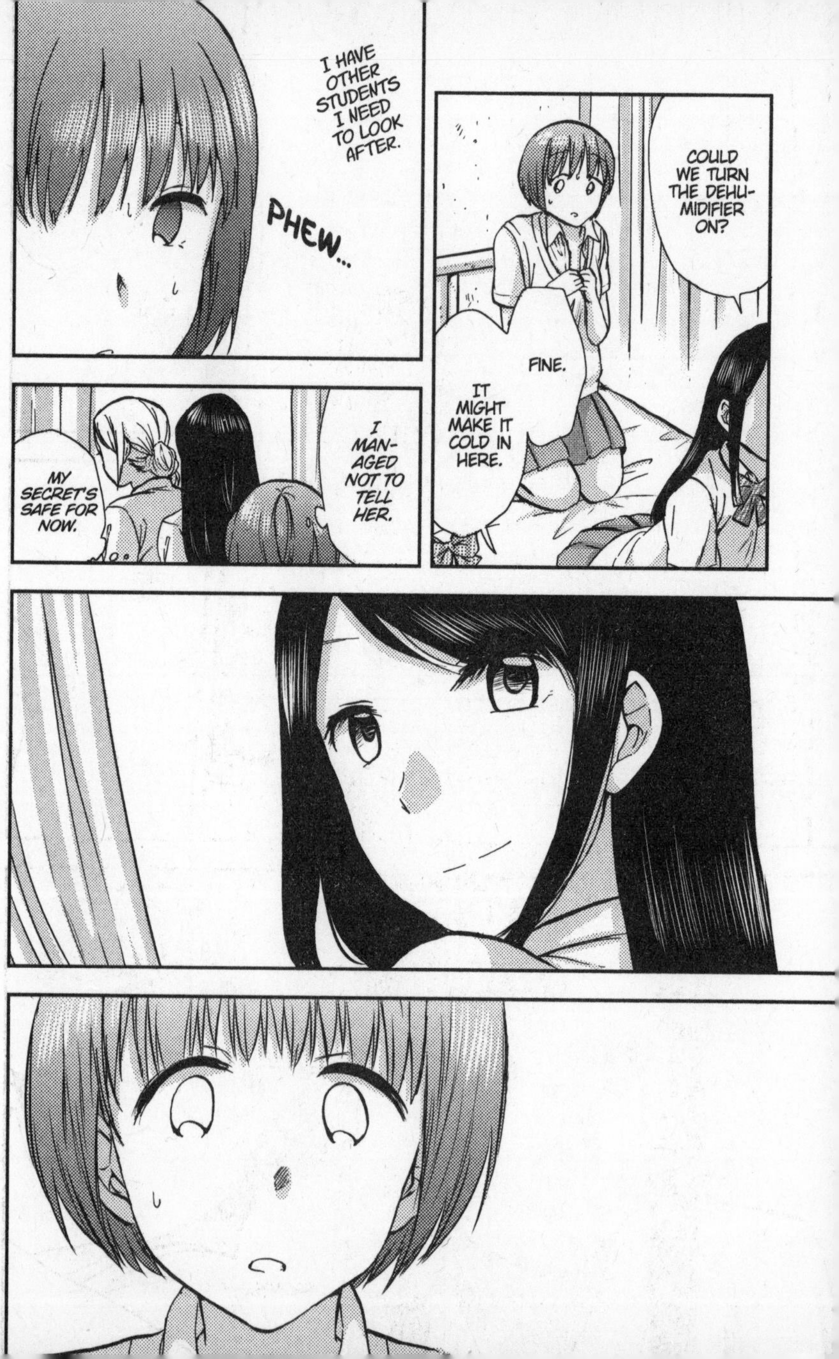
COULD WE TURN THE DEHUMIDIFIER ON?
FINE.
IT MIGHT MAKE IT COLD IN HERE.
I HAVE OTHER STUDENTS I NEED TO LOOK AFTER.
PHEW...
I MANAGED NOT TO TELL HER.
MY SECRET'S SAFE FOR NOW.

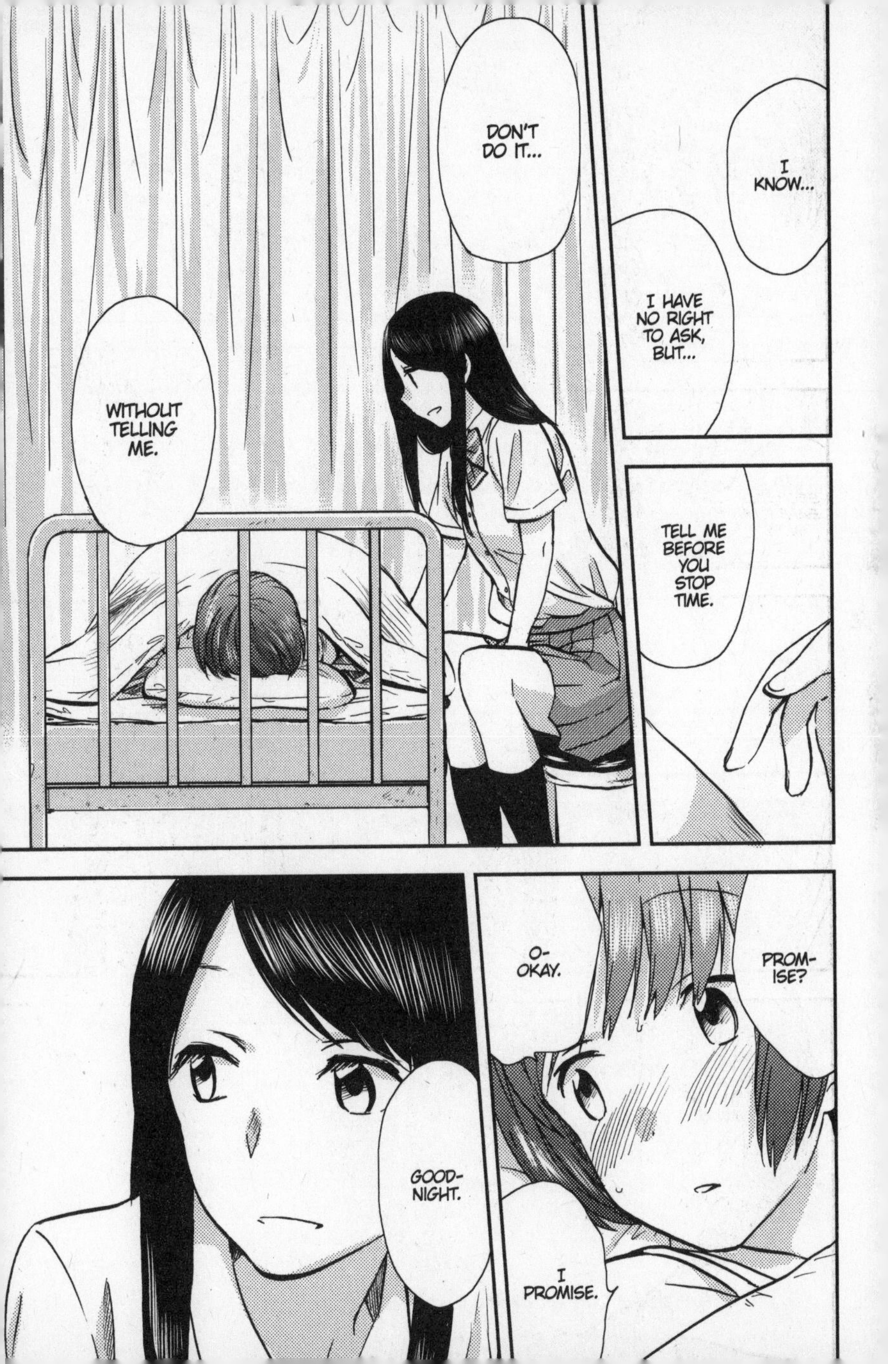
I KNOW...
I HAVE NO RIGHT TO ASK, BUT...
TELL ME BEFORE YOU STOP TIME.
DON'T DO IT...
WITHOUT TELLING ME.
PROM-ISE?
O-OKAY.
I PROMISE.
GOOD-NIGHT.

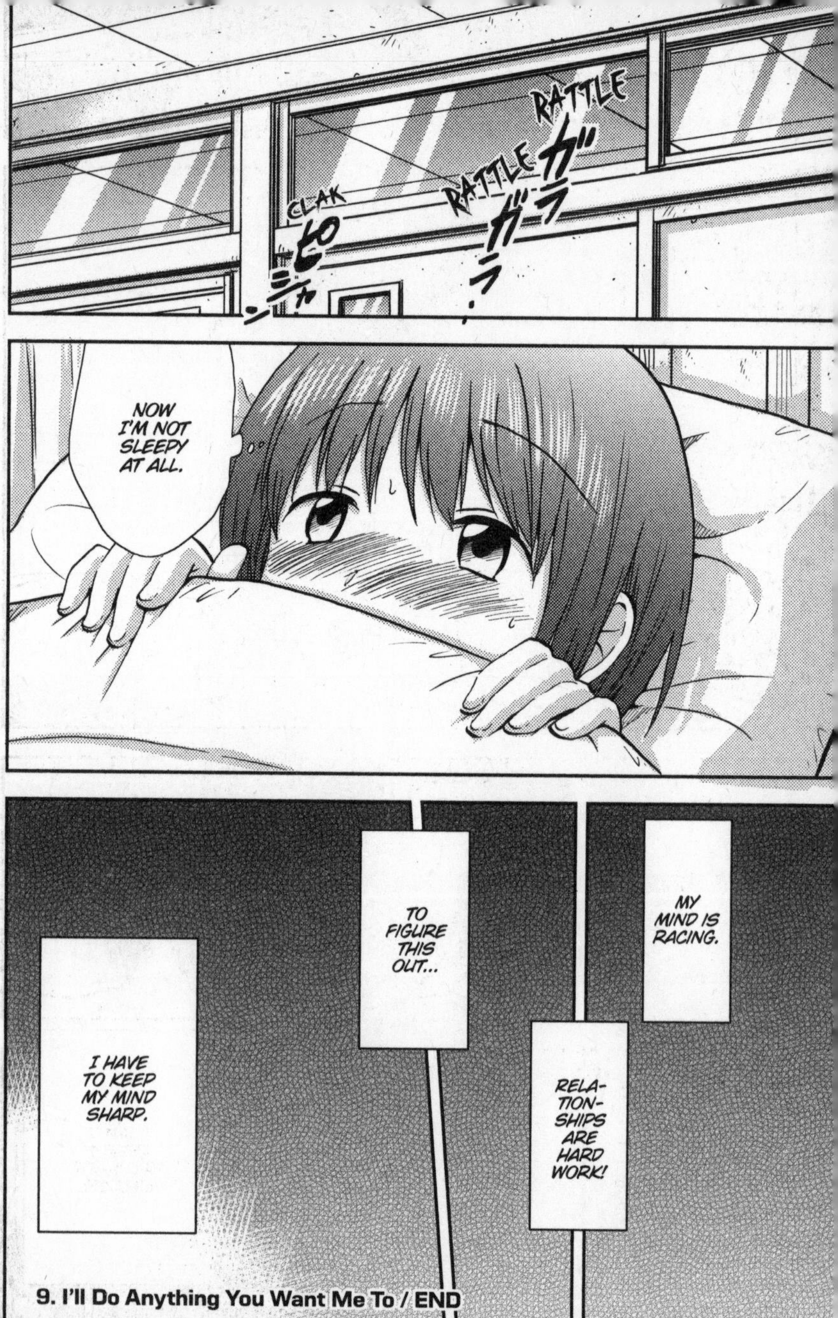
RATTLE
ガラ
RATTLE
ガラ
CLAK
ピシャン
NOW I'M NOT SLEEPY AT ALL.
MY MIND IS RACING.
RELA-TION-SHIPS ARE HARD WORK!
TO FIGURE THIS OUT...
I HAVE TO KEEP MY MIND SHARP.
9. I'll Do Anything You Want Me To / END

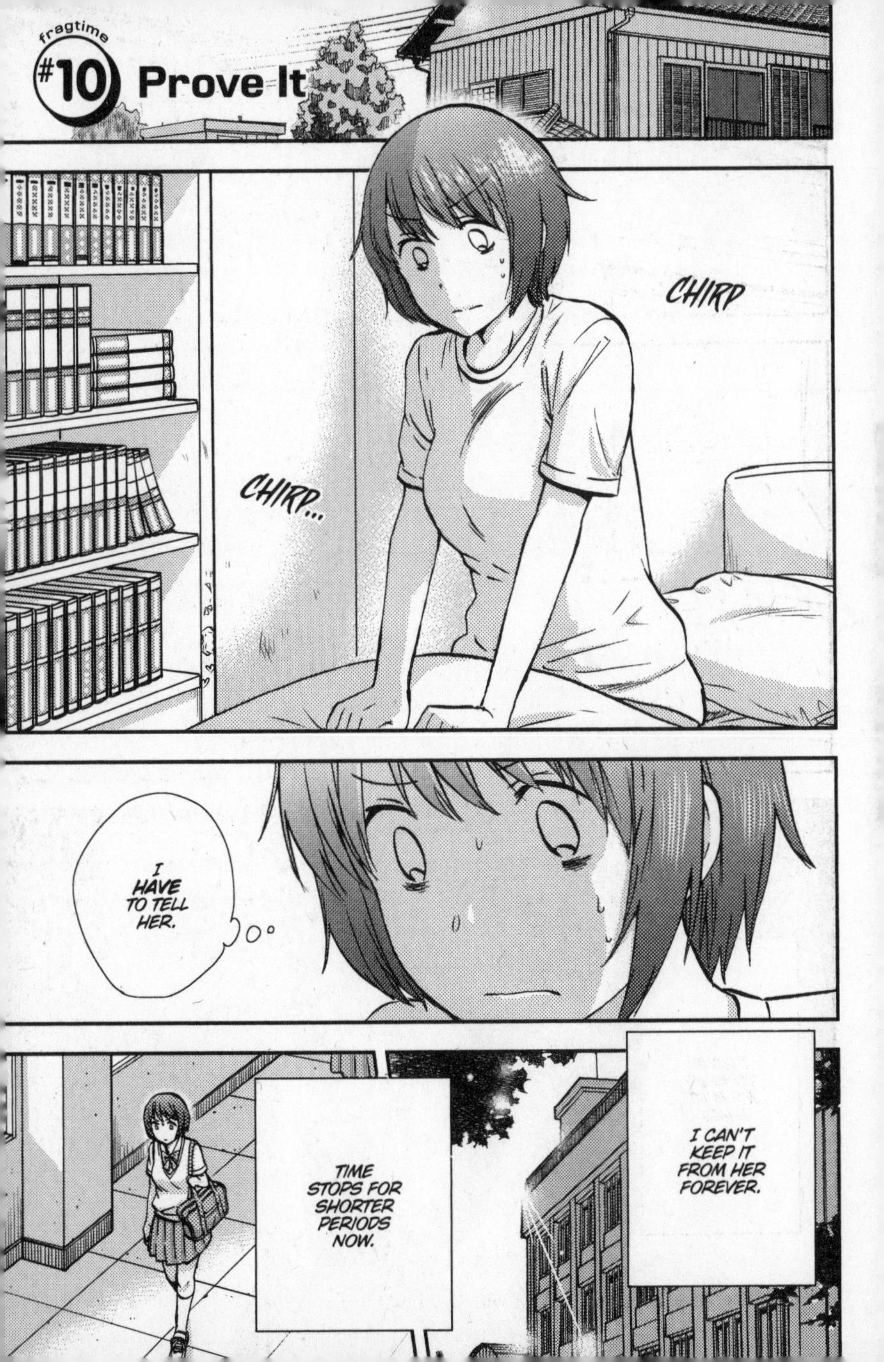
fragtime
#10 Prove It
CHIRP
CHIRP...
I HAVE TO TELL HER.
I CAN'T KEEP IT FROM HER FOREVER.
TIME STOPS FOR SHORTER PERIODS NOW.

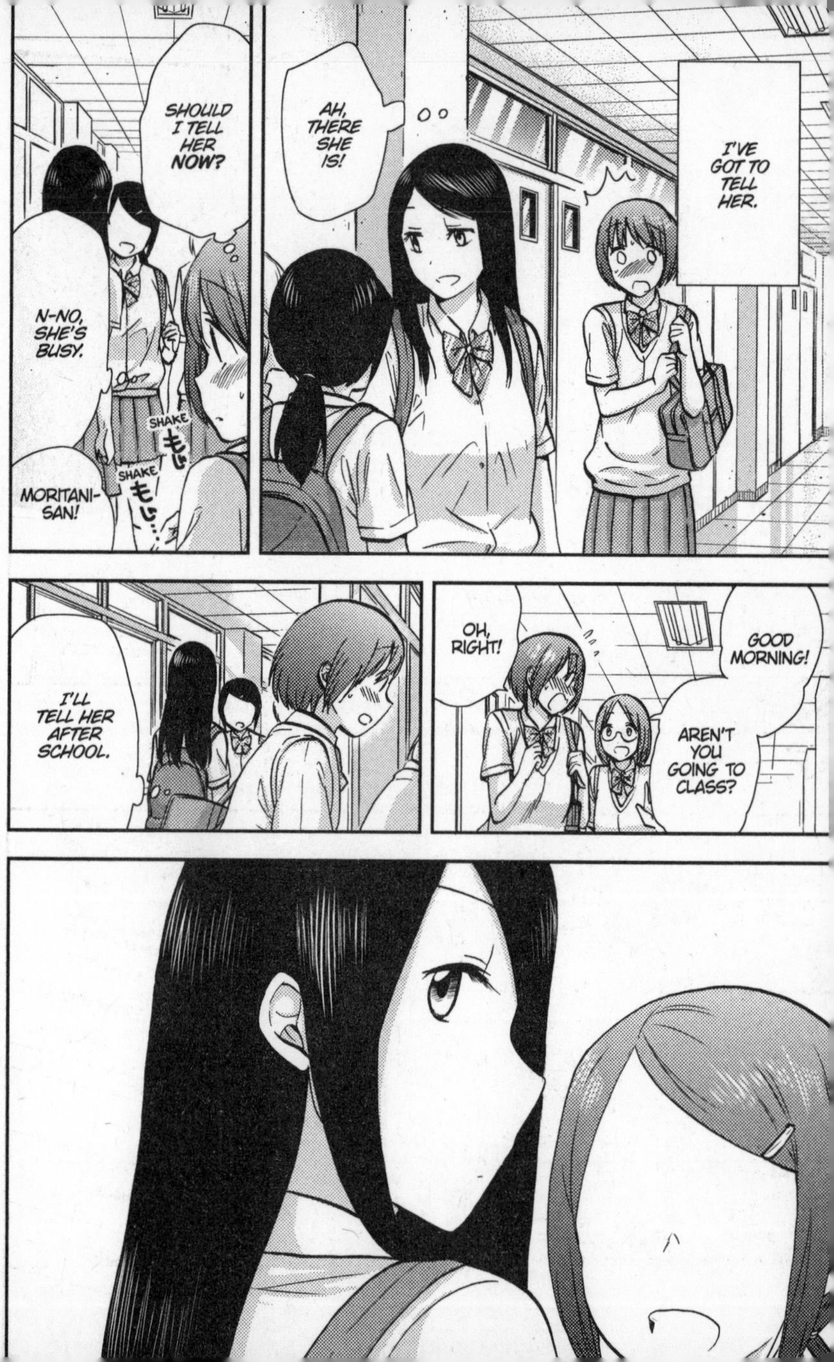
I'VE GOT TO TELL HER.
AH, THERE SHE IS!
SHOULD I TELL HER NOW?
N-NO, SHE'S BUSY.
SHAKE もじ
SHAKE もじ…
MORITANI-SAN!
GOOD MORNING!
OH, RIGHT!
AREN'T YOU GOING TO CLASS?
I'LL TELL HER AFTER SCHOOL.

WRITE YOUR TOP THREE CHOICES DOWN BEFORE MONDAY.

IT'S TIME TO THINK ABOUT THE FUTURE, PEOPLE!

Post-Secondary Interest Survey

HEY! DONE ALREADY?

I CAN BARELY HANDLE THE PRES-ENT.

THEY REALLY PUT US ON THE SPOT, EH?

N-NO, NOT YET.

I HAVEN'T THOUGHT ABOUT...

WHAT TO DO AFTER HIGH SCHOOL.

Post-Secondary Interest Survey

Grade:_____ Class:_____

Circle your desired post-secondary path.

University

Employment

Other

Ranked Choices	
1st Choice	
2nd Choice	
3rd Choice	

219

MANGA ARTIST?

YOU DRAW MANGA, KOBAYASHI-SAN?

SHH!

NOT SO LOUD!!

Post-Secondary Interest Survey
Grade: 2 Class: 2
Circle your desired post-secondary path.
University
Employment
Other

Ranked Choices		
	MANGA ARTIST
1st Choice	OTHER EMPLOYMENT
2nd Choice	
	ILLUSTRATOR
3rd Choice	

YEAH. I HAVE NO CLUE.

OH!

WELL, I HAVE SOME IDEAS.

DONE ALREADY?!

DA-DUN

TO BE HONEST...

IT'S THE ONLY PLAN I'VE GOT!

SHE'S REALLY THOUGHT THIS OUT.

I BET THEY WANT US TO GO TO UNIVERSITY, BUT I COME FROM A BIG FAMILY. WE DON'T HAVE MUCH MONEY, SO...

YOU'VE REALLY THOUGHT ABOUT THIS.

I ACTUALLY JOINED THE PING-PONG CLUB TO RESEARCH MY STORY.

ANYWAY, IT'S ALWAYS BEEN MY DREAM. I WANT TO DEBUT IN HIGH SCHOOL, BUT IF NOT, I'LL FIND ANOTHER JOB.

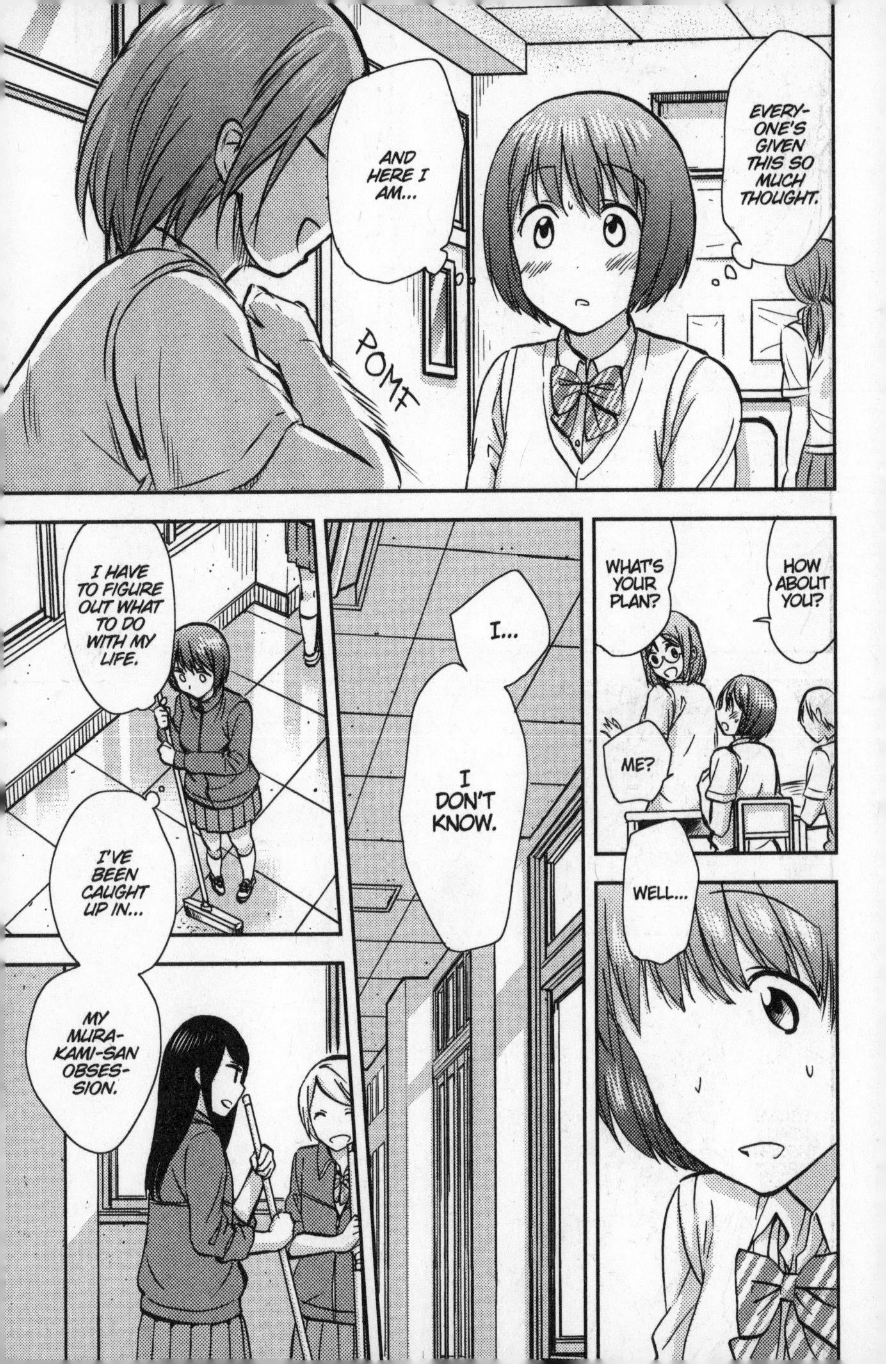
EVERYONE'S GIVEN THIS SO MUCH THOUGHT.
AND HERE I AM...
POMF
HOW ABOUT YOU?
WHAT'S YOUR PLAN?
ME?
WELL...
I...
I DON'T KNOW.
I HAVE TO FIGURE OUT WHAT TO DO WITH MY LIFE.
I'VE BEEN CAUGHT UP IN...
MY MURAKAMI-SAN OBSESSION.

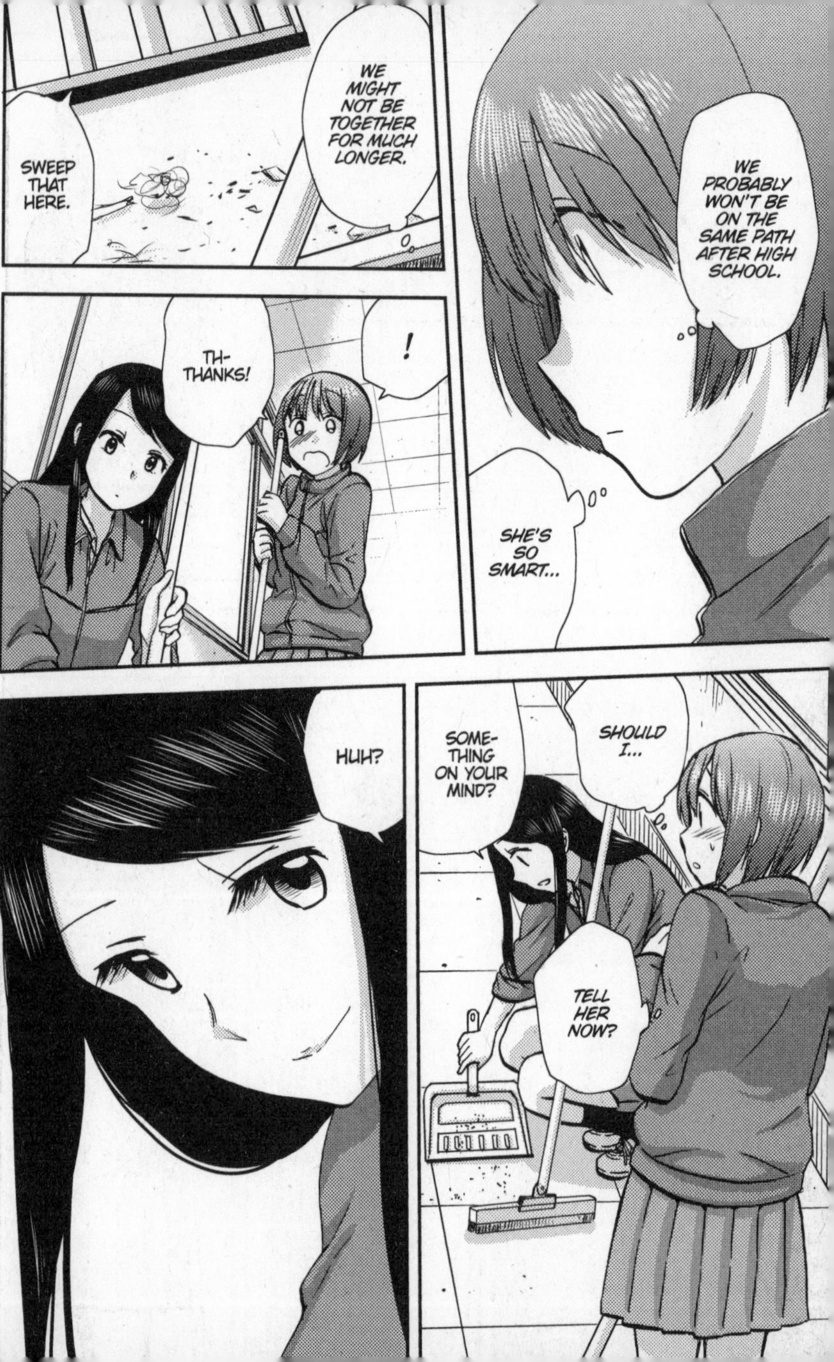
WE PROBABLY WON'T BE ON THE SAME PATH AFTER HIGH SCHOOL.
SHE'S SO SMART...
WE MIGHT NOT BE TOGETHER FOR MUCH LONGER.
SWEEP THAT HERE.
!
TH-THANKS!
SHOULD I...
SOME-THING ON YOUR MIND?
TELL HER NOW?
HUH?

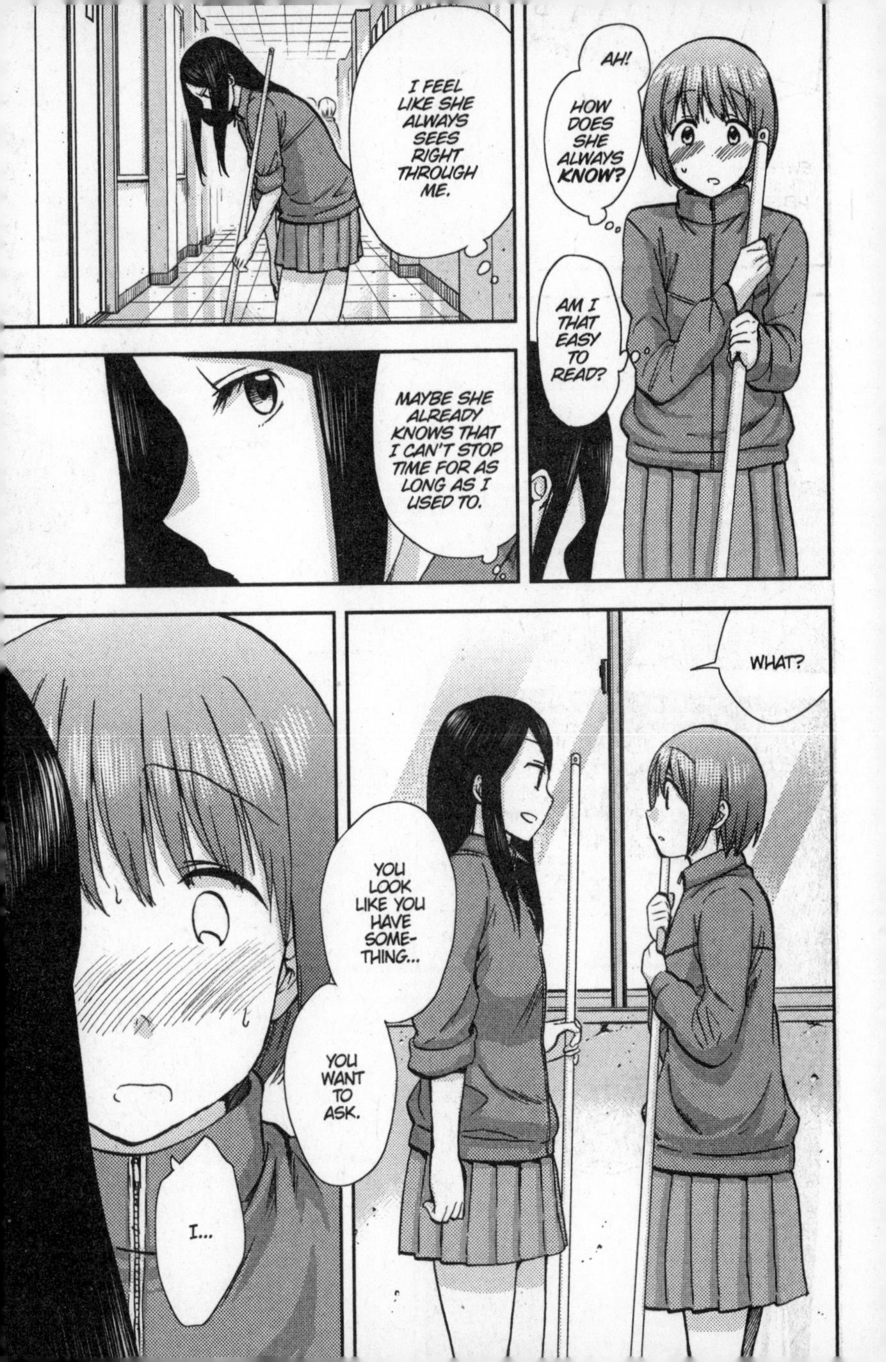

AH!
HOW DOES SHE ALWAYS KNOW?
AM I THAT EASY TO READ?
I FEEL LIKE SHE ALWAYS SEES RIGHT THROUGH ME.
MAYBE SHE ALREADY KNOWS THAT I CAN'T STOP TIME FOR AS LONG AS I USED TO.
WHAT?
YOU LOOK LIKE YOU HAVE SOME-THING...
YOU WANT TO ASK.
I...

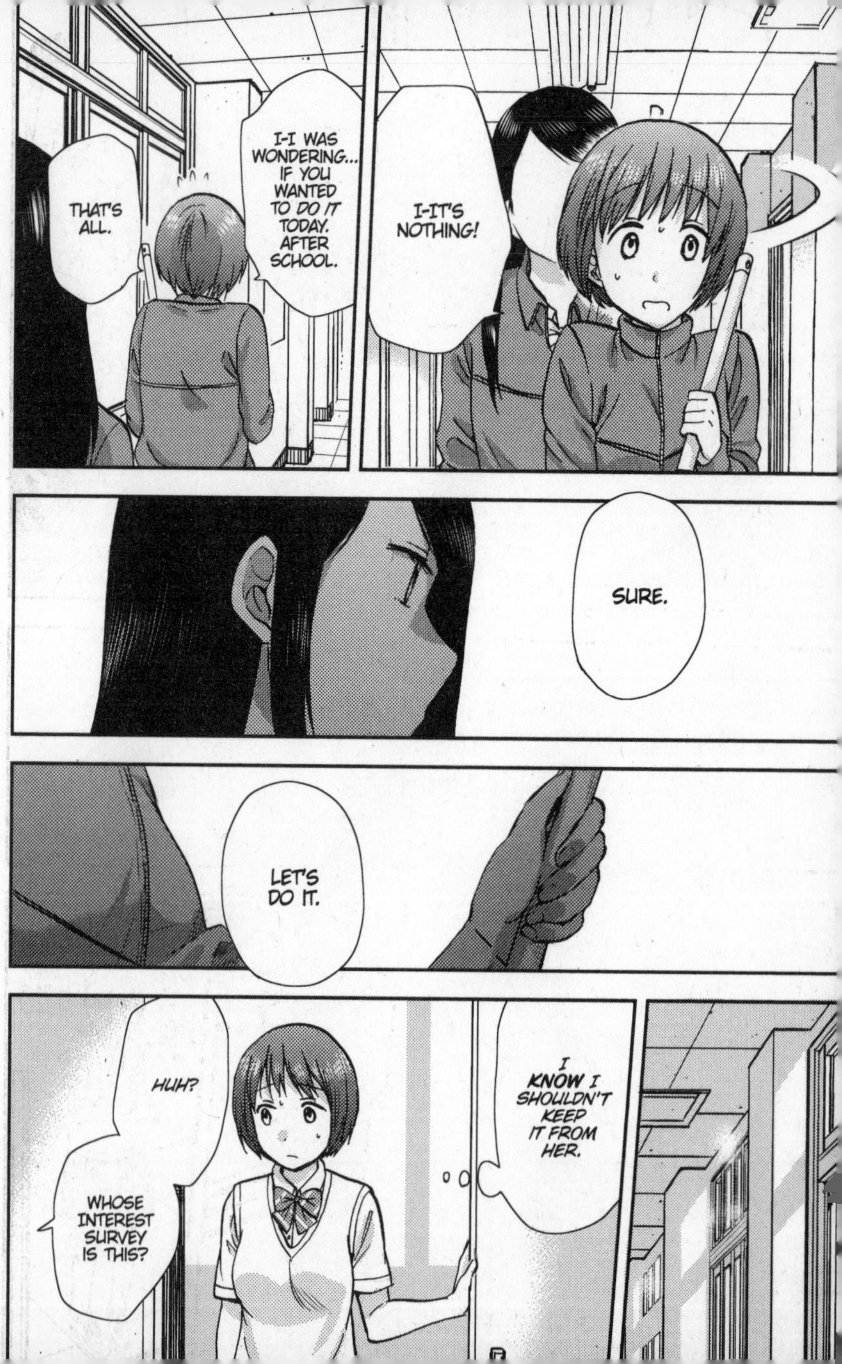
I-IT'S NOTHING!
I-I WAS WONDERING... IF YOU WANTED TO *DO IT* TODAY. AFTER SCHOOL.
THAT'S ALL.
SURE.
LET'S DO IT.
I *KNOW* I SHOULDN'T KEEP IT FROM HER.
HUH?
WHOSE INTEREST SURVEY IS THIS?

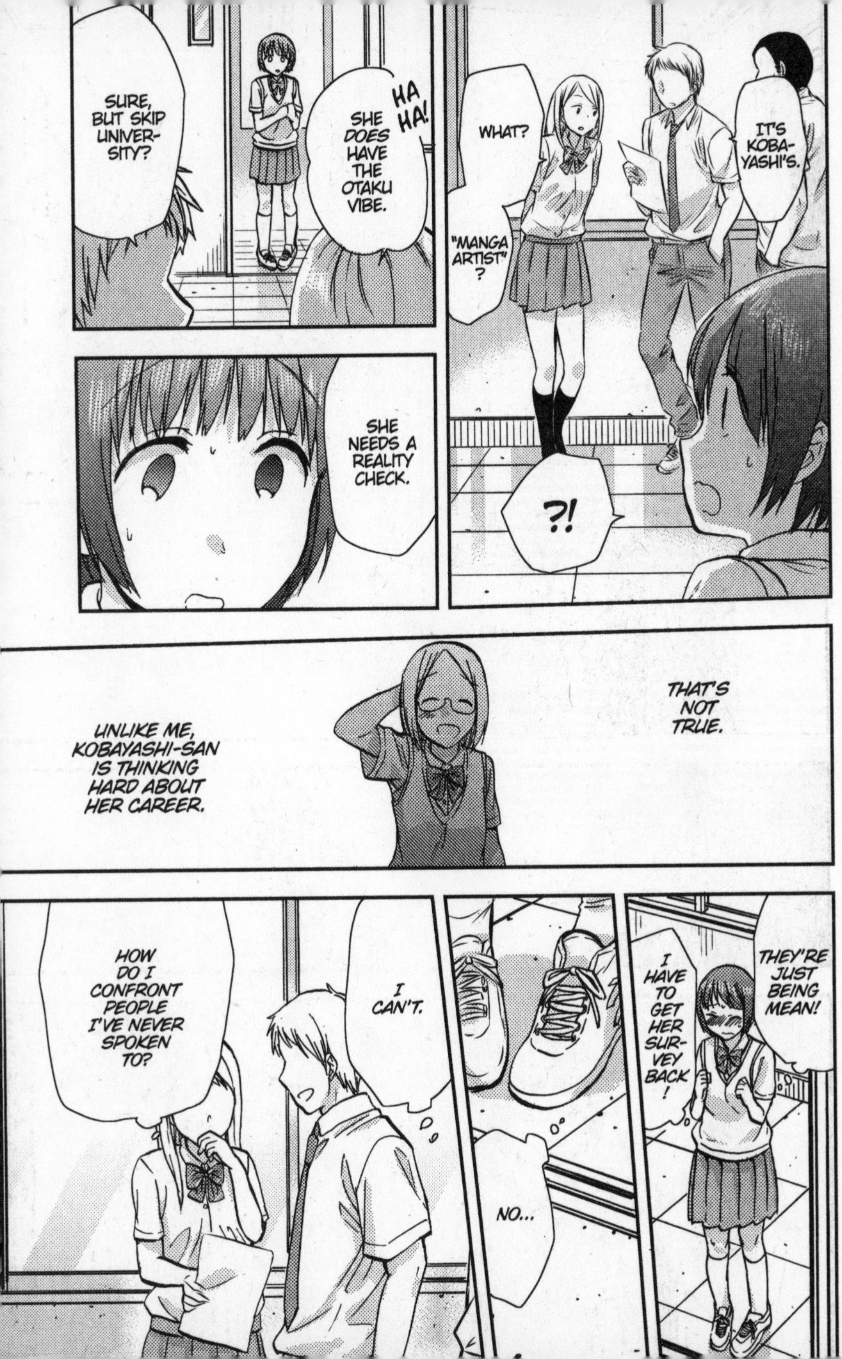
IT'S KOBA-YASHI'S.
WHAT?
"MANGA ARTIST"?
?!
HA HA!
SHE DOES HAVE THE OTAKU VIBE.
SURE, BUT SKIP UNIVER-SITY?
SHE NEEDS A REALITY CHECK.
THAT'S NOT TRUE.
UNLIKE ME, KOBAYASHI-SAN IS THINKING HARD ABOUT HER CAREER.
THEY'RE JUST BEING MEAN!
I HAVE TO GET HER SUR-VEY BACK!
NO...
I CAN'T.
HOW DO I CONFRONT PEOPLE I'VE NEVER SPOKEN TO?

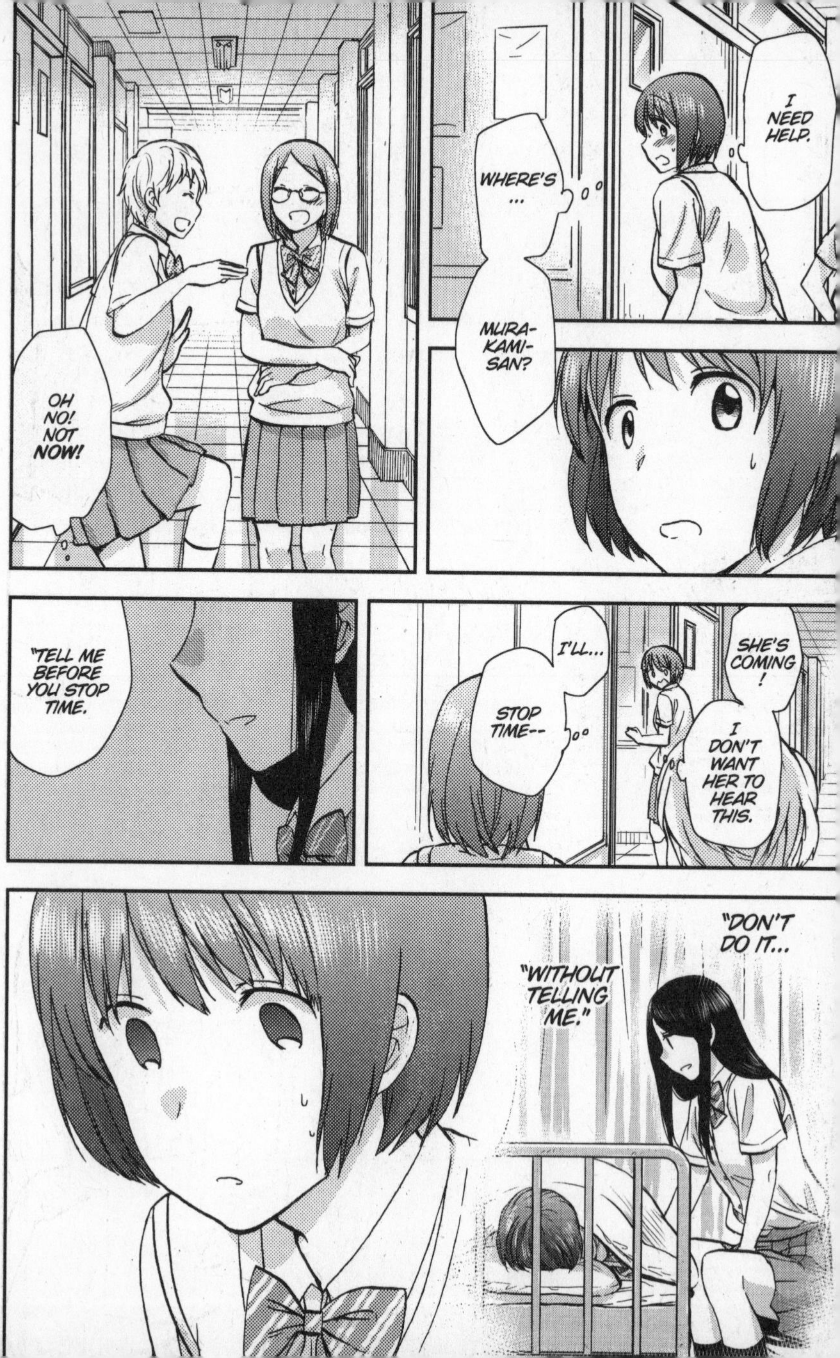
I NEED HELP.
WHERE'S ... MURAKAMI-SAN?
OH NO! NOT NOW!
SHE'S COMING!
I DON'T WANT HER TO HEAR THIS.
I'LL...
STOP TIME--
"TELL ME BEFORE YOU STOP TIME.
"DON'T DO IT...
"WITHOUT TELLING ME."

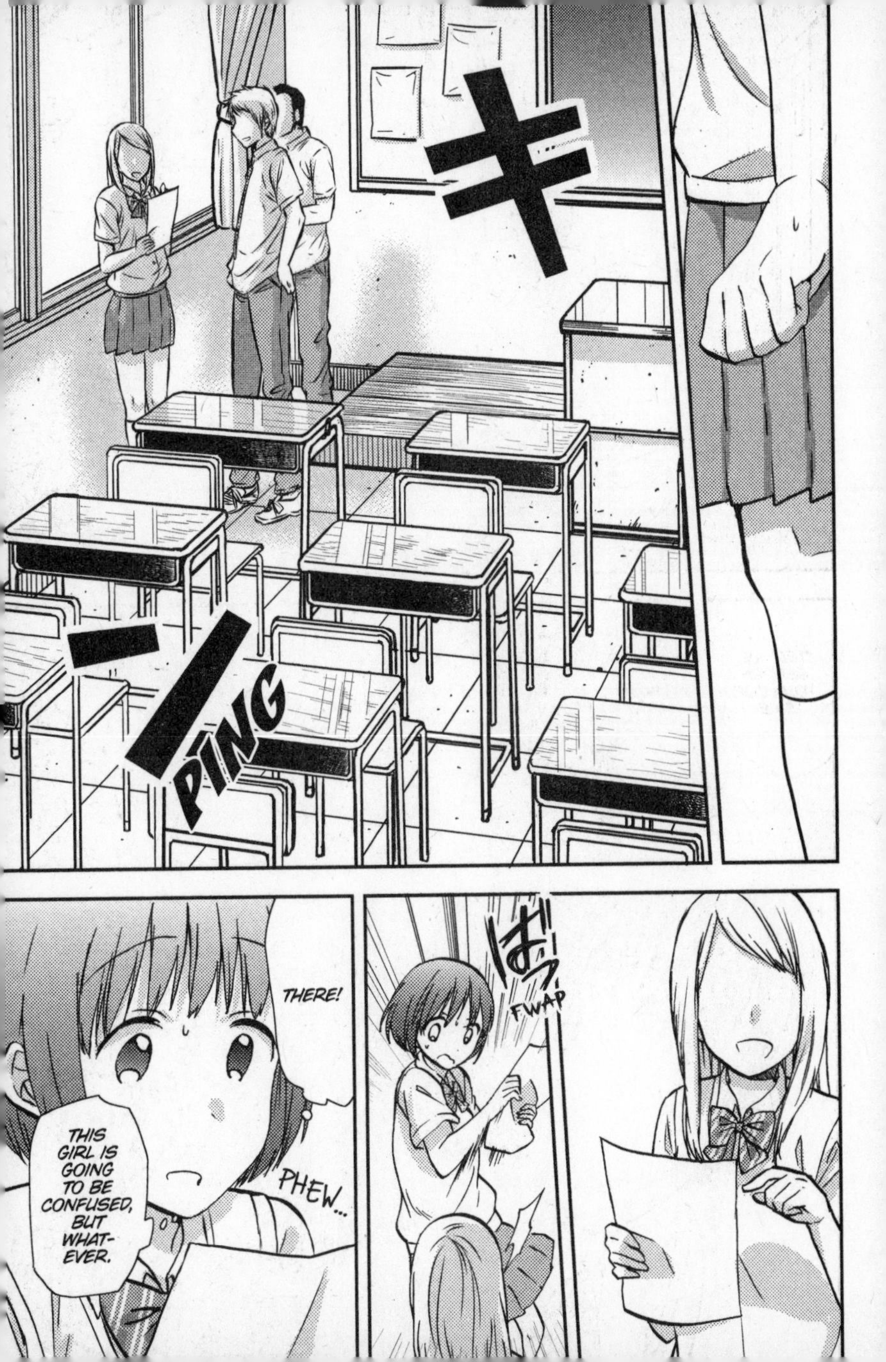
PING
ばっ
FWAP
THERE!
THIS GIRL IS GOING TO BE CONFUSED, BUT WHATEVER.
PHEW...

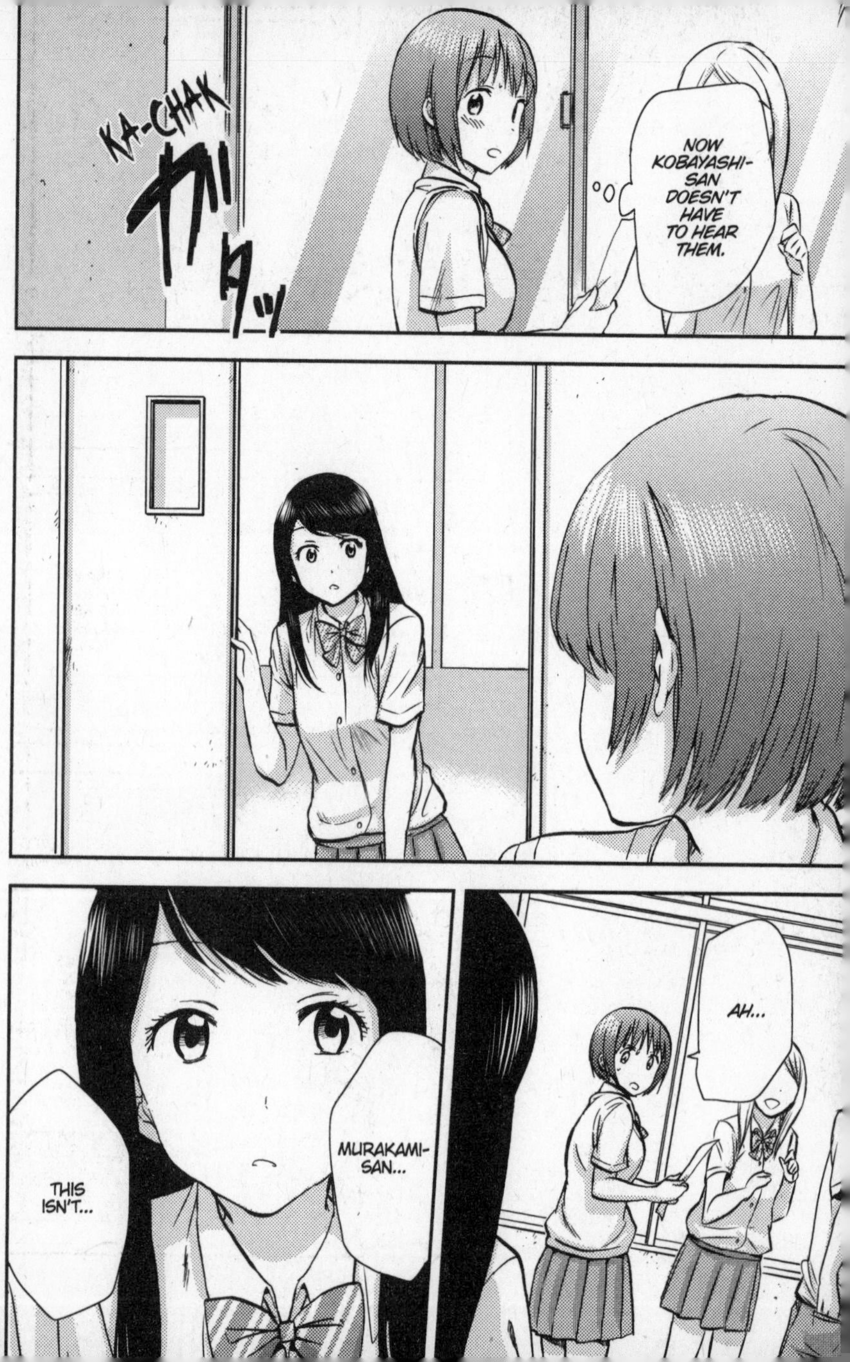
NOW KOBAYASHI-SAN DOESN'T HAVE TO HEAR THEM.
KA-CHAK
AH...
MURAKAMI-SAN...
THIS ISN'T...

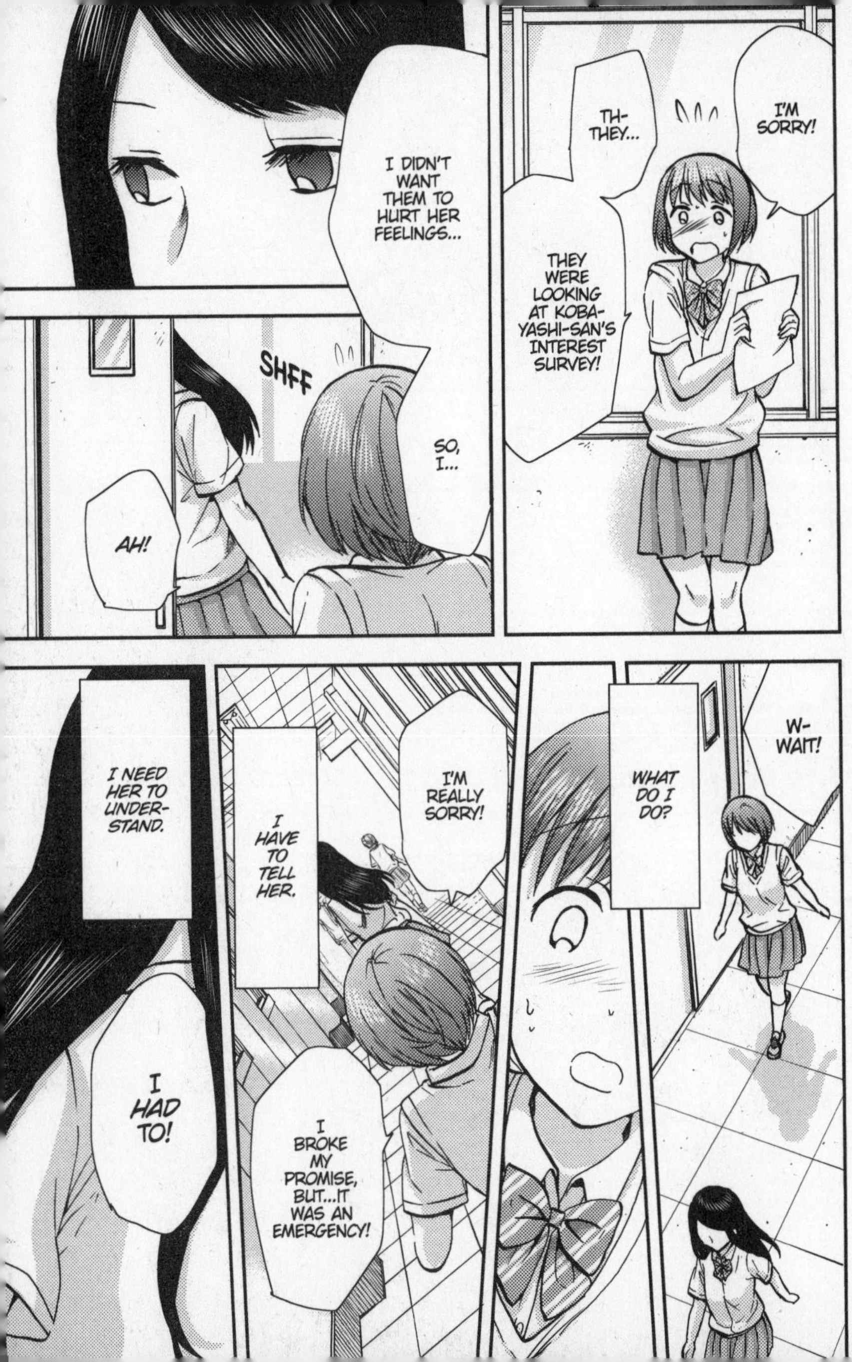
I'M SORRY!
TH- THEY...
THEY WERE LOOKING AT KOBA-YASHI-SAN'S INTEREST SURVEY!
I DIDN'T WANT THEM TO HURT HER FEELINGS...
SO, I...
SHFF
AH!
W- WAIT!
WHAT DO I DO?
I'M REALLY SORRY!
I HAVE TO TELL HER.
I BROKE MY PROMISE, BUT...IT WAS AN EMERGENCY!
I NEED HER TO UNDER-STAND.
I HAD TO!

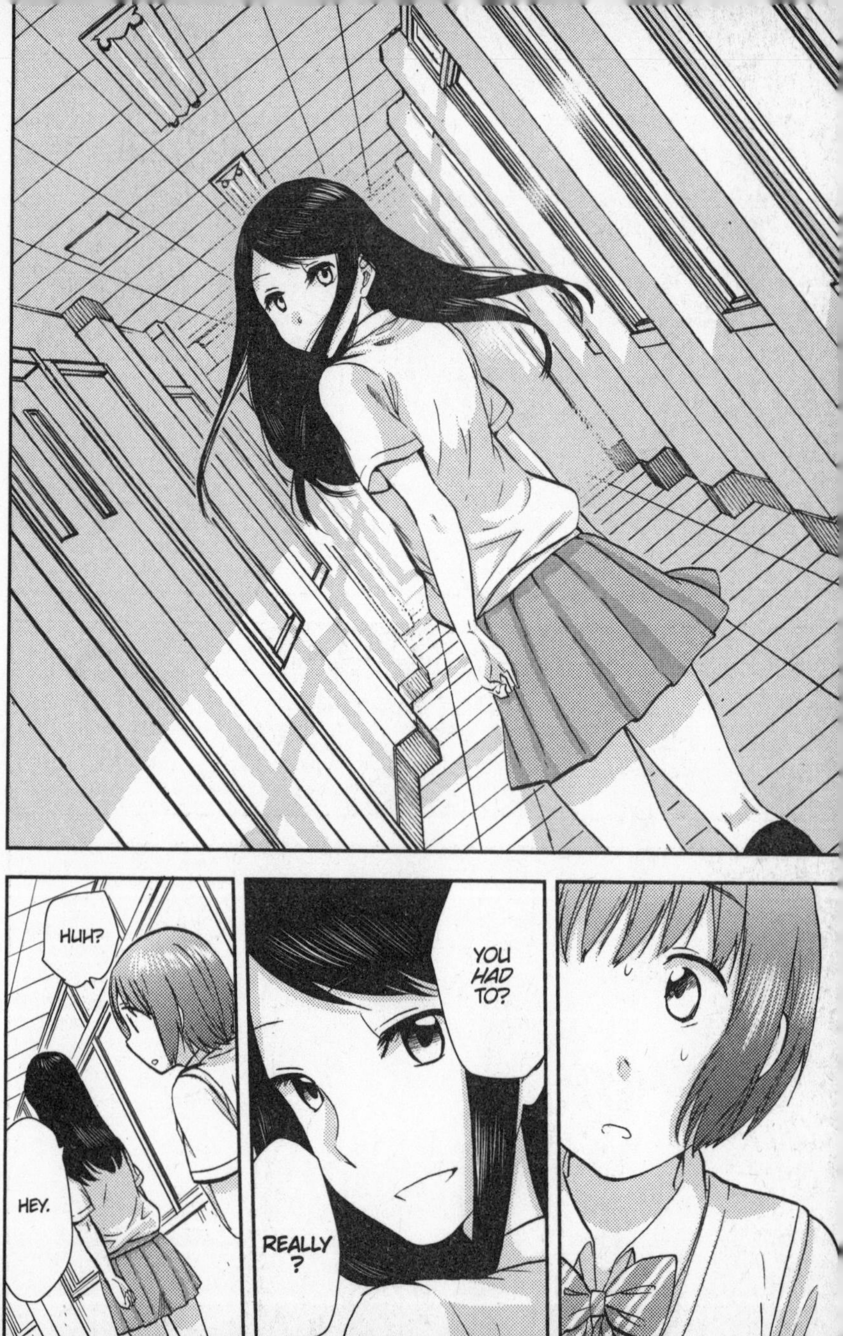
YOU HAD TO?
REALLY ?
HUH?
HEY.

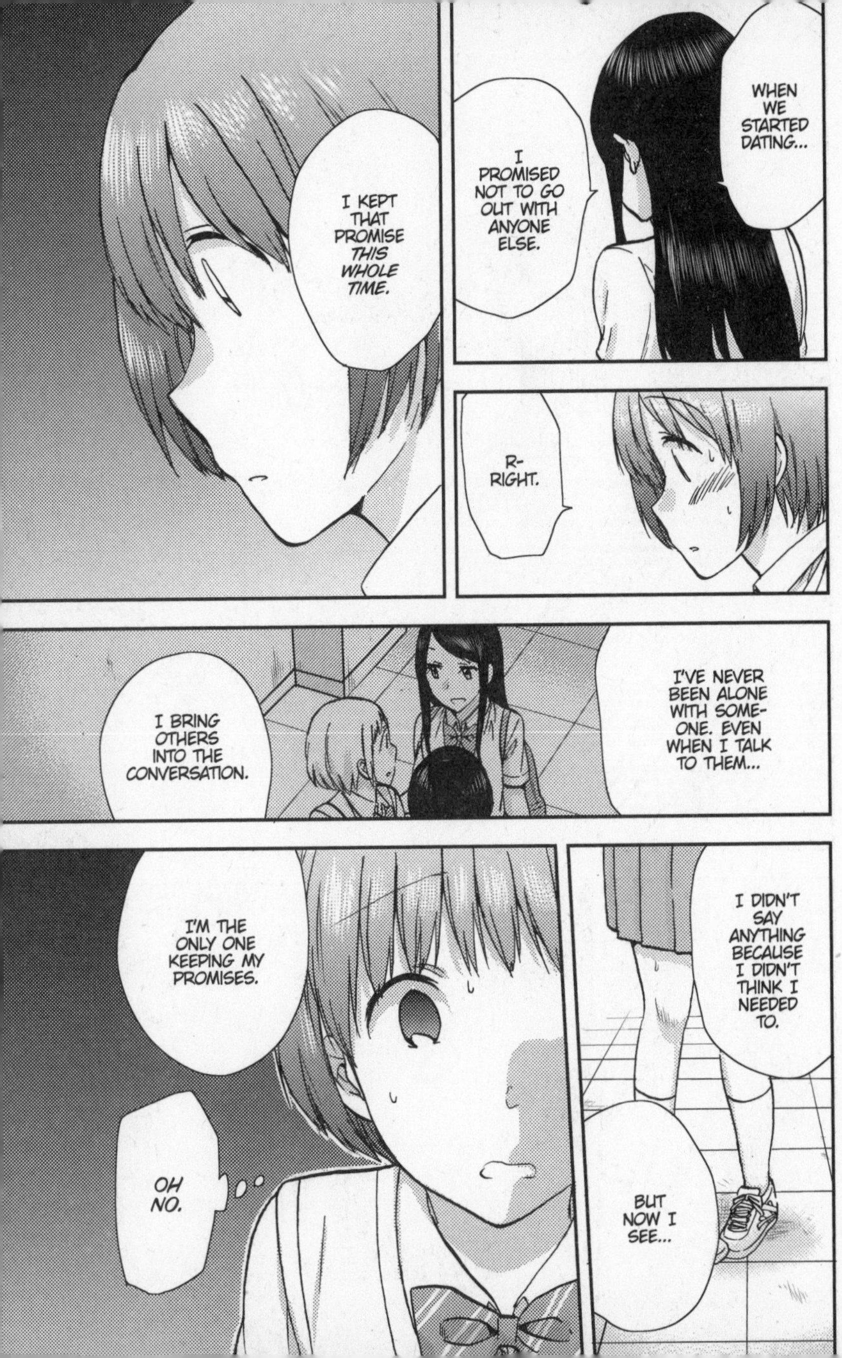
WHEN WE STARTED DATING...
I PROMISED NOT TO GO OUT WITH ANYONE ELSE.
R- RIGHT.
I KEPT THAT PROMISE *THIS WHOLE TIME.*
I'VE NEVER BEEN ALONE WITH SOME-ONE. EVEN WHEN I TALK TO THEM...
I BRING OTHERS INTO THE CONVERSATION.
I DIDN'T SAY ANYTHING BECAUSE I DIDN'T THINK I NEEDED TO.
BUT NOW I SEE...
I'M THE ONLY ONE KEEPING MY PROMISES.
OH NO.

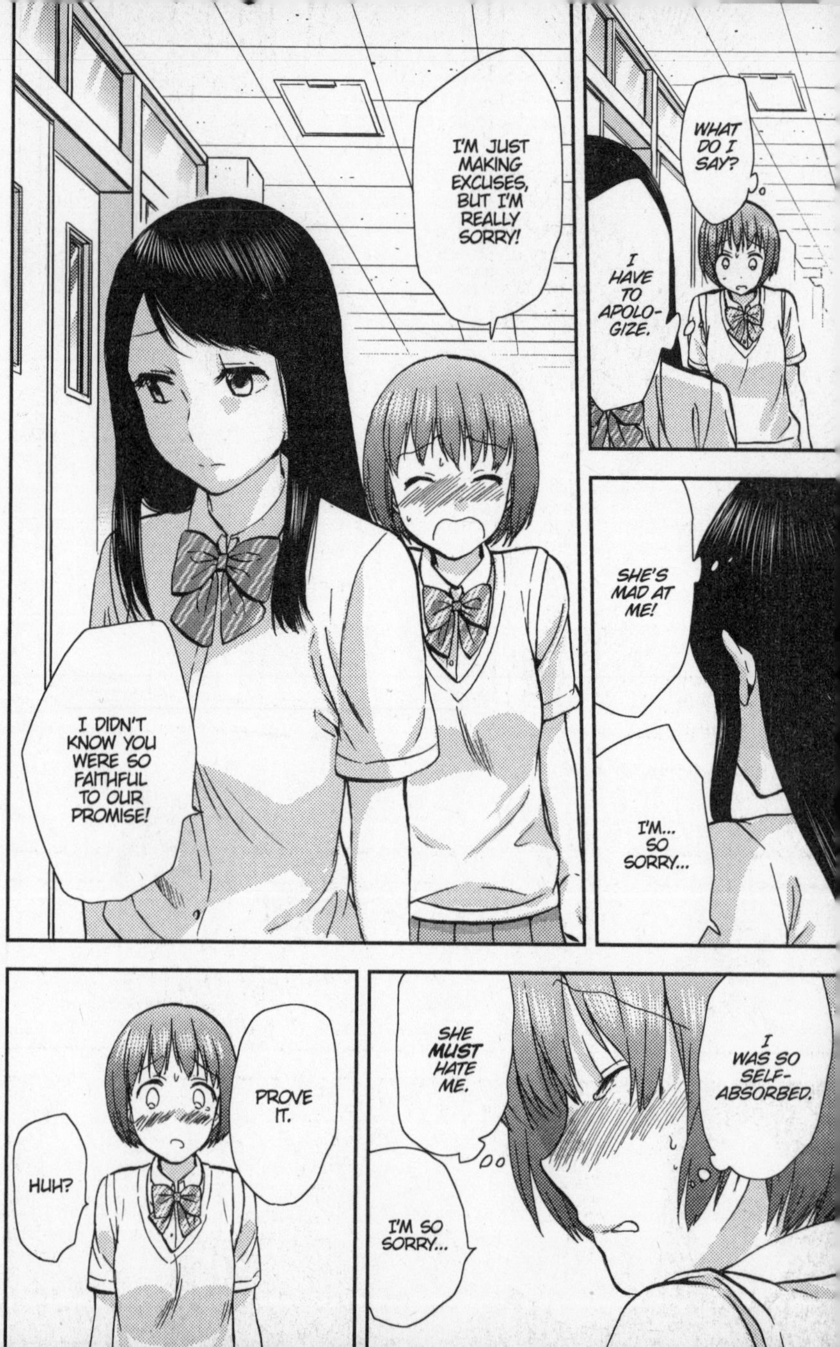
WHAT DO I SAY?
I HAVE TO APOLOGIZE.
SHE'S MAD AT ME!
I'M... SO SORRY...
I'M JUST MAKING EXCUSES, BUT I'M REALLY SORRY!
I DIDN'T KNOW YOU WERE SO FAITHFUL TO OUR PROMISE!
I WAS SO SELF-ABSORBED.
SHE **MUST** HATE ME.
I'M SO SORRY...
PROVE IT.
HUH?

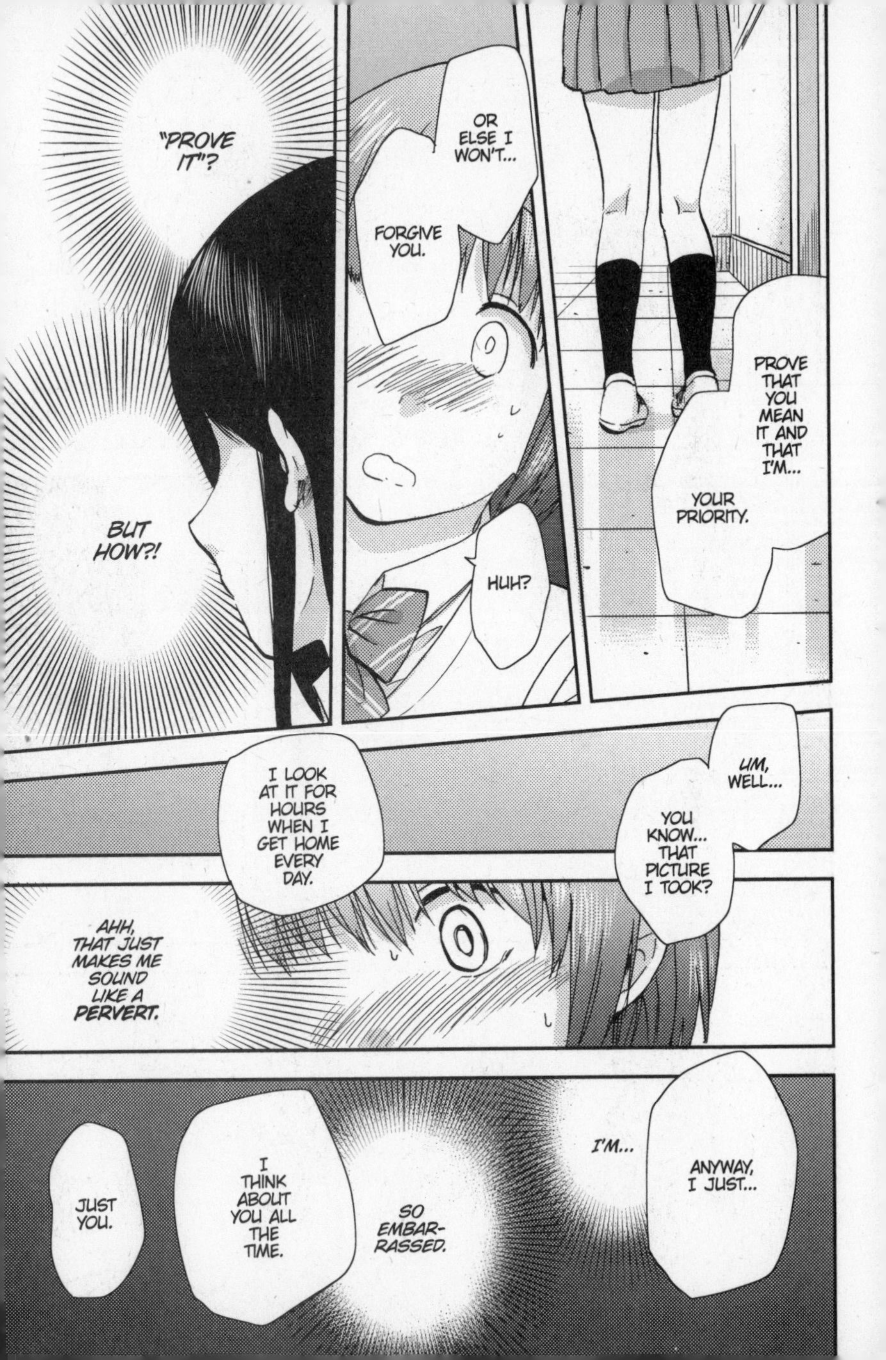

PROVE THAT YOU MEAN IT AND THAT I'M...
YOUR PRIORITY.
OR ELSE I WON'T...
FORGIVE YOU.
HUH?
"PROVE IT"?
BUT HOW?!
UM, WELL...
YOU KNOW... THAT PICTURE I TOOK?
I LOOK AT IT FOR HOURS WHEN I GET HOME EVERY DAY.
AHH, THAT JUST MAKES ME SOUND LIKE A PERVERT.
ANYWAY, I JUST...
I'M...
SO EMBARRASSED.
I THINK ABOUT YOU ALL THE TIME.
JUST YOU.

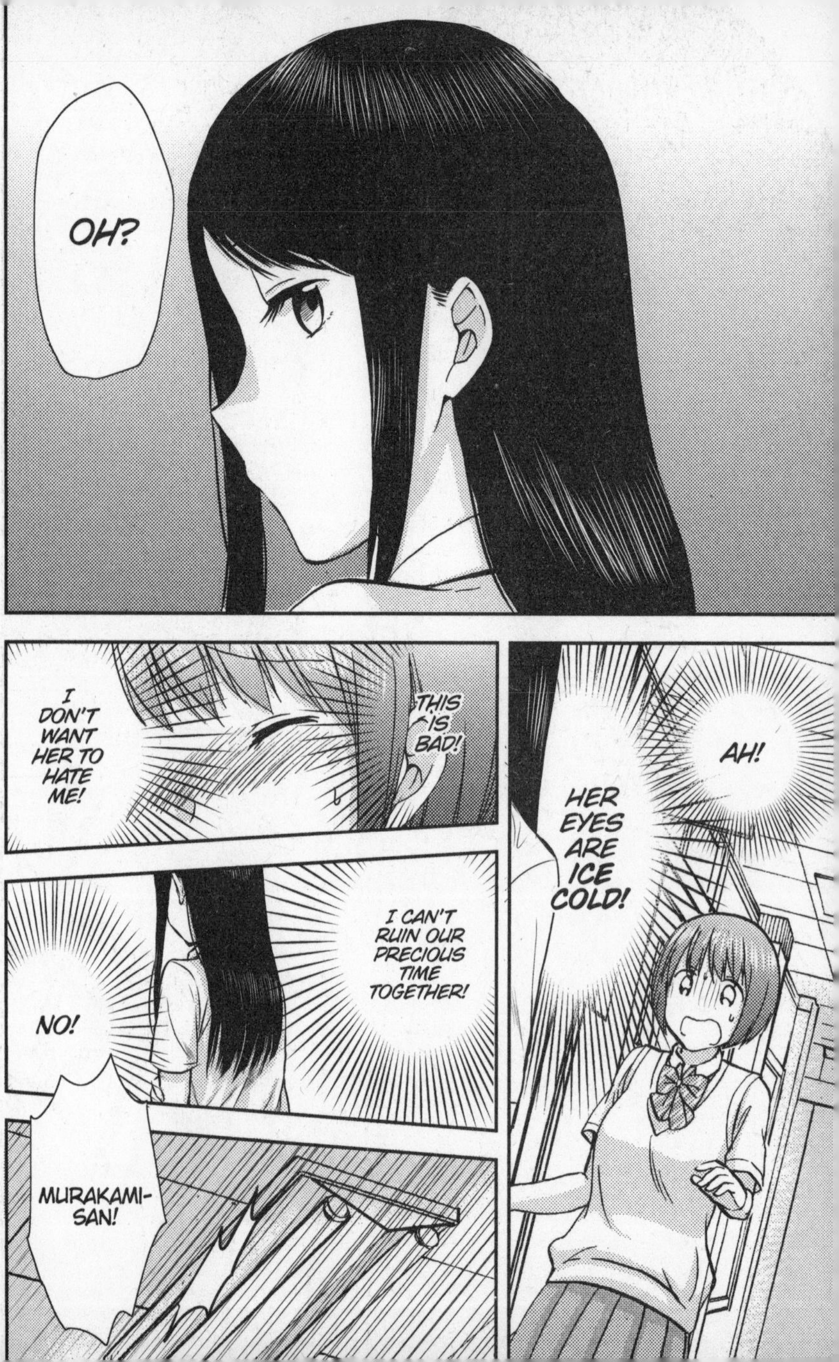
OH?
AH!
HER EYES ARE ICE COLD!
THIS IS BAD!
I DON'T WANT HER TO HATE ME!
I CAN'T RUIN OUR PRECIOUS TIME TOGETHER!
NO!
MURAKAMI-SAN!

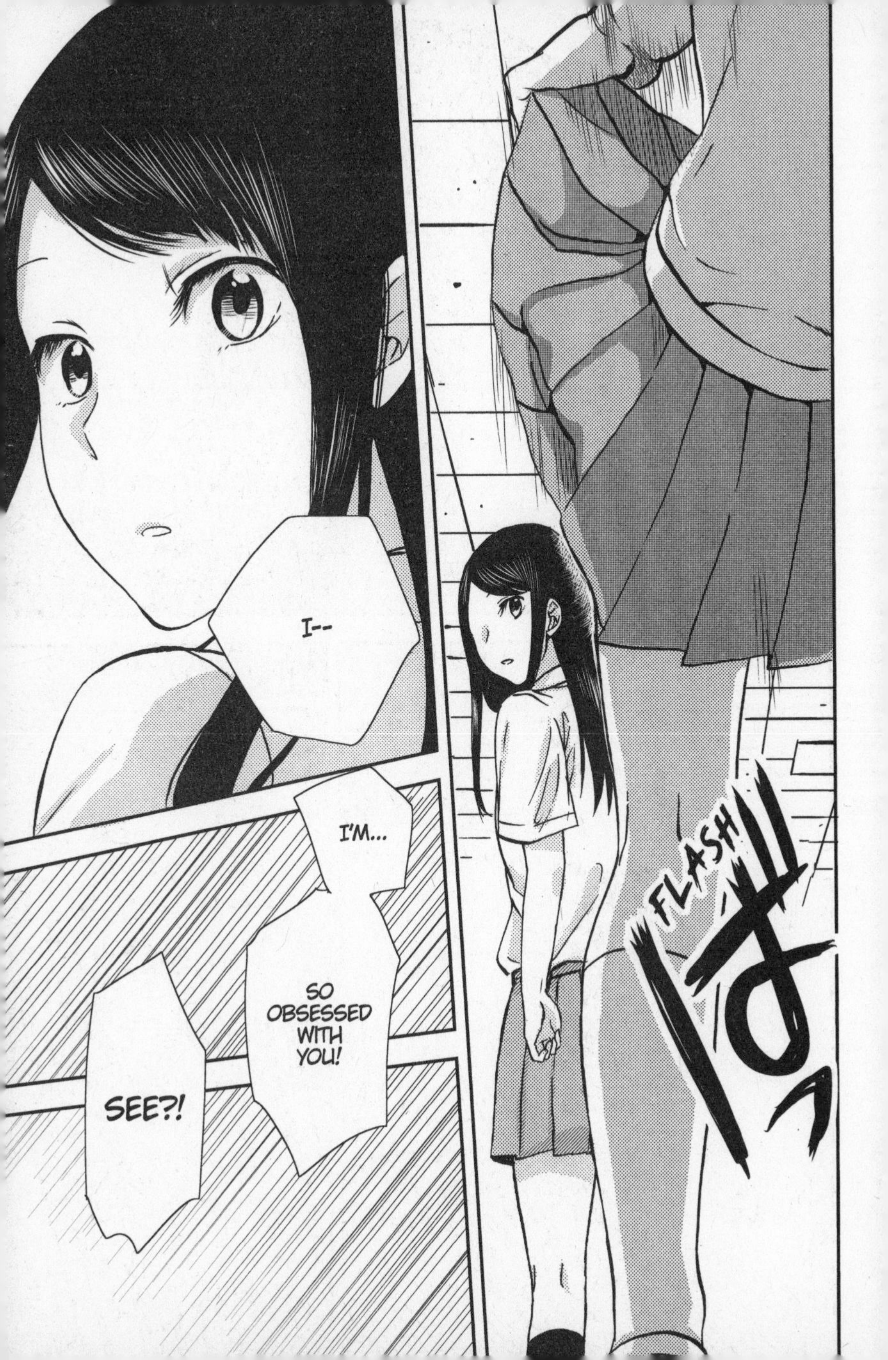
FLASH
I--
I'M...
SO OBSESSED WITH YOU!
SEE?!

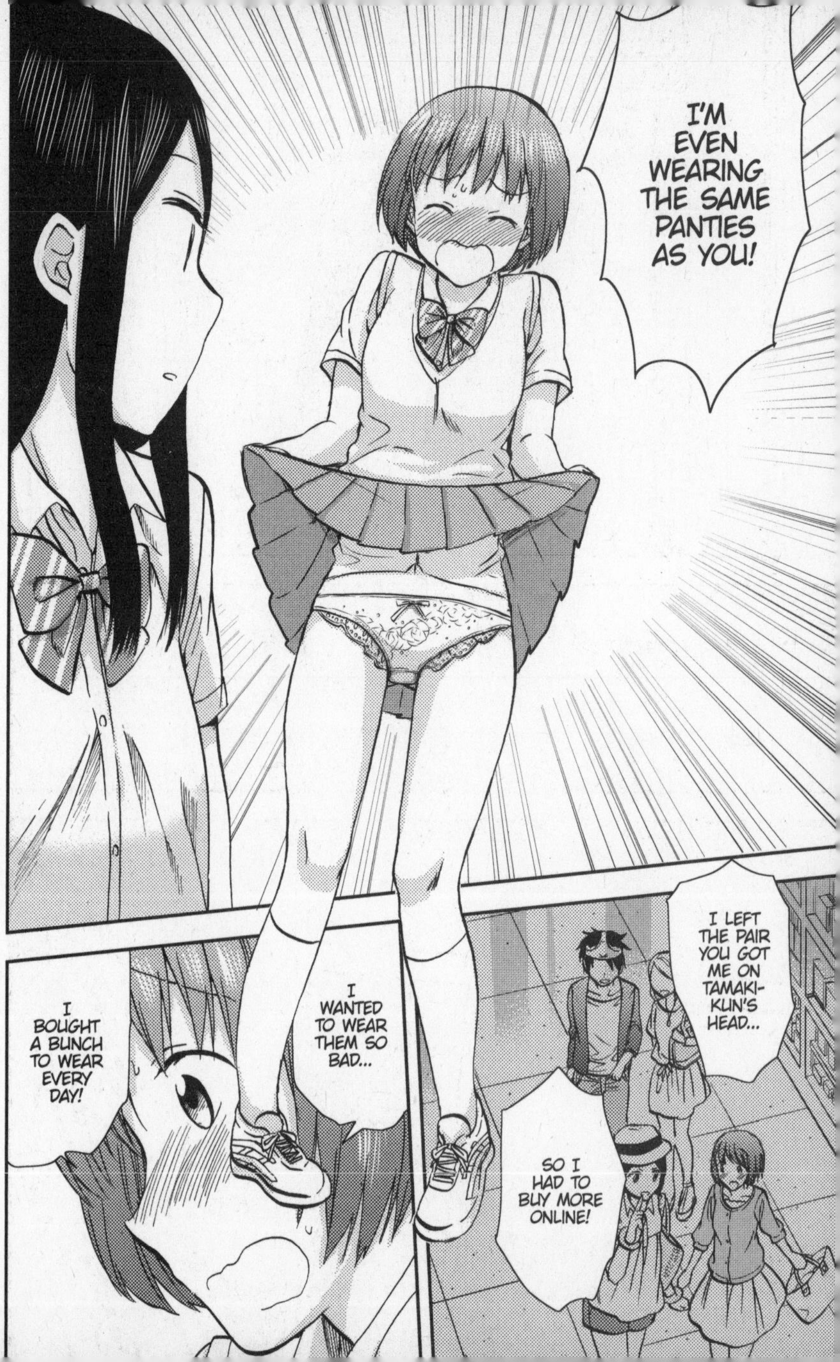
I'M EVEN WEARING THE SAME PANTIES AS YOU!
I LEFT THE PAIR YOU GOT ME ON TAMAKI-KUN'S HEAD...
SO I HAD TO BUY MORE ONLINE!
I WANTED TO WEAR THEM SO BAD...
I BOUGHT A BUNCH TO WEAR EVERY DAY!

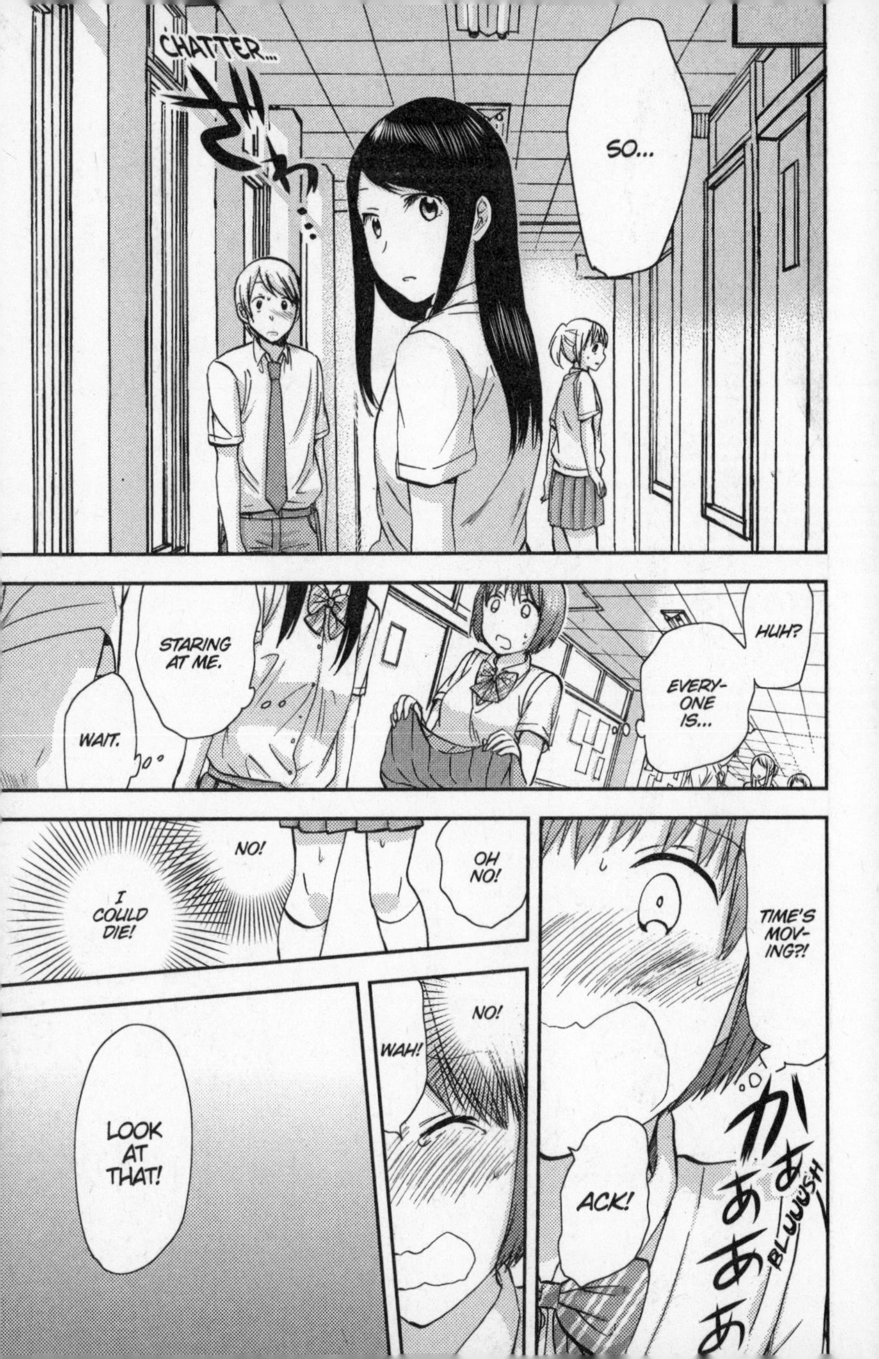
SO...
CHATTER...
HUH?
EVERY-ONE IS...
STARING AT ME.
WAIT.
TIME'S MOVING?!
OH NO!
NO!
I COULD DIE!
かあああ
BLUUUSH
ACK!
NO!
WAH!
LOOK AT THAT!

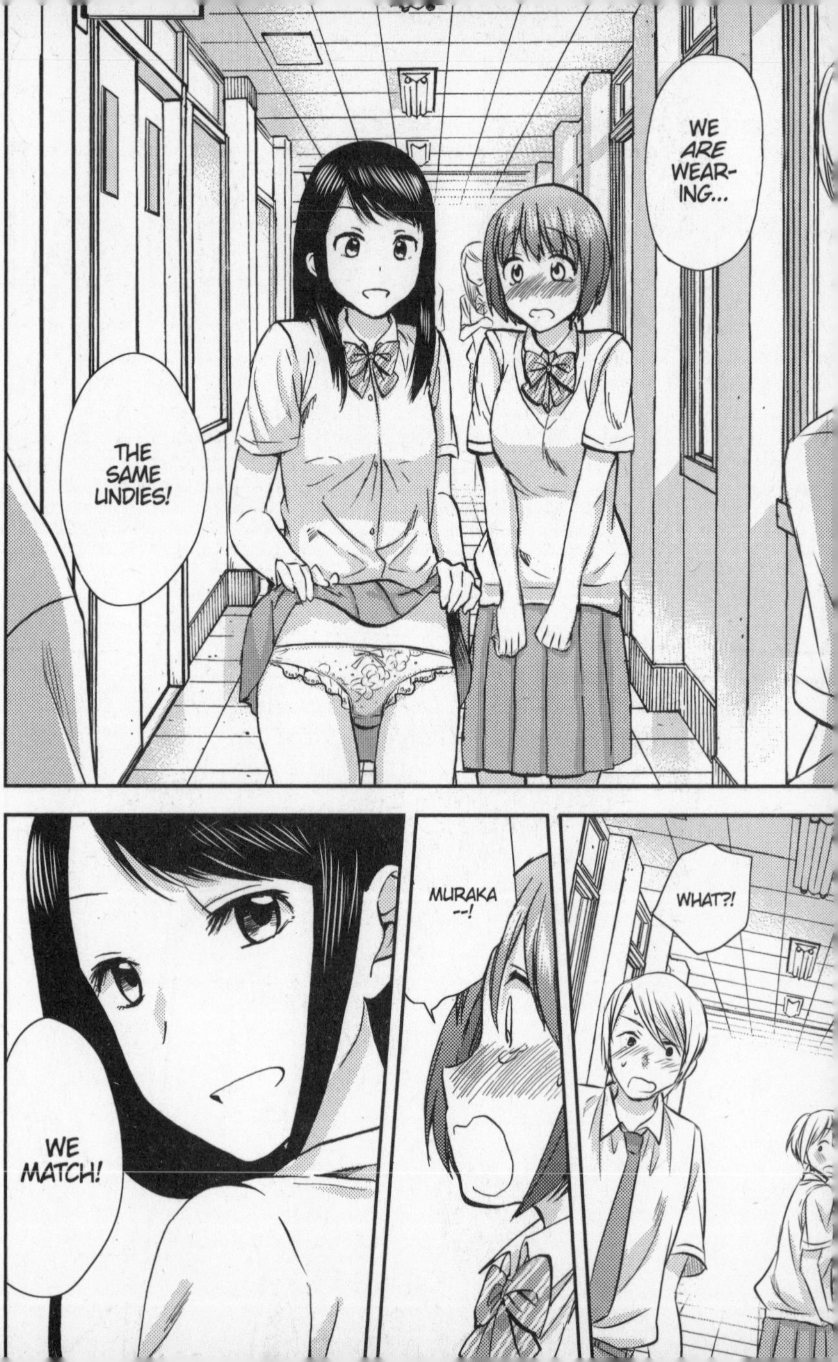
WE ARE WEAR- ING...
THE SAME UNDIES!
WHAT?!
MURAKA --!
WE MATCH!

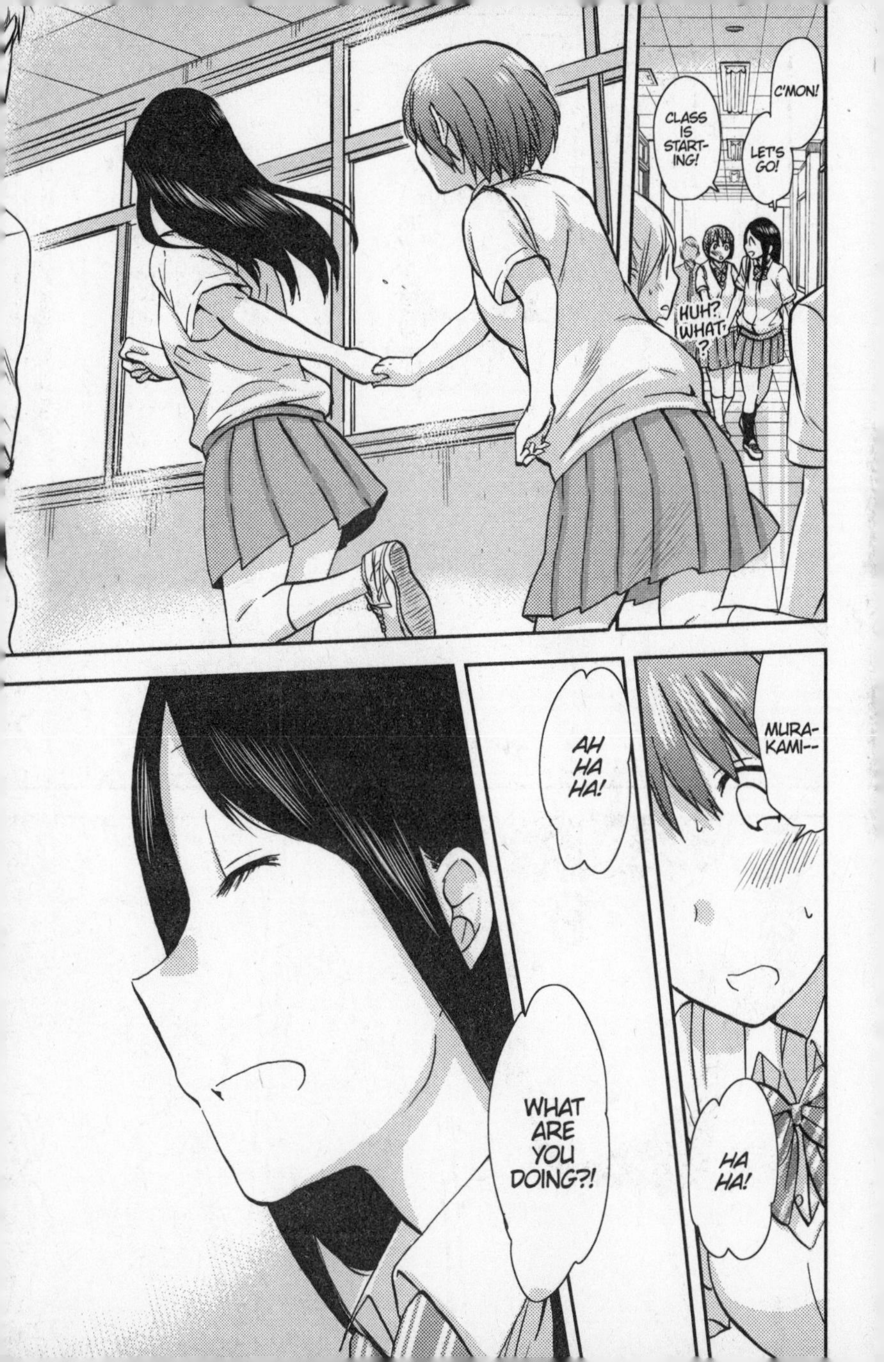
C'MON!
LET'S GO!
CLASS IS START-ING!
HUH? WHAT?
MURA-KAMI--
HA HA!
AH HA HA!
WHAT ARE YOU DOING?!

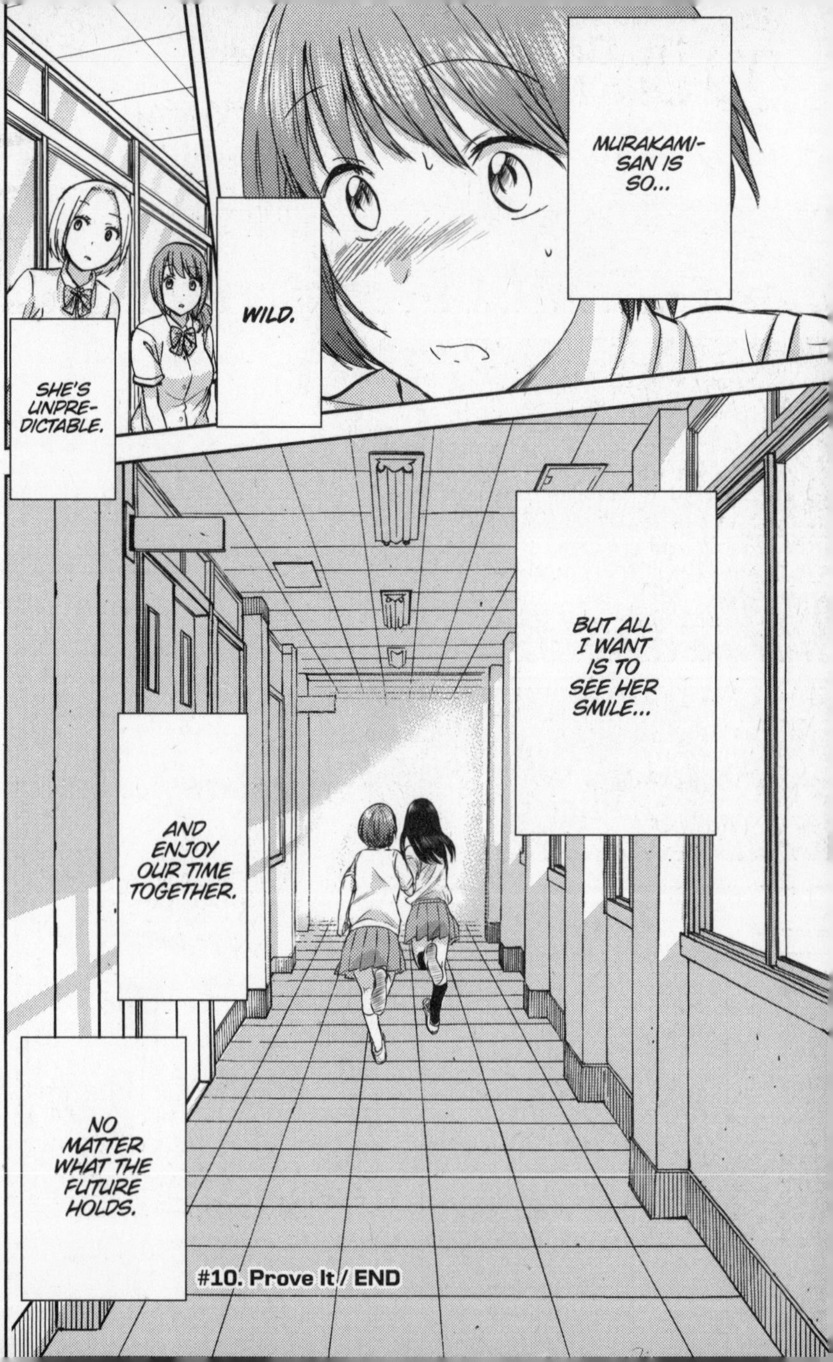
MURAKAMI-SAN IS SO...
WILD.
SHE'S UNPRE-DICTABLE.
BUT ALL I WANT IS TO SEE HER SMILE...
AND ENJOY OUR TIME TOGETHER.
NO MATTER WHAT THE FUTURE HOLDS.
#10. Prove It / END

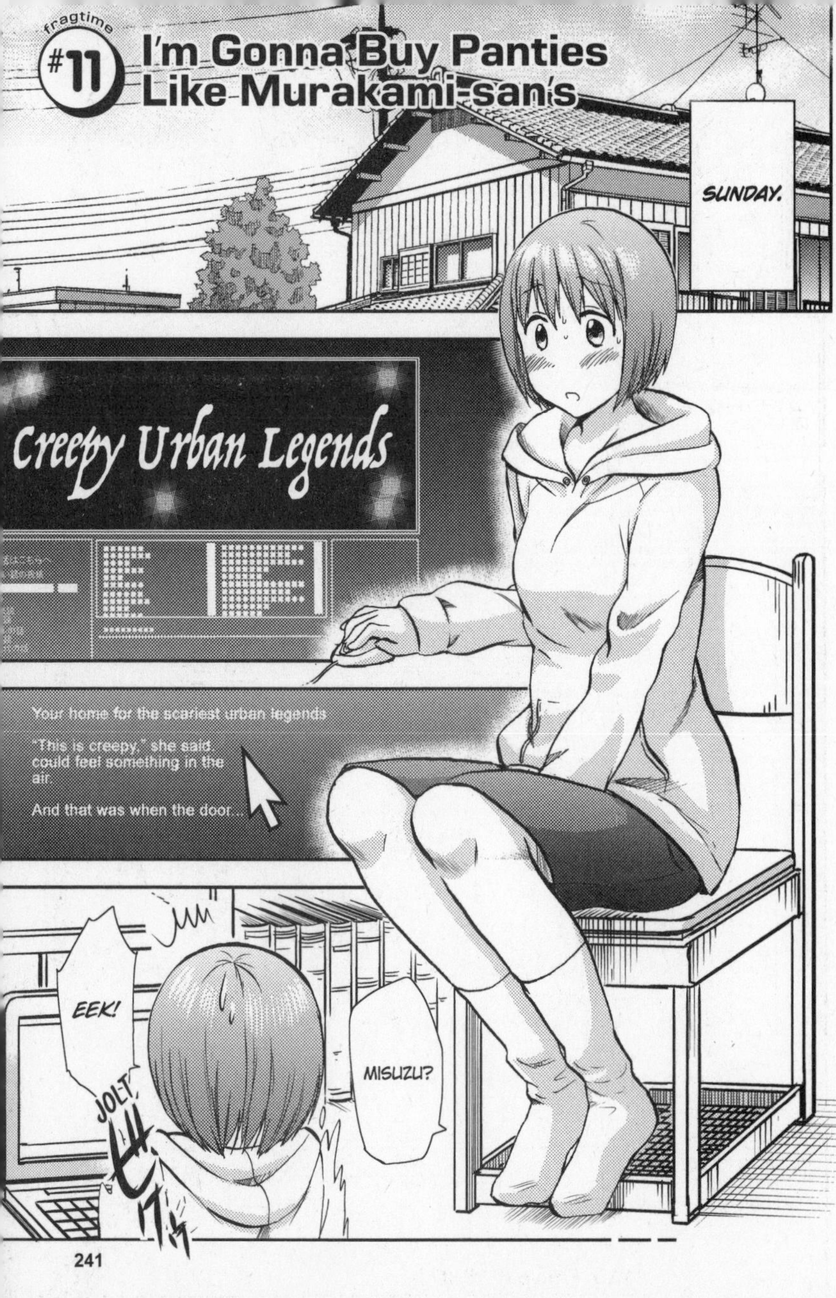
fragtime
#11 I'm Gonna Buy Panties Like Murakami-san's
SUNDAY.
Creepy Urban Legends
Your home for the scariest urban legends
"This is creepy," she said. could feel something in the air.
And that was when the door...
MISUZU?
EEK!
JOLT

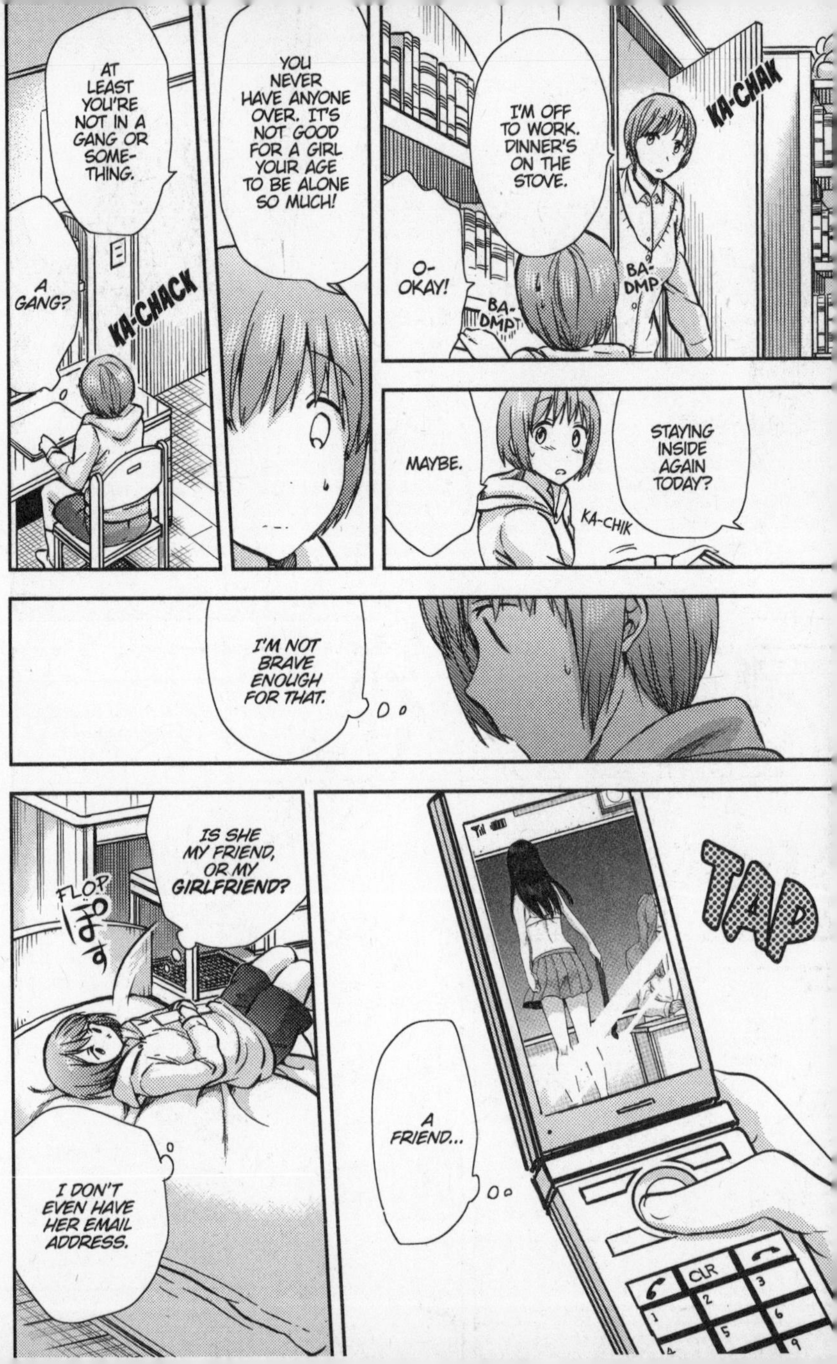
KA-CHAK
I'M OFF TO WORK. DINNER'S ON THE STOVE.
BA-DMP
BA-DMP
O-OKAY!
STAYING INSIDE AGAIN TODAY?
KA-CHIK
MAYBE.
YOU NEVER HAVE ANYONE OVER. IT'S NOT GOOD FOR A GIRL YOUR AGE TO BE ALONE SO MUCH!
AT LEAST YOU'RE NOT IN A GANG OR SOME-THING.
KA-CHACK
A GANG?
I'M NOT BRAVE ENOUGH FOR THAT.
TAP
A FRIEND...
CLR
IS SHE MY FRIEND, OR MY GIRLFRIEND?
FLOP ぽす
I DON'T EVEN HAVE HER EMAIL ADDRESS.

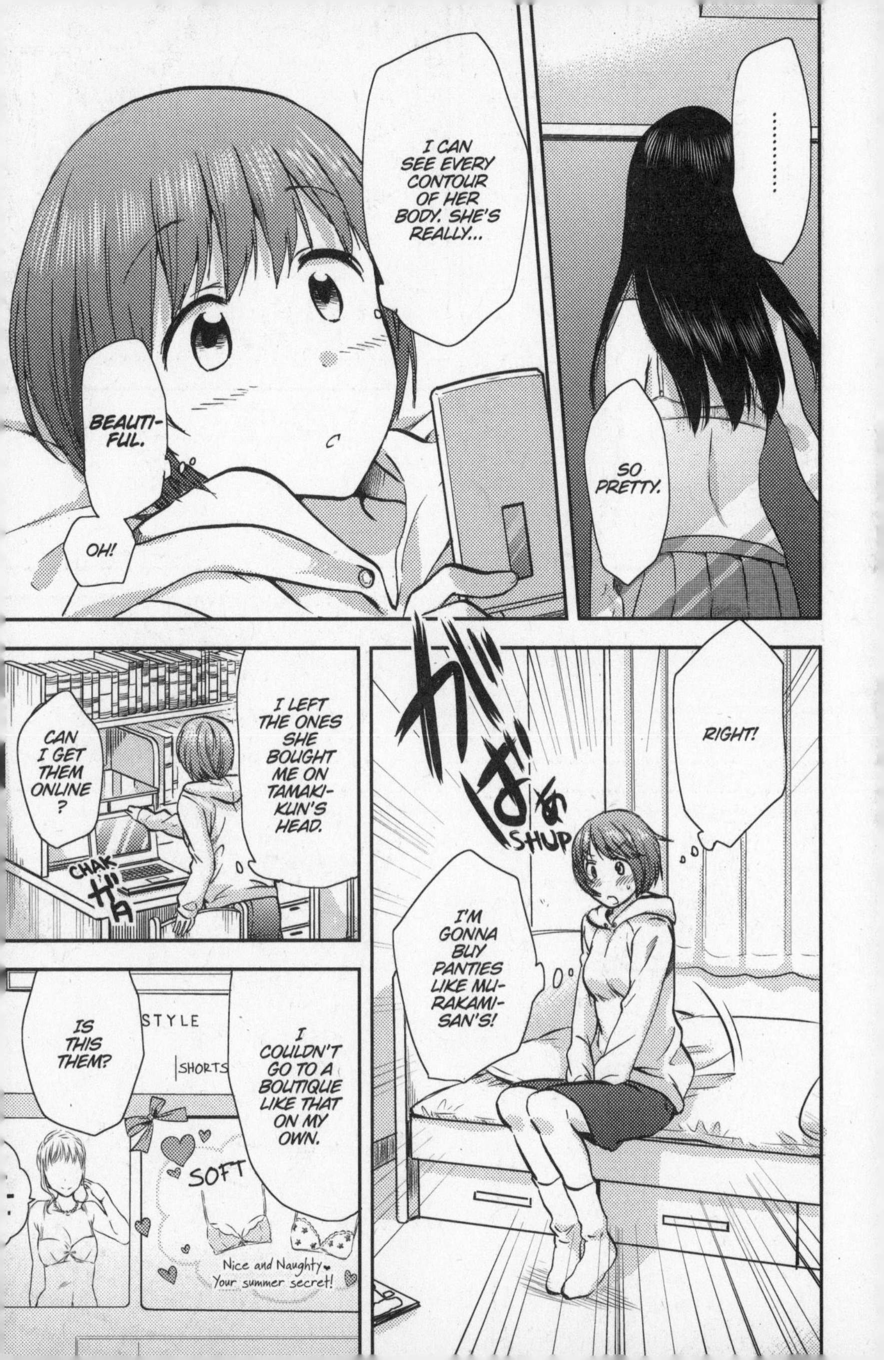
......
SO PRETTY.
I CAN SEE EVERY CONTOUR OF HER BODY. SHE'S REALLY...
BEAUTI-FUL.
OH!
SHUP
RIGHT!
I'M GONNA BUY PANTIES LIKE MU-RAKAMI-SAN'S!
I LEFT THE ONES SHE BOUGHT ME ON TAMAKI-KUN'S HEAD.
CAN I GET THEM ONLINE?
CHAK
I COULDN'T GO TO A BOUTIQUE LIKE THAT ON MY OWN.
IS THIS THEM?
STYLE
SHORTS
SOFT
Nice and Naughty
Your summer secret!

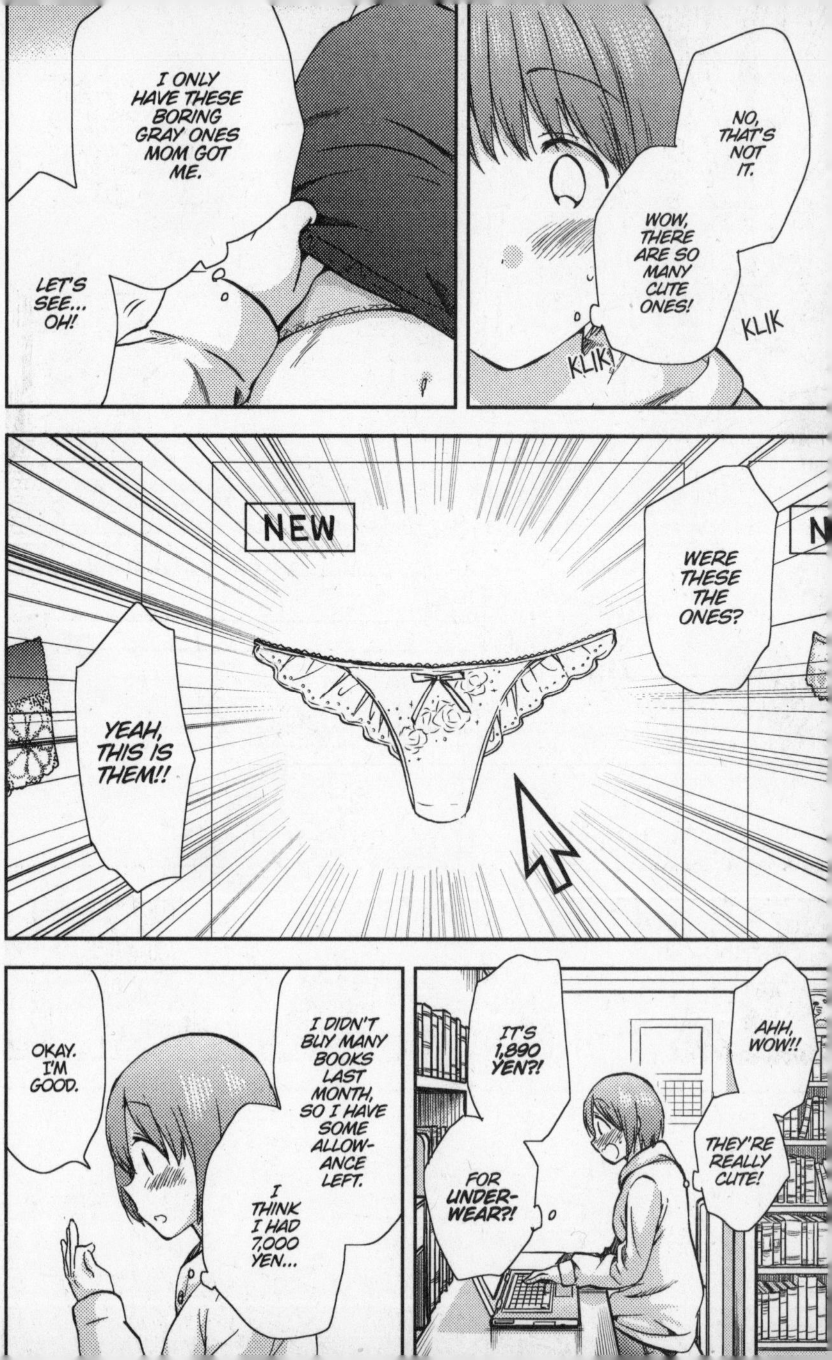

NO, THAT'S NOT IT.
WOW, THERE ARE SO MANY CUTE ONES!
KLIK
KLIK
I ONLY HAVE THESE BORING GRAY ONES MOM GOT ME.
LET'S SEE... OH!
WERE THESE THE ONES?
NEW
YEAH, THIS IS THEM!!
AHH, WOW!!
THEY'RE REALLY CUTE!
IT'S 1,890 YEN?!
FOR UNDER-WEAR?!
I DIDN'T BUY MANY BOOKS LAST MONTH, SO I HAVE SOME ALLOW-ANCE LEFT.
I THINK I HAD 7,000 YEN...
OKAY. I'M GOOD.

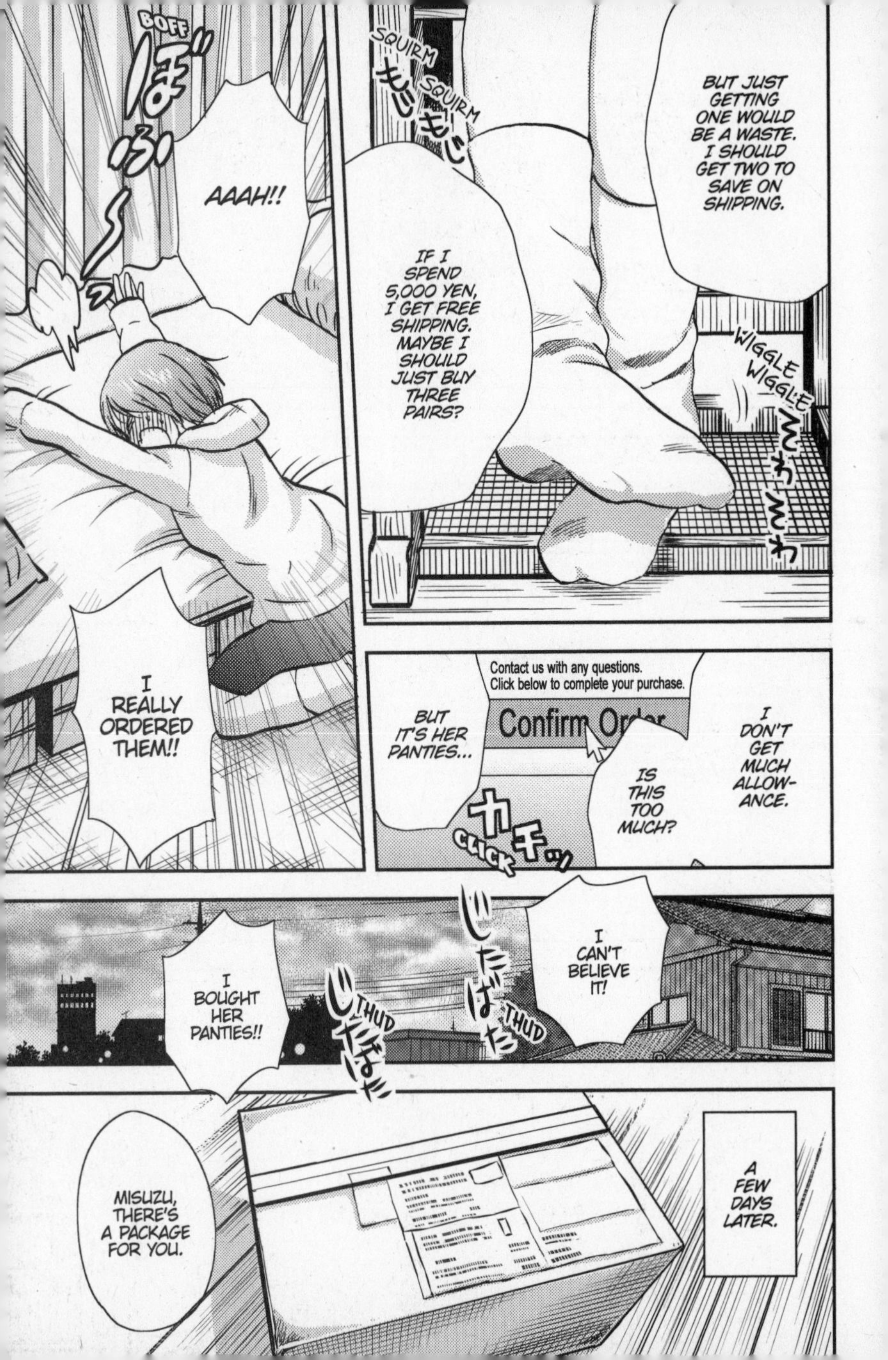
BUT JUST GETTING ONE WOULD BE A WASTE. I SHOULD GET TWO TO SAVE ON SHIPPING.
SQUIRM SQUIRM
もじもじ
WIGGLE WIGGLE
IF I SPEND 5,000 YEN, I GET FREE SHIPPING. MAYBE I SHOULD JUST BUY THREE PAIRS?
I DON'T GET MUCH ALLOWANCE.
Contact us with any questions.
Click below to complete your purchase.
Confirm Order
IS THIS TOO MUCH?
BUT IT'S HER PANTIES...
カチッ
CLICK
BOFF
AAAH!!
I REALLY ORDERED THEM!!
I CAN'T BELIEVE IT!
THUD THUD
I BOUGHT HER PANTIES!!
A FEW DAYS LATER.
MISUZU, THERE'S A PACKAGE FOR YOU.

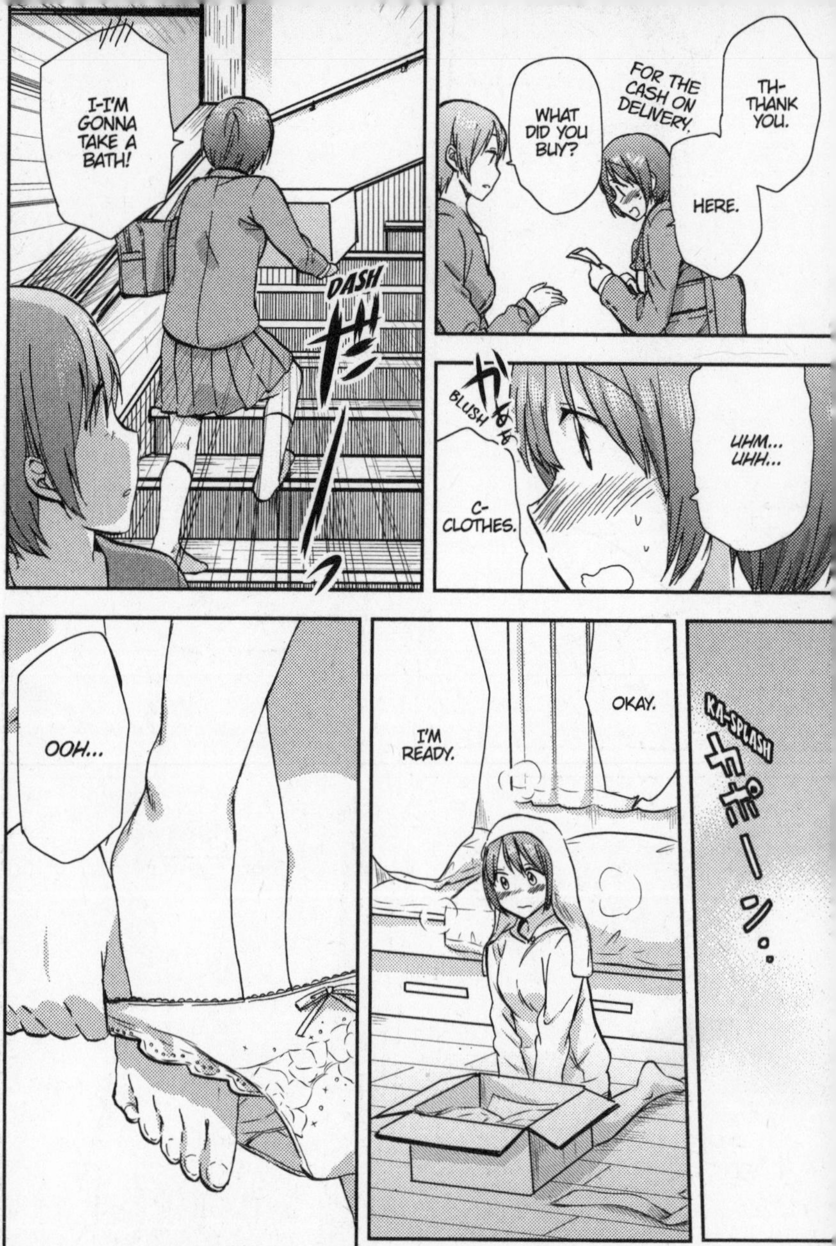
TH-THANK YOU.
FOR THE CASH ON DELIVERY.
HERE.
WHAT DID YOU BUY?
UHM... UHH...
BLUSH
C-CLOTHES.
DASH
I-I'M GONNA TAKE A BATH!
KA-SPLASH
OKAY.
I'M READY.
OOH...

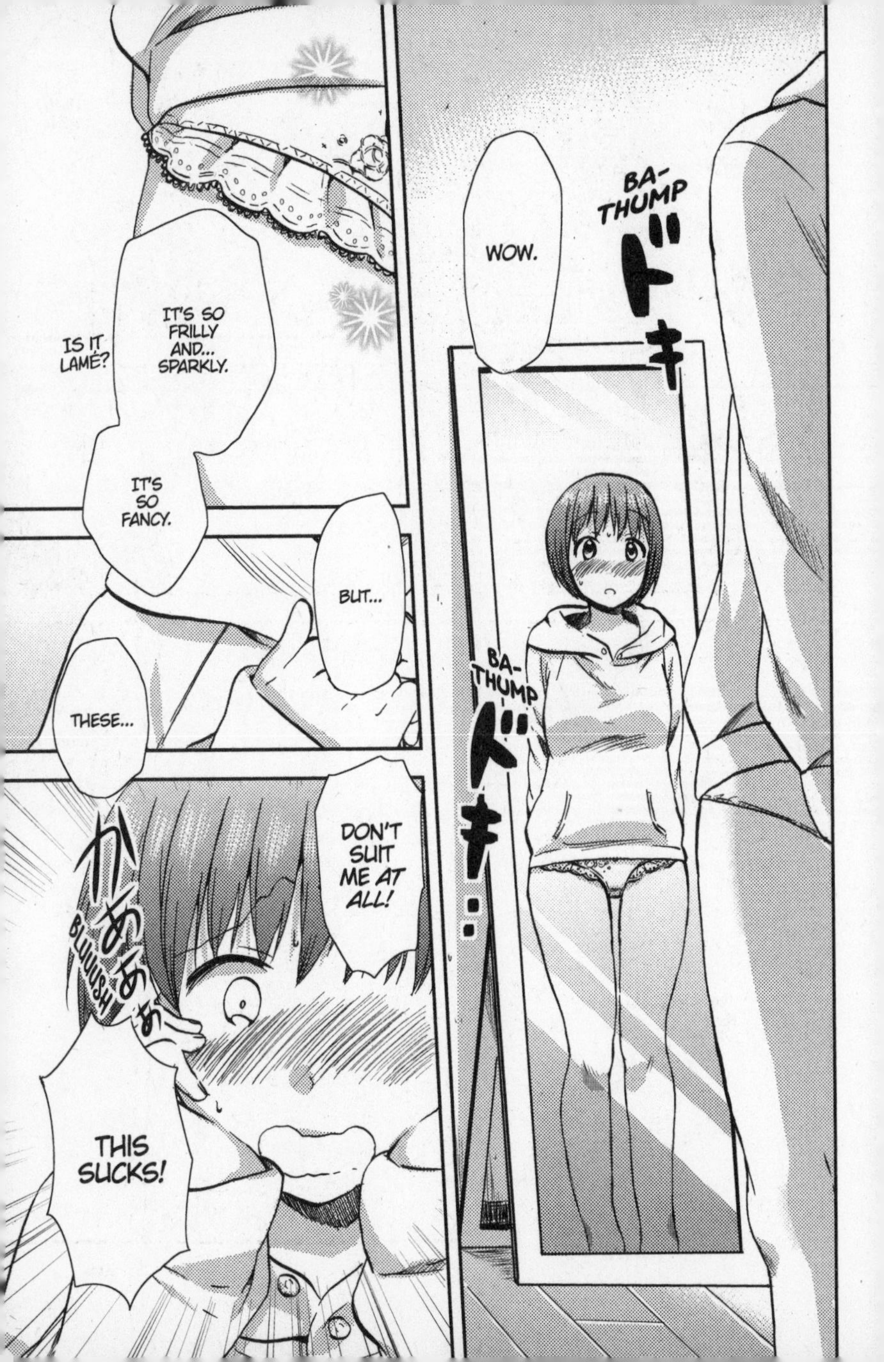
BA-THUMP
ドキ
WOW.
BA-THUMP
ドキ
IT'S SO FRILLY AND... SPARKLY.
IS IT LAMÉ?
IT'S SO FANCY.
BUT...
THESE...
DON'T SUIT ME AT ALL!
かぁぁぁ
BLUUUSH
THIS SUCKS!

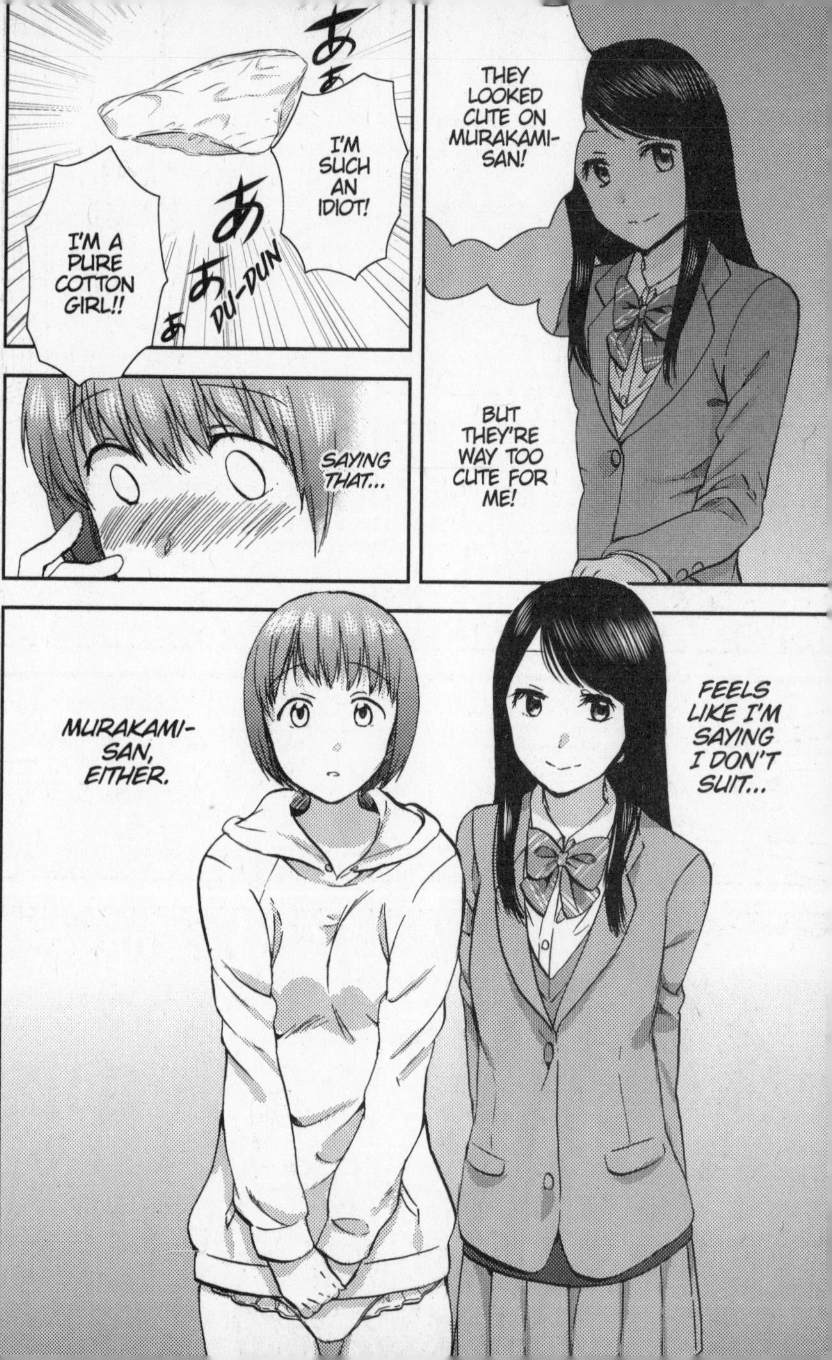
THEY LOOKED CUTE ON MURAKAMI-SAN!
BUT THEY'RE WAY TOO CUTE FOR ME!
あぁ
I'M SUCH AN IDIOT!
あぁぁ
DU-DUN
I'M A PURE COTTON GIRL!!
SAYING THAT...
FEELS LIKE I'M SAYING I DON'T SUIT...
MURAKAMI-SAN, EITHER.

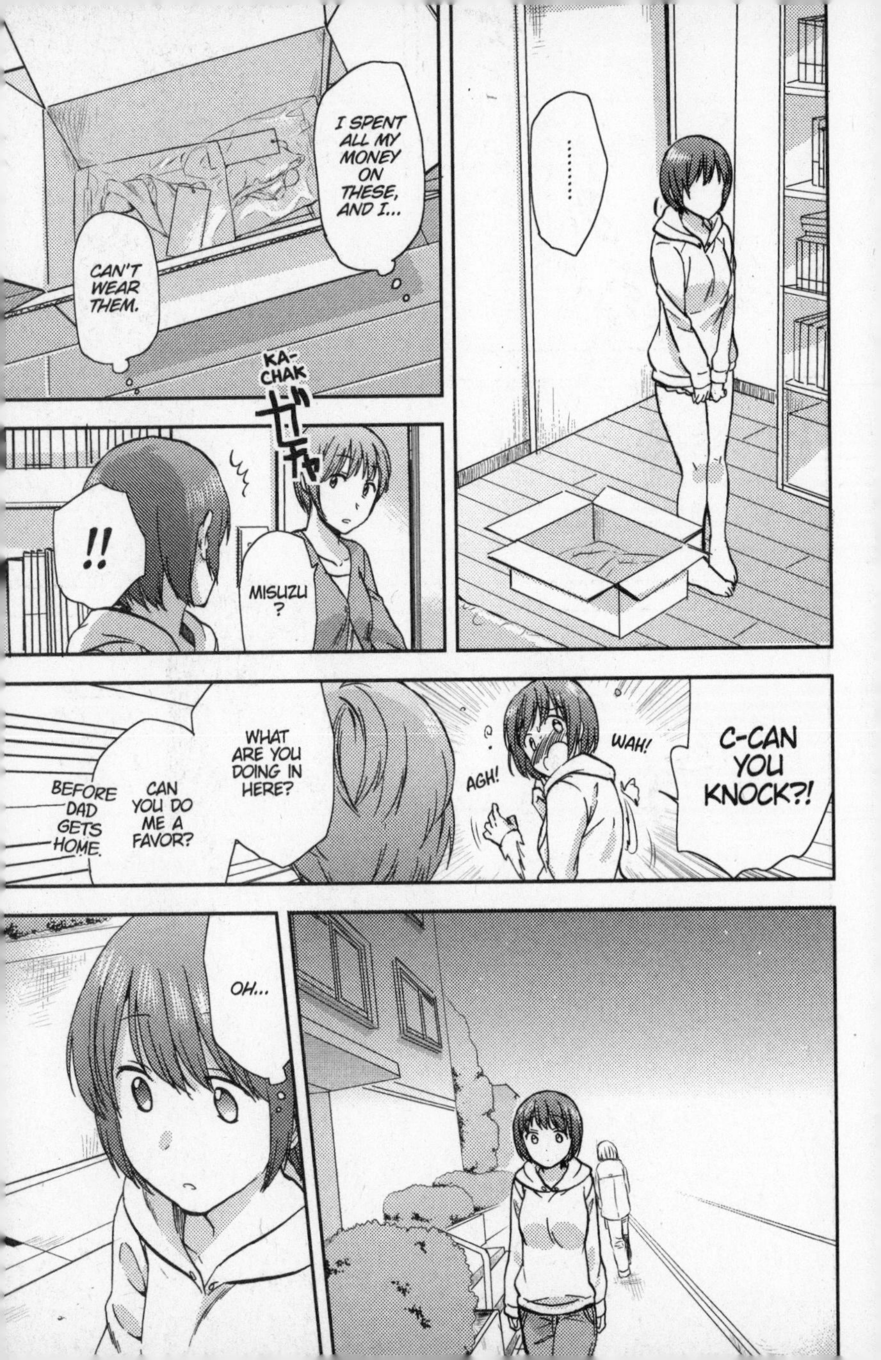
......
I SPENT ALL MY MONEY ON THESE, AND I...
CAN'T WEAR THEM.
KA-CHAK
ガチャ
MISUZU?
!!
C-CAN YOU KNOCK?!
WAH!
AGH!
WHAT ARE YOU DOING IN HERE?
CAN YOU DO ME A FAVOR?
BEFORE DAD GETS HOME.
OH...

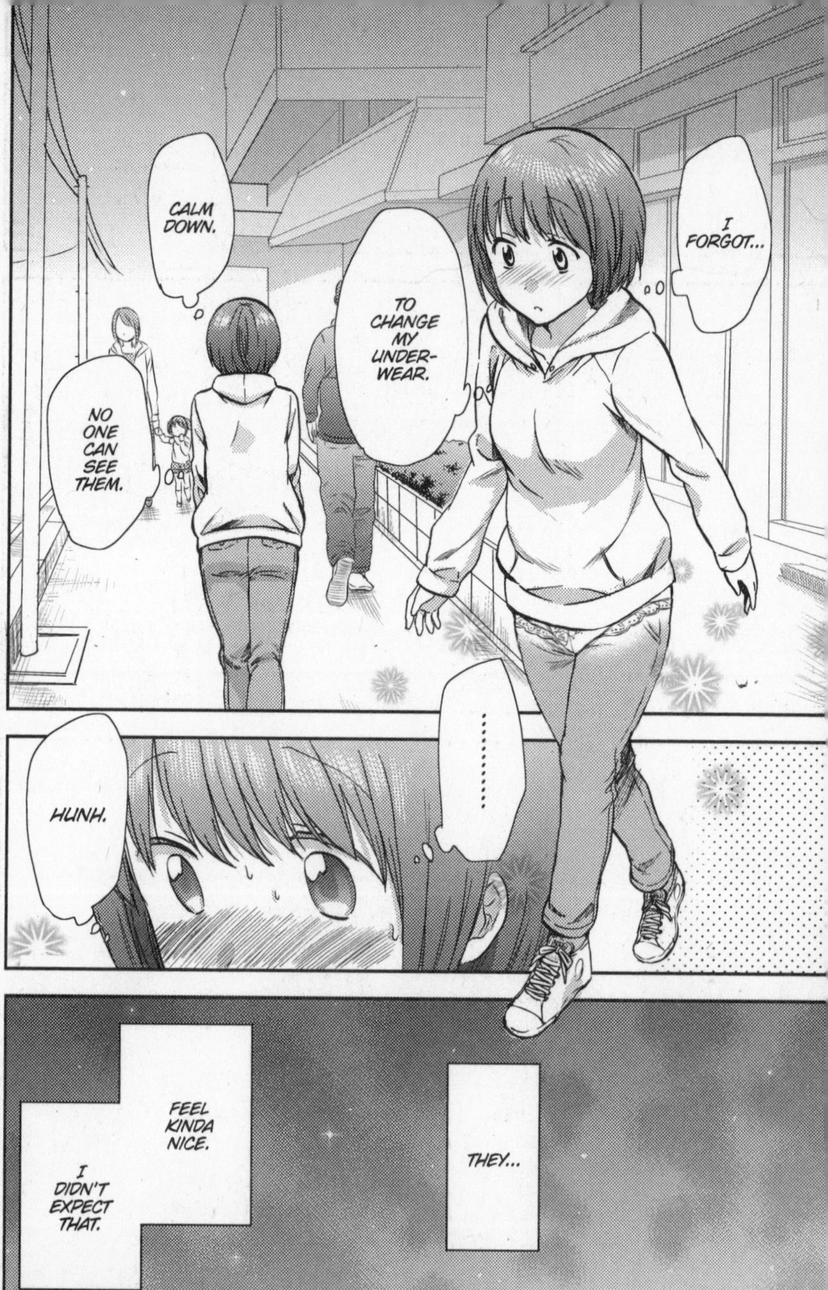
I FORGOT...
TO CHANGE MY UNDER-WEAR.
CALM DOWN.
NO ONE CAN SEE THEM.
......
HUNH.
THEY...
FEEL KINDA NICE.
I DIDN'T EXPECT THAT.

#11. I'm Gonna Buy Panties Like Murakami-san's / END

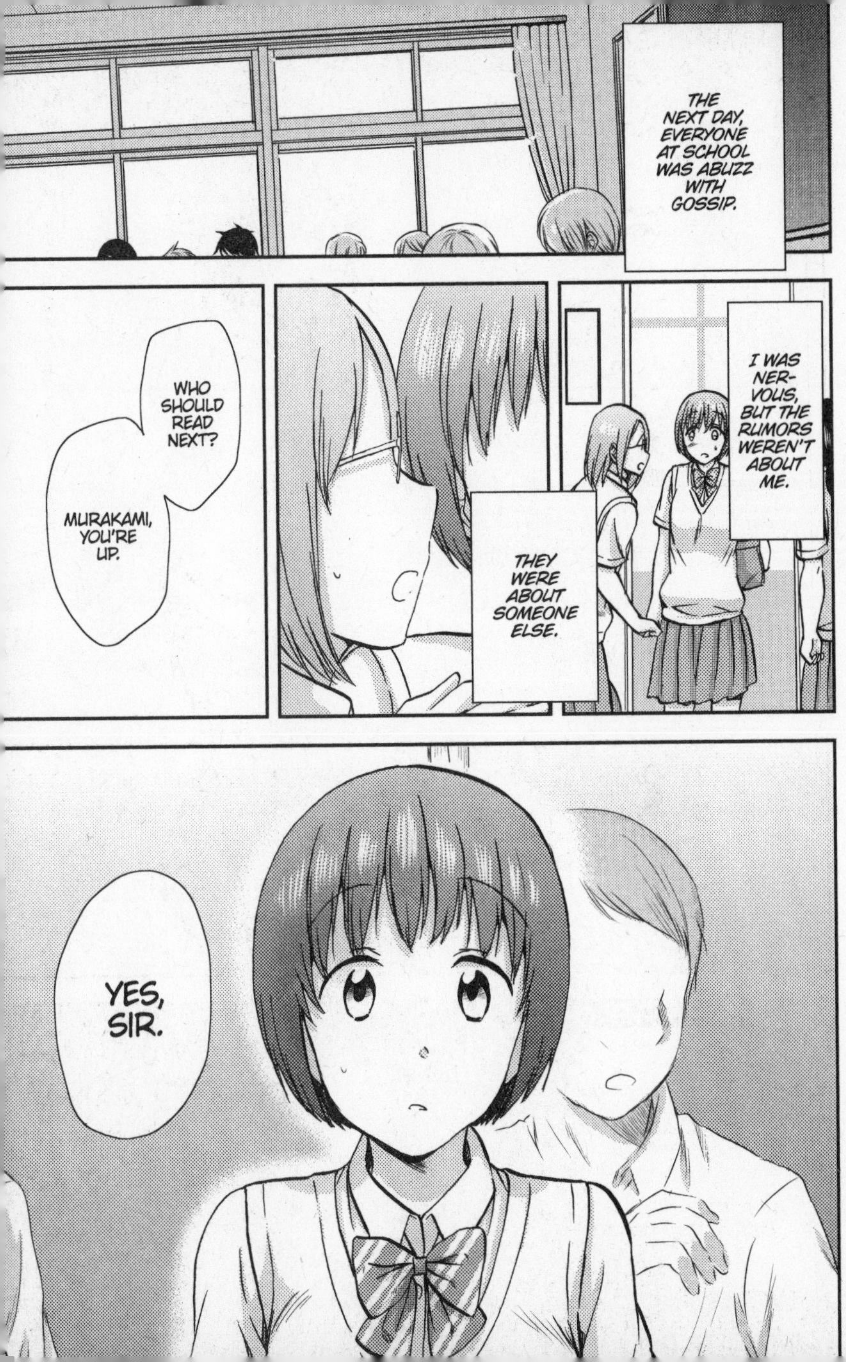
THE NEXT DAY, EVERYONE AT SCHOOL WAS ABUZZ WITH GOSSIP.
I WAS NER-VOUS, BUT THE RUMORS WEREN'T ABOUT ME.
THEY WERE ABOUT SOMEONE ELSE.
WHO SHOULD READ NEXT?
MURAKAMI, YOU'RE UP.
YES, SIR.

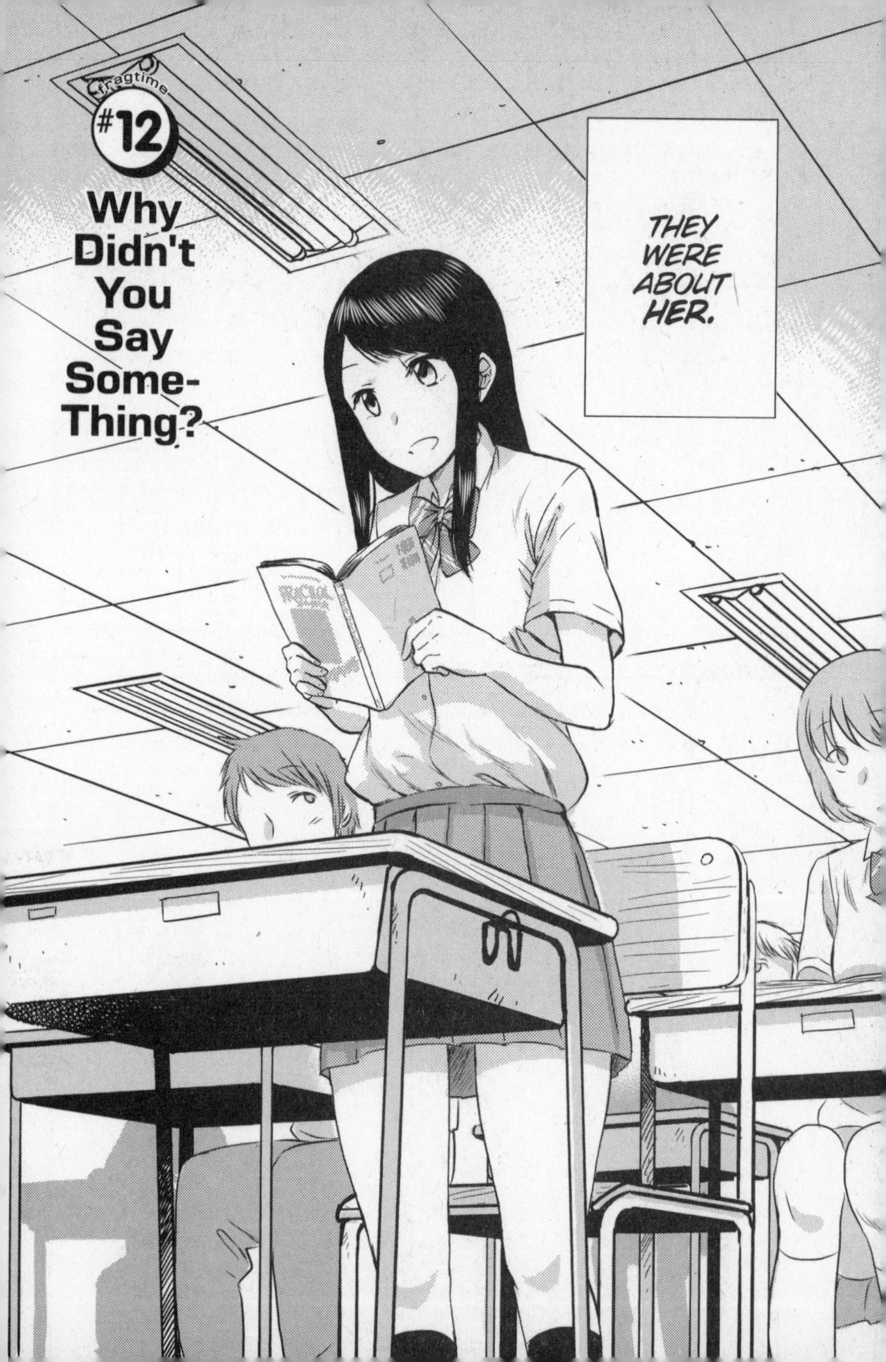
fragtime
#12
Why Didn't You Say Some-Thing?
THEY WERE ABOUT HER.

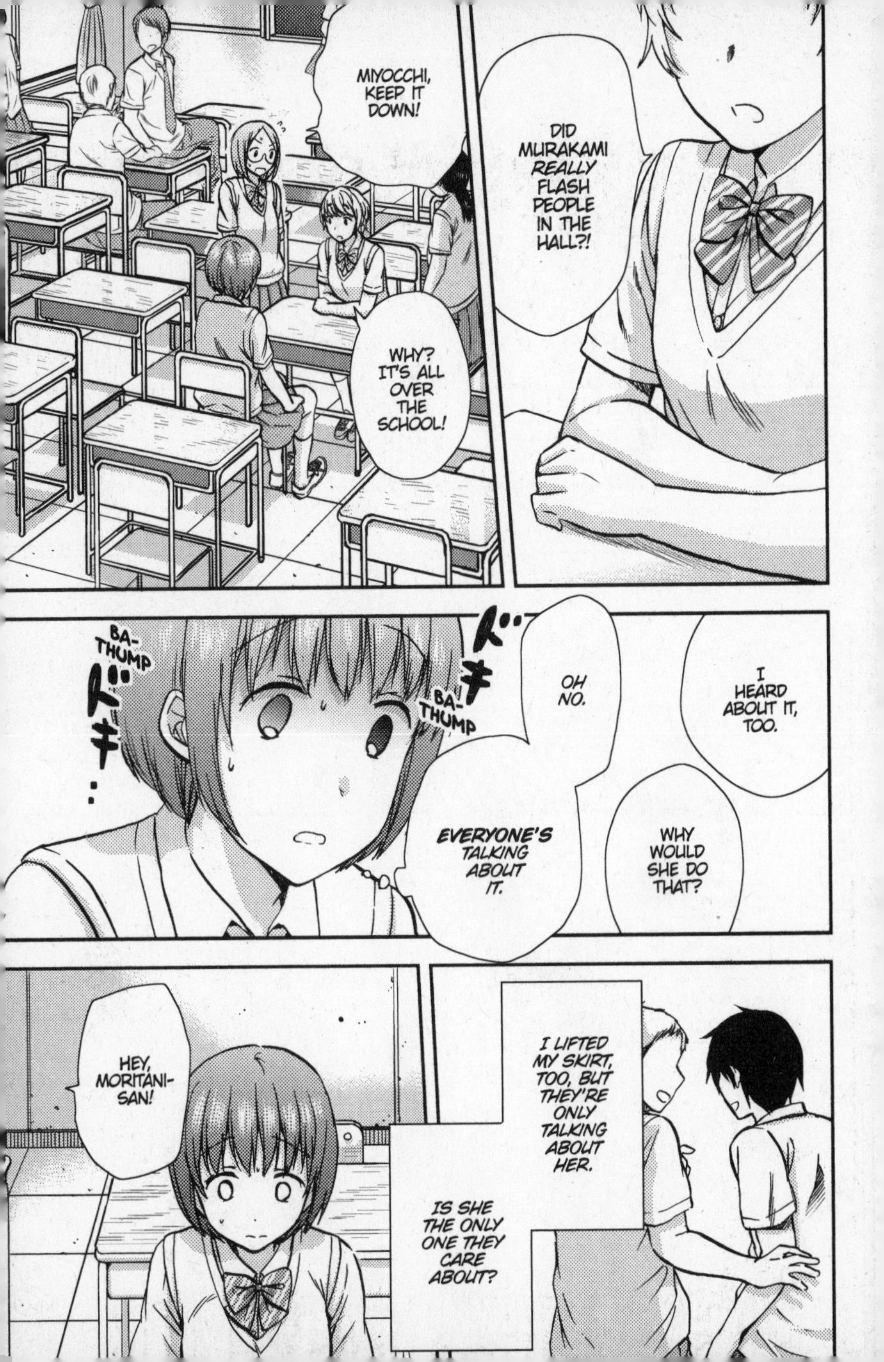
DID MURAKAMI REALLY FLASH PEOPLE IN THE HALL?!
MIYOCCHI, KEEP IT DOWN!
WHY? IT'S ALL OVER THE SCHOOL!
I HEARD ABOUT IT, TOO.
OH NO.
WHY WOULD SHE DO THAT?
EVERYONE'S TALKING ABOUT IT.
BA-THUMP
ドキ
BA-THUMP
ドキ
I LIFTED MY SKIRT, TOO, BUT THEY'RE ONLY TALKING ABOUT HER.
IS SHE THE ONLY ONE THEY CARE ABOUT?
HEY, MORITANI-SAN!

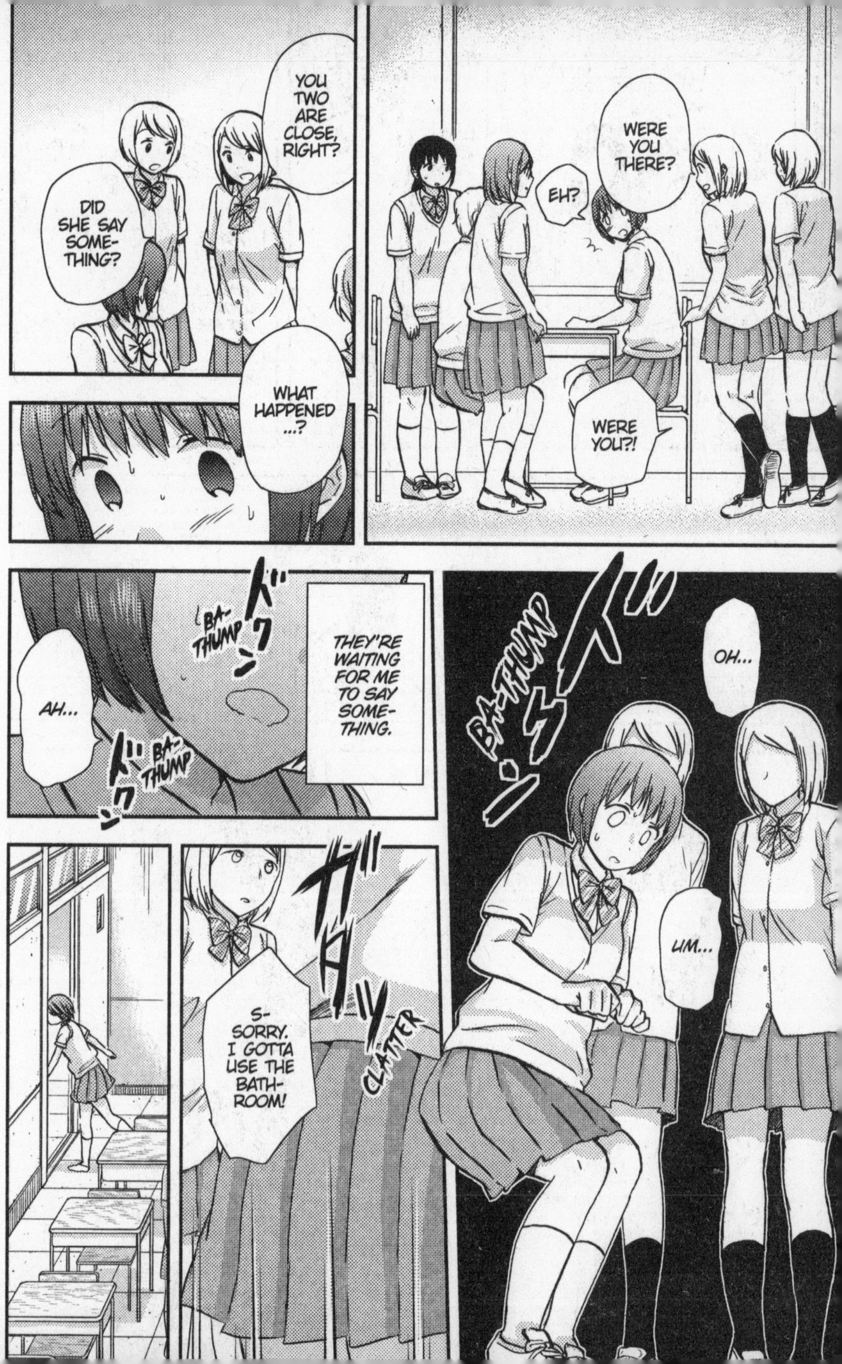
WERE YOU THERE?
EH?
WERE YOU?!
YOU TWO ARE CLOSE, RIGHT?
DID SHE SAY SOME-THING?
WHAT HAPPENED ...?
BA-THUMP
OH...
UM...
BA-THUMP
THEY'RE WAITING FOR ME TO SAY SOME-THING.
AH...
BA-THUMP
S-SORRY. I GOTTA USE THE BATH-ROOM!
CLATTER

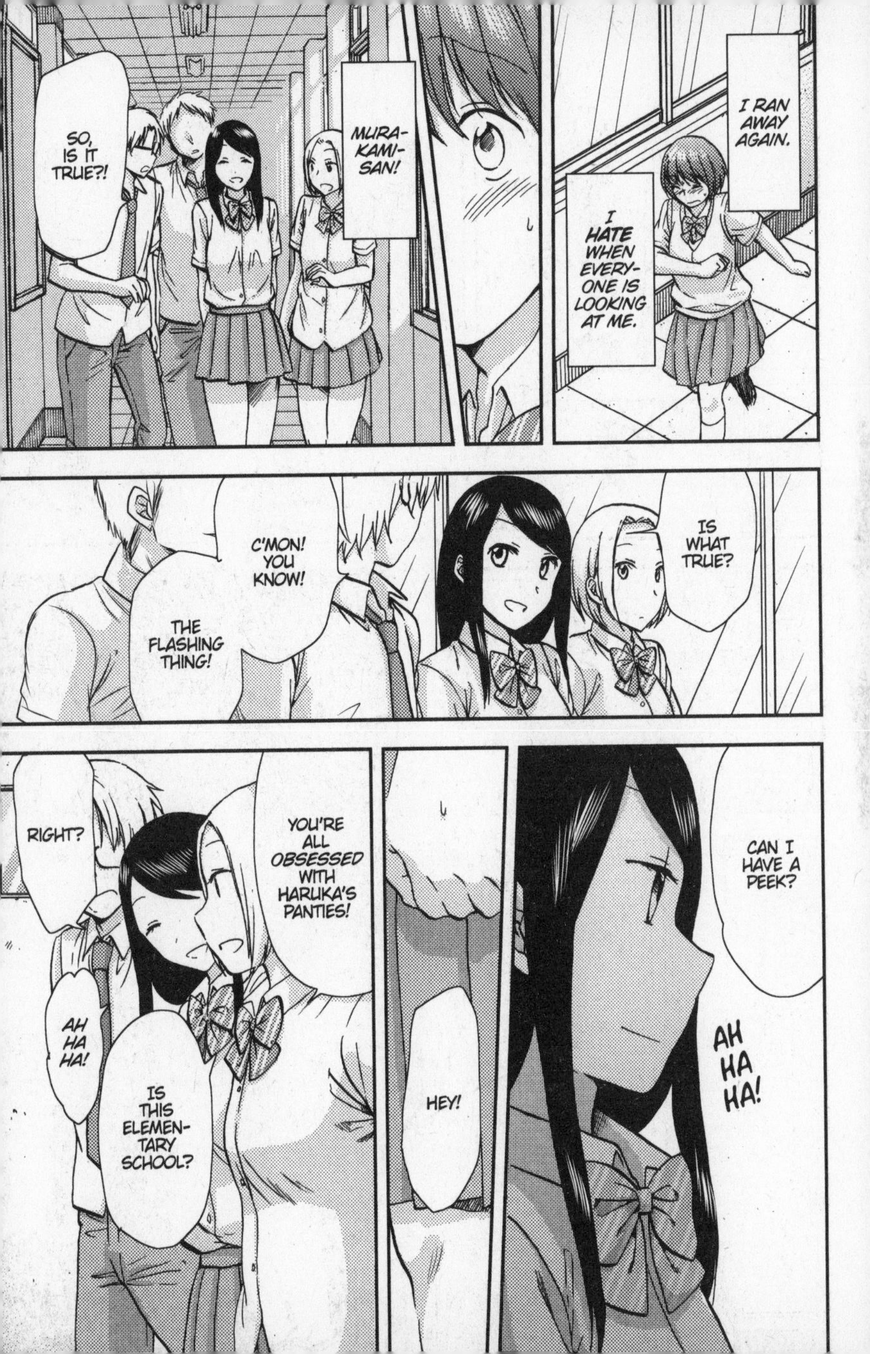
I RAN AWAY AGAIN.
I HATE WHEN EVERY-ONE IS LOOKING AT ME.
MURA-KAMI-SAN!
SO, IS IT TRUE?!
IS WHAT TRUE?
C'MON! YOU KNOW!
THE FLASHING THING!
CAN I HAVE A PEEK?
AH HA HA!
HEY!
YOU'RE ALL OBSESSED WITH HARUKA'S PANTIES!
RIGHT?
AH HA HA!
IS THIS ELEMENTARY SCHOOL?

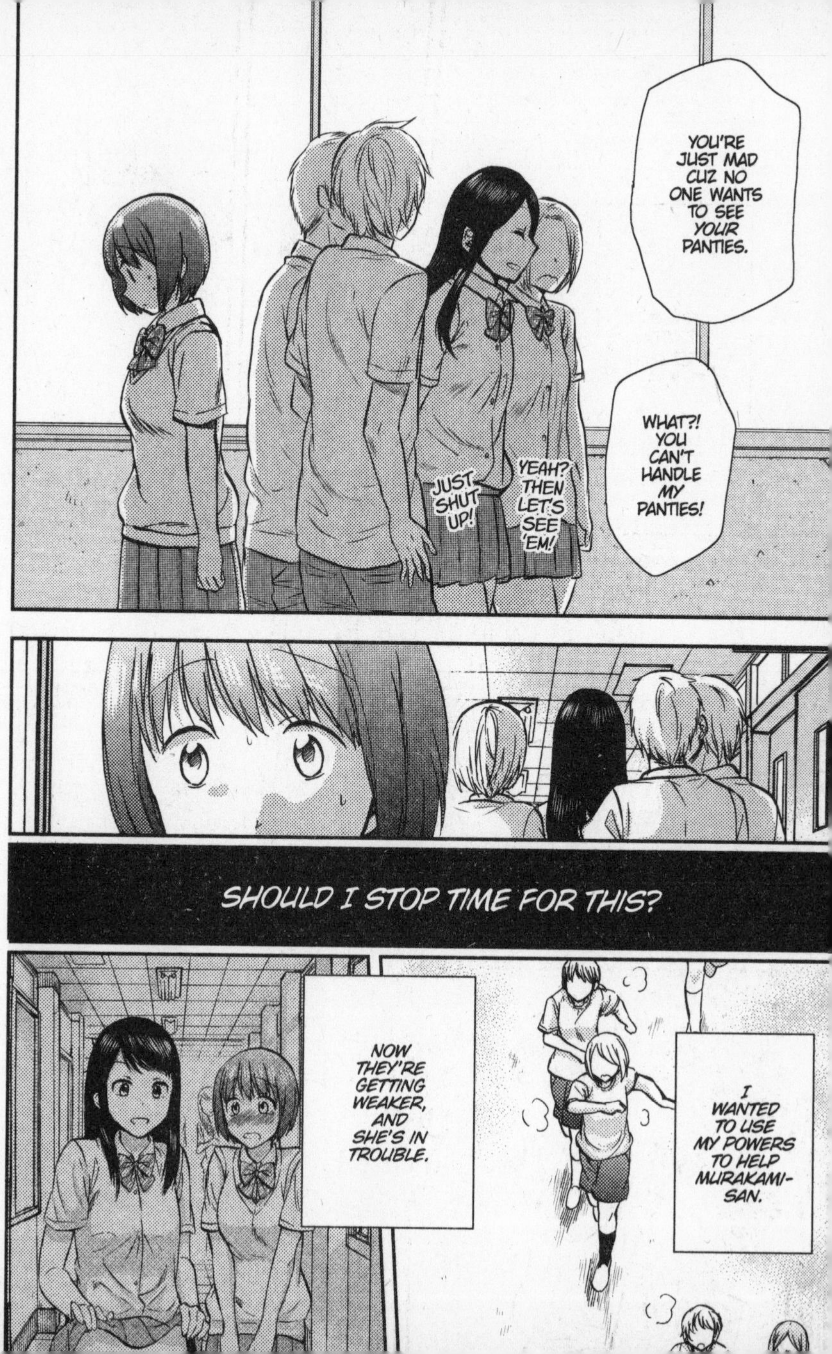
YOU'RE JUST MAD CUZ NO ONE WANTS TO SEE *YOUR* PANTIES.
WHAT?! YOU CAN'T HANDLE *MY* PANTIES!
YEAH? THEN LET'S SEE 'EM!
JUST SHUT UP!
SHOULD I STOP TIME FOR THIS?
I WANTED TO USE MY POWERS TO HELP MURAKAMI-SAN.
NOW THEY'RE GETTING WEAKER, AND SHE'S IN TROUBLE.

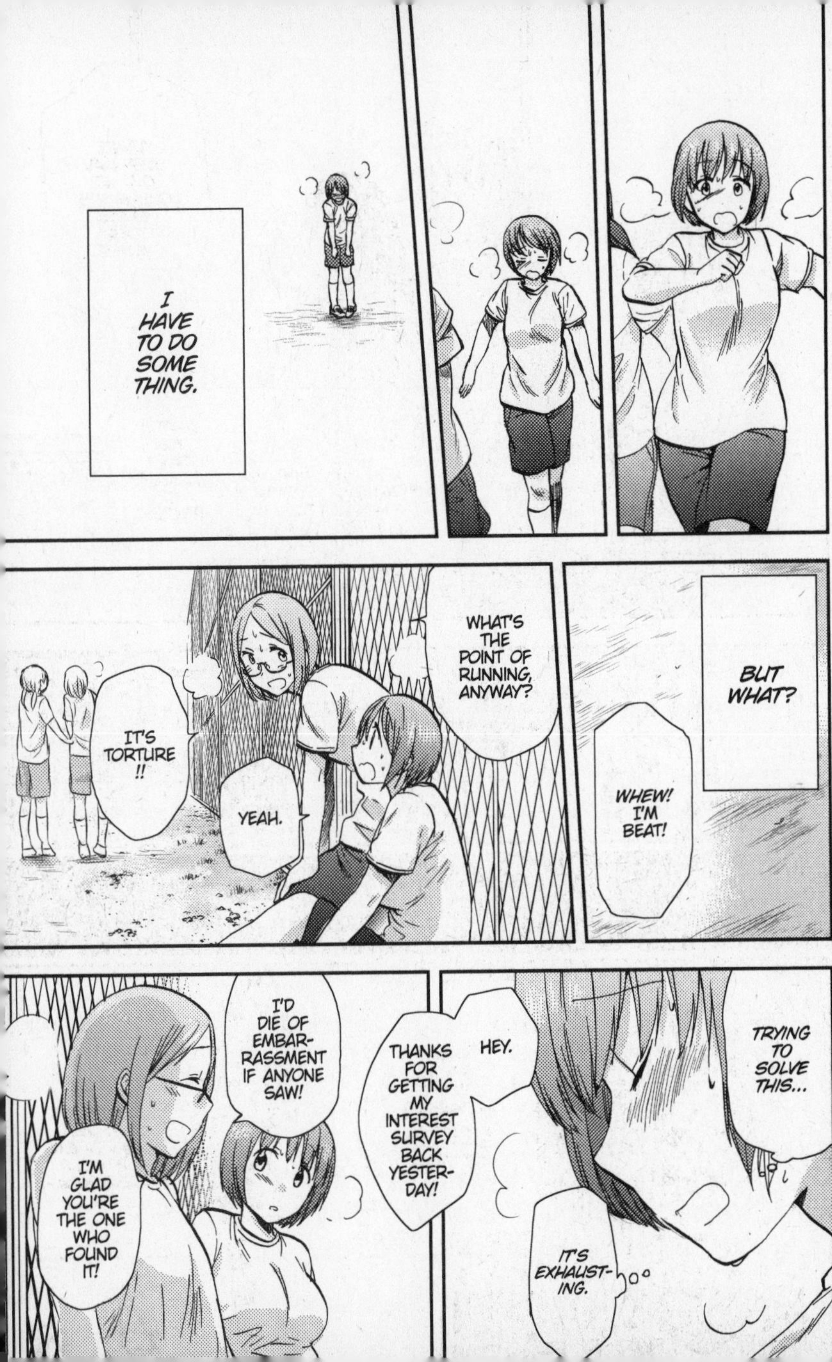
I HAVE TO DO SOME THING.
BUT WHAT?
WHEW! I'M BEAT!
WHAT'S THE POINT OF RUNNING, ANYWAY?
IT'S TORTURE !!
YEAH.
TRYING TO SOLVE THIS...
IT'S EXHAUSTING.
HEY.
THANKS FOR GETTING MY INTEREST SURVEY BACK YESTERDAY!
I'D DIE OF EMBARRASSMENT IF ANYONE SAW!
I'M GLAD YOU'RE THE ONE WHO FOUND IT!

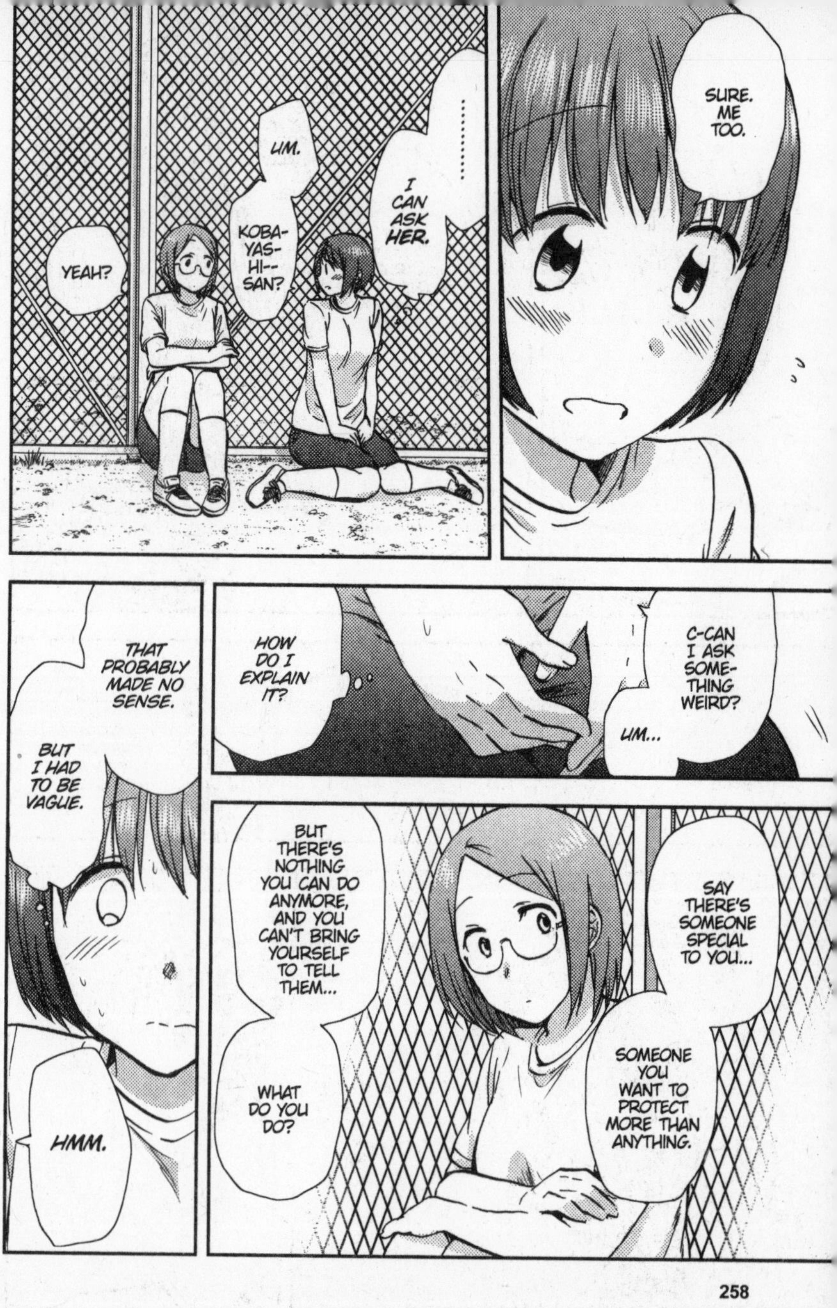
SURE. ME TOO.
...... I CAN ASK HER.
UM.
KOBA-YAS-HI--SAN?
YEAH?
C-CAN I ASK SOME-THING WEIRD?
UM...
HOW DO I EXPLAIN IT?
SAY THERE'S SOMEONE SPECIAL TO YOU...
SOMEONE YOU WANT TO PROTECT MORE THAN ANYTHING.
BUT THERE'S NOTHING YOU CAN DO ANYMORE, AND YOU CAN'T BRING YOURSELF TO TELL THEM...
WHAT DO YOU DO?
THAT PROBABLY MADE NO SENSE.
BUT I HAD TO BE VAGUE.
HMM.

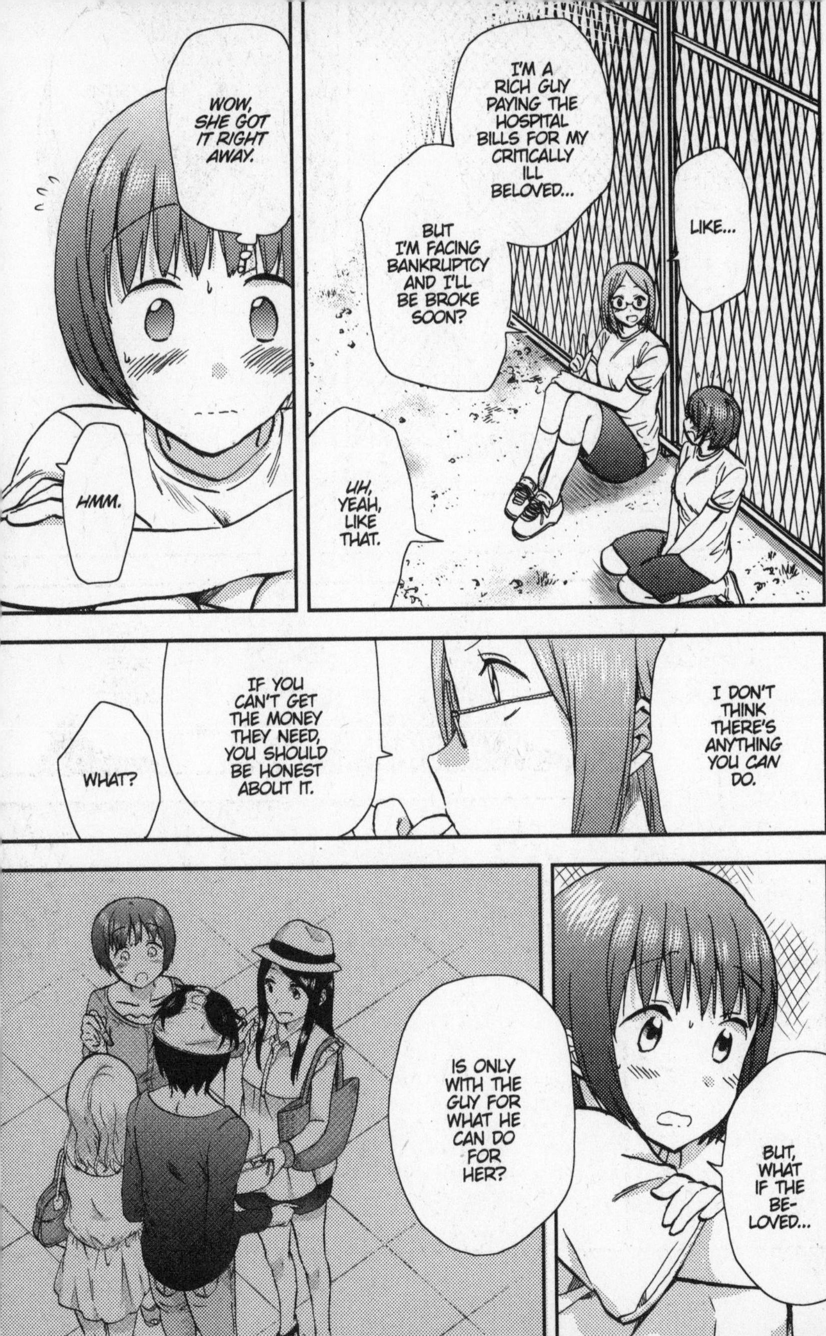
LIKE...
I'M A RICH GUY PAYING THE HOSPITAL BILLS FOR MY CRITICALLY ILL BELOVED...
BUT I'M FACING BANKRUPTCY AND I'LL BE BROKE SOON?
UH, YEAH, LIKE THAT.
WOW, SHE GOT IT RIGHT AWAY.
HMM.
I DON'T THINK THERE'S ANYTHING YOU CAN DO.
IF YOU CAN'T GET THE MONEY THEY NEED, YOU SHOULD BE HONEST ABOUT IT.
WHAT?
BUT, WHAT IF THE BE-LOVED...
IS ONLY WITH THE GUY FOR WHAT HE CAN DO FOR HER?

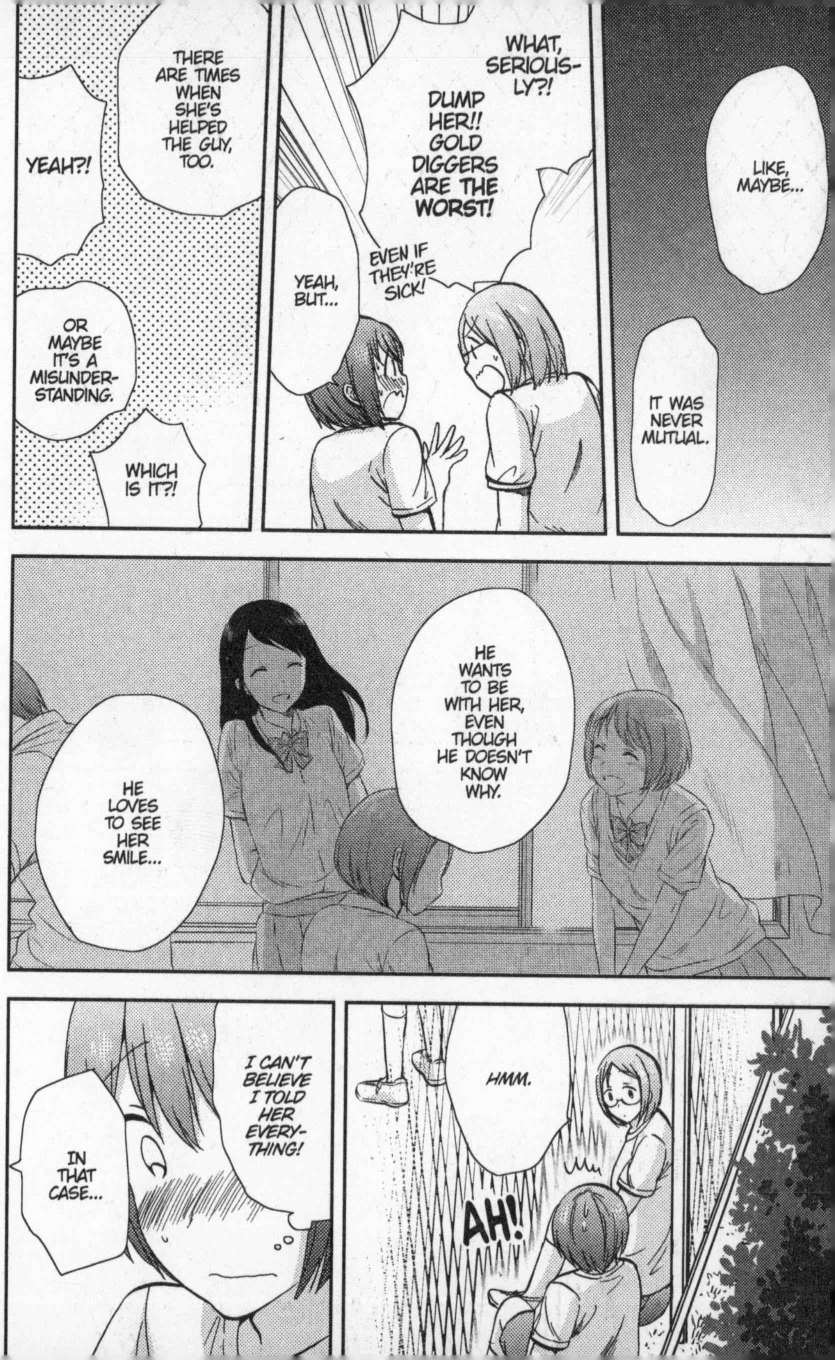
LIKE, MAYBE...
IT WAS NEVER MUTUAL.
WHAT, SERIOUSLY?!
DUMP HER!! GOLD DIGGERS ARE THE WORST!
EVEN IF THEY'RE SICK!
YEAH, BUT...
THERE ARE TIMES WHEN SHE'S HELPED THE GUY, TOO.
YEAH?!
OR MAYBE IT'S A MISUNDERSTANDING.
WHICH IS IT?!
HE WANTS TO BE WITH HER, EVEN THOUGH HE DOESN'T KNOW WHY.
HE LOVES TO SEE HER SMILE...
HMM.
AH!
I CAN'T BELIEVE I TOLD HER EVERYTHING!
IN THAT CASE...

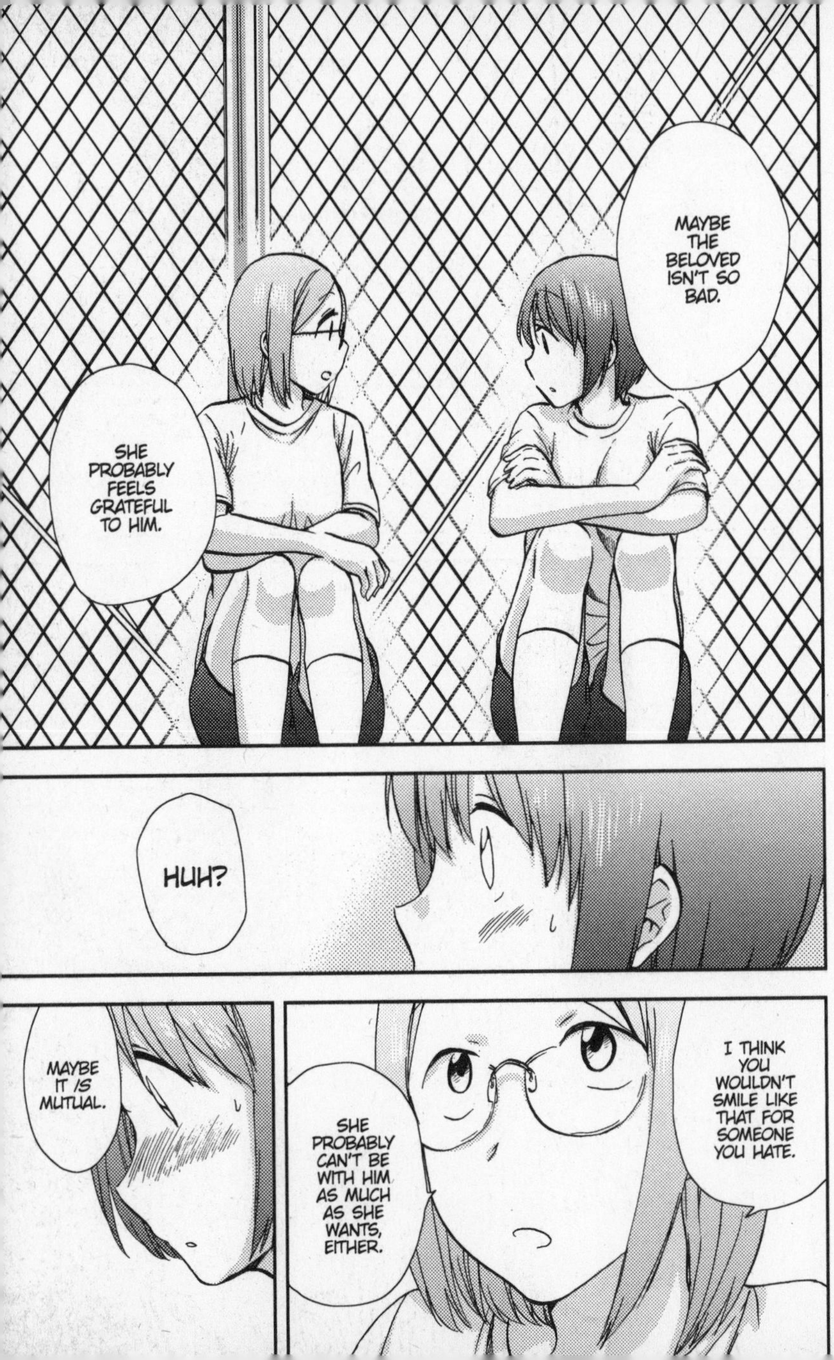
MAYBE THE BELOVED ISN'T SO BAD.
SHE PROBABLY FEELS GRATEFUL TO HIM.
HUH?
I THINK YOU WOULDN'T SMILE LIKE THAT FOR SOMEONE YOU HATE.
SHE PROBABLY CAN'T BE WITH HIM AS MUCH AS SHE WANTS, EITHER.
MAYBE IT *IS* MUTUAL.

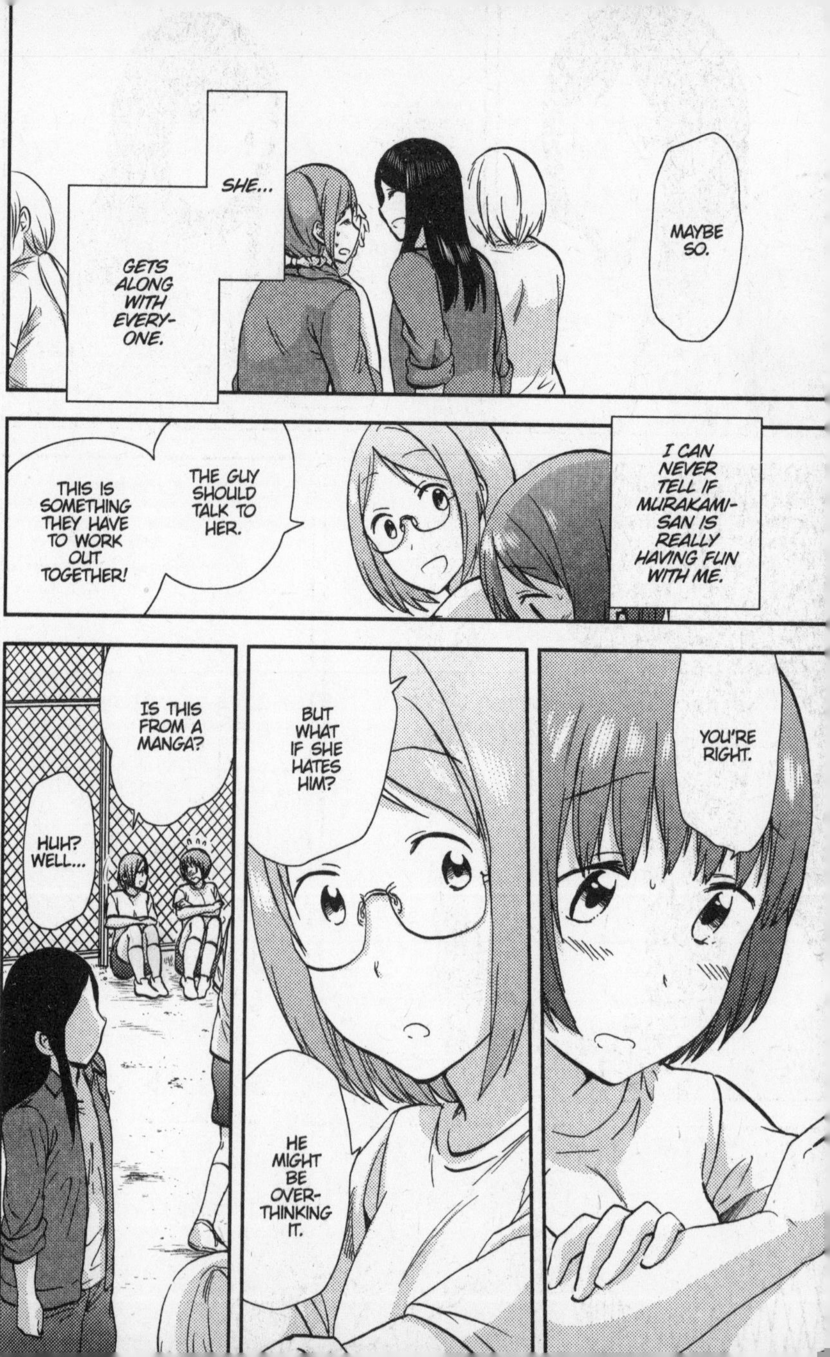
MAYBE SO.
SHE...
GETS ALONG WITH EVERYONE.
I CAN NEVER TELL IF MURAKAMI-SAN IS REALLY HAVING FUN WITH ME.
THE GUY SHOULD TALK TO HER.
THIS IS SOMETHING THEY HAVE TO WORK OUT TOGETHER!
YOU'RE RIGHT.
BUT WHAT IF SHE HATES HIM?
HE MIGHT BE OVER-THINKING IT.
IS THIS FROM A MANGA?
HUH? WELL...

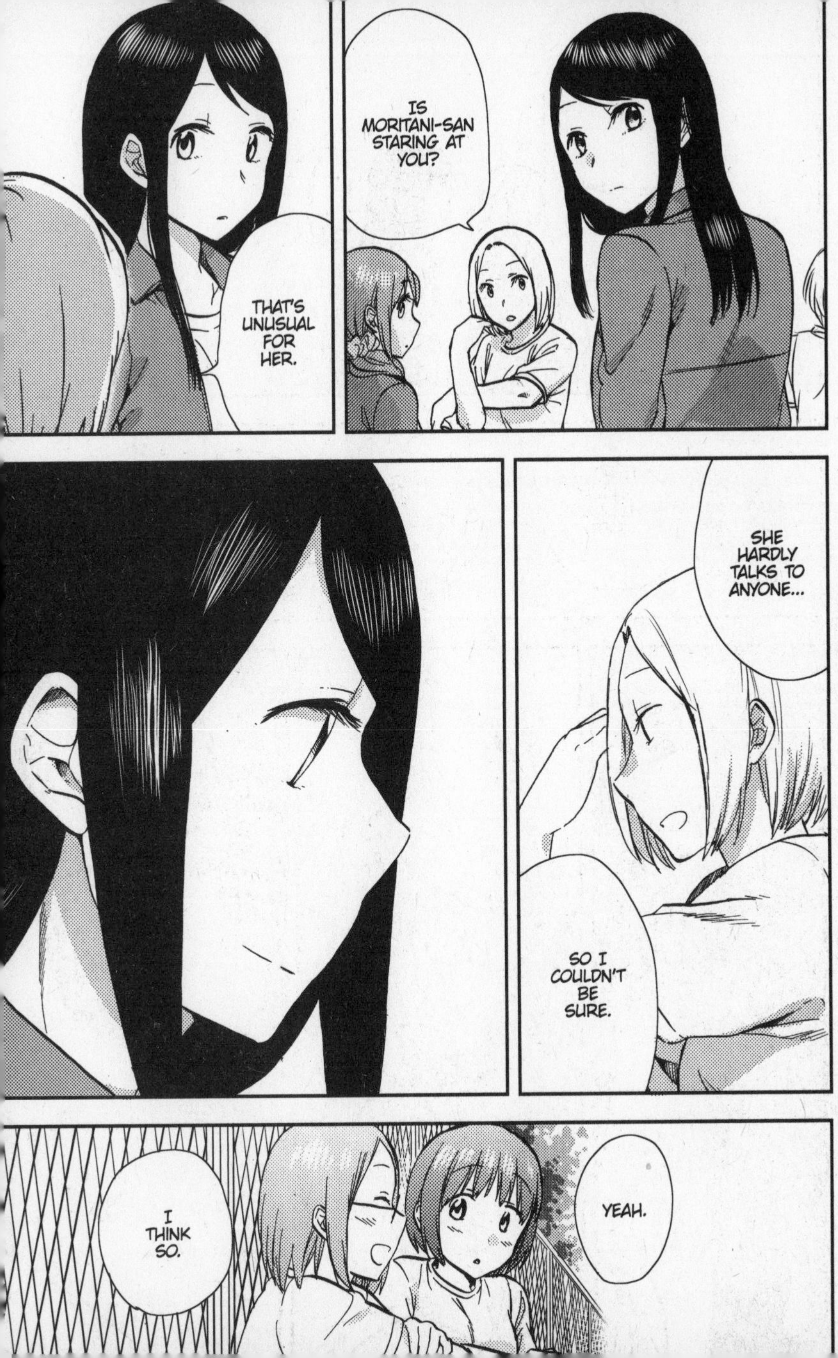
IS MORITANI-SAN STARING AT YOU?
THAT'S UNUSUAL FOR HER.
SHE HARDLY TALKS TO ANYONE...
SO I COULDN'T BE SURE.
YEAH.
I THINK SO.

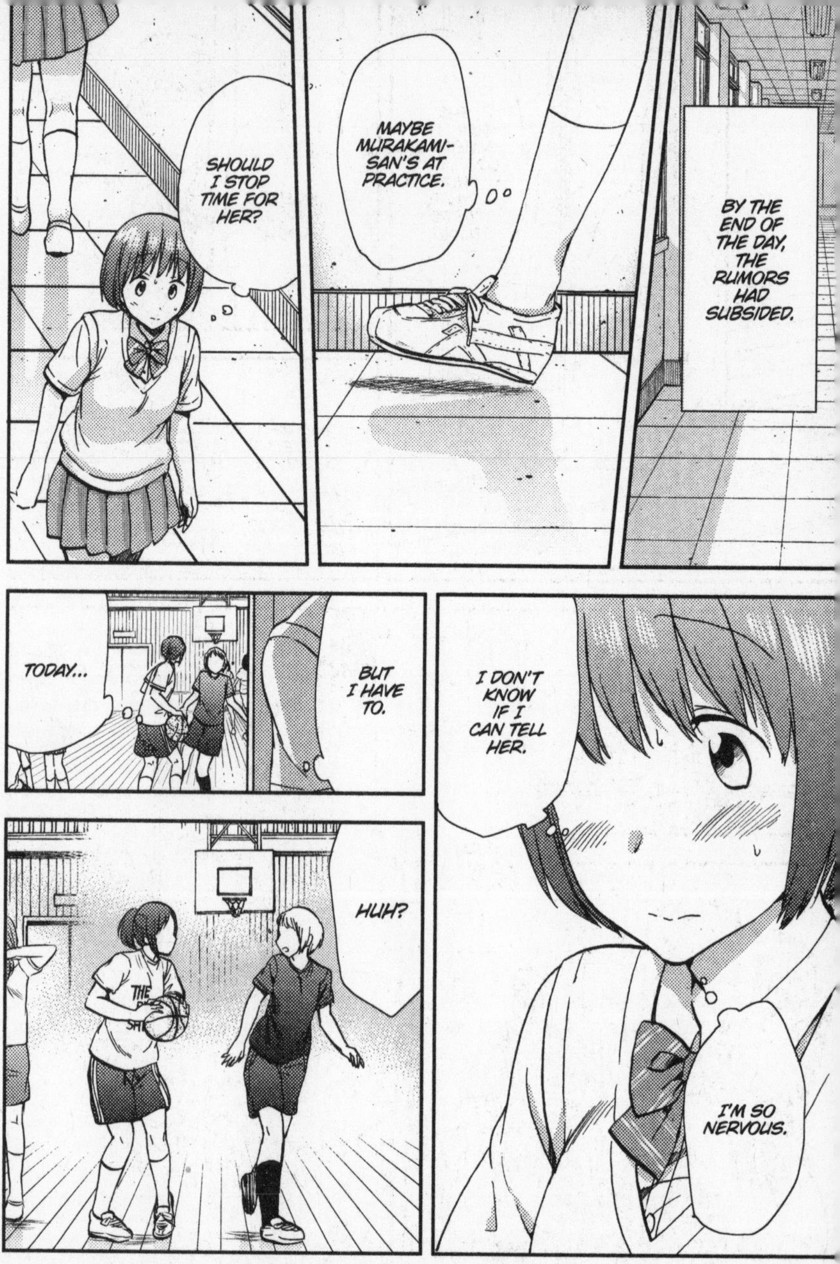
BY THE END OF THE DAY, THE RUMORS HAD SUBSIDED.
MAYBE MURAKAMI-SAN'S AT PRACTICE.
SHOULD I STOP TIME FOR HER?
I DON'T KNOW IF I CAN TELL HER.
I'M SO NERVOUS.
BUT I HAVE TO.
TODAY...
HUH?

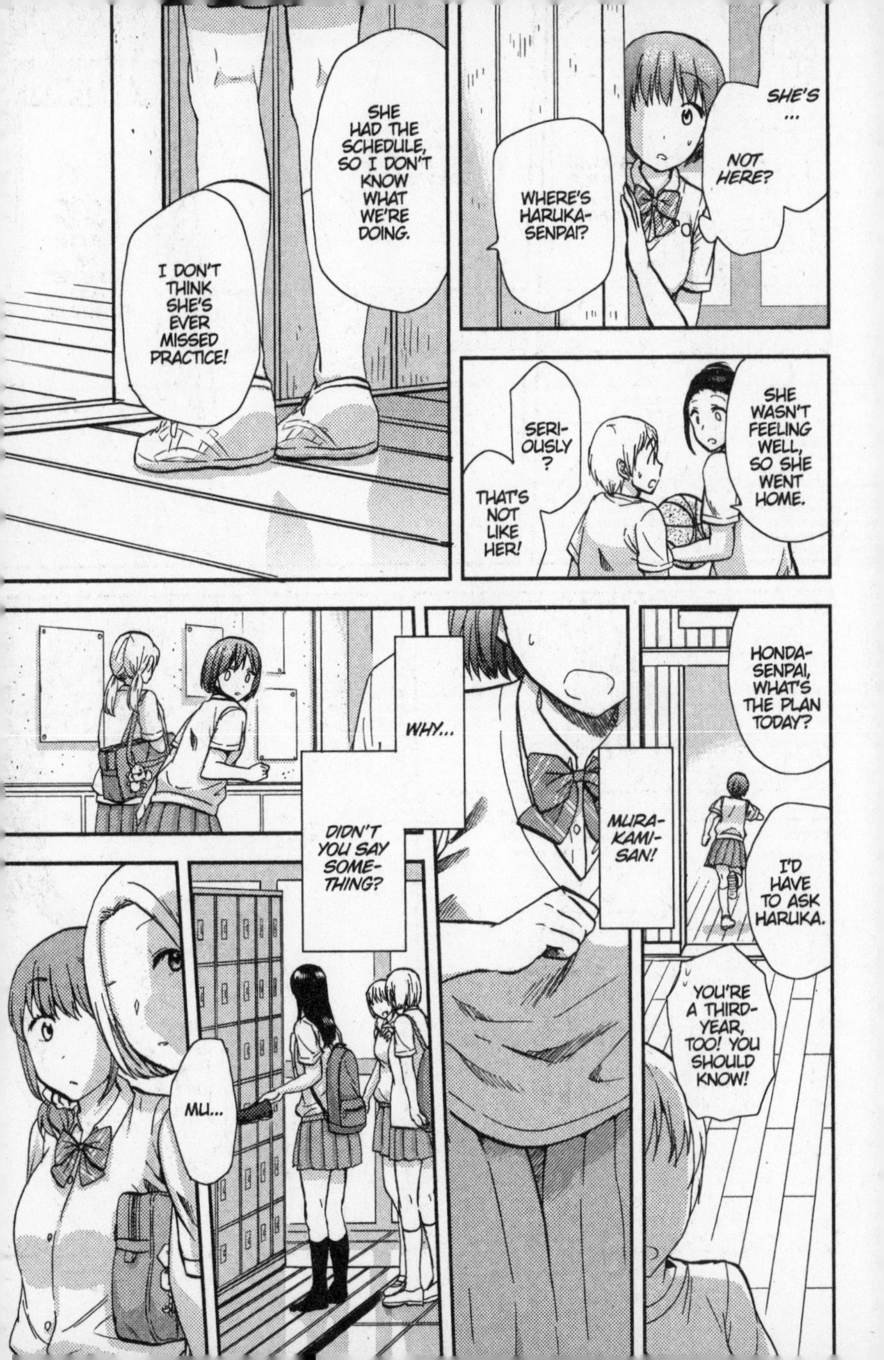
SHE'S ... NOT HERE?
WHERE'S HARUKA-SENPAI?
SHE WASN'T FEELING WELL, SO SHE WENT HOME.
SERIOUSLY? THAT'S NOT LIKE HER!
SHE HAD THE SCHEDULE, SO I DON'T KNOW WHAT WE'RE DOING.
I DON'T THINK SHE'S EVER MISSED PRACTICE!
HONDA-SENPAI, WHAT'S THE PLAN TODAY?
I'D HAVE TO ASK HARUKA.
YOU'RE A THIRD-YEAR, TOO! YOU SHOULD KNOW!
MURAKAMI-SAN!
WHY...
DIDN'T YOU SAY SOMETHING?
MU...

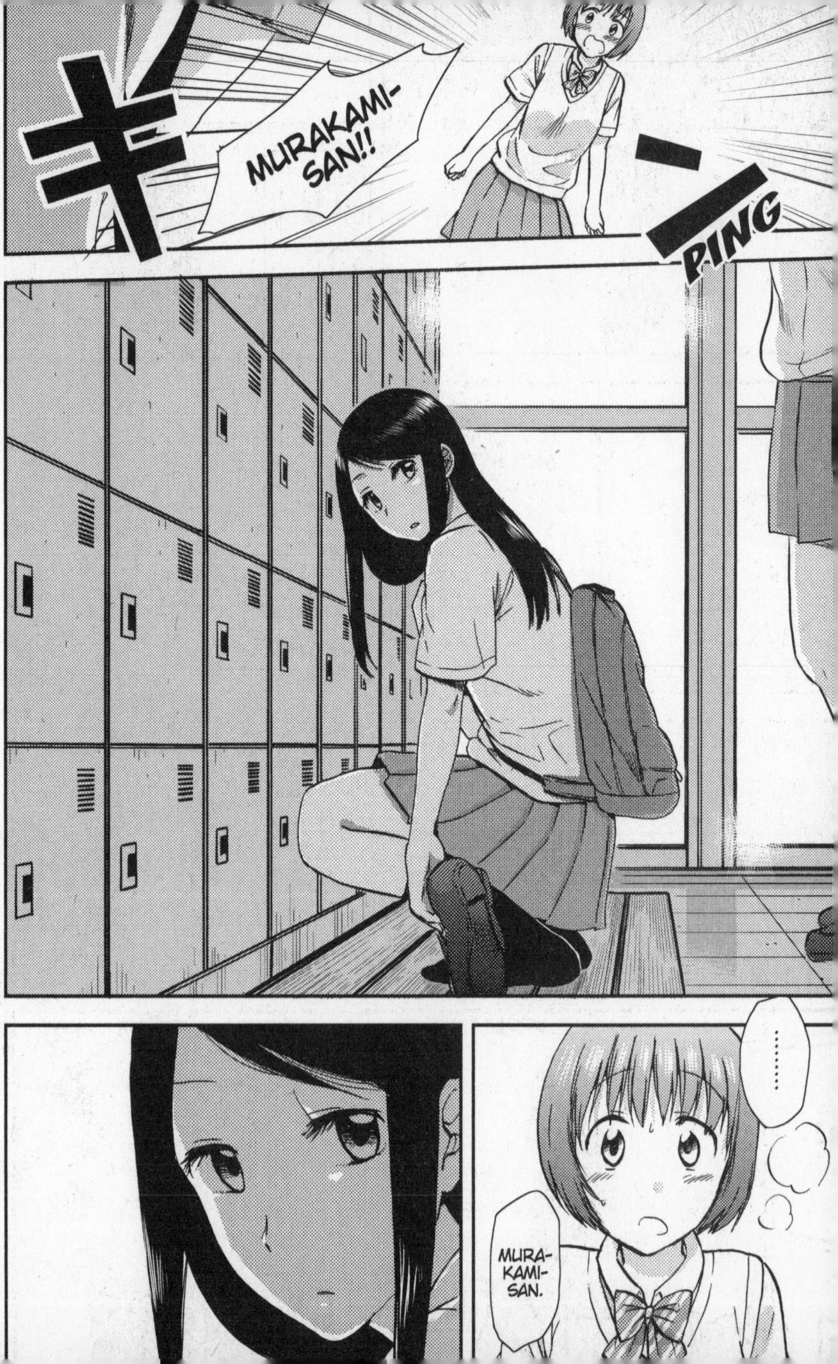
MURAKAMI-SAN!!
ギ
PING
......
MURAKAMI-SAN.

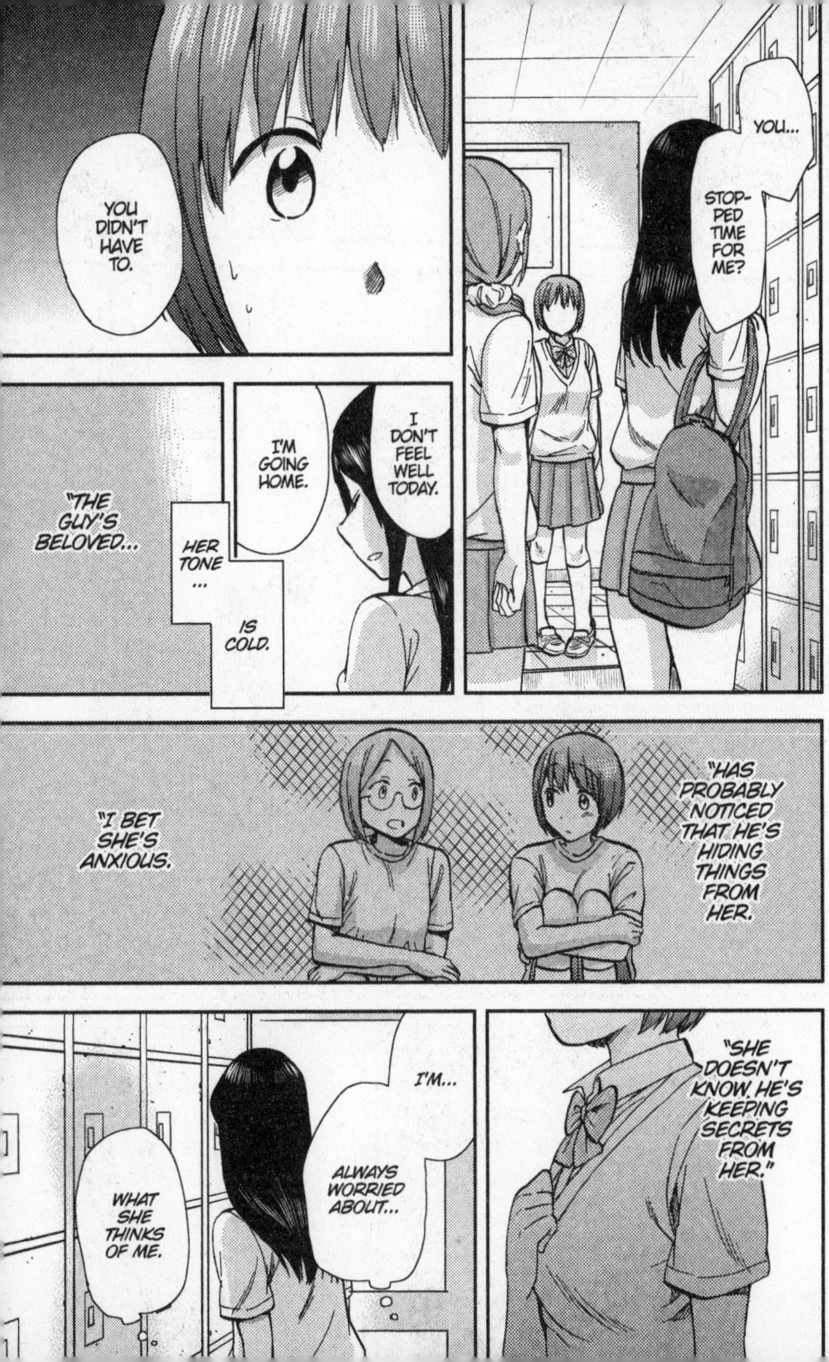
YOU...
STOP-PED TIME FOR ME?
YOU DIDN'T HAVE TO.
I DON'T FEEL WELL TODAY.
I'M GOING HOME.
HER TONE ...
IS COLD.
"THE GUY'S BELOVED...
"HAS PROBABLY NOTICED THAT HE'S HIDING THINGS FROM HER.
"I BET SHE'S ANXIOUS.
"SHE DOESN'T KNOW. HE'S KEEPING SECRETS FROM HER."
I'M...
ALWAYS WORRIED ABOUT...
WHAT SHE THINKS OF ME.

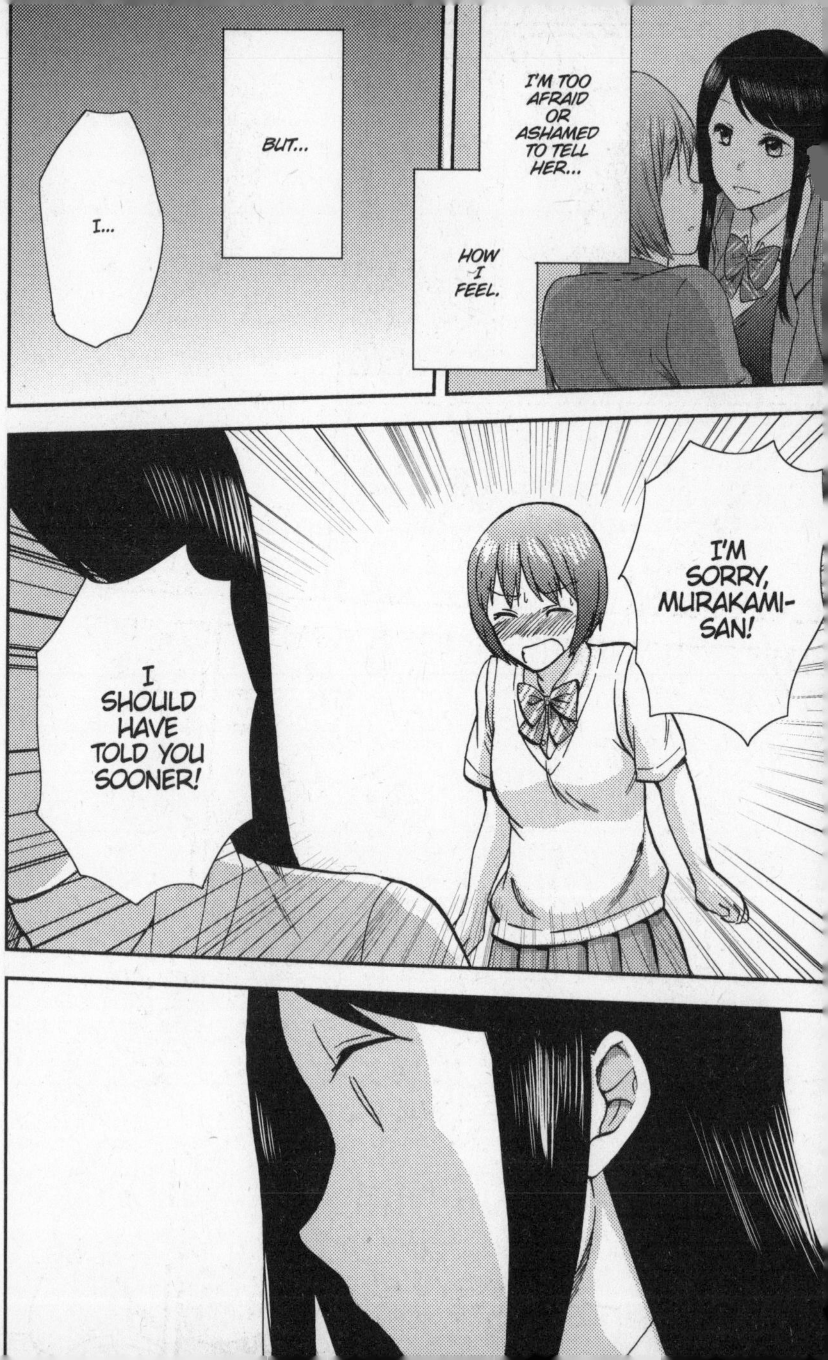
I'M TOO AFRAID OR ASHAMED TO TELL HER...
HOW I FEEL.
BUT...
I...
I'M SORRY, MURAKAMI-SAN!
I SHOULD HAVE TOLD YOU SOONER!

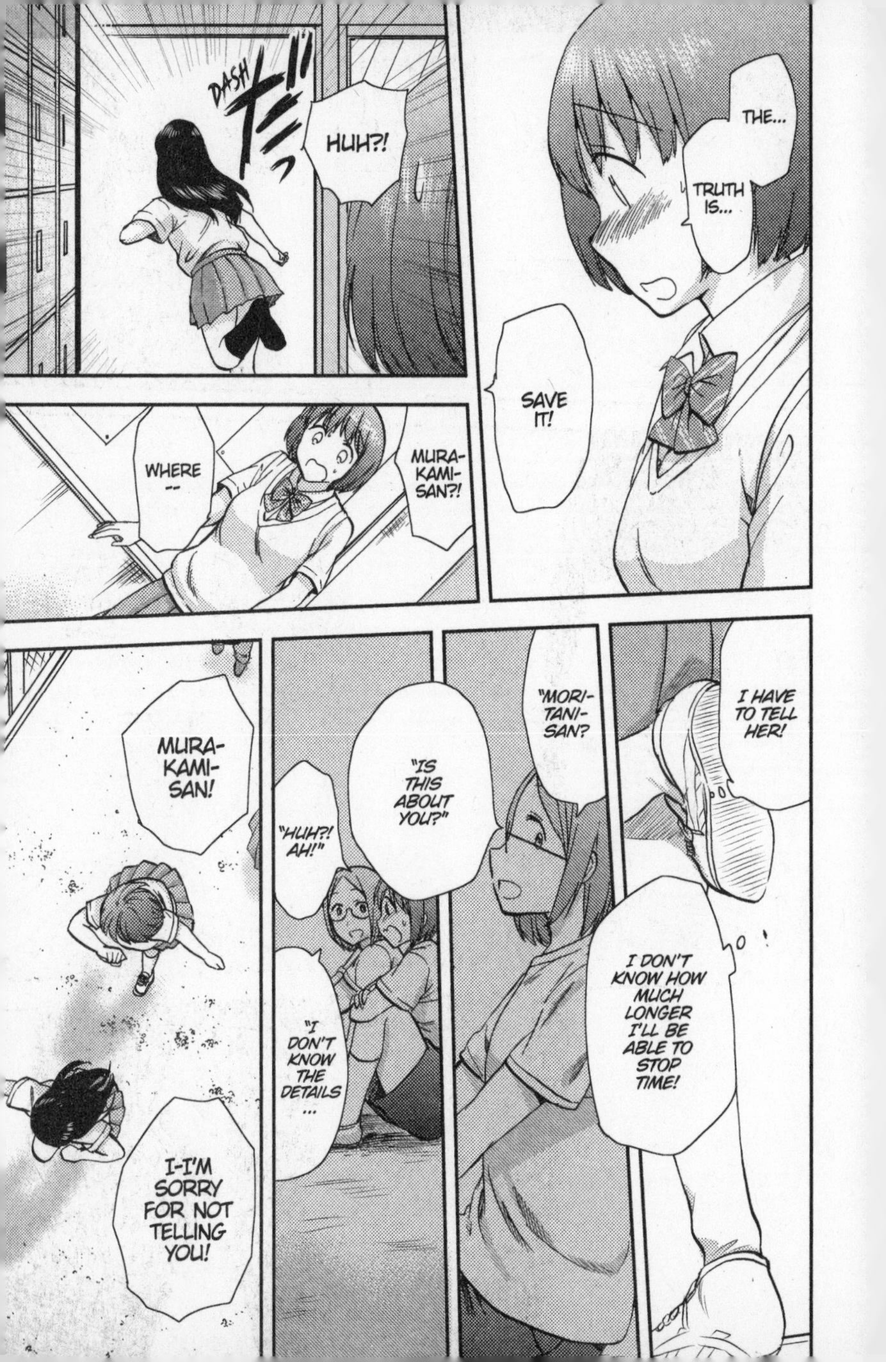
THE...
TRUTH IS...
SAVE IT!
DASH
HUH?!
MURA-KAMI-SAN?!
WHERE --
I HAVE TO TELL HER!
I DON'T KNOW HOW MUCH LONGER I'LL BE ABLE TO STOP TIME!
"MORI-TANI-SAN?
"IS THIS ABOUT YOU?"
"HUH?! AH!"
"I DON'T KNOW THE DETAILS...
MURA-KAMI-SAN!
I-I'M SORRY FOR NOT TELLING YOU!

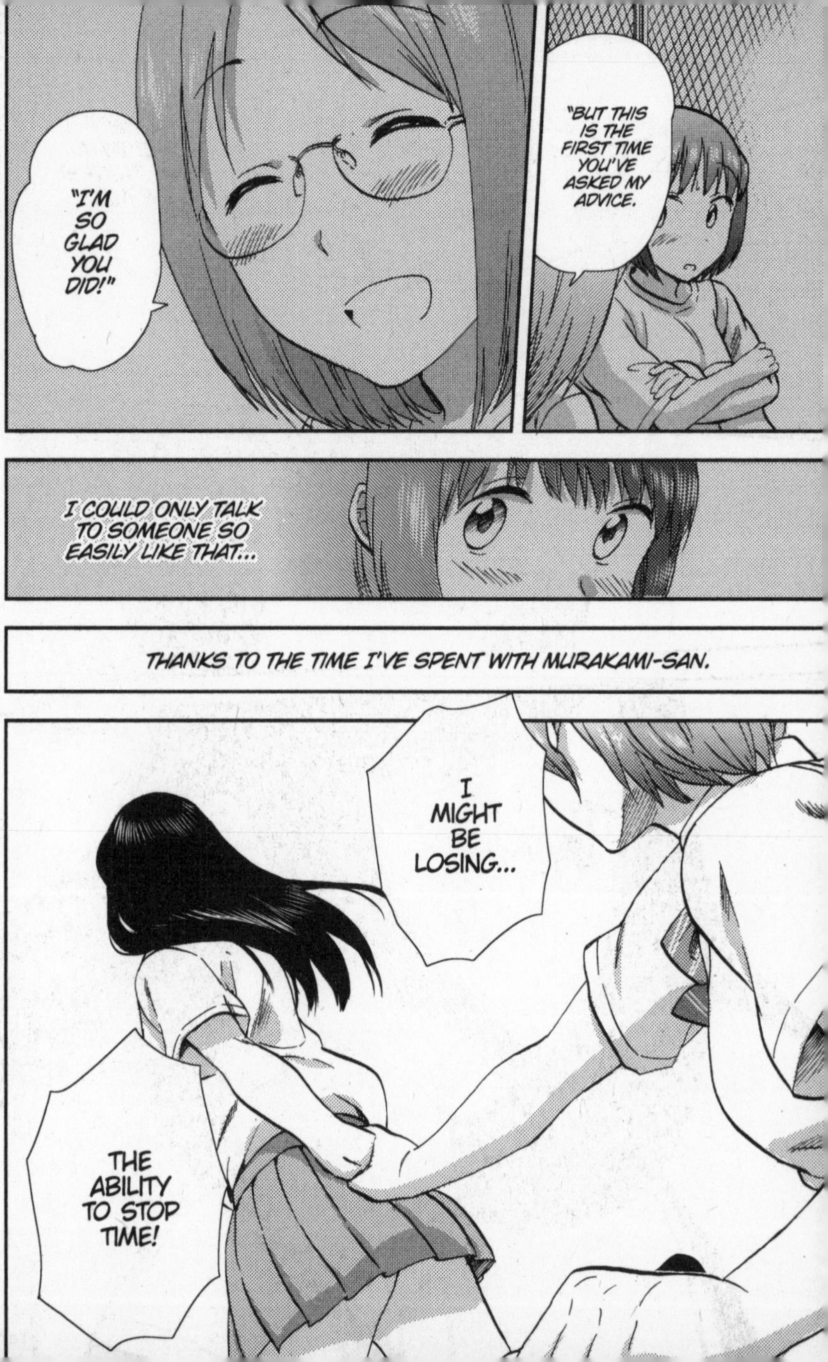
"BUT THIS IS THE FIRST TIME YOU'VE ASKED MY ADVICE.
"I'M SO GLAD YOU DID!"
I COULD ONLY TALK TO SOMEONE SO EASILY LIKE THAT...
THANKS TO THE TIME I'VE SPENT WITH MURAKAMI-SAN.
I MIGHT BE LOSING...
THE ABILITY TO STOP TIME!

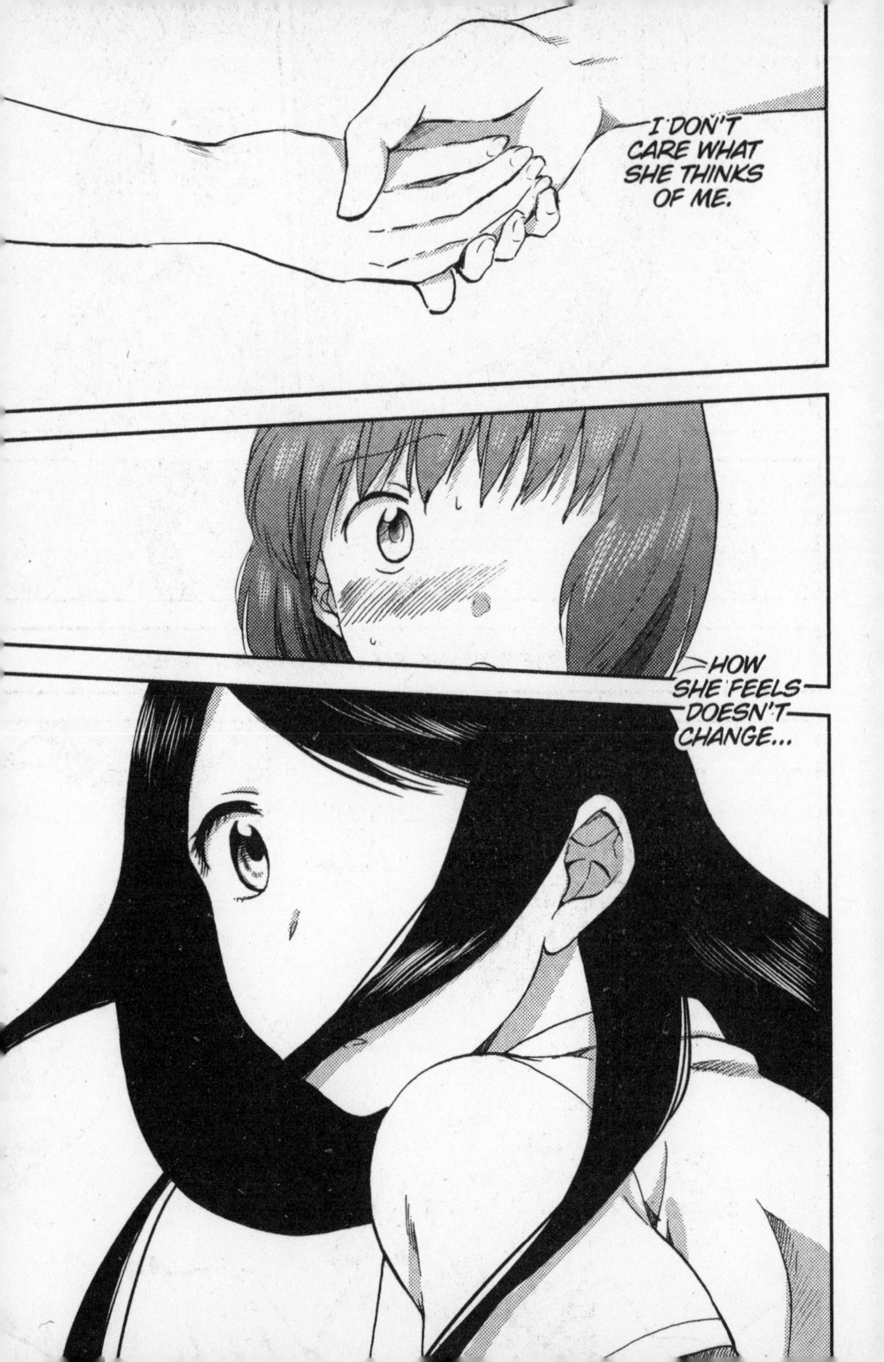
I DON'T CARE WHAT SHE THINKS OF ME.
HOW SHE FEELS DOESN'T CHANGE...

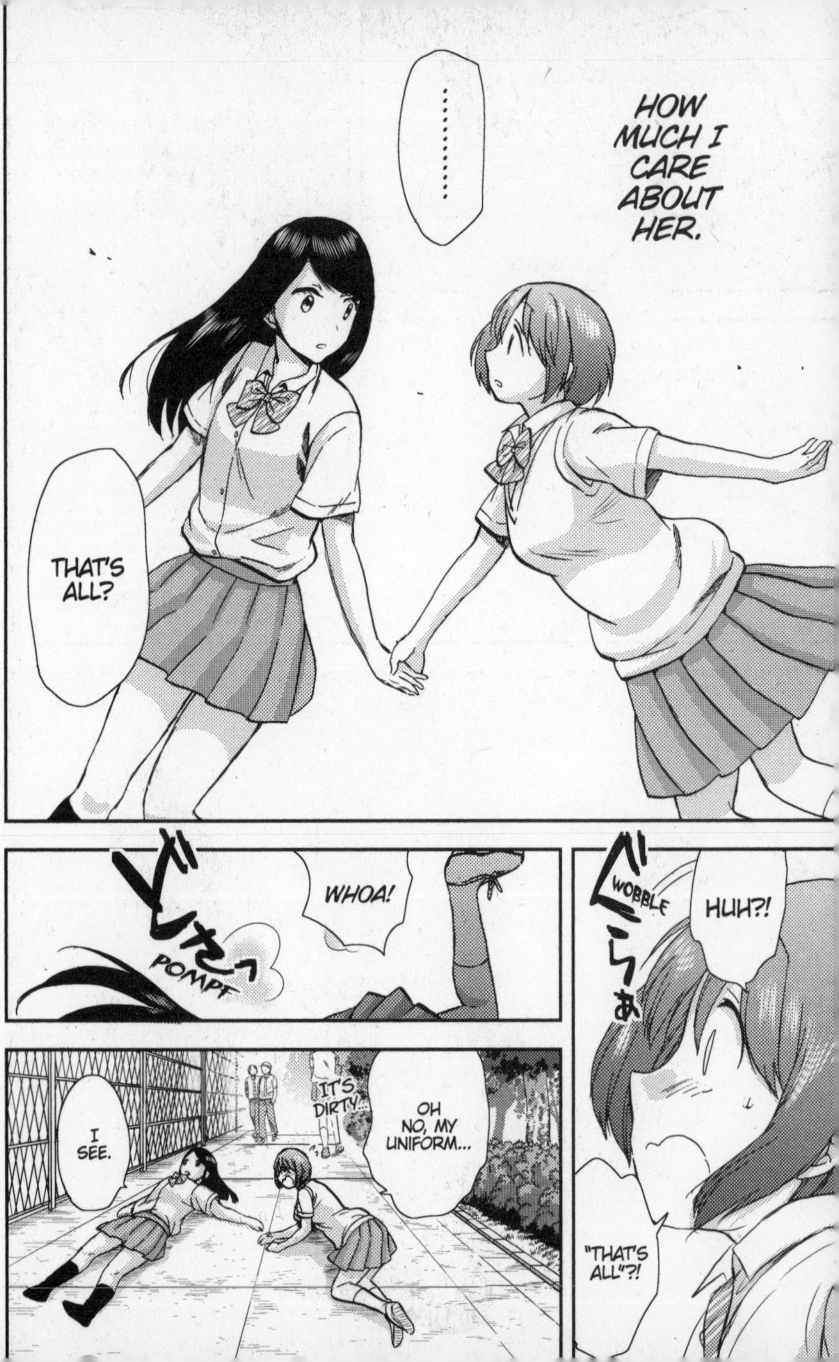
HOW MUCH I CARE ABOUT HER.
......
THAT'S ALL?
HUH?!
WOBBLE
"THAT'S ALL"?!
WHOA!
POMPF
OH NO, MY UNIFORM...
IT'S DIRTY...
I SEE.

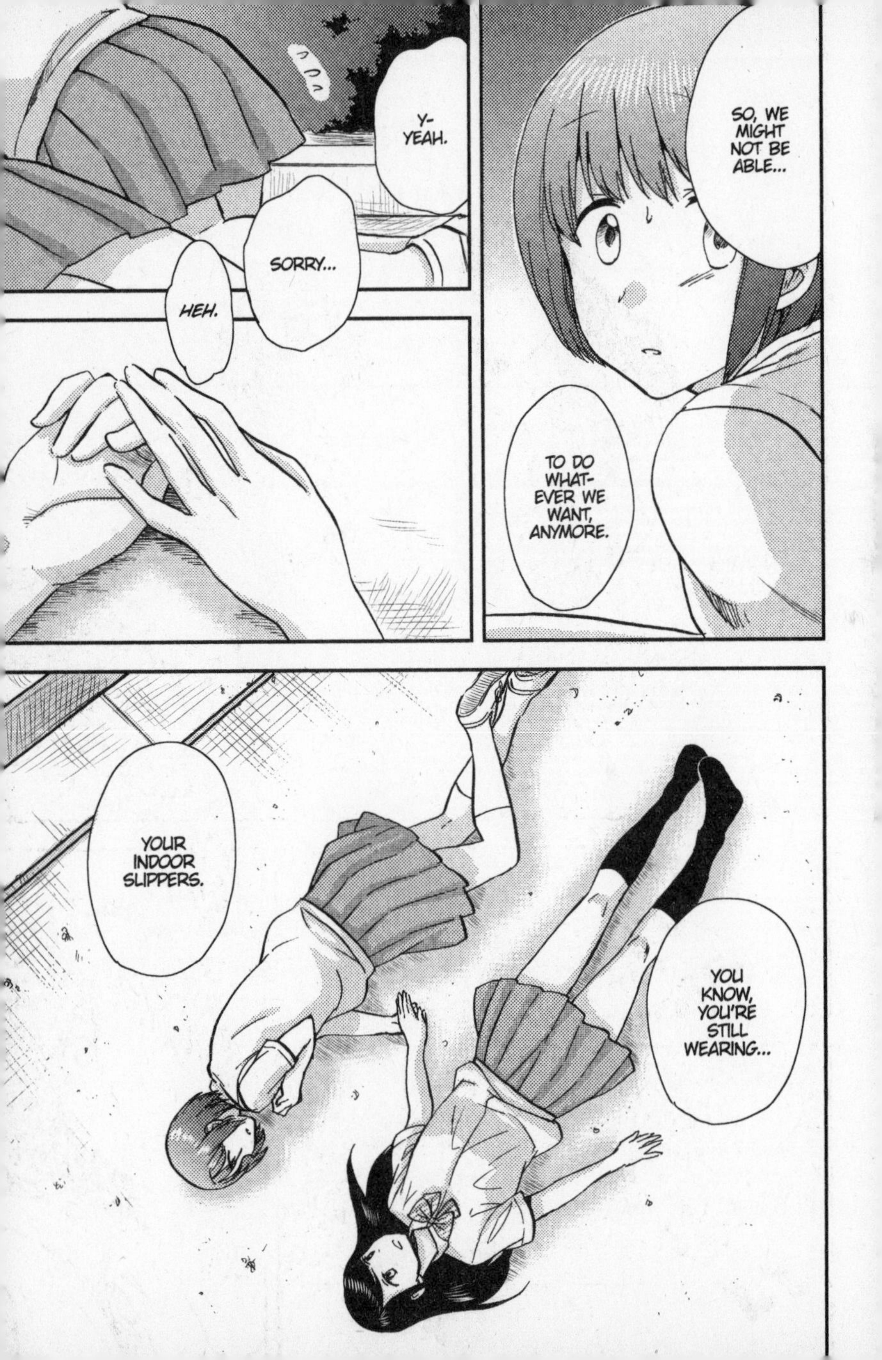
SO, WE MIGHT NOT BE ABLE...
TO DO WHAT-EVER WE WANT, ANYMORE.
Y-YEAH.
SORRY...
HEH.
YOU KNOW, YOU'RE STILL WEARING...
YOUR INDOOR SLIPPERS.

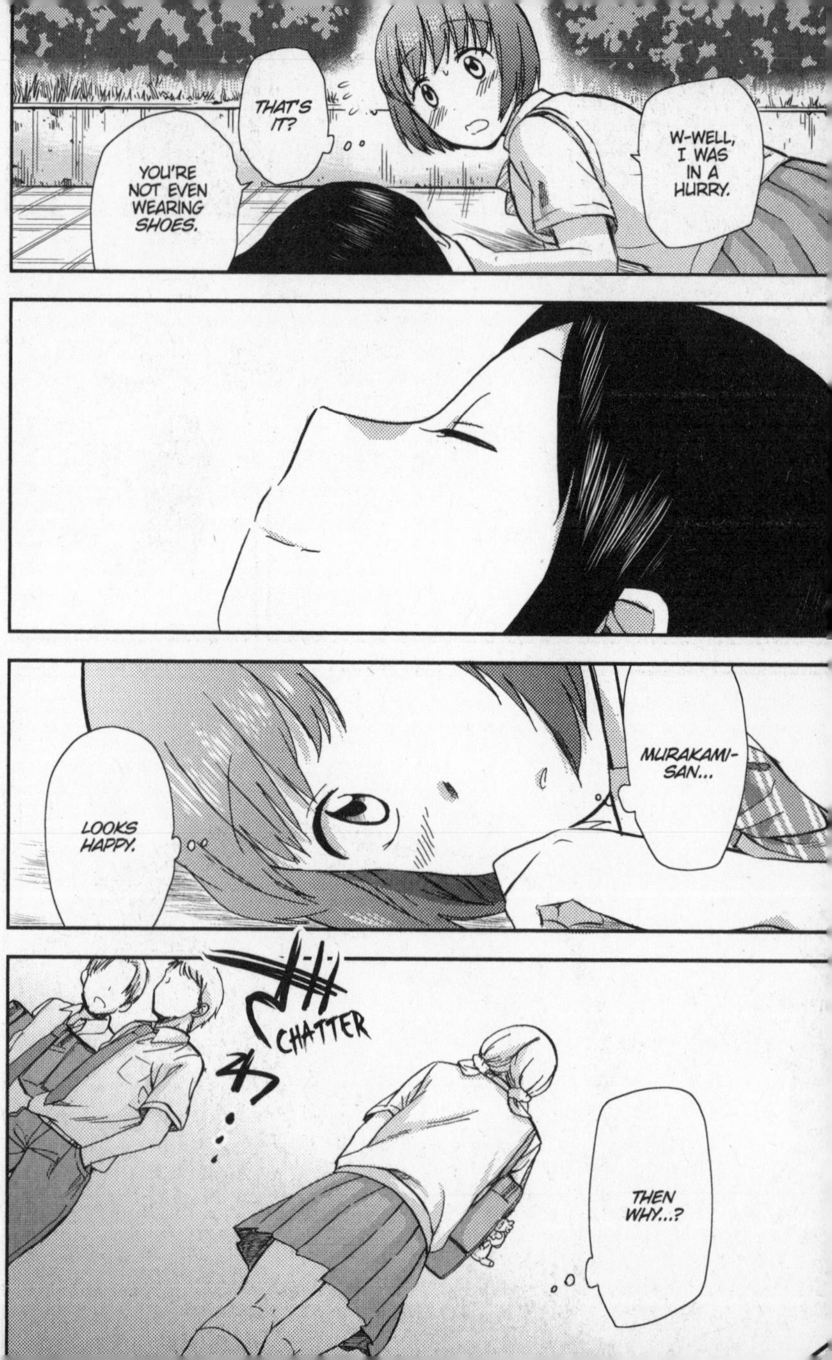
W-WELL, I WAS IN A HURRY.
THAT'S IT?
YOU'RE NOT EVEN WEARING SHOES.
MURAKAMI-SAN...
LOOKS HAPPY.
CHATTER
THEN WHY...?

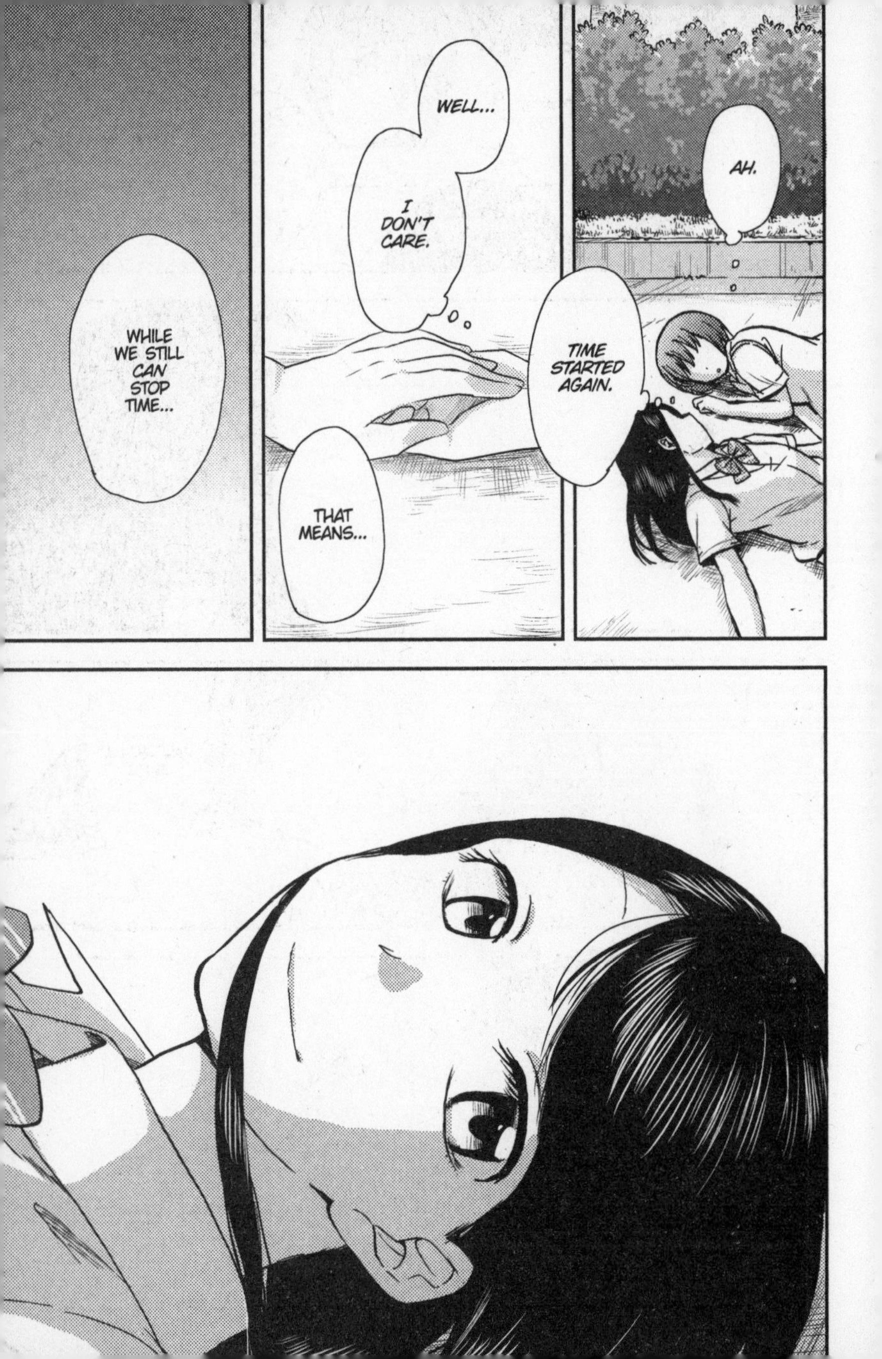
AH.
TIME STARTED AGAIN.
WELL...
I DON'T CARE.
THAT MEANS...
WHILE WE STILL CAN STOP TIME...

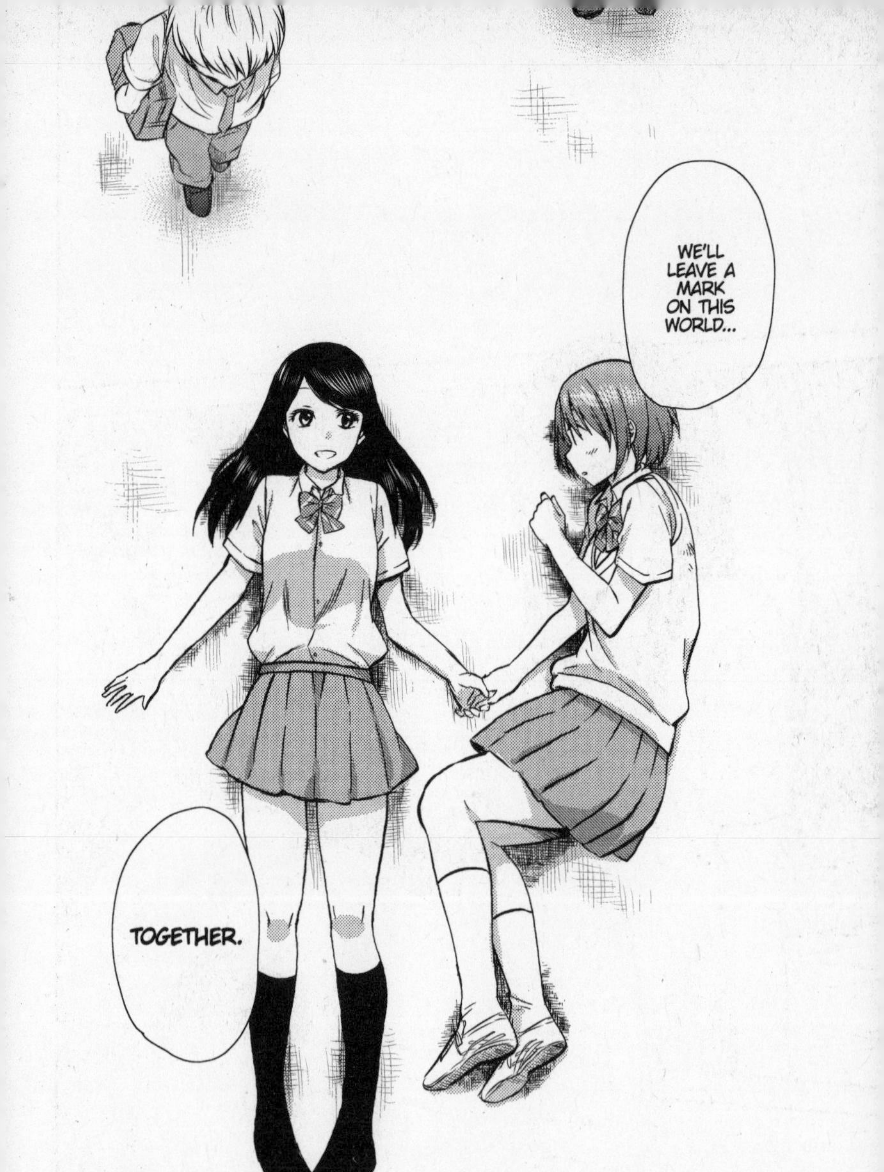
WE'LL LEAVE A MARK ON THIS WORLD...
TOGETHER.

#12. Why Didn't You Say Something? / END

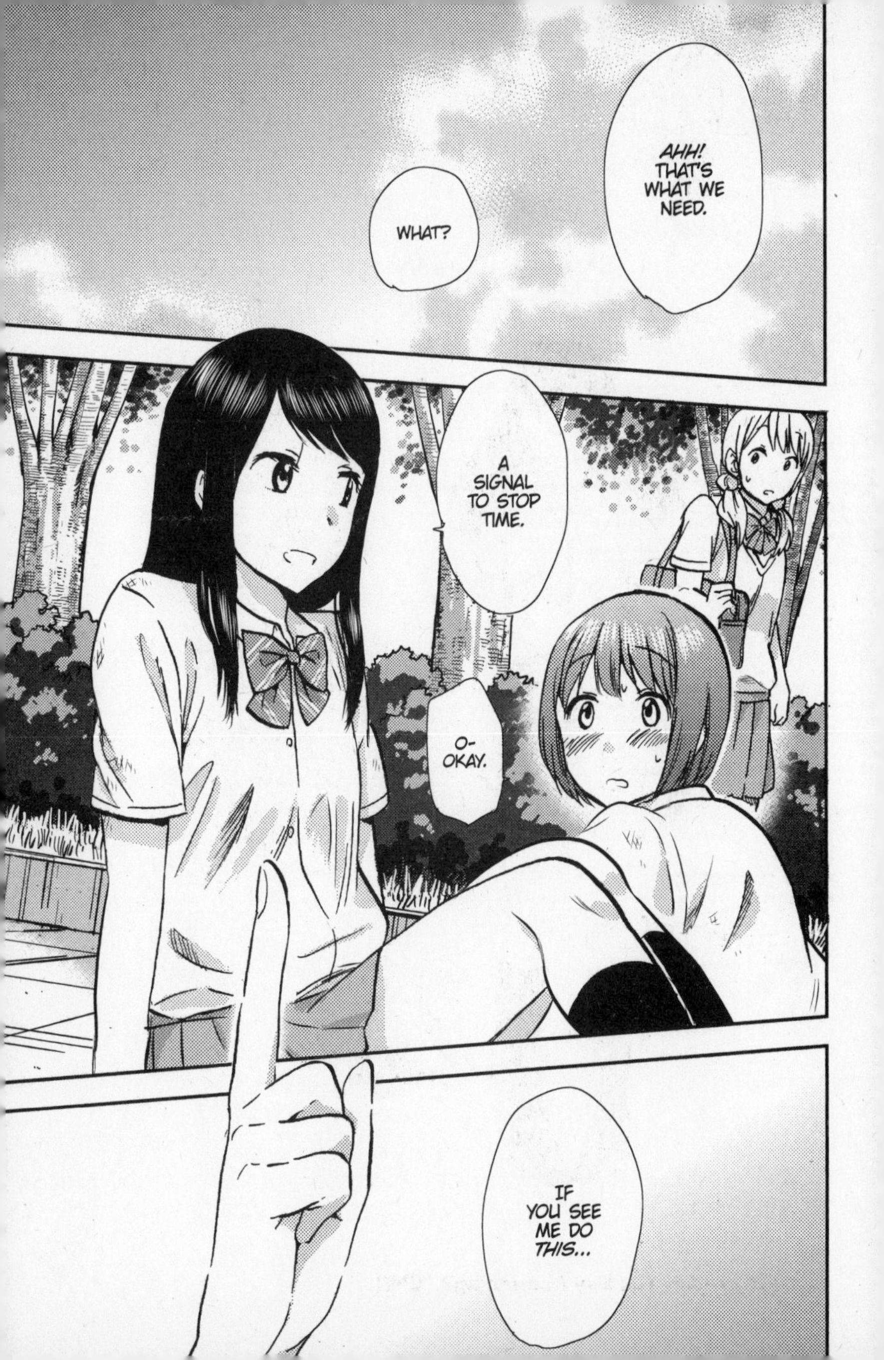
AHH! THAT'S WHAT WE NEED.
WHAT?
A SIGNAL TO STOP TIME.
O-OKAY.
IF YOU SEE ME DO *THIS*...

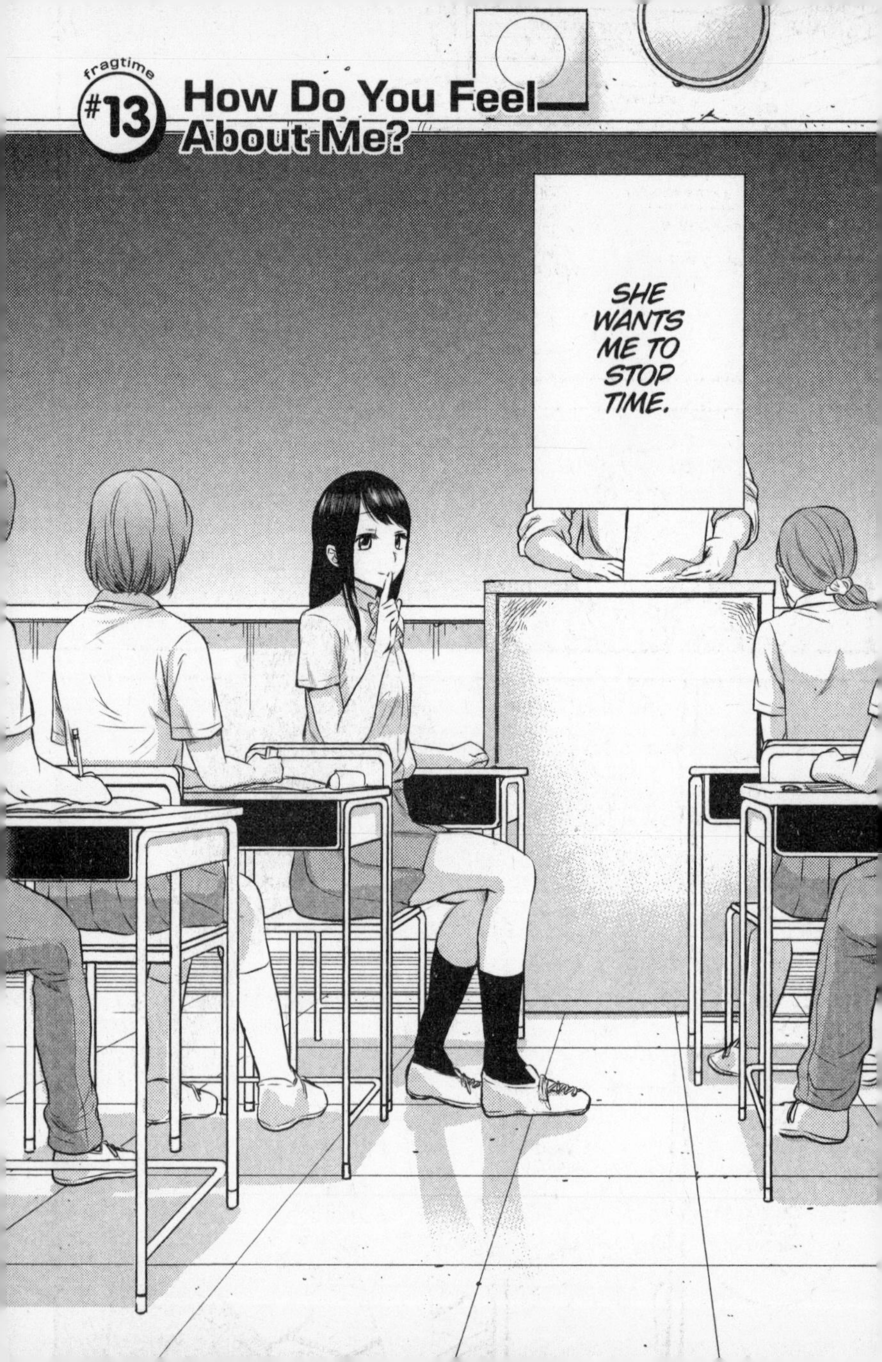
fragtime
#13 How Do You Feel About Me?
SHE WANTS ME TO STOP TIME.

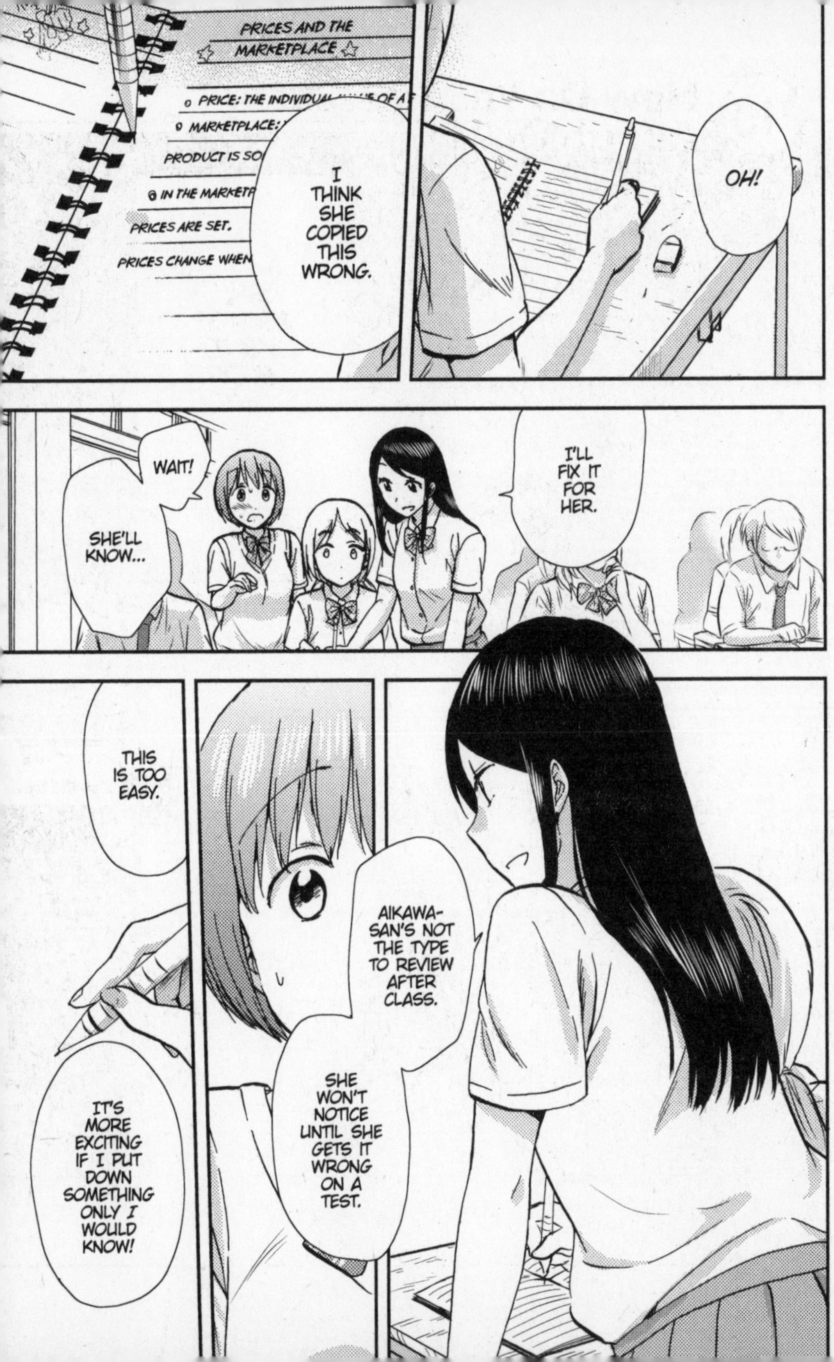
OH!
I THINK SHE COPIED THIS WRONG.
PRICES AND THE MARKETPLACE
PRICE: THE INDIVIDUAL
MARKETPLACE:
PRODUCT IS SO
IN THE MARKETP
PRICES ARE SET.
PRICES CHANGE WHEN
I'LL FIX IT FOR HER.
WAIT!
SHE'LL KNOW...
AIKAWA-SAN'S NOT THE TYPE TO REVIEW AFTER CLASS.
SHE WON'T NOTICE UNTIL SHE GETS IT WRONG ON A TEST.
THIS IS TOO EASY.
IT'S MORE EXCITING IF I PUT DOWN SOMETHING ONLY I WOULD KNOW!

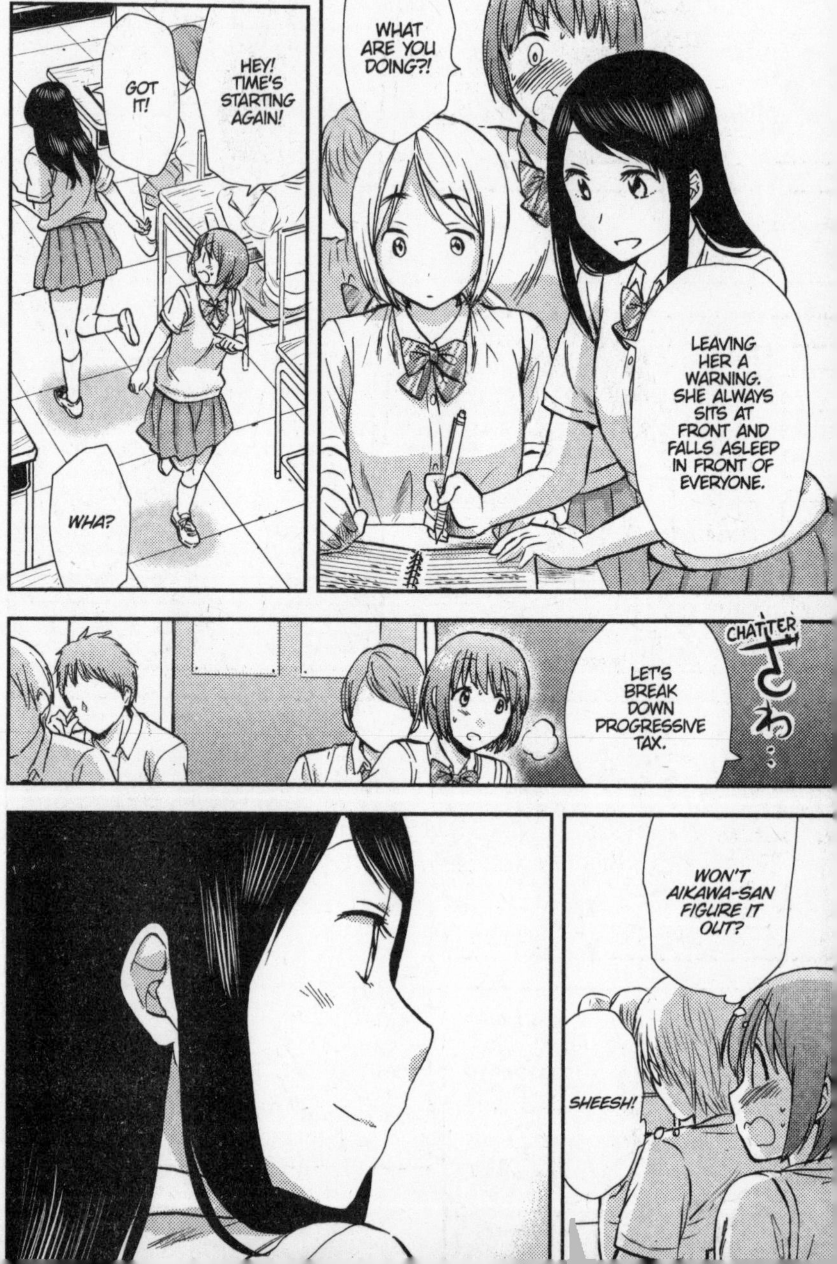
WHAT ARE YOU DOING?!
LEAVING HER A WARNING. SHE ALWAYS SITS AT FRONT AND FALLS ASLEEP IN FRONT OF EVERYONE.
HEY! TIME'S STARTING AGAIN!
GOT IT!
WHA?
CHATTER
LET'S BREAK DOWN PROGRESSIVE TAX.
WON'T AIKAWA-SAN FIGURE IT OUT?
SHEESH!

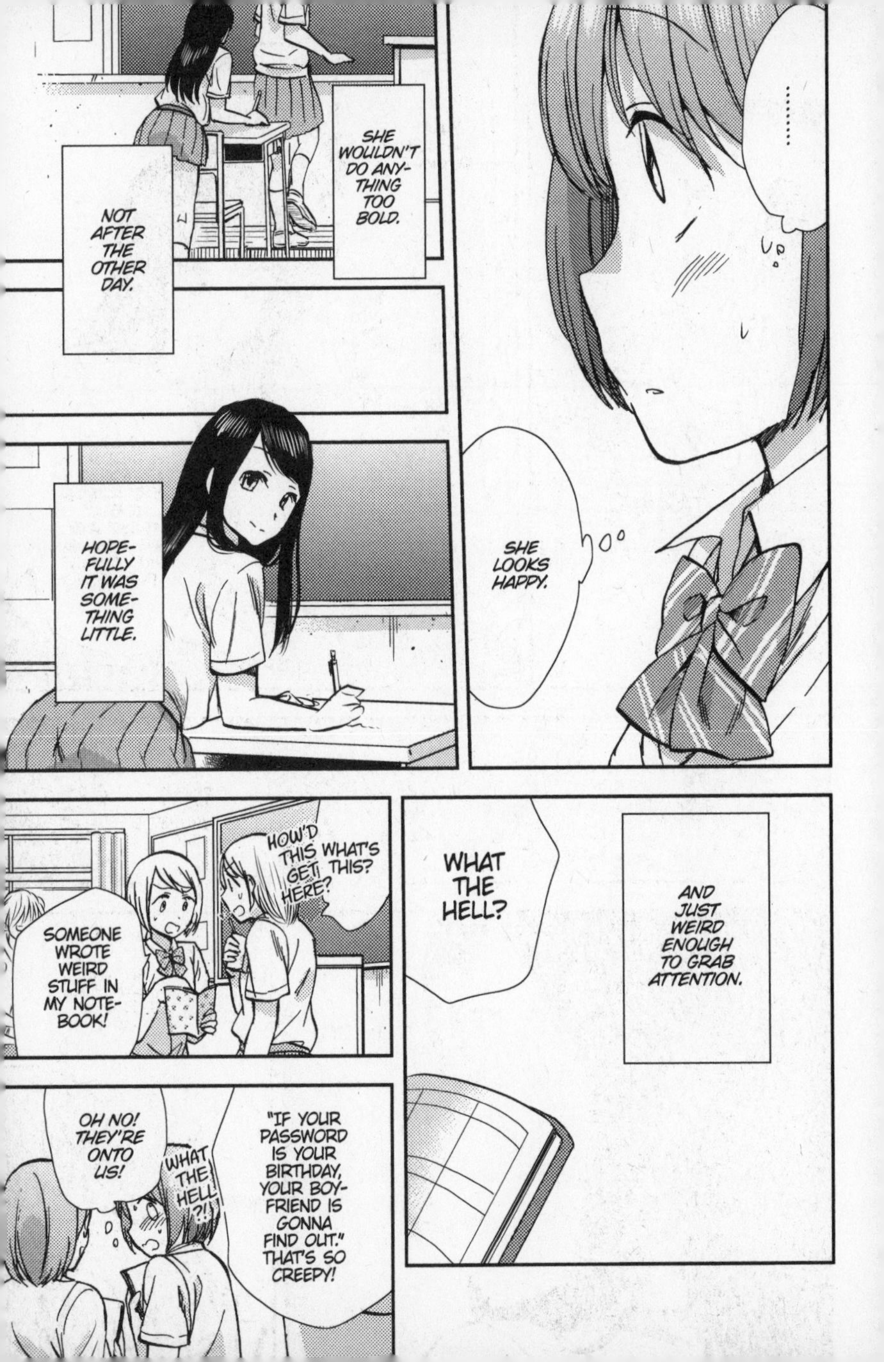
......
SHE LOOKS HAPPY.
SHE WOULDN'T DO ANYTHING TOO BOLD.
NOT AFTER THE OTHER DAY.
HOPEFULLY IT WAS SOMETHING LITTLE.
AND JUST WEIRD ENOUGH TO GRAB ATTENTION.
WHAT THE HELL?
WHAT'S THIS?
HOW'D THIS GET HERE?
SOMEONE WROTE WEIRD STUFF IN MY NOTEBOOK!
"IF YOUR PASSWORD IS YOUR BIRTHDAY, YOUR BOYFRIEND IS GONNA FIND OUT." THAT'S SO CREEPY!
OH NO! THEY'RE ONTO US!
WHAT THE HELL?!

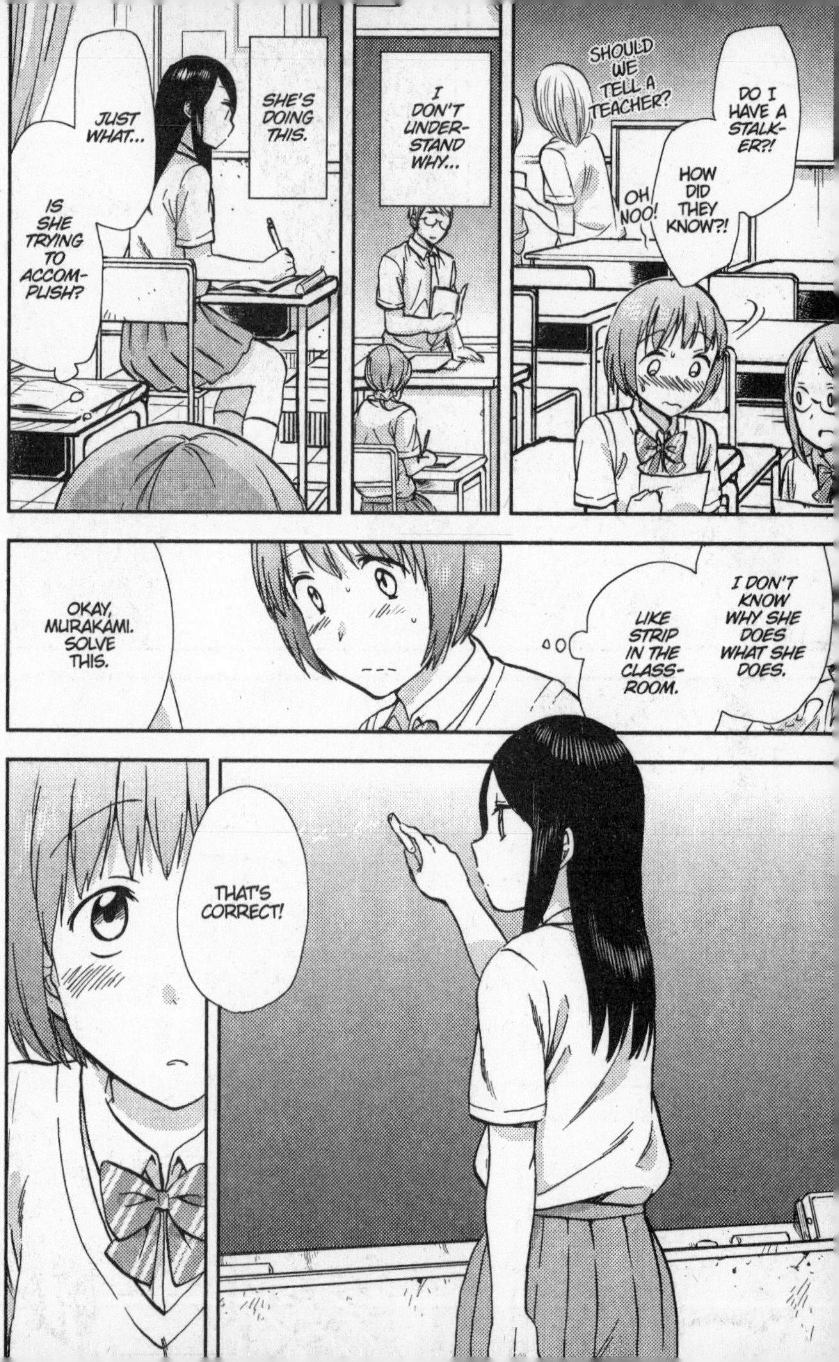
DO I HAVE A STALKER?!
SHOULD WE TELL A TEACHER?
HOW DID THEY KNOW?!
OH NOO!
I DON'T UNDERSTAND WHY...
SHE'S DOING THIS.
JUST WHAT...
IS SHE TRYING TO ACCOMPLISH?
I DON'T KNOW WHY SHE DOES WHAT SHE DOES.
LIKE STRIP IN THE CLASSROOM.
OKAY, MURAKAMI. SOLVE THIS.
THAT'S CORRECT!

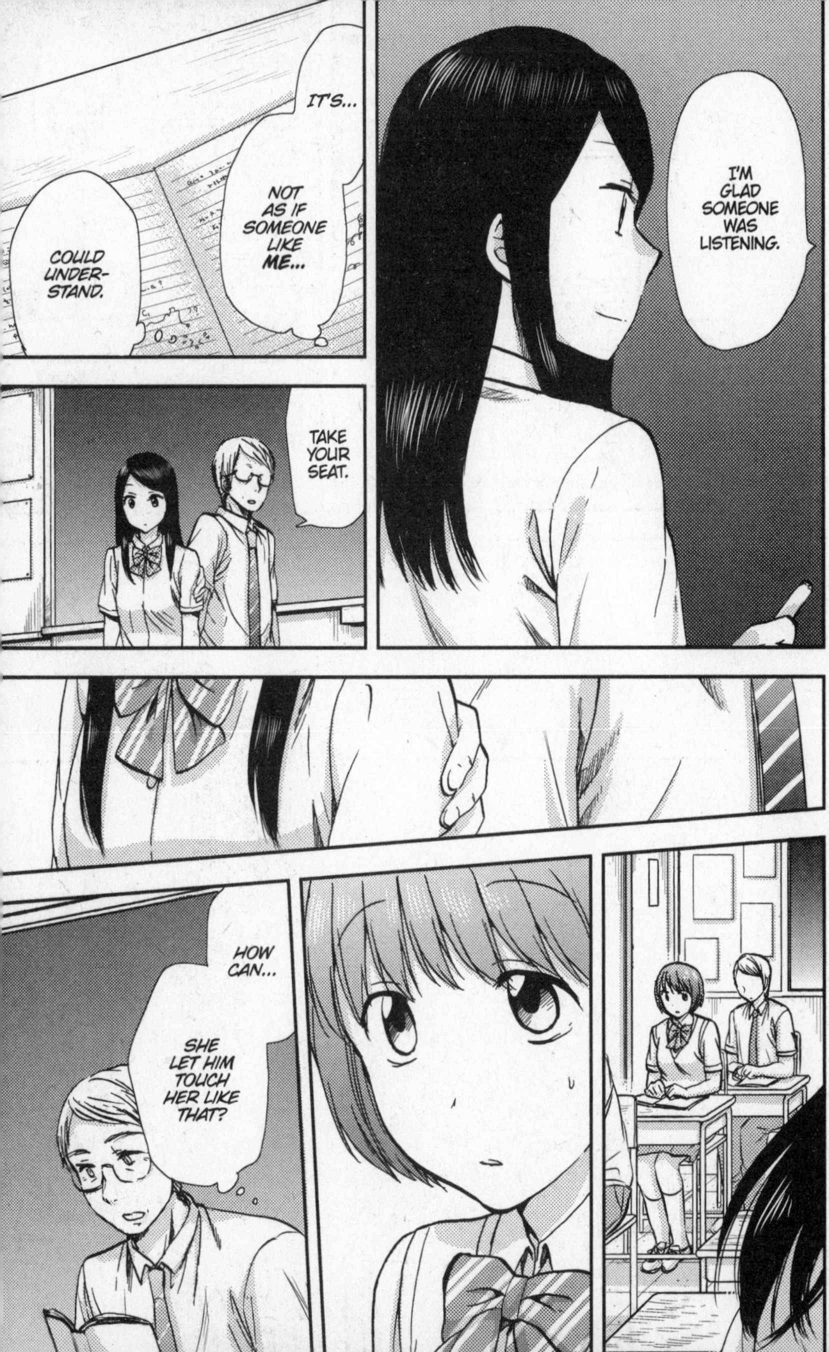
I'M GLAD SOMEONE WAS LISTENING.
IT'S...
NOT AS IF SOMEONE LIKE ME...
COULD UNDER-STAND.
TAKE YOUR SEAT.
HOW CAN...
SHE LET HIM TOUCH HER LIKE THAT?

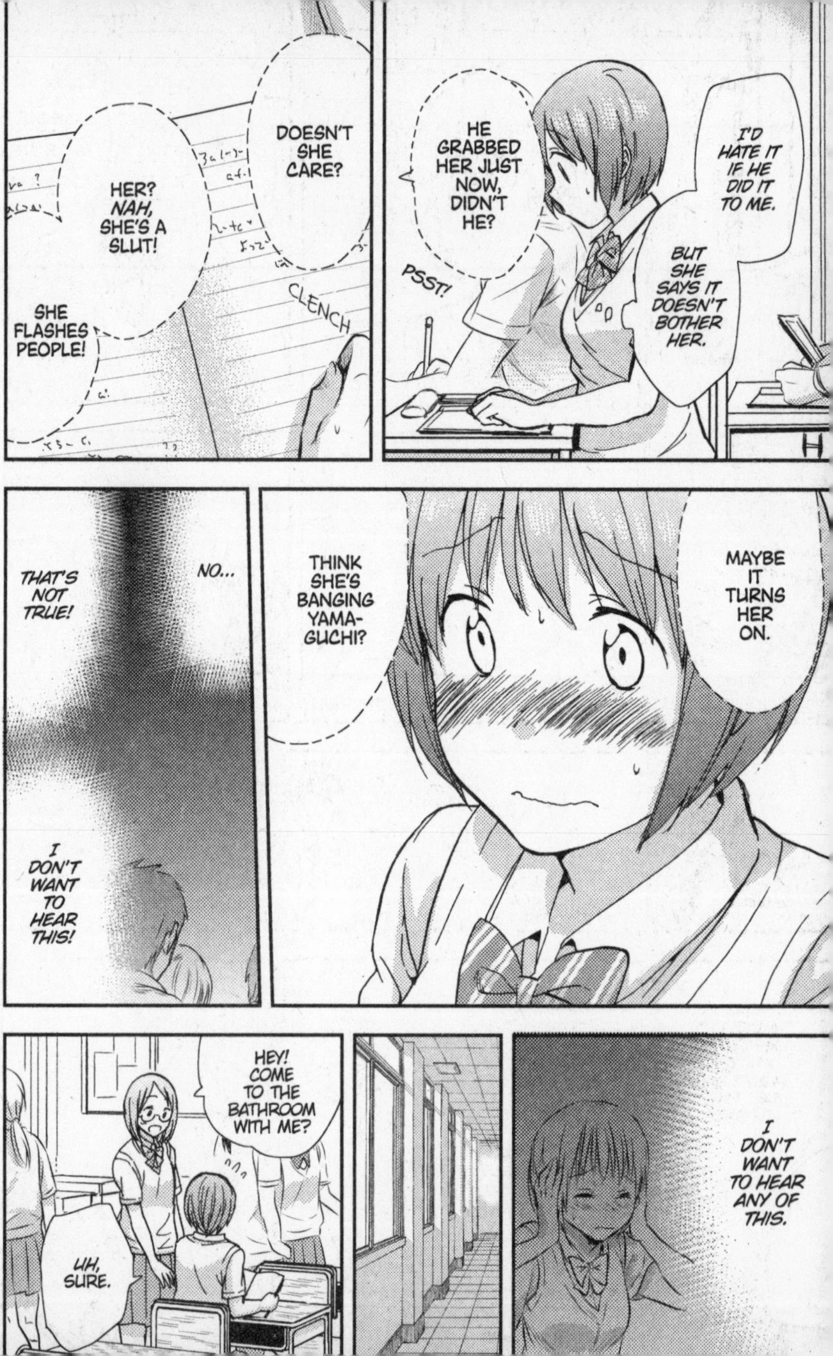
I'D HATE IT IF HE DID IT TO ME.
BUT SHE SAYS IT DOESN'T BOTHER HER.
HE GRABBED HER JUST NOW, DIDN'T HE?
PSST!
DOESN'T SHE CARE?
HER? NAH, SHE'S A SLUT!
CLENCH
SHE FLASHES PEOPLE!
MAYBE IT TURNS HER ON.
THINK SHE'S BANGING YAMA-GUCHI?
NO...
THAT'S NOT TRUE!
I DON'T WANT TO HEAR THIS!
I DON'T WANT TO HEAR ANY OF THIS.
HEY! COME TO THE BATHROOM WITH ME?
UH, SURE.

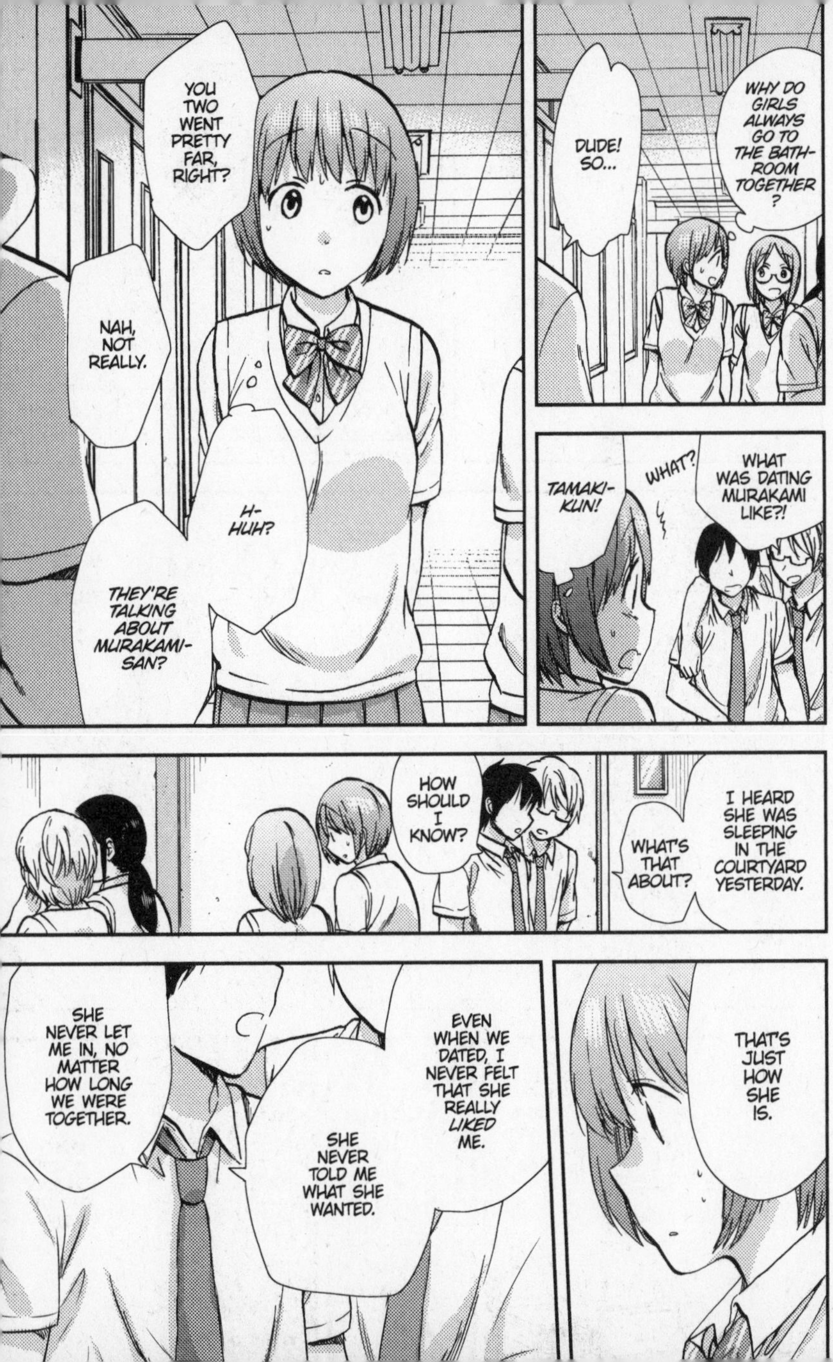
WHY DO GIRLS ALWAYS GO TO THE BATH-ROOM TOGETHER?
DUDE! SO...
WHAT WAS DATING MURAKAMI LIKE?!
WHAT?
TAMAKI-KUN!
YOU TWO WENT PRETTY FAR, RIGHT?
NAH, NOT REALLY.
H-HUH?
THEY'RE TALKING ABOUT MURAKAMI-SAN?
I HEARD SHE WAS SLEEPING IN THE COURTYARD YESTERDAY.
WHAT'S THAT ABOUT?
HOW SHOULD I KNOW?
THAT'S JUST HOW SHE IS.
EVEN WHEN WE DATED, I NEVER FELT THAT SHE REALLY LIKED ME.
SHE NEVER LET ME IN, NO MATTER HOW LONG WE WERE TOGETHER.
SHE NEVER TOLD ME WHAT SHE WANTED.

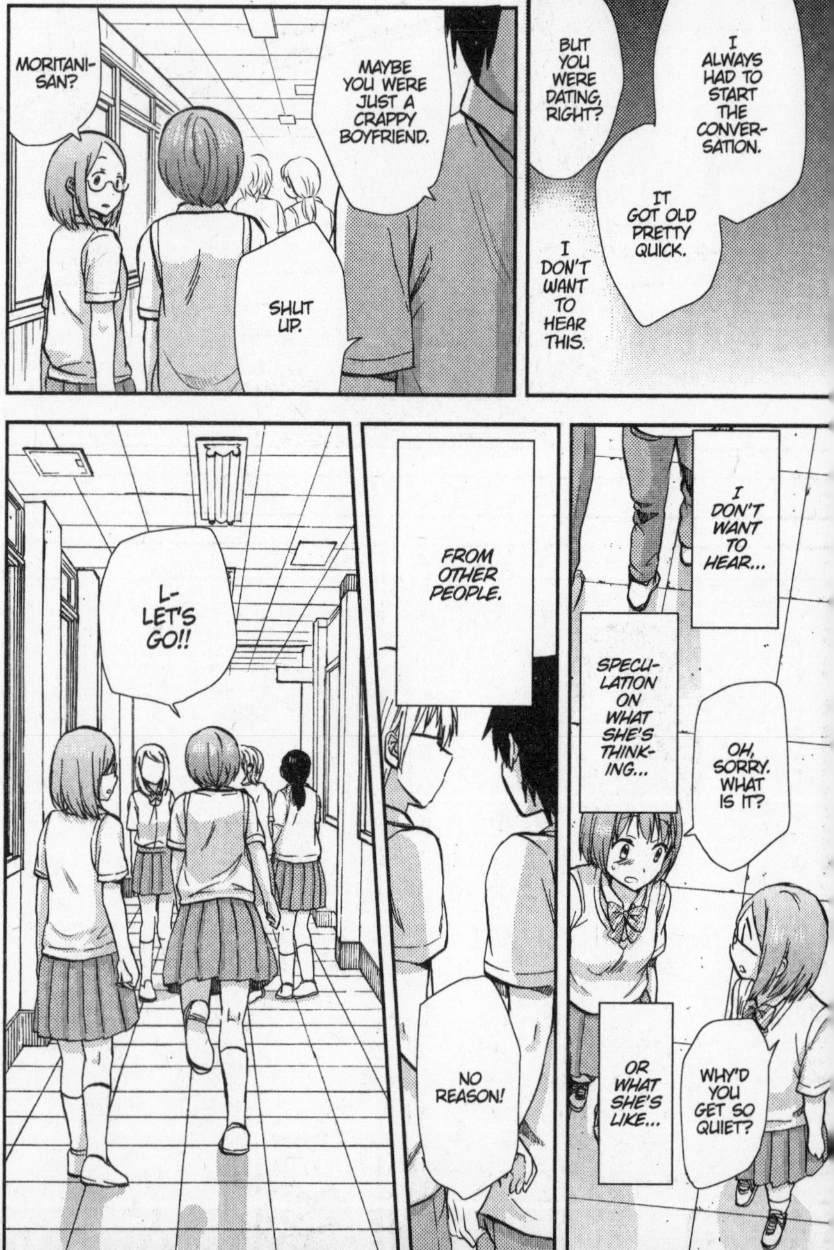
I ALWAYS HAD TO START THE CONVER-SATION.
BUT YOU WERE DATING, RIGHT?
IT GOT OLD PRETTY QUICK.
I DON'T WANT TO HEAR THIS.
MAYBE YOU WERE JUST A CRAPPY BOYFRIEND.
MORITANI-SAN?
SHUT UP.
I DON'T WANT TO HEAR...
SPECU-LATION ON WHAT SHE'S THINK-ING...
OH, SORRY. WHAT IS IT?
WHY'D YOU GET SO QUIET?
OR WHAT SHE'S LIKE...
FROM OTHER PEOPLE.
NO REASON!
L-LET'S GO!!

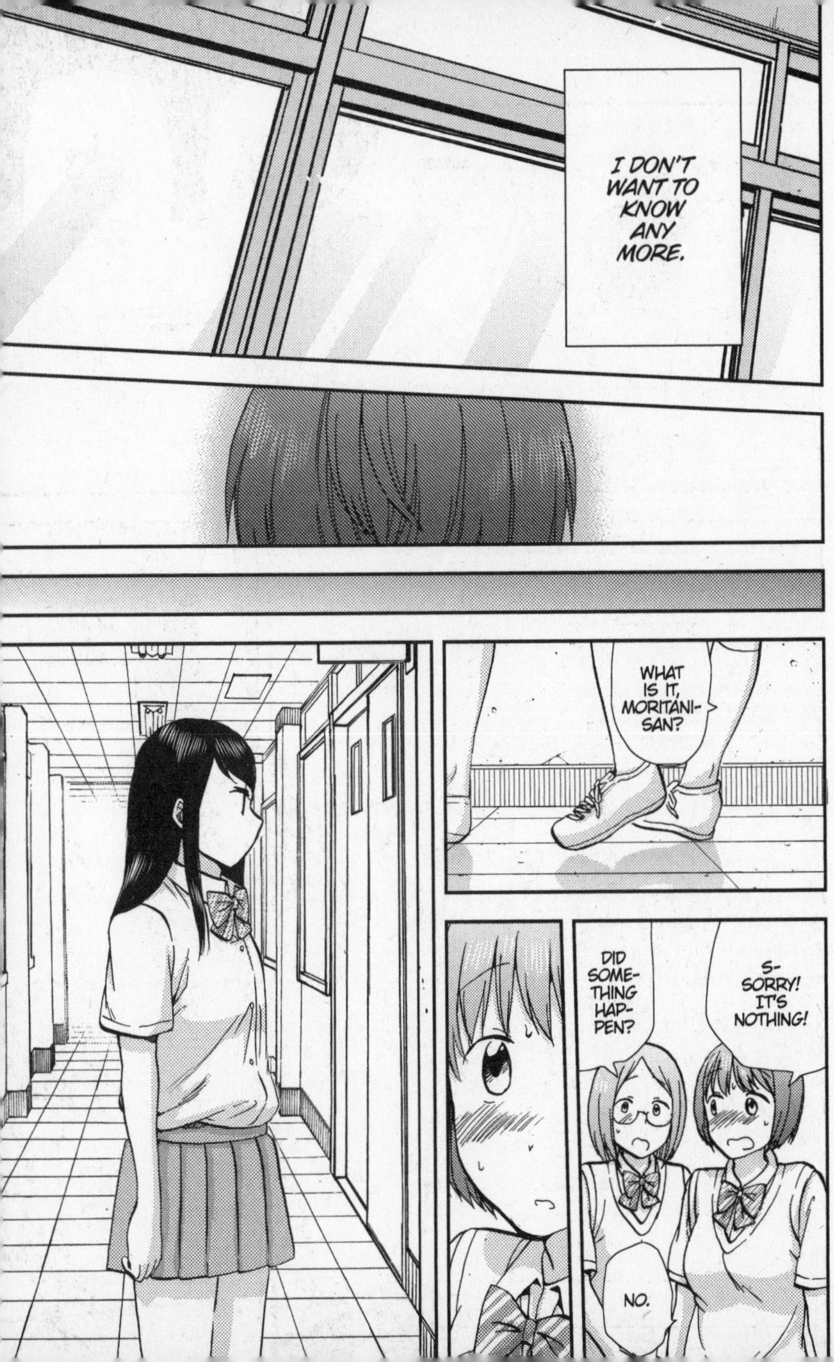
I DON'T WANT TO KNOW ANY MORE.
WHAT IS IT, MORITANI-SAN?
S-SORRY! IT'S NOTHING!
DID SOMETHING HAPPEN?
NO.

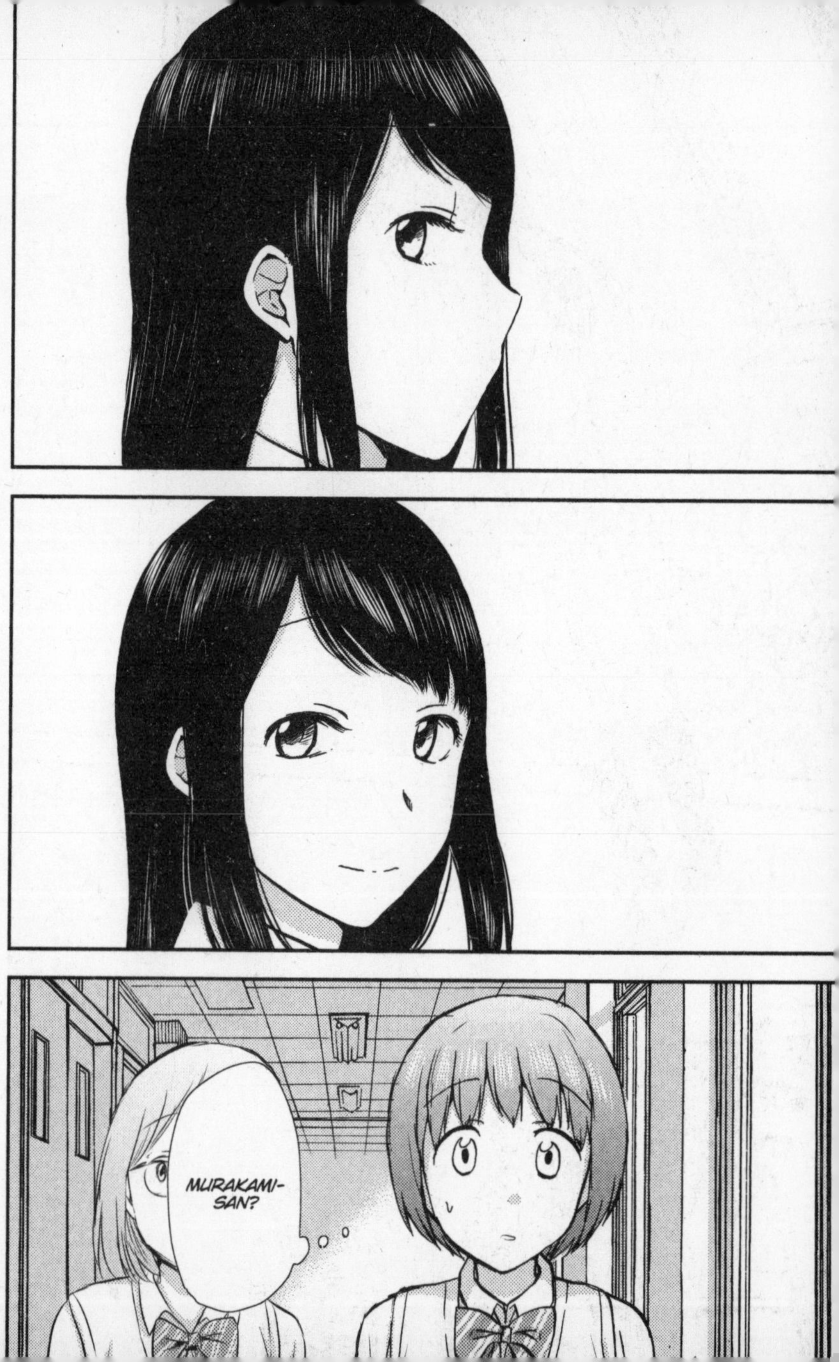
MURAKAMI-SAN?

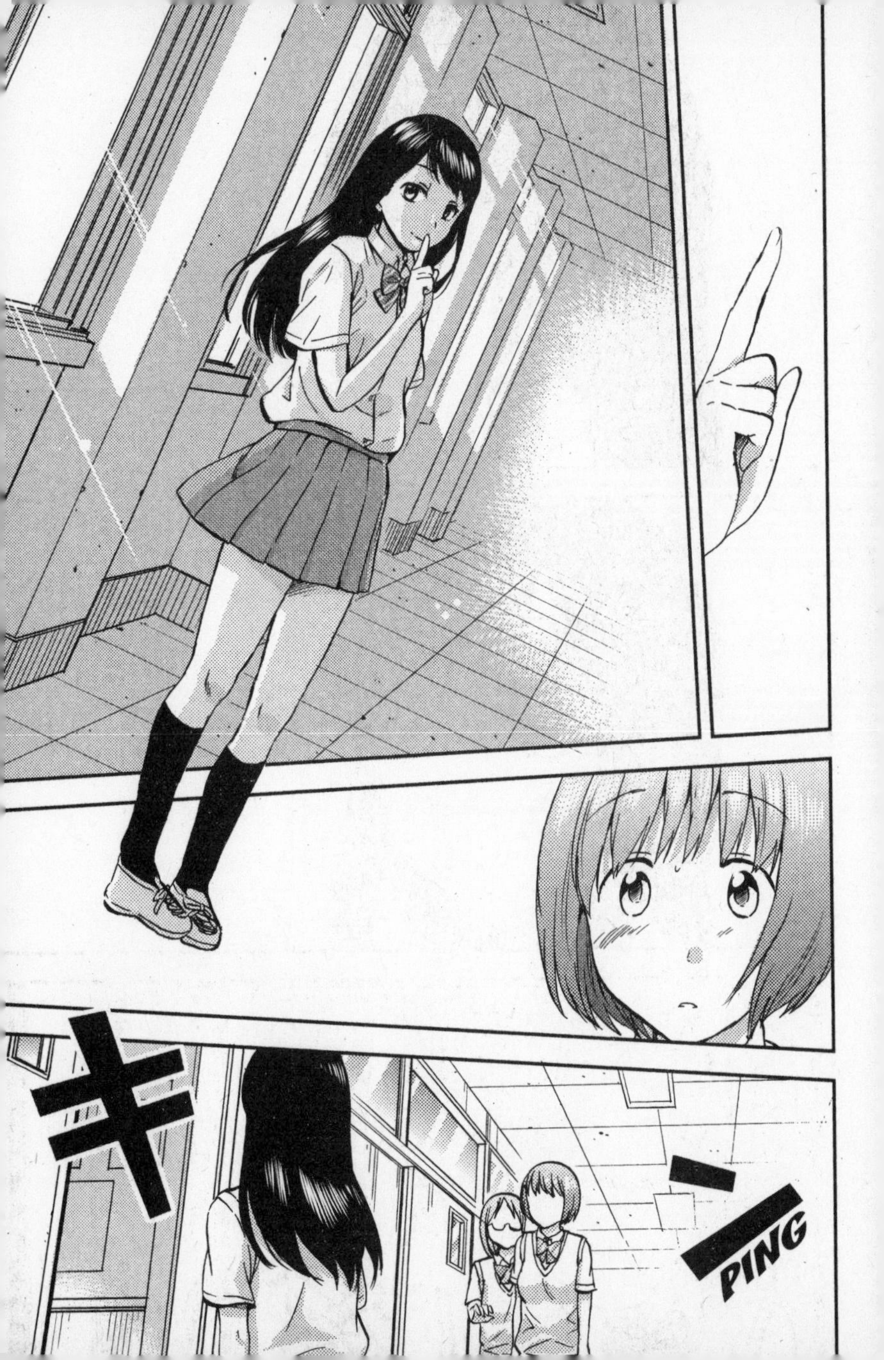
PING

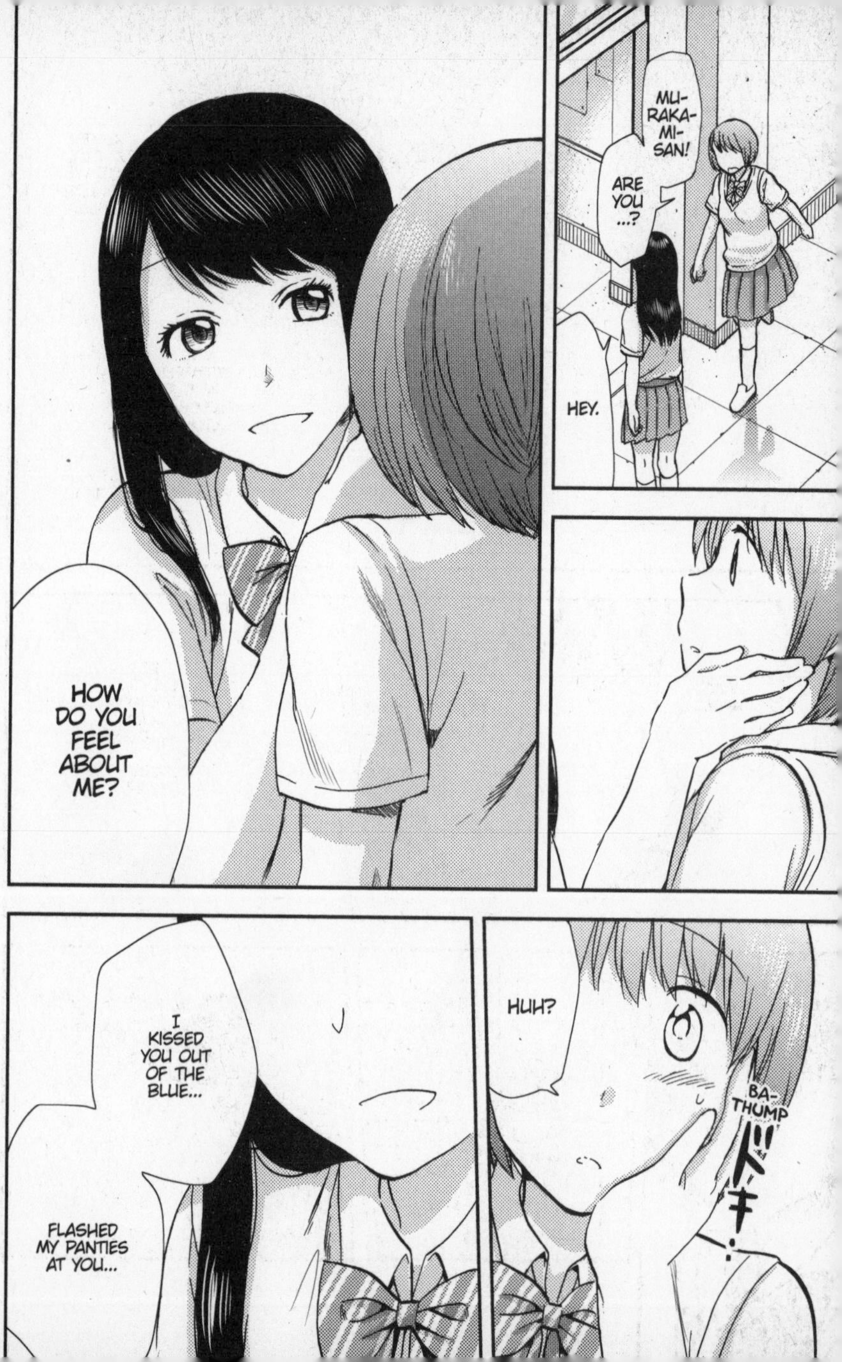
MU-RAKA-MI-SAN!
ARE YOU ...?
HEY.
HOW DO YOU FEEL ABOUT ME?
HUH?
BA-THUMP
ドキ!
I KISSED YOU OUT OF THE BLUE...
FLASHED MY PANTIES AT YOU...

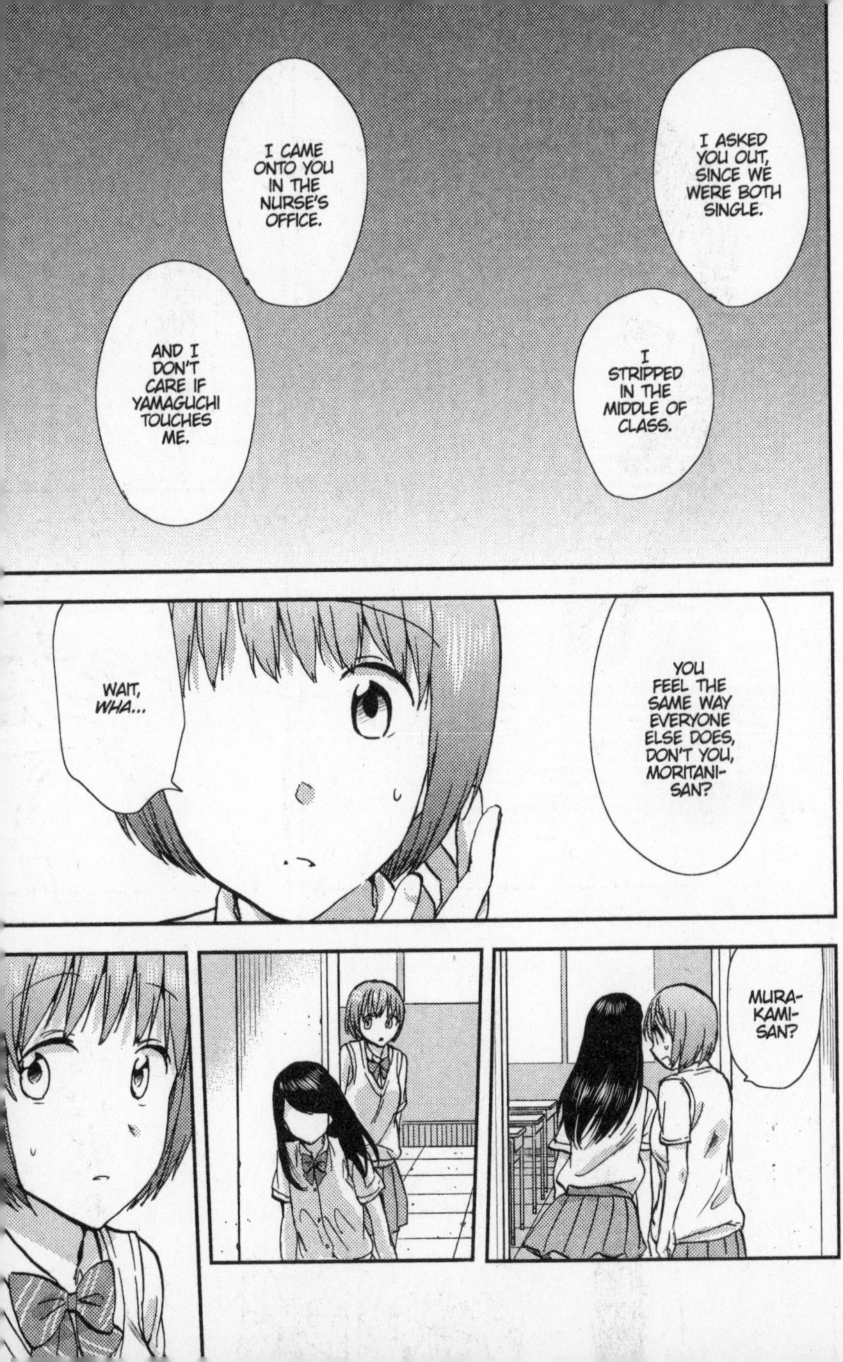
I ASKED YOU OUT, SINCE WE WERE BOTH SINGLE.
I CAME ONTO YOU IN THE NURSE'S OFFICE.
I STRIPPED IN THE MIDDLE OF CLASS.
AND I DON'T CARE IF YAMAGUCHI TOUCHES ME.
YOU FEEL THE SAME WAY EVERYONE ELSE DOES, DON'T YOU, MORITANI-SAN?
WAIT, WHA...
MURA-KAMI-SAN?

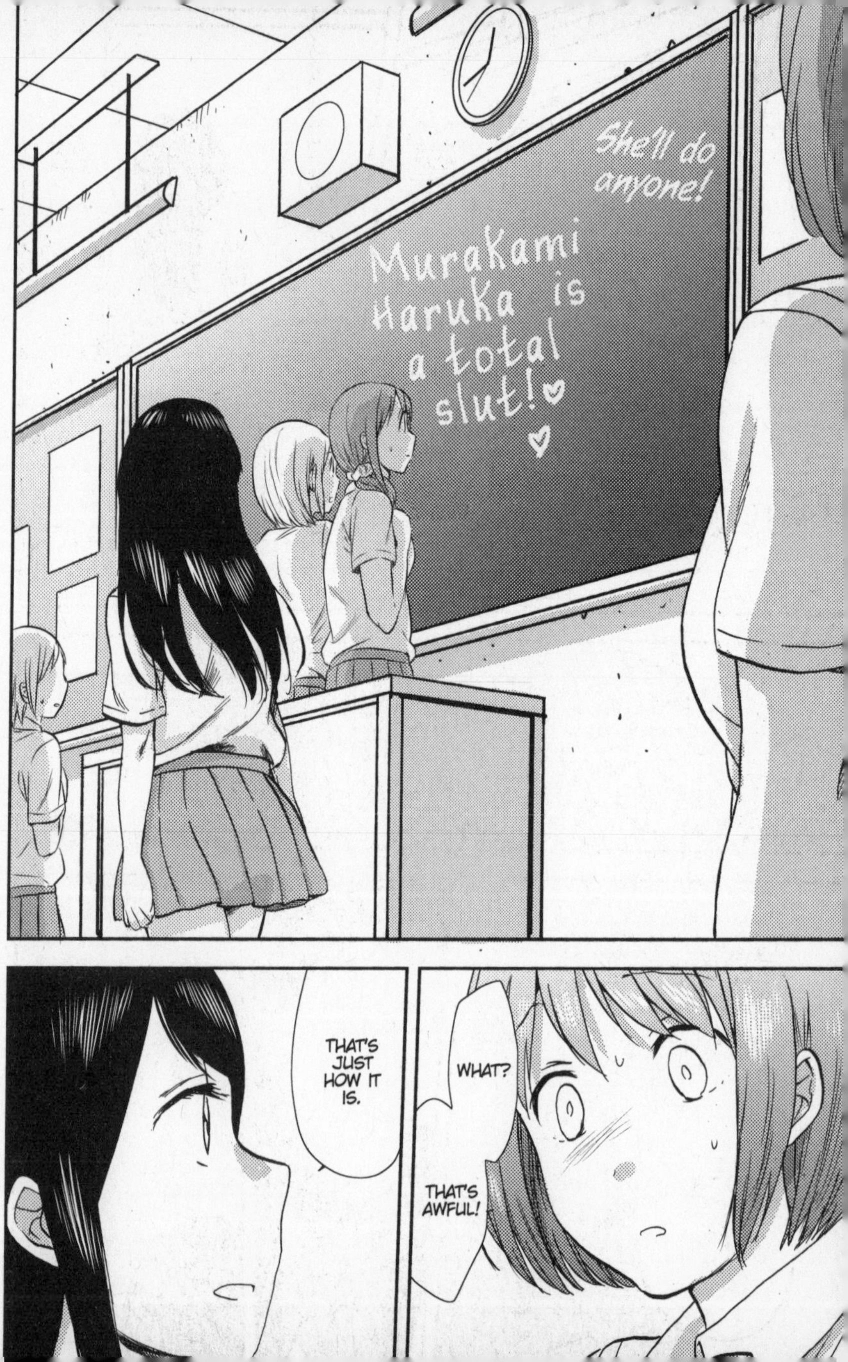
She'll do anyone!
Murakami Haruka is a total slut!
WHAT?
THAT'S AWFUL!
THAT'S JUST HOW IT IS.

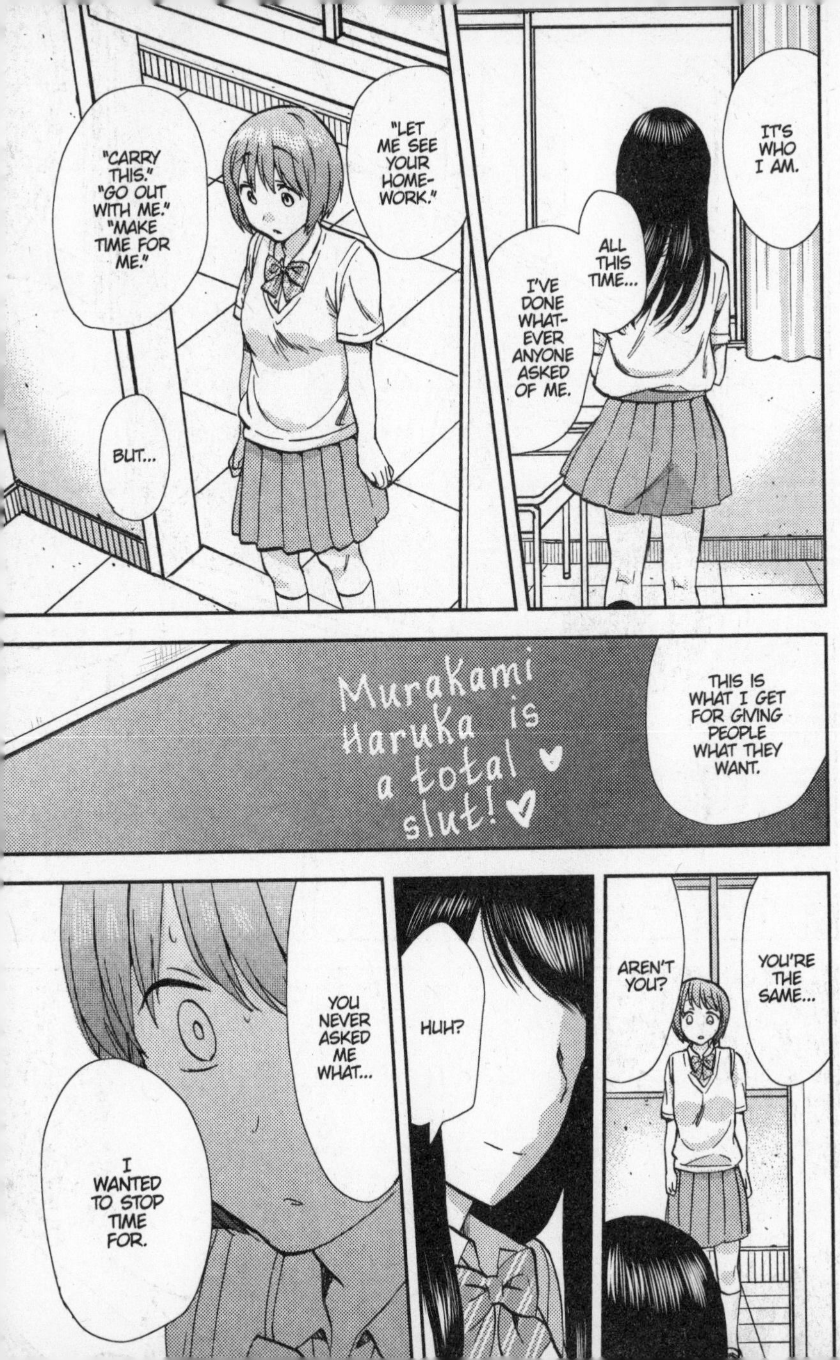
IT'S WHO I AM.
ALL THIS TIME...
I'VE DONE WHATEVER ANYONE ASKED OF ME.
"LET ME SEE YOUR HOMEWORK."
"CARRY THIS." "GO OUT WITH ME." "MAKE TIME FOR ME."
BUT...
THIS IS WHAT I GET FOR GIVING PEOPLE WHAT THEY WANT.
Murakami Haruka is a total slut!
YOU'RE THE SAME...
AREN'T YOU?
HUH?
YOU NEVER ASKED ME WHAT...
I WANTED TO STOP TIME FOR.

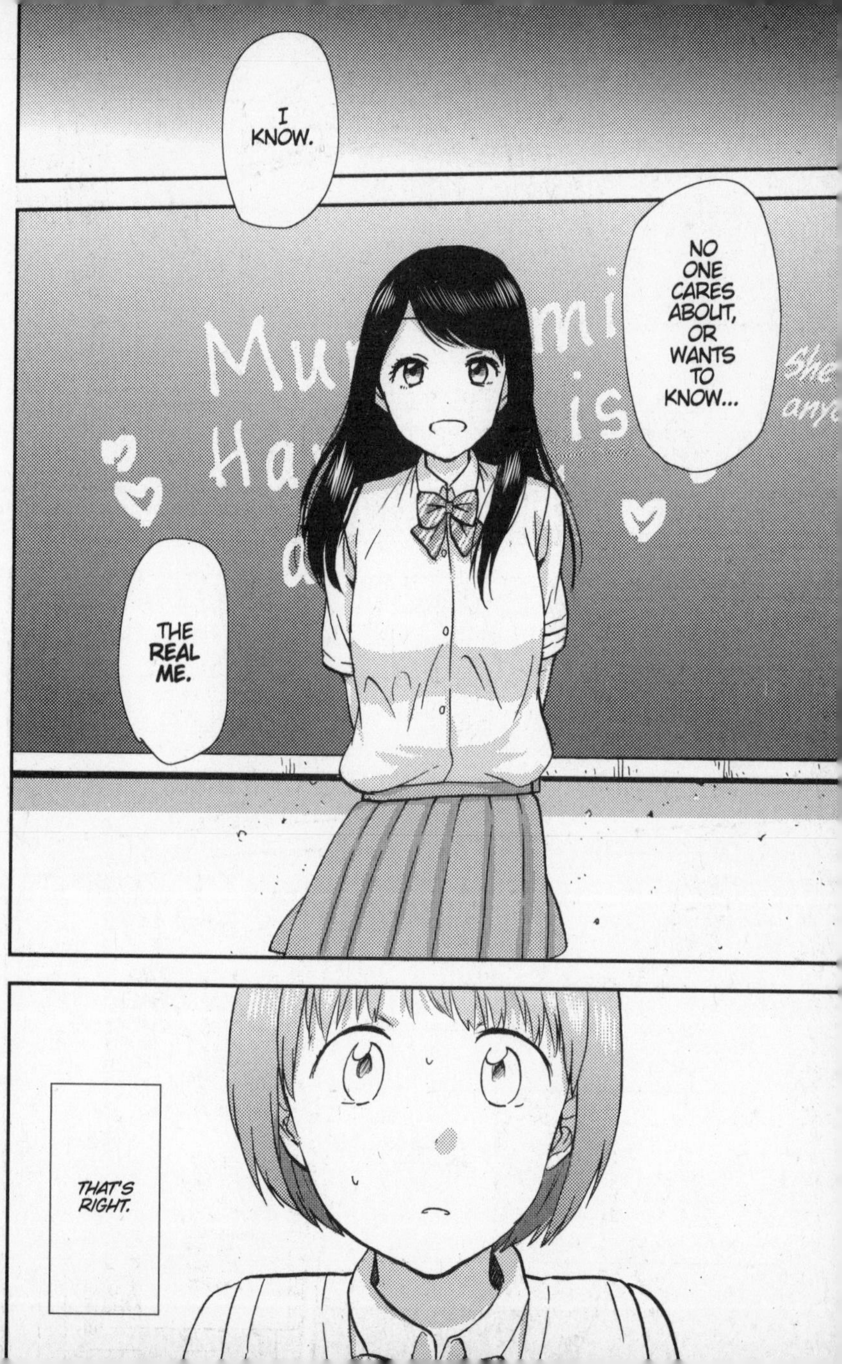
I KNOW.
NO ONE CARES ABOUT, OR WANTS TO KNOW...
THE REAL ME.
THAT'S RIGHT.

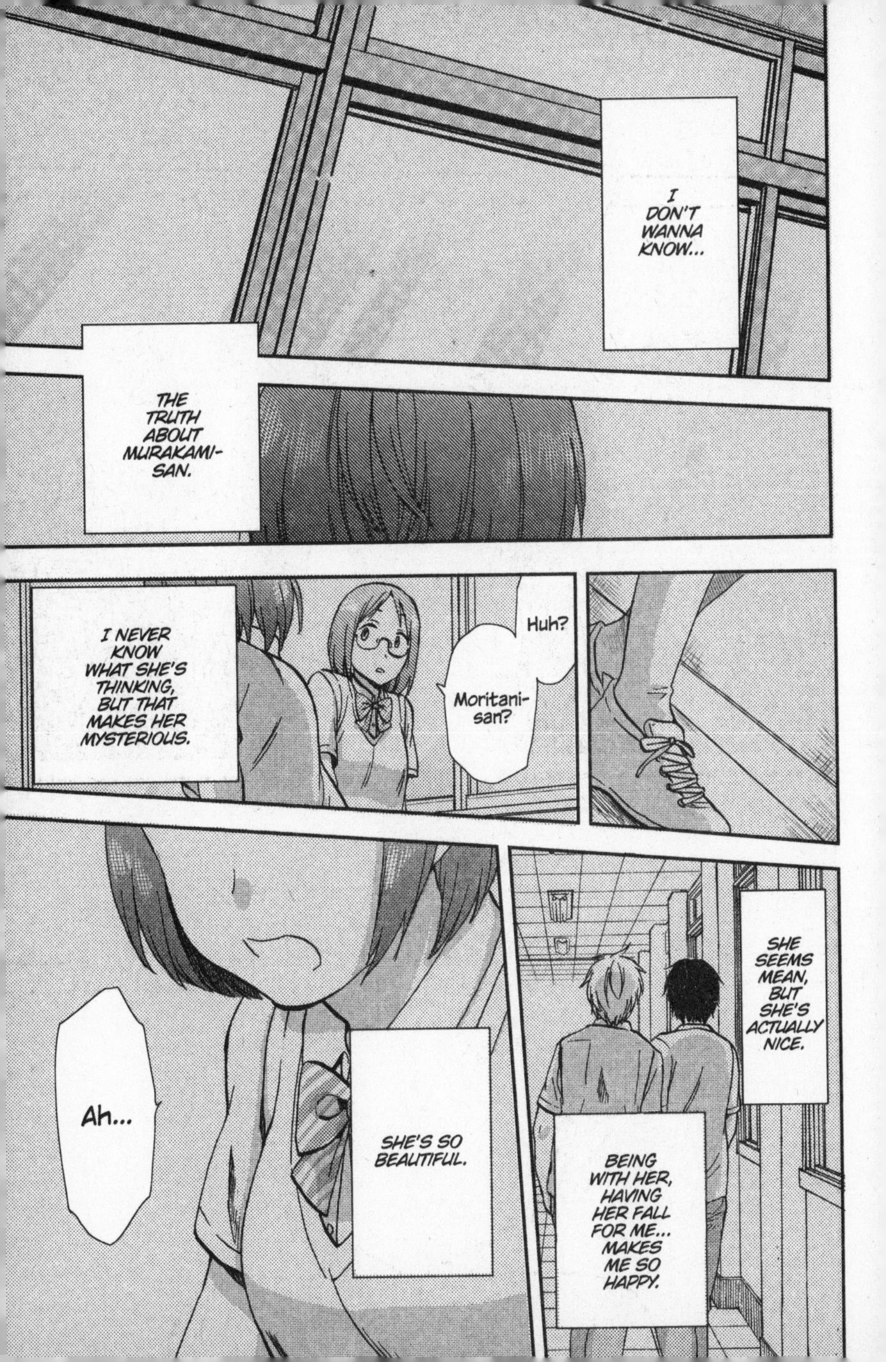
I DON'T WANNA KNOW...
THE TRUTH ABOUT MURAKAMI-SAN.
Huh? Moritani-san?
I NEVER KNOW WHAT SHE'S THINKING, BUT THAT MAKES HER MYSTERIOUS.
SHE SEEMS MEAN, BUT SHE'S ACTUALLY NICE.
BEING WITH HER, HAVING HER FALL FOR ME... MAKES ME SO HAPPY.
SHE'S SO BEAUTIFUL.
Ah...

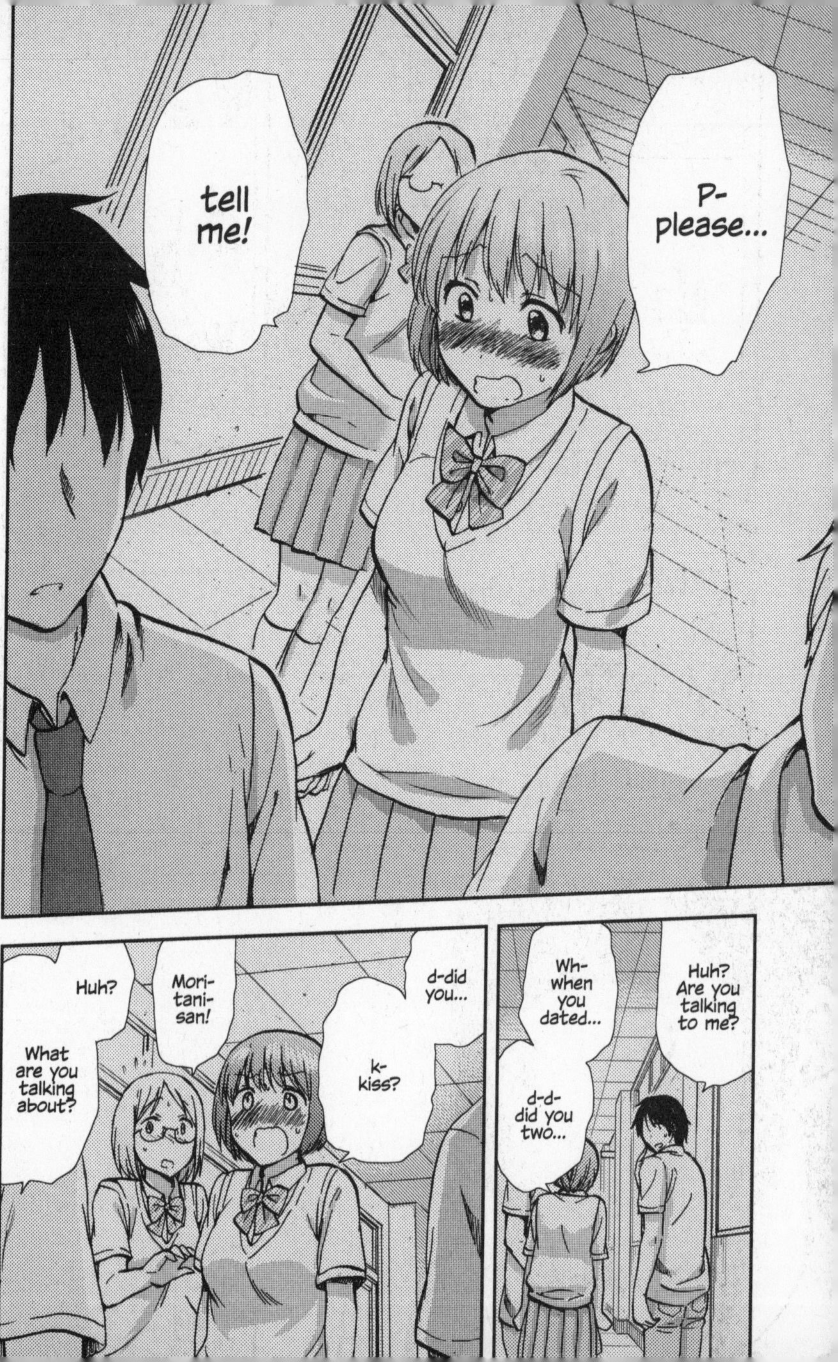
P-please...
tell me!
Huh? Are you talking to me?
Wh-when you dated...
d-d-did you two...
d-did you...
k-kiss?
Mori-tani-san!
Huh?
What are you talking about?

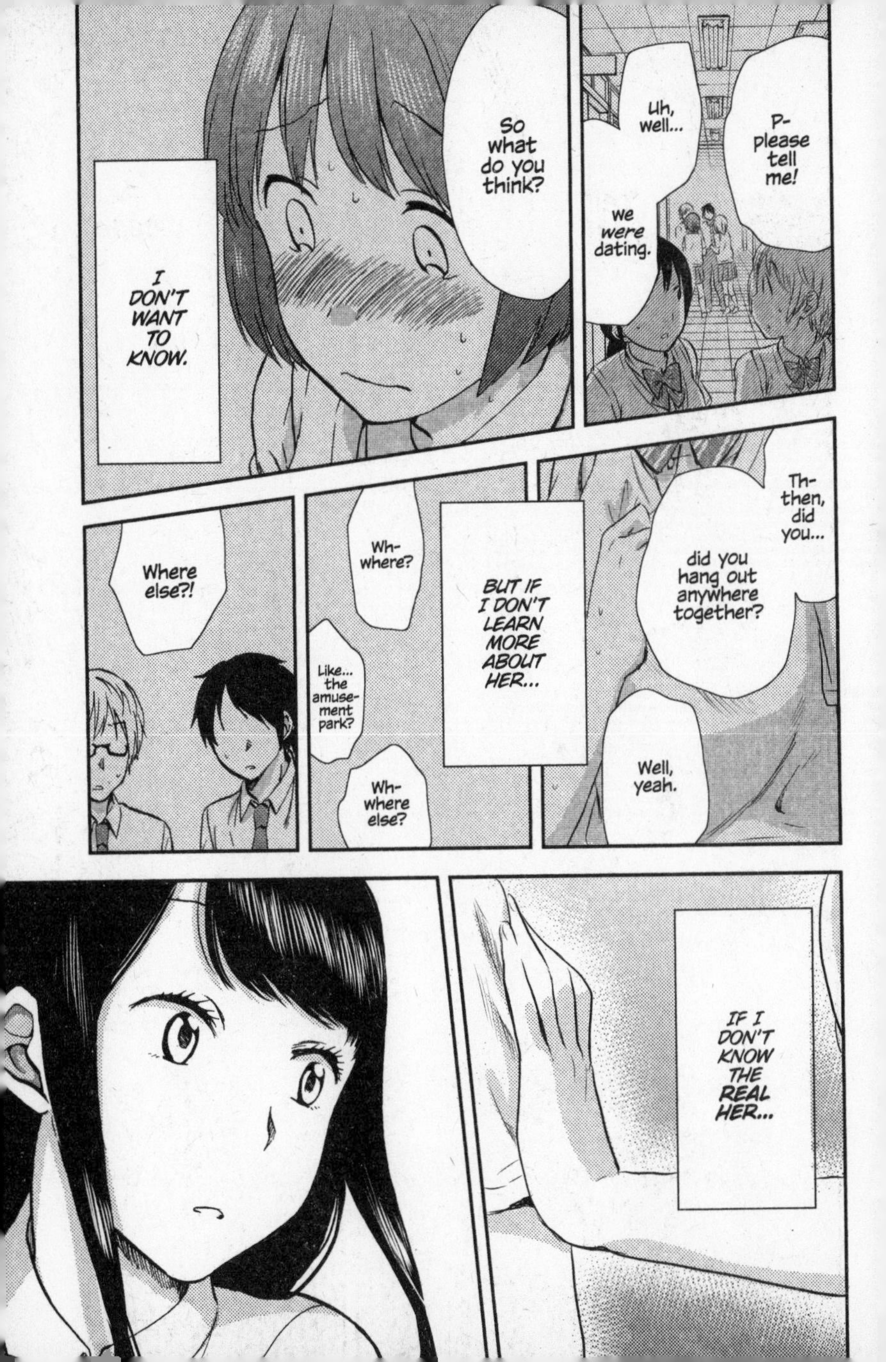
P- please tell me!
Uh, well...
we were dating.
So what do you think?
I DON'T WANT TO KNOW.
Th- then, did you...
did you hang out anywhere together?
Well, yeah.
BUT IF I DON'T LEARN MORE ABOUT HER...
Wh- where?
Like... the amuse- ment park?
Wh- where else?
Where else?!
IF I DON'T KNOW THE REAL HER...

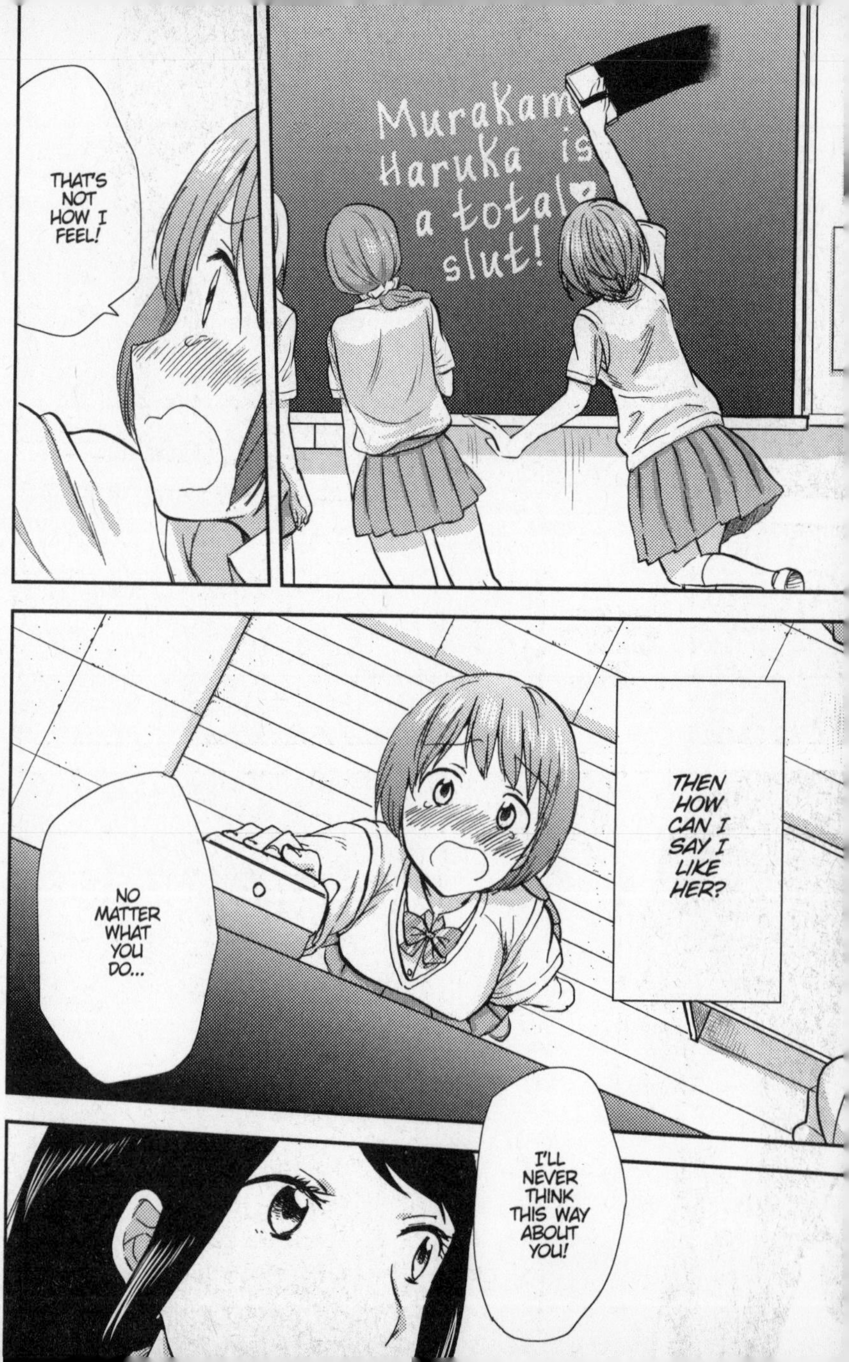
MuraKam Haruka is a total slut!
THAT'S NOT HOW I FEEL!
THEN HOW CAN I SAY I LIKE HER?
NO MATTER WHAT YOU DO...
I'LL NEVER THINK THIS WAY ABOUT YOU!

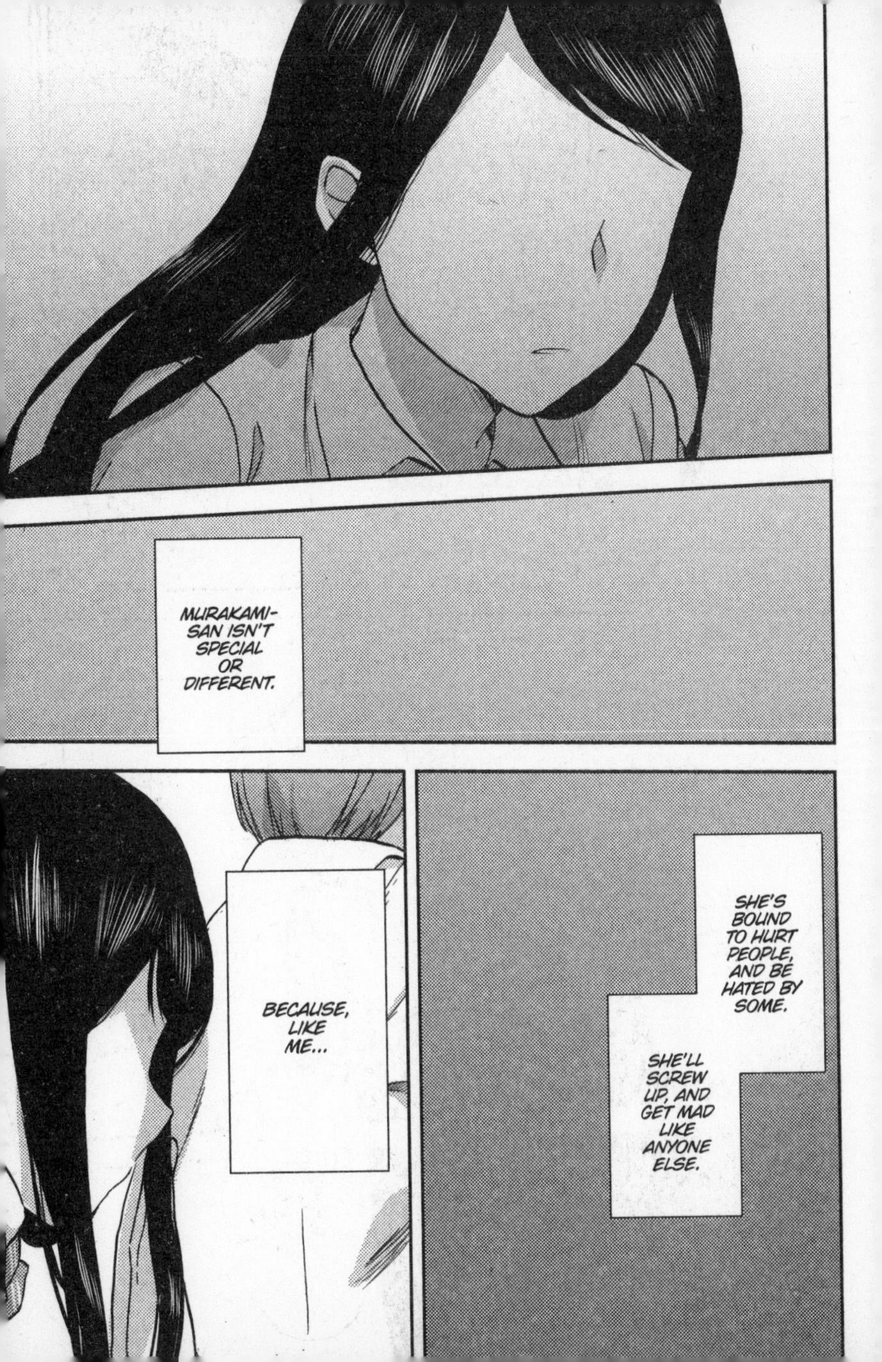
MURAKAMI-SAN ISN'T SPECIAL OR DIFFERENT.
SHE'S BOUND TO HURT PEOPLE, AND BE HATED BY SOME.
SHE'LL SCREW UP, AND GET MAD LIKE ANYONE ELSE.
BECAUSE, LIKE ME...

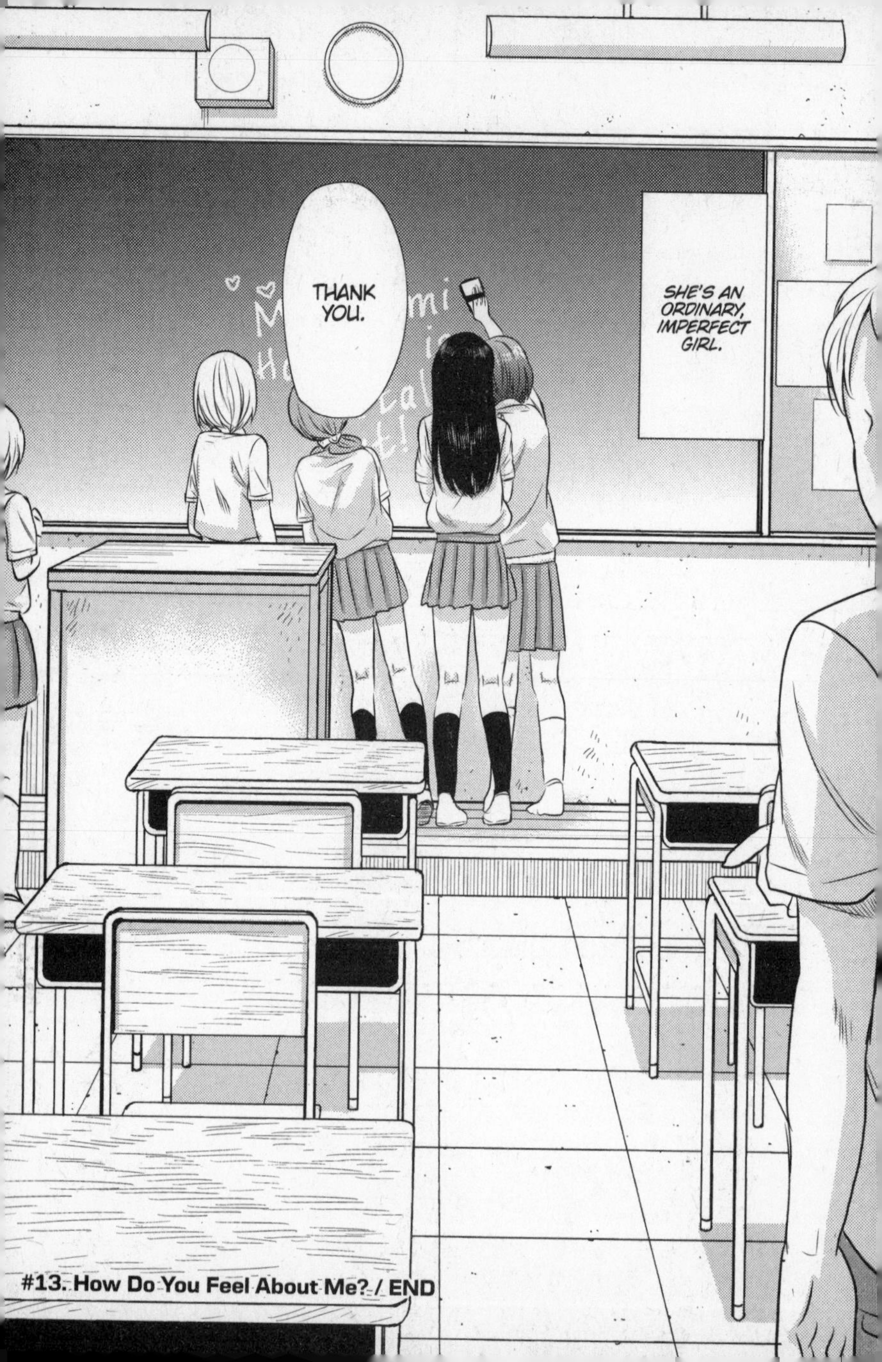
SHE'S AN ORDINARY, IMPERFECT GIRL.
THANK YOU.
#13. How Do You Feel About Me? / END

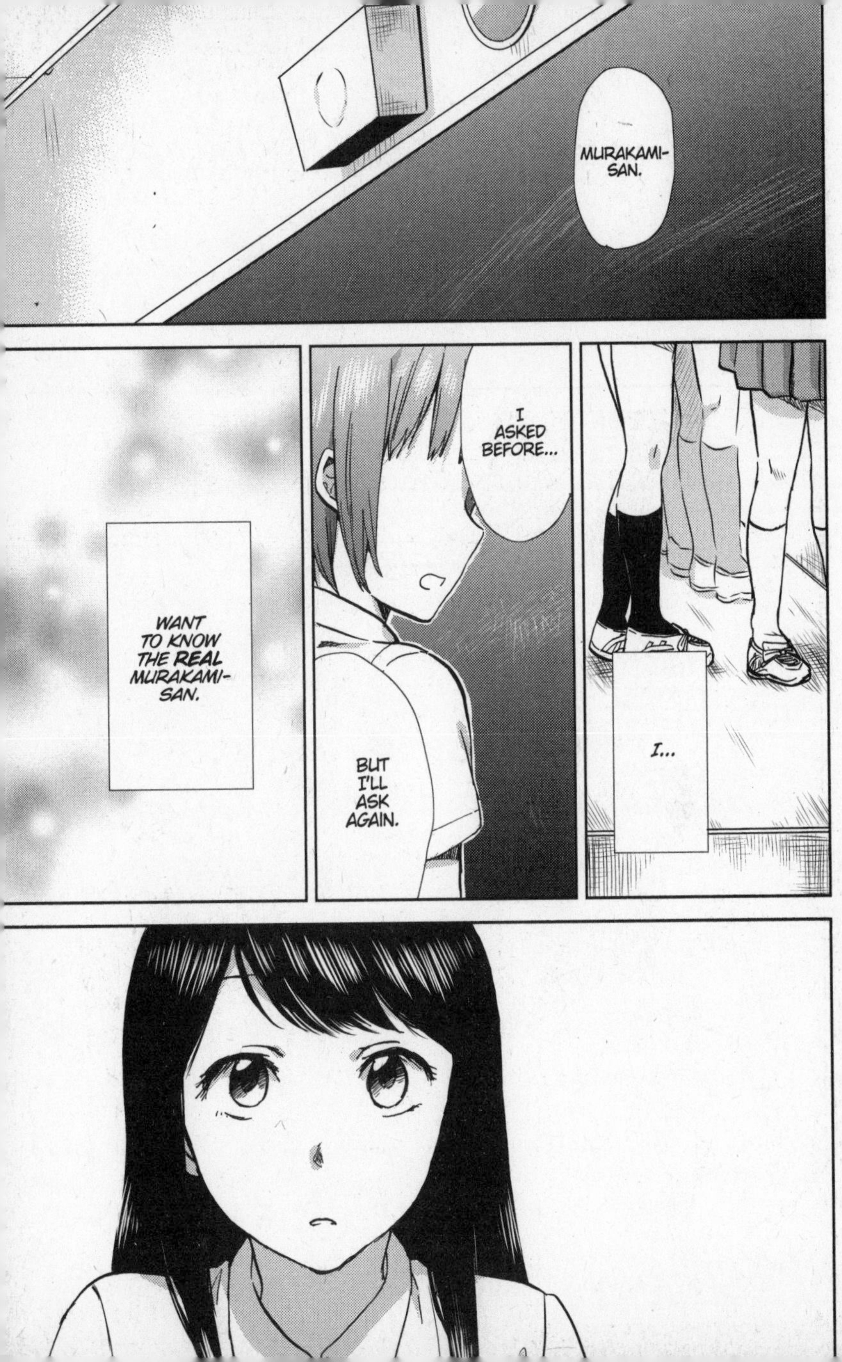
MURAKAMI-SAN.
I...
I ASKED BEFORE...
BUT I'LL ASK AGAIN.
WANT TO KNOW THE REAL MURAKAMI-SAN.

fragtime #14 You Want to Get To Know Me, Right?

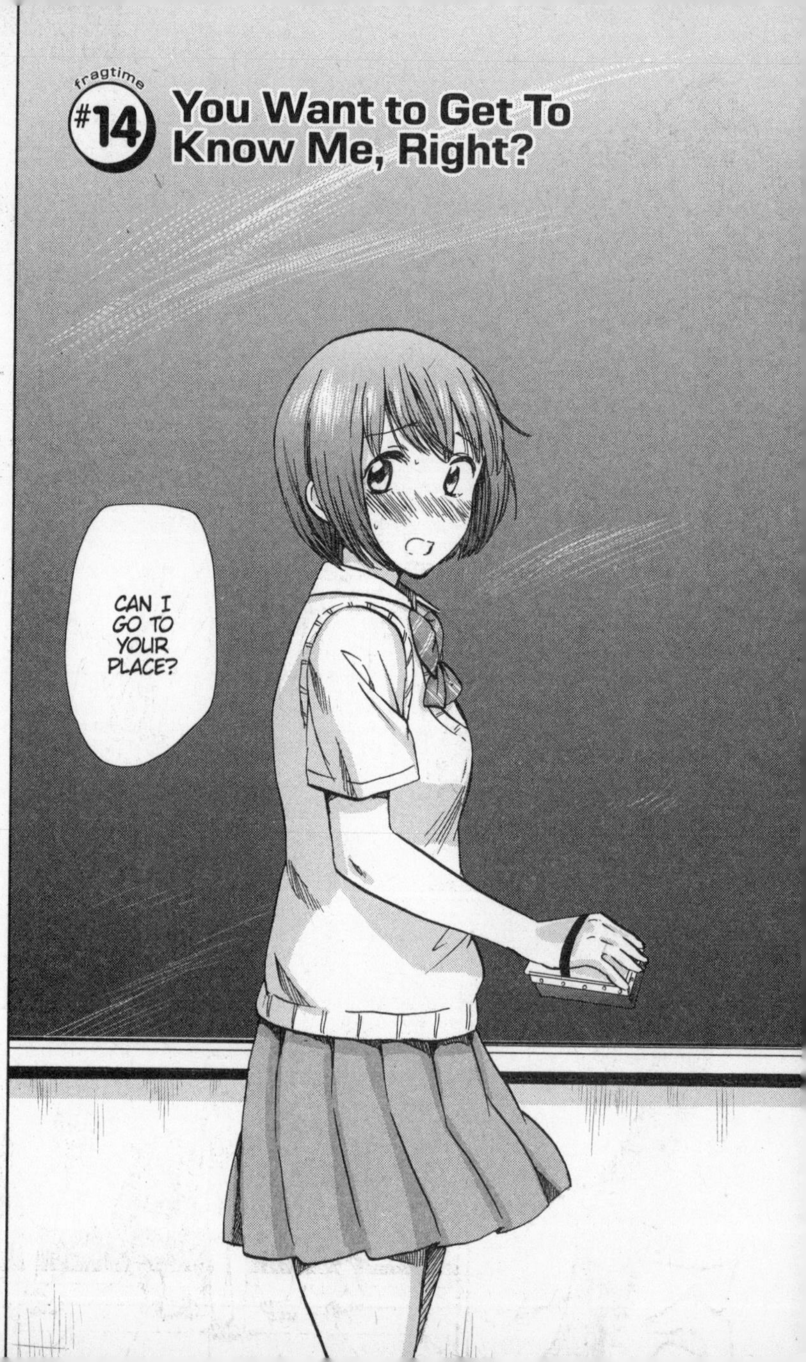
CAN I GO TO YOUR PLACE?

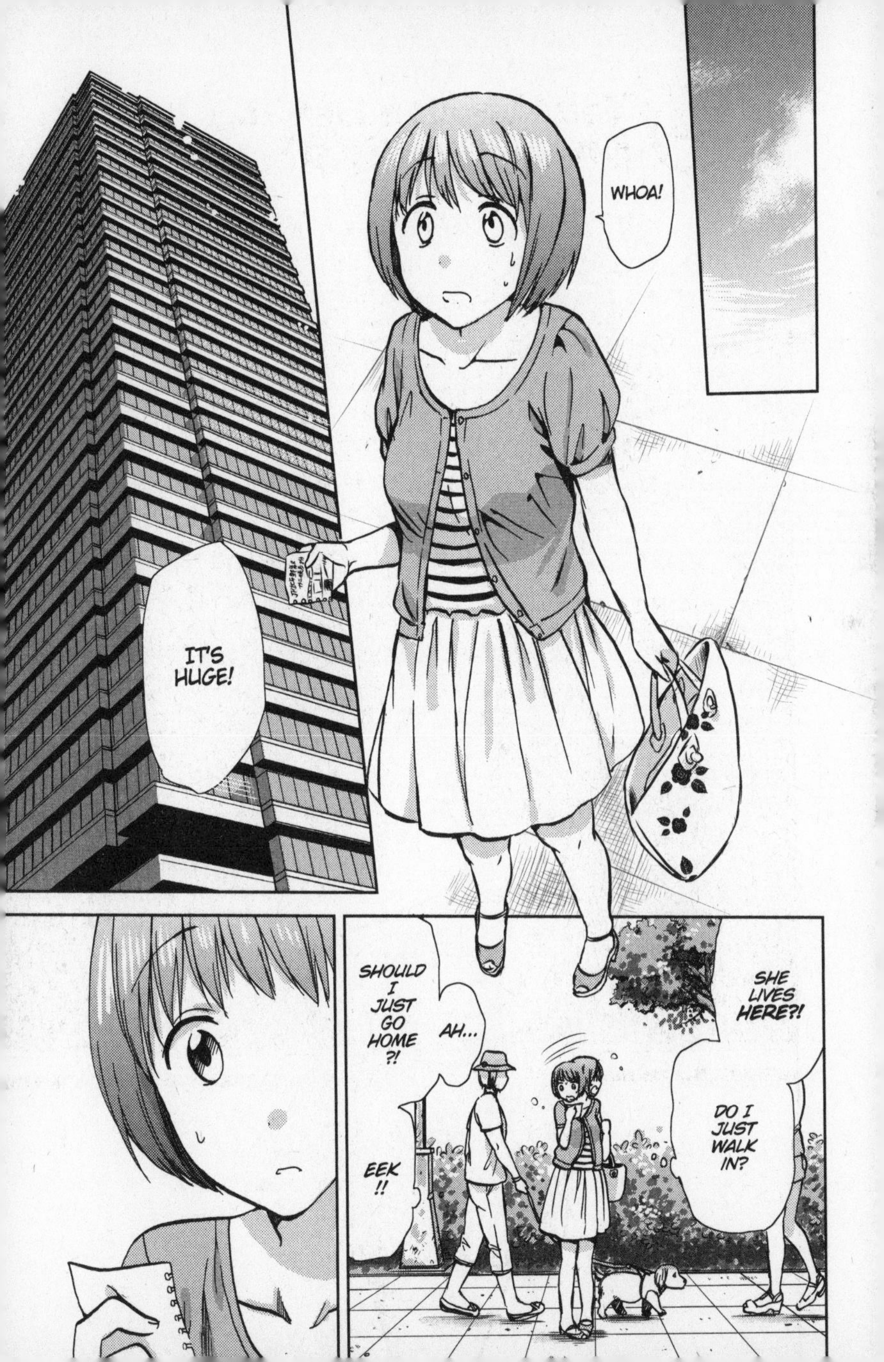
WHOA!
IT'S HUGE!
SHE LIVES HERE?!
DO I JUST WALK IN?
SHOULD I JUST GO HOME ?!
AH...
EEK !!

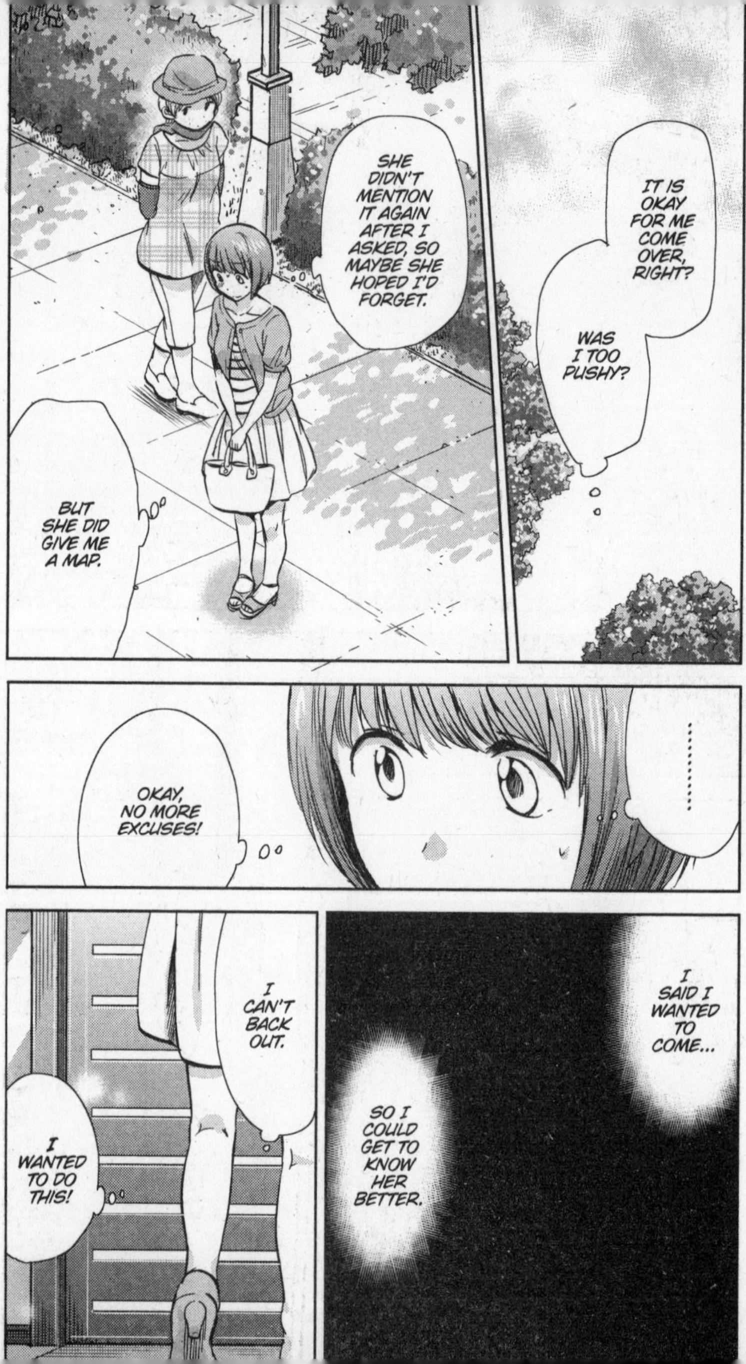
IT IS OKAY FOR ME COME OVER, RIGHT?
WAS I TOO PUSHY?
SHE DIDN'T MENTION IT AGAIN AFTER I ASKED, SO MAYBE SHE HOPED I'D FORGET.
BUT SHE DID GIVE ME A MAP.
......
OKAY, NO MORE EXCUSES!
I SAID I WANTED TO COME...
SO I COULD GET TO KNOW HER BETTER.
I CAN'T BACK OUT.
I WANTED TO DO THIS!

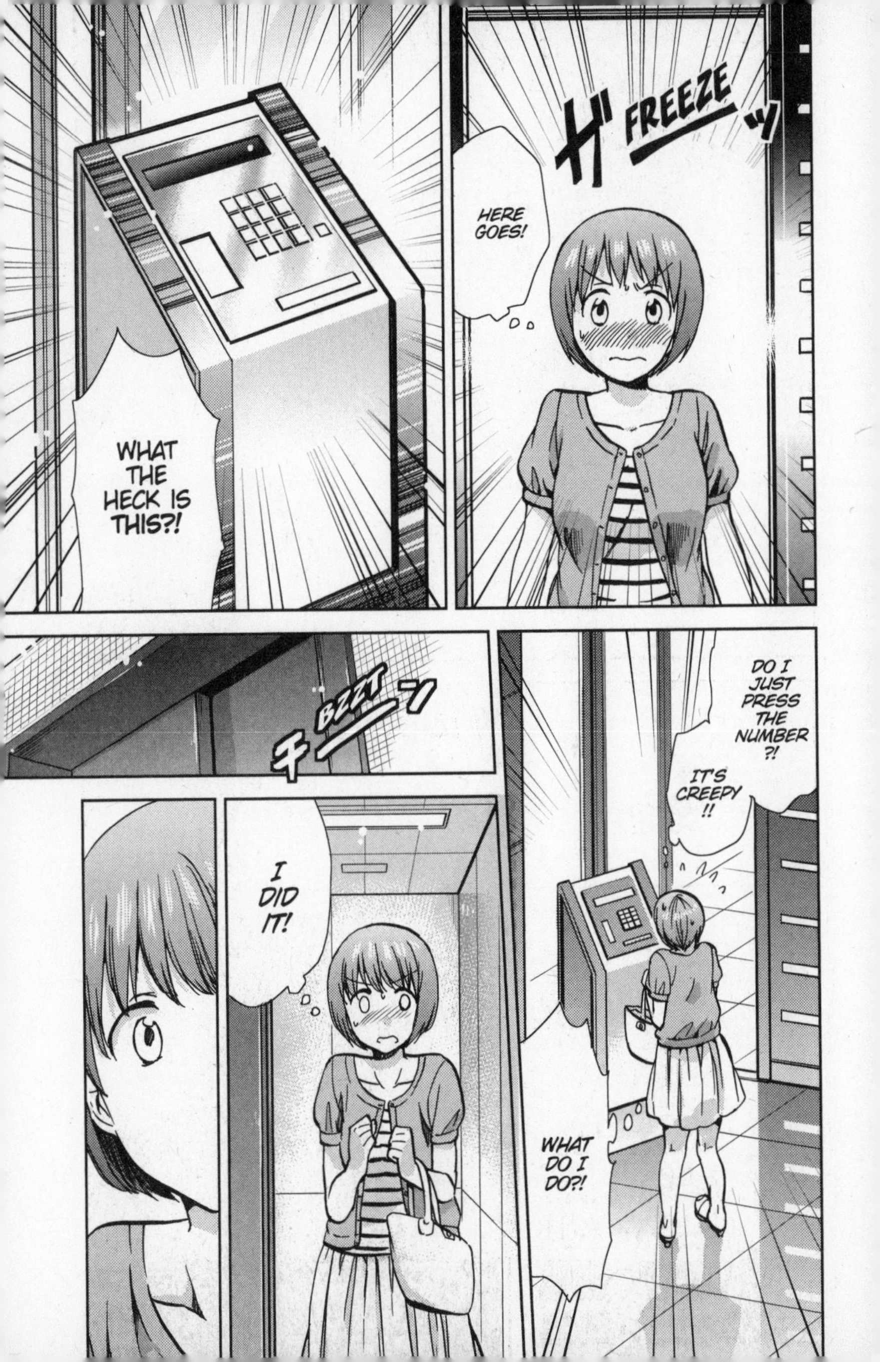
FREEZE
HERE GOES!
WHAT THE HECK IS THIS?!
DO I JUST PRESS THE NUMBER?!
IT'S CREEPY!!
WHAT DO I DO?!
BZZT
I DID IT!

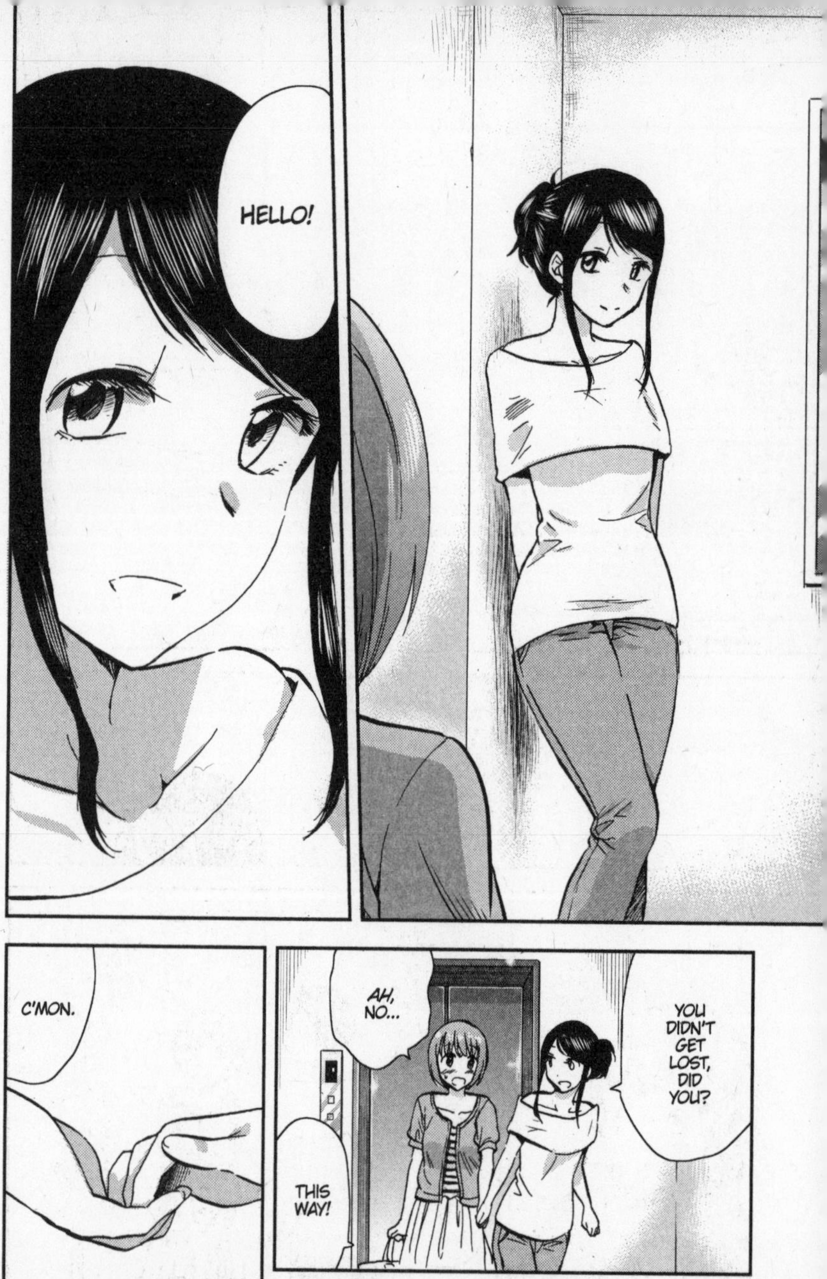
HELLO!
YOU DIDN'T GET LOST, DID YOU?
AH, NO...
THIS WAY!
C'MON.

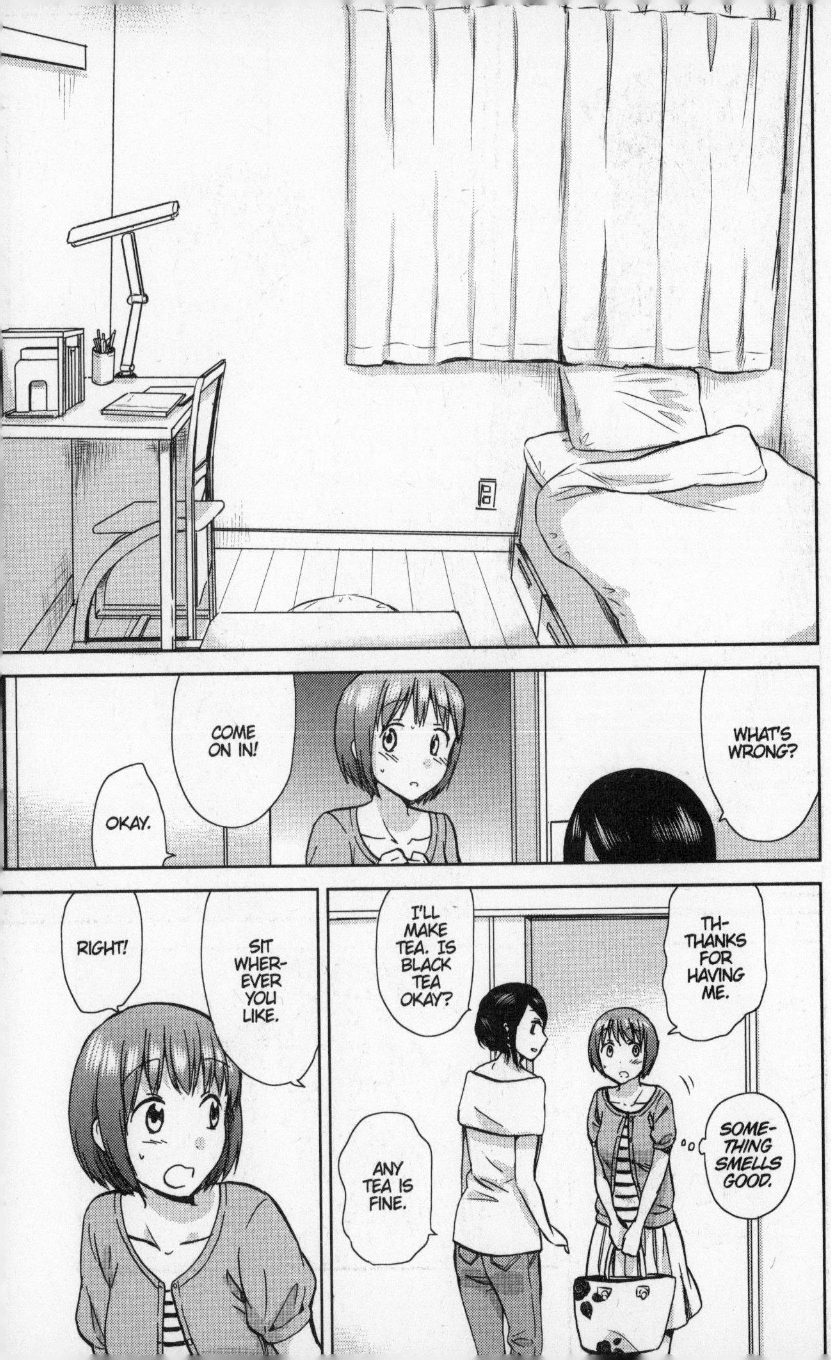
WHAT'S WRONG?
COME ON IN!
OKAY.
TH-THANKS FOR HAVING ME.
I'LL MAKE TEA. IS BLACK TEA OKAY?
SOME-THING SMELLS GOOD.
ANY TEA IS FINE.
SIT WHER-EVER YOU LIKE.
RIGHT!

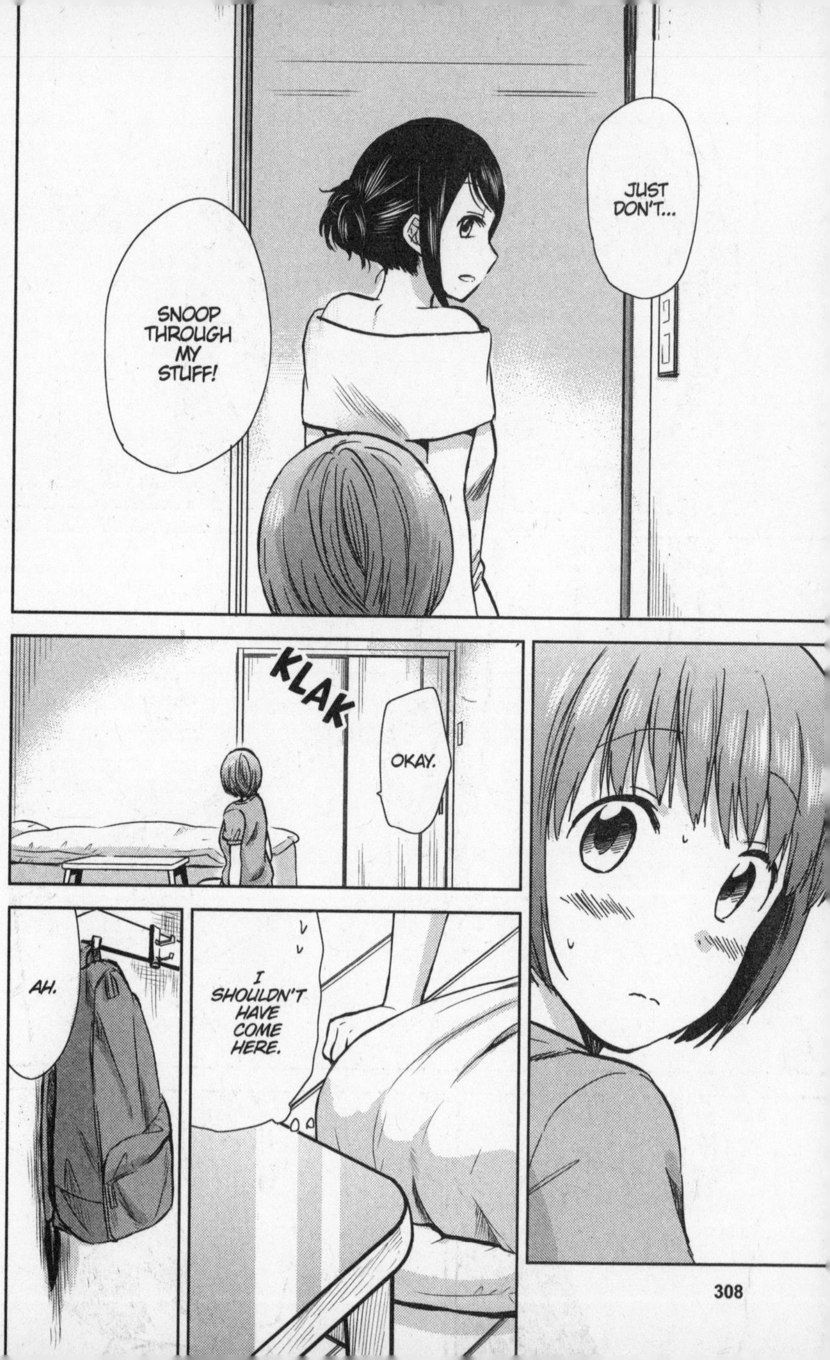
JUST DON'T...
SNOOP THROUGH MY STUFF!
KLAK
OKAY.
I SHOULDN'T HAVE COME HERE.
AH.

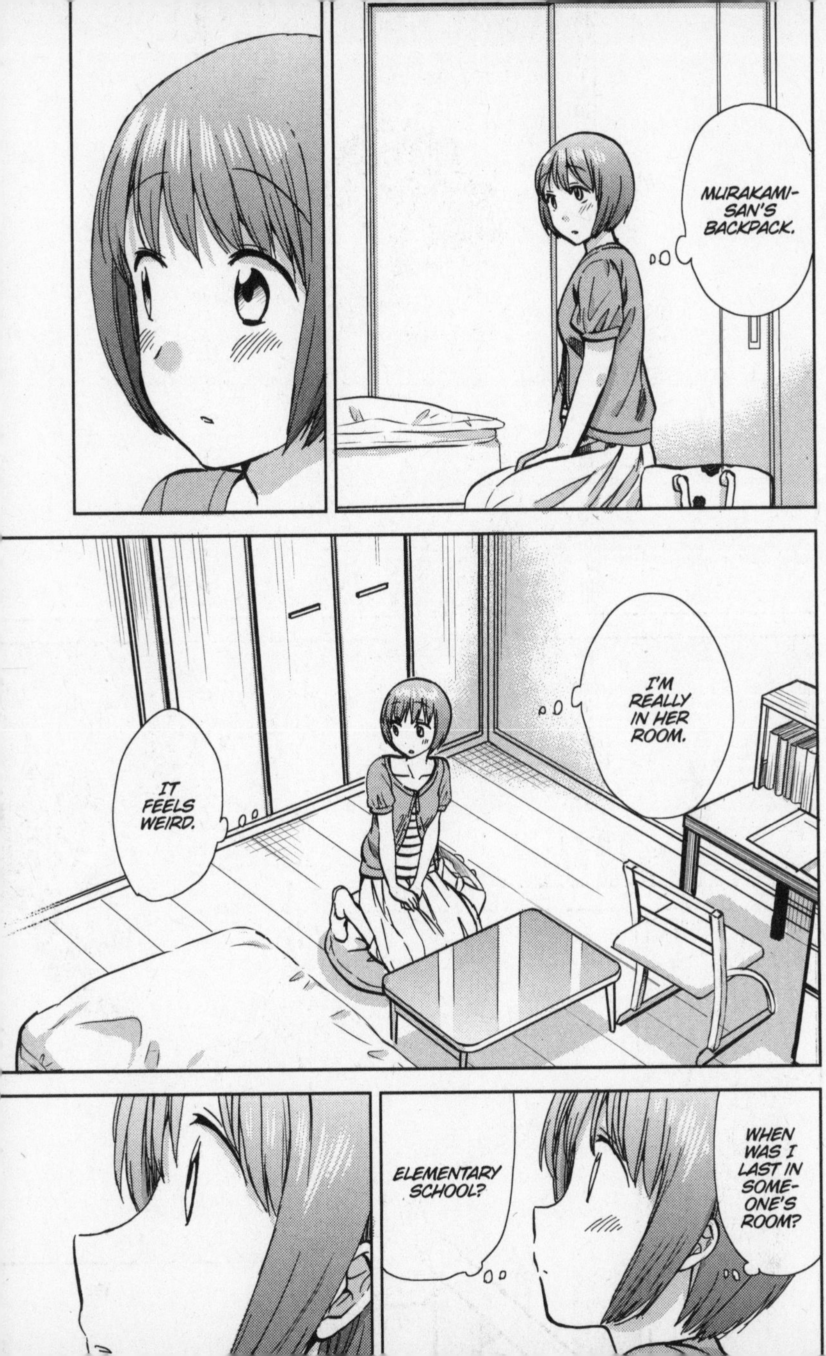
MURAKAMI-SAN'S BACKPACK.
I'M REALLY IN HER ROOM.
IT FEELS WEIRD.
WHEN WAS I LAST IN SOME-ONE'S ROOM?
ELEMENTARY SCHOOL?

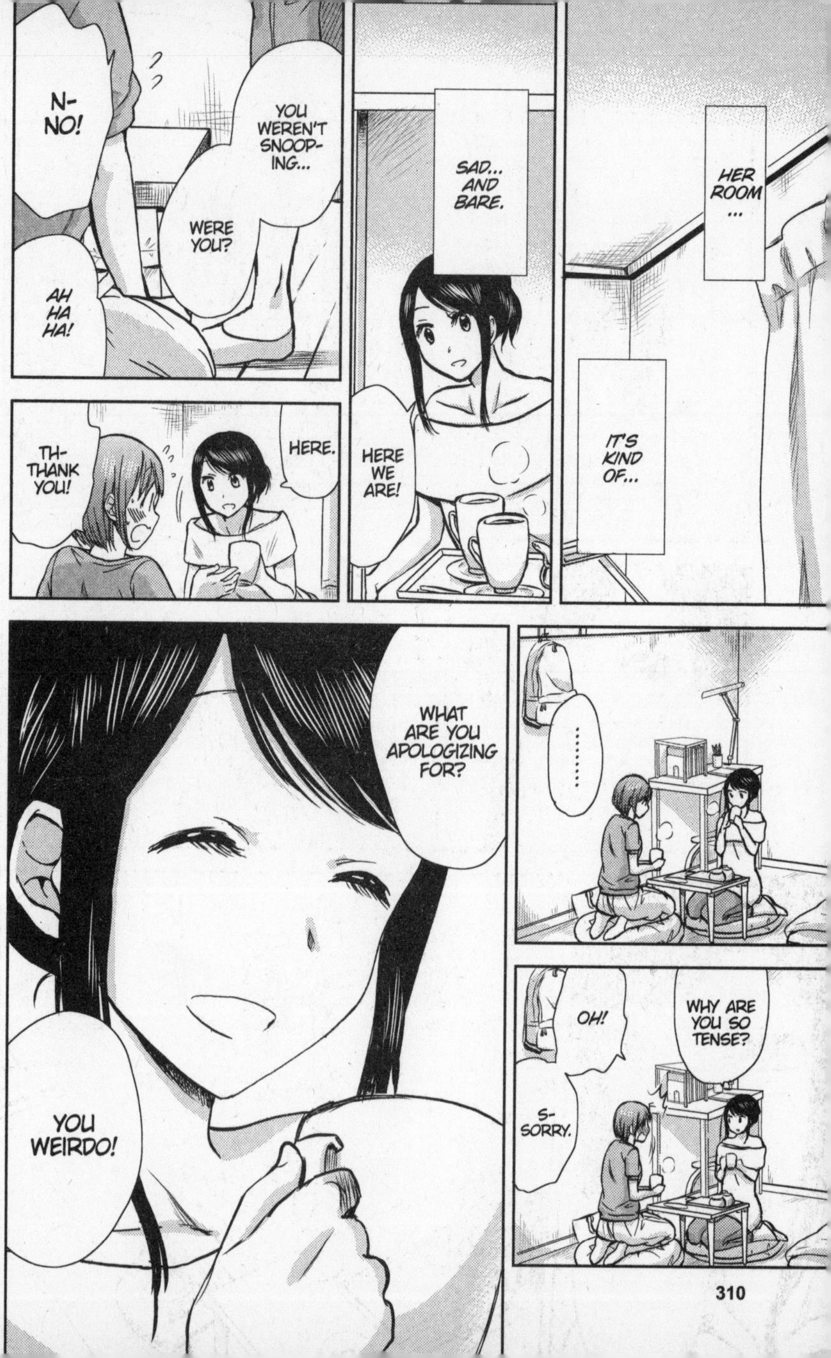
HER ROOM...
IT'S KIND OF...
SAD... AND BARE.
HERE WE ARE!
YOU WEREN'T SNOOPING... WERE YOU?
N-NO!
AH HA HA!
HERE.
TH-THANK YOU!
....
WHY ARE YOU SO TENSE?
OH!
S-SORRY.
WHAT ARE YOU APOLOGIZING FOR?
YOU WEIRDO!

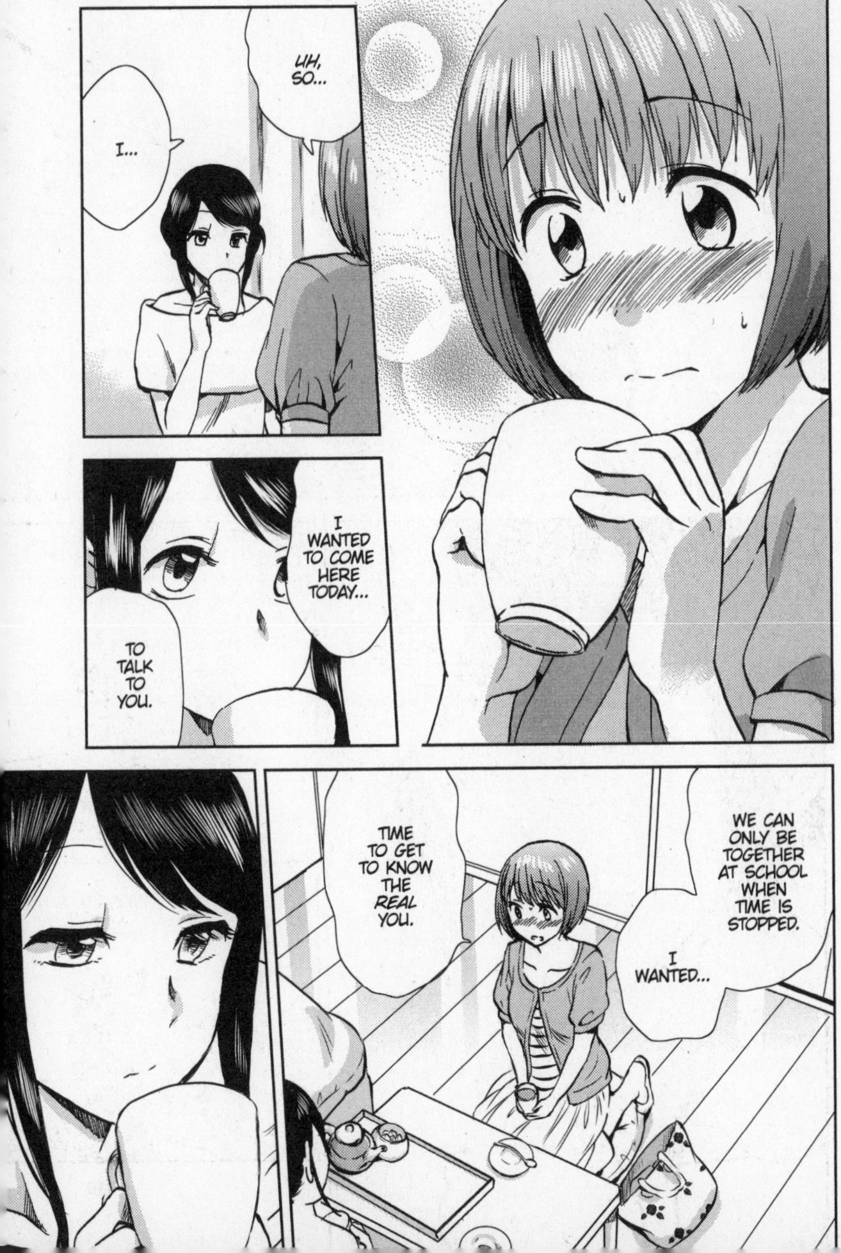
UH, SO...
I...
I WANTED TO COME HERE TODAY...
TO TALK TO YOU.
WE CAN ONLY BE TOGETHER AT SCHOOL WHEN TIME IS STOPPED.
I WANTED...
TIME TO GET TO KNOW THE *REAL* YOU.

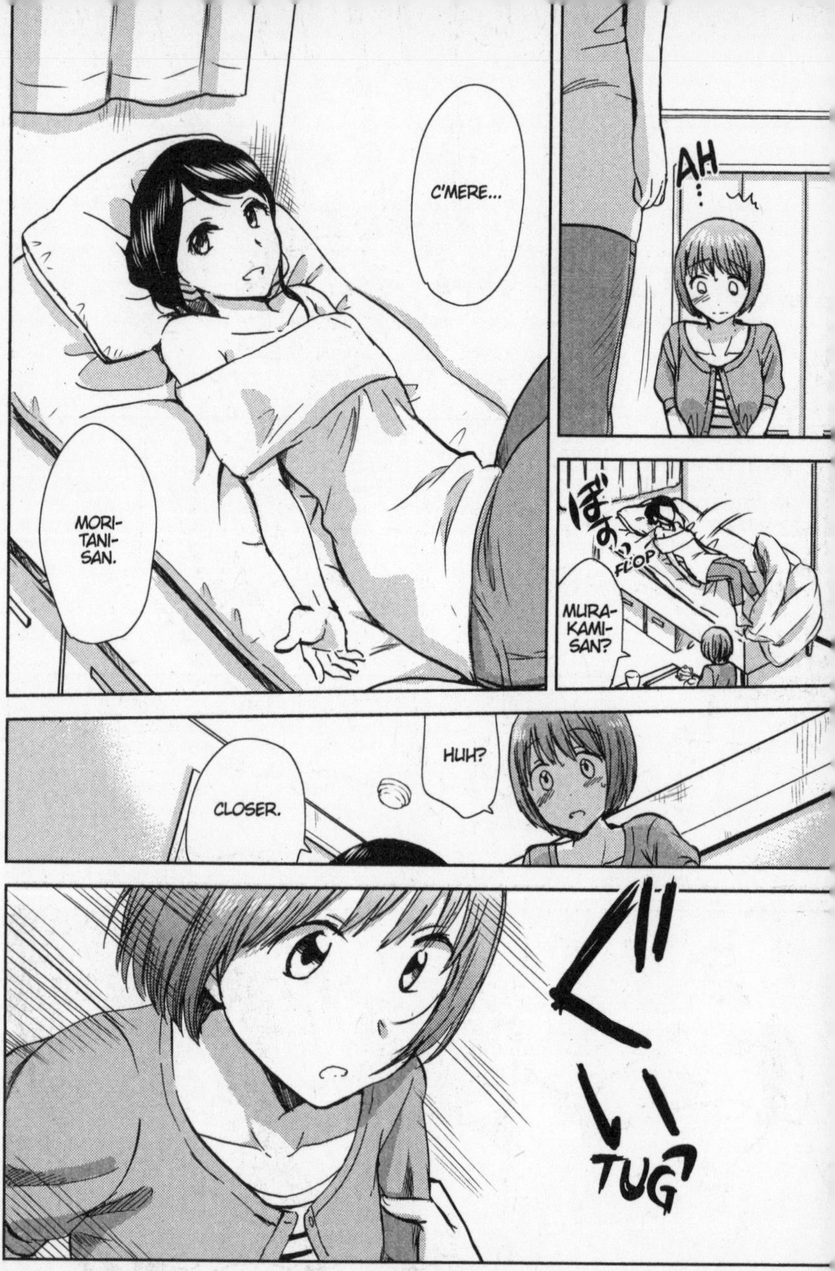
AH...
FLOP
MURA-KAMI-SAN?
C'MERE...
MORI-TANI-SAN.
HUH?
CLOSER.
ぐい
TUG

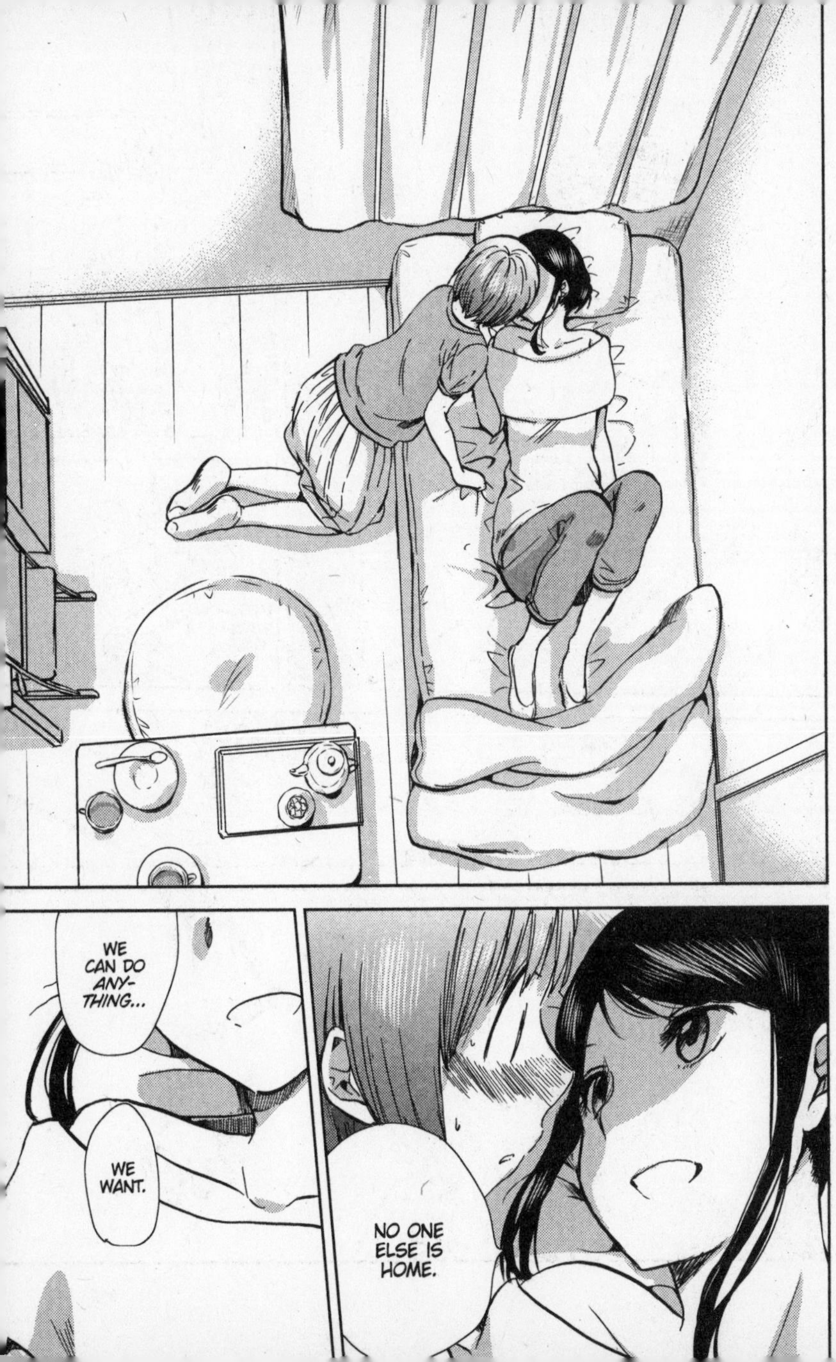
NO ONE ELSE IS HOME.
WE CAN DO ANYTHING...
WE WANT.

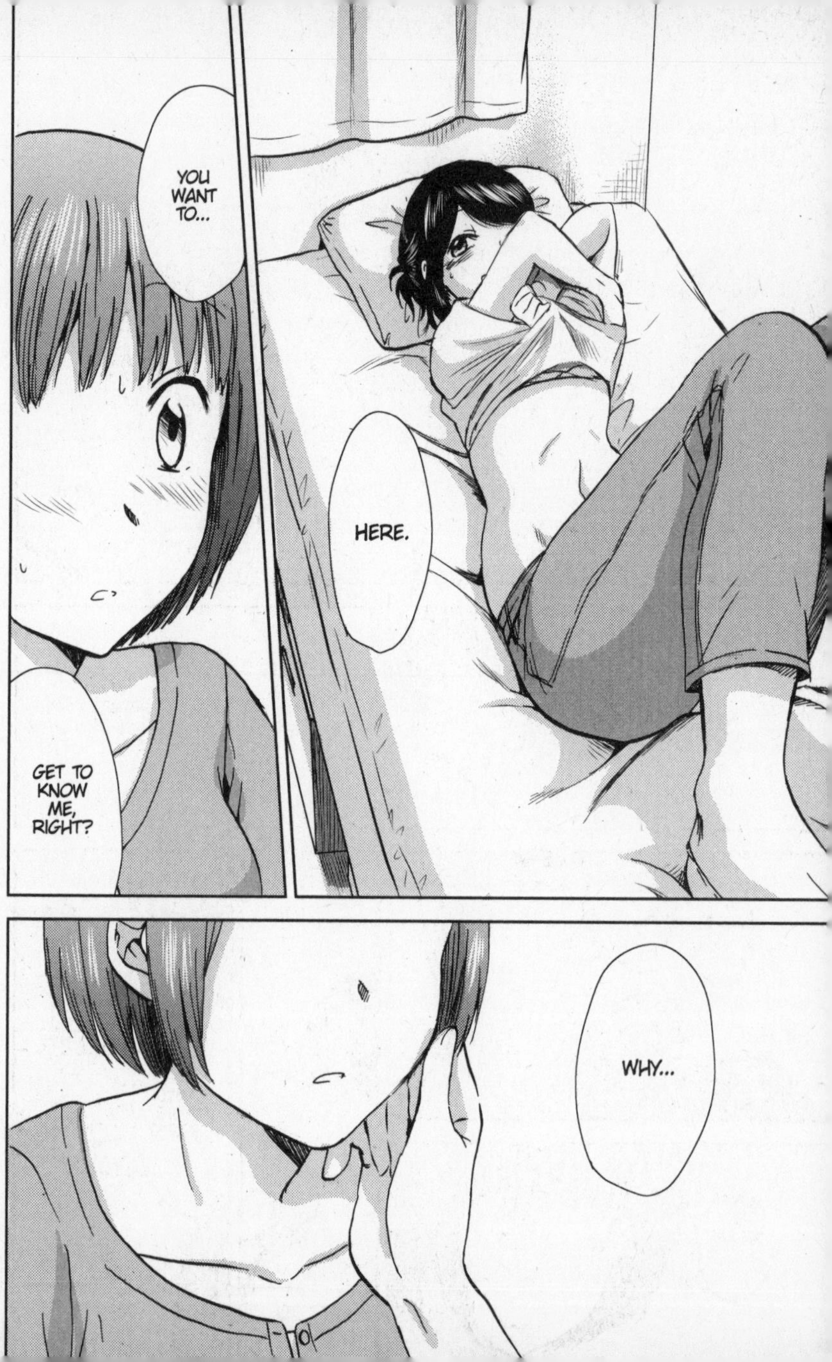
HERE.
YOU WANT TO...
GET TO KNOW ME, RIGHT?
WHY...

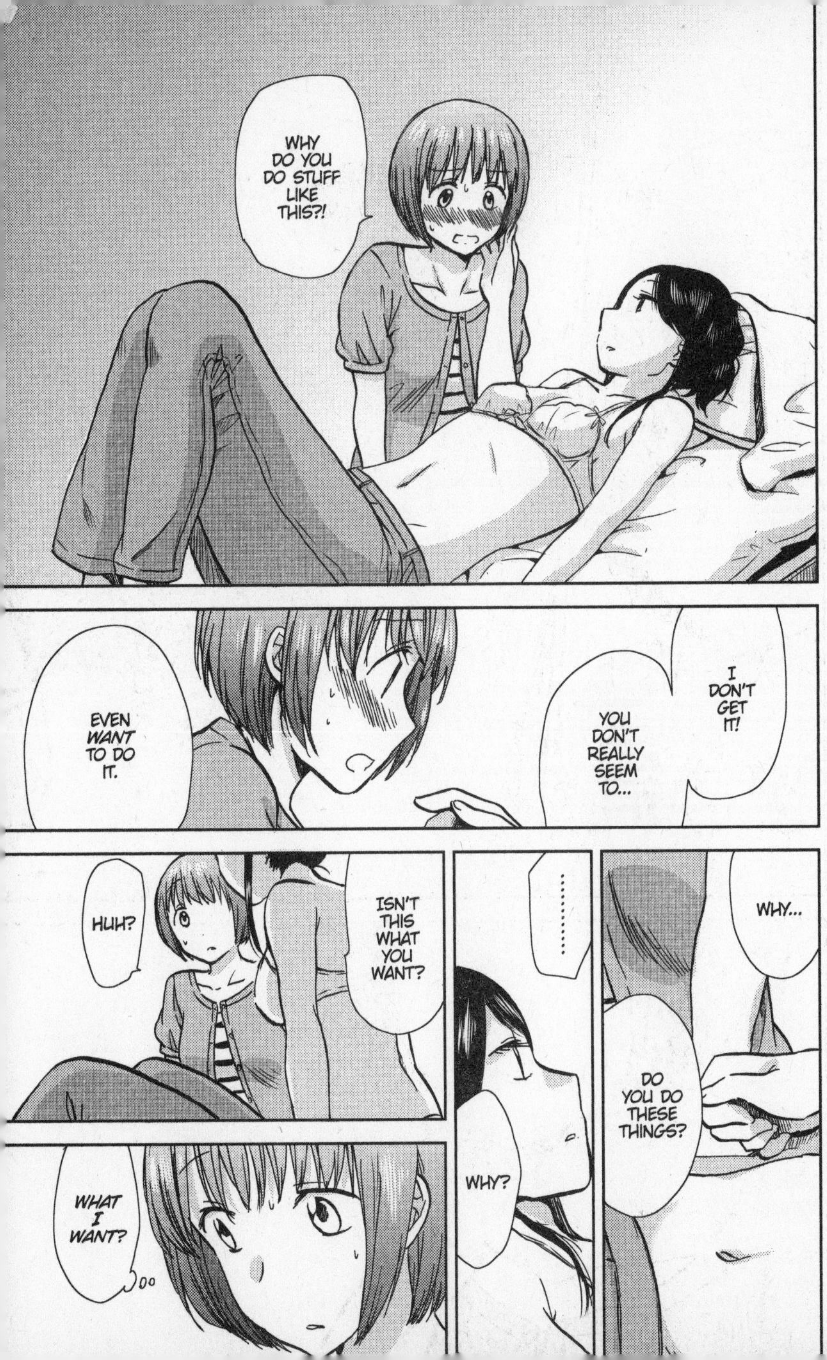
WHY DO YOU DO STUFF LIKE THIS?!
I DON'T GET IT!
YOU DON'T REALLY SEEM TO...
EVEN WANT TO DO IT.
WHY...
DO YOU DO THESE THINGS?
......
WHY?
ISN'T THIS WHAT YOU WANT?
HUH?
WHAT I WANT?

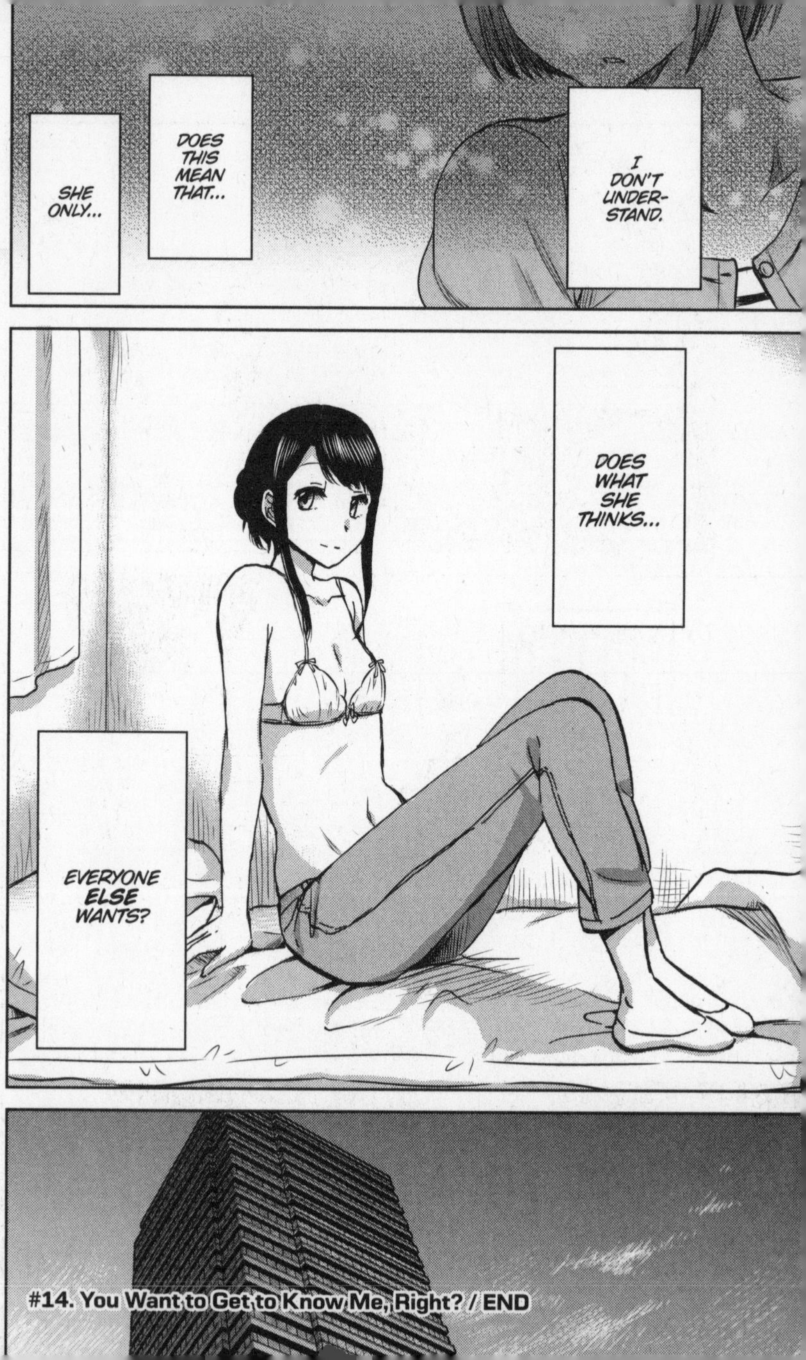
I DON'T UNDER-STAND.
DOES THIS MEAN THAT...
SHE ONLY...
DOES WHAT SHE THINKS...
EVERYONE ELSE WANTS?
#14. You Want to Get to Know Me, Right? / END

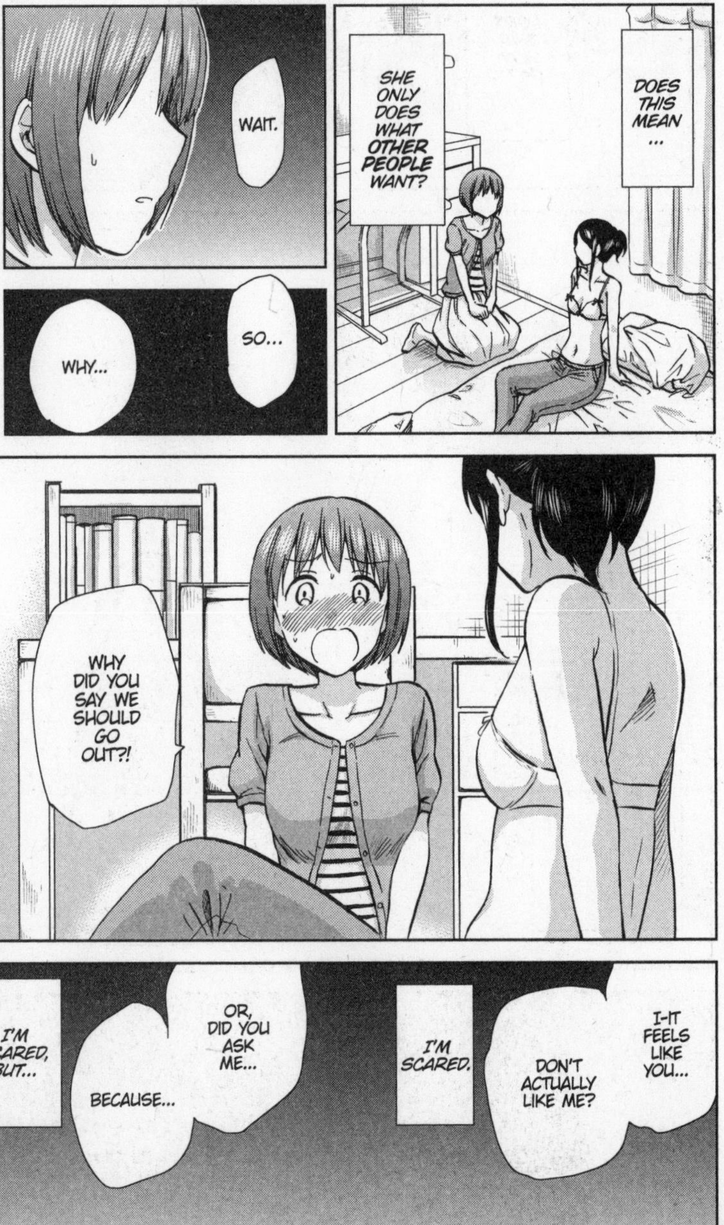
DOES THIS MEAN...
SHE ONLY DOES WHAT OTHER PEOPLE WANT?
WAIT.
SO...
WHY...
WHY DID YOU SAY WE SHOULD GO OUT?!
I-IT FEELS LIKE YOU...
DON'T ACTUALLY LIKE ME?
I'M SCARED.
OR, DID YOU ASK ME...
BECAUSE...
I'M SCARED, BUT...

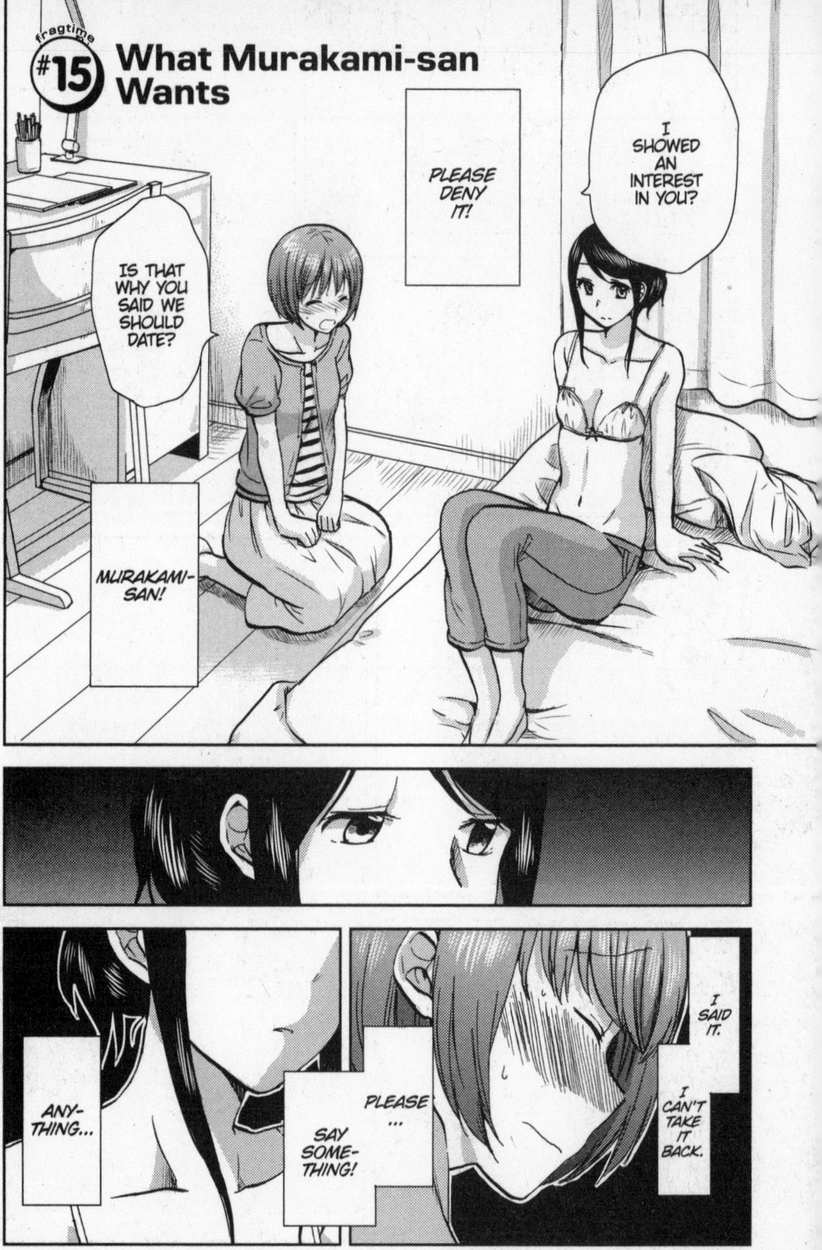
fragtime
#15 What Murakami-san Wants
I SHOWED AN INTEREST IN YOU?
PLEASE DENY IT!
IS THAT WHY YOU SAID WE SHOULD DATE?
MURAKAMI-SAN!
I SAID IT.
I CAN'T TAKE IT BACK.
PLEASE...
SAY SOME-THING!
ANY-THING...

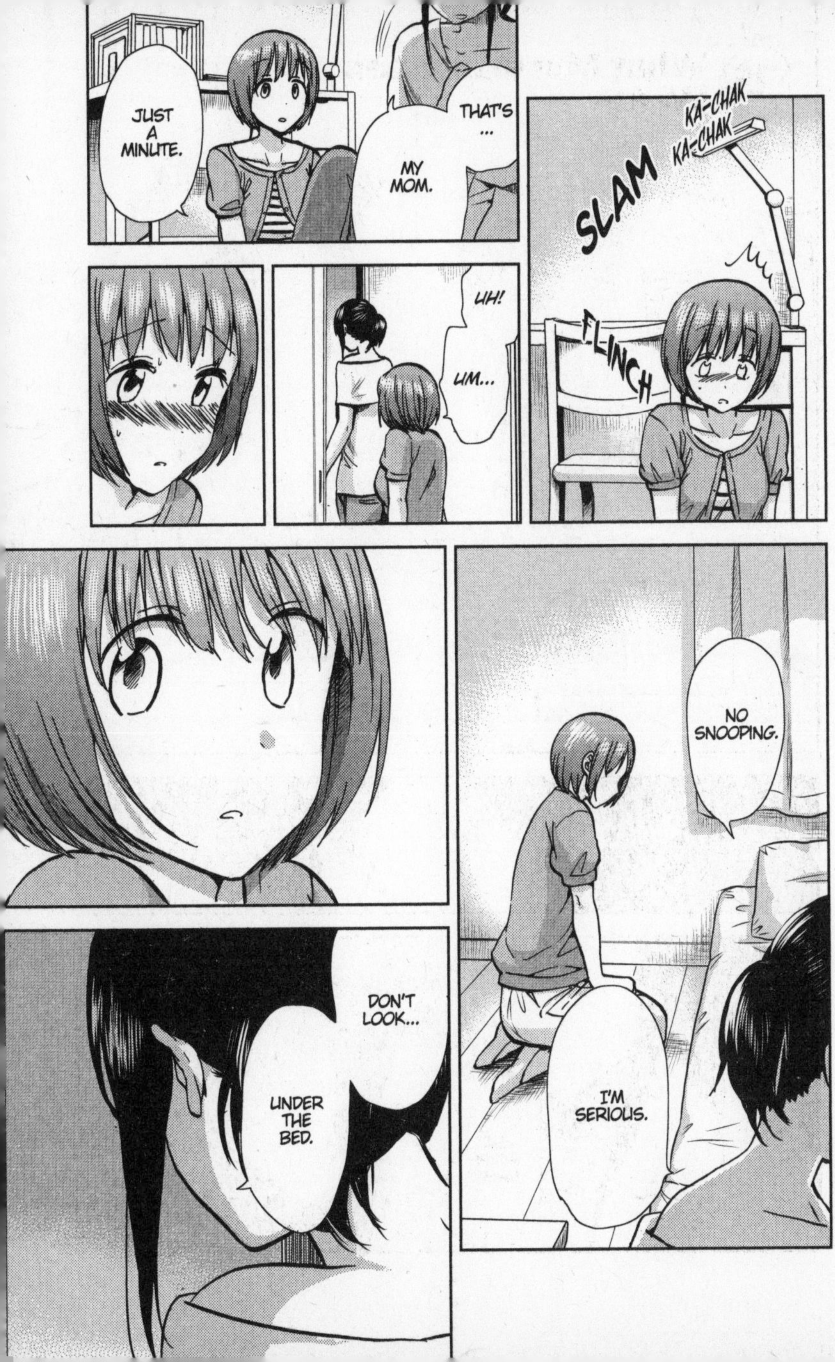
THAT'S ...
MY MOM.
JUST A MINUTE.
KA-CHAK KA-CHAK
SLAM
FLINCH
UH!
UM...
NO SNOOPING.
I'M SERIOUS.
DON'T LOOK...
UNDER THE BED.

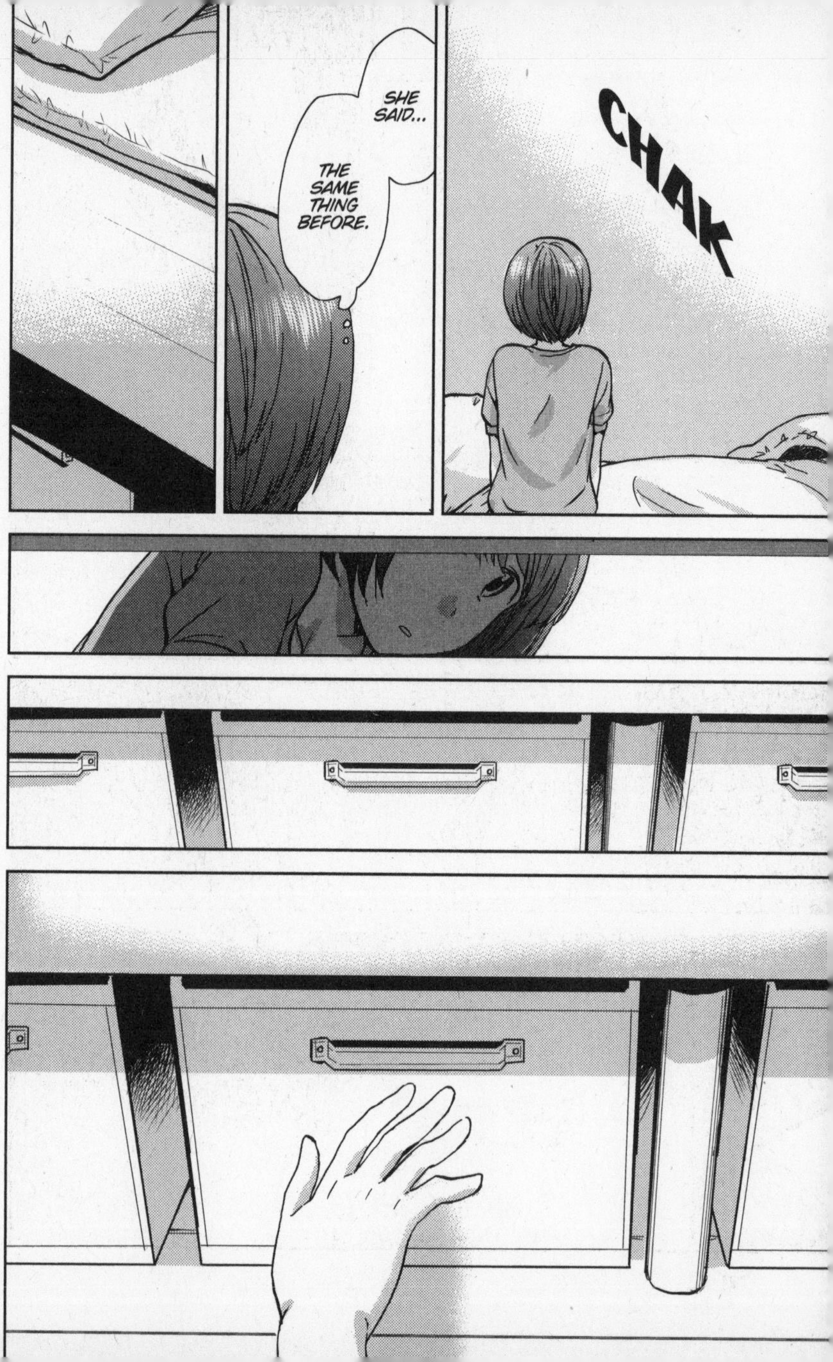
CHAK
SHE SAID...
THE SAME THING BEFORE.

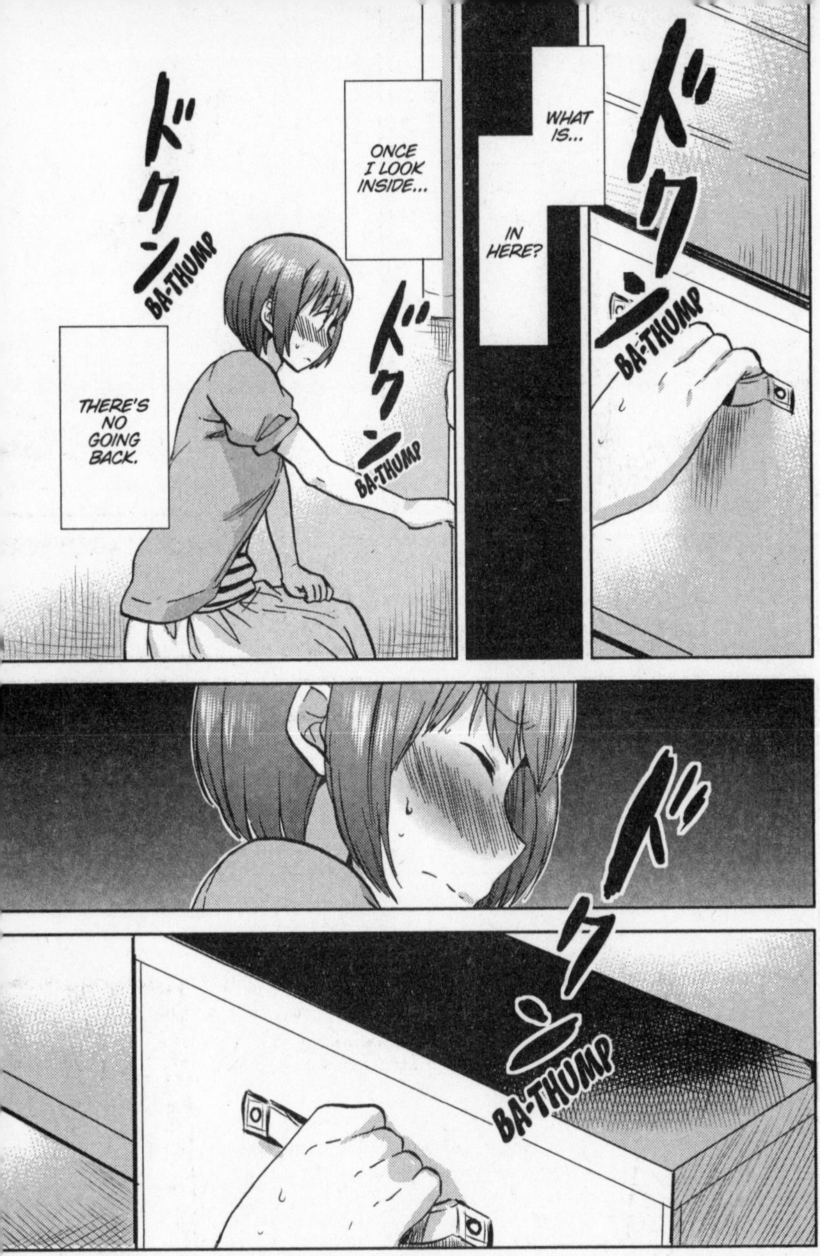
WHAT IS...
IN HERE?
ドクン
BA-THUMP
ONCE I LOOK INSIDE...
ドクン
BA-THUMP
ドクン
BA-THUMP
THERE'S NO GOING BACK.
ドクン
BA-THUMP

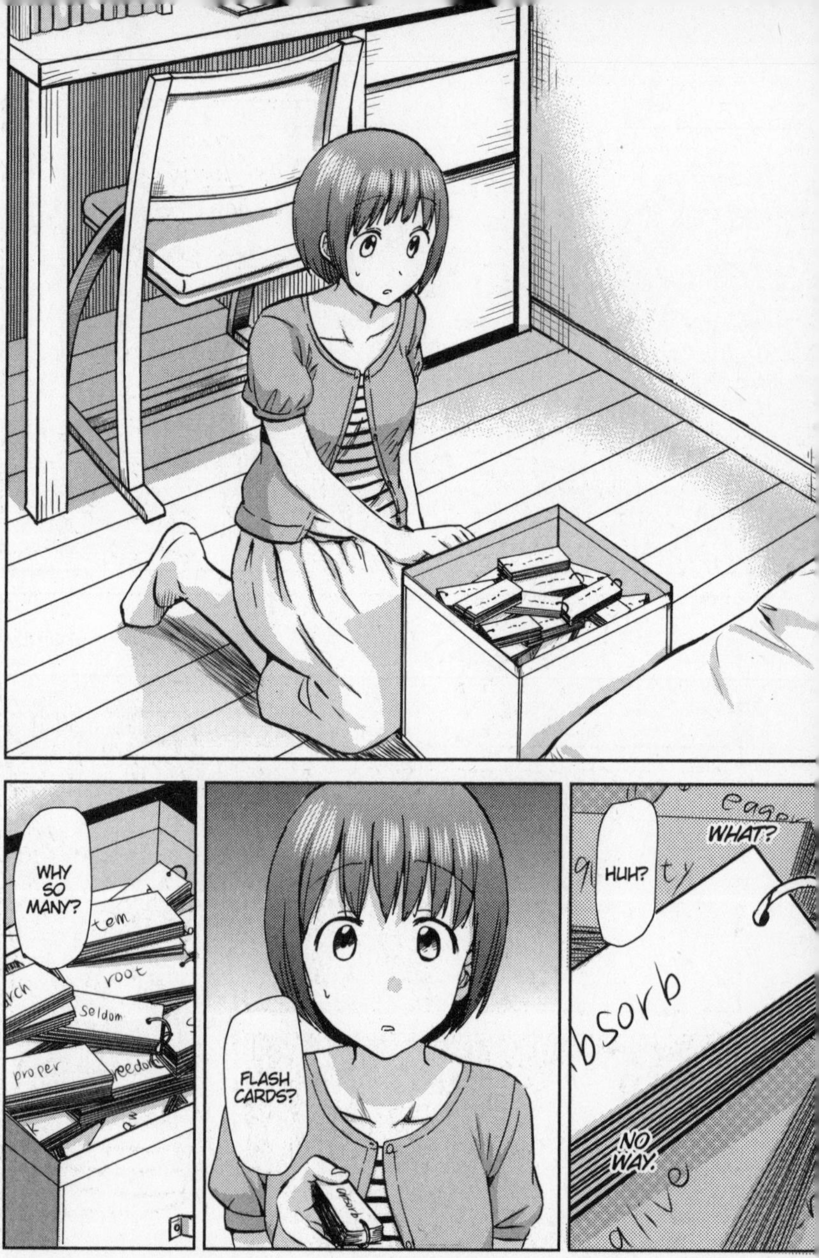
WHAT?
HUH?
NO WAY.
FLASH CARDS?
WHY SO MANY?

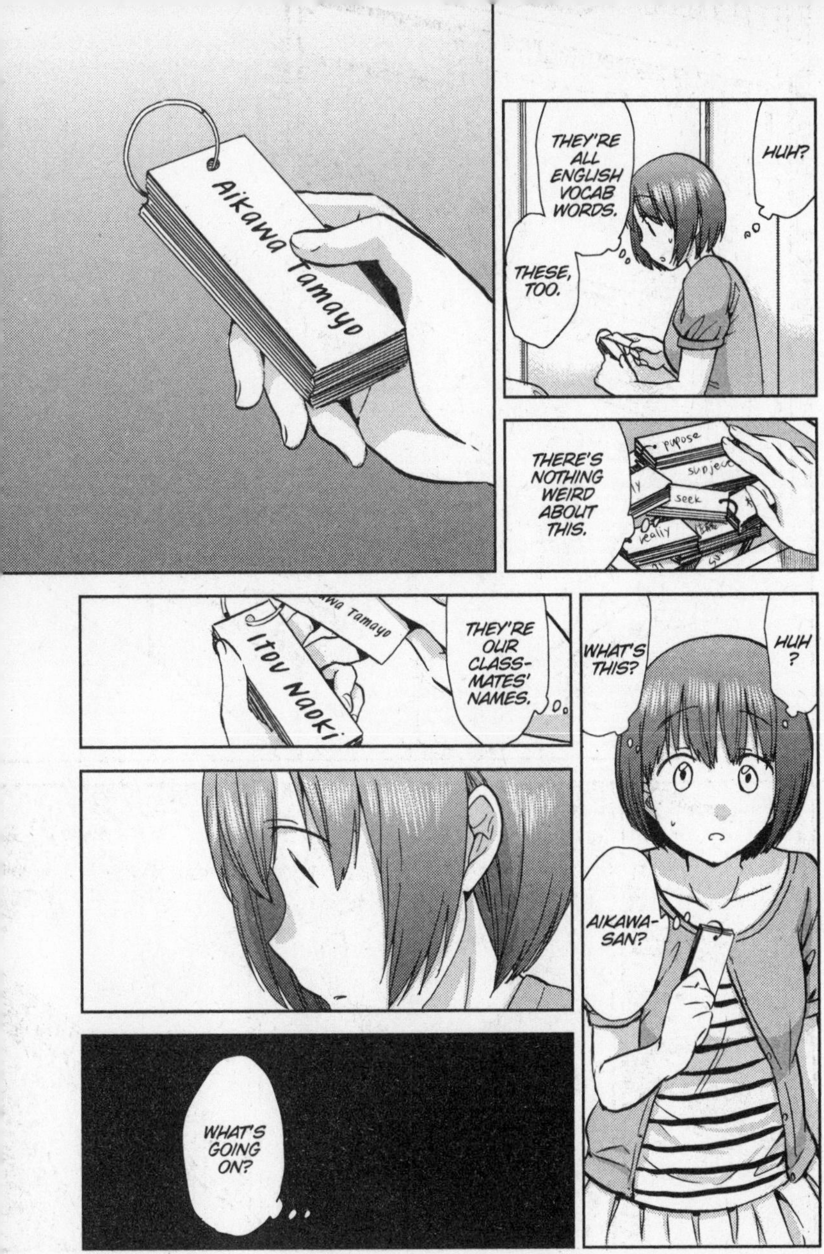
HUH?
THEY'RE ALL ENGLISH VOCAB WORDS.
THESE, TOO.
THERE'S NOTHING WEIRD ABOUT THIS.
seek
really
Aikawa Tamayo
HUH?
WHAT'S THIS?
AIKAWA-SAN?
THEY'RE OUR CLASS-MATES' NAMES.
Itou Naoki
WHAT'S GOING ON?
...

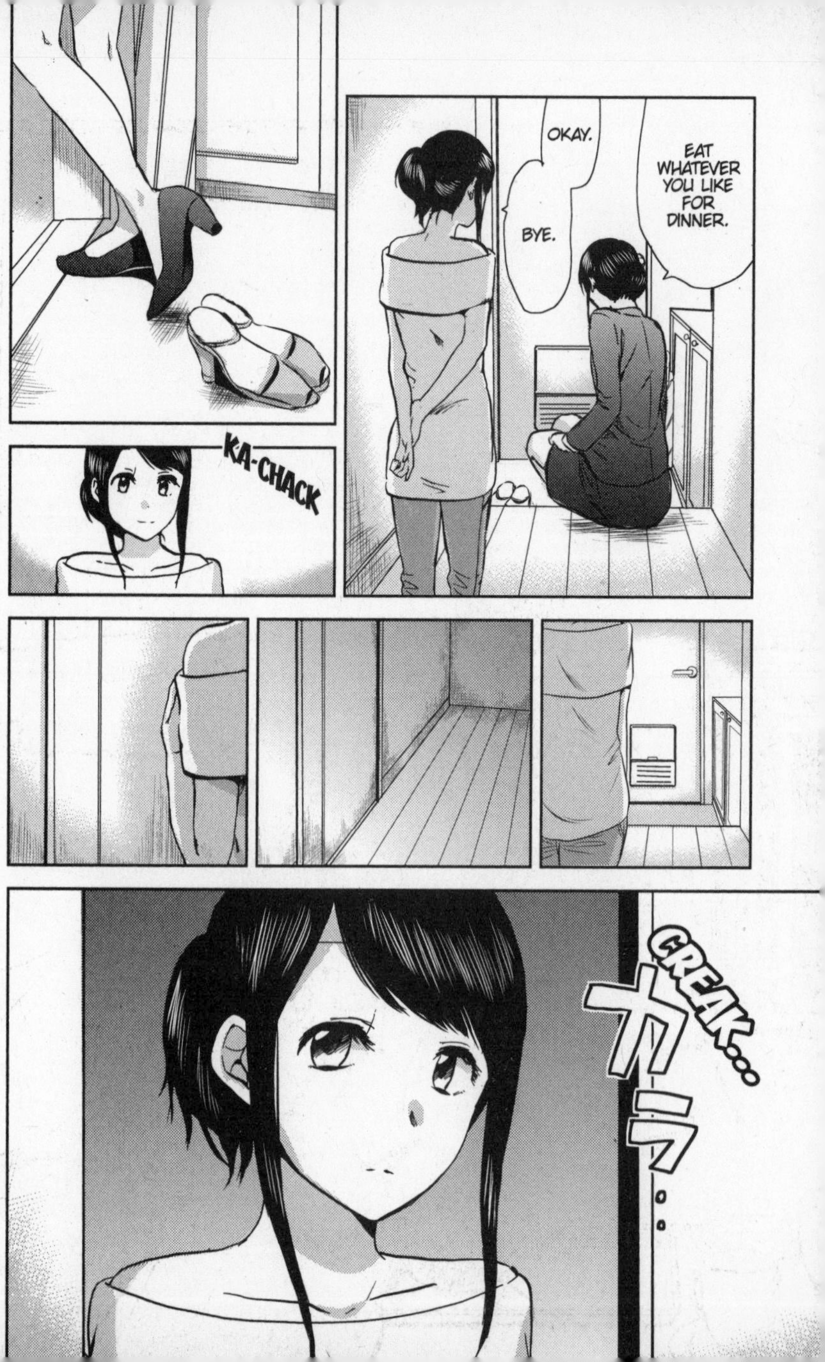
EAT WHATEVER YOU LIKE FOR DINNER.
OKAY.
BYE.
KA-CHACK
CREAK...
カラ...

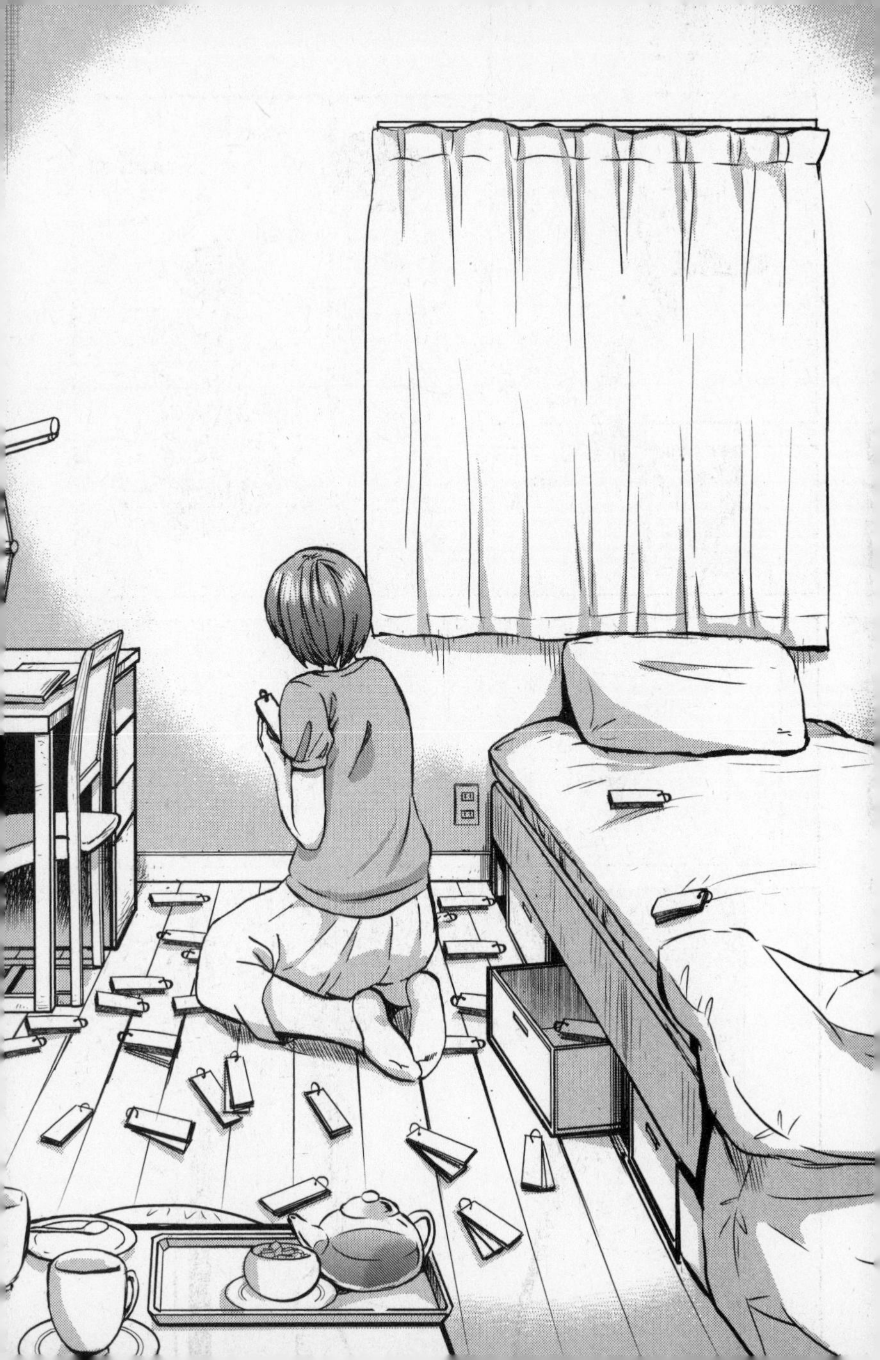

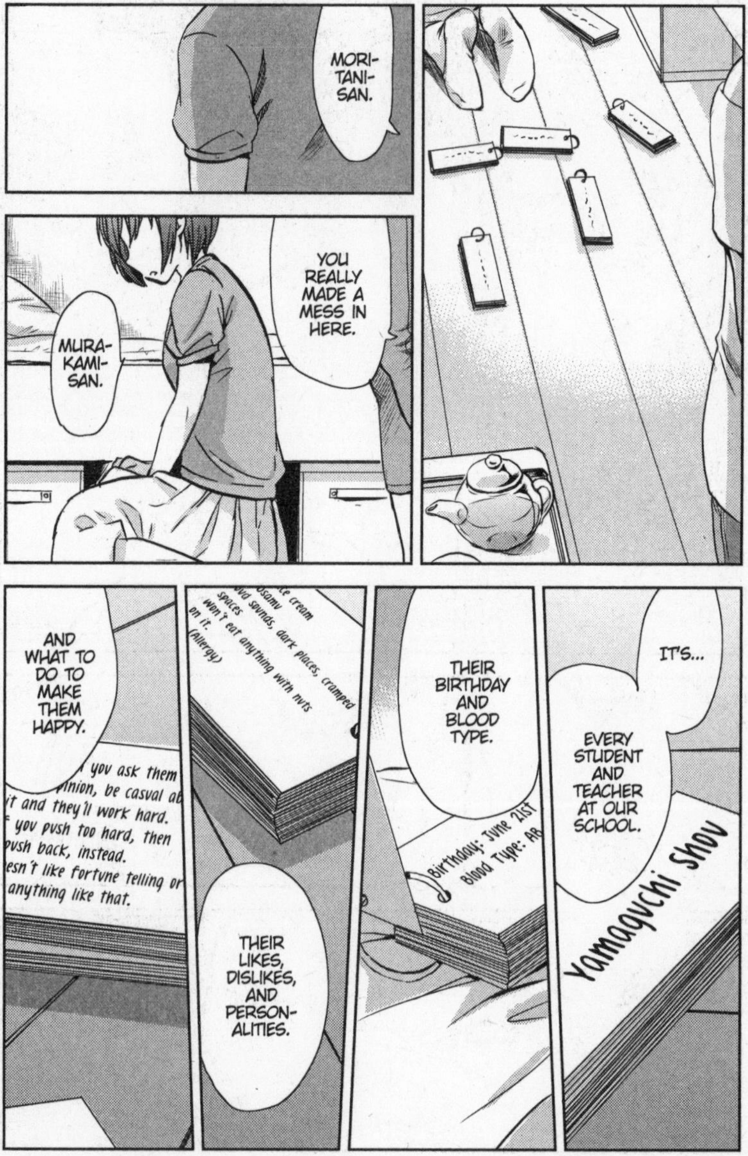
MORI-TANI-SAN.
YOU REALLY MADE A MESS IN HERE.
MURA-KAMI-SAN.
IT'S...
EVERY STUDENT AND TEACHER AT OUR SCHOOL.
Yamaguchi Shou
THEIR BIRTHDAY AND BLOOD TYPE.
Birthday: June 21st
THEIR LIKES, DISLIKES, AND PERSON-ALITIES.
spaces
won't eat anything with nuts
on it.
(Allergy)
AND WHAT TO DO TO MAKE THEM HAPPY.
you ask them
it and they'll work hard.
you push too hard, then
push back, instead.
anything like that.

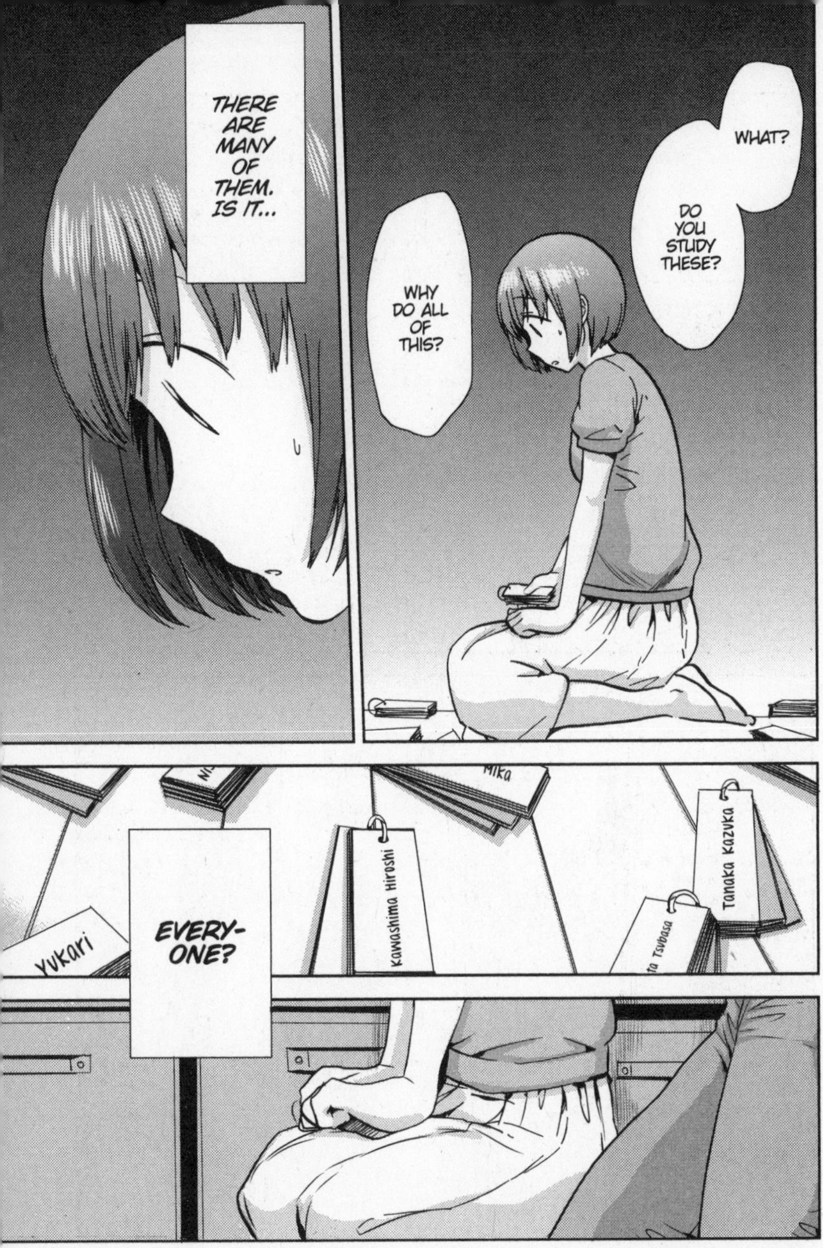
WHAT?
DO YOU STUDY THESE?
WHY DO ALL OF THIS?
THERE ARE MANY OF THEM. IS IT...
Mika
Tanaka Kazuka
Kawashima Hiroshi
Yukari
EVERY-ONE?

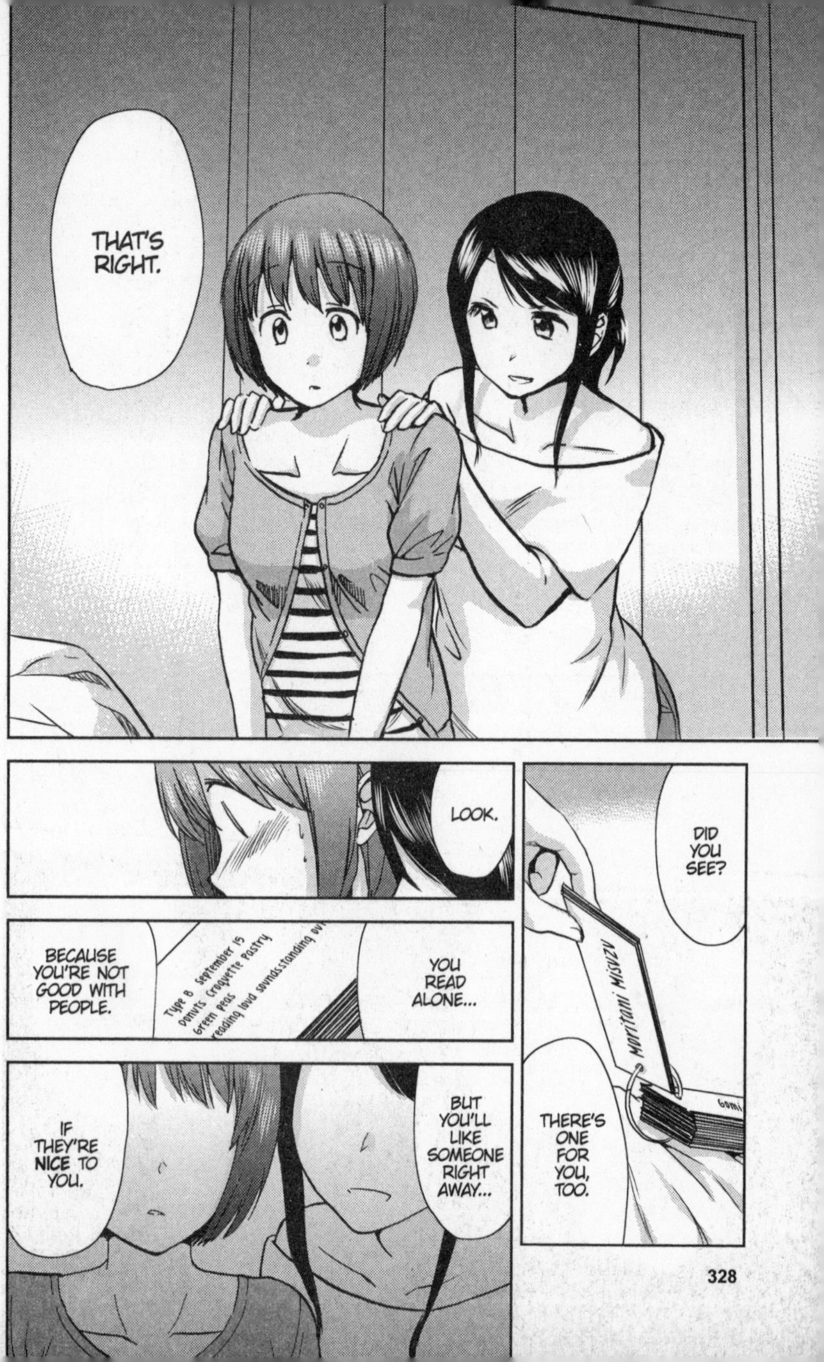
THAT'S RIGHT.
DID YOU SEE?
Moritani Misuzu
Gomi
THERE'S ONE FOR YOU, TOO.
LOOK.
YOU READ ALONE...
Type B September 15
Donuts Croquette Pastry
Green peas
reading loud sounds standing
BECAUSE YOU'RE NOT GOOD WITH PEOPLE.
BUT YOU'LL LIKE SOMEONE RIGHT AWAY...
IF THEY'RE NICE TO YOU.

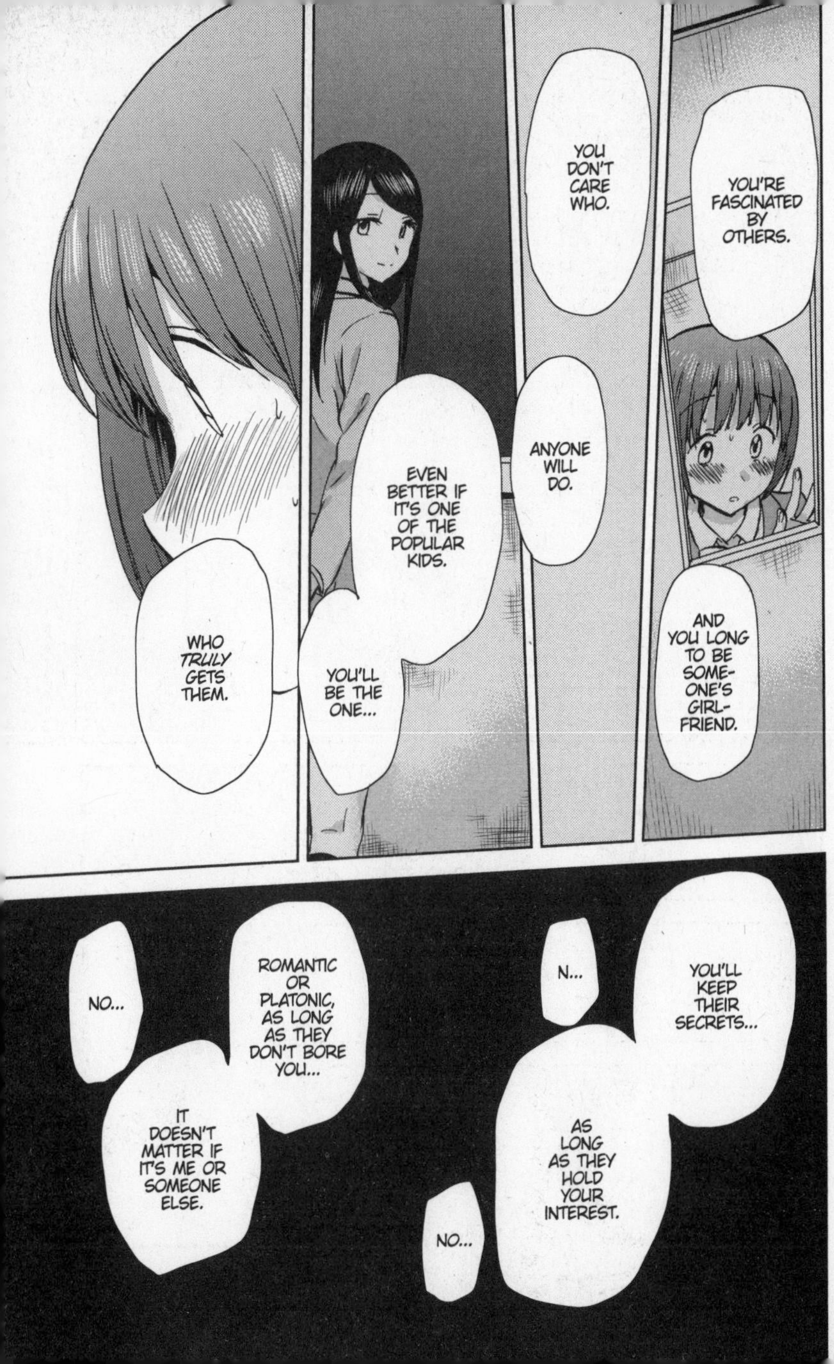
YOU'RE FASCINATED BY OTHERS.
AND YOU LONG TO BE SOME-ONE'S GIRL-FRIEND.
YOU DON'T CARE WHO.
ANYONE WILL DO.
EVEN BETTER IF IT'S ONE OF THE POPULAR KIDS.
YOU'LL BE THE ONE...
WHO *TRULY* GETS THEM.
YOU'LL KEEP THEIR SECRETS...
N...
AS LONG AS THEY HOLD YOUR INTEREST.
NO...
ROMANTIC OR PLATONIC, AS LONG AS THEY DON'T BORE YOU...
NO...
IT DOESN'T MATTER IF IT'S ME OR SOMEONE ELSE.

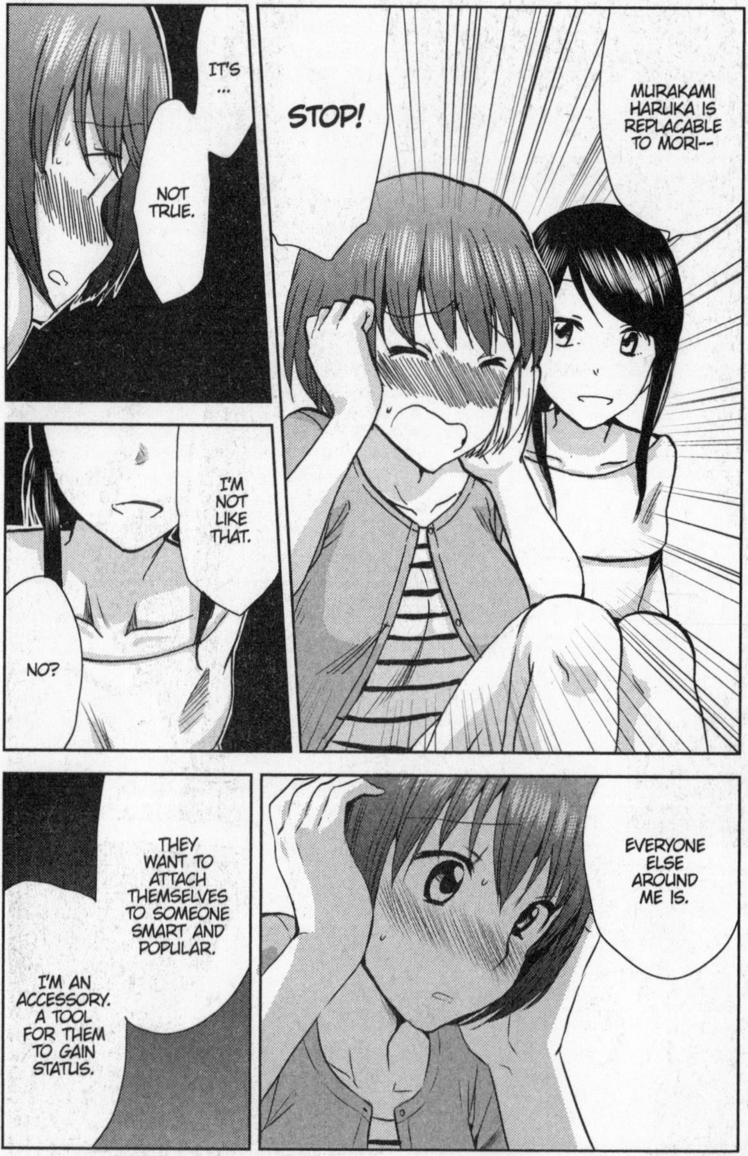
MURAKAMI HARUKA IS REPLACABLE TO MORI--
STOP!
IT'S ...
NOT TRUE.
I'M NOT LIKE THAT.
NO?
EVERYONE ELSE AROUND ME IS.
THEY WANT TO ATTACH THEMSELVES TO SOMEONE SMART AND POPULAR.
I'M AN ACCESSORY. A TOOL FOR THEM TO GAIN STATUS.

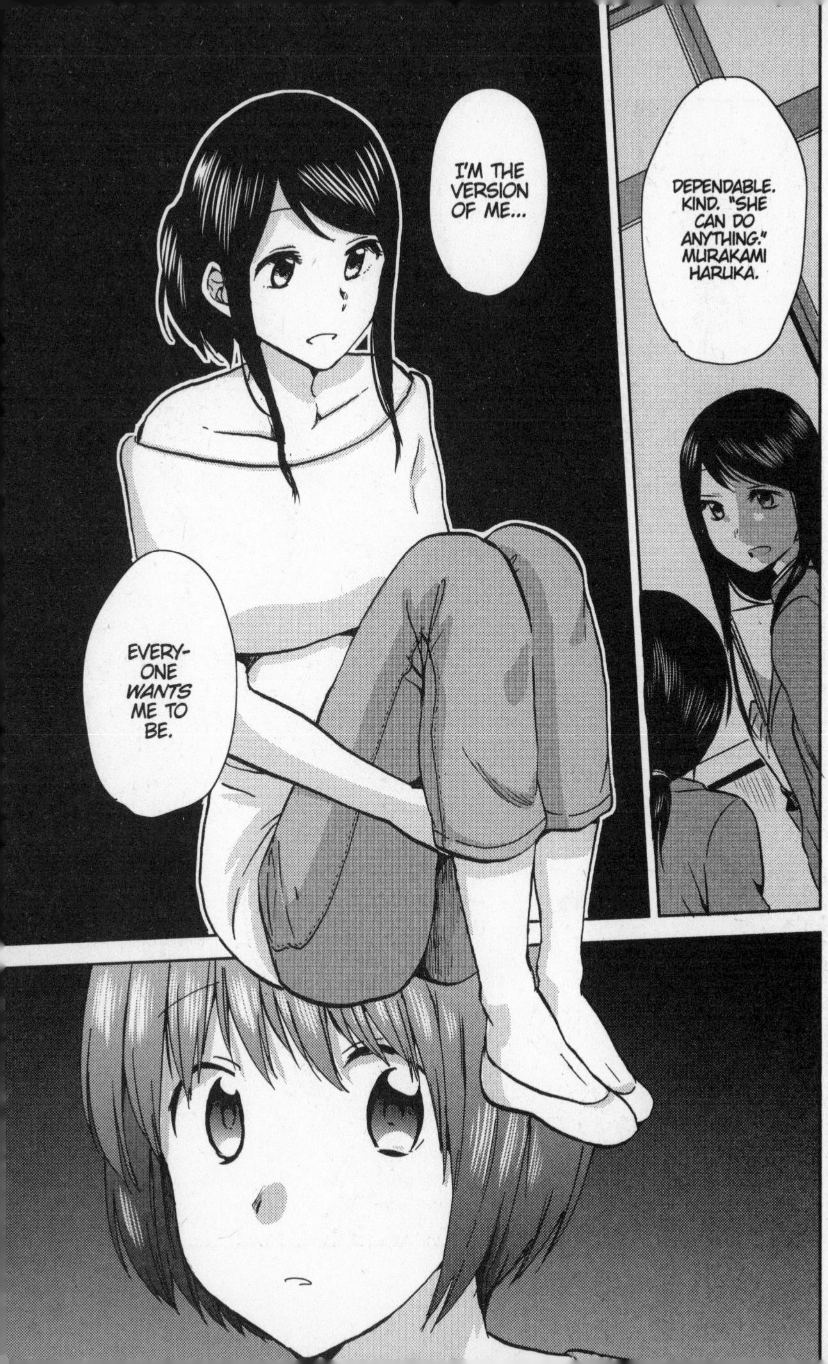
DEPENDABLE. KIND. "SHE CAN DO ANYTHING." MURAKAMI HARUKA.
I'M THE VERSION OF ME...
EVERY-ONE WANTS ME TO BE.

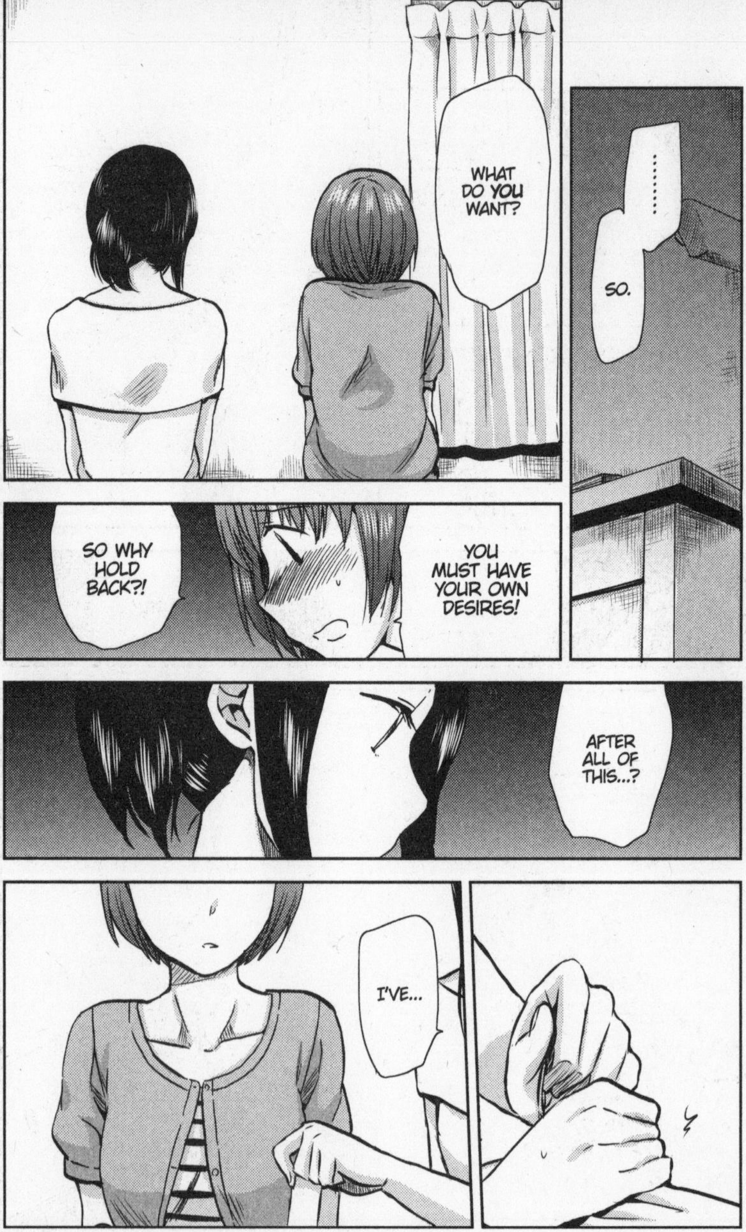
......
SO.
WHAT DO YOU WANT?
YOU MUST HAVE YOUR OWN DESIRES!
SO WHY HOLD BACK?!
AFTER ALL OF THIS...?
I'VE...

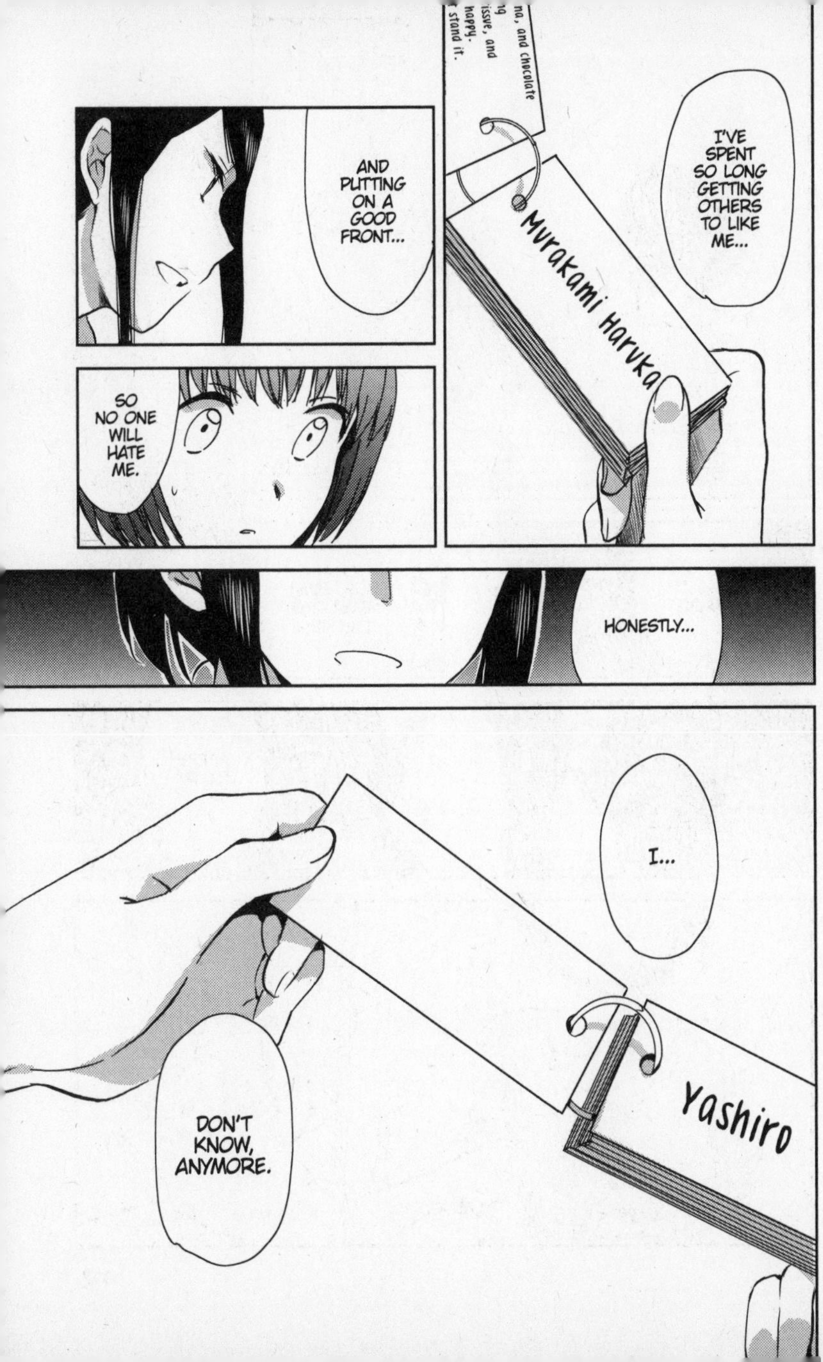
I'VE SPENT SO LONG GETTING OTHERS TO LIKE ME...
Murakami Haruka
AND PUTTING ON A GOOD FRONT...
SO NO ONE WILL HATE ME.
HONESTLY...
I...
Yashiro
DON'T KNOW, ANYMORE.

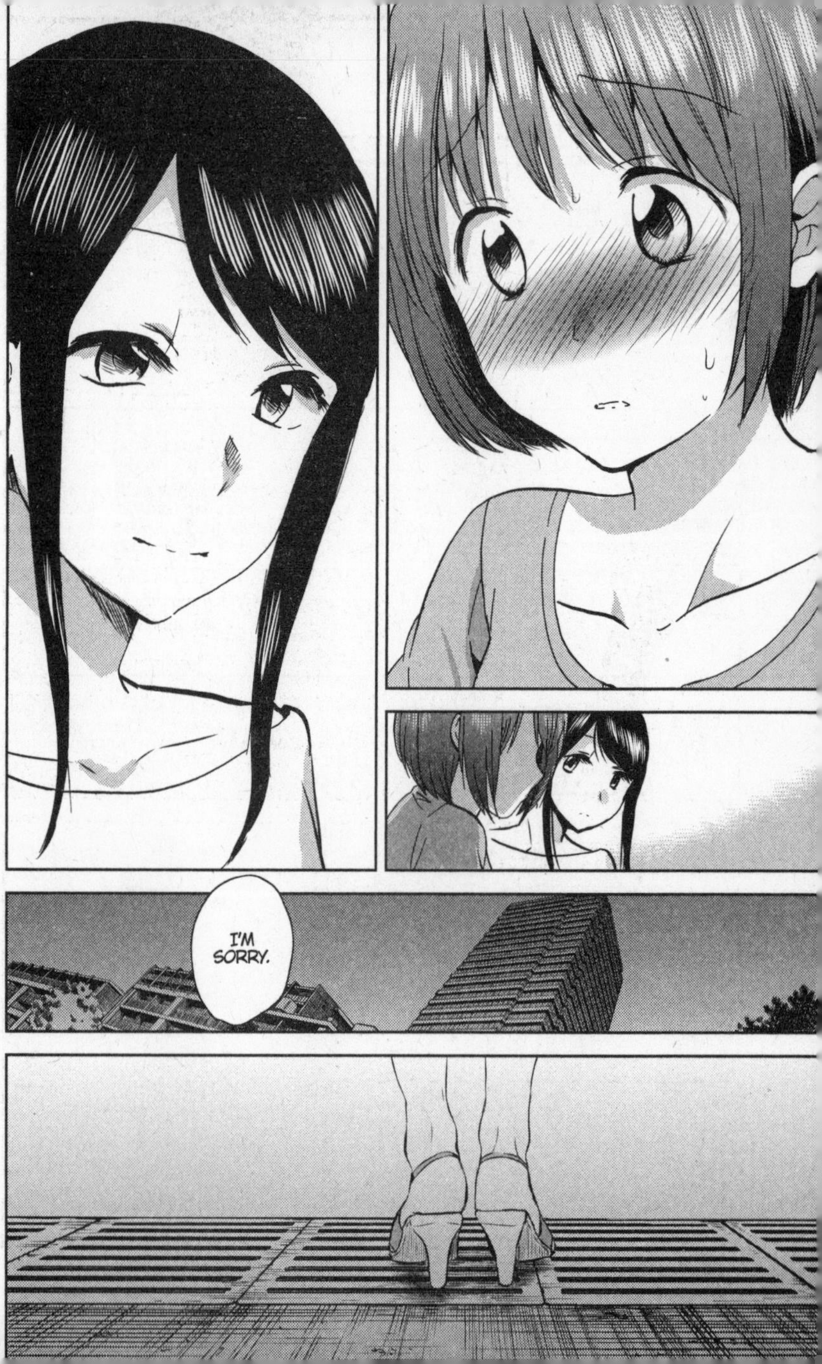
I'M SORRY.

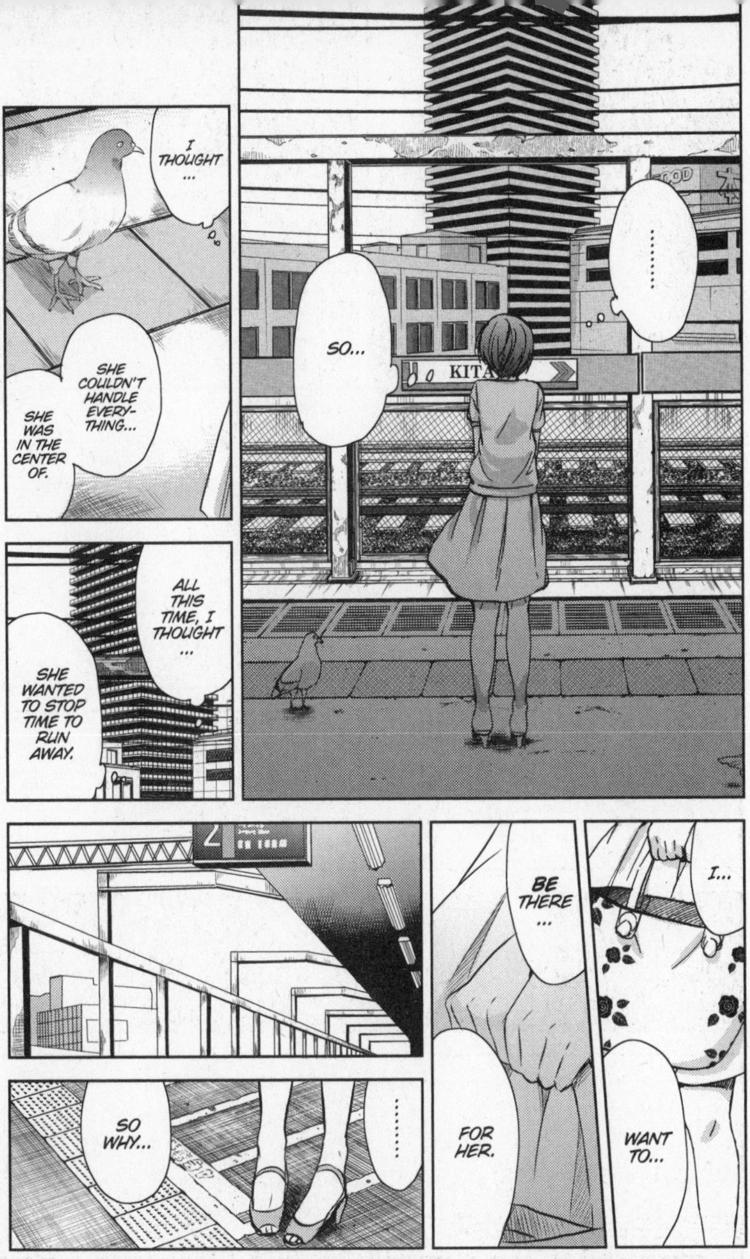
......
SO...
KITA
I THOUGHT...
SHE COULDN'T HANDLE EVERYTHING...
SHE WAS IN THE CENTER OF.
ALL THIS TIME, I THOUGHT...
SHE WANTED TO STOP TIME TO RUN AWAY.
I...
WANT TO...
BE THERE...
FOR HER.
......
SO WHY...

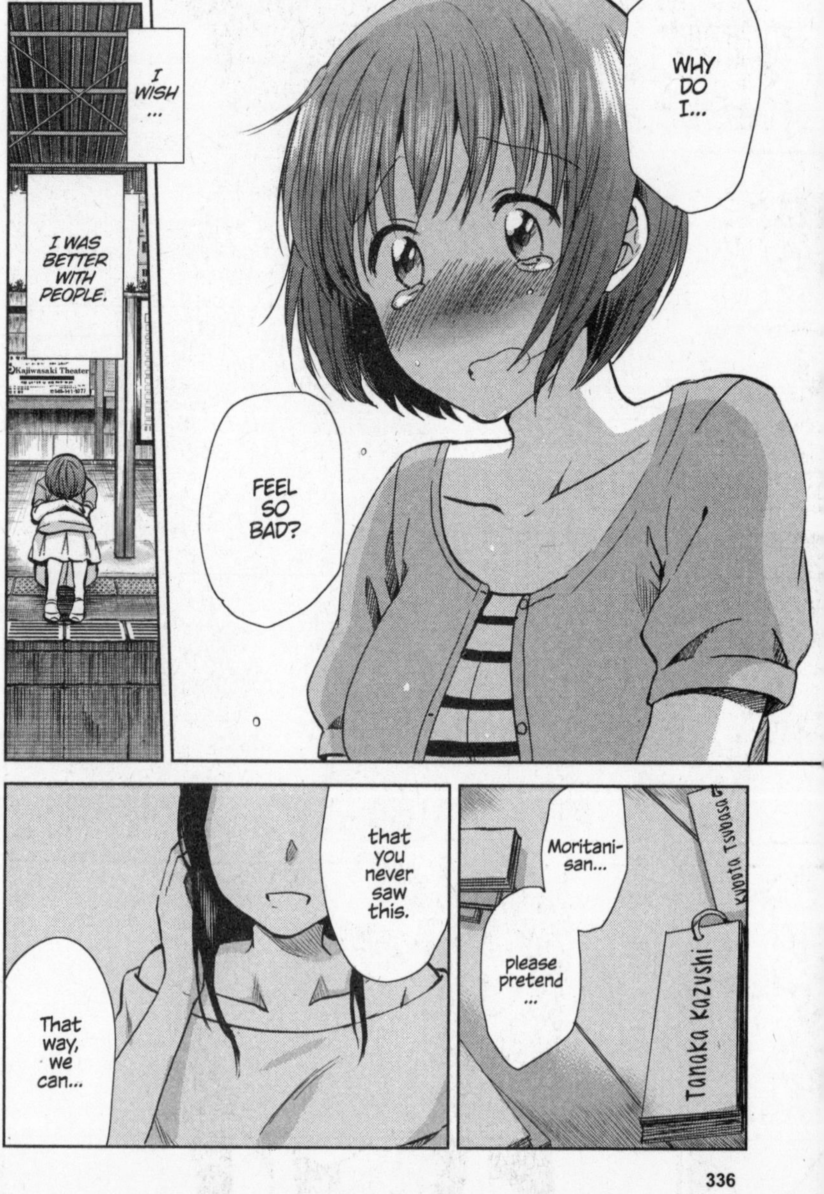
WHY DO I...
FEEL SO BAD?
I WISH ...
I WAS BETTER WITH PEOPLE.
Kajiwasaki Theater
Moritani-san...
please pretend ...
Tanaka Kazushi
that you never saw this.
That way, we can...

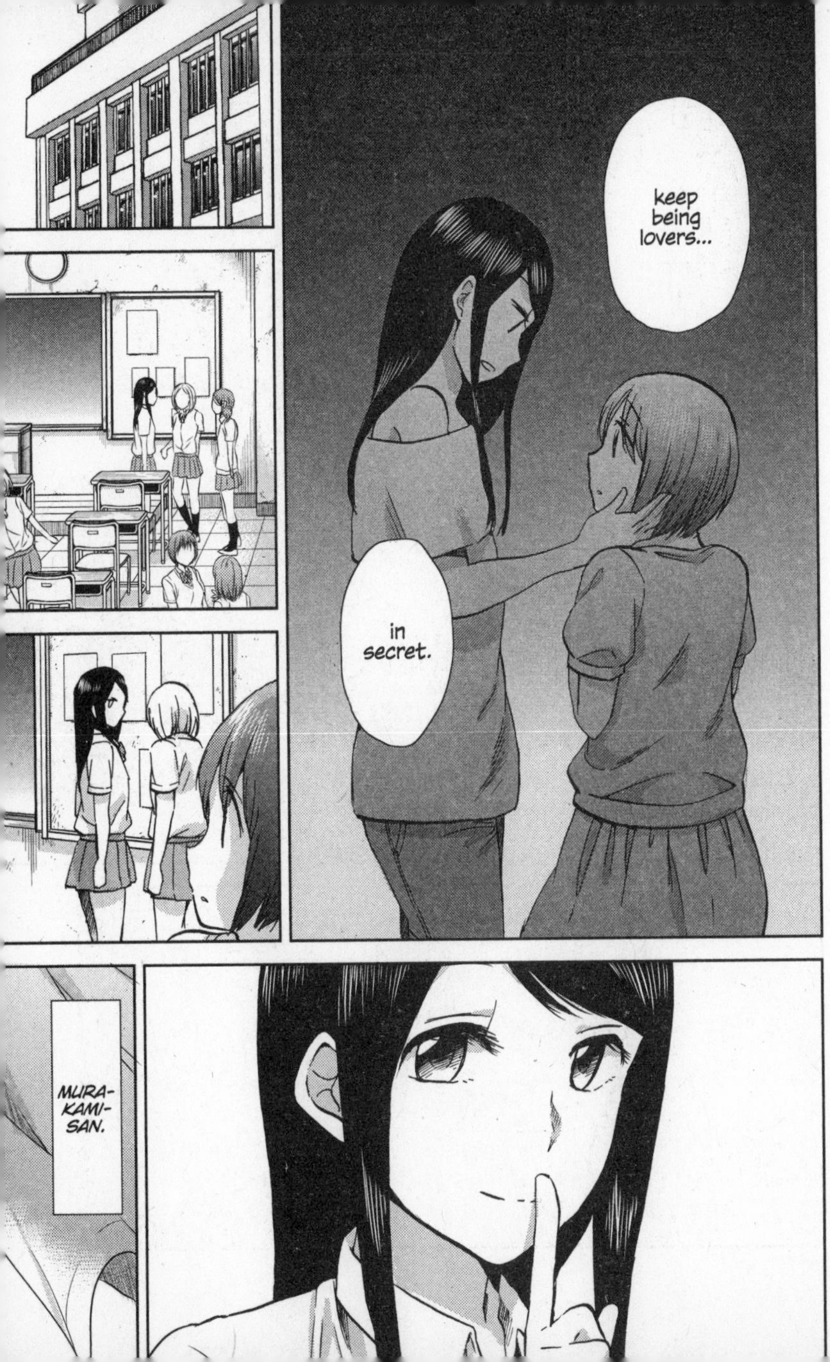
keep being lovers...
in secret.
MURA-KAMI-SAN.

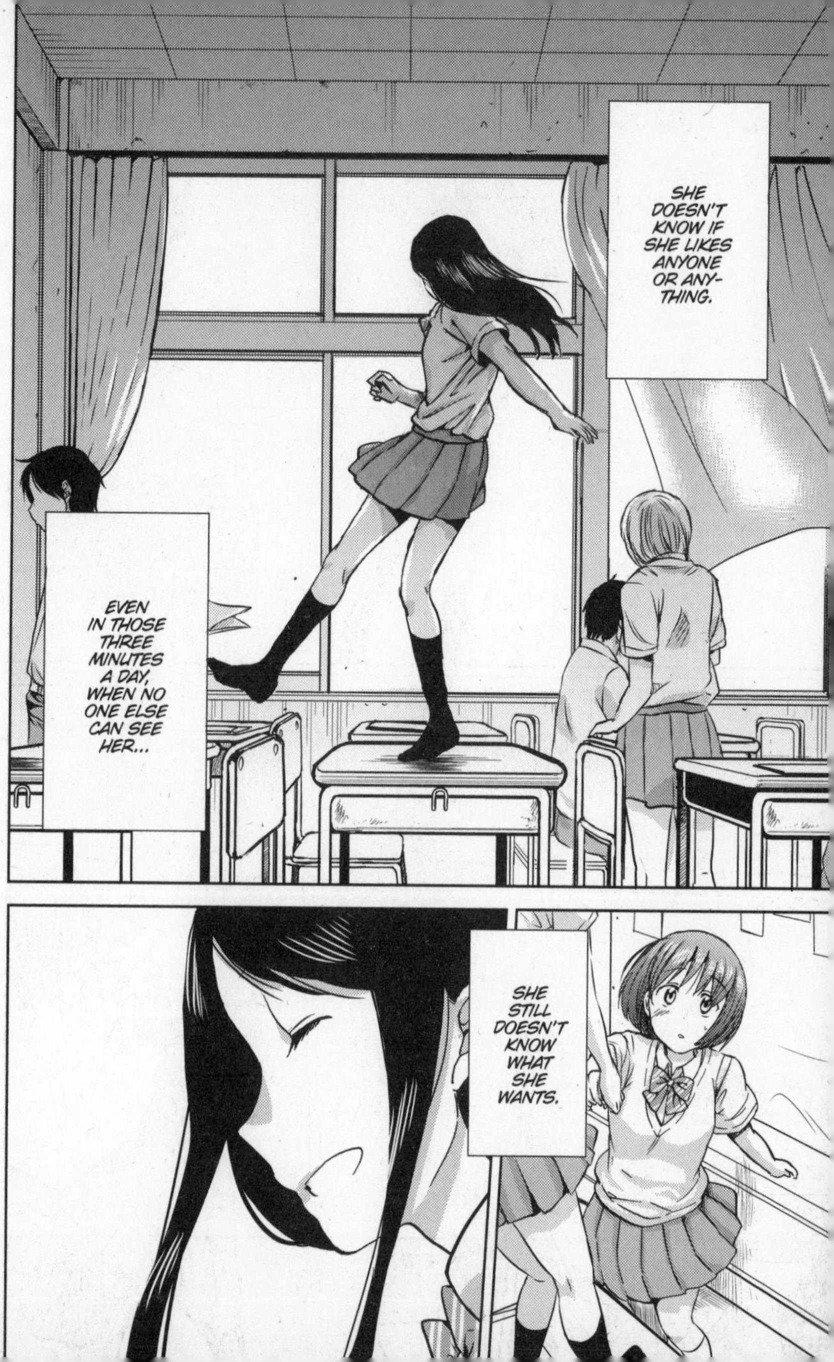
SHE DOESN'T KNOW IF SHE LIKES ANYONE OR ANY-THING.
EVEN IN THOSE THREE MINUTES A DAY, WHEN NO ONE ELSE CAN SEE HER...
SHE STILL DOESN'T KNOW WHAT SHE WANTS.

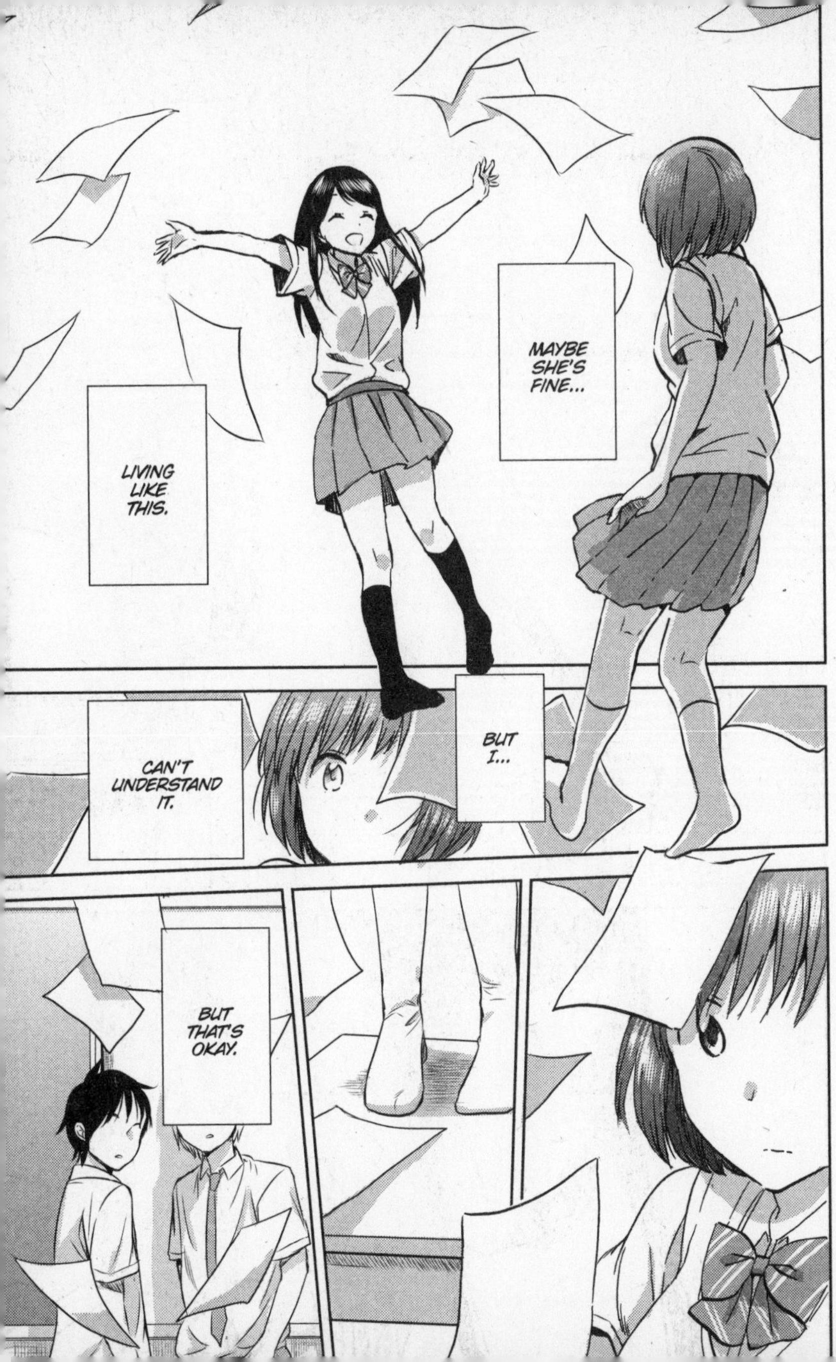
MAYBE SHE'S FINE...
LIVING LIKE THIS.
BUT I...
CAN'T UNDERSTAND IT.
BUT THAT'S OKAY.

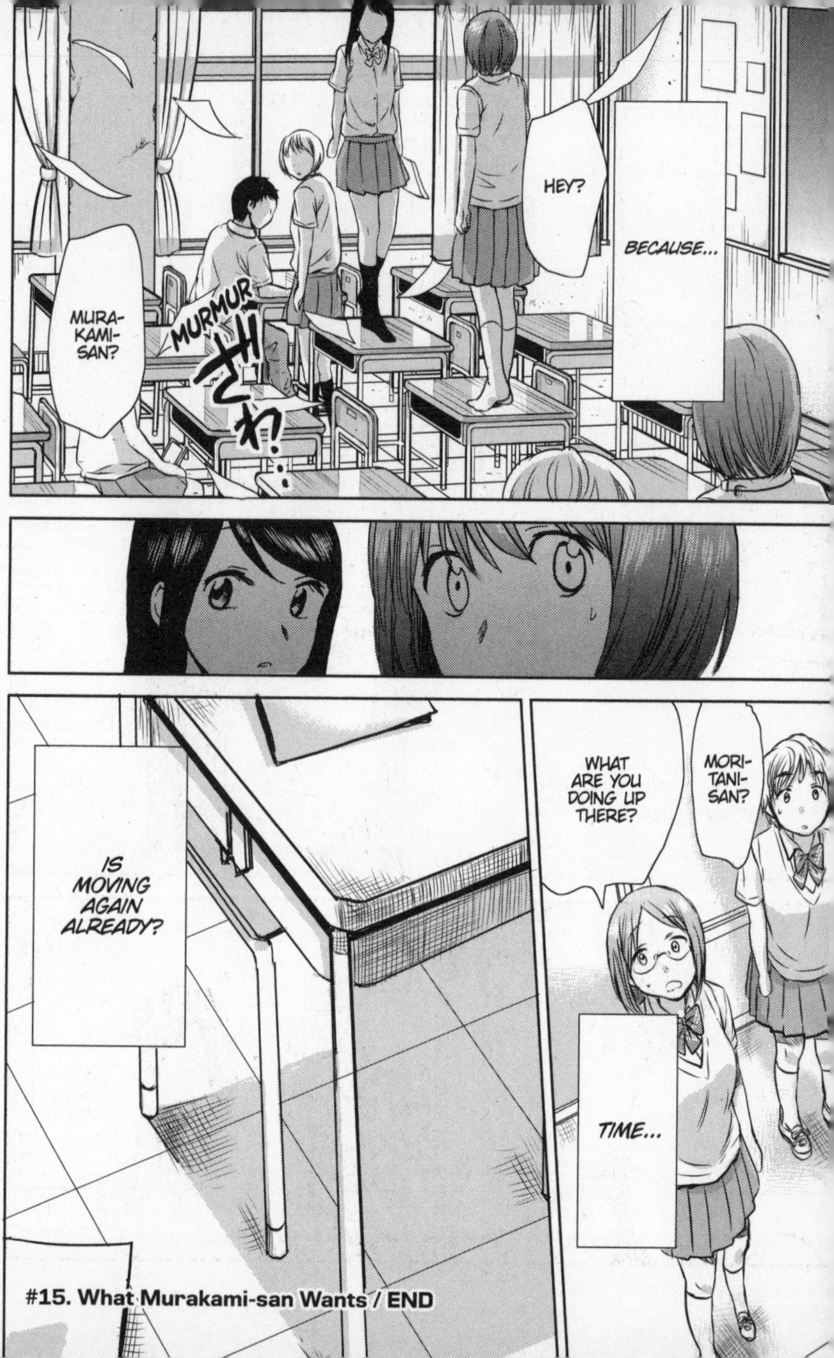
BECAUSE...
HEY?
MURMUR
ざわ!
MURA-KAMI-SAN?
MORI-TANI-SAN?
WHAT ARE YOU DOING UP THERE?
TIME...
IS MOVING AGAIN ALREADY?

#15. What Murakami-san Wants / END

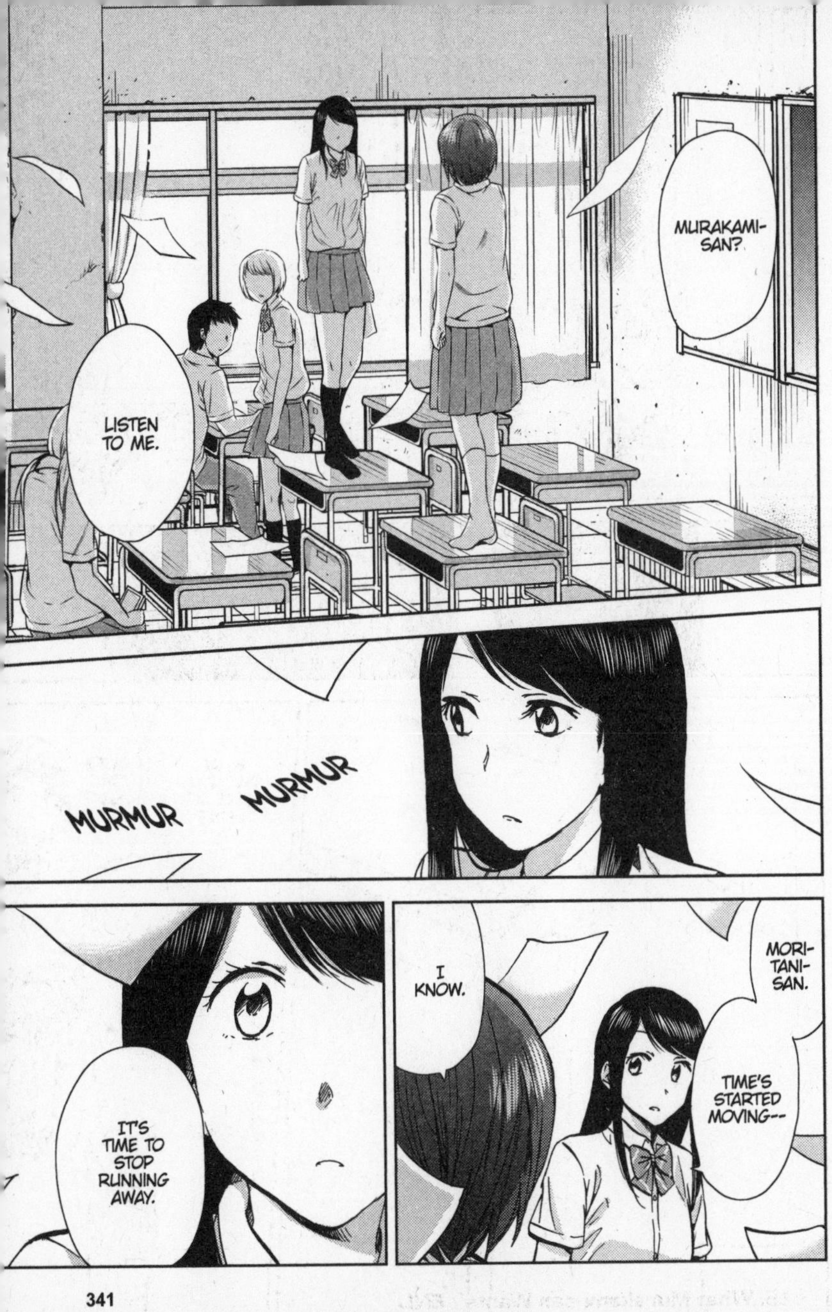
MURAKAMI-SAN?
LISTEN TO ME.
MURMUR
MURMUR
MORI-TANI-SAN.
TIME'S STARTED MOVING--
I KNOW.
IT'S TIME TO STOP RUNNING AWAY.

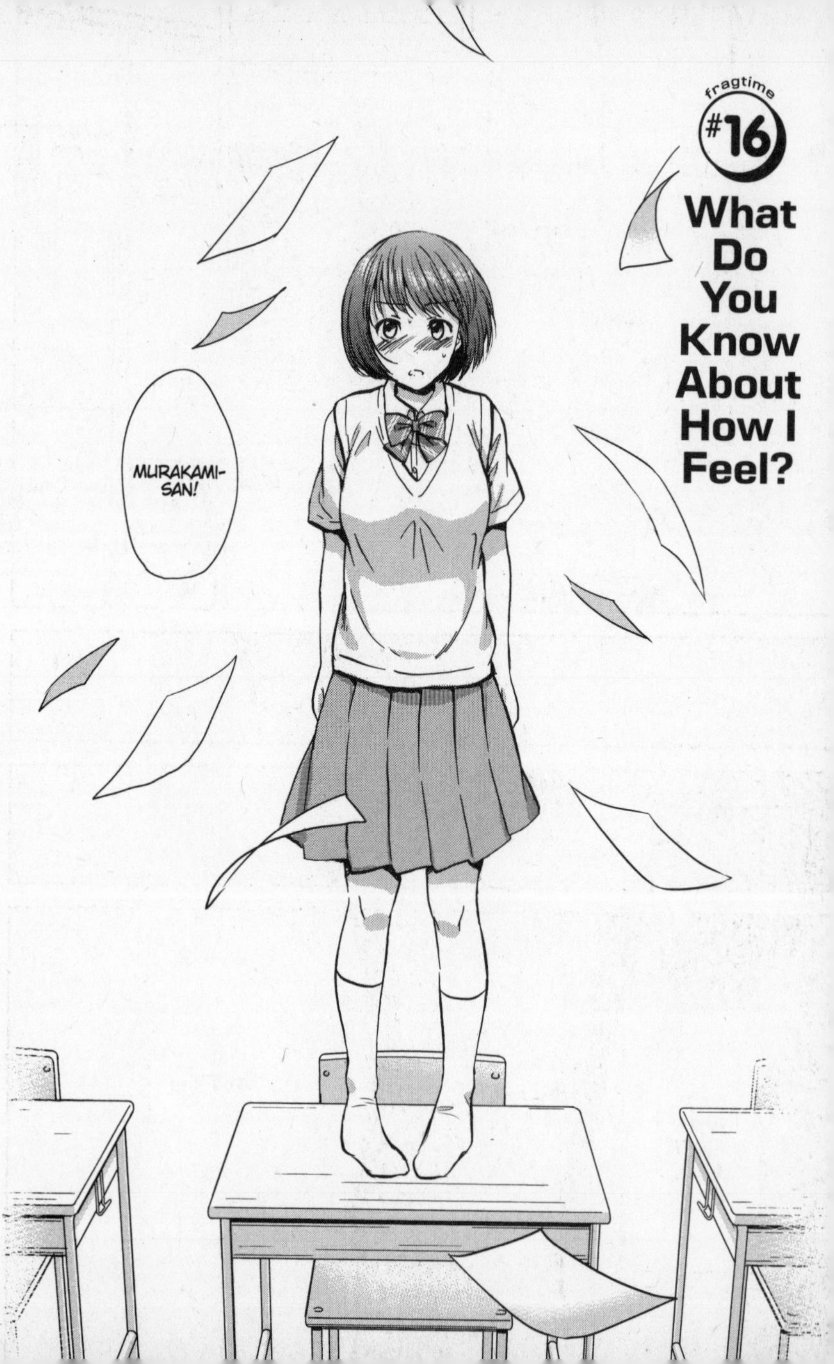
fragtime
#16
What Do You Know About How I Feel?
MURAKAMI-SAN!

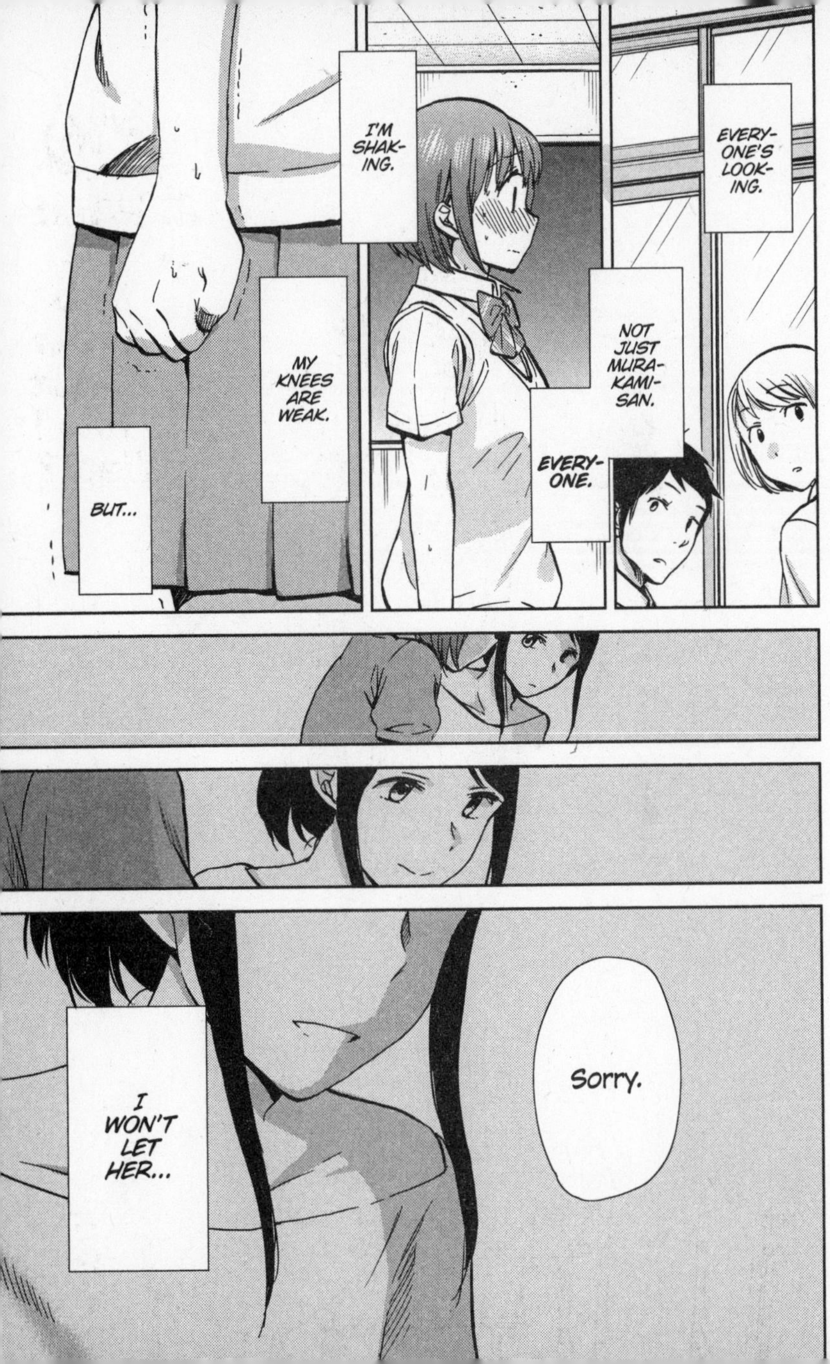
EVERY-ONE'S LOOK-ING.
NOT JUST MURA-KAMI-SAN.
EVERY-ONE.
I'M SHAK-ING.
MY KNEES ARE WEAK.
BUT...
Sorry.
I WON'T LET HER...

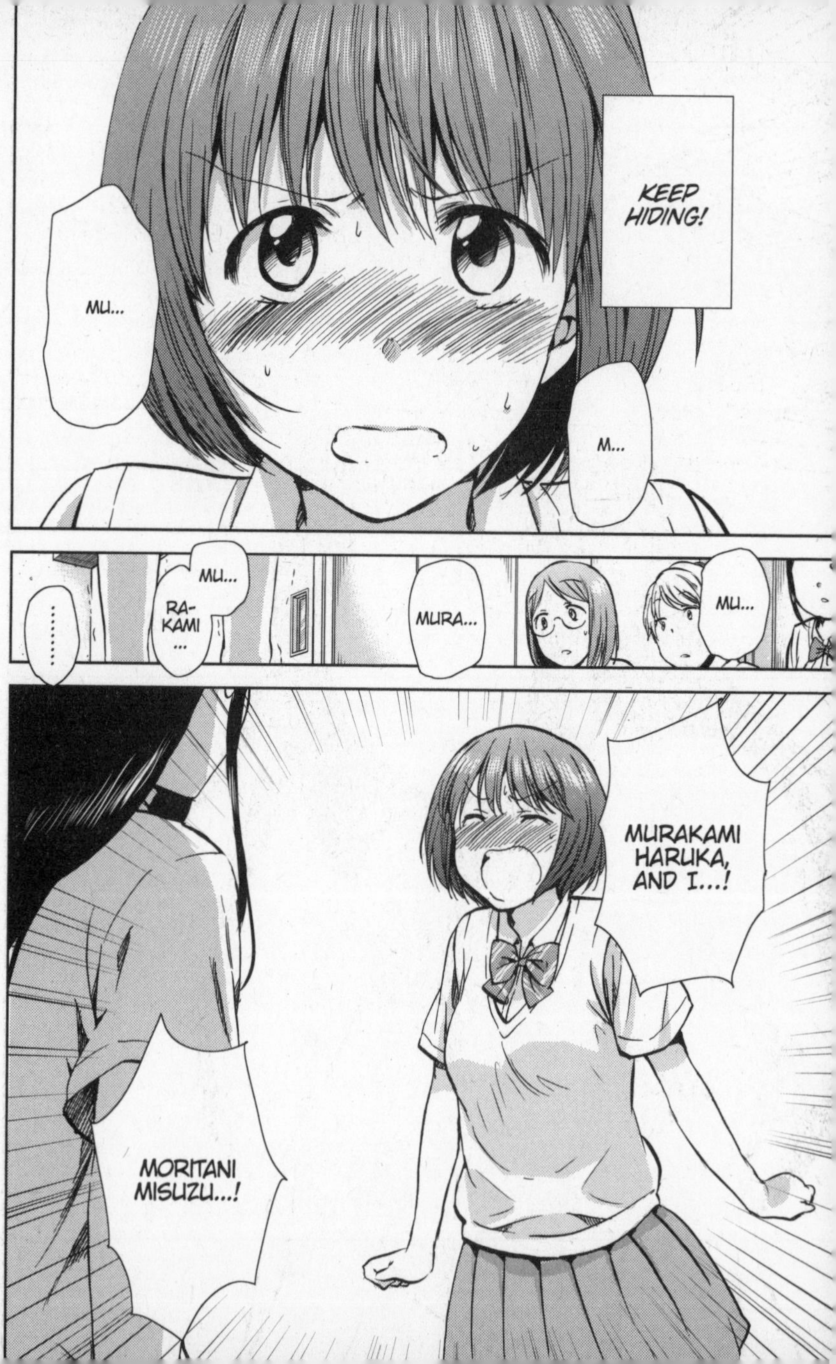
KEEP HIDING!
M...
MU...
MU...
MURA...
MU... RA-KAMI ...
......
MURAKAMI HARUKA, AND I...!
MORITANI MISUZU...!

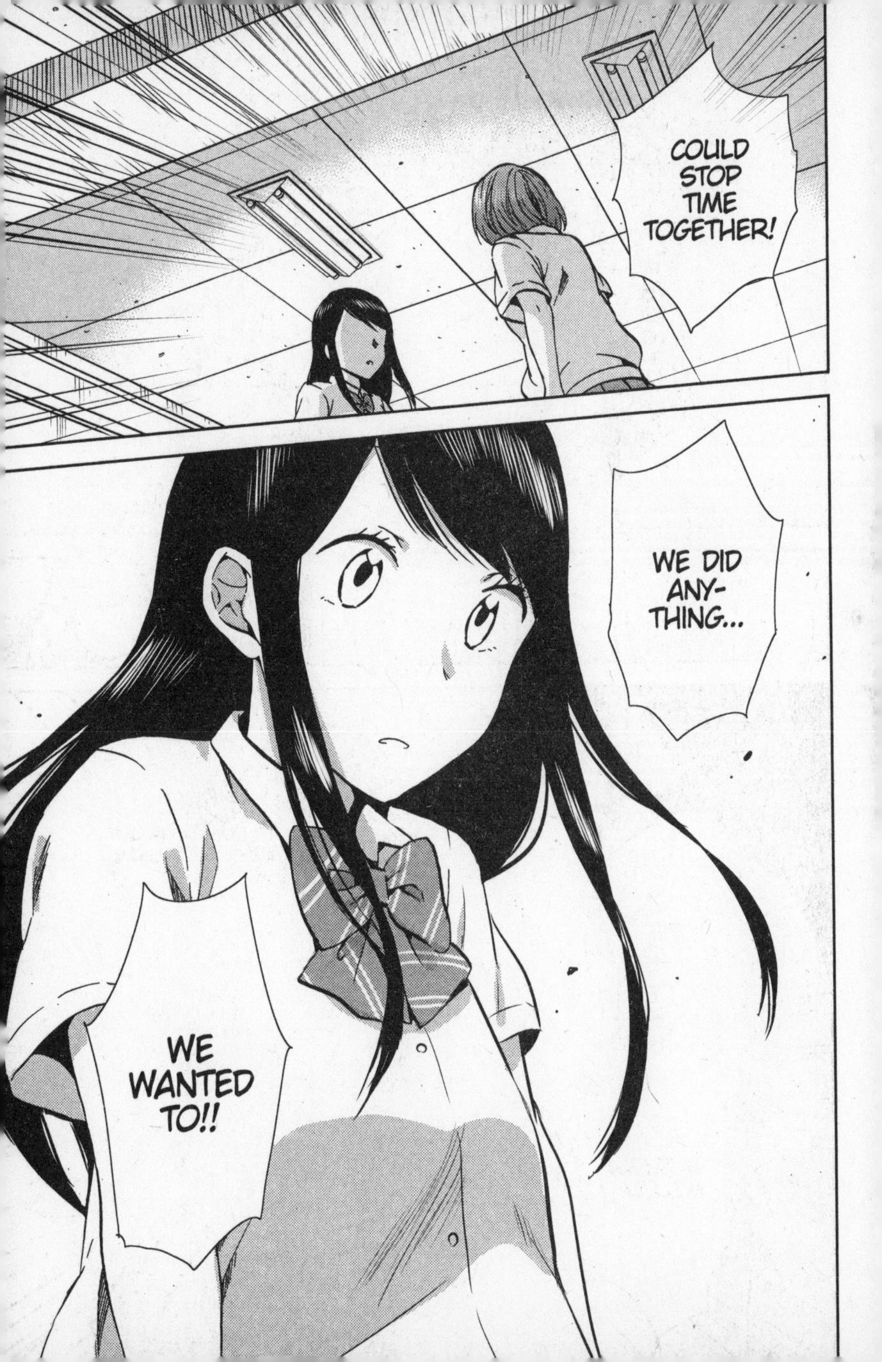
COULD STOP TIME TOGETHER!
WE DID ANY-THING...
WE WANTED TO!!

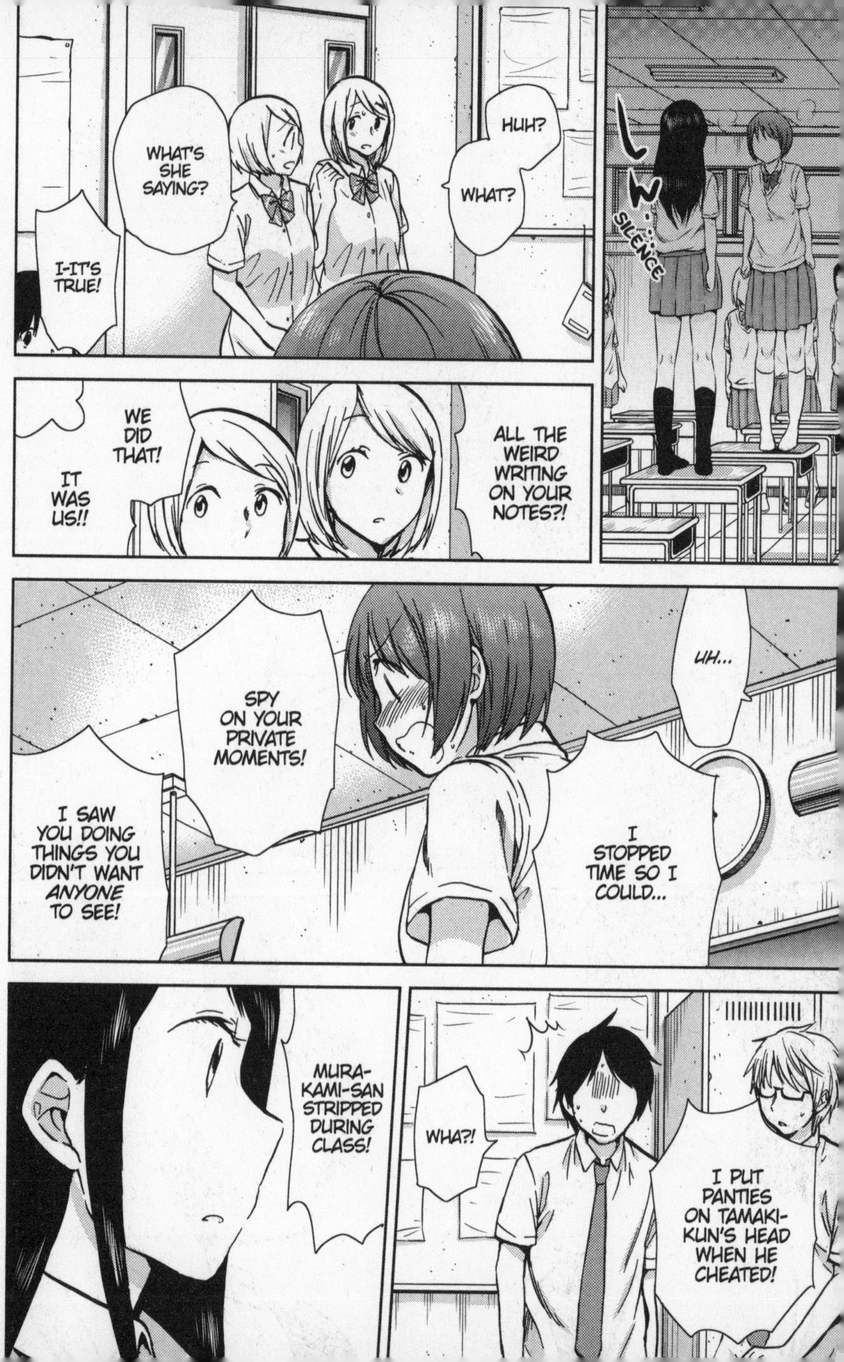
SILENCE
HUH?
WHAT?
WHAT'S SHE SAYING?
I-IT'S TRUE!
ALL THE WEIRD WRITING ON YOUR NOTES?!
WE DID THAT!
IT WAS US!!
UH...
I STOPPED TIME SO I COULD...
SPY ON YOUR PRIVATE MOMENTS!
I SAW YOU DOING THINGS YOU DIDN'T WANT *ANYONE* TO SEE!
I PUT PANTIES ON TAMAKI-KUN'S HEAD WHEN HE CHEATED!
WHA?!
MURAKAMI-SAN STRIPPED DURING CLASS!

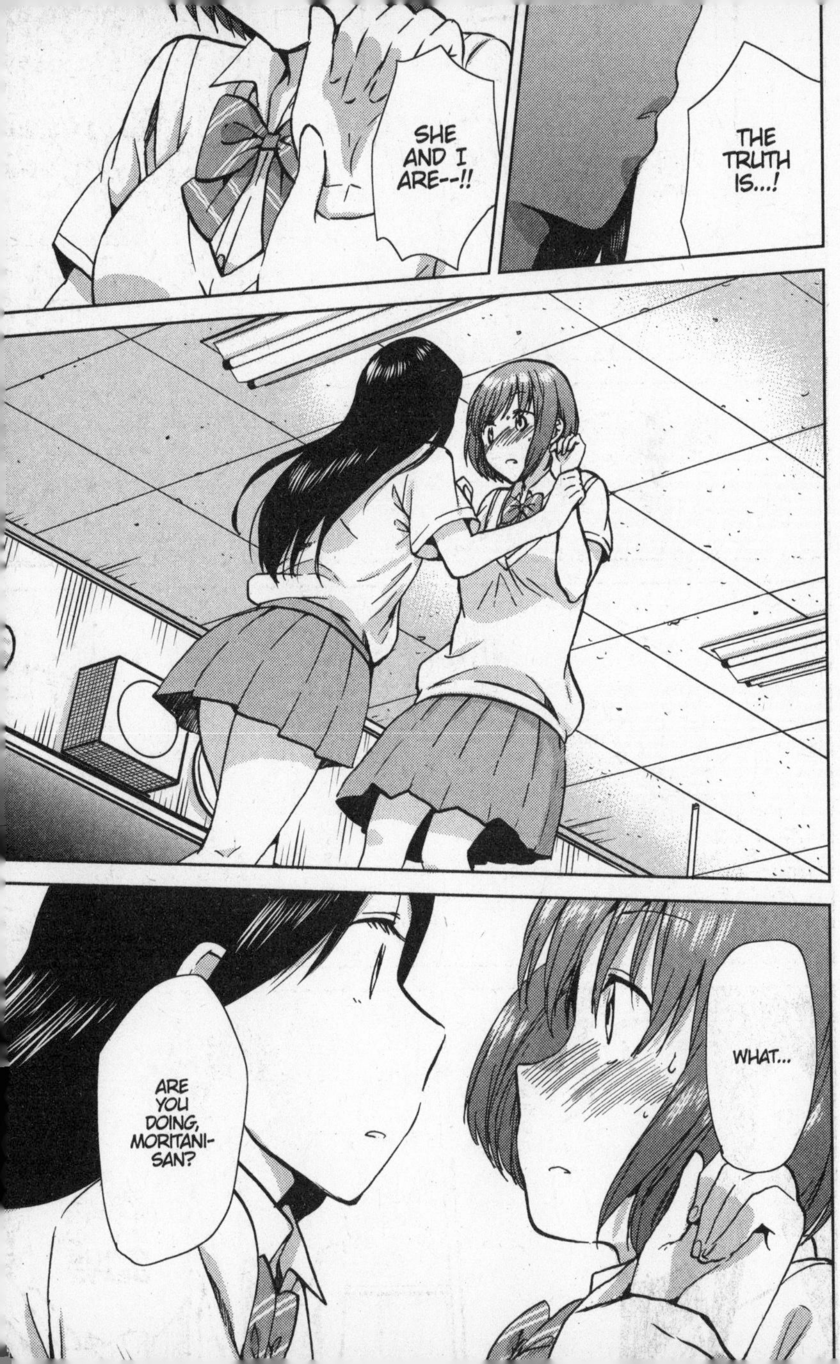
THE TRUTH IS...!
SHE AND I ARE--!!
WHAT...
ARE YOU DOING, MORITANI-SAN?

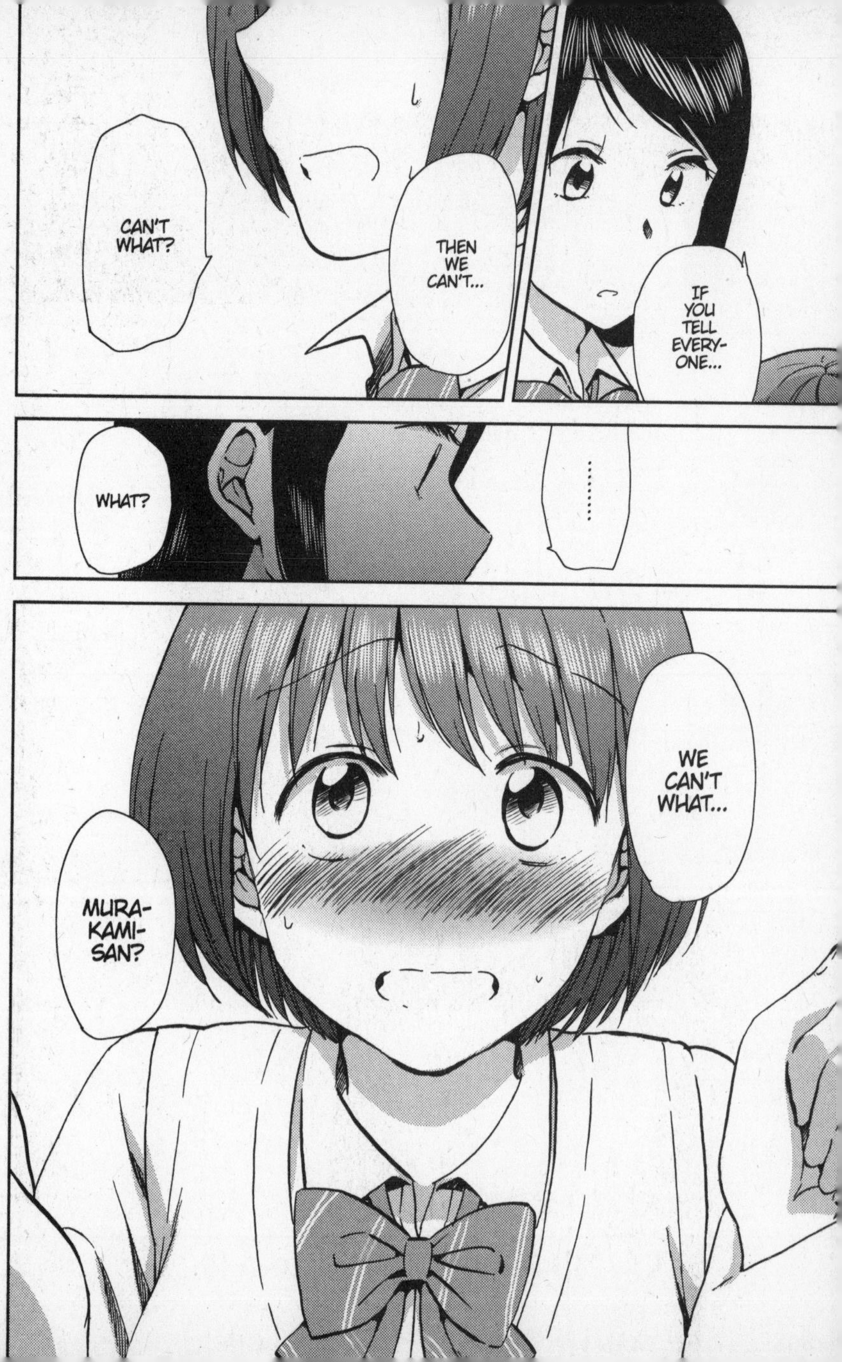
IF YOU TELL EVERYONE...
THEN WE CAN'T...
CAN'T WHAT?
......
WHAT?
WE CAN'T WHAT...
MURAKAMI-SAN?

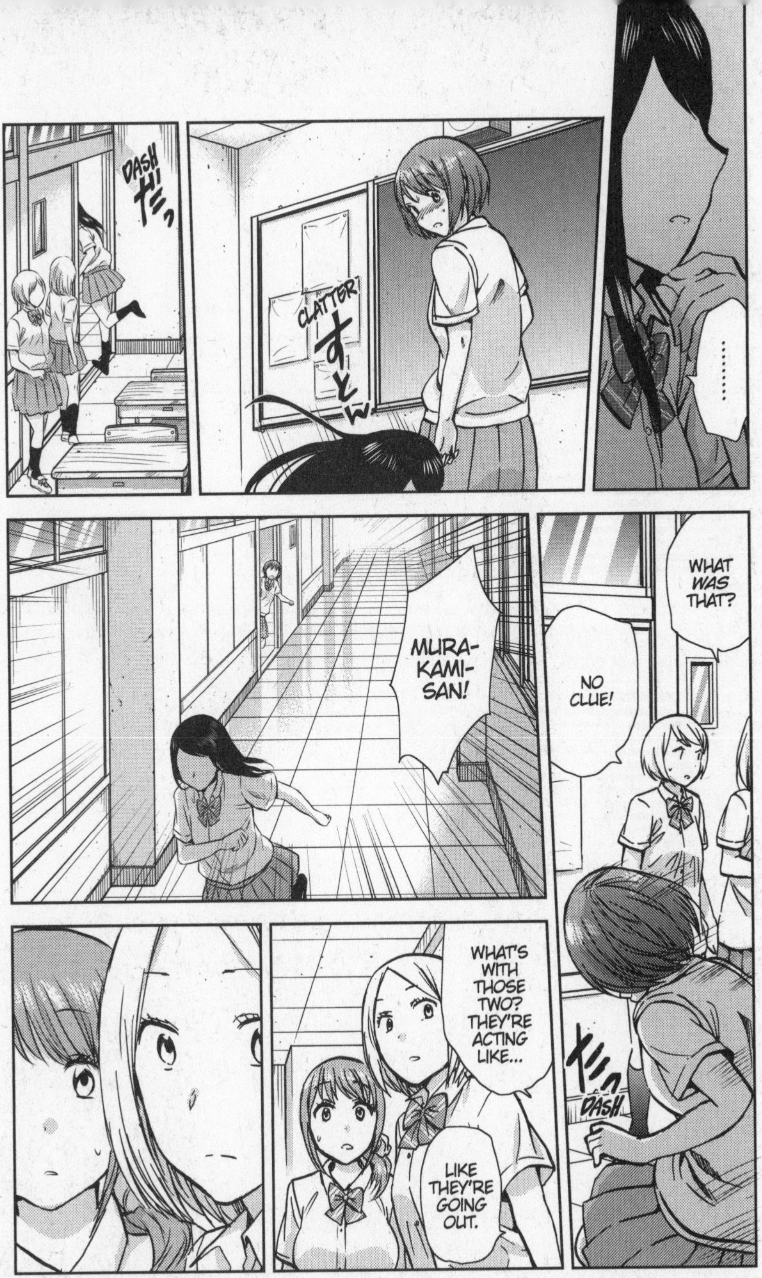
……
CLATTER
すとん
DASH
ダッ
WHAT WAS THAT?
NO CLUE!
ダッ
DASH
MURA-KAMI-SAN!
WHAT'S WITH THOSE TWO? THEY'RE ACTING LIKE…
LIKE THEY'RE GOING OUT.

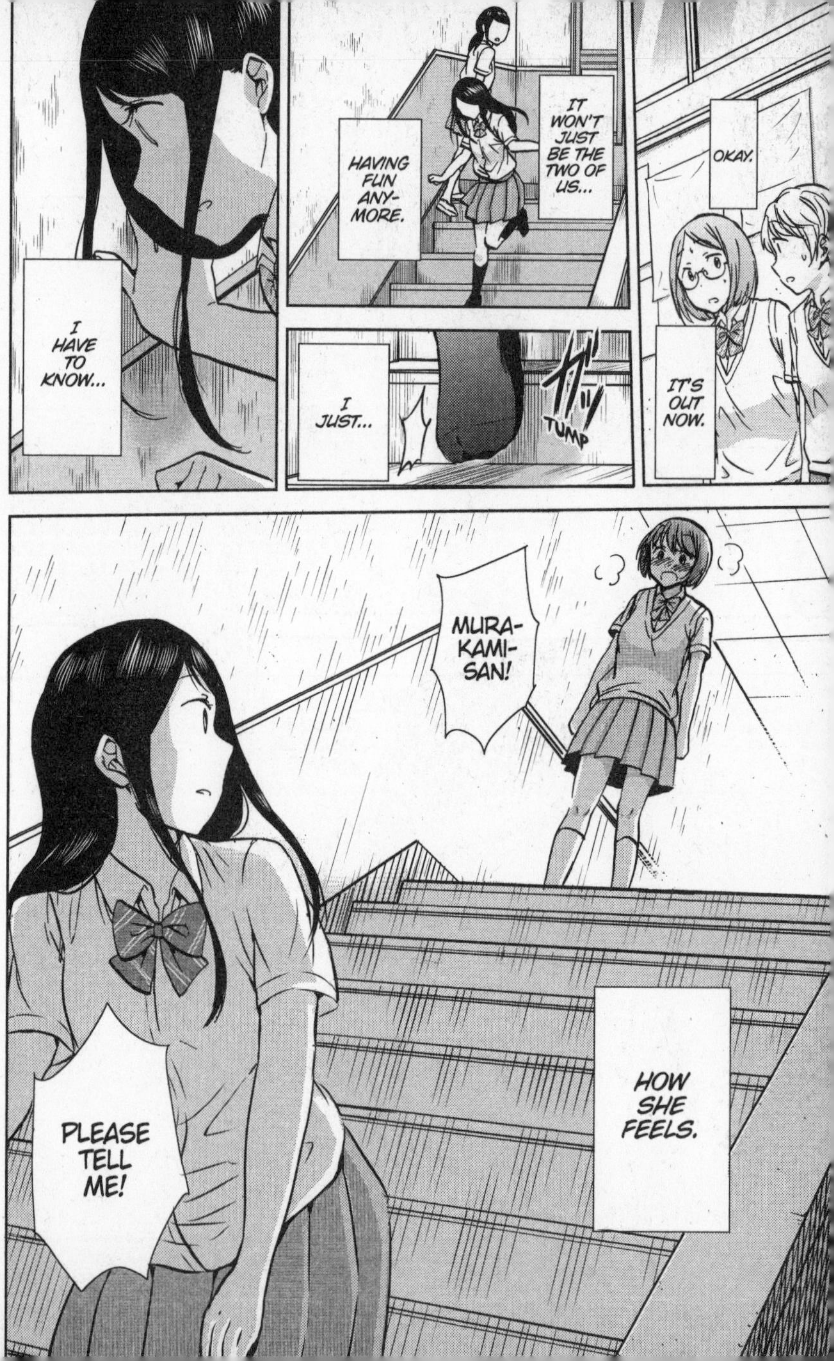
OKAY.
IT'S OUT NOW.
IT WON'T JUST BE THE TWO OF US...
HAVING FUN ANYMORE.
ガッ
TUMP
I JUST...
I HAVE TO KNOW...
MURA-KAMI-SAN!
HOW SHE FEELS.
PLEASE TELL ME!

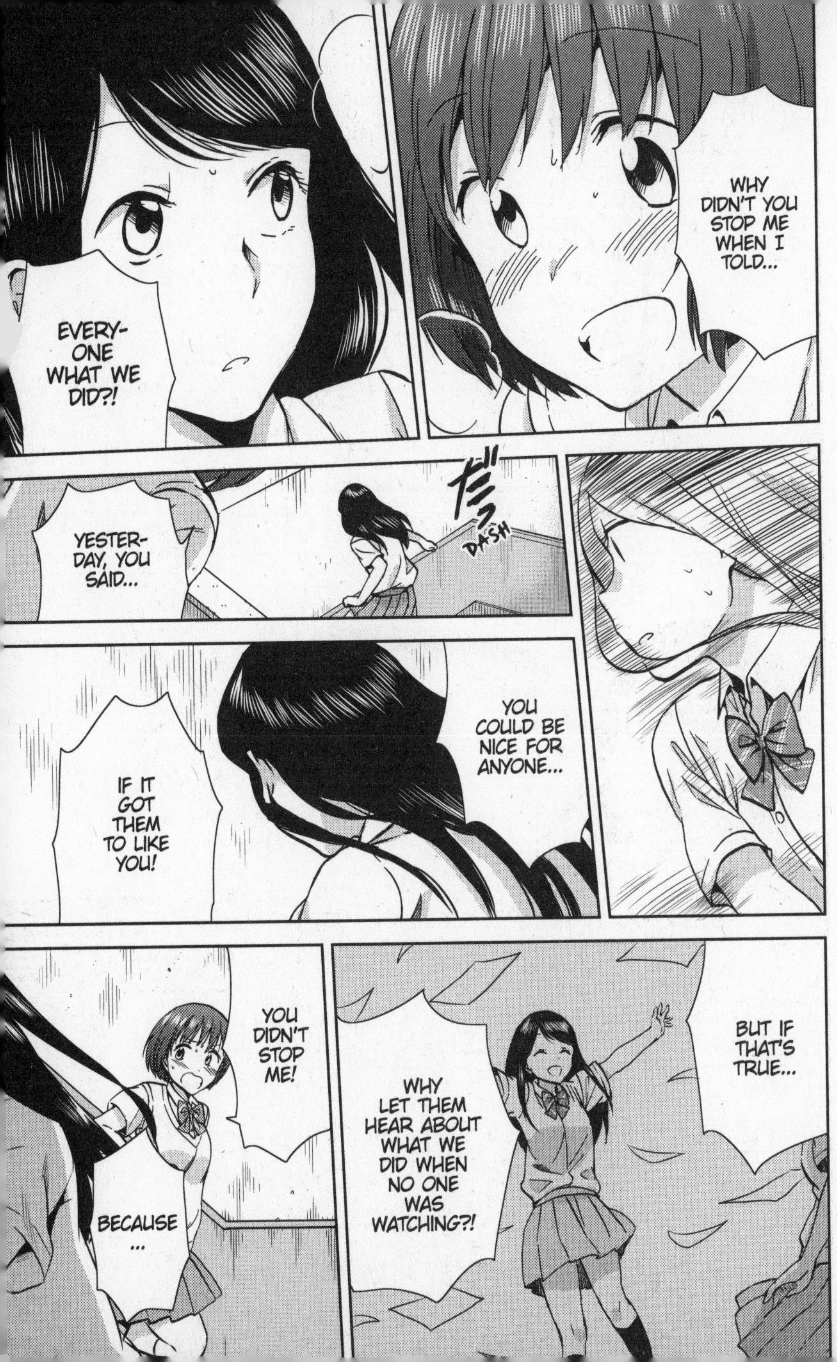
WHY DIDN'T YOU STOP ME WHEN I TOLD...
EVERY-ONE WHAT WE DID?!
DASH
YESTER-DAY, YOU SAID...
YOU COULD BE NICE FOR ANYONE...
IF IT GOT THEM TO LIKE YOU!
BUT IF THAT'S TRUE...
WHY LET THEM HEAR ABOUT WHAT WE DID WHEN NO ONE WAS WATCHING?!
YOU DIDN'T STOP ME!
BECAUSE ...

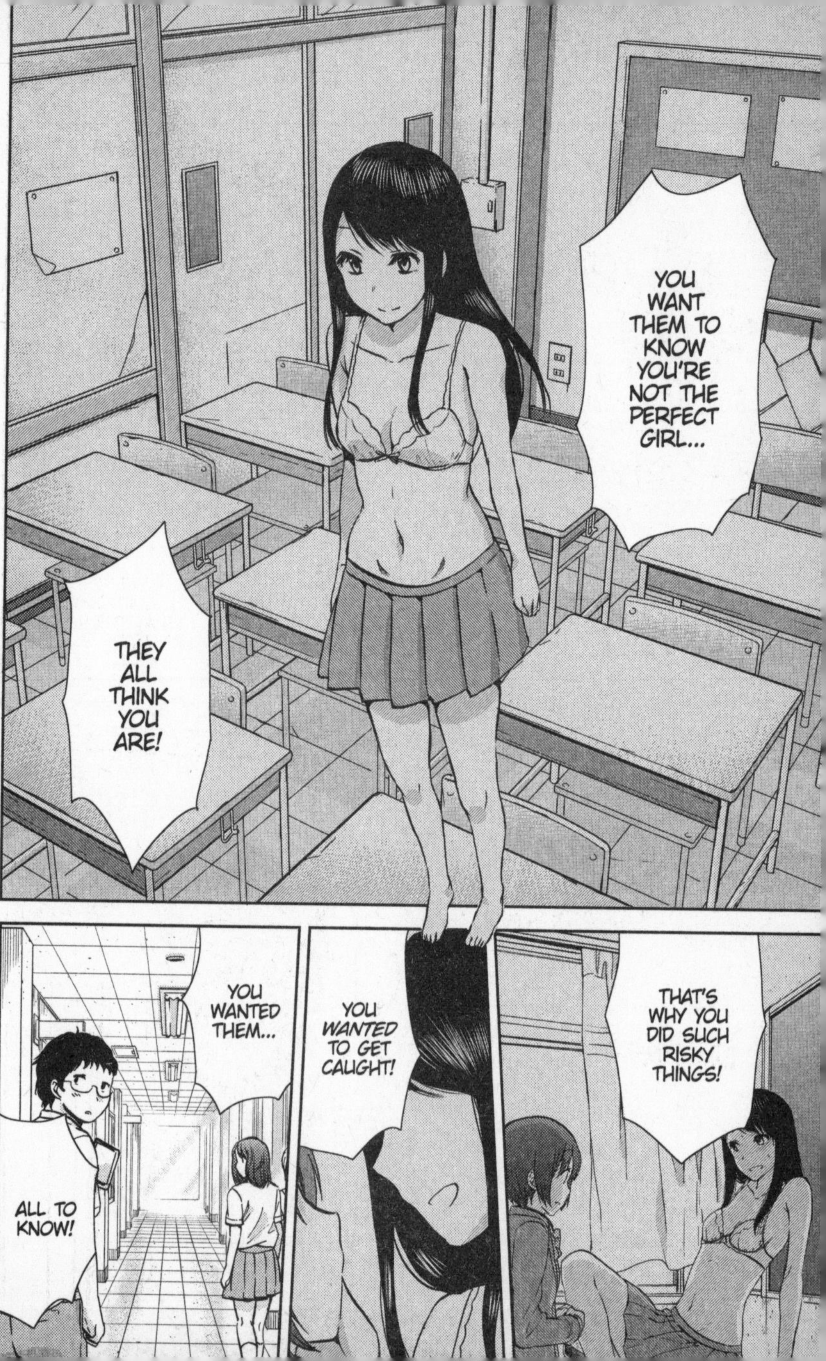
YOU WANT THEM TO KNOW YOU'RE NOT THE PERFECT GIRL...
THEY ALL THINK YOU ARE!
THAT'S WHY YOU DID SUCH RISKY THINGS!
YOU *WANTED* TO GET CAUGHT!
YOU WANTED THEM...
ALL TO KNOW!

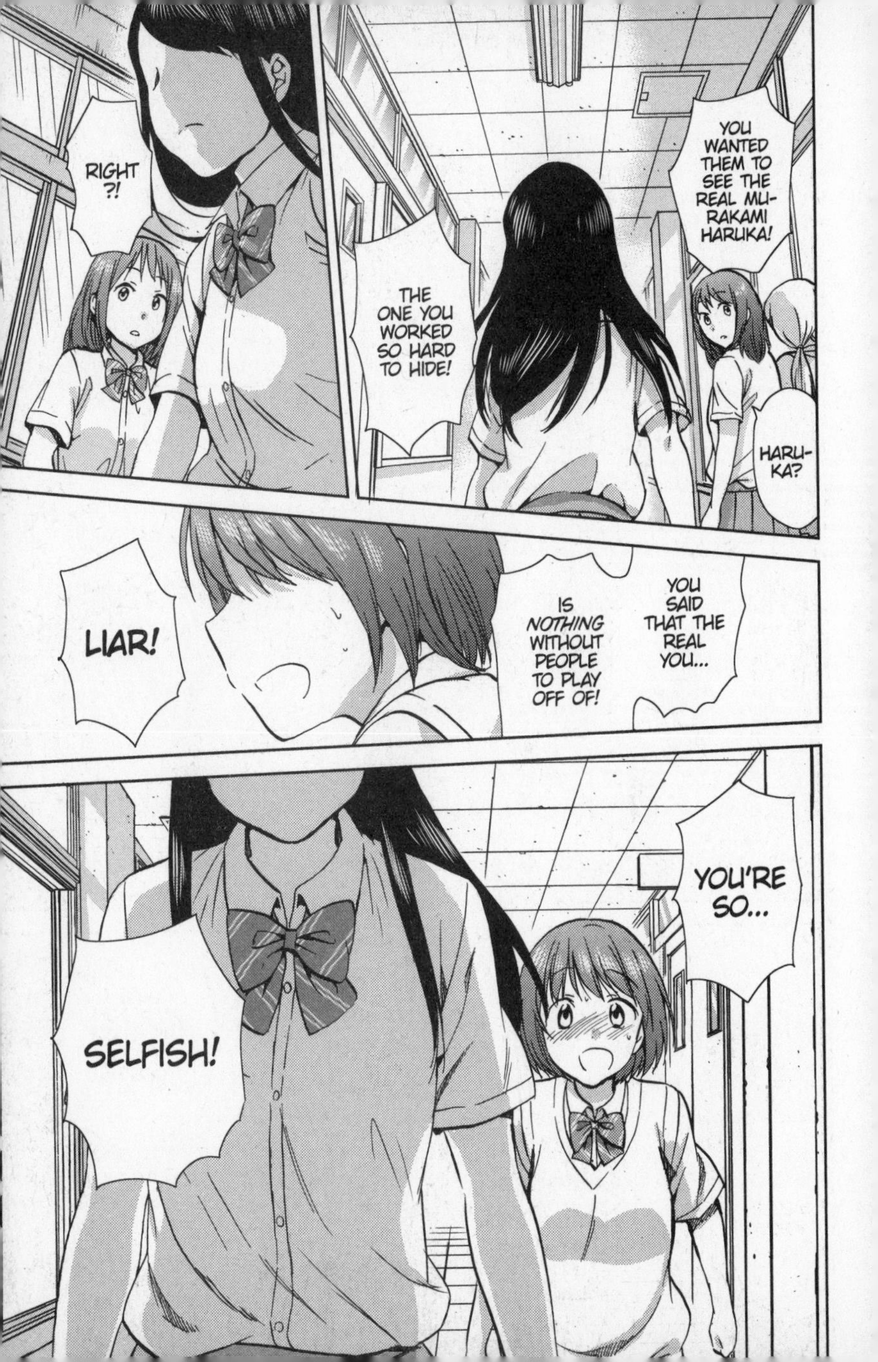
YOU WANTED THEM TO SEE THE REAL MU-RAKAMI HARUKA!
THE ONE YOU WORKED SO HARD TO HIDE!
HARU-KA?
RIGHT ?!
YOU SAID THAT THE REAL YOU...
IS *NOTHING* WITHOUT PEOPLE TO PLAY OFF OF!
LIAR!
YOU'RE SO...
SELFISH!

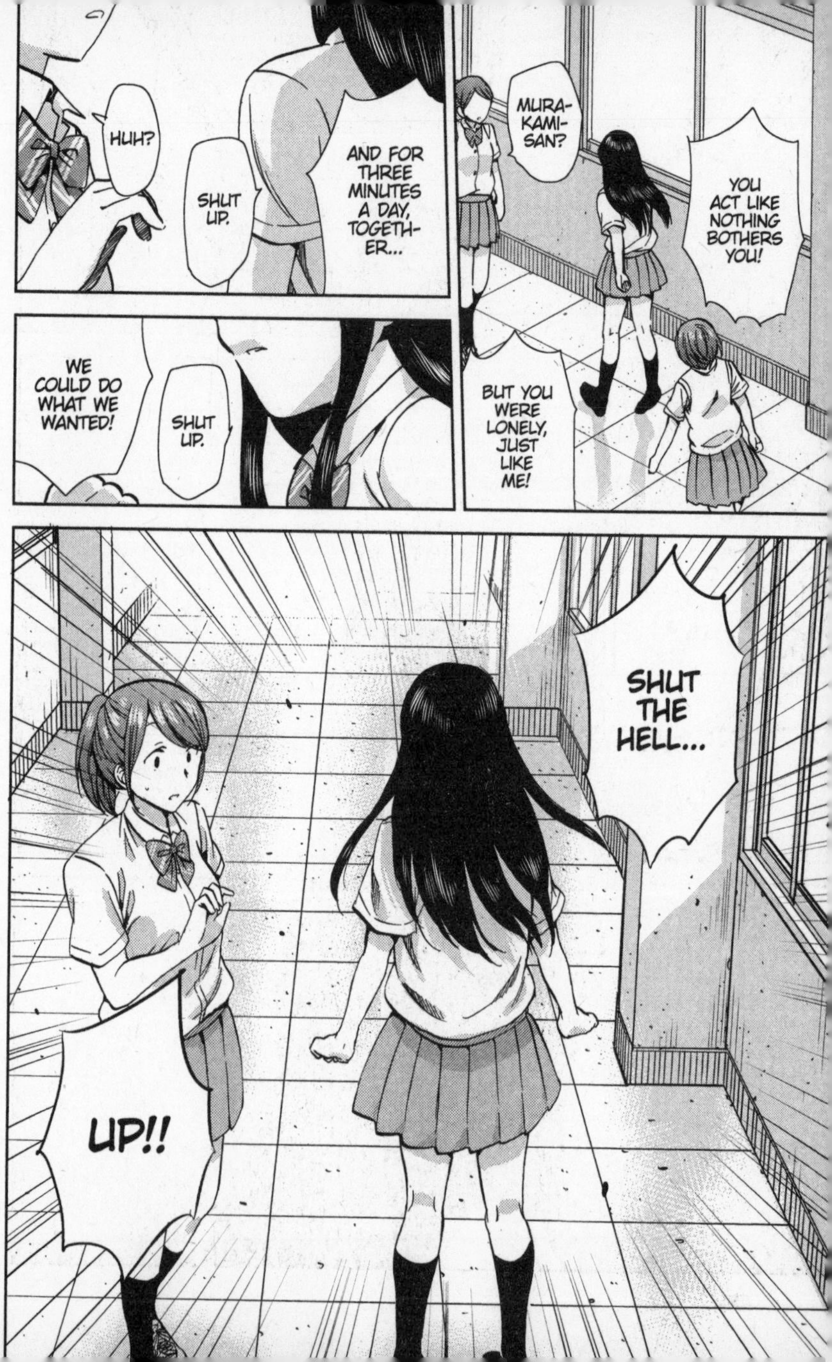
MURA-KAMI-SAN?
YOU ACT LIKE NOTHING BOTHERS YOU!
BUT YOU WERE LONELY, JUST LIKE ME!
AND FOR THREE MINUTES A DAY, TOGETH-ER...
SHUT UP.
HUH?
WE COULD DO WHAT WE WANTED!
SHUT UP.
SHUT THE HELL...
UP!!

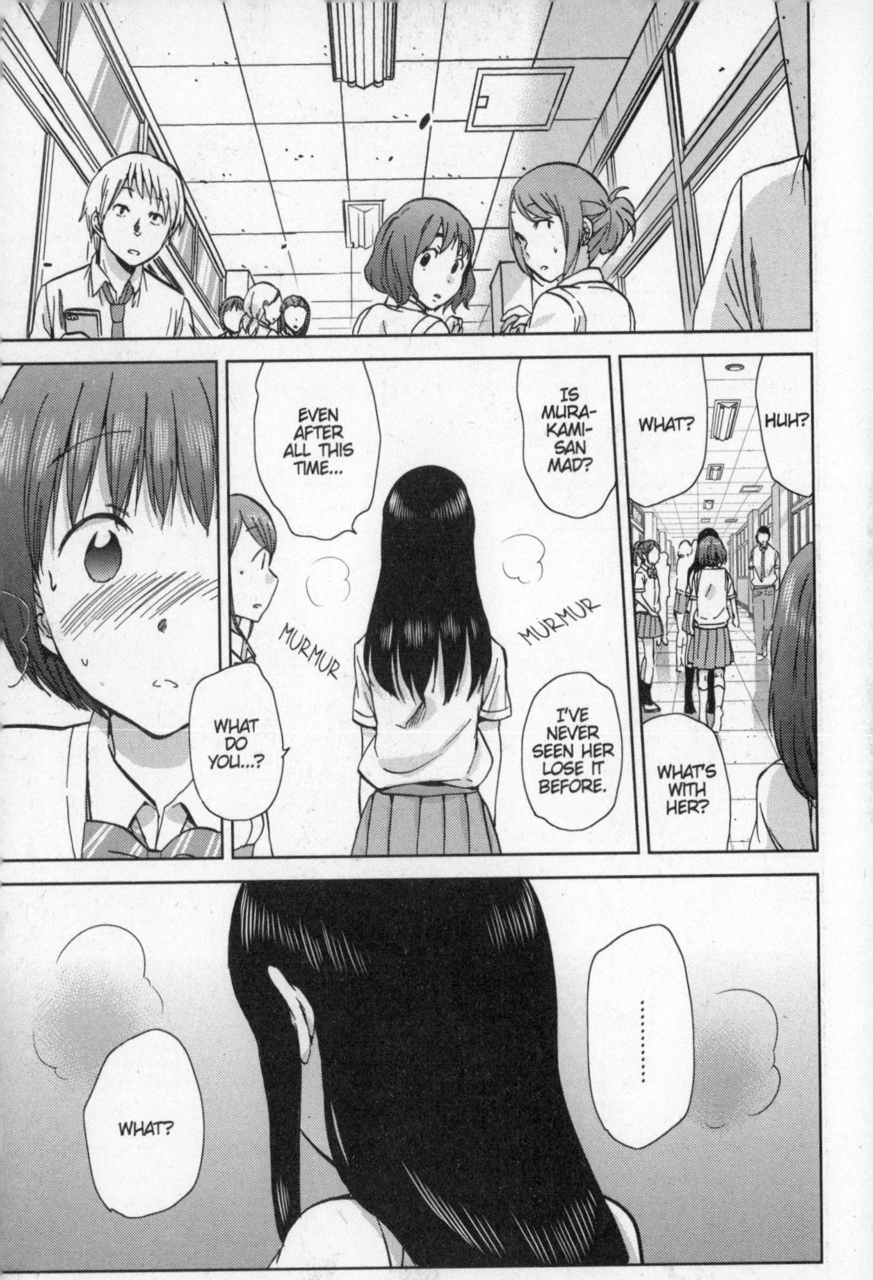
HUH?
WHAT?
WHAT'S WITH HER?
IS MURA-KAMI-SAN MAD?
EVEN AFTER ALL THIS TIME...
MURMUR
MURMUR
I'VE NEVER SEEN HER LOSE IT BEFORE.
WHAT DO YOU...?
......
WHAT?

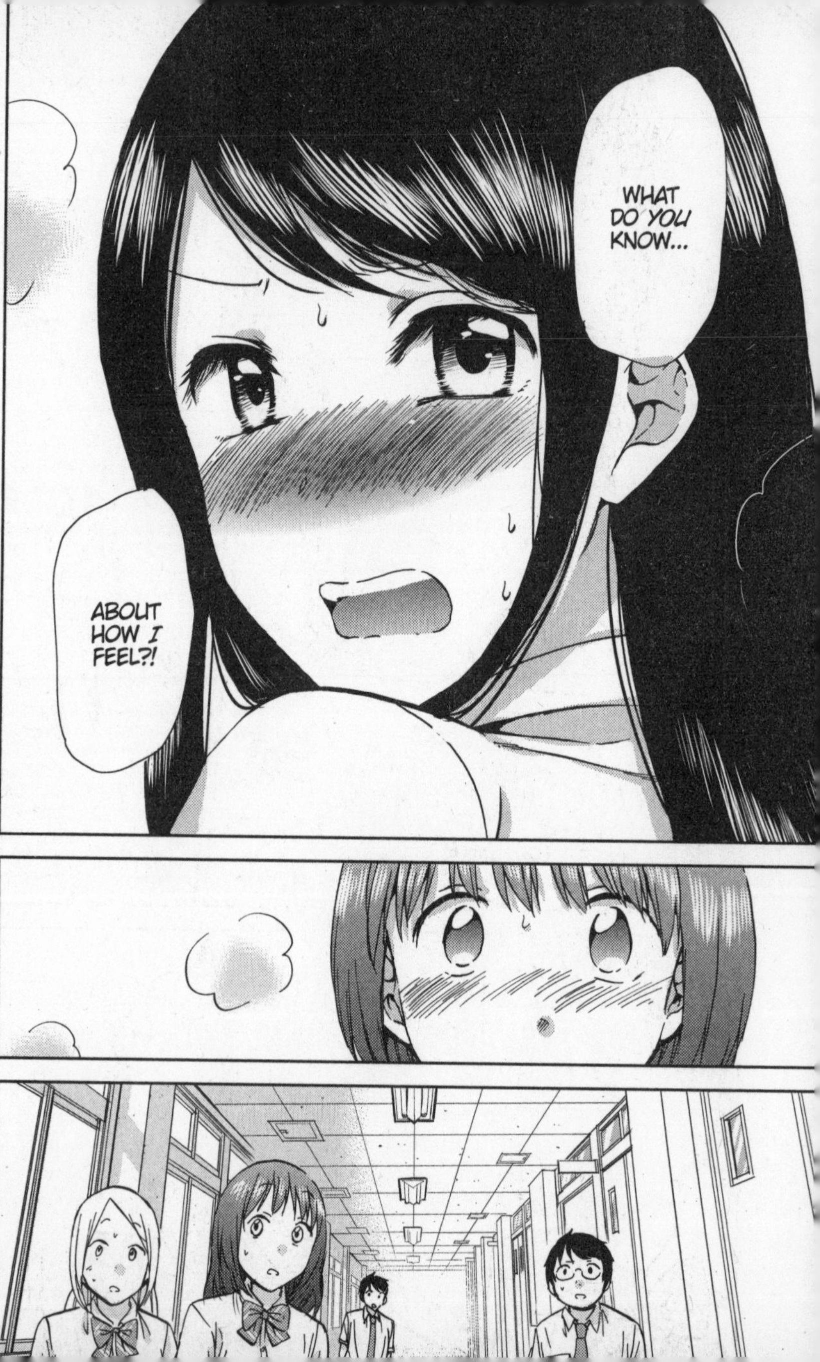
WHAT DO YOU KNOW...
ABOUT HOW I FEEL?!

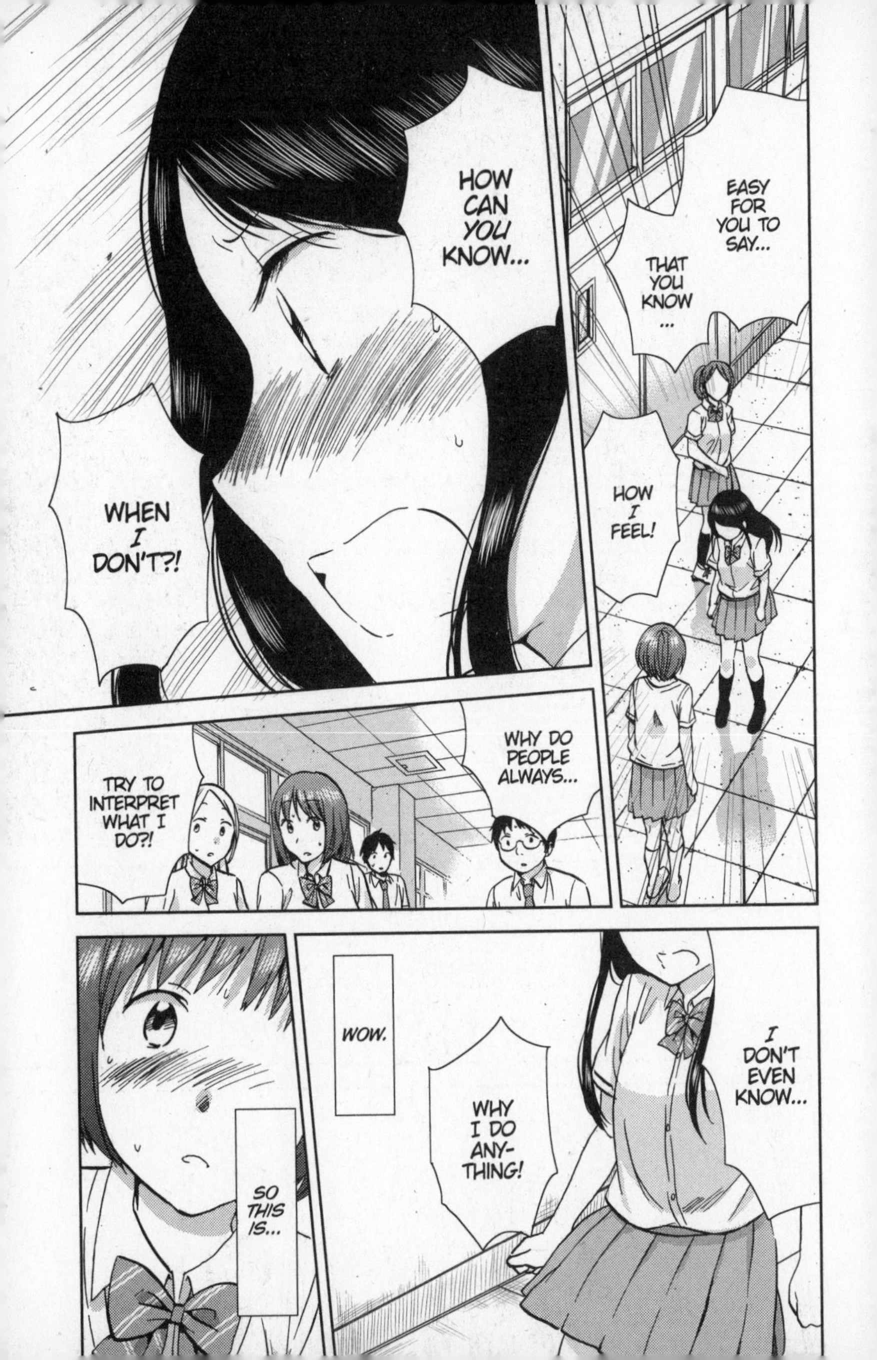
EASY FOR YOU TO SAY...
THAT YOU KNOW...
HOW I FEEL!
HOW CAN YOU KNOW...
WHEN I DON'T?!
WHY DO PEOPLE ALWAYS...
TRY TO INTERPRET WHAT I DO?!
I DON'T EVEN KNOW...
WHY I DO ANYTHING!
WOW.
SO THIS IS...

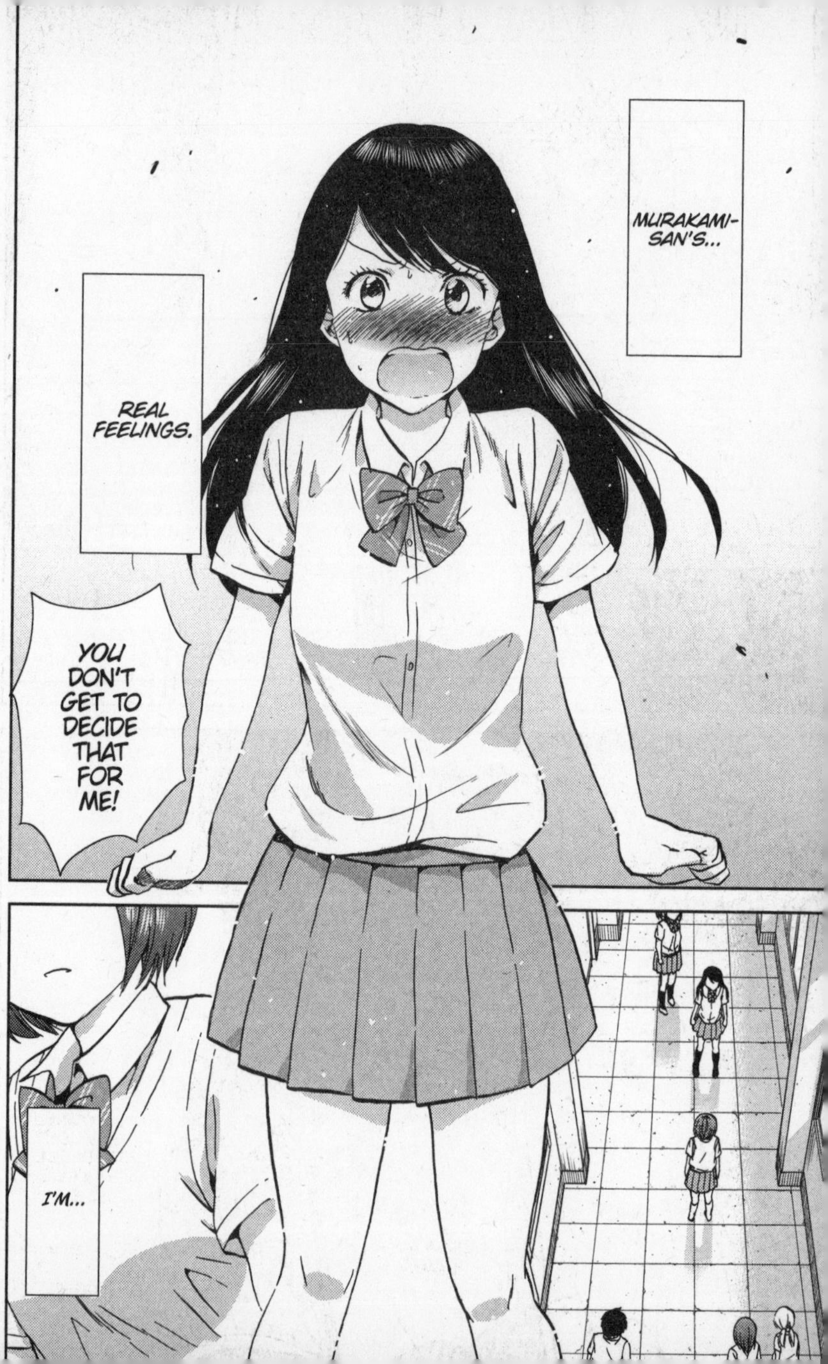
MURAKAMI-SAN'S...
REAL FEELINGS.
YOU DON'T GET TO DECIDE THAT FOR ME!
I'M...

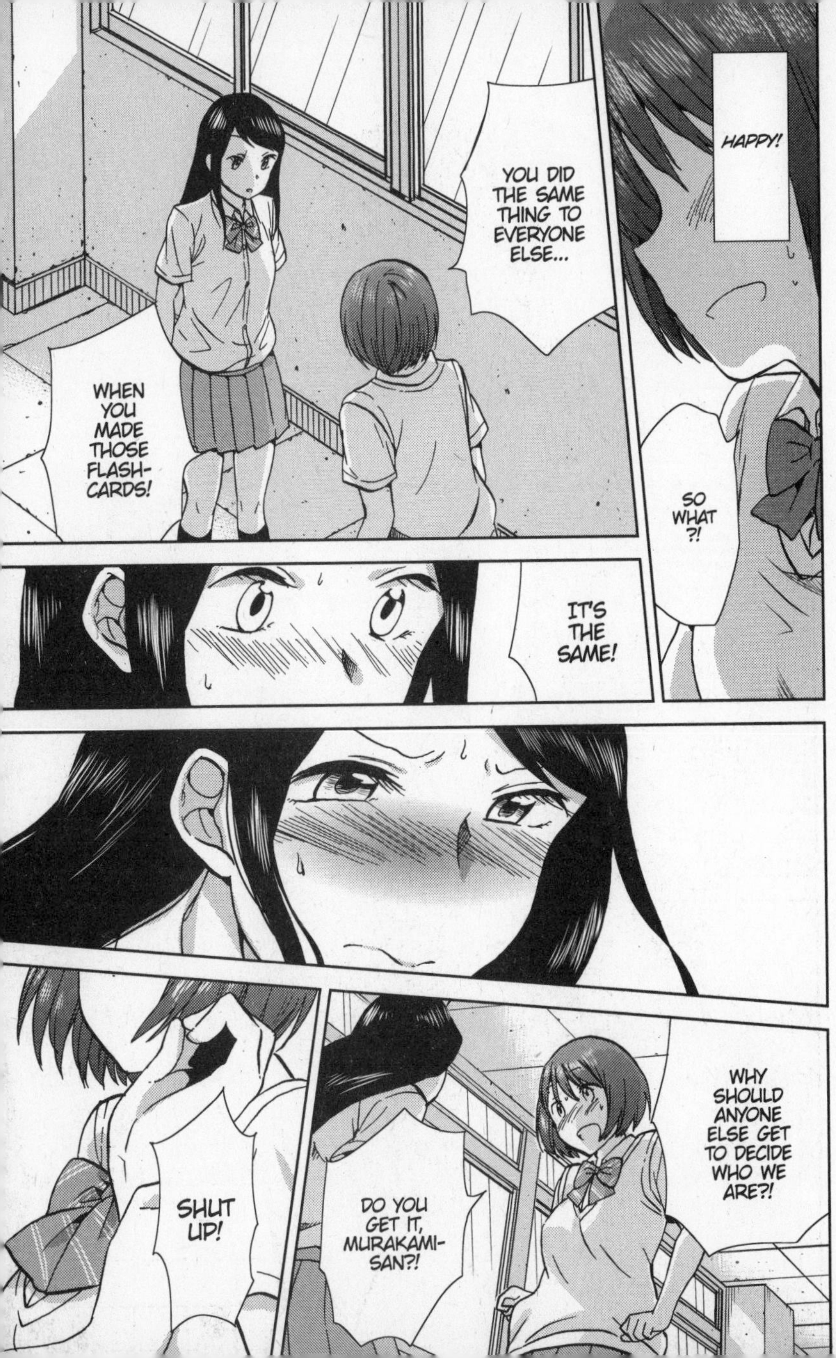
HAPPY!
SO WHAT?!
YOU DID THE SAME THING TO EVERYONE ELSE...
WHEN YOU MADE THOSE FLASH-CARDS!
IT'S THE SAME!
WHY SHOULD ANYONE ELSE GET TO DECIDE WHO WE ARE?!
DO YOU GET IT, MURAKAMI-SAN?!
SHUT UP!

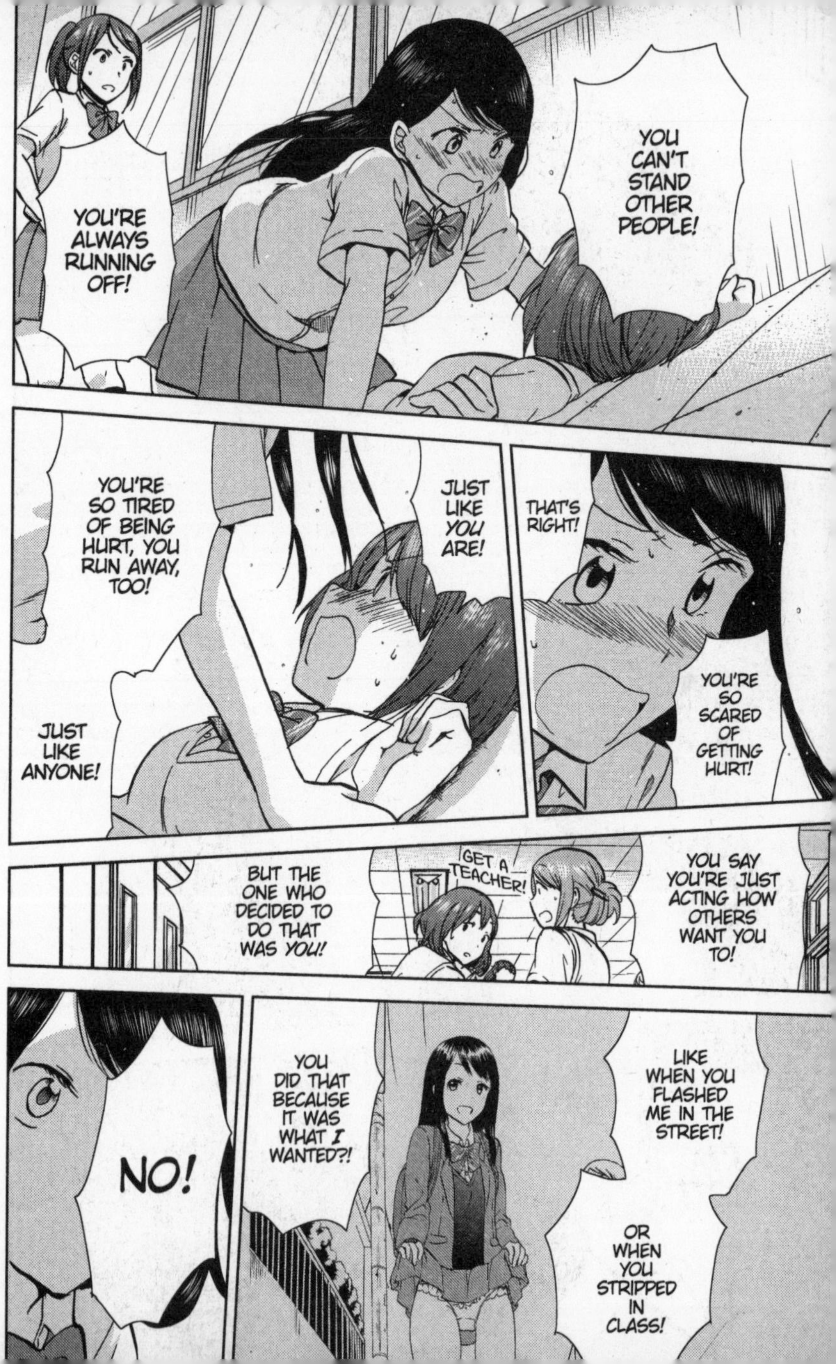
YOU CAN'T STAND OTHER PEOPLE!
YOU'RE ALWAYS RUNNING OFF!
THAT'S RIGHT!
YOU'RE SO SCARED OF GETTING HURT!
JUST LIKE YOU ARE!
YOU'RE SO TIRED OF BEING HURT, YOU RUN AWAY, TOO!
JUST LIKE ANYONE!
YOU SAY YOU'RE JUST ACTING HOW OTHERS WANT YOU TO!
GET A TEACHER!
BUT THE ONE WHO DECIDED TO DO THAT WAS YOU!
LIKE WHEN YOU FLASHED ME IN THE STREET!
OR WHEN YOU STRIPPED IN CLASS!
YOU DID THAT BECAUSE IT WAS WHAT I WANTED?!
NO!

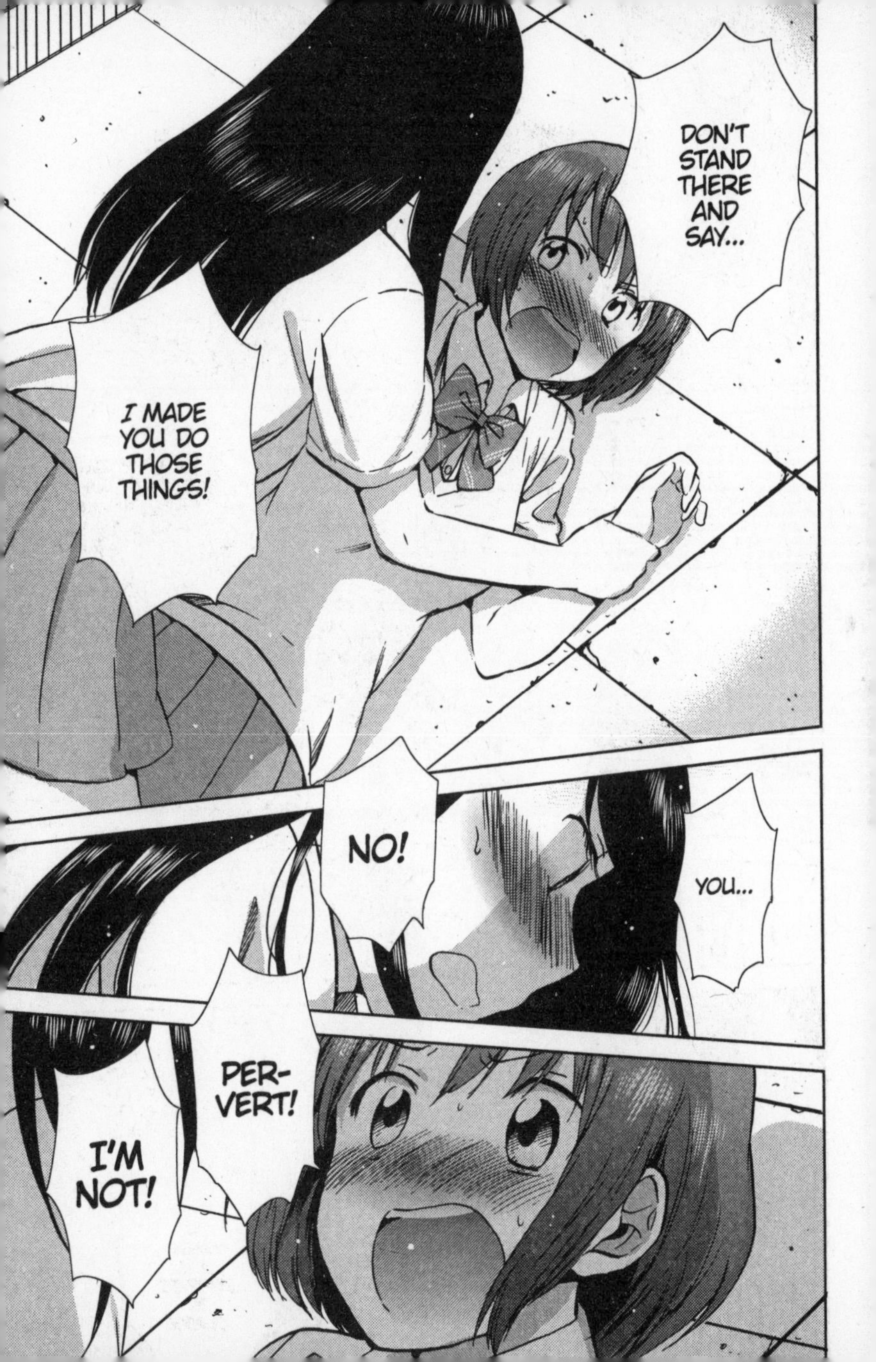
DON'T STAND THERE AND SAY...
I MADE YOU DO THOSE THINGS!
YOU...
NO!
PER-VERT!
I'M NOT!

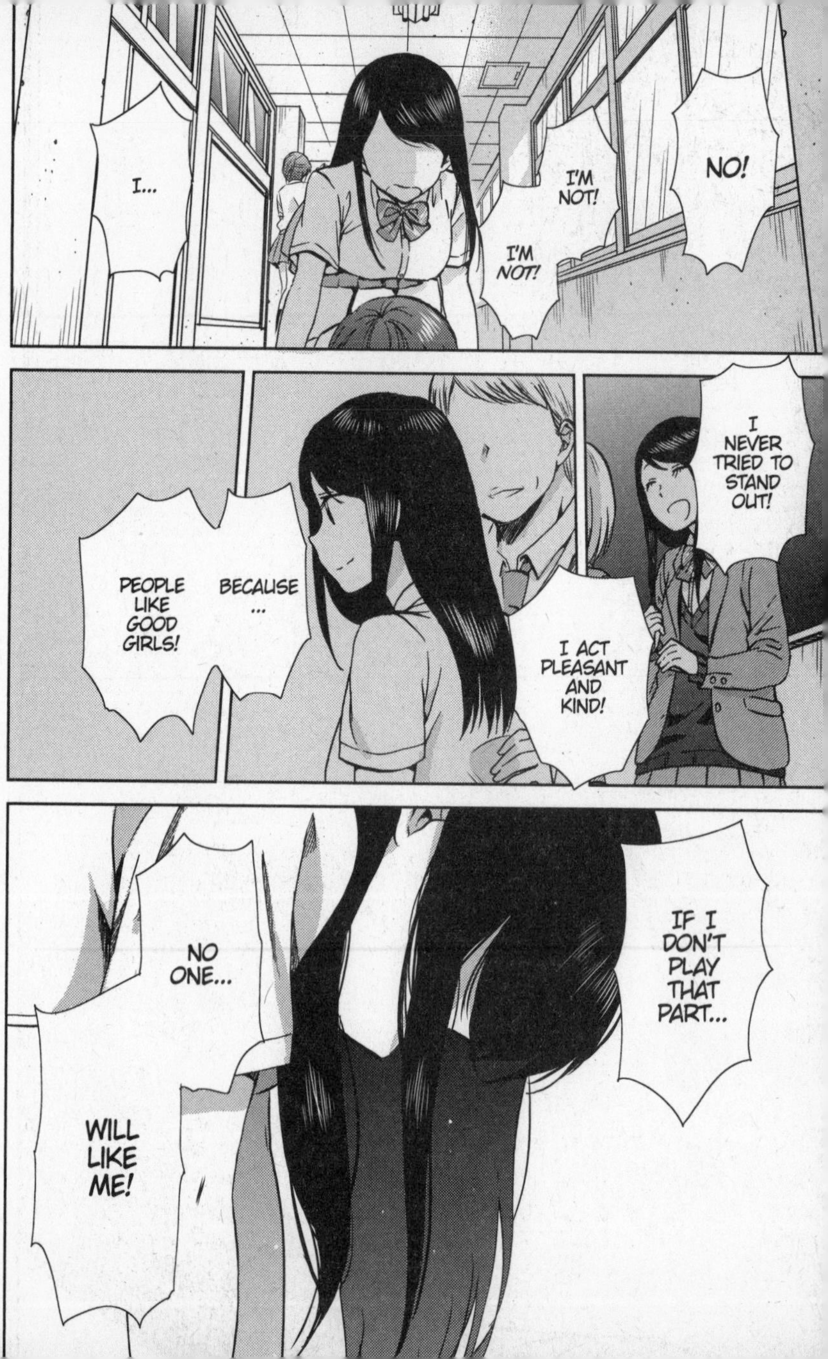
NO!
I'M NOT!
I'M NOT!
I...
I NEVER TRIED TO STAND OUT!
I ACT PLEASANT AND KIND!
BECAUSE ...
PEOPLE LIKE GOOD GIRLS!
IF I DON'T PLAY THAT PART...
NO ONE...
WILL LIKE ME!

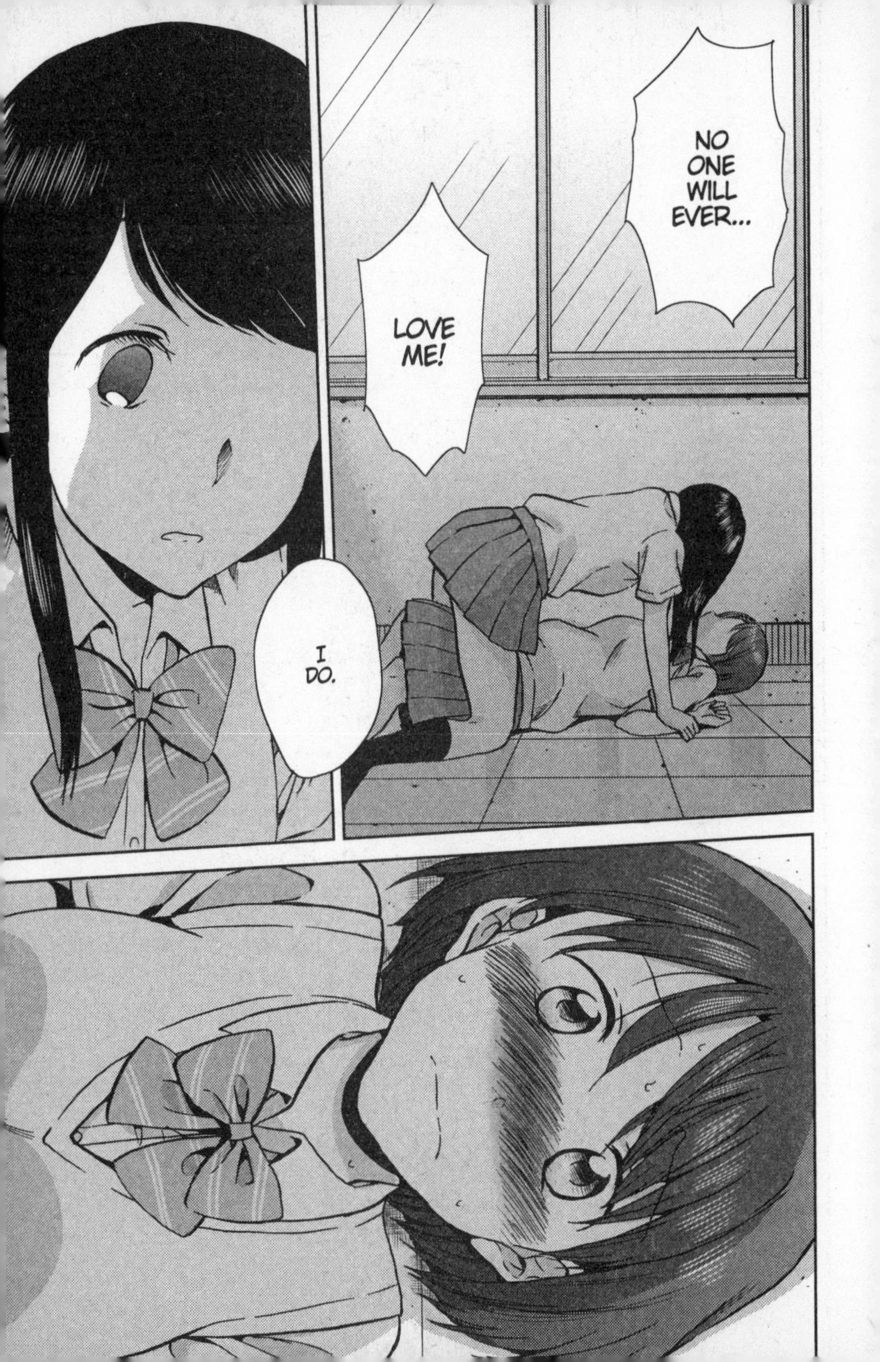
NO ONE WILL EVER...
LOVE ME!
I DO.

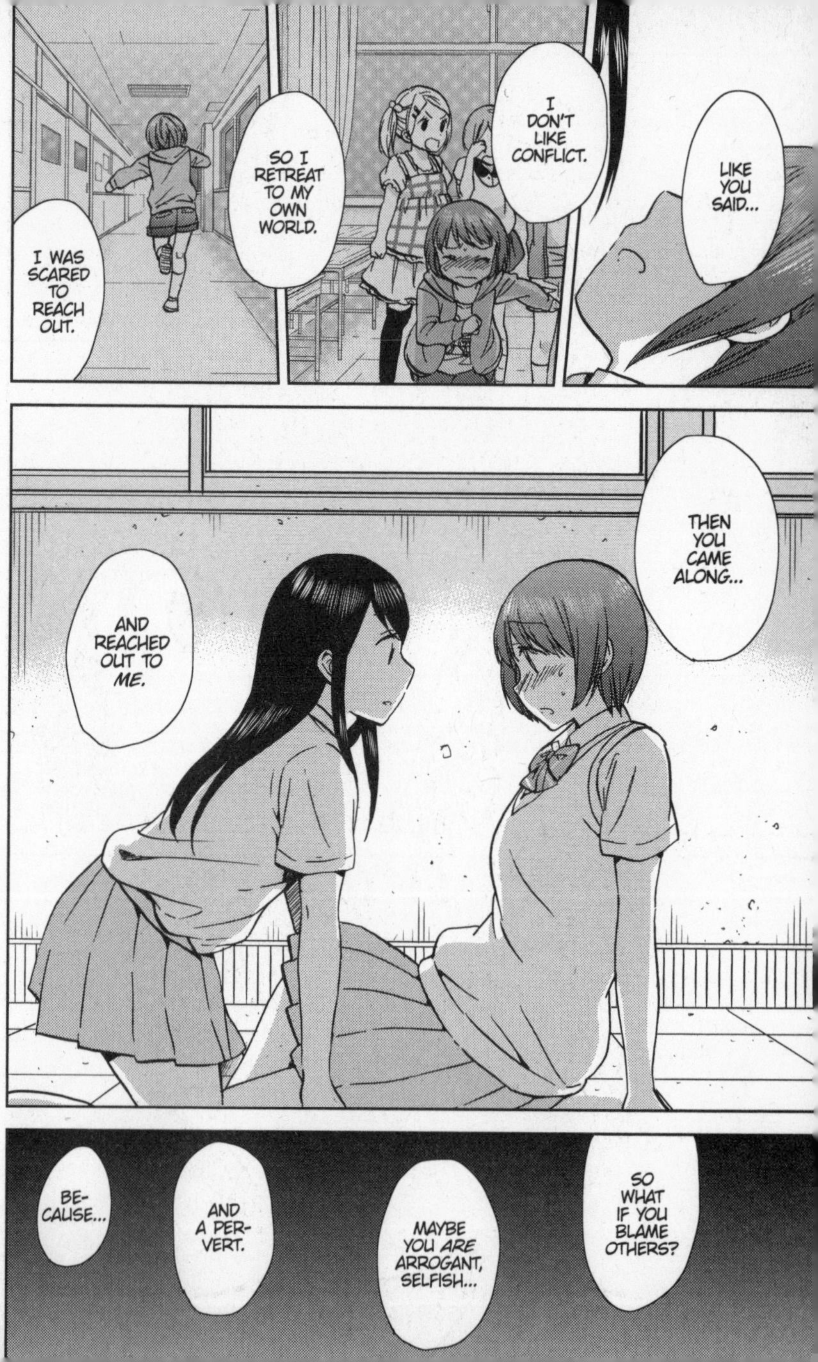
LIKE YOU SAID...
I DON'T LIKE CONFLICT.
SO I RETREAT TO MY OWN WORLD.
I WAS SCARED TO REACH OUT.
THEN YOU CAME ALONG...
AND REACHED OUT TO ME.
SO WHAT IF YOU BLAME OTHERS?
MAYBE YOU ARE ARROGANT, SELFISH...
AND A PER-VERT.
BE-CAUSE...

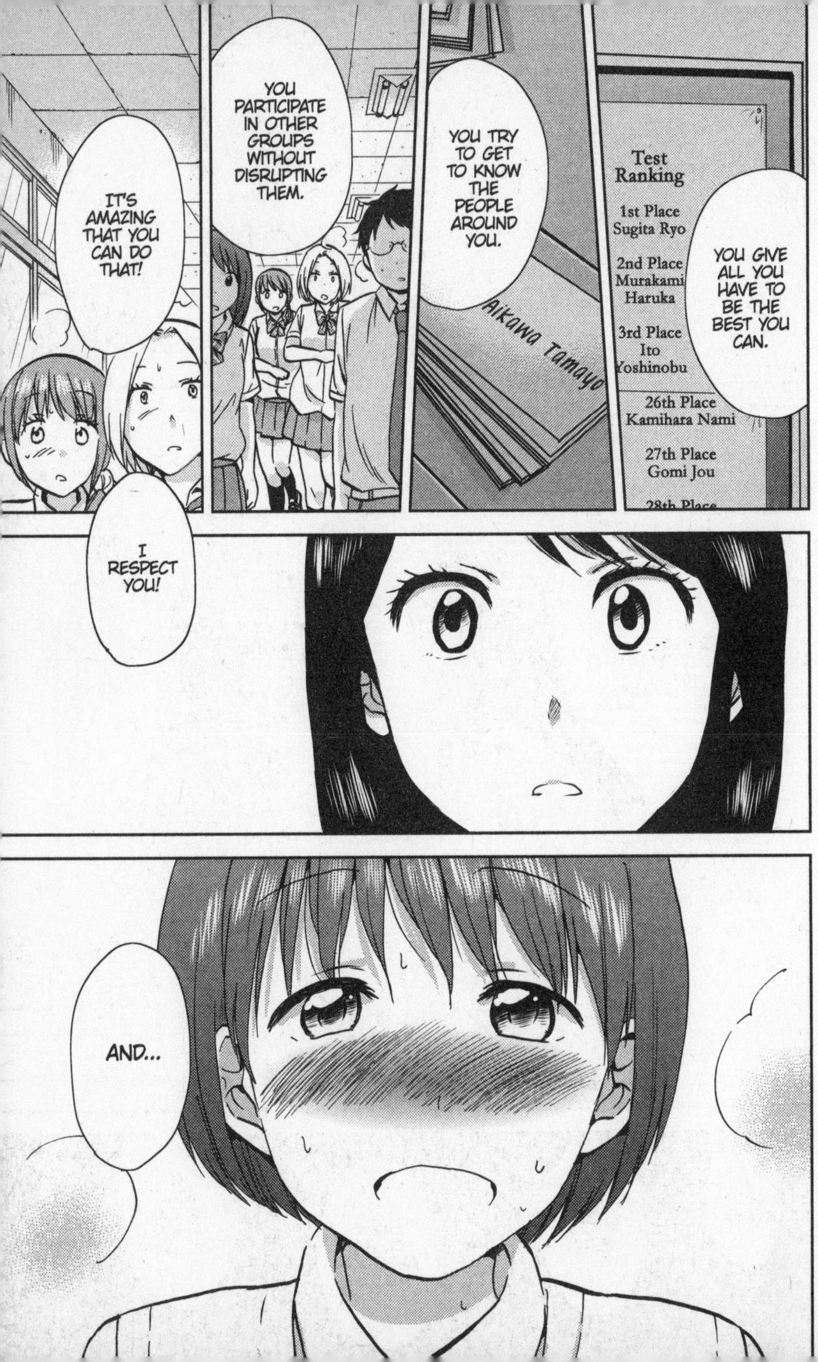

YOU GIVE ALL YOU HAVE TO BE THE BEST YOU CAN.
Test Ranking
1st Place Sugita Ryo
2nd Place Murakami Haruka
3rd Place Ito Yoshinobu
26th Place Kamihara Nami
27th Place Gomi Jou
YOU TRY TO GET TO KNOW THE PEOPLE AROUND YOU.
Aikawa Tamayo
YOU PARTICIPATE IN OTHER GROUPS WITHOUT DISRUPTING THEM.
IT'S AMAZING THAT YOU CAN DO THAT!
I RESPECT YOU!
AND...

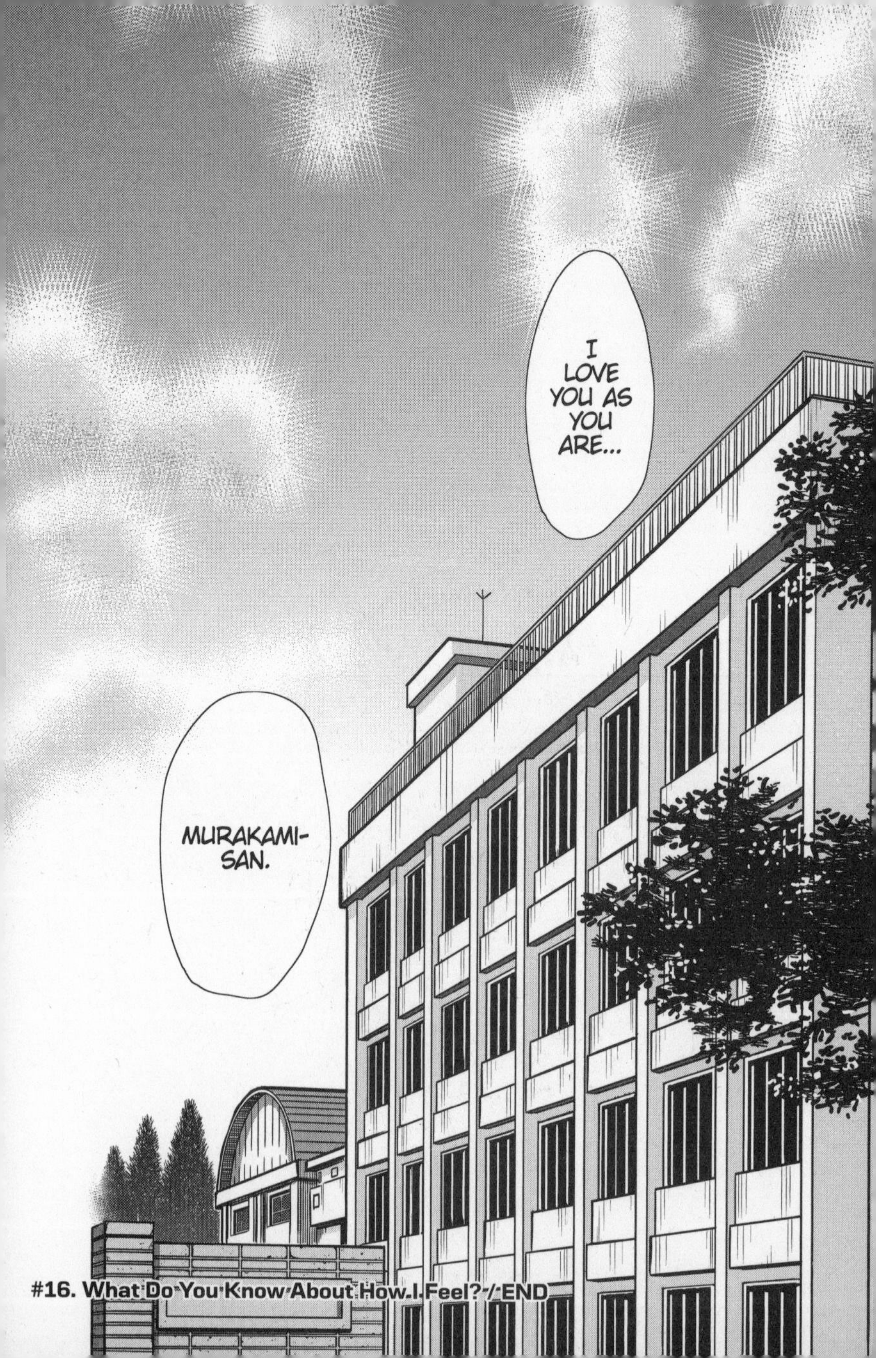
I LOVE YOU AS YOU ARE...
MURAKAMI-SAN.

#16. What Do You Know About How I Feel? / END

fragtime

Final I Love You

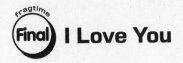

"YOU'RE SO BEAUTIFUL, HARUKA-CHAN! SOMETHING LIKE THIS WILL SUIT YOU."

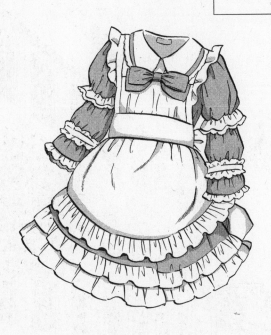

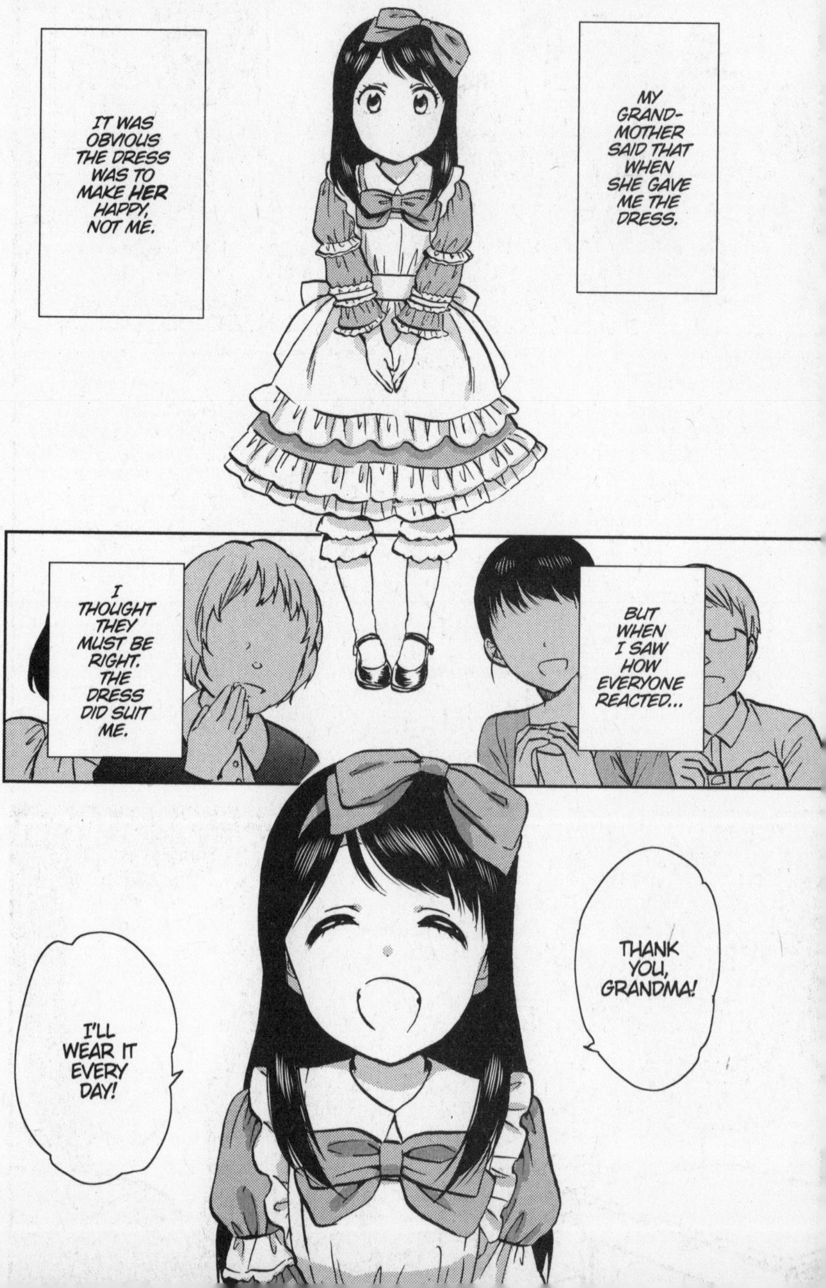
MY GRANDMOTHER SAID THAT WHEN SHE GAVE ME THE DRESS.
IT WAS OBVIOUS THE DRESS WAS TO MAKE HER HAPPY, NOT ME.
BUT WHEN I SAW HOW EVERYONE REACTED...
I THOUGHT THEY MUST BE RIGHT. THE DRESS DID SUIT ME.
THANK YOU, GRANDMA!
I'LL WEAR IT EVERY DAY!

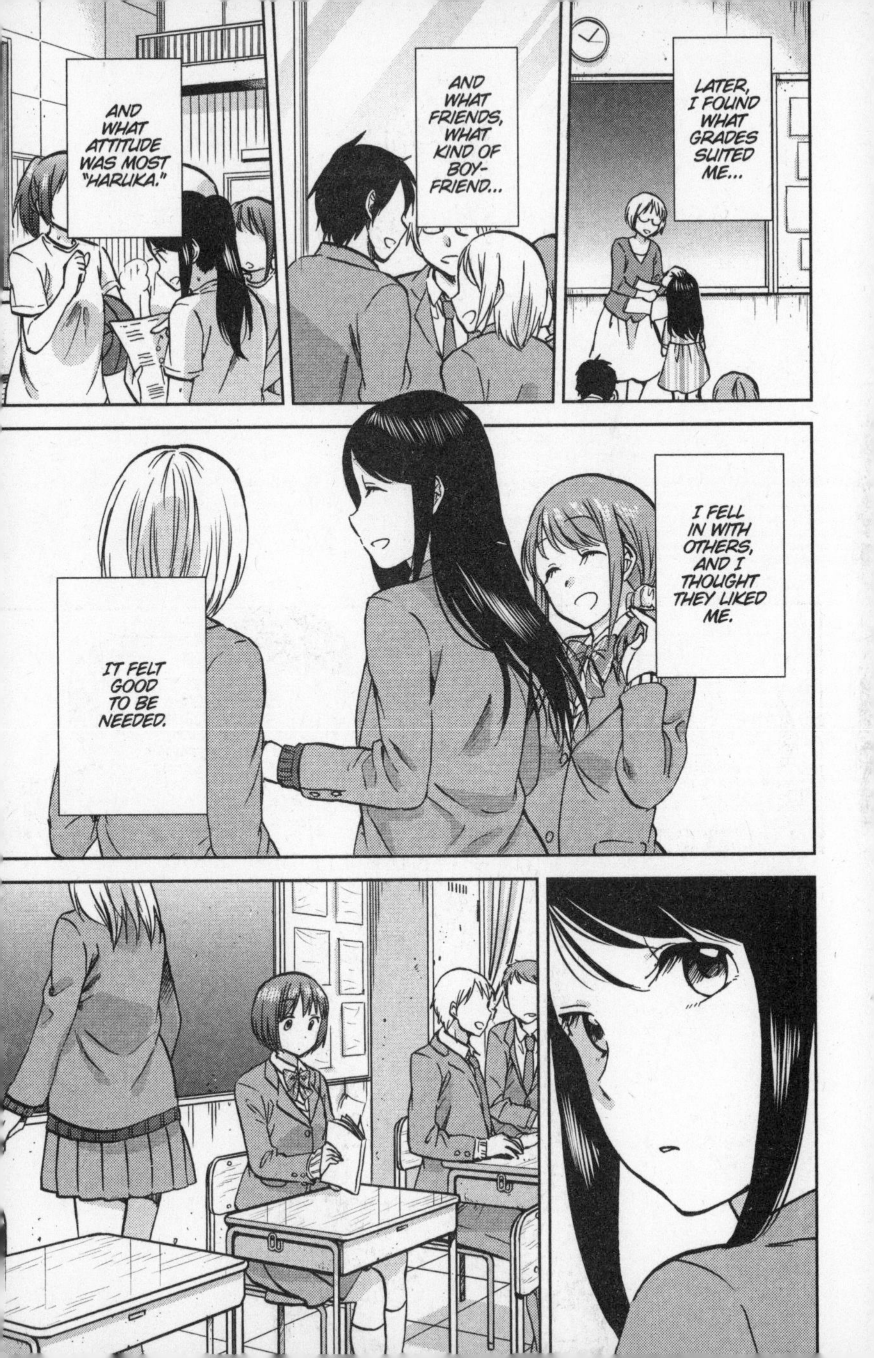
LATER, I FOUND WHAT GRADES SUITED ME...
AND WHAT FRIENDS, WHAT KIND OF BOY-FRIEND...
AND WHAT ATTITUDE WAS MOST "HARUKA."
I FELL IN WITH OTHERS, AND I THOUGHT THEY LIKED ME.
IT FELT GOOD TO BE NEEDED.

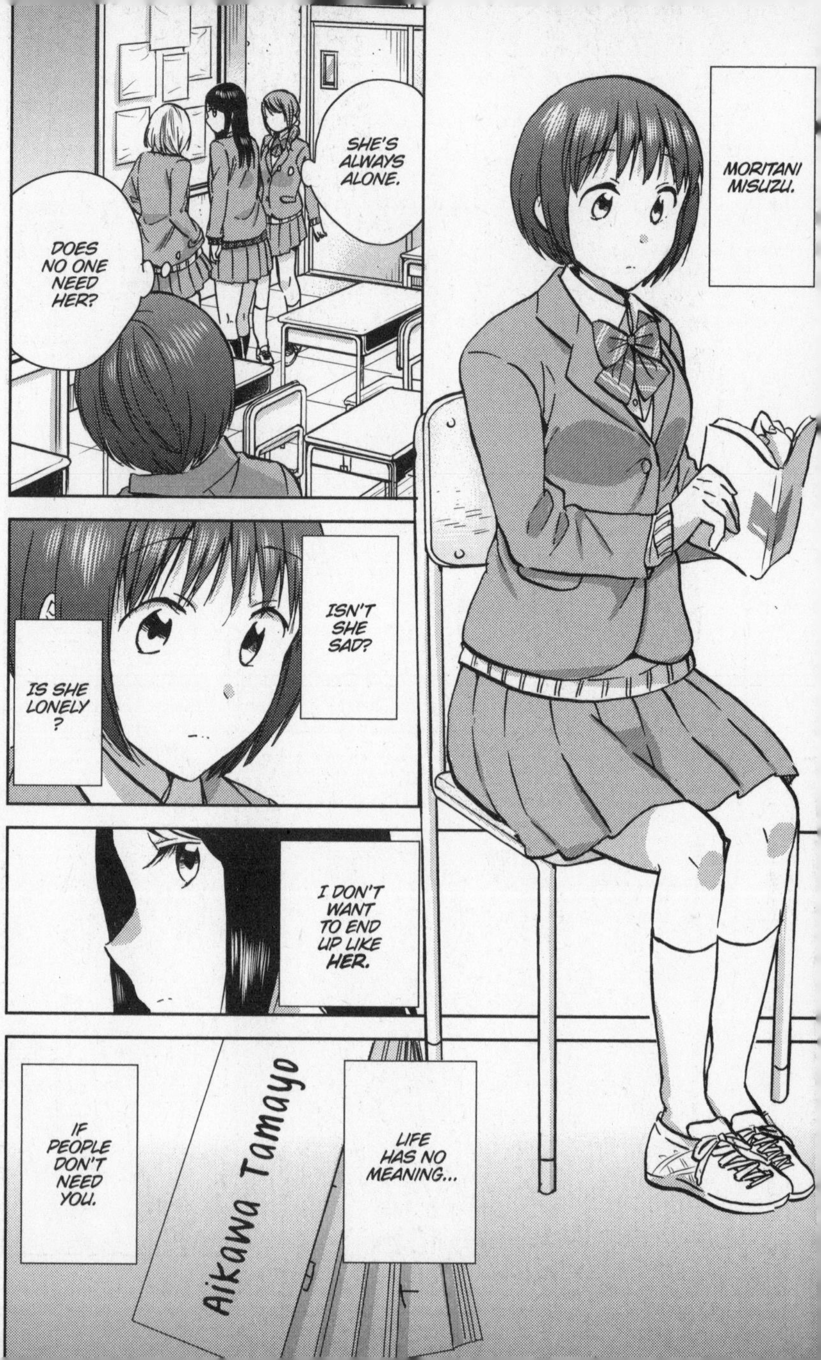
MORITANI MISUZU.
SHE'S ALWAYS ALONE.
DOES NO ONE NEED HER?
ISN'T SHE SAD?
IS SHE LONELY ?
I DON'T WANT TO END UP LIKE HER.
LIFE HAS NO MEANING...
Aikawa Tamayo
IF PEOPLE DON'T NEED YOU.

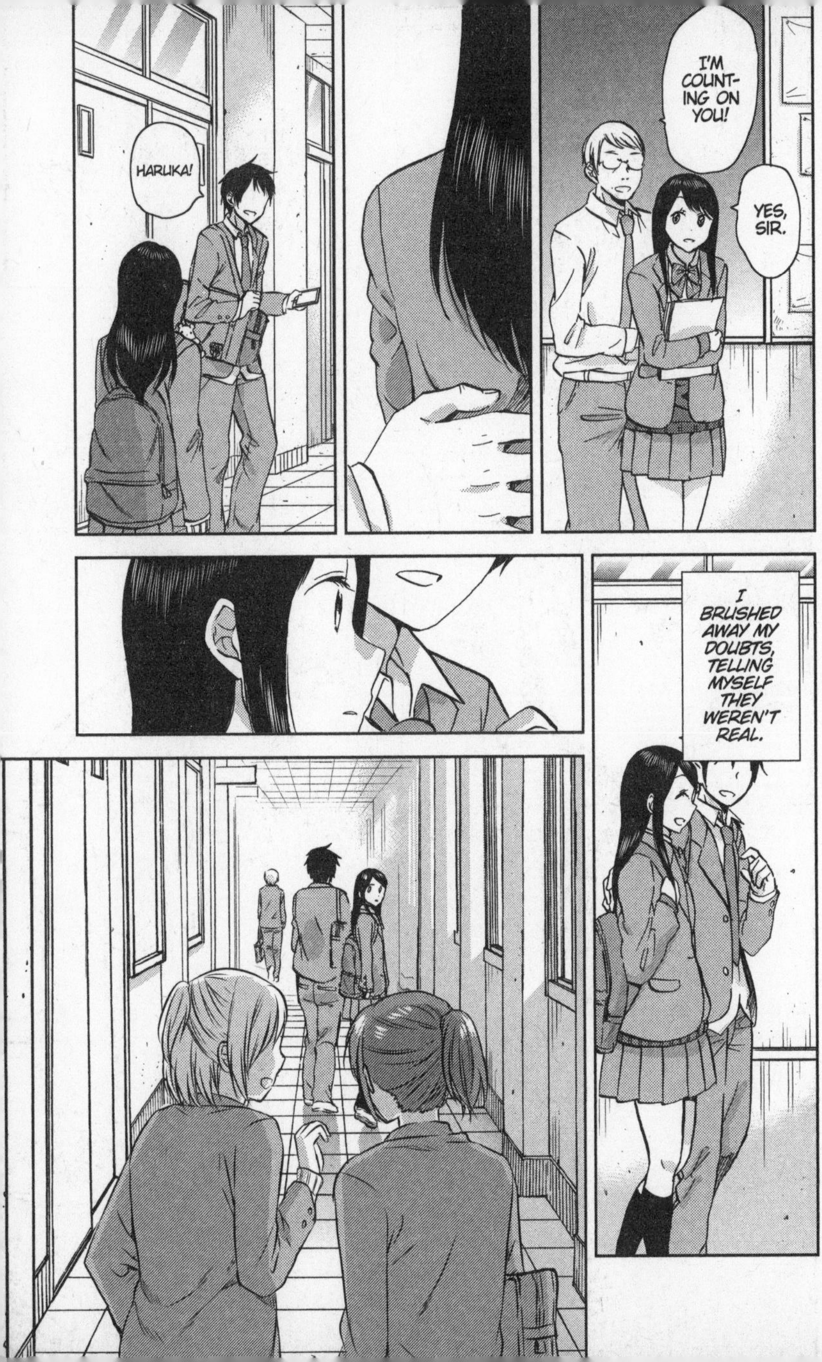
I'M COUNTING ON YOU!
YES, SIR.
HARUKA!
I BRUSHED AWAY MY DOUBTS, TELLING MYSELF THEY WEREN'T REAL.

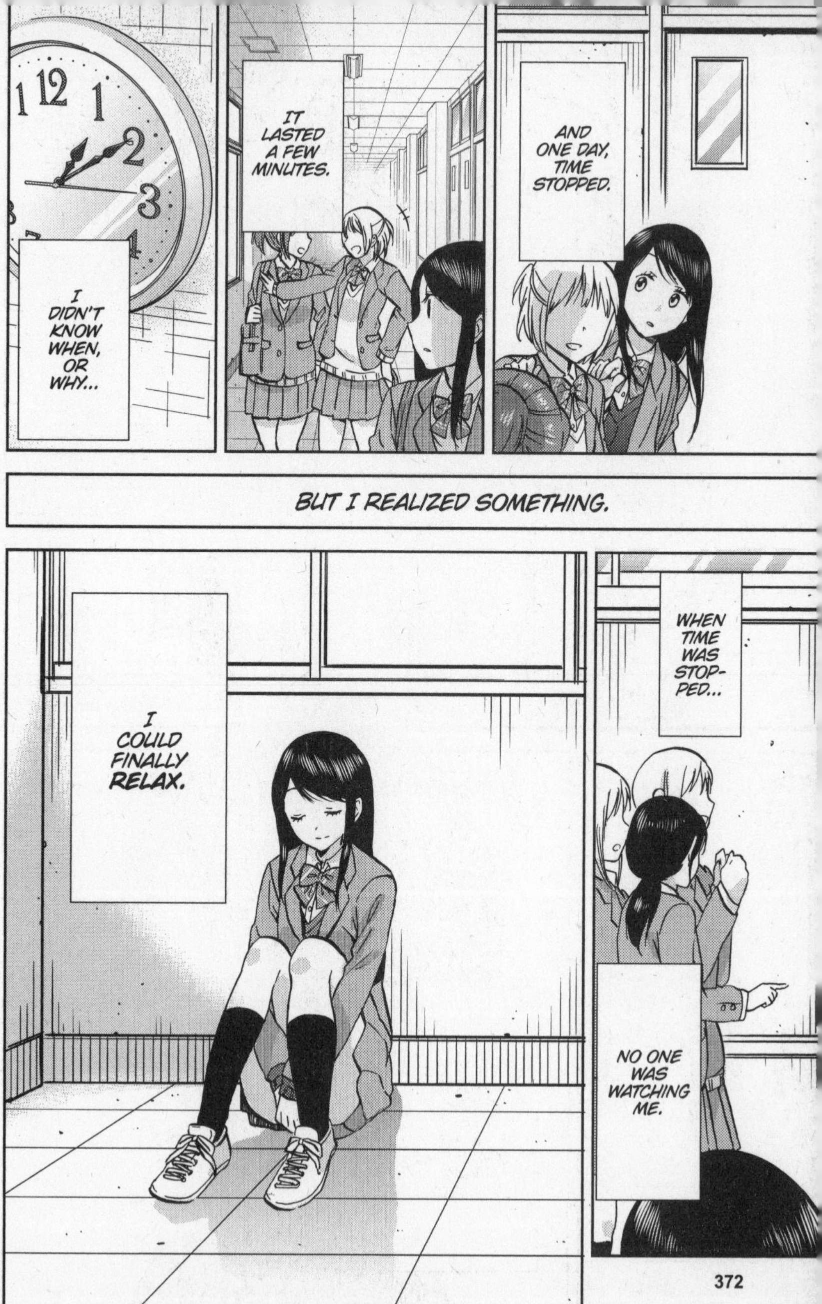
AND ONE DAY, TIME STOPPED.
IT LASTED A FEW MINUTES.
I DIDN'T KNOW WHEN, OR WHY...
BUT I REALIZED SOMETHING.
WHEN TIME WAS STOP-PED...
NO ONE WAS WATCHING ME.
I COULD FINALLY RELAX.

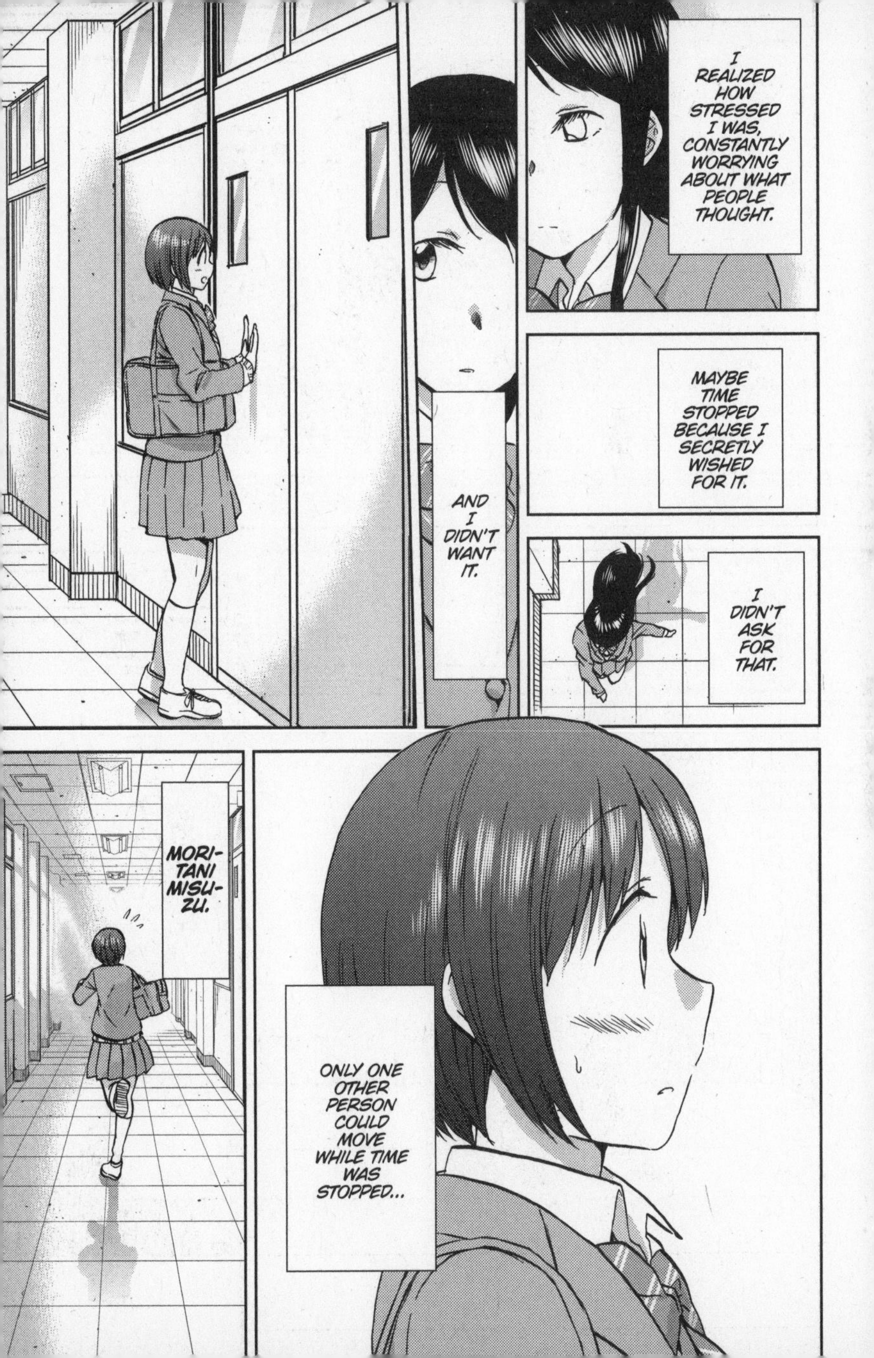
I REALIZED HOW STRESSED I WAS, CONSTANTLY WORRYING ABOUT WHAT PEOPLE THOUGHT.
MAYBE TIME STOPPED BECAUSE I SECRETLY WISHED FOR IT.
I DIDN'T ASK FOR THAT.
AND I DIDN'T WANT IT.
ONLY ONE OTHER PERSON COULD MOVE WHILE TIME WAS STOPPED...
MORI-TANI MISU-ZU.

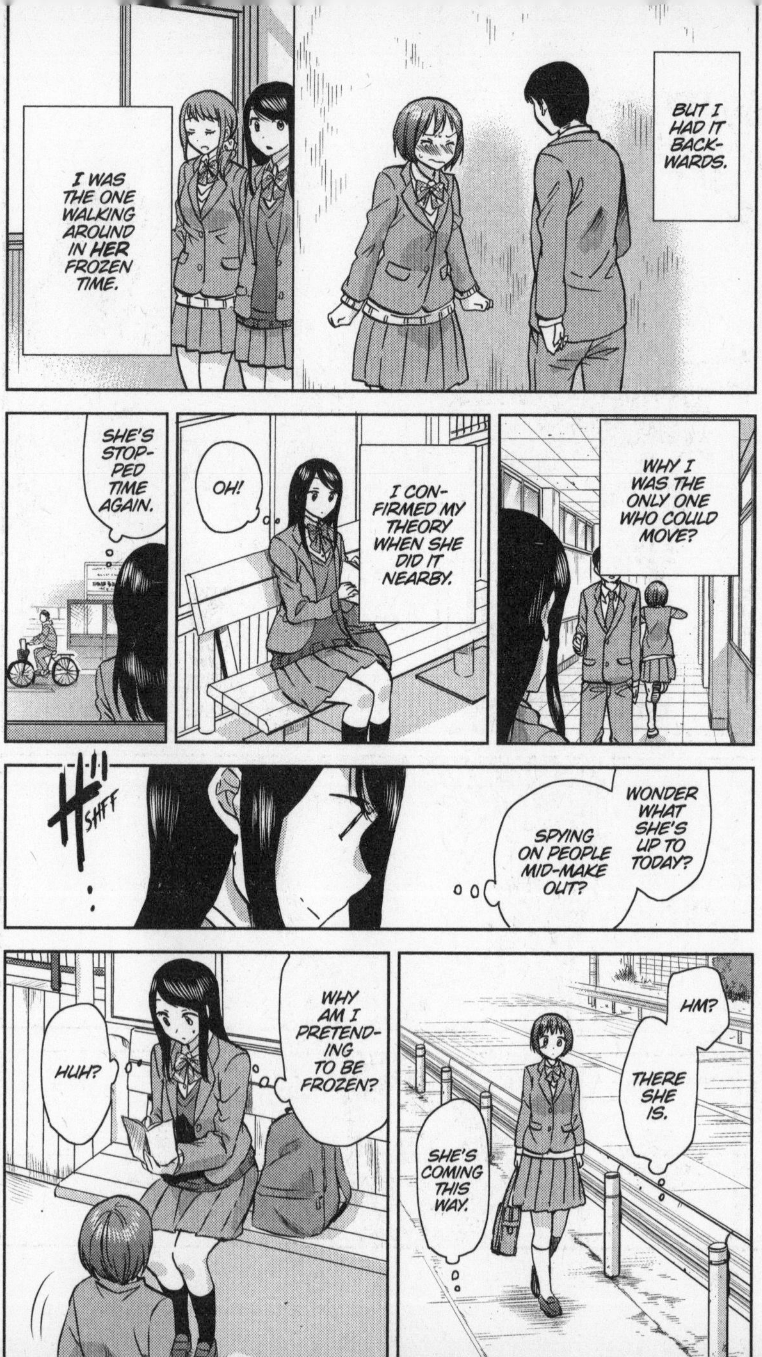
BUT I HAD IT BACKWARDS.
I WAS THE ONE WALKING AROUND IN HER FROZEN TIME.
WHY I WAS THE ONLY ONE WHO COULD MOVE?
I CONFIRMED MY THEORY WHEN SHE DID IT NEARBY.
OH!
SHE'S STOPPED TIME AGAIN.
WONDER WHAT SHE'S UP TO TODAY?
SPYING ON PEOPLE MID-MAKE OUT?
SHFF
HM?
THERE SHE IS.
SHE'S COMING THIS WAY.
WHY AM I PRETENDING TO BE FROZEN?
HUH?

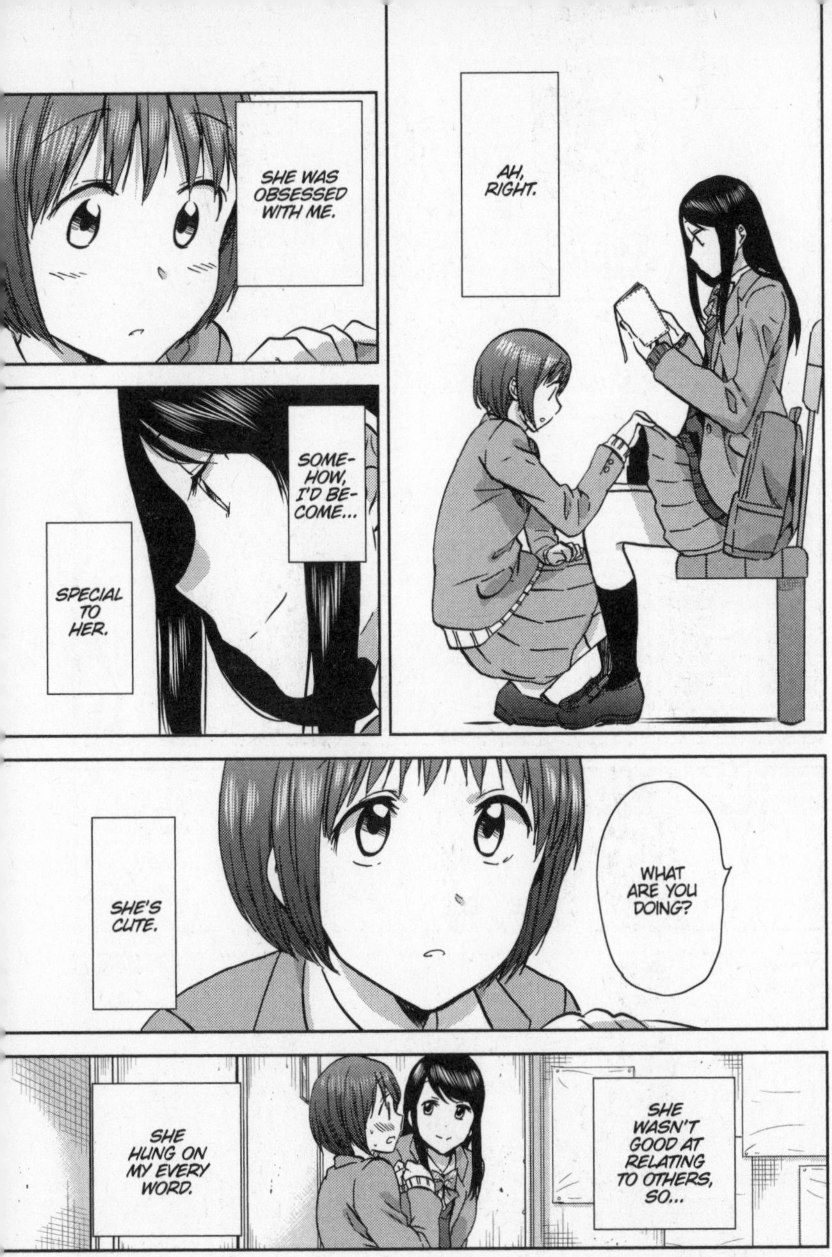
AH, RIGHT.
SHE WAS OBSESSED WITH ME.
SOME-HOW, I'D BE-COME...
SPECIAL TO HER.
WHAT ARE YOU DOING?
SHE'S CUTE.
SHE WASN'T GOOD AT RELATING TO OTHERS, SO...
SHE HUNG ON MY EVERY WORD.

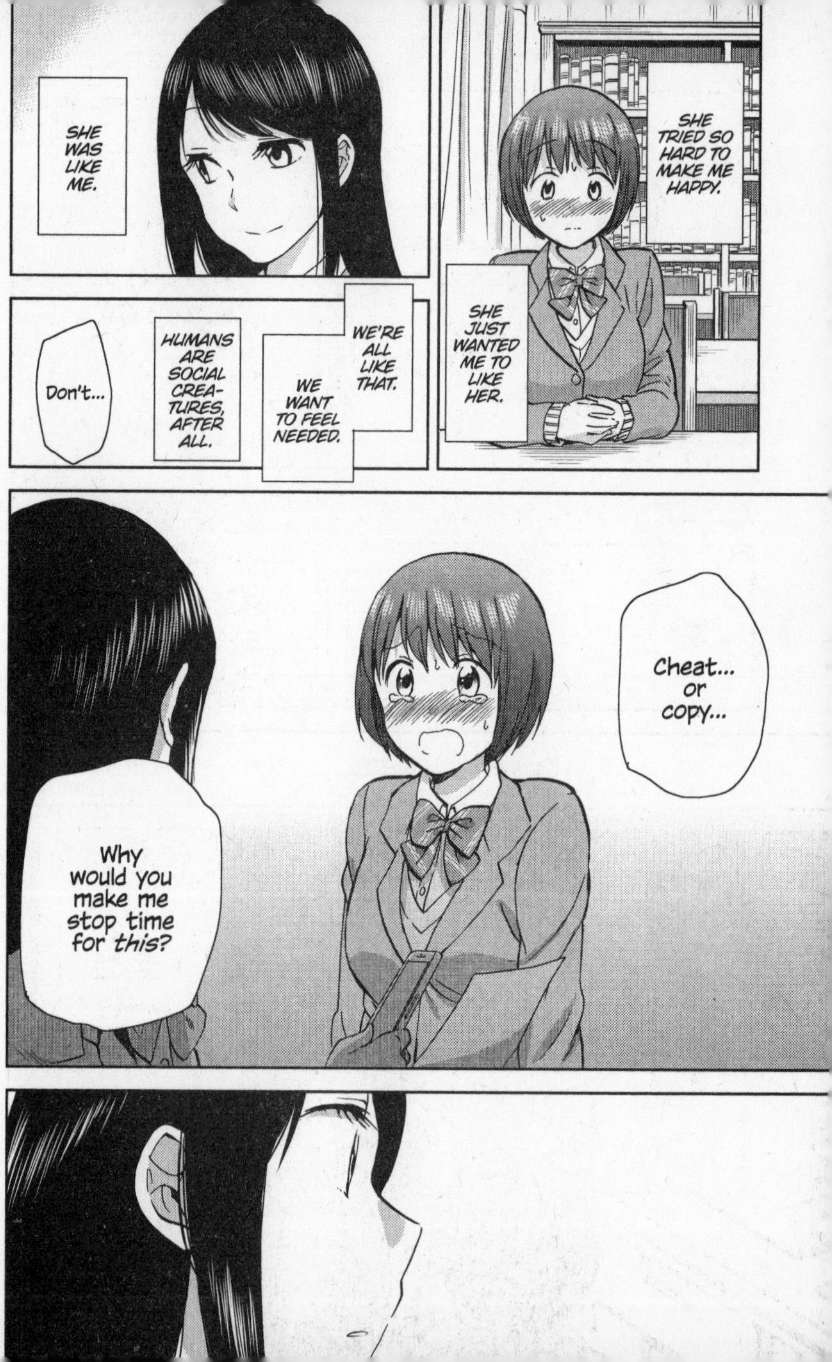
SHE TRIED SO HARD TO MAKE ME HAPPY.
SHE JUST WANTED ME TO LIKE HER.
SHE WAS LIKE ME.
WE'RE ALL LIKE THAT.
WE WANT TO FEEL NEEDED.
HUMANS ARE SOCIAL CREA-TURES, AFTER ALL.
Don't...
Cheat... or copy...
Why would you make me stop time for *this*?

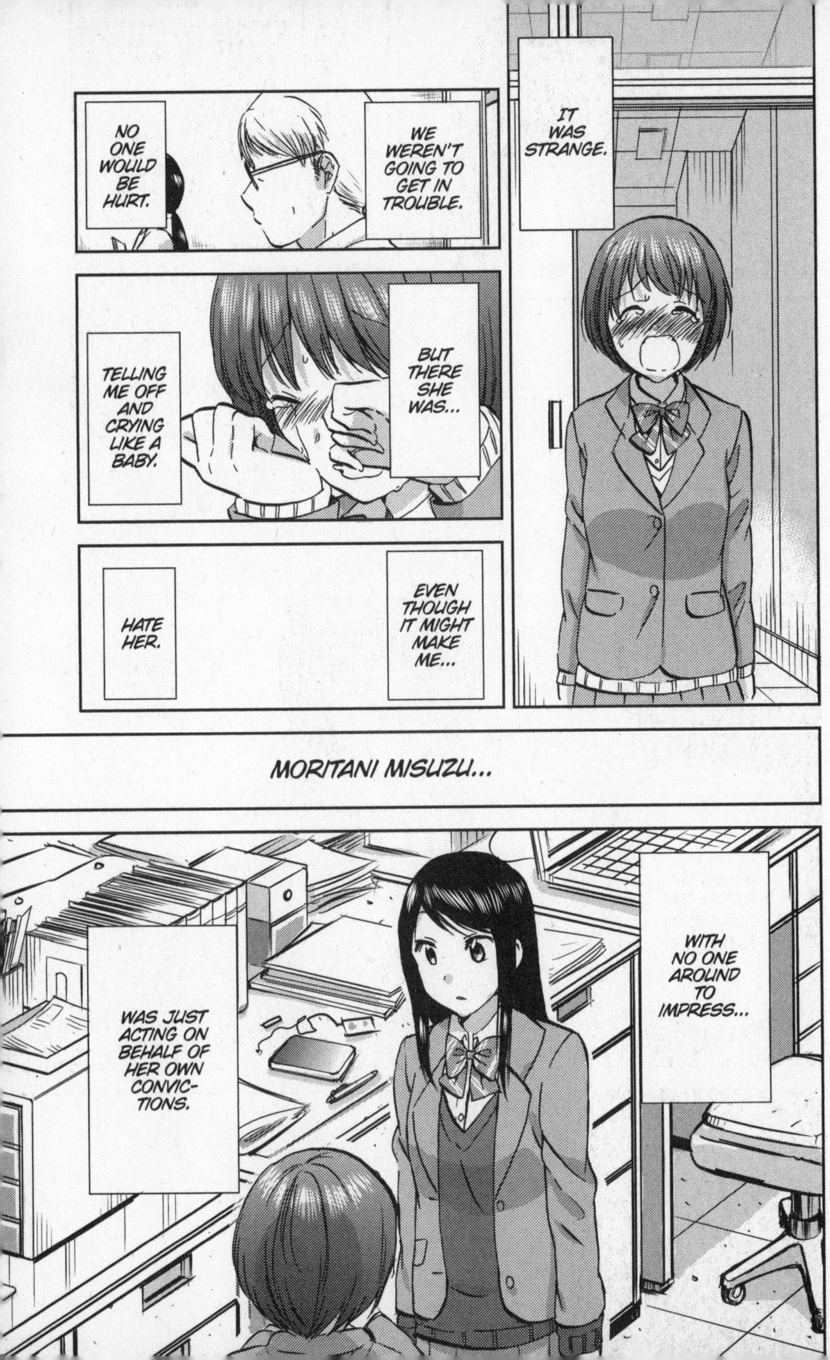
IT WAS STRANGE.
WE WEREN'T GOING TO GET IN TROUBLE.
NO ONE WOULD BE HURT.
BUT THERE SHE WAS...
TELLING ME OFF AND CRYING LIKE A BABY.
EVEN THOUGH IT MIGHT MAKE ME...
HATE HER.
MORITANI MISUZU...
WITH NO ONE AROUND TO IMPRESS...
WAS JUST ACTING ON BEHALF OF HER OWN CONVIC-TIONS.

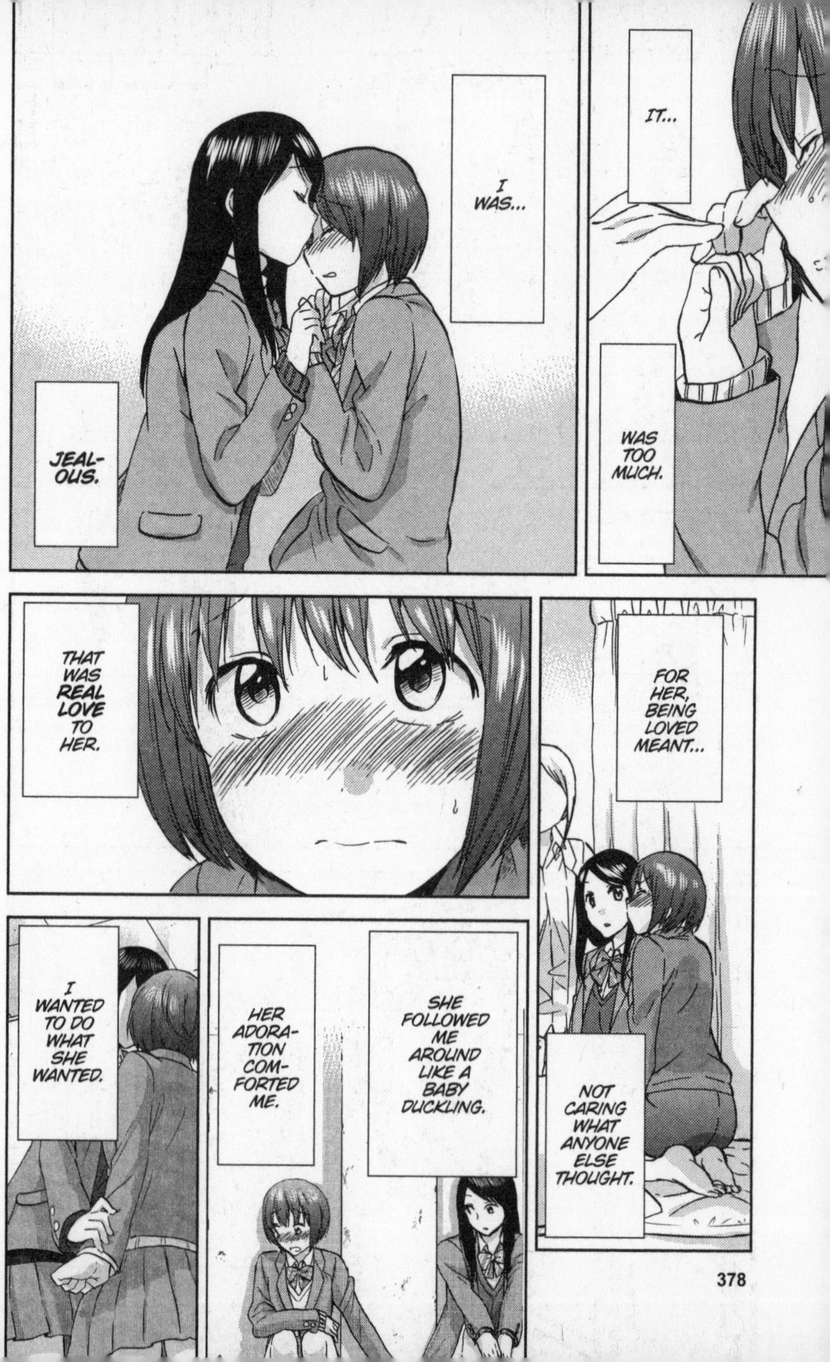
IT...
WAS TOO MUCH.
I WAS...
JEAL-OUS.
FOR HER, BEING LOVED MEANT...
NOT CARING WHAT ANYONE ELSE THOUGHT.
THAT WAS REAL LOVE TO HER.
SHE FOLLOWED ME AROUND LIKE A BABY DUCKLING.
HER ADORA-TION COM-FORTED ME.
I WANTED TO DO WHAT SHE WANTED.

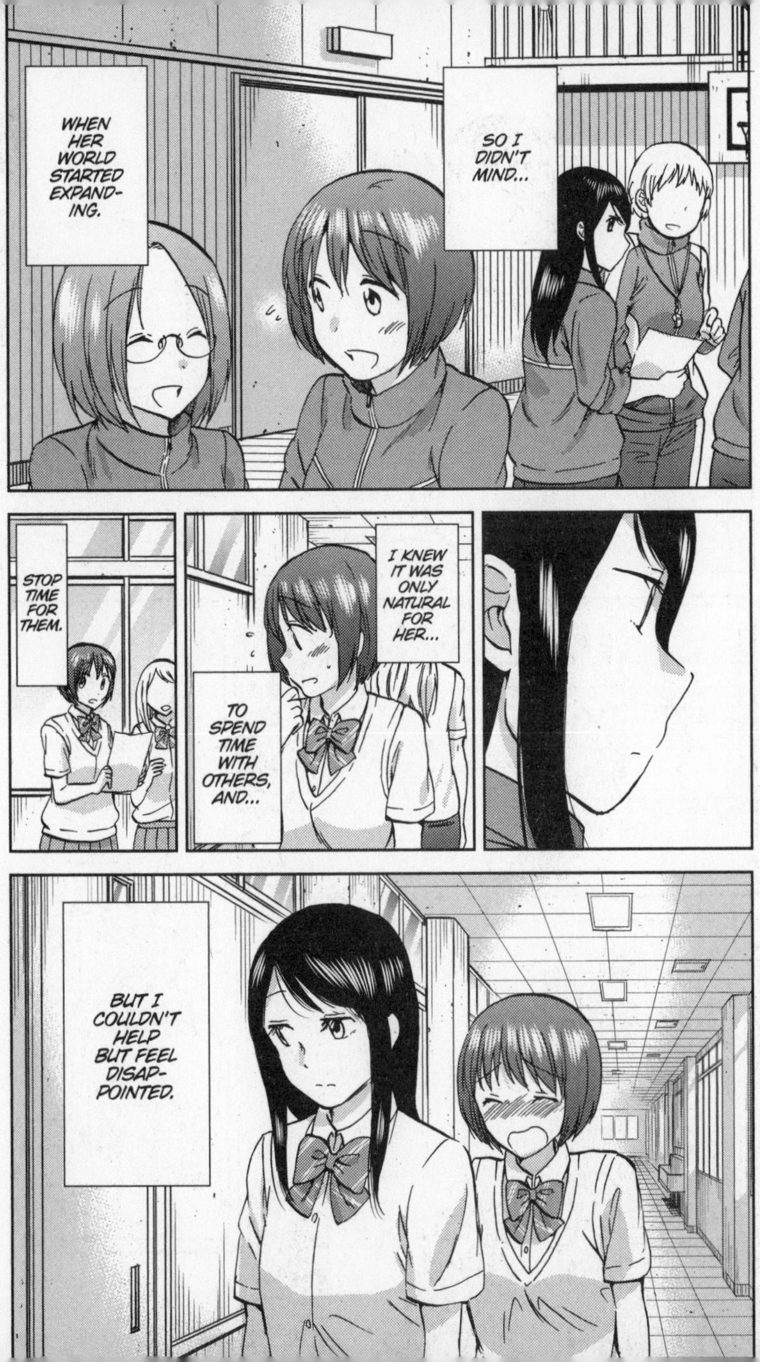
SO I DIDN'T MIND...
WHEN HER WORLD STARTED EXPAND-ING.
I KNEW IT WAS ONLY NATURAL FOR HER...
TO SPEND TIME WITH OTHERS, AND...
STOP TIME FOR THEM.
BUT I COULDN'T HELP BUT FEEL DISAP-POINTED.

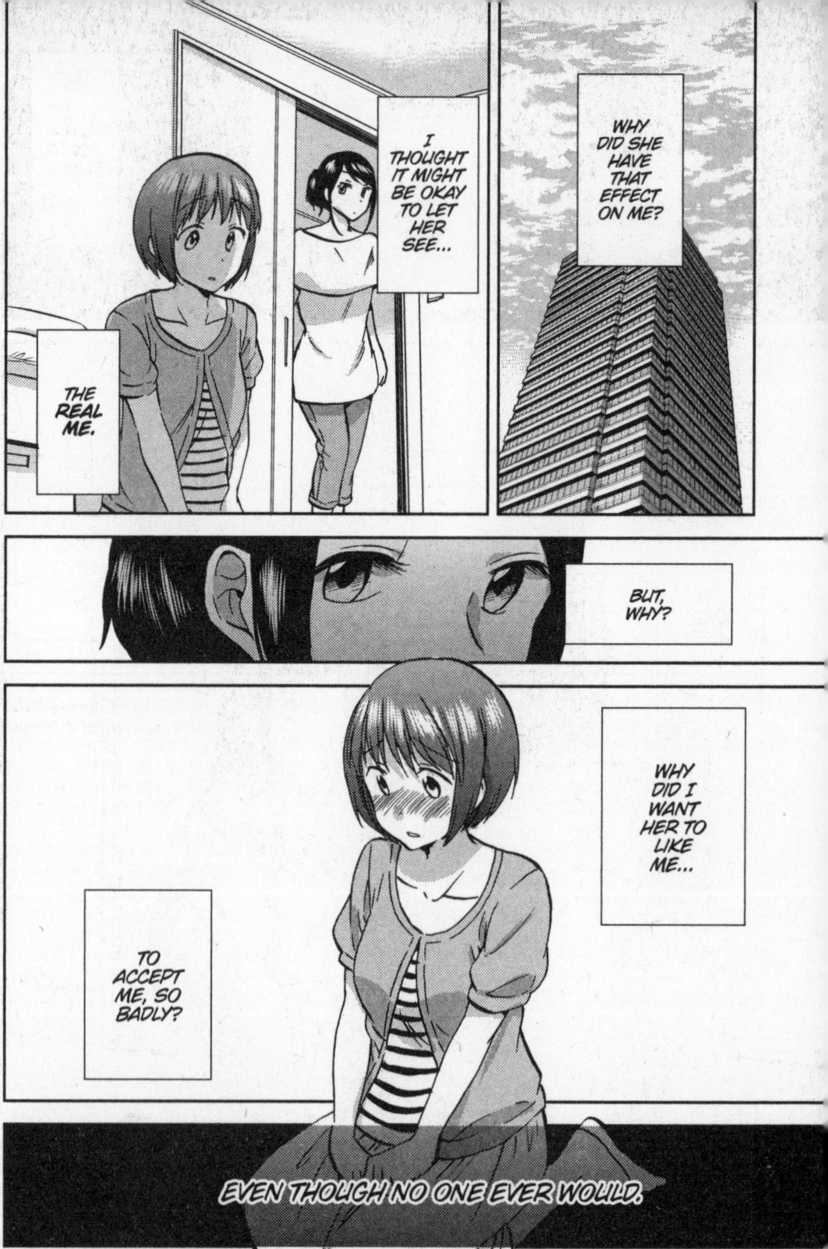
WHY DID SHE HAVE THAT EFFECT ON ME?
I THOUGHT IT MIGHT BE OKAY TO LET HER SEE...
THE REAL ME.
BUT, WHY?
WHY DID I WANT HER TO LIKE ME...
TO ACCEPT ME, SO BADLY?
EVEN THOUGH NO ONE EVER WOULD.

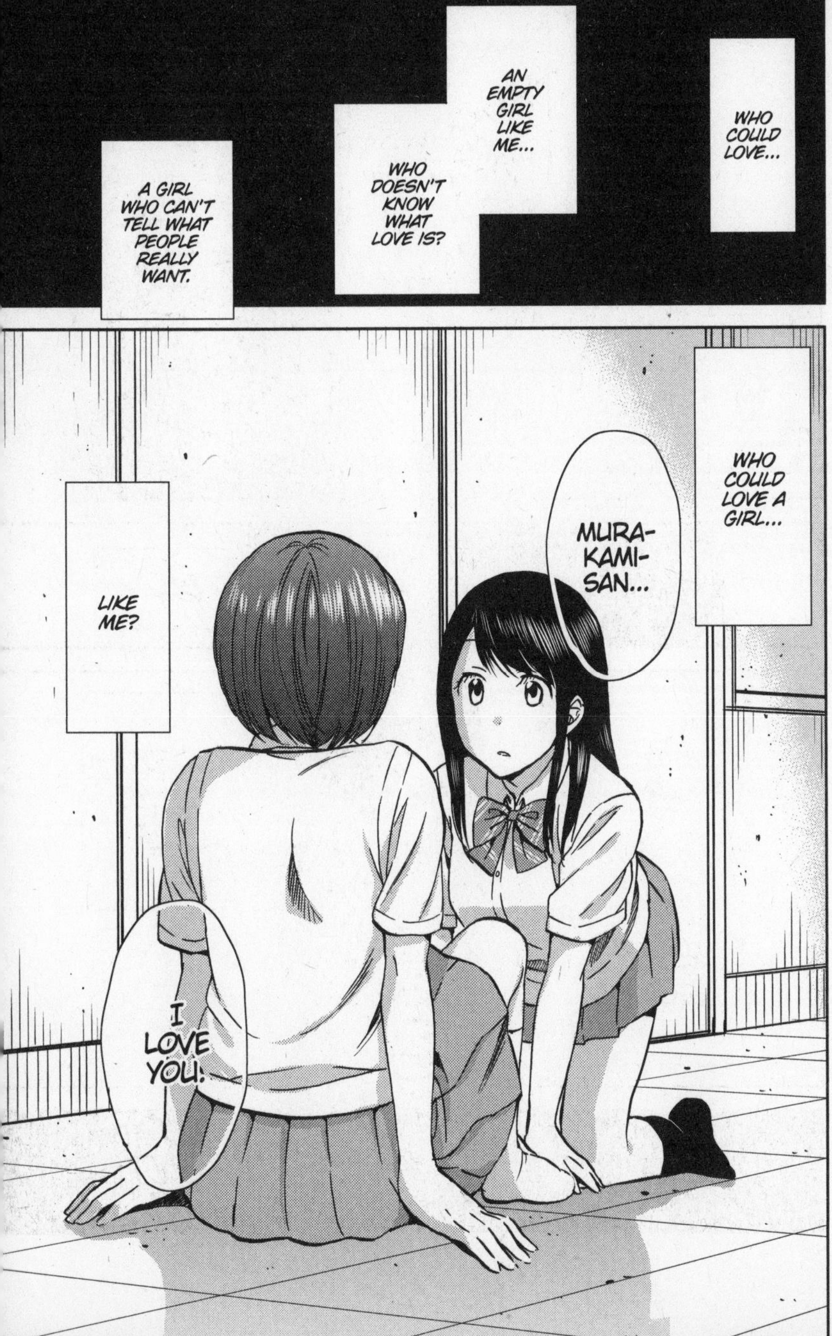
WHO COULD LOVE...
AN EMPTY GIRL LIKE ME...
WHO DOESN'T KNOW WHAT LOVE IS?
A GIRL WHO CAN'T TELL WHAT PEOPLE REALLY WANT.
WHO COULD LOVE A GIRL...
MURA-KAMI-SAN...
LIKE ME?
I LOVE YOU!

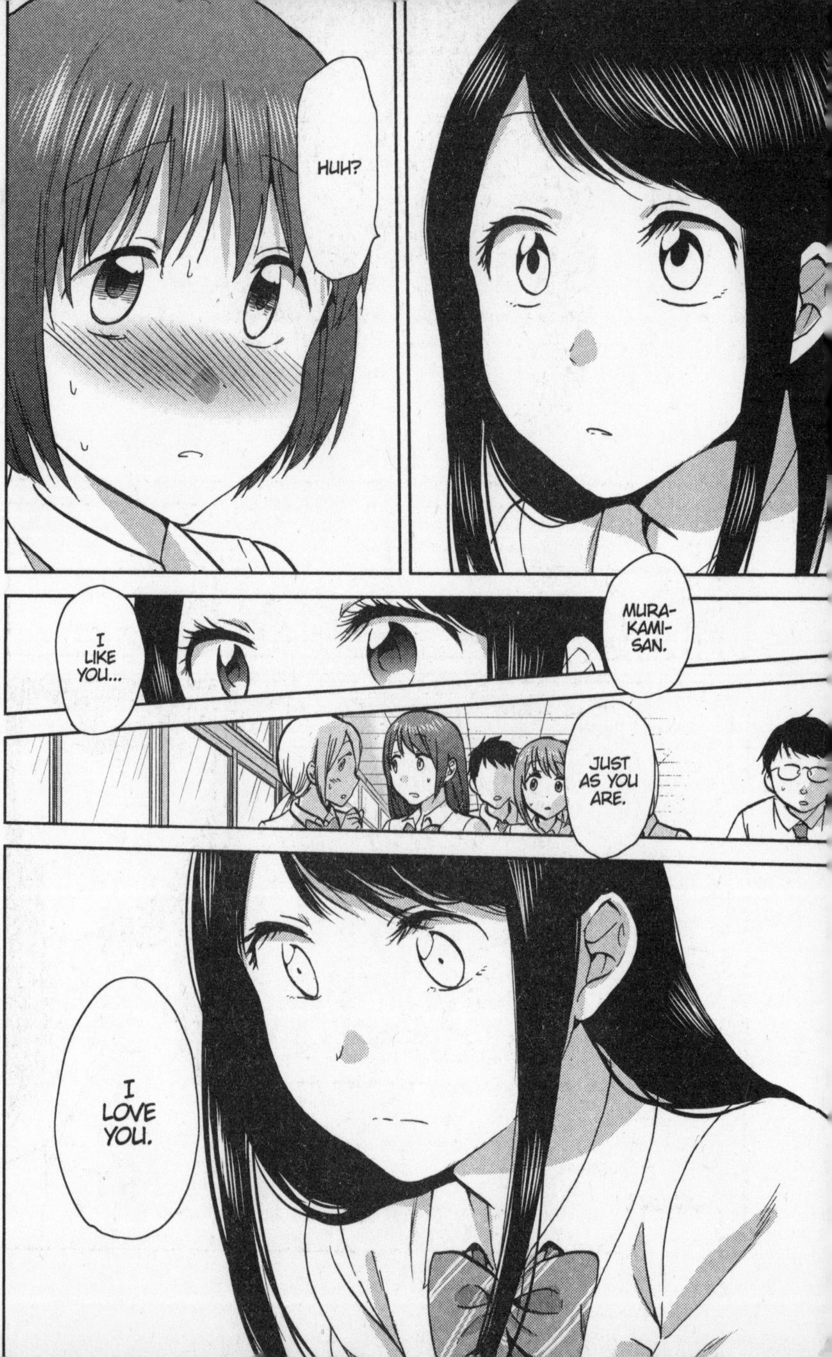
HUH?
MURA-KAMI-SAN.
I LIKE YOU...
JUST AS YOU ARE.
I LOVE YOU.

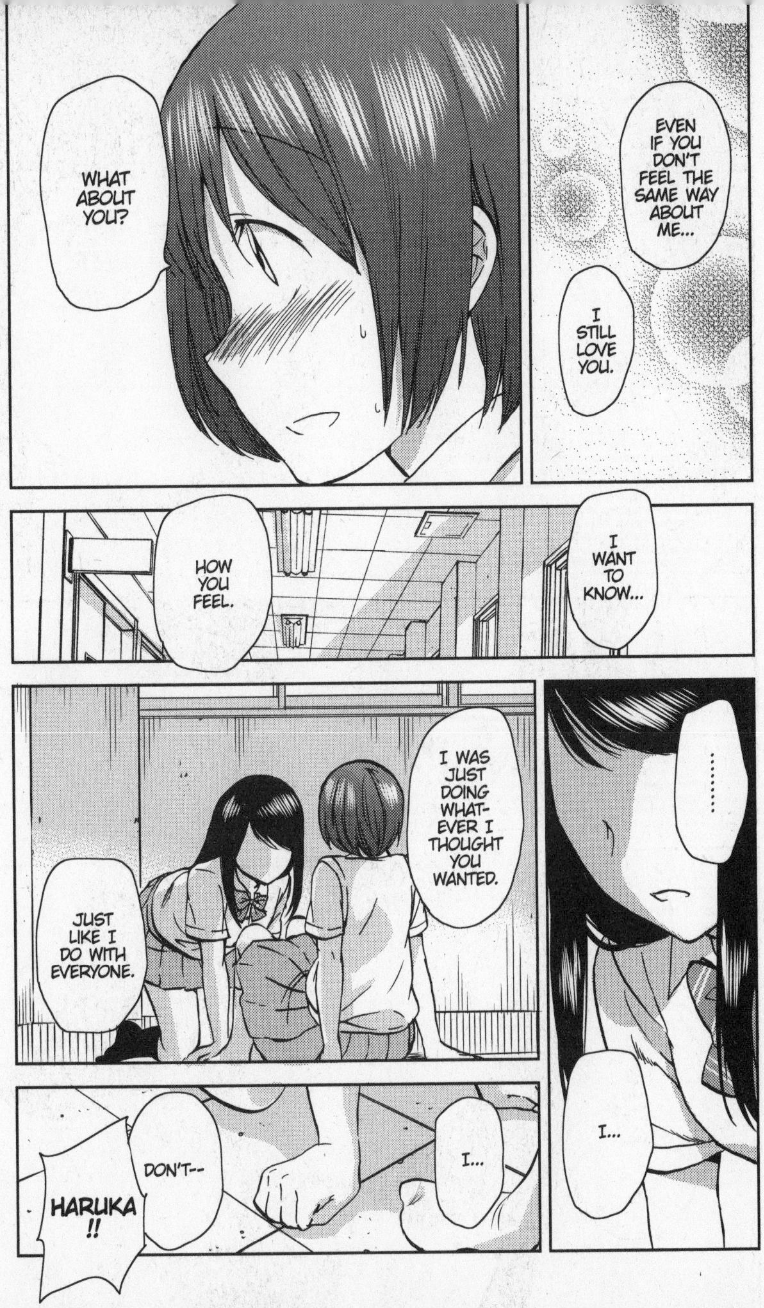
EVEN IF YOU DON'T FEEL THE SAME WAY ABOUT ME...
I STILL LOVE YOU.
WHAT ABOUT YOU?
I WANT TO KNOW...
HOW YOU FEEL.
......
I...
I WAS JUST DOING WHAT-EVER I THOUGHT YOU WANTED.
JUST LIKE I DO WITH EVERYONE.
I...
DON'T--
HARUKA!!

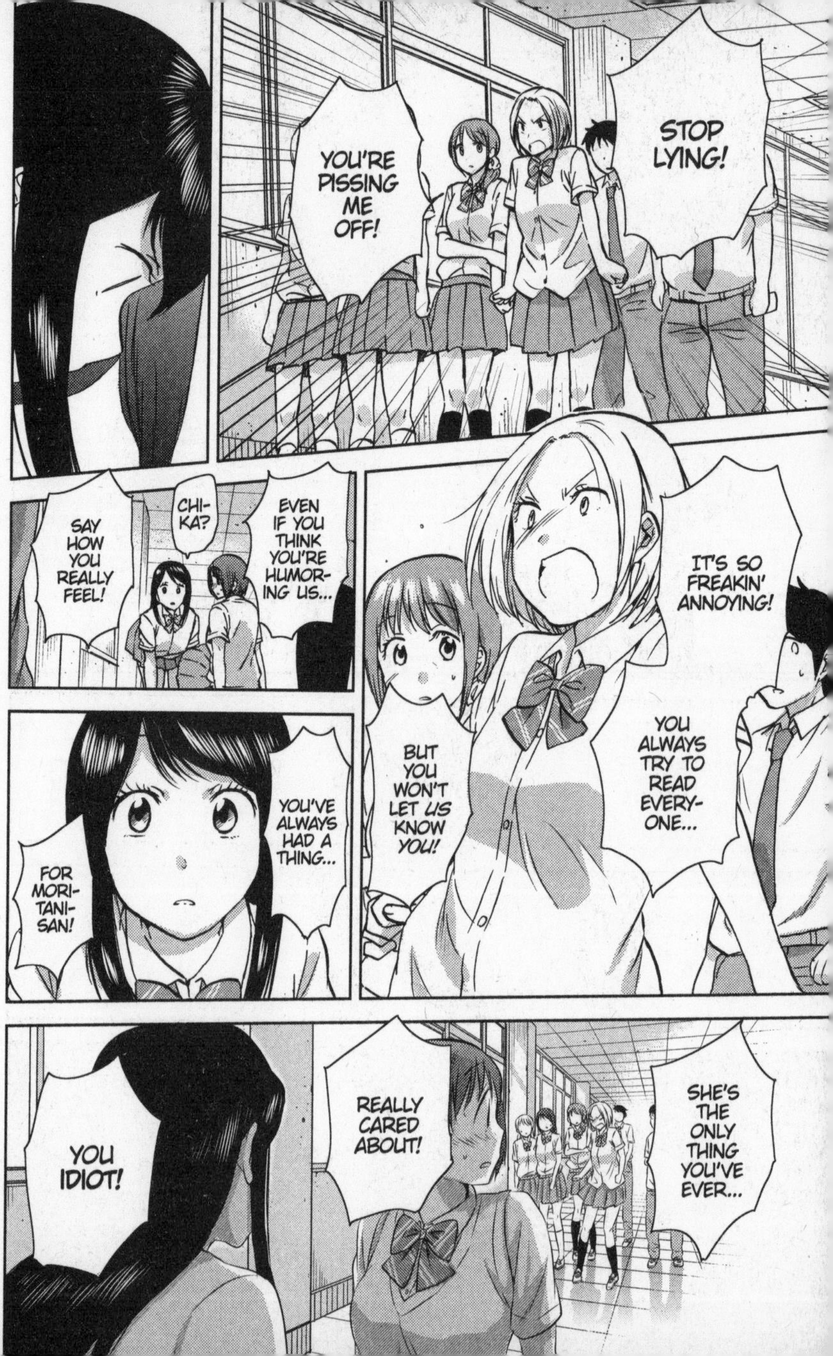
STOP LYING!
YOU'RE PISSING ME OFF!
IT'S SO FREAKIN' ANNOYING!
YOU ALWAYS TRY TO READ EVERY-ONE...
BUT YOU WON'T LET *US* KNOW *YOU*!
EVEN IF YOU THINK YOU'RE HUMOR-ING US...
CHI-KA?
SAY HOW YOU REALLY FEEL!
YOU'VE ALWAYS HAD A THING...
FOR MORI-TANI-SAN!
SHE'S THE ONLY THING YOU'VE EVER...
REALLY CARED ABOUT!
YOU IDIOT!

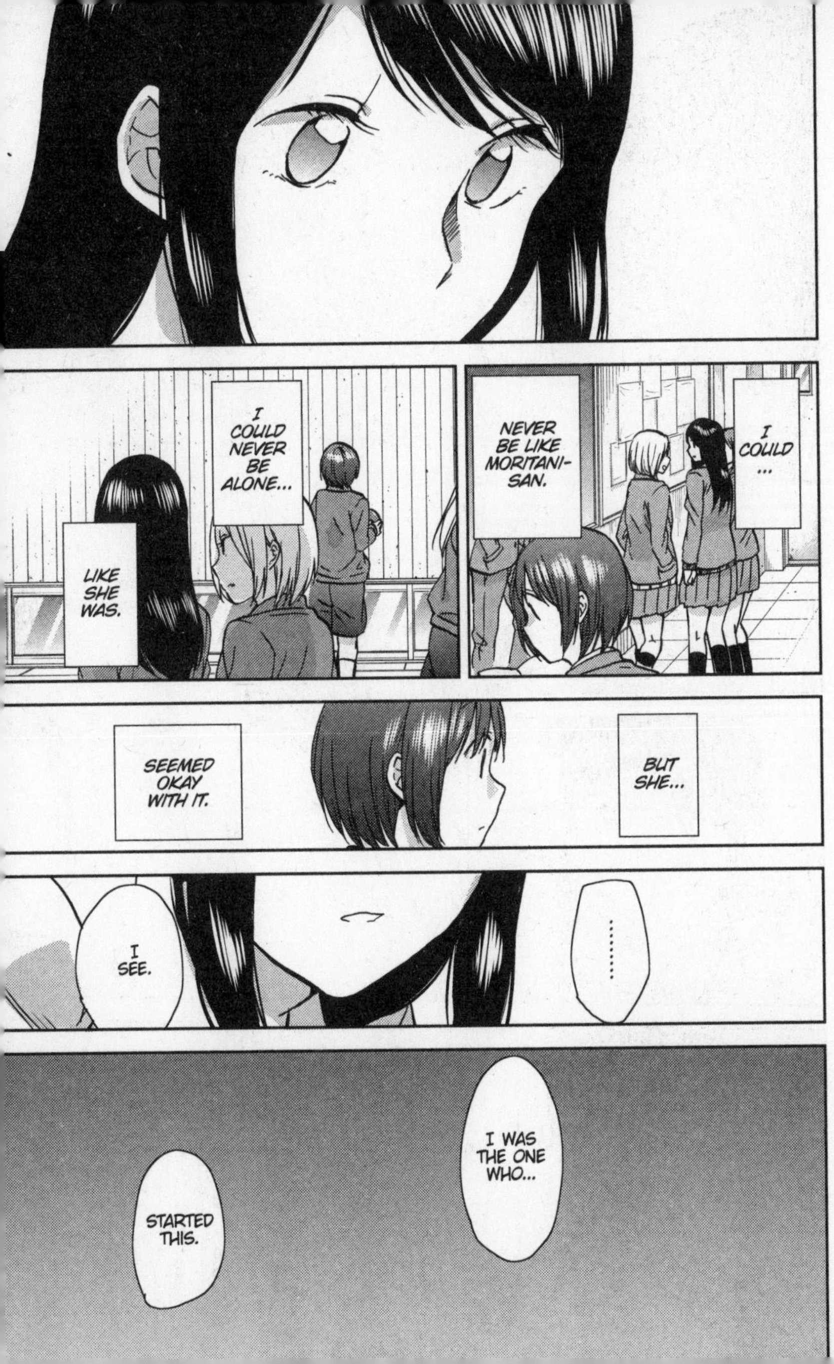
I COULD...
NEVER BE LIKE MORITANI-SAN.
I COULD NEVER BE ALONE...
LIKE SHE WAS.
BUT SHE...
SEEMED OKAY WITH IT.
......
I SEE.
I WAS THE ONE WHO...
STARTED THIS.

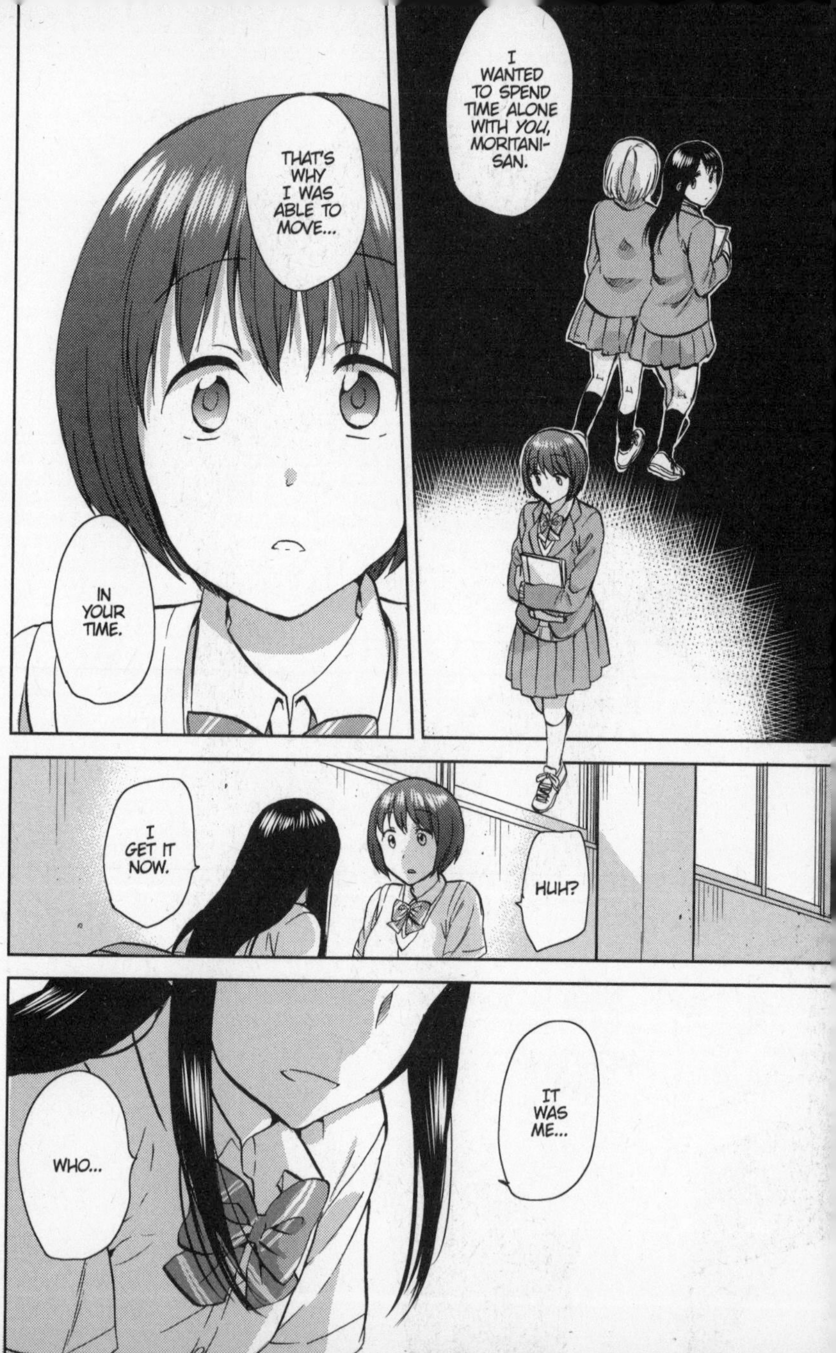
I WANTED TO SPEND TIME ALONE WITH *YOU*, MORITANI-SAN.
THAT'S WHY I WAS ABLE TO MOVE...
IN YOUR TIME.
HUH?
I GET IT NOW.
IT WAS ME...
WHO...

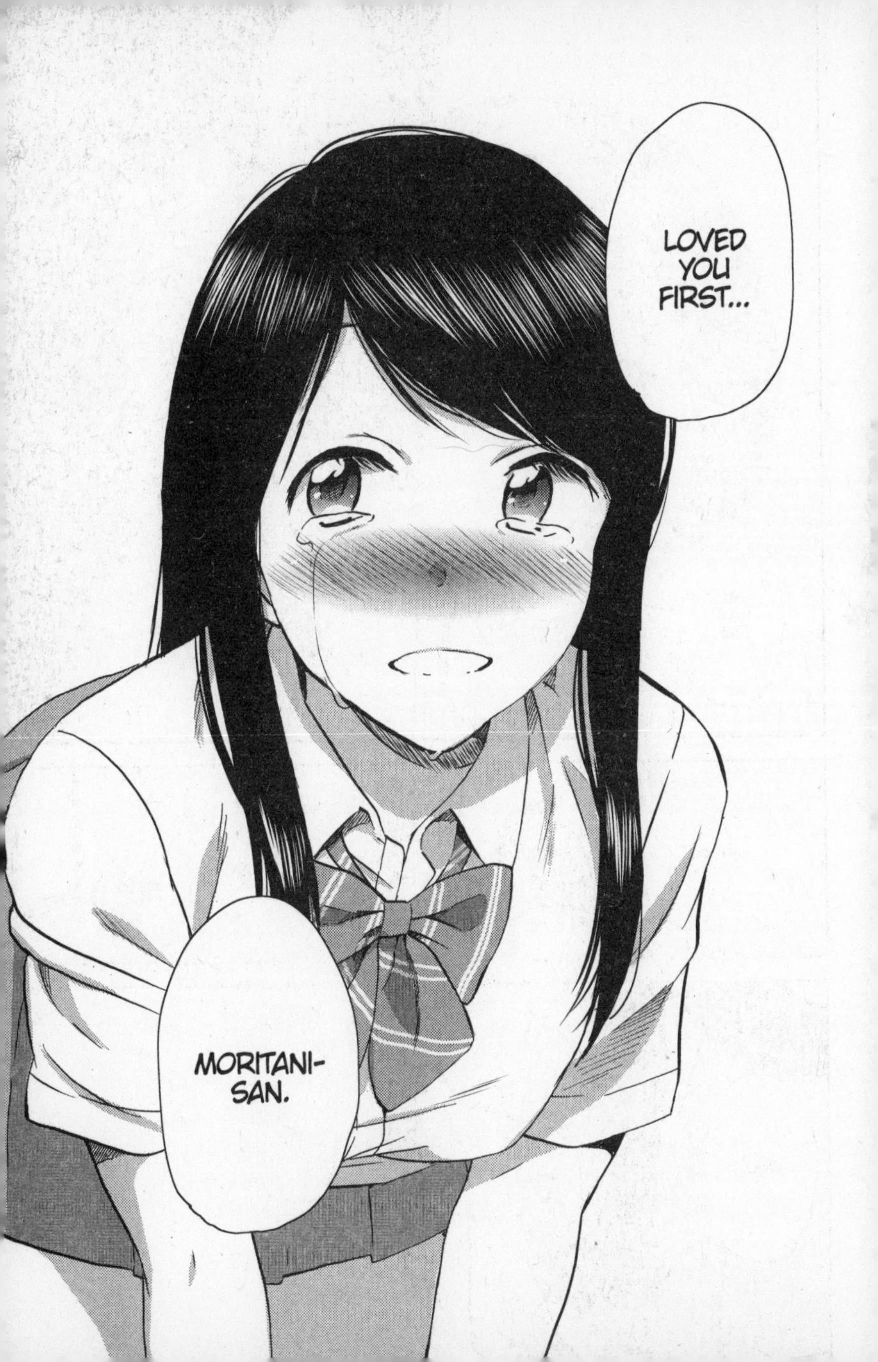
LOVED YOU FIRST...
MORITANI-SAN.

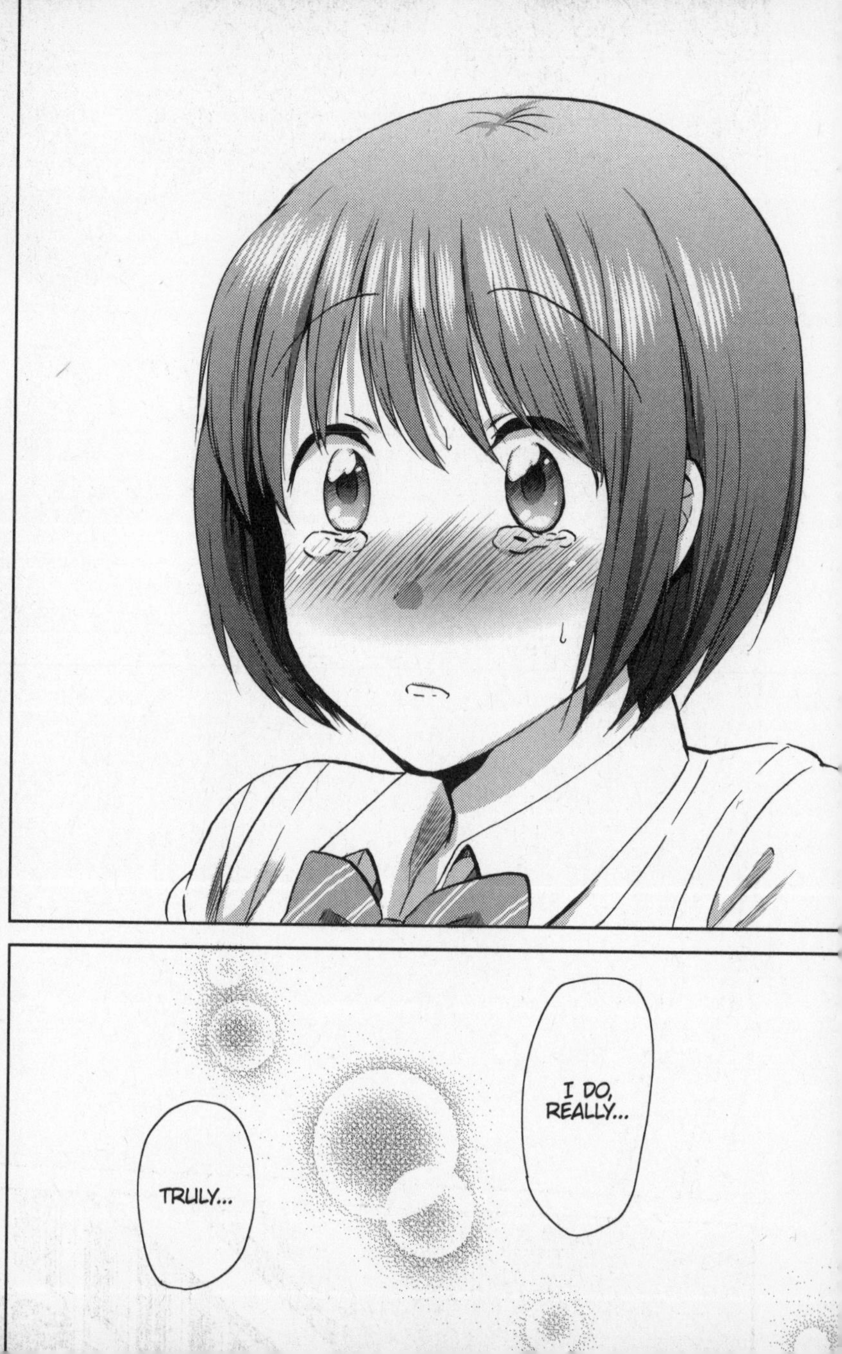
I DO, REALLY...
TRULY...

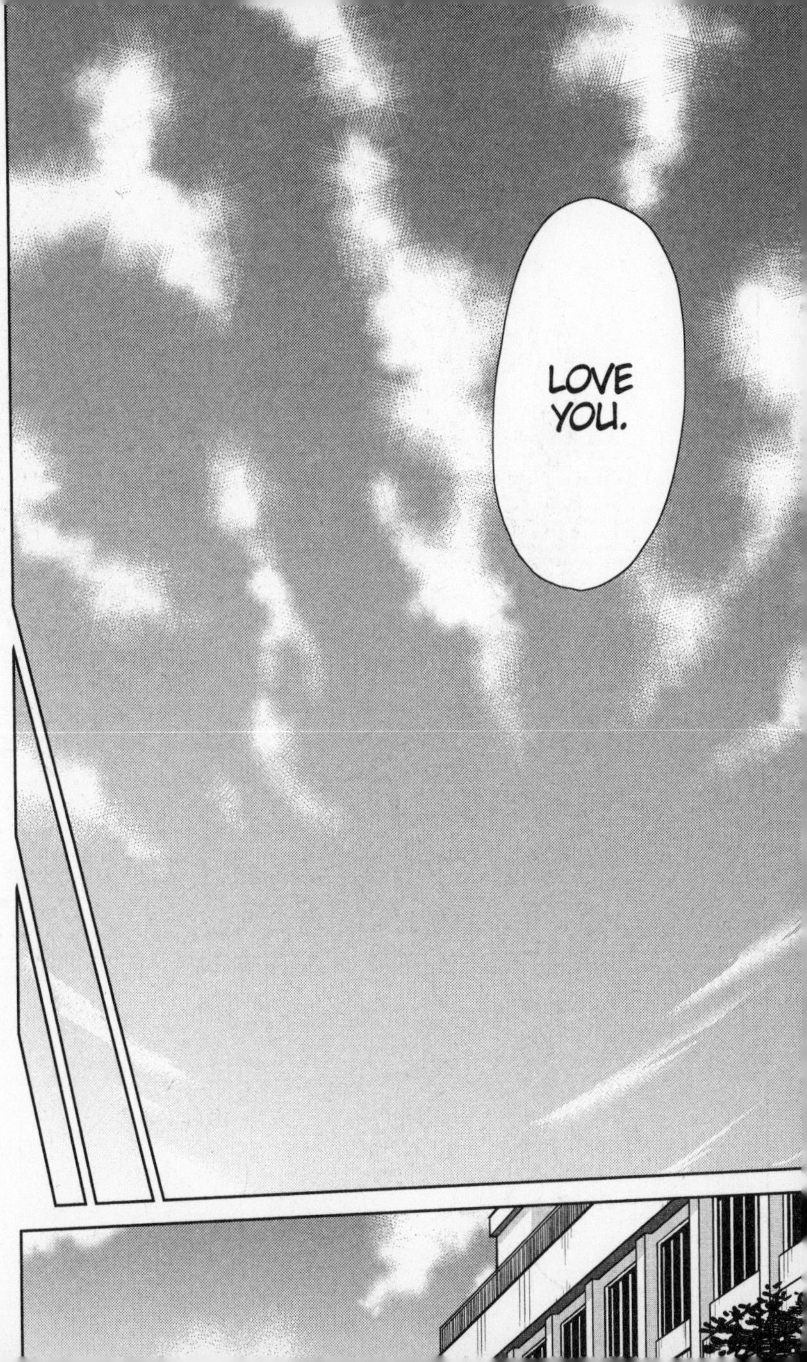
LOVE YOU.

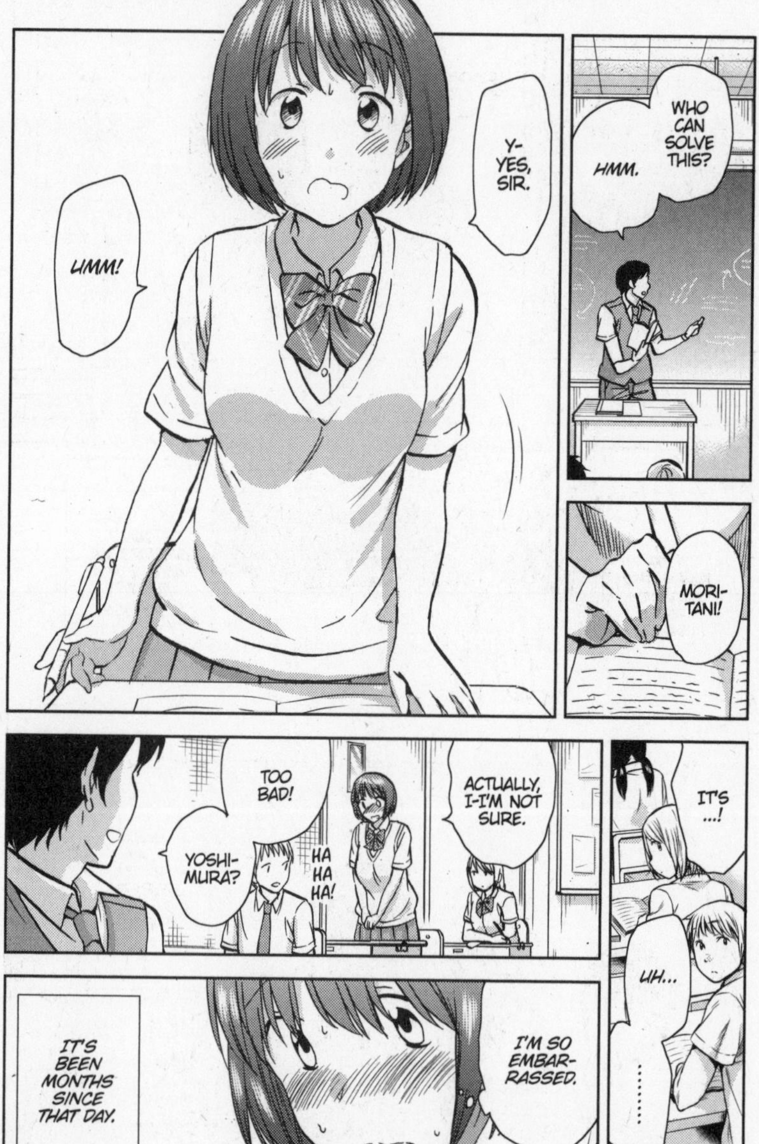
WHO CAN SOLVE THIS?
HMM.
MORI-TANI!
Y-YES, SIR.
UMM!
IT'S ...!
UH...
......
ACTUALLY, I-I'M NOT SURE.
TOO BAD!
HA HA HA!
YOSHI-MURA?
I'M SO EMBAR-RASSED.
IT'S BEEN MONTHS SINCE THAT DAY.

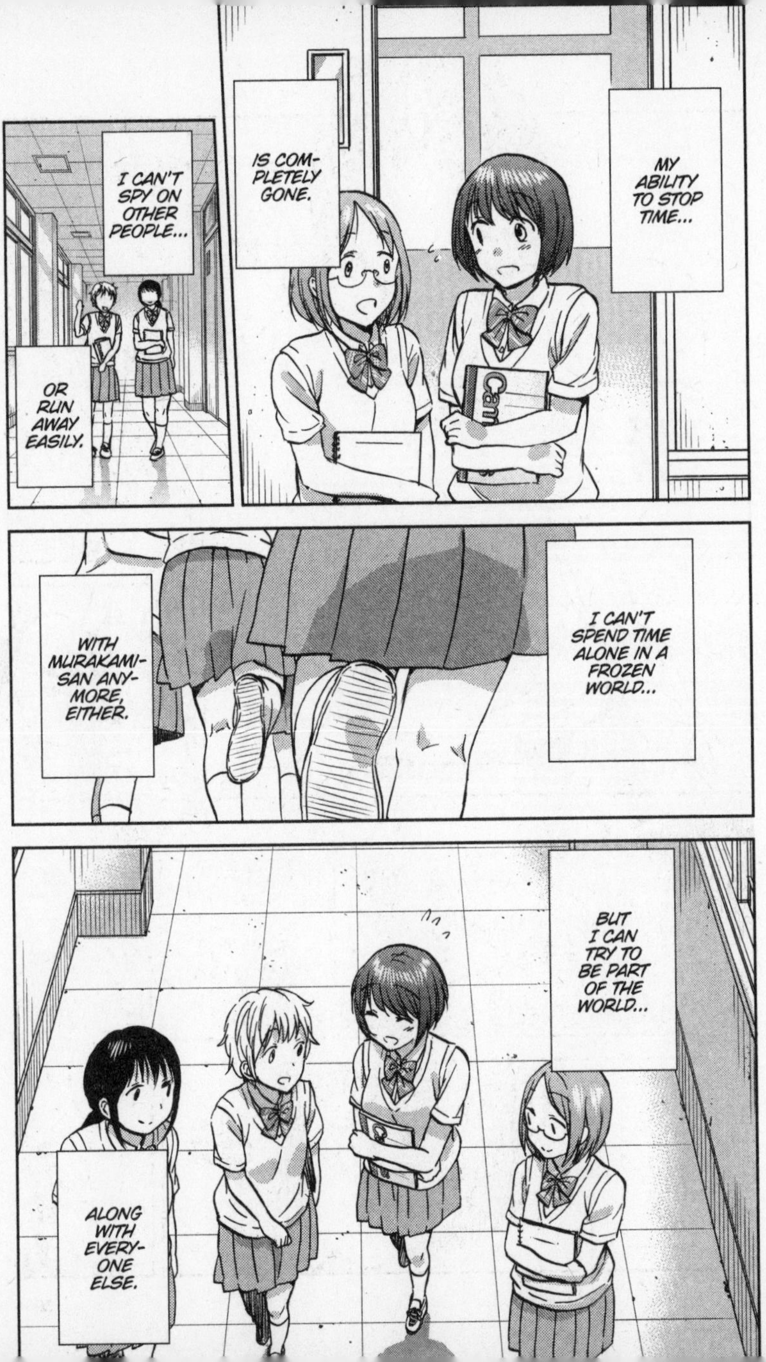
MY ABILITY TO STOP TIME...
IS COMPLETELY GONE.
I CAN'T SPY ON OTHER PEOPLE...
OR RUN AWAY EASILY.
I CAN'T SPEND TIME ALONE IN A FROZEN WORLD...
WITH MURAKAMI-SAN ANYMORE, EITHER.
BUT I CAN TRY TO BE PART OF THE WORLD...
ALONG WITH EVERYONE ELSE.

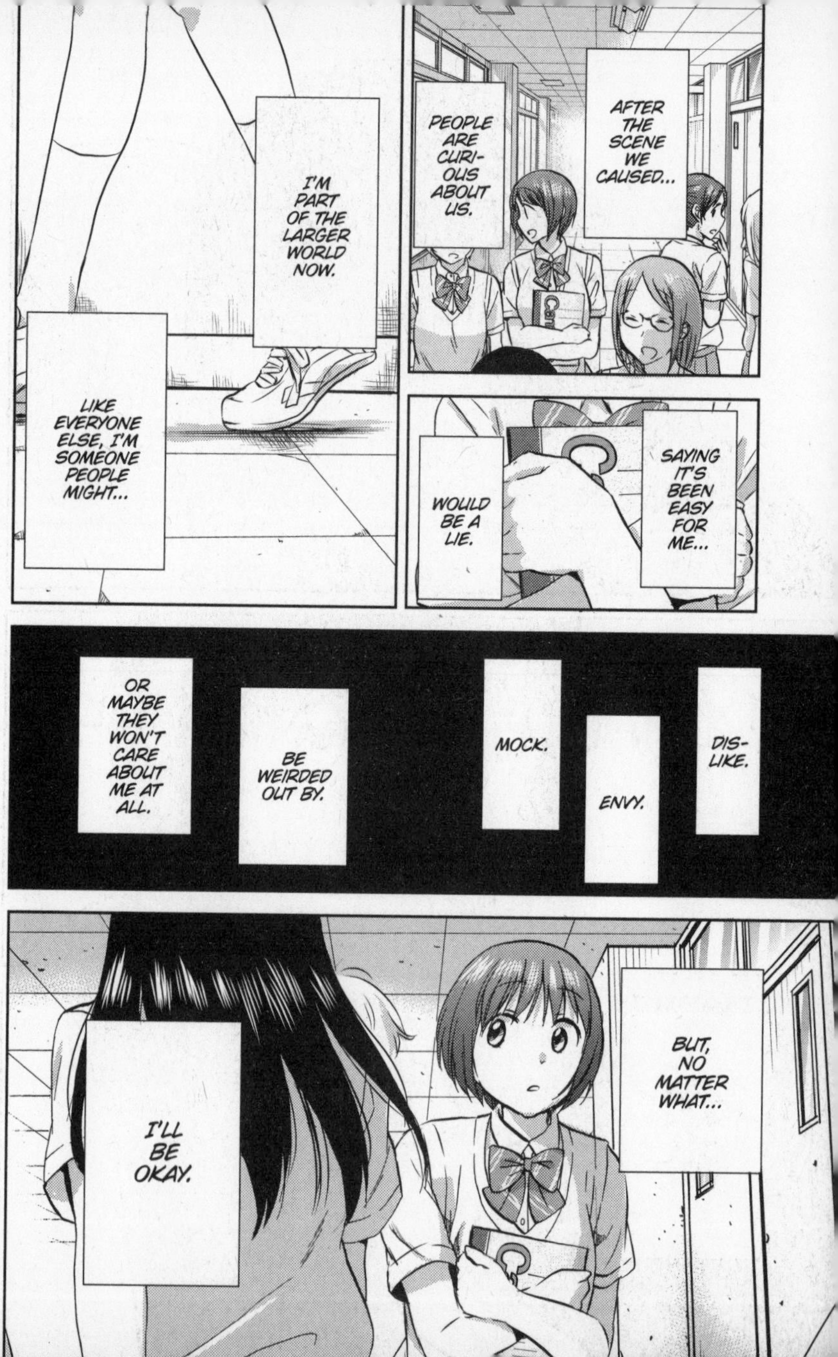
AFTER THE SCENE WE CAUSED...
PEOPLE ARE CURI-OUS ABOUT US.
SAYING IT'S BEEN EASY FOR ME...
WOULD BE A LIE.
I'M PART OF THE LARGER WORLD NOW.
LIKE EVERYONE ELSE, I'M SOMEONE PEOPLE MIGHT...
DIS-LIKE.
ENVY.
MOCK.
BE WEIRDED OUT BY.
OR MAYBE THEY WON'T CARE ABOUT ME AT ALL.
BUT, NO MATTER WHAT...
I'LL BE OKAY.

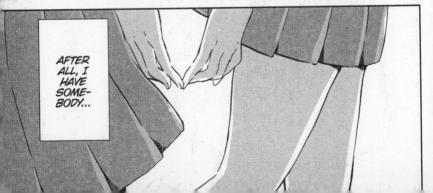

AFTER ALL, I HAVE SOME-BODY...

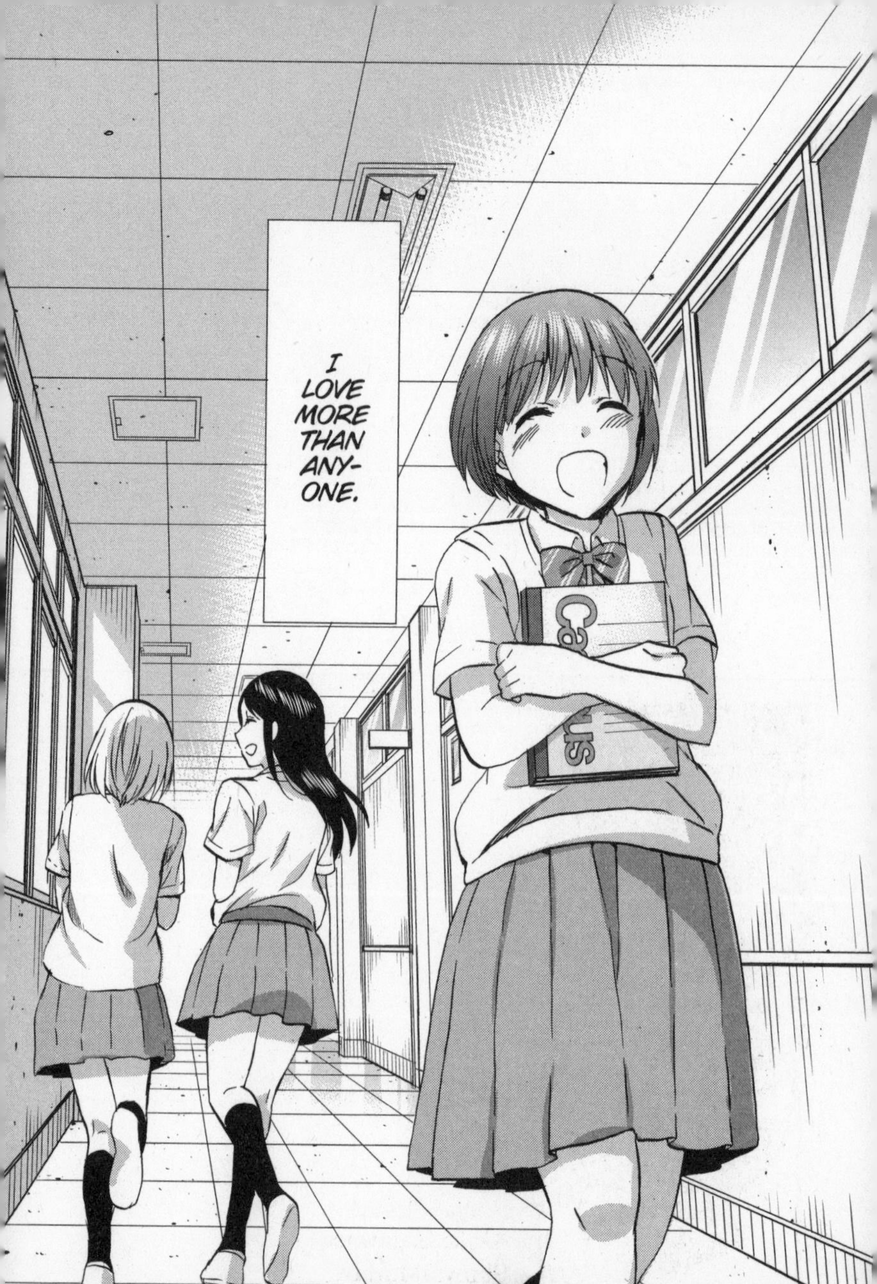
I LOVE MORE THAN ANY-ONE.

Final Chapter: I Love You / END

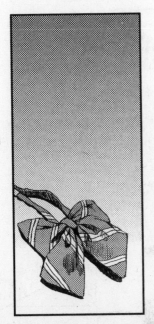

Special Thanks

Kaduo Ogathu
Akiko Sugawara
Shinya Murata

SEVEN SEAS ENTERTAINMENT PRESENTS

FRAGTIME

THE COMPLETE MANGA COLLECTION

story and art by **SATO**

TRANSLATION
Amber Tamosaitis

ADAPTATION
Dawn Davis

LETTERING AND RETOUCH
Laura Heo

COVER DESIGN
Nicky Lim

PROOFREADER
Stephanie Cohen
B. Lana Guggenheim

EDITOR
Shannon Fay

PREPRESS TECHNICIAN
Rhiannon Rasmussen-Silverstein

PRODUCTION MANAGER
Lissa Pattillo

MANAGING EDITOR
Julie Davis

ASSOCIATE PUBLISHER
Adam Arnold

PUBLISHER
Jason DeAngelis

FRAG TIME VOLUMES 1-2

Originally published in Japan in 2014 by Akita Publishing Co., Ltd.
English translation rights arranged with Akita Publishing Co., Ltd.
through TOHAN CORPORATION, Tokyo.

Seven Seas press and purchase enquiries can be sent to Marketing Manager Lianne Sentar at press@gomanga.com. Information regarding the distribution and purchase of digital editions is available from Digital Manager CK Russell at digital@gomanga.com.

ISBN: 978-1-64505-465-8

Printed in Canada

First Printing: April 2020

10 9 8 7 6 5 4 3 2 1

READING DIRECTIONS

This book reads from ***right to left***, Japanese style. If this is your first time reading manga, you start reading from the top right panel on each page and take it from there. If you get lost, just follow the numbered diagram here. It may seem backwards at first, but you'll get the hang of it! Have fun!!

1
2
3
4
5
6
7
8
9

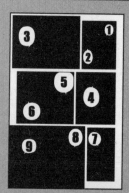